No. **13**

This textbook has been purchased under the
NEW YORK STATE TEXTBOOK LAW
It is the property of the:

BOARD OF EDUCATION
South Colonie Central Schools
102 Loralee Drive
Albany, New York 12205
It is loaned to you in the condition indicated below. It
is your responsibility to care for this book and to return it
in a satisfactory condition.

DATE	Signature of Student	Condition of Book

Scott Foresman - Addison Wesley
MIDDLE SCHOOL MATH
Course 3

Randall I. Charles   John A. Dossey   Steven J. Leinwand
Cathy L. Seeley   Charles B. Vonder Embse

L. Carey Bolster • Janet H. Caldwell • Dwight A. Cooley • Warren D. Crown
Linda Proudfit • Alma B. Ramírez • Jeanne F. Ramos • Freddie Lee Renfro
David Robitaille • Jane Swafford

Scott Foresman
Addison Wesley

Editorial Offices: Menlo Park, California • Glenview, Illinois
Sales Offices: Reading, Massachusetts • Atlanta, Georgia • Glenview, Illinois
Carrollton, Texas • Menlo Park, California

http://www.sf.aw.com

Cover artist: Robert Silvers, 28, started taking photographs and playing with computers at the same time, about 19 years ago. He always thought of computer programming as a way to express himself much as he does with photography. Silvers has melded his interests to produce the image on this cover.

FROM THE AUTHORS

Dear Student,

We have designed a unique mathematics program that answers the question students your age have been asking for years about their math lessons: "When am I ever going to use this?"

In *Scott Foresman - Addison Wesley Middle School Math*, you'll learn about math in your own world and develop problem-solving techniques that will work for you in everyday life. The chapters have two or three sections, each with a useful math topic and an interesting theme. For example, you'll relate ratios to special effects, linear equations to pets, and rational numbers to water.

Each section begins with an opportunity to explore new topics and make your own conjectures. Lessons are presented clearly with examples and chances to try the math yourself. Then, real kids like you and your friends say what they think about each concept and show how they understand it. And every section contains links to the World Wide Web, making your math book a dynamic link to an ever-expanding universe of knowledge.

You will soon realize how mathematics is not only useful, but also connected to you and your life as you continue to experience the real world. We trust that each of you will gain the knowledge necessary to be successful and to be everything you want to be.

Randall I. Charles   *John A. Dossey*   *Steven J. Leinwand*
            Cathy L. Seeley   *Charles B. Vonder Embse*

L. Carey Bolster   *Janet H. Caldwell*   *Dwight A. Cooley*   *Warren D. Crown*   *Linda Proudfit*
Alma B. Ramirez   *Jeanne F. Ramos*   *Freddie Lee Renfro*   *David Robitaille*   *Jane Swafford*

Authors

L. Carey Bolster
Public Broadcasting System
Alexandria, Virginia

Randall I. Charles
San Jose State University
San Jose, California

Warren D. Crown
Rutgers, the State University of New Jersey
New Brunswick, New Jersey

Steven J. Leinwand
Connecticut Department of Education
Hartford, Connecticut

Alma B. Ramírez
Oakland Charter Academy
Oakland, California

Freddie Lee Renfro
Fort Bend Independent School District
Sugarland, Texas

Cathy L. Seeley
Texas SSI in Math and Science
Austin, Texas

Charles B. Vonder Embse
Central Michigan University
Mount Pleasant, Michigan

Janet H. Caldwell
Rowan College of New Jersey
Glassboro, New Jersey

Dwight A. Cooley
M. L. Phillips Elementary School
Fort Worth, Texas

John A. Dossey
Illinois State University
Normal, Illinois

Linda Proudfit
Governors State University
University Park, Illinois

Jeanne F. Ramos
Nobel Middle School
Los Angeles, California

David Robitaille
University of British Columbia
Vancouver, British Columbia, Canada

Jane Swafford
Illinois State University
Normal, Illinois

Problem Solving
in Chapter 1

Use real-world data to solve problems involving money and surveys.

TECHNOLOGY

• Spreadsheet
• Calculator
• World Wide Web
• Interactive CD-ROM

x Algebra

Make and use scatterplots to look for trends by plotting the data points.

CHAPTER

1	2	3	4	5	6	7	8	9	10	11	12

DATA ANALYSIS...2

SECTION 1A
Data Presentations

SECTION 1B
Using Data to Answer Questions

Problem Solving
in Chapter 2

Use positive and negative numbers to solve problems about currency and our changing earth.

TECHNOLOGY

- Scientific Calculator
- Spreadsheet
- World Wide Web
- Interactive CD-ROM

Algebra

Solve equations with positive and
negative numbers using your
knowledge of operations.

CHAPTER

| 1 | **2** | 3 | 4 | 5 | 6 | 7 | 8 | 9 | 10 | 11 | 12 |

INTEGERS...58

Problem Solving in Chapter 3

Use formulas and algebra to solve problems about flight, energy, and electricity.

TECHNOLOGY

- Graphing Utility
- Spreadsheet
- World Wide Web
- Interactive CD-ROM

Algebra

Learn methods for solving algebraic expressions and equations involving variables.

CHAPTER

1	2	**3**	4	5	6	7	8	9	10	11	12

THE LANGUAGE OF ALGEBRA: VARIABLES, EXPRESSIONS, AND EQUATIONS...118

SECTION 3A
Formulas and Expressions

SECTION 3B
Writing and Solving Equations and Inequalities

Problem Solving
in Chapter 4

Use algebra to solve problems
about pets and outdoor recreation.

TECHNOLOGY

• Graphing Utility
• Spreadsheet
• World Wide Web
• Interactive CD-ROM

x **Algebra**

Solve and graph two-variable
equations and inequalities.

CHAPTER

| 1 | 2 | 3 | **4** | 5 | 6 | 7 | 8 | 9 | 10 | 11 | 12 |

ALGEBRA: LINEAR EQUATIONS AND INEQUALITIES...168

Problem Solving in Chapter 5	TECHNOLOGY	X Algebra
Solve problems about communication and special effects by using ratios and proportions.	• Geometry Software • Calculator • World Wide Web • Interactive CD-ROM	Use ratios and proportions to solve algebraic equations.

CHAPTER

| 1 | 2 | 3 | 4 | 5 | 6 | 7 | 8 | 9 | 10 | 11 | 12 |

RATIO AND PROPORTION...218

Problem Solving
in Chapter 6

Solve problems about food, nutrition, and advertising using percents.

TECHNOLOGY

• Scientific Calculator
• Spreadsheet
• World Wide Web
• Interactive CD-ROM

x Algebra

Find unknown percents by using your equation-solving skills.

CHAPTER

| 1 | 2 | 3 | 4 | 5 | **6** | 7 | 8 | 9 | 10 | 11 | 12 |

PERCENT...270

Problem Solving in Chapter 7

Solve problems about codes, water, and houses by performing operations involving rational and irrational numbers.

TECHNOLOGY

• Spreadsheet
• Calculator
• World Wide Web
• Interactive CD-ROM

𝑥 Algebra

Solve equations involving rational and irrational numbers, square roots, and the Pythagorean Theorem.

CHAPTER

| 1 | 2 | 3 | 4 | 5 | 6 | **7** | 8 | 9 | 10 | 11 | 12 |

NUMBER SENSE, RATIONAL NUMBERS, AND IRRATIONAL NUMBERS...320

Learn how the Global Positioning System uses measurement and position. Investigate the geometry of shapes found in nature.

- Geometry Software
- World Wide Web
- Interactive CD-ROM

Use formulas to find areas and perimeters of geometric shapes.

CHAPTER

| 1 | 2 | 3 | 4 | 5 | 6 | 7 | **8** | 9 | 10 | 11 | 12 |

GEOMETRY AND MEASUREMENT...386

Problem Solving in Chapter 9

Solve problems about perimeter, area, and volume in the theater and package delivery.

TECHNOLOGY

• Geometry Software
• Spreadsheet
• World Wide Web
• Interactive CD-ROM

X Algebra

Find the area and volume of three-dimensional shapes by using geometric formulas.

CHAPTER

| 1 | 2 | 3 | 4 | 5 | 6 | 7 | 8 | **9** | 10 | 11 | 12 |

AREA AND VOLUME...440

SECTION 9A

Perimeter, Area, and Surface Area

SECTION 9B

Volume

**Problem Solving
in Chapter 10**

Work with polynomials and functions to solve problems involving motion and birds.

TECHNOLOGY

• Graphing Utility
• Scientific Calculator
• World Wide Web
• Interactive CD-ROM

 Algebra

Use your equation-solving skills to solve problems involving functions and relationships.

CHAPTER

| 1 | 2 | 3 | 4 | 5 | 6 | 7 | 8 | 9 | **10** | 11 | 12 |

ALGEBRA: FUNCTIONS AND RELATIONSHIPS...504

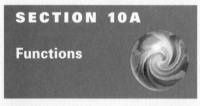

Problem Solving in Chapter 11

Identify similar and congruent figures in bridges and investigate the use of transformations in Native American arts and crafts.

TECHNOLOGY

• Geometry Software
• World Wide Web
• Interactive CD-ROM

x Algebra

Solve for unknown values to determine if figures are similar or congruent.

CHAPTER

| 1 | 2 | 3 | 4 | 5 | 6 | 7 | 8 | 9 | 10 | **11** | 12 |

SIMILARITY, CONGRUENCE, AND TRANSFORMATIONS...560

SECTION 11A

Similarity and Congruence

SECTION 11B

Transformations

Problem Solving
in Chapter 12

The Olympics and birthdays provide situations where counting and probability are used.

TECHNOLOGY

• Graphing Utility
• Scientific Calculator
• World Wide Web
• Interactive CD-ROM

Ⓧ Algebra

Solve algebraic equations to determine probability.

| 1 | 2 | 3 | 4 | 5 | 6 | 7 | 8 | 9 | 10 | 11 |

CHAPTER 12

COUNTING AND PROBABILITY...622

Internet Connections

The world of math is connected to the world around you in so many interesting ways. We'd like to invite you to explore these connections on the World Wide Web.

To begin your journey, you will need a web browser. Use your browser to visit the home page for *Mathsurf* by typing in *http://www.mathsurf.com.*

You'll find more web addresses at the top of each chapter opener and section opener that send you directly to pages that relate to your chapter or section.

Problem Solving and Applications

Math is all around you. Having good math skills can help you solve problems every day. What types of problems can you solve using mathematics?

Problem Solving
Understand
Plan
Solve
Look Back

Problem Solving
STRATEGIES

Problem Solving TIP

WHAT DO YOU THINK?

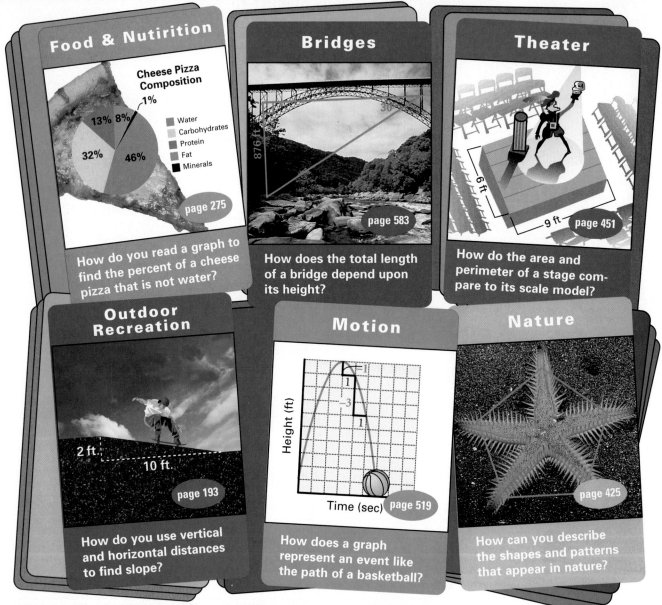

Food & Nutrition

Cheese Pizza Composition

- 1%
- 13%
- 8%
- 32%
- 46%

Water
Carbohydrates
Protein
Fat
Minerals

page 275

How do you read a graph to find the percent of a cheese pizza that is not water?

Bridges

876 ft

page 583

How does the total length of a bridge depend upon its height?

Theater

6 ft
9 ft

page 451

How do the area and perimeter of a stage compare to its scale model?

Outdoor Recreation

2 ft
10 ft.

page 193

How do you use vertical and horizontal distances to find slope?

Motion

Height (ft)
Time (sec)

page 519

How does a graph represent an event like the path of a basketball?

Nature

page 425

How can you describe the shapes and patterns that appear in nature?

Math is also connected to the other subjects you are studying.
Look on these pages to find examples of how math is connected to:

Science				History				Geography			
p. 44	p. 92	p. 152	p. 174	p. 71	p. 125	p. 144	p. 255	p. 9	p. 13	p. 15	p. 30
p. 253	p. 257	p. 276	p. 284	p. 282	p. 292	p. 303	p. 304	p. 65	p. 93	p. 99	p. 102
p. 328	p. 351	p. 391	p. 397	p. 329	p. 346	p. 349	p. 370	p. 112	p. 153	p. 158	p. 260
p. 412	p. 417	p. 422	p. 483	p. 372	p. 378	p. 395	p. 405	p. 289	p. 333	p. 353	p. 359
p. 520	p. 524	p. 586	p. 607	p. 415	p. 431	p. 458	p. 478	p. 372	p. 375	p. 394	p. 401

PROBLEM SOLVING HAND BOOK

Problems, problems, problems. We run into them every day. We can solve some problems easily and quickly, but there will always be problems that require more effort. If you have ever asked the question, "What do you think?" you'd know that everyone has his or her own way of solving problems.

If you are looking for a job and you're a creative problem solver, then you've got it made—you can think through problems logically, work with others cooperatively, and communicate your thoughts effectively.

Right now your teacher and textbook will guide you to becoming a creative problem solver. In this course you'll explore challenging problems independently and in groups. You'll use problem solving tools such as calculators, computers, even pencil and paper.

The students shown here will be sharing their thoughts with you throughout this textbook. But the key question will always be,

"What do you think?"

1. What do you think creative problem solving is?

2. Give examples of problems that people have to solve every day.

Solving Problems

▶ Lesson Link You've solved many problems in your previous math classes. Now you'll look more closely at well-known methods you can use to solve problems. ◀

Problem Solving

You solve problems every day. A problem such as "how much change should you receive?" is straightforward. Often you can use mathematics to find quick solutions. For example, you can add, subtract, multiply, or divide to find a quick numerical answer.

Problems that involve more thought may have many possible solutions. Finding any solution may be easy, but finding the best solution requires thorough knowledge of the problem. You solve these problems the best way you can. Sometimes it helps to have more than one person solving the same problem because everyone is a unique problem solver.

No matter what problem you are tackling, you need a plan or a strategy for solving it. A plan or strategy will help you to understand the problem, work out a creative solution, and check to see that the solution makes sense.

Problem Solving

Understand
Plan
Solve
Look Back

PROBLEM SOLVING GUIDELINES

❶ UNDERSTAND the Problem
- What do you know?
- What do you need to find out?

❷ Develop a PLAN
- Have you ever solved a similar problem?
- What strategies can you use?
- What is an estimate for the answer?

❸ SOLVE the Problem
- Do you need to try another strategy?
- What is the solution?

❹ LOOK BACK
- Did you answer the right question?
- Is your answer reasonable?

Example

The Arguello's are driving from Denver to Kansas City, a distance of 605 mi. They've been traveling for 5 hr at 55 mi/hr. If they increase their speed to 60 mi/hr, how much longer will it take them to reach their destination?

① UNDERSTAND the Problem

You know that the family has completed part of their drive. *You need to find* out how long the rest of the trip will take.

② Develop a PLAN

You've solved similar problems involving distance, time, and rate. You need to recall that these quantities are related by the formulas $t = d \div r$ and $d = r \times t$, where $d =$ distance, $r =$ average speed, and $t =$ time.

Estimate the answer. After 5 hr, the Arguellos have gone about $5 \times 60 = 300$ mi. They have about 300 mi to go. They need about 5 hr to complete the trip.

One *strategy* is to draw a diagram to help you solve the problem.

③ SOLVE the Problem

After you draw the diagram, you might need to compare it to the formula.

$$
\begin{array}{c}
t = 5 \qquad t = ? \\
r = 55 \qquad r = 60 \\
\xrightarrow{\hspace{1cm}} \\
\text{Denver} \qquad \qquad \text{Kansas City}
\end{array}
$$

You know that $t = 5$ hr $r = 55$ mi/hr

$d = r \times t = 5 \times 55 = 275$ The family has traveled 275 mi.

Remaining distance $= 605 - 275 = 330$ mi

$t = d \div r = 330 \div 60 = 5.5$ hr needed to complete the trip.

The *solution* is that it will take 5.5 hr. You don't need to *try another strategy*.

④ LOOK BACK

You answered the right question. Because your answer is close to your estimate of 5 hr, *your answer makes sense.*

Check | Your Understanding

1. What other strategies could you have used to solve the problem?

2. Why is it important to have a plan before you begin a solution?

3. When would you have to *try another strategy* when solving a problem?

Look for a Pattern

Sometimes the numbers in a problem form a pattern. To solve the problem, you can find the rule that creates the pattern and use the rule to find the answer. ◄

Example

A display of gift boxes has 1 box in the top row, 3 boxes in the next row, 5 boxes in the next row, and so on. There are 10 rows in all. How many gift boxes are in the display?

Look for a pattern using the number of rows and the number of boxes in each row of the gift-box display.

1 row uses **1** box.

2 rows use $1 + 3 = $ **4** boxes.

3 rows use $1 + 3 + 5 = $ **9** boxes.

4 rows use $1 + 3 + 5 + 7 = $ **16** boxes.

Notice the pattern: The total number of boxes is the number of rows multiplied by itself. Use this rule to solve the problem.

The number of boxes in 10 rows is $10 \times 10 = 100$ boxes.

Try It

a. A basketball drops from a height of 76 in. On bounce 1, it rebounds to a height of 38 in. On bounce 2, it rebounds to a height of 19 in. How high does the basketball rebound on bounce 4?

b. The 8 members of a science club are recruiting new members by calling other students. Each science club member calls 12 people. How many phone calls would be made if there were 20 members?

Make an Organized List

Problem Solving

STRATEGIES

- Look for a Pattern
- **Make an Organized List**
- Make a Table
- Guess and Check
- Work Backward
- Use Logical Reasoning
- Draw a Diagram
- Solve a Simpler Problem

Sometimes a problem asks you to find the number of ways in which something can be done. To solve the problem, list all of the ways and then count them. The key to a correct solution is to organize your list carefully so you do not overlook any possibilities. ◄

Example

Dale and Ali play *Rock, Paper, Scissors.* Each player plays by putting out either a fist (rock), a flat hand (paper), or two fingers (scissors). Paper defeats (covers) rock, rock defeats (dulls) scissors, and scissors defeats (cuts) paper. No one wins if each person plays the same item. How many different ways can Dale and Ali play one game?

Dale	Ali	Winner
Rock	Rock	None
Rock	Paper	Ali
Rock	Scissors	Dale
Paper	Rock	Dale
Paper	Paper	None
Paper	Scissors	Ali
Scissors	Rock	Ali
Scissors	Paper	Dale
Scissors	Scissors	None

- First, list all the results that can occur if Dale plays rock. Ali can play rock, paper, or scissors.

- Next, list all the results that can occur if Dale plays paper. Keep Ali's plays in the same order.

- Finally, list all the results that can occur if Dale plays scissors.

There are 9 possible ways that Dale and Ali can play one game.

Try It

a. A spinner has 3 colors—red, yellow, and blue. If you spin two times, how many different color orders can you get?

b. Neal subscribes to 3 daily newspapers. In how many different orders can he read them?

<table>
<tr><td>

Problem Solving

STRATEGIES

- Look for a Pattern
- Make an Organized List
- **Make a Table**
- Guess and Check
- Work Backward
- Use Logical Reasoning
- Draw a Diagram
- Solve a Simpler Problem

</td></tr>
</table>

Make a Table

A problem involving a relationship between two sets of numbers can often be solved by making a table. A table helps you organize data so you can see the numerical relationship and find the answer. ◄

Example

In 1990, Beth bought a 6 ft tall redwood seedling. The tree grew 2 ft each year. In 1990, she bought a 2 ft tall willow seedling. The tree grew 3 ft each year. In what year were the trees the same height?

Make a table to organize data about the heights of the trees.

| | **Year** | | | | |
	1990	1991	1992	1993	1994
Redwood Height (ft)	6	8	10	12	14
Willow Height (ft)	2	5	8	11	14

The table shows that the amount by which the height of the redwood exceeded the height of the willow decreased each year.

In 1994, both trees were the same height.

Try It

a. Water from an 8,550 ft^3 water tank is used at a rate of 475 ft^3 per day. Water from a 7,200 ft^3 tank is used at a rate of 250 ft^3 per day. If no water is replaced, how much water will be in each tank when the two tanks hold equal amounts?

b. Quality-control personnel in a blue jean sewing plant check every sixteenth pair of jeans for color and every twenty-eighth pair for size. How often is a pair of jeans checked for both color and size?

Guess and Check

Problem Solving

STRATEGIES

• Look for a Pattern
• Make an Organized List
• Make a Table
• Guess and Check
• Work Backward
• Use Logical Reasoning
• Draw a Diagram
• Solve a Simpler Problem

If you're not sure how to solve a problem, make an educated guess at the answer. Check your guess. If it's wrong, revise your first guess by adding or subtracting. Repeat the pattern of *guess-check-revise* until you find the answer. ◄

Example

At a library book sale, Marika used an equal number of quarters and nickels to buy a $1.20 book. How many of each coin did she use?

Guess: Make an educated guess.

3 quarters and 3 nickels

$(3 \times \$0.25) + (3 \times \$0.05) = \$0.90$

Check: The total is too low.

Revise: Add to the first guess.

5 quarters and 5 nickels

$(5 \times \$0.25) + (5 \times \$0.05) = \$1.50$

Check: The total is too great.

Revise: The number is between 3 and 5.

4 quarters and 4 nickels

$(4 \times \$0.25) + (4 \times \$0.05) = \$1.20$

Check: It works.

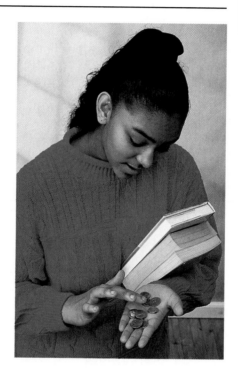

Marika used 4 quarters and 4 nickels.

Try It

a. In the championship basketball game, Corey scored 25 points total on 2-point goals and 3-point goals. He hit 5 more 2-pointers than 3-pointers. How many of each did he hit?

b. Yolanda drove 600 mi from Castleton to Monroe. She returned to Castleton at a 10 mi/hr slower average speed. She drove 22 hr total. Find her average speed in each direction.

Problem Solving

STRATEGIES

• Look for a Pattern
• Make an Organized List
• Make a Table
• Guess and Check
• **Work Backward**
• Use Logical Reasoning
• Draw a Diagram
• Solve a Simpler Problem

Work Backward

A problem may give the result of a series of steps and ask you to find the initial value. To solve the problem, you can work backward step-by-step until you get to the beginning. ◄

Example

Laura, Seth, and Keena volunteered to wash a box of test tubes in the chemistry lab. Laura took half the total, Seth took two-thirds of what was left, and Keena took the remaining 8. How many test tubes were in the box?

The problem describes three steps occurring in order:

1. Laura took half the test tubes.

2. Seth took test tubes.

3. Keena took test tubes.

It also tells you the end result of 0 test tubes remaining. To solve the problem, work backward to the beginning.

Step	What Happened	Conclusion
3	Keena took 8 test tubes, leaving none.	Before this step, Seth left 8 test tubes.
2	Seth took two-thirds of the test tubes, leaving 8.	Before this step, Laura left 24 test tubes because 8 is *one-third* of the number Laura left.
1	Laura took half the test tubes, leaving 24.	Before this step, the number of test tubes was *twice* 24, or 48.

The box must have contained 48 test tubes.

Try It

a. Max, Holly, and Kim divided a carton of tennis balls among themselves. Max took half the balls. Holly took three-fourths of what was left. Kim took the remaining 3 balls. How many balls were in the carton?

b. Art is running in a 10 km race. When he has run three times as far as he has already run, he'll be 4 km from the end. How far has he run?

Use Logical Reasoning

Problem Solving
STRATEGIES

• Look for a Pattern
• Make an Organized List
• Make a Table
• Guess and Check
• Work Backward
• Use Logical Reasoning
• Draw a Diagram
• Solve a Simpler Problem

To solve a problem using logical reasoning, decide how the facts relate to each other. Then work your way step-by-step to a sensible solution. Be careful not to make conclusions that are not based on facts. ◄

Example

Polly, Ike, and Fred have a dog, a cat, and a parakeet for pets, though not necessarily in that order. Ike is allergic to feathers. The dog owner is Polly's friend and Ike's classmate. Match the owners with their pets.

Take clues one at a time. Use a grid to keep track of your conclusions.

1. Ike is allergic to feathers.

	Dog	Cat	Parakeet
Polly			
Ike			No
Fred			

2. The dog owner is Polly's friend and Ike's classmate.

	Dog	Cat	Parakeet
Polly	No		
Ike	No		No
Fred			

Fred must be the dog owner.

Ike must be the cat owner.

That means Polly owns the parakeet.

	Dog	Cat	Parakeet
Polly	No	No	Yes
Ike	No	Yes	No
Fred	Yes	No	No

Try It

a. Jane, Gus, and Tim visited Canada, Peru, and France. Jane has never been to Europe. Tim plays bridge with the person who visited Canada but not the one who went to France. Match the people with their vacation spots.

b. Tom, Zeno, and Rosa are a farmer, a pilot, and a doctor. Zeno can't tell a pig from a hog. Neither he nor Rosa is a pilot. Match each person with his or her occupation.

→

Draw a Diagram

Some problems may involve objects or positions. To solve the problem, draw a diagram and use it to visually identify relationships between the data. Then use the relationships to find the answer. ◄

Example

The Hawaiian volcano Mauna Kea is 33,480 ft tall. Also in Hawaii, the volcano Kilauea rises 4,077 ft above sea level. Mauna Kea has 19,684 ft of its height below sea level. How much taller than Kilauea is Mauna Kea?

Draw a sketch to compare the heights.

By looking at the sketch, we can determine by substracting that 13,796 ft of Mauna Kea is above sea level.

$33,480 - 19,684 = 13,796$

Also, $13,796 - 4,077 = 9,719$

Mauna Kea is 9,719 ft taller than Kilauea.

Try It

a. A pilot is 3,800 ft below the clouds. A plane at a lower altitude is 5,500 ft above the ground. The clouds are at 12,000 ft altitude. Find the difference in altitude between the planes.

b. A tree branch divides into 2 branches. Each smaller branch divides into 3 branches. Each of these divides into 5 branches. How many branches of all sizes are there?

Solve a Simpler Problem

Problem Solving

STRATEGIES

• Look for a Pattern
• Make an Organized List
• Make a Table
• Guess and Check
• Work Backward
• Use Logical Reasoning
• Draw a Diagram
• Solve a Simpler Problem

A problem may seem very complex. It may contain large numbers or appear to require many steps to solve. Instead of solving the complex problem, try a similar problem that is simpler to solve. After solving the simpler problem, look for shortcuts, patterns, or relationships to solve the original problem. ◄

Example

At the Oh, Grow Up! Nursery, tree seedlings are raised in square plots that are side by side. Each square side is a 1 m section of fence. What is the total length of fence needed for a row of 25 tree plots?

You could sketch all 25 plots and then count the number of 1 m fence sections. That would be very time-consuming. So instead solve the simpler problem for 1, 2, and 3 tree plots.

1 square: □ 4 m of fence sections are needed.

2 squares: □□ 7 m of fence sections are needed.

3 squares: □□□ 10 m of fence sections are needed.

Notice that 4 fence sections are needed for the first square. For all tree plots after that, only three 1 m fence sections are needed.

Of the 25 tree plots, 1 tree plot requires 4 m of fence. The other 24 tree plots will each require 3 m of fence.

$4 + (24 \times 3) = 4 + 72 = 76$

76 m of fence are needed.

Try It

a. When 3 points are marked on a line segment, as in the figure, 3 line segments can be identified. How many segments can be counted if you mark 12 points on a line segment?

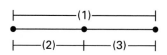

b. Suppose you earned $1 on your first day at a job, $2 the second day, $4 the third day, $8 the fourth day, and so on. How much would your total earnings be after 15 days?

1 Data Analysis

Cultural Link
www.mathsurf.com/8/ch1/people

Entertainment Link
www.mathsurf.com/8/ch1/ent

People of the World

Swahili is a trade and governmental language that is spoken in the Congo region and in East Africa. Swahili number words are shown.

1	moja
2	mbili
3	tatu
4	nne
5	tano
6	sita
7	saba
8	nane
9	tisa
10	kumi

Arts & Literature

Horace was a Roman poet who wrote odes and odes of poems and had something to say about statistics.

"We are just statistics, born to consume resources."

Entertainment

Television makes big bucks on advertising things from what we wear to what we eat. Almost $2 billion was spent on television ads for clothing and food in 1990.

Science

Between 1980 and 1990 the occurance of measles increased by 14,300 cases. Measles are caused by a virus and usually cause red circular spots on the skin.

KEY MATH IDEAS

Data can be useful and informative when presented in charts, tables, diagrams, and graphs.

Sometimes a single number, such as the mean, median, or mode, can help you understand the meaning of a set of data.

Surveys are used to collect data for a variety of purposes, such as political elections, advertising, and taste tests.

A sample is the part of the population that participates in a survey.

Social Studies

To show numbers, Mayans drew dots, lines, and ovals. When an oval is below a number, the result is 20 times larger.

For instance: • = 1;
🔔 = 1 × 20 = 20.

CHAPTER PROJECT

Problem Solving
Understand
Plan
Solve
Look Back

In this project, you will create a profile of the typical 13- or 14-year-old. You will design a survey to collect all the data needed to draw this profile. Data collected might include favorite subject, teacher, sports, games, hobbies, clubs, music, movies, or food.

3

**Problem
Solving**

Understand
Plan
Solve
Look Back

Problem Solving Focus

Read each problem and
answer the questions
about the problem.

Reading the Problem

As you read a
problem, you may
be overwhelmed by
information. Breaking
the information into
small parts can help
you understand what
the problem is say-
ing. Ask yourself
questions to be
sure you understand
each part.

1 In skateboard competitions,
5 judges give scores based on
100 points and the highest
and lowest scores are thrown
out. The remaining 3 scores
are averaged to determine the
skater's score for the run.
Tess' scores were 82, 85, 87,
85, and 84. Mario's scores
were 83, 84, 85, 84, and 88.
Who won the race?

a. What is the problem about?

b. What is the problem asking?

c. What is the highest score for
Tess? For Mario?

d. What is the lowest score for
Tess? For Mario?

e. Write and answer a question
of your own.

2 The skateboard shop sells
custom-made skateboard
decks for $50, four wheels for
$29, bearings for $16, and
trucks for $35. They give a
20% discount on the custom-
made board. Ready-made
boards cost $99. Which skate-
board is less expensive?

a. What is the problem about?

b. What is the problem asking?

c. What is the total cost of the
custom-made skateboard
before the discount?

d. What is the discount on the
custom-made skateboard?

e. Write and answer a question
of your own.

4

Money In Money Out

ant to make a lot of money? Want to run a successful business? Then invent, make, or produce a product that teenagers will buy. Why? Because teens in the United States spend almost $100 billion each year. Not only do they spend a lot of money, teens also influence how their friends and families spend money.

What do teens spend their money on? It may be the latest music, fashions, or technology—all items that teens frequently know as much, if not more, about than adults.

Where do teens typically get their money? They get it the old-fashioned way—they earn it, by baby-sitting, mowing lawns, delivering newspapers, and doing household chores.

The really amazing thing is that the population of teens in the United States is increasing and has been since 1992. Experts expect the teen population to be about 34,900,000 by the year 2010. That's a lot of teenagers with a lot of money to spend.

1 How do you influence what is purchased for your household?

2 How do you think experts forecasted the teen population for the year 2010?

Line Plots and Stem-and-Leaf Diagrams

You'll Learn ...

■ how to understand data with line plots and stem-and-leaf diagrams

... How It's Used

Movie theater managers use stem-and-leaf diagrams to analyze the price of movie tickets across the nation.

Vocabulary

range

line plot

stem-and-leaf diagram

double stem-and-leaf diagram

▶ **Lesson Link** You have seen how data are used in newspapers and magazines. In this lesson, you will learn ways of using and comparing data. ◀

Explore Line Plots

Summer's Blockbusters

Summertime isn't just swimming and lemonade, it's also movies. Movie theaters and video stores do their best business in the summer. How many movies did you see this summer?

1. How many movies did each person in your group see in a movie theater? Plot your data as shown in the diagram (one X for each movie).

Movies in a Theater

```
                        x
        x               x
        x               x
     _____
      Damion          Shauna
```

Shauna saw 3 movies in a theater.

2. How many movies on video did each person see? Make a similar plot for this data.

3. Make another plot showing the total number of movies seen by each person in your group.

4. How many students in your group saw fewer than five movies? Between five and ten movies? More than ten movies?

5. Without counting, describe how you can determine by looking at your plot who saw the fewest movies? The most movies?

6. What can you report by looking at your line plots?

Learn Line Plots and Stem-and-Leaf Diagrams

When working with data it is useful to know the range of the set. The **range** of a data set is the difference between the highest and lowest values.

Between 1950 and 1990, the yearly number of tropical storms worldwide was as low as 2 (in 1982) and as high as 12 (in 1969).

The range of yearly tropical storms is 2 to 12, or 10.

A **line plot** is a display of data that shows how many times each data value occurs. Each time a data value occurs, a mark is made above that value on a number line.

Example 1

A media club had a quiz with the question, "How many cable television networks can you name?" The results were 8, 12, 16, 14, 17, 6, 6, 12, and 13. Make a line plot for the media club's data and report the results.

The range 6 to 17 is used to draw the axis.

Plot 2 Xs above 6 because 2 people each answered "6."

One student got a high score of 17.

Media Club's Cable TV Knowledge

Television networks

A **stem-and-leaf diagram** uses the digits of the data numbers to show the shape and distribution of a data set. Each data number is separated into a stem and leaf.

Example 2

In the 1995–1996 season, the total number of games won by each team of the Atlantic division of the Eastern National Hockey League (NHL-East) was 45, 41, 41, 39, 38, 37, and 22. Create a stem-and-leaf diagram to see how the Atlantic teams did.

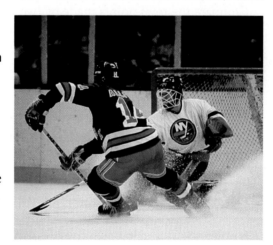

Use the tens digit as the stem. The range of wins is 22 to 45 so stems are 2 to 4. Use the ones digit as the leaf.

Stem	Leaf	
2	2	List ones digits of each stem in increasing order.
3	7 8 9	37 has a stem of **3** and a leaf of **7**.
4	1 1 5	Two teams had 41 wins.

The three strongest teams of the Atlantic NHL division each won over 40 games. The weakest team in the league won only 22 games.

A **double stem-and-leaf diagram** compares two sets of data in one diagram.

Remember

In the number 37, 3 is in the tens place and 7 is in the ones place.
(Previous course)

Example 3

In the 1995–1996 season, the Pacific NHL-West teams had win totals of 47, 32, 24, 30, 20, 34, and 35. Create a double stem-and-leaf diagram to compare the Atlantic and Pacific NHL teams.

Use the stem-and-leaf diagram from Example 2.

Add a new leaf column to the left of the stem. For each stem list ones digits of Pacific NHL wins in *decreasing* order in the new leaf column.

Stem	Leaf
2	2
3	7 8 9
4	1 1 5

Leaf	Stem	Leaf
4 0	2	2
5 4 2 0	3	7 8 9
7	4	1 1 5

The range of Pacific NHL wins is 20 to 47.

30 has a stem of 3 and a leaf of 0.

The double stem-and-leaf diagram shows that out of both NHL divisions the Atlantic NHL teams won the most games with scores greater than 40 in the 1995–1996 season.

Try It

Compare the total points made by two NBA Chicago Bulls starters, Michael Jordan and Scottie Pippen, during the six-game 1996 finals series. Use a double stem-and-leaf diagram.

Game	1	2	3	4	5	6
Jordan	28	29	36	23	26	22
Pippen	21	21	12	9	14	17

Check Your Understanding

1. When would you use a line plot? A stem-and-leaf diagram?

2. How can you determine the range of a set of data? Give two ways the range can be expressed.

Practice and Apply

Students in an Eighth Grade Class

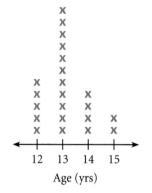

1. Getting Started

   a. The line plot represents the ages of students in an eighth grade class. How many 12-year-olds are there?

   b. What is the range of ages in this eighth grade class?

   c. What student age is most frequent? Least frequent?

State the range and draw a line plot for each data set.

2. A mother called some piano teachers in the Houston area to ask about prices for half-hour lessons. The prices quoted were $18, $20, $15, $17, $18, $21, and $17.

3. Kids in an arcade were asked, "How much money do you spend in an arcade each week?" Their answers, rounded to the nearest dollar, were $2.00, $3.00, $7.00, $5.00, $2.00, $4.00, $3.00, and $2.00.

4. Test Prep Eight gymnastics judges gave Kim scores of 8.9, 9.2, 9.0, 8.8, 9.1, 8.9, 9.2, and 9.1 for her performance on the uneven bars. Which of the following expresses the range of her scores?

   Ⓐ 8   Ⓑ 5   Ⓒ 0.4   Ⓓ 9.2

State the range and draw a stem-and-leaf diagram for each data set.

5. Science An aquarium has several species of tropical fish. The populations of each species are 23, 16, 8, 12, 18, 22, and 33.

6. Geography The table shows the number of school days per year. (The stem can have two digits.)

Country	Belgium	U.S.	Sweden	Mexico	Scotland	Israel	South Korea	Japan
School Days	160	180	180	180	200	215	220	243

7. Create a double stem-and-leaf diagram to compare nonschool days to school days of the countries listed in Exercise 6. To find the nonschool days of each country, subtract the number of school days from 365.

Problem Solving and Reasoning

8. Math Reasoning When the city schools take a two-week winter holiday, a skating rink gives students under 18 a discount to skate on weekdays. Make a stem-and-leaf diagram using a table which shows the daily number of students that take advantage of this discount. What days are represented in the stem with the most leaves?

Mon.	Tue.	Wed.	Thur.	Fri.	Mon.	Tue.	Wed.	Thur.	Fri.
64	52	57	51	42	44	39	42	52	55

9. Communicate Vicious pooches across the country bite mail carriers. Make a stem-and-leaf diagram of the serious dog bite counts. Write a paragraph about preventing these dog crimes.

> **Problem Solving TIP**
>
> Simply listing data in numerical order can give you a good start.

Houston	117	Chicago	75
Santa Ana	101	Fort Worth	66
South Florida	81	Long Beach	57
Central Florida	76	San Francisco	53
San Jose	75	Oakland	50

10. Critical Thinking Suppose a stem-and-leaf diagram has 2, 3, 4, and 5 listed in the stem column. What can you determine if there is nothing in the leaf column next to the 4?

11. 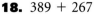 A double stem-and-leaf diagram compares two sets of data. Provide a specific situation and reasonable data that would be appropriate to display in a double stem-and-leaf diagram.

Mixed Review

Write each as a number. [*Previous course*]

12. eight million   **13.** four hundred thirty-seven   **14.** two thousand six hundred

15. fifty thousand   **16.** six thousand twenty-two   **17.** seven million thirty thousand

Add. [*Previous course*]

18. $389 + 267$ **19.** $295 + 430$ **20.** $439 + 27 + 64$ **21.** $8325 + 478$

22. $8376 + 8756$ **23.** $3740 + 2369$ **24.** $7345 + 3648$ **25.** $2669 + 7831$

Measures of Central Tendency

▶ **Lesson Link**   You know how to display data using line plots and stem-and-leaf diagrams. Now you will learn how to represent data with just one number. ◀

Explore   Mode, Median, and Mean

Middle America

The number of U.S. representatives each state sends to Congress depends on the state's population size. The map shows the number of representatives from the states between the Rocky Mountains and the Mississippi River.

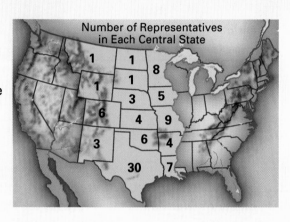

Number of Representatives in Each Central State

1. Use the map to create a line plot that shows how many states have the same number of representatives (for example, four states have one representative). Discuss your results.

2. What is the total number of representatives in this central region?

3. What is the greatest number of representatives in one state within this region? The least number of representatives?

4. What would you say is a typical number of representatives for a state in this region of the United States?

5. Suppose each of these 15 states had the same number of representatives and there were a total of 89 representatives in this region. How many representatives would each state have?

You'll Learn ...

■ how to analyze and represent data using mean, median, and mode

... How It's Used

Real estate agents use these numbers to determine how the housing market is behaving.

Vocabulary

measure of central tendency

mean

median

outlier

mode

Learn   Measures of Central Tendency

A **measure of central tendency** is a single value that summarizes a set of numerical data. The **mean**, or *average*, is the sum of a set of data divided by the number of data.

Example 1

Galileo discovered four large moons of Jupiter in 1610. The diameters of these moons are shown in the table. What is the mean diameter of these moons?

Moon	Moon's Diameter
Europa	3130 km
Io	3640 km
Callisto	4840 km
Ganymede	5270 km

$$\frac{3130 + 3640 + 4840 + 5270}{4} = 4220$$ Add all data. Divide by number of data.

The mean diameter of Jupiter's large moons is 4220 km.

The **median**, another measure of central tendency, is the middle value of a data set. It is identified when the data are arranged in numerical order. If there is an even number of data values, the median is the mean of the two middle values.

The median can be a better measure of central tendency than the mean when the data set has **outliers**, extreme values separated from most of the data set.

Example 2

An electronics store that wants more young customers sells CD players at the following prices: $350, $275, $500, $325, $100, $375, and $300. What is the median price? Are there any outlier prices?

Problem Solving TIP

It can be easier to see an outlier if you plot the data on a number line drawn to scale.

List values in numerical order.

The middle value is $325.

$100 and $500 are outliers.

Prices of CD Players

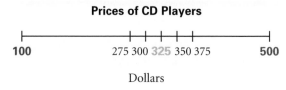

Dollars

The median price for a CD player is $325. The outlier prices are $100 and $500. The store should sell less expensive CD players so young people can afford them.

Example 3

Ten popular brands of berry-flavored sorbet have the following prices per cup: 69¢, 70¢, 59¢, 61¢, 66¢, 67¢, 70¢, 73¢, 66¢, and 93¢. Find the median price of these popular brands.

59, 61, 66, 66, 67, 69, 70, 70, 73, 93   List values in numerical order.

59, 61, 66, 66, *67*, *69*, 70, 70, 73, 93   There are two middle values.

$\dfrac{67 + 69}{2} = 68$ Find the mean of the two middle values.

68¢ is the median price per cup of popular brands of berry sorbet.

Example 4

Use your calculator to determine the mean per capita annual income of the following countries.

Guatemala	Tanzania	Indonesia	India	Hungary
$3,350	$580	$3,150	$1,220	$6,050

> **▶ Language Link**
>
> "Per capita" means "by heads" in Latin. "Per capita" can mean per person.

Enter 3350 [+] 580 [+] 3150 [+] 1220 [+] 6050 [=] *14350*

Enter [÷] 5 [=] *2870*

The mean per capita income is $2,870.

Try It

Ten people ages 12 to 15 were asked, "How much of your own money do you spend each week?"

The responses were $2, $10, $5, $15, $3, $5, $5, $15, $10, and $20.

Find the mean and median money spent per week by this group.

The **mode** is the *most common* data value. If no value occurs more than once, there is no mode.

The data in Example 3 has two modes, 66¢ and 70¢.

If every value in a set of data only occurs once then there is no mode.

The data in Example 1 has no mode.

Barry Bonds' yearly home run totals from 1987 to 1995 are listed. Would you find the mean, median, or mode to give a summary of his nine year performance?

Year	'87	'88	'89	'90	'91	'92	'93	'94	'95
Home Runs	25	24	19	33	25	34	46	37	33

Sarah thinks ...

I'll find the mean. First I'll add the number of home runs. Then I'll divide by 9, because I added 9 numbers.

$$\frac{25 + 24 + 19 + 33 + 25 + 34 + 46 + 37 + 33}{9} \approx 30.67$$

If I round the answer, the mean is 31 home runs per year.

Daniel thinks ...

I'll find the median and the mode. All I need to do is write the number of home runs in numerical order.

19, 24, 25, 25, 33, 33, 34, 37, 46

It looks like there are two modes: 25 and 33. They both appear twice.

The middle number is 33, so the median is 33.

What do you think?

1. Which mode is closer to the *center* of the data? Explain.

2. Why do you think the mean and median were almost the same?

Check | Your Understanding

1. What effect do outliers have on the mean and median of a data set?

2. Describe how to find the median of a data set that has an even number of values.

1-2 Exercises and Applications

Practice and Apply

1. **Getting Started** Jerry's test scores for last year's English class were 95, 70, 85, 88, 100, 71, 95, 80, and 90. Find the mean of his test grades.

   a. Find the sum of all of the scores.

   b. How many tests did Jerry take?

   c. Divide the sum by the number of tests to calculate the mean.

Find the mean, median, and mode of each data set.

2. Various brands of skateboards sell for $19.99, $22.99, $59.98, $39.98, $24.99, $27.99, and $29.99.

3. In a stack of paperback books, the total pages of each book are 139, 253, 130, 174, and 204.

4. **Science** Some of the longest times spent in space are 439 days, 115 days, 115 days, and 169 days.

5. **Science** During 1982–1990, the annual number of oil tanker spills worldwide was 9, 17, 15, 9, 8, 12, 13, 31, and 8. Identify the outlier and calculate the mean and median as if the outlier were not in the data set.

Geography The table shows the areas and 1992 populations for five east Asian countries. Use the table in Exercises 6–8.

Country	Area (thousands of mi^2)	Population (millions)
Indonesia	735	197
Japan	146	125
North Korea	47	22
Philippines	116	67
South Korea	38	44

6. What is the mean area of these countries? Is there an outlier?

7. What is the mean population size?

8. What is the mean population density— that is, population ÷ area?

9. **Test Prep** If a store manager says, "Size 10 is our best-selling women's coat size," what measure of central tendency is being used?

Ⓐ Mean   Ⓑ Median   Ⓒ Mode   Ⓓ Outlier

Problem Solving and Reasoning

10. **Communicate** The top ten American movies from 1980 to 1990 and their gross earnings (to the nearest million dollars) are shown in the table. Is there a relationship between the year of the movie and the movie's gross earnings? Explain.

E.T. (1982)	$400 mil	Back to the Future (1985)	$208 mil
Home Alone (1990)	$286 mil	Beverly Hills Cop (1984)	$235 mil
Ghostbusters (1984)	$221 mil	Raiders of the Lost Ark (1981)	$242 mil
Batman (1989)	$251 mil	The Empire Strikes Back (1980)	$223 mil
Ghost (1990)	$217 mil	Return of the Jedi (1983)	$263 mil

11. **Choose a Strategy** Last year the junior high spirit squad sold five items as homecoming souvenirs to raise money. They sold 61 pom-pons for $1 each, 57 pins for $1 each, 19 cups for $2 each, 45 key chains for $3 each, and 3 T-shirts for $22 each. What was the mean price for a homecoming souvenir? How did outlier prices affect the mean?

12. **Critical Thinking** Create sets of data with at least three values that will make each statement true.

   a. The mode is larger than the mean.

   b. The mean is larger than the median.

   c. The median is larger than the mean.

Problem Solving
STRATEGIES

• Look for a Pattern
• Make an Organized List
• Make a Table
• Guess and Check
• Work Backward
• Use Logical Reasoning
• Draw a Diagram
• Solve a Simpler Problem

Mixed Review

Write each number in words. *[Previous course]*

13. 856   **14.** 378   **15.** 4826   **16.** 2360

17. 45,600   **18.** 23,867   **19.** 3,746,700   **20.** 2,735,752

Subtract. *[Previous course]*

21. 768 − 42   **22.** 463 − 345   **23.** 634 − 236   **24.** 900 − 678

25. 4637 − 783   **26.** 6040 − 2783   **27.** 7823 − 2975   **28.** 4378 − 3774

Box-and-Whisker Plots

▶ **Lesson Link**   Now you will use your knowledge of the median to display data graphically. ◀

Explore   Quartiles

Rolling Sums

Materials: 2 number cubes

1. Roll both number cubes 20 times. Record the sum of each roll.

2. Find the median by listing the data in numerical order. Draw a double line where the median occurs. The ten lowest numbers should be on the left side of this line.

3. Find the median of the ten lowest numbers. Draw a straight line to show where this number would appear. Do the same for the ten highest numbers.

4. You have drawn three lines that divide your data into four parts. Discuss the significance of these four parts.

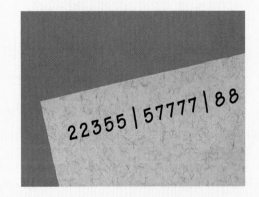

22355 | 57777 | 88

… How It's Used

Teachers use box-and-whisker plots to understand how students perform on national tests like the PSAT.

Learn   Box-and-Whisker Plots

A **box-and-whisker plot** is a visual way of showing median values for a set of data.

Quartiles are three numbers that divide a data set into four equal parts. The median is the middle quartile. Take the median of the upper and lower halves of the data set to find the other two quartiles.

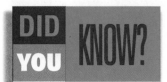
Suppose a student scores 97, 80, 85, 72, 65, 94, and 76, on seven quizzes.

| 65 | 72 | 76 | 80 | 85 | 94 | 97 |

↓ 72   ↓ 80   ↓ 94

The **lower quartile**, 72, is the median of the lower half of the data set.

The **upper quartile**, 94, is the median of the upper half of the data set.

The whiskers show the range to be 65 to 97.

The median is 80.

The box shows that the middle half of the grades are between **72** and **94**.

Math Quiz Grades

Lower quartile — Median — Upper quartile

65   72 80 94   97

Example 1

Below is a box-and-whisker plot showing the gross earnings of the top 50 movies in 1994. Give the range and median. What does the whisker left of the median show?

1994 Movie Earnings ($ millions)

38.8 91.1
50.9
26.4   298.9

The range is $26.4 million to $298.9 million.   Look at the whiskers.

The median is $50.9 million.   Look at the middle line in the box.

The whisker left of the median shows that one-quarter of the movies grossed between $26.4 million and $38.8 million.

Try It

One hundred 12 to 15 year olds were asked how many times they had been in a music store within the past 30 days. The results are shown in the box-and-whisker plot.

Number of Times Teens Browse Music Stores

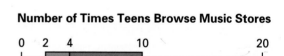

0 2 4   10   20

a. What is the range of the data?   **b.** What is the median?

c. What are the lower and upper quartiles?

d. What does the whisker to the right of the median show?

Example 2

When businesses look for employees they often post a classified ad in a big newspaper. The daily price for one line of an ad can vary. Some possible prices are:

$4.20 $4.49 $4.83 $5.24 $5.72 $6.29

$7.01 $7.97 $8.49 $9.73 $10.38 $13.79

$15.31 $16.77

JOB OPPORTUNITIES

HELP WANTED
Great after school job
serving ice cream
M – F,   4 – 6 p m
Call 555-CONE

HELP WANTED

▶ **Career Link**

Looking at the help-wanted ads will keep you informed about the jobs that are available.

Create a box-and-whisker plot of these prices. Between what values does the middle half of the prices fall?

The range of prices is from $4.20 to $16.77.   Find the range.

$$\frac{\$7.01 + \$7.97}{2} = \$7.49 \text{ is the median price}$$ Find the median.

$4.20, $4.49, $4.83, $5.24, $5.72, $6.29, $7.01   Find median of lower half.

$7.97, $8.49, $9.73, $10.38, $13.79, $15.31, $16.77   Find median of upper half.

The lower quartile price is $5.24 and the upper quartile price is $10.38.

The middle half of the prices are between $5.24 and $10.38.

Draw a line showing the range.

Plot the median and the quartiles.

Draw a box between the quartiles.

Write a title.

Daily Prices for an Employment Classified Ad ($)

Lower   Median   Upper
quartile   quartile
5.24   7.49   10.38
4.20   16.77

Try It

Ten 12 to 15 year olds were asked, "What age would you rather be?" The results were 17, 18, 16, 20, 15, 18, 17, 16, 17, 16. Create a box-and-whisker plot of these desired ages. Between what values does the middle half of the data fall?

ESTIMATION

When you mark the median and quartiles on a box-and-whisker plot, round the numbers so they are easier to plot.

Check | Your Understanding

1. How do outliers affect the size of the whiskers on a box-and-whisker plot?

2. In a box-and-whisker plot, how much of the data is in the box? In each whisker? Explain.

Practice and Apply

1. **Getting Started** At a local school's mathematics competition, one team's members obtained scores, in ascending order, of 90, 93, 94, 95, 96, 99, and 100. Follow the steps to prepare a box-and-whisker plot for this data.

   a. Find the highest and lowest scores and draw a line covering the entire range.

   b. Identify the median on the number line.

   c. Identify the lower quartile by finding the median of the lower half of the scores.

   d. Identify the upper quartile by finding the median of the upper half of the scores.

   e. Draw a box from the lower quartile to the upper quartile. Then draw the whiskers.

Sketch a box-and-whisker plot for each set of data. Between what values does the middle half of the data fall?

2. **Science** During the 1980s, the largest major earthquakes around the world registered 7.3, 7.2, 7.7, 7.1, 7.8, 8.1, 7.3, 6.5, 7.3, 6.8, and 6.9 on the Richter Scale.

3. **Consumer** In a mail-order clothing retailer's summer catalog, different models of girls' swimsuits sell for $25, $16, $20, $23, $22, $25, $24, and $20.

4. **Test Prep** What is the upper quartile of the data whose box-and-whisker plot is shown?

   Ⓐ 28   Ⓑ 31   Ⓒ 36   Ⓓ 45

Ages of People in a Ballroom Dancing Class

23   28   31   36   45

5. In 1991, the ten largest U.S. cities had the following burglary rates (per 100,000 people): 1524, 1615, 1858, 2385, 1344, 1507, 2515, 3064, 2432, and 2609. Draw a box-and-whisker plot and discuss the results.

PRACTICE 1-3

6. The following numbers represent the number of gallons of gas used per automobile in 1993 for each of ten U.S. states: 918, 698, 771, 624, 688, 760, 731, 789, 644, and 614. Draw a box-and-whisker plot. What states might one expect to find at the upper end of the plot?

Problem Solving and Reasoning

7. **Communicate** Which box-and-whisker plot would typically have longer whiskers: one for a data set with or without outliers? Explain.

8. **Medicine** Doctors often test for allergies by scratching some of the test substance into the patient's skin and later measuring the size of the resulting wheal, or bump. In one study, a substance produced different-sized bumps on different people. The data are summarized in this plot.

Wheal Size (mm²)

```
3    12   21        38                          77
|----[====|=========]-----------------------------|
```

What does this plot suggest? Give more than one interpretation of the data.

9. **Journal** For a box-and-whisker plot, describe in your own words what information you can get from the box, and what information you can get from the whiskers.

10. **Number Sense** Suppose a box-and-whisker plot displays a data set with 48 values. How many values are represented in the box?

Mixed Review

Multiply. *[Previous course]*

11. 237×78 12. 863×43 13. 326×61 14. 4362×47

15. 7348×76 16. 375×789 17. 432×636 18. 934×765

Round as indicated. *[Previous course]*

19. 43,644, nearest ten   20. 78,326, nearest hundred

21. 36,604, nearest thousand   22. 63,649, nearest ten

23. 46,351, nearest hundred   24. 87,486, nearest thousand

Bar Graphs and Line Graphs

You'll Learn ...

■ how to understand data using bar graphs and line graphs

... How It's Used

News reporters use graphs to help communicate important situations that involve numbers.

Vocabulary

bar graph

double bar graph

line graph

double line graph

▶ **Lesson Link** Last year you learned how to create bar graphs and line graphs. Now you will learn some variations of these graphs. ◀

Explore **Line Graphs**

Federal Minimum Wages

Year	1955	1960	1965	1970	1975	1980	1985	1990	1995
Wage	$0.75	$1.00	$1.25	$1.45	$2.10	$3.10	$3.35	$3.80	$4.25

The Fair Labor Standards Act of 1938 and its amendments are the reasons our country has a minimum hourly wage.

There have been different minimum wages for different jobs. For example, the wages for farm workers were lower than those of nonfarm workers.

This data shows the minimum wage every five years from 1955 to 1995.

1. In what year was the federal minimum wage the lowest? The highest?

2. What happened to the minimum wage from 1960 to 1965?

3. What was the minimum wage increase between 1975 and 1980?

4. What is the minimum wage now? Did it decrease or increase since 1995? By how much?

5. Discuss how the federal minimum wage might change in the future.

A **bar graph** uses bars to represent the values of a data set. Bar graphs are used to compare data from several situations. Each bar represents a category of data labeled on the horizontal axis. The height of the bars correlate with a number on the vertical axis.

Example 1

People ages 12 to 19 were asked when buying certain products did brand names matter to them.

A bar graph shows the results.

What percent of people prefer a specific brand of jeans? Gum?

Loyalty to Brand Names

About 50% think a brand name is important when buying jeans.

About **20%** think a brand name is important when buying gum.

> ► **Industry Link**
>
> Many companies hope that young people will be loyal to their brand. Companies think that when teenagers become adults they will still be loyal to the same brand name.

Try It

The bar graph shows the number of cellular phone subscribers (in thousands) from 1990 through 1994.

a. What year had the least number of subscribers?

b. What year had the greatest number of subscribers?

Cellular Phone Subscribers

A **double bar graph** shows two bar graphs together and compares two related data sets.

Example 2

Teenagers who buy music have different tastes from those who don't. Create a double bar graph to see what music style they disagree about most.

Music Style	Rap	Alternative	Country	Top 40
Buyers	81	61	41	61
Nonbuyers	73	46	51	57

The range of both data sets is from 41 to 81.

The bars for buyers and non-buyers are different colors.

Teenagers Talk Music

The greatest difference in taste is shown for alternative music. Buyers prefer it more than nonbuyers do.

A **line graph** is a line drawn through pairs of associated numbers on a grid. It is usually used to show changes over time.

Example 3

The table displays U.S. teenagers' income from 1986 to 1994. Display the data in a line graph to determine the year with the most dramatic increase.

Year	'86	'87	'88	'89	'90	'91	'92	'93	'94
Billions of Dollars	$65	$68	$73	$78	$94	$95	$88	$86	$96

The values, $65 billion to $96 billion, must be included in the vertical axis. Draw a break in the vertical axis because it does not start at zero.

Scale vertical axis with dollars and horizontal axis with years.

Plot the income for each year and draw a line through each point.

Label each axis and title the graph.

Teen income increased dramatically from 1989 to 1990.

Teen Income

A **double line graph** shows two line graphs together to compare two related data sets.

Example 4

The table shows some yearly median earnings for men and women (in thousands of dollars). Make a double line graph from the data.

Year	1988	1989	1990	1991	1992
Men	26.7	27.3	27.7	29.4	30.4
Women	17.6	18.8	19.8	20.6	21.4

The range of earnings, 17.6 to 30.4, is used to fit both line graphs.

The lines for men and women are different colors.

Men's salaries were higher than women's. Women's salaries show a slight increase since 1988.

Salaries of Men and Women

Try It

The table shows the number of Soviet and U.S. space launches. Make a double bar graph from the data.

Year	1980	1981	1982	1983	1984	1985
Soviet	89	98	191	98	97	98
United States	13	18	18	22	22	17

Check Your Understanding

1. Display the data of Example 4 in a double bar graph.

2. How is the range of data used in creating a line or bar graph? A double line or double bar graph?

3. Describe why the contrasts in a graph appear so dramatic when the vertical axis does not start at zero.

Practice and Apply

1. **Getting Started** Using the bar graph shown, create a line graph that shows the amount of money made by book publishing from 1988 through 1994.

   a. Draw a grid using the same scale on the vertical axis.

   b. Draw and label gridlines for the horizontal axis.

   c. Plot the points from the top of each bar.

   d. Connect the points with a line.

   e. Label the axes and title the line graph.

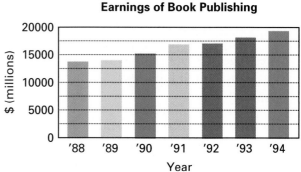

Earnings of Book Publishing

2. **Science** Create a bar graph to represent the data. Draw a conclusion about the relationship between life-span and size of animal based on the data.

Animal	Dog	Cat	Rabbit	Guinea Pig	Mouse
Average Life-Span (yr)	12	12	5	4	3

3. **Career** Create a line graph to represent the data. Draw a conclusion about the number of U.S. postmasters after 1994.

Year	1988	1989	1990	1991	1992	1993	1994
Thousands of Postmasters in U.S.	28	27	27	27	26	25	27

4. **Industry** Draw a line graph of the average monthly production of cars (in thousands) in the U.S. from 1986 to 1992. About how many cars were made in 1990?

Year	1986	1987	1988	1989	1990	1991	1992
Cars	474	451	504	567	592	590	626

5. **Test Prep** Which graph would be most appropriate to compare the amounts of money spent by high school boys and girls on food, clothes, transportation, and entertainment?

   Ⓐ Mean   Ⓑ Double line graph

   Ⓒ Bar graph   Ⓓ Double bar graph

Problem Solving and Reasoning

6. **Journal** Explain why a line graph would not be an appropriate choice for displaying the animal life-span data in Exercise 2.

7. **Critical Thinking** The percent of women competing in the Olympic Games has increased since the Games opened in 1896. Data from selected Olympiads are presented in the graph below.

Olympic Competitions

Great Britain's Charlotte Cooper. 1900 Paris Olympics.

United States' Monica Seles. 1996 Atlanta Olympics.

What if someone wanted to present the data using a bar graph instead? Would this method be just as appropriate as a line graph? Explain.

8. **Communicate** What type of graph would be appropriate to present the population of the ten largest states in the United States? Explain.

Mixed Review

Divide. *[Previous course]*

9. 208 ÷ 8   **10.** 259 ÷ 7   **11.** 504 ÷ 14   **12.** 923 ÷ 13   **13.** 522 ÷ 73

Order from least to greatest. *[Previous course]*

14. 879, 789, 897, 798   **15.** 735, 4321, 578, 2378   **16.** 1121, 1211, 1112

17. 4725, 4257, 4527   **18.** 3100, 3010, 301, 3000   **19.** 684, 654, 642, 664

Project Progress

Use your survey to prove something about the people in your age group. Ask questions that will give you numerical results and consider the kind of graph that would be most appropriate for your data.

Problem Solving

Understand
Plan
Solve
Look Back

T E C H N O L O G Y

Using a Spreadsheet • Creating Graphs From Data

Problem: Given the following data set of minimum wages from 1955 to 1997, how could you create a graph that would help you see a trend in the data? Note that the data is given in year-wage pairs.

Data set: 1955, 0.75; 1956, 1.00; 1961, 1.15; 1963, 1.25; 1967, 1.40; 1968, 1.60; 1974, 2.00; 1975, 2.10; 1978, 2.65; 1979, 2.90; 1980, 3.10; 1981, 3.35; 1990, 3.80; 1991, 4.25; 1996, 4.75; 1997, 5.15.

You can use your spreadsheet program to help you create the necessary graph.

1 Enter the data in your spreadsheet as shown.

	A	B
1	Yr.	Minimum wage
2	1955	0.75
3	1956	1.00
4	1961	1.15
5	1963	1.25

Solution: A line or bar graph will show a trend of increasing minimum wages over the years.

2 Using your spreadsheet's built-in graphing capabilities, choose a graph for your data.

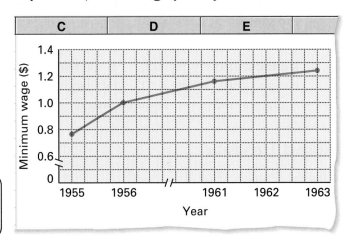

TRY IT

Using your spreadsheet, create a reasonable graph for each of the following data sets:

a. Weekly earnings: Week 1, $12; Week 2, $15; Week 3, $18; Week 4, $21; Week 5, $24.

b. Test Scores: Test 1, 100; Test 2, 95; Test 3, 85; Test 4, 70; Test 5, 60.

ON YOUR OWN

▶ Do you think a spreadsheet automatically gives you the most reasonable graph of your data? Explain.

▶ Which is easier, to generate a graph using a spreadsheet or by hand? Explain.

▶ What kinds of information can you obtain from your graphs?

In this section, you have learned how to create graphs and use them to understand data. In the Connect, you will have a chance to answer a question of your own choosing.

Money in Money out

Materials: Calculator, graph paper

Many people stop at convenience stores to buy soda, gum, candy, or a sandwich. Often people buy things they didn't plan to purchase; this is called "impulse buying."

In a group, talk about how you shop. What do you usually buy when you go shopping? Why would you buy an item on impulse?

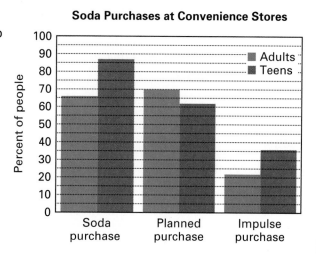

Soda Purchases at Convenience Stores

1. What conclusions can your group draw from the bar graph?

2. Make two lists of purchases you made in convenience stores in the past month: one of things you bought on impulse and another of things you planned to buy. (Try to list at least five items in each list.)

3. Estimate the price of each item in the lists. Use your calculator to calculate the measures of central tendency for each list. Create a box-and-whisker plot for both of your lists.

4. Create a double bar graph that compares the total you spent on planned purchases and impulse purchases. Compare your graph to those of other members in your group.

5. Use data from the most impulsive and least impulsive shoppers in your group to create a double bar graph.

1. The table shows how the Detroit Tigers placed in the American League baseball teams in the 1930s. Find their mean, median, and mode place finishes during the 1930s. Draw a line plot to show the mode.

Year	1930	1931	1932	1933	1934	1935	1936	1937	1938	1939
Place	5th	7th	5th	5th	1st	1st	2nd	2nd	5th	5th

2. Create a stem-and-leaf diagram for the data: 11, 64, 11, 53, 29, 43, 46.

Geography The table shows data on ten nations of the west African coast.

3. Find the mean area and population of these countries.

4. Create a box-and-whisker plot for the area of these countries.

5. Create a box-and-whisker plot and bar graph for the population of these countries.

6. **Communicate** Describe a possible relationship between the area of one of these African countries and its population. Use your results from Exercises 2–5.

Country	Area (thousands of km²)	Population (millions)
Senegal	197	8.2
Gambia	11	1.1
Guinea-Bissau	36	1.1
Guinea	246	6.4
Sierra Leone	72	4.6
Liberia	111	2.9
Côte d'Ivoire	322	13.9
Ghana	239	16.9
Togo	57	4.3
Benin	113	5.3

7. **Journal** In 1994, the mean attendance of the Colorado Silver Bullets baseball team's first 44 games was 6595 fans. There were 7462 fans at game 45, the final game. What was the mean attendance for all games? Describe how you solved this problem.

Test Prep

On a multiple choice test, you need to understand the question in order to choose the correct answer.

8. Given the data set 3, 14, 26, 30, 22, 78, 7, and 12, which of the following numbers would best represent the mean of this data?

Ⓐ 24   Ⓑ 8   Ⓒ 40.5   Ⓓ 14

Who Asked You ANYWAY?

Yes   No

You are alone in the shopping mall, window-shopping, minding your own business. In the store window you see the reflection of a stranger approaching you with something in his hand. He taps you on the shoulder and you whirl around, your eyes resting on the object in his hand—a clipboard. The stranger is conducting a survey and wants to know what you think.

Your answers and the answers of others surveyed will become data and decisions will be made based on that data. Who makes those decisions and what do they want to know?

One kind of survey is called a product test in which you try a new product and report what you think of it. A taste test is one kind of product test in which you sample different foods and give your reactions. Sometimes you may be paid to participate in a product test.

A good survey requires careful planning beforehand. Sometimes there are questions that research cannot answer, and in those cases, people conducting the survey must use their best judgment.

1 What difficulties might you encounter conducting a survey?

2 What else do you think a survey can be used for?

3 If you've been part of a survey, describe what you did. What questions did you answer?

31

Understanding Surveys

▶ **Lesson Link** You learned how to use graphs to interpret data. Now you will see how data can be collected from a survey. ◀

You'll Learn ...

■ to understand surveys and consider how a sample affects survey results

... How It's Used

Legislators draw possible conclusions from survey results.

Vocabulary

survey

population

sample

random sample

Explore | A Survey

Radio or Magazine?

You're on an advertising team and designing a new ad campaign. The team asks people, "Do you spend more of your free time listening to the radio or reading magazines?"

1. In a column, write the names of ten classmates. Who do you think spends more of their free time listening to the radio? Write *radio* next to their names. Write *magazine* next to the names of those you think spend more free time reading magazines.

2. Make a bar graph that compares the radio people to the magazine people.

3. What other questions would you ask to help design an ad campaign? Discuss why you chose those questions.

4. What answers would you expect for each question? Would those answers differ if you only asked adults? Only senior citizens?

5. As a group, create a slogan for a radio ad and another for a magazine to promote a product of your choice.

Learn | Understanding Surveys

If you need data to answer a question then you should conduct a **survey**, a study that requires collecting information and analyzing it.

A survey is taken of a **population**, the collection of all things to be studied. A survey usually uses a **sample**, a part of the population.

Example 1

Two days before the election results, a telephone survey of 2000 town residents was taken and they were asked, "Who do you think will win the mayoral election?"

HINT

When you subtract more than one number, you don't have to press $=$ more than once.

$2000 - 16 - 52$

would be entered as:

$2000 \; \boxed{-} \; 16 \; \boxed{-} \; 52 \; \boxed{=}$

There were 16 busy signals and 52 answering machines. The surveyors did not have enough time to call these people back.

What is the population of this survey? The size of the sample?

The population of the survey is all the town residents.

$2000 - 16 - 52 = 1932$ Calculate the total people surveyed.

The sample size of the survey is 1932 people.

When designing a survey, the sample size is an important consideration. For example, if a survey of the nation's taste in music were taken, then a sample size of 100 people may not be representative of the entire country.

A sample that is representative of the population is often called a random sample. A **random sample** is a sample chosen in such a way that everyone in the population has an equal chance of being in the sample.

Example 2

Determine whether or not the following are random samples.

a. A leading beeper company selects every seventy-fifth pager from the assembly line to be tested.

All of the first beepers do not have a chance of being in the sample. This is not a random sample.

b. A disc jockey writes ten song titles on separate cards, shuffles them, and chooses one card.

This is a random sample (if the DJ can't see the song titles).

Now that it's easy to get "cool" graphics on a computer, there are many opportunities for people to design Web sites for companies.

Example 3

2746 people visited a World Wide Web site for a recent movie. Only 585 people answered a questionnaire. The results of the survey indicated that 447 of these people rated the movie a 10.

What is the sample size? Is the sample random?

The sample is the group that answered the questionnaire. The sample size is 585 people.

The sample for this survey is not random, because people who do not use computers or the Web did not have equal opportunity to participate in the survey.

Try It

3786 people visited the home page for a television show. Out of these visitors, 679 people answered a questionnaire on the home page.

a. What is the sample size?

b. Is the sample random?

Check Your Understanding

1. Describe how you can distinguish between a random sample and a sample that is not random.

2. Give examples of a random sample and a sample that is not random.

3. Can you think of some ways a survey is used?

4. How do you think sample size affects a survey's results?

Practice and Apply

1. **Getting Started** A door-to-door survey of city households was conducted. After one week, 2567 homes were visited. There were 252 homes with no one home, and 14 with only out-of-town house guests. What is the population of this survey? The sample size?

2. **Consumer** Eight boys and 13 girls between the ages of 12 and 14 were asked how much of their own money they spend every week. The boys' mean answer was $10, the girls' $6. Are these results representative of all people aged 12–14? Justify your answer.

For Exercises 3–6, state the population and whether or not the sample is random.

3. **Social Studies** For the population of U.S. state governors: five cards are drawn from a deck of 50 that have a different governor's name on each.

4. **Consumer** For the population of potential car buyers: a dealership specializing in sport utility vehicles asks every visitor what he or she wants from a car.

5. **Music** For the population of country music fans: randomly chosen attendees of a country music concert are asked about their favorite performers.

6. **Science** A biologist samples the number of flowers on fruit trees that are 1, 2, 3, and 4 years old.

7. **Industry** A food manufacturer is developing a new barbecue sauce. After revising the recipe a couple of times, the people in the test kitchen—a crew of four— agree that they have a winner. Is this representative of the sauce's national success? Explain.

8. To fine-tune its recipe, the same food manufacturer conducted a blind taste test at a Texas county fair, using its sauce and a competitor's. 481 tasters participated. How useful will the data be to the manufacturer in deciding whether the sauce will sell well nationally? Explain.

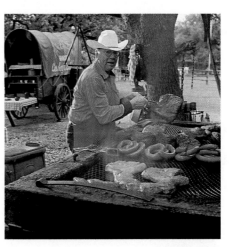

9. **Consumer** A cosmetic company gave out 9120 free jars of *anti-aging wrinkle fighter* cream to women who would use the cream for ten days and complete a questionnaire. Only 7244 questionnaires were returned.

   a. What is the population of this survey?

   b. What is the sample size of the survey?

10. **Test Prep** Rex wants to find out what the students at his school think about pop quizzes. Which of the samples is most representative?

    Ⓐ 22 students at random   Ⓑ 26 students in his math class

    Ⓒ Everyone in his chess club   Ⓓ 12 students on his bus

Problem Solving and Reasoning

11. **Critical Thinking** A research group mailed a questionnaire with a $1 bill to 15,000 adults. This survey technique got an 82 percent response rate. Was the sample random? Explain.

12. **Journal** The two bar graphs below show the same data. Describe the difference between the graphs and how each graph would be used.

13. **Communicate** A research group found that of 529 purchases of flu medication, only 145 were made by the person using the product. Describe how this might affect the advertising of the medication.

14. **Choose a Strategy** To help school officials prepare for a "Say No To Drugs" campaign, you are asked to survey students on their feelings about drugs. How would you conduct this survey, keep all information confidential, and obtain a high rate of response?

Problem Solving STRATEGIES

- Look for a Pattern
- Make an Organized List
- Make a Table
- Guess and Check
- Work Backward
- Use Logical Reasoning
- Draw a Diagram
- Solve a Simpler Problem

Mixed Review

Add or subtract. *[Previous course]*

15. $32,897 + 23,563$ 16. $73,734 - 29,823$ 17. $736,629 + 237,723$

Make a line plot for each set of data. *[Lesson 1-1]*

18. 45, 49, 53, 54, 57, 49, 58, 52   19. 3, 4, 5, 3, 2, 4, 3, 4, 5, 3, 5, 2, 4, 2

20. 8, 12, 9, 11, 13, 10, 9, 10, 8, 10   21. 24, 26, 25, 28, 24, 25, 21, 25, 24

Recording and Organizing Data

▶ **Lesson Link** You've learned about different ways of presenting data. Now you will learn how to organize collected data. ◀

Explore Organizing Data

Music for the Masses

Materials: Graph paper

1. Instruct each member of your group to answer all of the questions to the right.

2. Have every member of your group record this information.

3. Compare how each of you organized the data. Notice the similarities and differences.

4. Exchange data with another group by trading one set of recorded data. Now your sample is larger.

5. Use this larger sample to calculate the mean and median of (1) the number of audio CDs purchased per month; (2) the number of audio cassettes purchased per month; and (3) the number of both purchased per month.

6. Have each group member create a display of the data (for example, a bar graph, line graph, box-and-whisker plot, and so on) using the data from your larger sample.

7. Make a conclusion based on each group member's display of data.

8. Can you make a conclusion representative of your class? Representative of your school? Your town? Why or why not?

How many audio CDs do you buy each month?

How many audio cassettes?

What is your favorite type of music?

Who is your favorite musical performer?

You'll Learn ...

■ to organize data and choose an appropriate method of organization

... How It's Used

Pollsters, people who take polls and surveys, understand the purpose of their data in order to organize their data appropriately.

Vocabulary

tally

frequency

frequency table

histogram

Learn | Recording and Organizing Data

No matter what you're investigating, collecting data is likely to involve a lot of counting. A **tally** is used as a quick way to record the counting. Tallies are used to determine **frequency**, how often something happens.

A **frequency table** shows classes of things, a tally, and the frequency at which they occur.

The frequency table here shows car colors seen in a parking lot.

The tally marks are used to count the cars.

Line plots or stem-and-leaf diagrams are useful for counting data values (for example, age, grade).

Color of Car	Tally	Frequency
Blue	ⵜⵜ⎟⎟	7
White	⎟⎟⎟⎟	4
Yellow	ⵜⵜ ⵜⵜ	10
Red	ⵜⵜ ⎟⎟	7

Histograms are useful for equal intervals (for example, decades, age groups).

Example 1

Magazines have many ads. The number of full-page ads in 13 issues of a popular magazine is shown in the table. Display the data shown in the frequency table as a line plot.

Number of Full-Page Ads	Frequency
32	2
33	7
35	3
37	1

Number of Full-Page Ads

```
      X
      X
      X
      X
      X     X
 X    X     X
 X    X     X        X
 ←─┼──┼──┼──┼──┼──┼─→
  32 33 34 35 36 37
```

The number of full-page ads is used to make the horizontal axis.

The frequency is shown by the number of Xs.

Try It

Use the data in the table to make a line plot showing the age of people who said, "I would buy more chewing gum if the design on the package changed."

Age	Frequency
14	9
15	7
16	4

Example 2

At the end of each episode of a TV talk show, viewers are invited to write to the show's producers. They are asked to give their age and state the topics they'd like to see addressed on the show.

Use the frequency table to create a histogram.

All of the intervals are equal (ten years).

Drawing a histogram is just like drawing a bar graph.

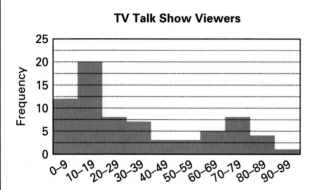

TV Talk Show Viewers

Interval (ages)	Frequency
0–9	12
10–19	20
20–29	8
30–39	7
40–49	3
50–59	3
60–69	5
70–79	8
80–89	4
90–99	1

By looking at the histogram, you can see that the 10–19 age group is a very responsive audience for this talk show.

Try It

Greenlee Street is a 30 mi/hr traffic zone. The frequency chart shows the speeds (to the nearest mi/hr) for which people received tickets on Greenlee Street. Create a histogram from the chart.

Speed Range	Tally	Frequency
36-40 mi/hr	⦀⦀	5
41-45 mi/hr	⦀⦀ ⦀⦀⦀	8
46-50 mi/hr	⦀⦀ ⦀⦀ ⦀⦀	12
51-55 mi/hr	⦀⦀ ⦀	6
56-60 mi/hr	⦀⦀⦀	3

SPEED LIMIT 30

Check   Your Understanding

1. Make a list of situations where knowing the frequency is important.

2. When have you used a tally in the past? How did you use your tally?

3. Why would you organize the data in Example 2 in a histogram rather than a line plot?

Practice and Apply

1. **Getting Started** The table gives a breakdown by age of the 1993 U.S. population.

   a. Construct a histogram using the given data.

   b. Could you use this data to construct a line plot? Explain.

   c. What kind of graph would address the question, "What is the relationship between age and number of people in the U.S. population?"

Age	Number (millions)
0–9	38
10–19	36
20–29	38
30–39	44
40–49	35
50–59	23
60–69	20
70–79	15
80–89	6
90–99	1
100+	< 0.5

2. **Science** Asteroids are chunks of rock orbiting the sun. Most of them are between the orbits of Mars and Jupiter. Astronomers have studied 105 of them to see how fast they rotate. The data is rounded to the nearest rotation and summarized in this histogram.

   a. How many asteroids have rotation speeds of four per day?

   b. Make a frequency table for this histogram.

   c. What is the mode?

Rotations of Asteroids

Rotations per day

3. **Social Studies** The table shows the 1980 Native American populations of ten states. Create a histogram, using intervals of 1000 on the vertical axis.

Cherokee basketry

State	Population	State	Population
Arkansas	9411	South Carolina	5758
Virginia	9336	Connecticut	4533
Nebraska	9197	Rhode Island	2898
Maine	4087	Hawaii	2778
Iowa	5453	Pennsylvania	9459

4. **Test Prep** A(n) _____ is a number of data values corresponding to one bar in a histogram.

Ⓐ Mode   Ⓑ Stem   Ⓒ Interval   Ⓓ Frequency

Problem Solving and Reasoning

5. Math Reasoning A small survey of people ages 12 to 19 was taken. The question was, "What is your number-one worry?" Each person gave one answer. The tallies were taken separately for males and females. Create a double bar graph and make a conclusion based on the frequencies.

#1 Worry	Females	Males
Grades	⦀⦀ ‖	⦀⦀
Having enough money	‖‖	⦀⦀
How I look	⦀⦀ ‖‖	‖‖
Planning my future	‖‖	‖
Parents	‖‖	‖‖
Being talked about	‖‖	‖‖

6. Communicate If you were a manufacturer of a product of your choice for young people, how would you use the "number-one worry" data from Exercise 5 to plan your advertising campaign for the next ten years? What is your product and how does it affect your ad campaign?

Mixed Review

Multiply or divide. *[Previous course]*

7. 7828×264 **8.** $2262 \div 87$ **9.** 9236×647 **10.** $3682 \div 78$

11. 7237×243 **12.** $7437 \div 105$ **13.** 6392×214 **14.** $9724 \div 173$

Find the mean and median of each data set. *[Lesson 1-2]*

15. 68, 39, 64, 52, 75, 64, 25, 34, 78   **16.** 167, 764, 375, 264, 763, 272

17. 78, 76, 79, 75, 74, 79, 68, 75   **18.** 4543, 4648, 4482, 2734, 4538

Scatterplots and Trends

You'll Learn ...

■ to make scatterplots and determine trends shown in the scatterplots

... How It's Used

Pediatricians use scatterplots and trend lines to determine whether a baby's growth is within normal ranges.

Vocabulary

scatterplot

trend

trend line

▶ **Lesson Link** You have used a grid to make line graphs. Now you will learn to show data on a grid and see trends in data. ◄

Explore Trend Lines

Value of a Dollar

Materials: Clear ruler, Graph paper

Over time, the dollar has gradually lost value (as have most other currencies around the world, because of inflation). The table shows the dollar's value, in 1994 terms, since 1980.

Year	'80	'82	'84	'86	'88	'90	'92	'94
Dollar Value	1.80	1.54	1.43	1.36	1.26	1.14	1.06	1.00

1. The scale of the horizontal axis should include the years 1980 to 1994.

2. The scale of the vertical axis should include $1.00 to $1.80. (This covers the entire range of data values.)

3. Plot each pair (year, dollar amount) as a point.

4. Use your ruler to draw the best straight line you can through or near all the points.

5. Compare your line to those of other people in your group.

6. Use your line to determine the expected value of the dollar (in 1994 terms) in the year 2000.

7. What are some reasons your expectation might not be accurate?

8. What kind of graph could you have drawn in Step 4, instead of drawing a straight line?

A **scatterplot** is a set of points that shows a relationship between two sets of data. Sometimes those points form a pattern. Such a pattern is called a **trend** . The line that approximately "fits" the points is the **trend line** . The trend line can be used to see expected future data values.

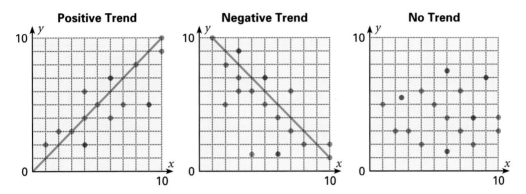

Positive Trend **Negative Trend** **No Trend**

The scatterplots and trend lines above show positive, negative, and no trend.

Example 1

The scatterplot shows the amount of waste we recycle or reuse compared to the total amount of waste we produce per year in the United States. Use the scatterplot and trend line to determine the trend between these two sets of data.

The trend line shows a positive trend.

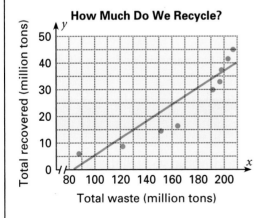

How Much Do We Recycle?

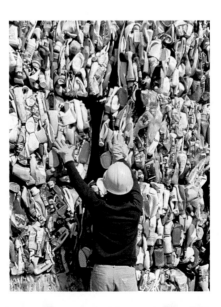

Problem Solving TIP

If a scatterplot appears to have a trend when you cover two points, then you can assume there is a trend.

Try It

State the relationship shown in the scatterplot.

When creating a scatterplot, you must first decide which data category to show on the horizontal axis and which category to show on the vertical axis. Then you must be sure to scale each axis to include all values that occur in the data set.

▶ **Science Link**

The temperature of the human body is normally 98.6° Fahrenheit.

Example 2

Create a scatterplot for the given data and determine a trend line between age and body temperature.

Use age to label the horizontal axis. Use body temperature to scale the vertical axis.

Plot the points.

There is no clear trend between age and body temperature.

Age	Body Temperature (°F)	Time in Morning
18	98.2	7:00
18	99.2	9:00
19	97.7	8:00
19	98.0	12:00
20	98.2	8:00
20	97.0	11:00
21	99.0	10:00
21	98.4	7:00
22	98.8	12:00
23	98.0	11:00
24	97.4	8:00
25	97.8	9:00
25	97.4	10:00
27	97.5	7:00
27	98.8	8:00

Try It

Use the data above to create a scatterplot and draw a trend line to determine a relationship between body temperature and time of day.

a. Is there a trend?

b. What is the relationship between body temperature and time of day?

Check Your Understanding

1. In your own words, define scatterplot. How can you tell the difference between a scatterplot and a line graph? Explain.

2. Describe how you can tell whether a scatterplot indicates a trend. When can it be useful to notice a trend?

3. If a portion of a scatterplot shows a trend, and a portion of it does not, can this still be useful? Explain.

Practice and Apply

1. **Getting Started** Determine a trend for each scatterplot. If the plot has a trend, state whether the trend is positive or negative.

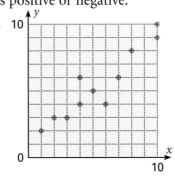

2. **Science** As people age, their sleeping habits change. Below is a table that displays daily sleep time (in hours) and age (in years). Create a scatterplot and draw a trend line for the data.

Age	1	4	6	12	10	22	18	67	82	43	51
Sleep Time	13	11	11	10.5	9	8	9	5.5	5	7.5	6

3. **Industry** The annual budget (in billions of dollars) for NASA (National Aeronautics and Space Administration) for the years 1977 to 1996 appears below. Create a scatterplot of the data and draw a trend line. Based on your scatterplot, what do you expect the budget to be in 2000?

Year	Budget	Year	Budget	Year	Budget
'77	3.9	'84	7.0	'91	13.9
'78	4.0	'85	7.3	'92	14.0
'79	4.2	'86	7.4	'93	14.3
'80	4.8	'87	7.6	'94	14.6
'81	5.4	'88	9.1	'95	14.3
'82	6.0	'89	11.0	'96	14.1
'83	6.7	'90	12.4		

Orion Nebula photographed using the Hubble Space Telescope (NASA Science Photo Library).

4. Health In a lifetime, the average person goes to the doctor over 200 times. The table at the right shows the average number of doctor visits per person each year in relationship to their ages. Create a scatterplot for this data. Determine a trend and draw a trend line.

Age Range	Doctor Visits
0–9	3.6
10–19	2.7
20's	2.1
30's	2.6
40's	3.2
50's	3.9
60's	4.9
70's	6.3

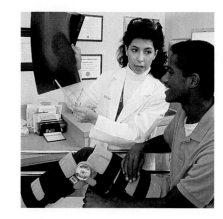

5. **Test Prep** To estimate a future data value, one looks at:

Ⓐ The mean of known data values. Ⓑ The median of known data values.

Ⓒ The last known data value. Ⓓ The trend line.

Problem Solving and Reasoning

6. Communicate When would you choose to use a line graph? A scatterplot? Explain.

7. **Journal** Write about where you have seen or would see scatterplots and trend lines.

8. Math Reasoning Suppose the points (3, 4); (5, 4); (3, 7); (5, 2); and (2, 3) are part of a data set. Would a scatterplot be more appropriate than a line graph for this data set? Explain.

9. Critical Thinking Suppose a scatterplot showed 10 points of a data set with a decreasing trend line. Is it possible for the trend to change if more data were collected? Give an example.

10. Communicate If you had to make a scatterplot from a data set that included (5, 3) more than once, how would you show that the point occurred more than once on the scatterplot? How would you show a point that occurred more than twice on a scatterplot?

Mixed Review

Add, subtract, multiply, or divide. [Previous course]

11. 728,726 + 162,762   **12.** 762,727 − 263,986   **13.** 173,736 × 87,783

14. 697,126 ÷ 32,163   **15.** 273,873 × 283,827   **16.** 782,728 ÷ 78,312

Sketch a box-and-whisker plot for each set of data. [Lesson 1-3]

17. 76, 74, 39, 47, 52, 78, 64, 67, 26   **18.** 3, 6, 4, 6, 8, 1, 5, 4, 7, 4, 5, 4, 5, 2

19. 19, 25, 11, 18, 16, 17, 16, 13, 15   **20.** 8, 12, 11, 16, 7, 9, 8, 15, 21, 14, 12

Designing a Survey

▶ **Lesson Link** Having learned how to organize and present data to answer a specific question, you will now learn how to plan a survey. ◀

Explore Take Part in a Survey

Web Site Questionnaire

Materials: On-line computer

Visit Scott Foresman/Addison Wesley's Web site to take part in a survey of the students across the country who are using this textbook. Go to www.mathsurf.com/8/ch1

Follow the directions given to reach the questionnaire. Answer the questionnaire and analyze the results of the survey.

Scott Foresman • Addison Wesley

© Addison Wesley Longman. All Rights Reserved.

1. What is the population being studied in the survey?

2. Will the survey be based on a random sample of the population?

3. How large is the current sample? Is it large enough to represent the population being surveyed?

4. What data are being collected? Describe the results for each question asked in the survey.

5. How are the data presented? Discuss why you think the data are presented as shown.

You'll Learn …

■ to design a survey and to decide the purpose and population of a survey

… How It's Used

Advertising researchers conduct surveys to find out what appeals to most customers.

Learn Designing a Survey

The first step in designing a survey is to know what you want to find out. When that is clear, choose a way to collect data, trying to get a representative sample of your population and an appropriate sample size.

Finally, decide how to analyze and display your data.

Test Prep

It's good planning to know when the next test will be and what will be on it.

Example

You're thinking of starting a school astronomy club, and you want to know how many people would join. You have only half an hour a day for five days to conduct this survey.

a. What question would you ask?

You can ask, "Would you join a school astronomy club if there were one?"

b. Whom would you ask?

For a random sample, you could get a list of all students and choose randomly from the list, but there isn't enough time to get this information.

You could approach students in a location everyone gathers, such as the lunch area (people who skip lunch would get left out).

c. How would you display your data?

To record the data, you should make a tally of various answers. When the survey is complete, a bar graph can be made.

Would you join a school astronomy club if there were one?

Yes	No	Other

Try It

A teacher wants to know how many hours of homework per week the students in her class are doing.

a. What question should she ask?

b. How should she select her sample?

c. How should she display the data?

Study TIP

Don't forget to keep up with your homework assignments. Keeping a schedule for assignments works for some people.

Check | Your Understanding

1. Would the survey in the example be representative of all people in your school?

2. What difference would it have made in the example if the survey had just asked, "Would you be interested in an astronomy club?"

Practice and Apply

1. **Getting Started** A shoe company plans to make a TV commercial to target young people in the United States. It wants to know what kind of music and images appeal to American teenagers. To find out, the company will take a survey.

   a. Who is the population of the survey?

   b. What is the company's goal?

   c. Would a sample of people from New York City be a representative sample?

2. Cards similar to the one shown are enclosed with items such as CD players, computers, and fax machines.

   a. Who is the population of the survey?

   b. What are the manufacturers trying to find out by distributing this questionnaire?

   c. If some people who buy the product do not fill out the card, how will it affect the results of the survey?

   d. What kind of decisions will be made after the results of the questionnaires are considered?

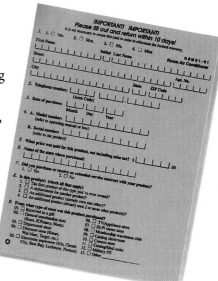

3. Provide a possible question that would appear on a survey card that comes with a new pair of athletic shoes.

4. Provide a possible question that would appear on a survey card that comes with a bottle of cologne.

5. Provide a possible question that would appear on a survey card that comes with a new VCR.

6. Provide a possible question that would appear on a survey card that comes with a new video game.

7. **Test Prep** The bar graph shows the results of a survey that asked, "How many kinds of cereal do you usually have to choose from in the morning?" Choose the most appropriate conclusion.

   Ⓐ There were 12 people surveyed.

   Ⓑ The most frequent answer was "0–5 kinds of cereal."

   Ⓒ 6–10 people have 4 kinds of cereal.

   Ⓓ None of the above

Breakfast Cereal

Number of people / Number of cereal choices (0–5, 6–10, 11–15)

Problem Solving and Reasoning

8. **Journal** Depending on the survey population, a sample size that is representative of that population may vary. Discuss the difference between the survey population sizes for a national cola taste test and for a middle school student body election poll. What do you think the sample size would be for each of these surveys?

9. **Communicate** Many groups send surveys to people through the mail. Sometimes results from these surveys are used to influence lawmakers. Discuss how you would react if you were a legislator and a group used results from a survey conducted through the mail to influence you. Explain your reasoning.

10. **Critical Thinking** For each of the following questions, name both the kind of company that would use the question in a survey and the population of the survey. Explain your reasoning for each.

    a. Approximately how many times per year do you get a sunburn?

    b. How many headaches do you get per year?

    c. How many computer video games do you play each week?

    d. How long has it been since you've had a burger?

Mixed Review

Multiply. *[Previous course]*

11. $8 \times 8 \times 8 \times 8 \times 8$ **12.** $6 \times 6 \times 6 \times 6$ **13.** $11 \times 11 \times 11 \times 11 \times 11$

14. $30 \times 30 \times 30$ **15.** $52 \times 52 \times 52 \times 52$ **16.** $123 \times 123 \times 123$

Sketch a line graph to represent each set of data. *[Lesson 1-4]*

17.

Year	1987	1988	1989	1990	1991
Profit ($)	6205	7823	8190	8573	8469

18.

Year	1975	1980	1985	1990	1995
Number	253	221	189	269	354

Project Progress

Using what you know about surveys and presenting data, state your population, sample size, and how you'll present your data. Also, describe how you would have collected your data to make your sample random.

Problem Solving

Understand
Plan
Solve
Look Back

Section 1B Connect

In this section, you learned about the basics of conducting surveys. Now you will have the chance to do a survey of your own.

Who Asked You Anyway?

Materials: Spreadsheet software

Many schools across the country have a student government. Students vote for their classmates to be president, treasurer, secretary, or a class representative.

To make an effective campaign, people running in student elections should be familiar with the issues that most concern the student body.

A political campaign is similar to advertising. You need to know your population.

1. As a group, think of three issues in your own school that should be addressed by your student government.

2. State exactly what you want to know and write the questions for your survey. The question should be one that can be answered with a number (for example, "How many _____ ?" or "How would you rate _____ ?").

3. Have two groups answer your survey. Organize the resulting data.

4. What kind of graph would best display your data? Explain and describe how this graph will be useful.

5. Enter your data into the data analysis application and generate the appropriate graph.

6. What are the results of your survey for this sample? Is this sample representative of your population? Explain.

7. Suppose a member of your group is running for student body president. Write a few campaign slogans that are based on your survey issues.

8. Describe how your group could make a successful advertising campaign for your student body candidate. What issues would be addressed and why?

1. Identify the following surveys as random or not random. If the sample is not random, state the part of the population that is not represented.

a. A car manufacturer inspects every fiftieth car that comes off the assembly line.

b. A student conducting a survey asks all of her friends, "Who is your favorite teacher?"

2. Science The climate of our planet changes gradually. During the past century, scientists have measured the average temperature of Earth. A scatterplot of these temperatures is shown. What trend is evident in the years 1865 to 1915? What trend is evident since then?

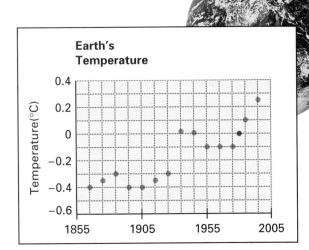

Earth's Temperature

3. Communicate A fast-food chain claims that the average customer waits only two minutes in line. The data shown give the wait times, in seconds, of 15 customers. Make a frequency table from this data. Organize customers by length of wait: those who waited 0–60 seconds, 61–120 seconds, 121–180 seconds, 181–240 seconds, and 241+ seconds. Is the claim reasonable? Explain.

Time Customers Wait in Line (sec)			
94	150	100	360
32	43	76	135
84	121	15	210
48	114	93	

4. Now that you've learned about designing a survey, describe how you would conduct your own survey. What would be the purpose of your survey? What would your population be?

Test Prep

Multiple choice tests often include the possibility of "none of the above." Just because "none of the above" is shown, it isn't necessarily the answer.

5. A survey mailed 2000 questionnaires to people in the largest U.S. cities. Of all the letters, 132 were "returned to sender." What is the sample size of the survey?

   Ⓐ 132   Ⓑ 2000   Ⓒ 1545   Ⓓ None of the above

Double Box-and-Whisker Plots

Double box-and-whisker plots allow you to compare two separate sets of data at a glance.

Math Test Scores

From the plot above, you can determine the following information.

- The scores in Maria's class ranged from about 43 to 92.
- The score range for Wong's class was 40.
- Out of both classes, the highest score was about 92 in Maria's class.
- Out of both classes, the lowest score was about 40 in Wong's class.
- The median score for Maria's class was 70.
- The median score for Wong's class was 75.

Math Test Scores

Analyze the above double box-and-whisker plot to determine the following for **A** and **B**.

1. Median
2. The range
3. The lower quartile
4. Draw a double box-and-whisker plot for the following data.
   X = 20, 35, 10, 30, 15, 5, 25
   Y = 23, 60, 18, 42, 10, 36, 55

Chapter 1 Summary and Review

Graphic Organizer

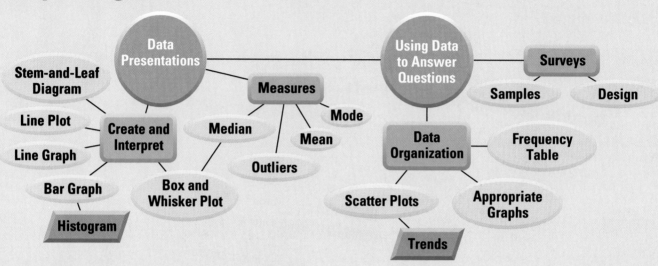

Section 1A Data Presentations

Summary

- **Line plots** and **stem-and-leaf diagrams** show how many times each value in a data set occurs.

- The **mean** is the sum of all values divided by the number of values. The **median** is the middle value; half the data is above and half is below. The **mode** is the value that occurs most frequently.

- A **box-and-whisker plot** shows the median, quartiles, and range of the data set.

- A **line graph** connects pairs of numbers with a line.

- A **bar graph** compares data of several categories.

Review

1. Construct a line plot for the data set 22, 35, 30, 27, 26, 22, 31, 27, 22, 23, 26, 29, 30.

2. Make a stem-and-leaf diagram for the data set 6, 22, 27, 14, 13, 7, 13, 21, 22.

3. Find the mean, median, and mode of the data values 17.5, 15.7, 14.9, 17.0, and 14.9.

4. Construct a box-and-whisker plot for the data set 4, 8, 5, 3, 1, 0, 5, 6, 3, 7.

5. Make a bar graph to show that a hardcover book costs $25.00, a paperback $6.50, a magazine $3.00, and a newspaper $0.50.

6. Make a line graph for the following manager salaries: $12,000 in 1980, $25,000 in 1990, $29,000 in 1993, and $31,000 in 1996.

Summary

- A **survey** is a detailed study of a **population**. The part of the population that is used in the survey is the **sample**.

- If every member of the population has an equal chance of being selected for the sample, then the sample is a **random sample**.

- A **tally** and **frequency table** are ways to count and organize data.

- A **trend line** can be drawn through the points of a **scatterplot** to show a trend.

- A **histogram** is a type of bar graph where the categories are numeric.

Review

7. Describe a method for taking a random sample of households listed in your local phone book.

8. Would a random selection of 10,000 *TV Guide* readers be a random sample of the population of adult Americans?

9. Read the bar graph to determine the number of each item in the library.

10. Read the line graph to determine the number of fiction books acquired by the library each year.

What's in the Library?

How Many Books the Library Bought

11. Create a frequency table for the data set 7, 2, 6, 7, 6, 5, 4, 2, 5, 1, 0, 2, 5.

12. Create a frequency table for the data set 3, 6, 9, 3, 1, 7, 5, 5, 7, 9, 2, 3, 7.

13. Make a frequency table showing three occurrences of 5.35, two of 1.57, and one each of 2.74, 2.45, and 7.39.

14. Create a scatterplot and draw a trend line for the data set ('86, 1.7), ('87, 8.0), ('88, 10.4), ('89, 9.5), ('90, 9.5), ('91, 15.1), and ('92, 21).

15. The U.S. national debt (in trillions of dollars) was 0.5 in 1975, 0.9 in 1980, 1.8 in 1985, and 3.2 in 1990. Create a scatterplot and draw a trend line if possible.

16. At an auction, the price for a brass chicken was $34 at 10 A.M., $32 at 11 A.M., $29 at 12 P.M., $33 at 1 P.M., $36 at 2 P.M., $31 at 3 P.M., and $33 at 4 P.M. Create a scatterplot.

Four people have telephone charge cards. The weekly charges accumulated on each card are shown. Use this data for Questions 1–4.

Card Owner	Week 1	Week 2	Week 3	Week 4	Week 5	Week 6	Week 7	Week 8
Amanda	$3.25	$3.00	$7.75	$6.45	$5.95	$5.70	$4.90	$4.90
Devon	$10.30	$8.50	$8.00	$7.17	$6.68	$5.31	$4.01	$2.10
Monique	$1.11	$0.45	$0.20	$0.20	$0.20	$5.20	$4.95	$2.13
Paolo	$5.05	$5.05	$4.80	$3.22	$0.04	$19.00	$14.89	$12.13

1. Find the mean and median weekly charges for Devon's card.

2. Make a box-and-whisker plot for all weekly charges on Amanda's card.

3. Construct a bar graph comparing the four weekly charges for Week 3.

4. Draw a line graph that shows all of the weekly charges on Paolo's card.

5. Make a stem-and-leaf diagram for the data: 19, 13, 16, 23, 33, 43, 27, 29, 22, 47, 19.

6. Mario writes the name of ten sports stores on separate cards. He mixes up the cards and chooses three. Mario calls the three stores and asks if they carry skateboards. Did Mario take a random sample of sports stores?

7. Gloria asked all of the smiling people coming out of a movie theater, "Did you like the movie?" Did she take a random sample for her survey?

An amusement park charged $12.00 for general admission in 1975, $15.00 in 1980, $16.50 in 1985, $21.00 in 1990, and $22.00 in 1995. Use this data for Questions 8–9.

8. Construct a scatterplot of the data.

9. Draw a possible trend line. Is the trend positive or negative?

Performance Task

The average monthly high temperatures (°F) for five major cities are shown. Present this data using one measure of central tendency and three graphs or plots.

City	January	April	July	October
Ottawa	21	51	81	54
Acapulco	85	87	89	88
Sydney	78	71	60	71
Rio de Janeiro	84	80	75	77
Rome	54	68	88	73

Performance Assessment

Choose one problem.

Just a Dash of Statistics

The table shows winning 400-m dash times (in seconds) for six recent Olympic Games.

1972	1976	1980	1984	1988	1992
44.66	44.26	44.60	44.27	43.87	43.50

Make a scatterplot, draw a trend line, and identify a trend. Explain why your method would not be appropriate for predicting results in the 2020 Olympics.

A Fair Exchange?

The European Currency Unit (ECU) is a unit of money like the dollar. In 1996, one ECU was worth 1.3 U.S. dollars. It was also worth 0.80 Irish pence, 13 Austrian schillings, 1.6 Swiss francs, 8.2 Norwegian kroner, 1.9 German marks, and 8.4 Swedish kronas. Construct a bar graph of the data. What questions can this graph be used to answer?

Bargain Sampling

Pick an item you buy regularly (for example, food, beverage, or gum) and collect a representative sample of prices for this item in your area. Ask a significant question about the price of your item. On a poster, present your data using a graph and explain how it answers your question.

CRYPTIC COMMENTS

From a book, pick a page at random and make a frequency table for each letter (A–Z) appearing on that page. Compare your results with your classmates. How do you think the kind of data you collected might be useful to code breakers?

2 Integers

➤ Entertainment Link
www.mathsurf.com/8/ch2/ent

➤ Arts & Literature Link
www.mathsurf.com/8/ch2/art

Entertainment

The greatest loss of yardage in a football game in a single play occurred during the 1929 Rose Bowl. Roy Riegels recovered a fumble and galloped 65 yards in the wrong direction (−65 yards).

People of the World

The average American travels 7753 miles each year by vehicle, not counting trains and planes, more than any other people of the world.

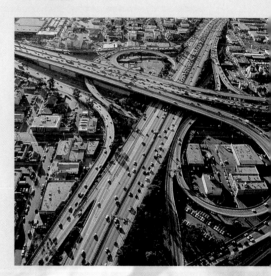

Arts & Literature

In his novel *20,000 Leagues Under the Sea,* written in 1870, Jules Verne describes a ship that could travel great distances under water and stay submerged for long periods of time.

Social Studies

The most expensive real estate in the world is found in Japan. A plot of land the size of a piece of notebook paper would cost about $12,000 in Tokyo's central business district, the Ginza.

KEY MATH IDEAS

Integers are whole numbers and their opposites.

The absolute value of a number is the distance it is from zero on a number line.

Integers can be added, subtracted, multiplied, and divided.

Integers can be plotted on a coordinate grid.

Scientific notation can be used to write very large and very small numbers.

Science

Death Valley, California, is the lowest point in the United States at 282 feet below sea level (−282) and has the highest recorded temperature in the United States at 134°F (+134).

CHAPTER PROJECT

Problem Solving

Understand
Plan
Solve
Look Back

In this project, you will create a time line with at least 20 events that have contributed to the development of mathematics throughout history. Use negative numbers to represent B.C. entries.

Problem Solving Focus

Some of the following problems have unnecessary information. For each problem, state any information that you think is unnecessary. Do not solve the problems.

1 The longest suspension bridge is Humber Bridge in Great Britain. It is 4626 ft long. The Verrazano-Narrows Bridge in New York is 4260 ft long. The Golden Gate Bridge in San Francisco is 4200 ft long. How much longer is the Humber Bridge than the Golden Gate Bridge?

2 In January 1989, the toll on the Golden Gate Bridge increased from $1 to $2. For the first 6 months, you could buy a book of 16 tickets for $20. How much did each ticket cost?

3 Since 1989 the toll on the Golden Gate Bridge increased from $2 to $3. To motivate the use of car pools, there is no toll if there are three or more people in a car. How much money can Pat save if she commutes to work with two other people?

4 The Lincoln Tunnel in New York is about twice as long as the Baytown Tunnel in Texas. Together they are about 12,300 ft long. About how long is each tunnel?

Operations Using Integers

Money Makes the World Go 'Round

Can you imagine our world without money? How would you buy food, clothes, heat, air conditioning? Would there be movies, computers, schools? We use money to purchase things we cannot produce ourselves. Money was developed primarily for trade.

When we think of money, we generally think of coins and paper bills, but early forms of money were quite different. In China, around 3000 B.C., knives and rice were used. In Babylonia, around 2500 B.C., cattle were used. American Indian tribes, in the 1500s and 1600s, used beads and beaver furs.

Paper money was used initially as IOUs or promissory notes. Merchants and goldsmiths would issue the notes. Today, throughout the world, only governments can issue money.

Until the mid 1900s, United States paper money included the words Silver Certificate at the top. This indicated that the bill could be redeemed for silver from the U.S. Treasury. The words Federal Reserve Note have since replaced Silver Certificate on these notes.

1 What are some of the ways your life would change if money did not exist?

2 Why do you think money can be issued only by governments?

3 What are some other forms of IOUs or promissory notes used today?

2-1 Integers and Absolute Value

You'll Learn ...

■ to compare and order integers

■ to find the absolute value of integers

... How It's Used

Bank loan officers must compare figures such as income, expenses, profits, and losses to determine whether to approve a loan.

Vocabulary

opposite

integers

positive numbers

negative numbers

absolute value

▶ **Lesson Link** In Chapter 1, you worked with data in the form of whole numbers, decimals, fractions, and percents. In this chapter you will work with positive and negative numbers. ◄

A number line can be used to display different types of numbers.

Zero is neither positive nor negative.

4 (or +4) is 4 units to the *right* of 0

4 is a positive number

−4 is 4 units to the *left* of 0

−4 is a **negative** number, read as "negative four"

−4 and 4 are opposites

Negative numbers   Positive numbers

$$\xleftarrow{\hspace{0.3cm}} \begin{array}{ccccccccc} \bullet & | & | & | & | & | & | & | & \bullet \\ -4 & -3 & -2 & -1 & 0 & 1 & 2 & 3 & 4 \end{array} \xrightarrow{\hspace{0.3cm}}$$

Two numbers are **opposites** of one another if they are on opposite sides of zero and the same distance from zero. The opposite of zero is zero.

Explore | Integers

Money Matters

Situations involving money are shown below.

1. For each of the situations, write an opposite event or action.

2. For each pair of opposites that you have noted, which event or action would you assign a negative number to? Why?

3. Name some events or actions that do not involve money that are opposites.

a. Profit of $10

b. Price increased by $4.50

c. Lost $6

d. Stock went up $\frac{1}{8}$ point

e. Markup of $30

f. Earned $0

g. Cut in pay of $25

h. Added $5 to savings

i. Saved $20

Learn | Integers and Absolute Value

Integers are whole numbers and their opposites. This is how we can write the set of all integers:

$$\{\ldots, -5, -4, -3, -2, -1, 0, 1, 2, 3, 4, 5, \ldots\}$$

Positive numbers are numbers greater than zero. **Negative numbers** are numbers less than zero.

Often you have to compare numbers involving integers—temperatures, heights and depths, withdrawals and deposits. Number lines can help you understand how to compare integers.

Integers are greater as you move from left to right on a horizontal number line.

$$-10\ -9\ -8\ -7\ -6\ -5\ -4\ -3\ -2\ -1\ \ 0\ \ 1\ \ 2\ \ 3\ \ 4\ \ 5\ \ 6\ \ 7\ \ 8\ \ 9\ \ 10$$

Integers are greater as you move up on a vertical number line.

70 is above 50, so 70 > 50

−10 is below 0, so −10 < 0

−30 is below 30, so −30 < 30

Example 1

Which number is greater? Use the number line above to compare.

a. −6 or 4   **b.** −4 or −2

−6 is to the left of 4, so 4 is greater. −2 is to the right of −4, so −2 is greater.

Try It

Which number is greater?

a. −6 or 3   **b.** −$3 or −$9   **c.** 0 or −7

Sometimes it is more important to know a number's size without its sign.

The **absolute value** of a number is the distance it is from zero. The symbol for absolute value is | |.

$$-5\ -4\ -3\ -2\ -1\ \ 0\ \ 1\ \ 2\ \ 3\ \ 4\ \ 5$$

$$|-4| = 4 \qquad\qquad |4| = 4$$

Some calculators have an absolute value key, [ABS]. To find |3|, enter [ABS] 3 [ENTER]. To find |−3|, enter [ABS] [(−)] 3 [ENTER].

Example 2

Which two numbers have an absolute value of 3?

Both 3 and −3 are 3 units from zero, so $|3| = 3$ and $|{-3}| = 3$.

Try It

What two numbers have an absolute value of 17?

Example 3

Countries' currencies are always fluctuating in relation to each other. The table shows the change in value of $100 in world currencies from 1982 to 1986 with respect to the U. S. dollar. Which two currencies showed the greatest change?

Belgium	3
Canada	−11
Denmark	3
France	−5
West Germany	12
Italy	−9
Japan	48
Netherlands	9
Norway	−13
Sweden	−12
United Kingdom	−16

The number with the largest absolute value is 48, so Japan's currency showed the greatest change.

The number with the next largest absolute value is −16, so the United Kingdom's currency showed the next greatest change.

Try It

Which three countries' currencies showed the least amount of change?

Check | Your Understanding

1. Does every integer have an opposite? Explain.

2. Do you think that a decimal number such as 5.4 has an opposite? Explain.

3. When is the absolute value of a number the number itself?

Practice and Apply

1. **Getting Started** Follow the steps below to order the following numbers from least to greatest: 2, −4, 0, −1, 3

   a. Draw a number line and graph each number.

   b. Find the number that is graphed farthest to the left. This is the smallest number.

   c. As you move to the right on the number line, the numbers are greater. Put the numbers in order.

Number Sense Name the opposite of each number.

2. 6   **3.** −42   **4.** −111   **5.** 0   **6.** 12

Describe a situation that could be represented by each integer.

7. −25°F   **8.** −10 seconds   **9.** −$60   **10.** 5   **11.** −75

12. What integer is described by the following? The absolute value is 5 and the number is to the left of 0 on a number line.

13. **Test Prep** Which number is an integer?

   Ⓐ $-\frac{1}{2}$ Ⓑ 6.2   Ⓒ 0.3   Ⓓ 5

Use >, <, or = to compare each set of numbers.

14. −6 _____ −8   **15.** |$10| _____ |−$10| **16.** −2 _____ 0   **17.** −25°F _____ −10°F

18. −75 _____ −|75| **19.** 8 _____ −14   **20.** −|−3| _____ 0   **21.** −85 _____ −86

Find each absolute value.

22. |218| **23.** |−18| **24.** |0| **25.** |7 − 5|

26. **Science** Temperatures in Verkhoyansk, Russia, have been as low as −90°F and as high as 98°F. Name a temperature lower than −90°F.

27. **Geography** Altitudes can be expressed as integers. For example, the altitude of Mt. Kilimanjaro in Tanzania, Africa, is 19,340 ft. The lowest point of the Dead Sea in Israel is −1312 ft, which means that it is 1312 ft below sea level. Which of these has the greatest absolute value?

28. Consumer This spreadsheet shows income versus expenses for 6 months. Note that expenses appear as negative numbers.

	A	B	C	D	E	F	G
1	Month	Jan.	Feb.	Mar.	Apr.	May	June
2	Income	$4,250	$8,645	$2,398	$4,589	$1,444	$1,624
3	Expenses	−$3,666	−$4,445	−$2,456	−$4,600	−$1,400	−$2,045
4	Profit	$584	$4,200	−$58	−$11	$44	−$421

a. In which months was income greater than expenses? (Hint: Use absolute value.)

b. For which 3 months were profits furthest from 0?

Problem Solving and Reasoning

29. Critical Thinking Suppose you have five positive integers and two negative integers. The mean is:

Ⓐ Negative   Ⓑ Positive   Ⓒ Not enough information

30. Journal Is there a greatest negative integer? Can you name it? Is there a smallest positive integer? Explain your answers.

31. Communicate A dollar today doesn't buy as much as it did a few years ago. If the photo accurately represents the value of the dollar, what negative quantity could be associated with the missing portion? Why?

Mixed Review

Identify each sampling as random or nonrandom. *[Lesson 1-5]*

32. For the population of Jonesville residents: A pollster knocks on the doors of all homes on Orchard Avenue.

33. For the population of Watson High School students: A card is made with each student's name, and 40 cards are chosen from a drum.

Construct a corresponding histogram for each stem-and-leaf diagram. *[Lesson 1-6]*

34.

Stem	Leaf
2	46778
3	002235556778
4	011222578
5	25

35.

Stem	Leaf
8	346689
9	012334668
10	24467
11	057

Addition of Integers

▶ Lesson Link In Lesson 2-1, you learned to compare and order integers. In this lesson, you will add integers. Algebra tiles can be used to model integers. Yellow tiles model positive numbers and red tiles model negative numbers. ◀

1   6   −1   −6   1 + (−1) = 0

These tiles form a *zero pair*.

The opposite of a number is called its **additive inverse**.

THE ZERO PROPERTY OF ADDITION

The sum of an integer and its additive inverse is 0.

$a + (-a) = 0$ and $-a + a = 0$

$6 + (-6) = 0$ and $-6 + 6 = 0$

You'll Learn ...
■ to add integers

... How It's Used

Professional golfers must know how to add integers when keeping score.

Vocabulary

additive inverse

commutative property

associative property

Explore Adding Integers

Opposites Attract

Materials: Algebra unit tiles
cup

To model addition of integers with algebra tiles, think of addition as putting tiles into a cup.

1. Start with 3 yellow tiles in the cup. Add 4 more yellow tiles. What is the sum? Try other combinations of positive tiles. What is the sign of the sum of two positive numbers?

2. Experiment with the red or negative tiles. Start with 3 red tiles in the cup. Add 4 more red tiles. What is the sum? Try other combinations of red tiles. What is the sign of the sum of two negative numbers?

3. Use both positive and negative tiles. Model the following using the tiles. (Don't forget to remove zero pairs.) What is the sign of your answer in each case?

   a. −5 + 2   **b.** 5 + (−2)   **c.** 2 + (−5)   **d.** −2 + 5

4. Try more examples of adding positive and negative numbers. Make a guess about the sign of the sum of any positive and negative number.

In Lesson 2-1, a number line was used to help you understand absolute value and compare and order integers. A number line is also useful when adding.

Example 1

Add.

a. $10 + (-4)$

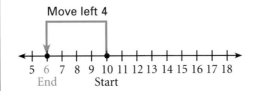

Move left 4

5 6 7 8 9 10 11 12 13 14 15 16 17 18
End   Start

$10 + (-4) = 6$

b. $-3 + 5$

Move right 5

$-8\ -7\ -6\ -5\ -4\ -3\ -2\ -1\ \ 0\ \ 1\ \ 2\ \ 3\ \ 4\ \ 5$
Start   End

$-3 + 5 = 2$

Try It

Add.

a. $5 + 3$ **b.** $5 + (-3)$ **c.** $-5 + 3$ **d.** $-5 + (-3)$

You can use absolute value to help you add.

ADDING INTEGERS WITH THE SAME SIGN

- Add the absolute value of the two numbers.
- Use the sign of the numbers.

ADDING INTEGERS WITH DIFFERENT SIGNS

- Subtract the number with the smaller absolute value from the number with the larger absolute value.
- Take the sign of the number with the larger absolute value.

Example 2

Jolice had a beginning balance of $125.25. Use a calculator to find her ending balance based on the following deposits and withdrawals: $22.50, −$4.50, $5.00, −$10.00.

Enter 125.25 ⊕ 22.50 ⊕ 4.50 ⊞ ⊕
5.00 ⊕ 10.00 ⊞ ⊜ *138.25*.
Her ending balance was $138.25.

When you added whole numbers, you learned the following properties. These properties hold true for integers.

COMMUTATIVE PROPERTY

$a + b = b + a$

ASSOCIATIVE PROPERTY

$(a + b) + c = a + (b + c)$

Example 3

Atoms contain charged particles called protons and electrons. Each proton has a charge of $+1$, each electron has a charge of -1. A sulfur ion has 16 protons and 18 electrons. Represent the net charge using integers.

The charge of the protons can be represented as $+16$ and the charge of the electrons can be represented as -18.

The net charge is found by adding $16 + (-18)$.

$16 + (-18) = -2$.

The net charge of the sulfur ion is -2.

▶ **Chemistry Link**

When an atom has the same number of protons and electrons, it has no charge and is said to be *neutral*.

Example 4

Find the sum of $7 + 3 + (-5) + (-7)$.

$7 + 3 + (-5) + (-7)$

$= 7 + (-7) + 3 + (-5)$ Use the commutative property to rewrite the problem.

$= 0 + 3 + (-5)$ 7 and -7 are additive inverses.

$= -2$

Try It

Add.

a. $17 + (-6)$ **b.** $(-9) + -22 + 9$

Check | Your Understanding

1. Does every integer have an additive inverse?

2. When is the sum of two integers with different signs negative?

3. Can the sum of two negative numbers ever be positive? Explain.

Practice and Apply

1. **Getting Started** Add by using the commutative and associative properties: $-2 + (-4) + 2 + (-3) + 5$.

  a. Group integers that are additive inverses.

  b. Group integers that have the same sign.

  c. Add the numbers in parentheses.

  d. Add the remaining numbers.

Write the addition problem for each model.

2.

3.

Add.

4. $34 + 28$	**5.** $-34 + (-28)$	**6.** $34 + (-28)$
7. $-34 + 28$	**8.** $95 + 47$	**9.** $-95 + (-47)$
10. $95 + (-47)$	**11.** $-95 + 47$	**12.** $-8 + 8 + (-8)$
13. $-24 + (-100) + (-1)$	**14.** $-75 + 85 + (-25)$	

15. **Test Prep** At 7:00 A.M. the temperature in Paradise, Michigan, was $-7°F$. By noon a front had moved through and the temperature went up $10°F$. What is the temperature at noon?

  Ⓐ $3°F$ Ⓑ $17°F$ Ⓒ $-3°F$ Ⓓ $-17°F$

16. Lee, David, and Bridgit often play miniature golf. Par is the number of strokes it should take you to complete each hole. 4 over par ($+4$) means it took 4 more strokes. 1 under par (-1) means it took 1 fewer stroke.

  a. Bridgit was 3 under par for the first hole and 1 over par for the second hole. David had scores of -2 and $+2$ for the first two holes, and Lee had scores of $+3$ and par. Compare each of their scores to par for the first two holes.

  b. The person with the lowest total is winning after two holes. Who is winning?

Number Sense Decide whether the sum is always, sometimes, or never positive.

17. Two negative numbers

18. Three positive, one negative number

19. Two positive numbers

20. Two positive, two negative numbers

21. **History** In the 1800s, money could not be transferred electronically. Gold bars had to be traded and transported. The North Hope Bank had owed Cheyenne Security Bank 412 gold bars. North Hope sent 85 bars on a stagecoach to Cheyenne Security. Use addition to show how much North Hope still owes.

22. **Science** The Kelvin temperature scale is sometimes used in science. The formula $K = 273 + C$ relates degrees Kelvin (K) to degrees Celsius (C). Find the Kelvin temperature for each of the following.

    a. $-25°C$ **b.** $0°C$ **c.** $25°C$ **d.** $-32°C$

Problem Solving and Reasoning

23. Explain to a classmate how you can tell, before actually calculating, whether the sum of two integers is positive or negative.

24. **Critical Thinking** The sum of two integers is -6. One integer is 10 more than the other. What are the integers?

25. **Communicate** An elevator on the tenth floor goes down 9 floors. Then it goes up 19 floors, down 3, and finally up 12. What floor does it end up on? Explain how you arrived at your answer.

PROBLEM SOLVING 2-2

Mixed Review

Make a scatterplot for each data set. Decide whether there is an increasing trend, a decreasing trend, or no trend at all. *[Lesson 1-7]*

26. $(3, 7), (8, 2), (5, 6), (8, 1), (9, 1), (2, 8), (4, 7), (6, 4), (5, 5)$

27. $(1, 6), (5, 6), (7, 4), (6, 5), (2, 5), (4, 5), (9, 6), (8, 5), (3, 4)$

What population would it make most sense to survey for each product?
[Lesson 1-8]

28. Home stereo equipment

29. Fingernail polish

30. Computer disk drives

31. Home air-conditioning equipment

Subtraction of Integers

You'll Learn ...

■ to subtract integers

... How It's Used

Oceanographers subtract integers when comparing numbers relating to sea level.

> ▶ **Lesson Link**   In Lesson 2-2, you learned to add integers. In this lesson, you will learn to subtract integers. ◀

Explore   Subtracting Integers

About Face!

1. Select 15 of your classmates to form a number line from left to right facing the class. Who in the line represents 0? What numbers do the two end students represent?

2. You will represent a point on the number line.

You will use the following rules for addition and subtraction.

Addition   Face the positive end of the number line

Subtraction   Face the negative end of the number line

If the number added or subtracted is positive   Walk forward

If the number added or subtracted is negative   Walk backward

3. To model −3 + 2, stand in front of the student who represents −3, face the *positive* end of the number line, and walk *forward* 2 students. What is the result?

4. Model −3 − 5. What is the result?

5. Model −1 + (−5). What is the result?

6. Model −1 − (−5). What is the result?

7. Explain how adding −5 and subtracting 5 are alike in this model. Explain how adding 5 and subtracting −5 are alike in this model.

Learn | Subtraction of Integers

In Lesson 2-2, you looked at addition of integers on a number line. Subtraction of integers can also be modeled on a number line.

Example 1

Juan owed Judy $6. She told him that he could subtract $2 of what he owed her if he would feed her dog. How does this result compare with Judy telling him she would pay him $2 for feeding her dog?

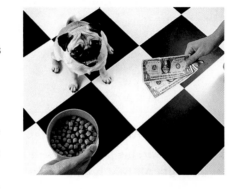

The first situation can be represented by $-6 - (-2)$. The second situation can be represented by $-6 + 2$.

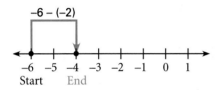

Either way Juan now owes her $4.

HINT

Enter 6 ⊞ 2 ⊬ ⊜.
Enter 6 ⊟ 2 ⊜.
Try a few other examples like this to see that adding the opposite of a number is the same as subtracting that number.

SUBTRACTING INTEGERS

Subtraction of integers is the same as adding the opposite.
$a - b = a + (-b)$.

Example 2

Subtract.

a. $4 - 7$

$= 4 + (-7)$ Add the opposite of 7.

$= -3$

b. $-8 - (-9)$

$= -8 + 9$ Add the opposite of -9.

$= 1$

Try It

Subtract.

a. $-7 - 5$ **b.** $-5 - 7$ **c.** $7 - (-5)$ **d.** $5 - (-7)$

In the National Hockey League, players have plus/minus ratings. When a goal is scored, each player on the ice for the goal-scoring team receives +1, and each player on the opposing team receives −1. These points are added through the season.

Example 3

Before the All-Star break, Henri had a plus/minus rating of −18. By the end of the year, his plus/minus rating was 14. What was his plus/minus rating after the All-Star break?

His rating at the end of the year minus his rating before the All-Star break:

$$14 - (-18)$$

His rating after the All-Star break was 32.

Try It

a. Sergei's plus/minus rating was 7 in the first half of the season, but −24 by the end of the season. What was his plus/minus rating in the second half of the season?

b. Early in the fall, the water level in a reservoir was −14 ft with respect to sea level. After the winter rains, the level was 11 ft. How many feet did the water level rise or fall?

MENTAL MATH

When you subtract a negative number, think of clicking a light switch once to subtract, and again for the minus sign. Two clicks turn the light back **on**, so "minus a minus" is a **plus**.

Check | Your Understanding

1. Describe what happens when you subtract the opposite of a number from itself. Use an example in your explanation.

2. Your friend says, "This is great. I don't ever have to subtract again!" Explain what she means.

3. Is the additive inverse used in the subtraction of integers? If so, how and when?

4. If you change a subtraction problem to an addition problem by adding the opposite, will the commutative property hold true? Explain.

2-3 Exercises and Applications

Practice and Apply

1. **Getting Started** Write each subtraction as an addition.

   a. $4 - 2 = 4 +$ _____   **b.** $-8 - (-9) = -8 +$ _____   **c.** $-5 - 10 = -5 +$ _____

2. Use your calculator to add or subtract.

   a. $125 - (-40)$ **b.** $125 + 40$ **c.** $-545 + 365$

   d. $-545 - (-365)$ **e.** $-428 + (-467)$ **f.** $-428 - 467$

   g. What do you notice about each pair of problems? Why is this true?

3. **Number Sense** Write each problem as an addition problem. Compute the answer.

   a. $12 - 24$ **b.** $-24 - 12$ **c.** $24 - (-12)$ **d.** $-12 - (-24)$

Add or subtract.

4. $12 - 13$

5. $-87 + (-61)$

6. $5 - (-1)$

7. $-55 - 55$

8. $-1 - 8$

9. $-18 + 987 - 2$

10. $50 - 80 - (-50)$

11. $0 - 2$

12. $101 + 4 - (-5)$

13. $-22 + (-22) - 4$

14. $7 - 17 - 10$

15. $400 + 23 + (-3)$

16. **Measurement** A fish finder helps locate fish in deep waters. Your line is at 90 feet, but the finder shows that the fish are 30 feet deeper. Do you let the line out 30 feet? 120 feet? Do you reel it in 30 feet? 60 feet? Explain.

90 ft.

17. **Consumer** Last week, Maria saw a dress priced at $53. The sign in the window said there was $5 off any purchase in the store. She decided to wait for a sale. This week, the dress was priced at $49 but there was no discount. She bought the dress. Should she have waited? Explain.

18. **Social Studies** The national debt, which is in the trillions of dollars, increases by about $650 million a day. It will soon reach $6 trillion. Approximately how much will the debt be one day later?

OUR NATIONAL DEBT:
$5,036,856,391.4 ▮▮
YOUR *Family share* $65,413.
THE NATIONAL DEBT CLOCK
NATIONAL DEBT INCREASE PER SECOND $ 10,000
1992 INTEREST COST – $292 BILLION

19. Science The planet Venus reaches a temperature of 864°F at the surface, whereas Mercury's temperature may drop to −301°F. What is the difference between the temperatures of the two planets?

20. Explain how it is possible to subtract a number from 100 and get a result that is greater than 100.

Mercury   Venus

21. **Test Prep** The temperature in Juneau, Alaska, was −10°F. It was predicted to drop 5 degrees. What temperature will it be then?

   Ⓐ −5°F   Ⓑ 5°F

   Ⓒ 15°F   Ⓓ −15°F

Problem Solving and Reasoning

22. Critical Thinking Find two integers whose difference is −18 and whose sum is 2.

23. Communicate Explain how to fill in the blanks with $<$, $>$, or $=$ without actually doing the computations.

   a. $28 - (-5)$ _____ $28 + (-5)$ **b.** $35 - 5$ _____ $35 - (-5)$

24. Critical Thinking The balance on a credit card is calculated monthly.

   a. Does a positive balance mean that you owe the company money or that the company owes you money?

   b. Does a negative balance mean that you owe the company money or the company owes you money? How might you get a negative balance?

   c. Your balance in May was $89.50. In June, $150.25 was charged and a payment of $75.00 was made. What is your June balance?

Mixed Review

Make a stem-and-leaf diagram for each set of data. *[Lesson 1-1]*

25. 32, 41, 53, 42, 46, 58, 34, 38, 42   **26.** 64, 73, 81, 92, 76, 93, 71, 74

Sketch a line graph to represent each set of data. *[Lesson 1-4]*

27.

Year	1990	1991	1992	1993	1994
Profit	483	521	693	875	798

28.

Year	1940	1950	1960	1970	1980
Number	30	42	23	37	32

Multiplication and Division of Integers

▶ Lesson Link In the last two lessons, you added and subtracted integers. In this lesson, you will learn to multiply and divide integers. ◀

Explore Multiplying Integers

Product Patterns

Materials: Algebra unit tiles

When modeling multiplication of integers, think of placing (positive) or removing (negative) sets of yellow (positive) or red (negative) tiles.

1. Place 2 sets of 3 red tiles on your layout. How many tiles are there? What is the sign of the product of a positive number and a negative number?

2. Add 2 sets of 3 yellow tiles to the layout to make "zero." Then *remove* 2 sets of 3 red tiles from the layout. How many tiles are left? What product is modeled? What is the sign of the product of two negative numbers?

3. Model each of the following using the tiles.

   a. -3×4 **b.** 3×4 **c.** -3×-4 **d.** 3×-4

You'll Learn ...

■ to multiply and divide integers

... How It's Used

Chemists must calculate with integers to determine whether a reaction will occur when solutions are mixed.

Vocabulary

multiplicative inverse

reciprocal

Learn Multiplication and Division of Integers

Patterns can often help you discover rules for mathematical computations.

The following patterns suggest rules for multiplying integers.

Because of the commutative property, 3×-3 is the same as -3×3.

$3 \times 2 = 6$
$3 \times 1 = 3$
$3 \times 0 = 0$
$3 \times -1 = -3$
$3 \times -2 = -6$

$-3 \times 2 = -6$
$-3 \times 1 = -3$
$-3 \times 0 = 0$
$-3 \times -1 = 3$
$-3 \times -2 = 6$

> The product of two numbers with the same sign is positive.
>
> $$(+)(+) = (+) \qquad (-)(-) = (+)$$
>
> The product of two numbers with different signs is negative.
>
> $$(+)(-) = (-) \qquad (-)(+) = (-)$$

Example 1

Earl has a bank account that is charged a $5 service fee for each month that the balance is below $500. Earl's balance was less than $500, and he forgot about the account for 4 months. What has been the overall change in the account balance?

For each of the 4 months, the change in the balance has been $-\$5$. $4 \times -5 = -\$20$. The change in the balance has been $-\$20$.

Try It

ATM withdrawal charges appear as $-\$1.25$ on Amy's bank statement. She made 8 ATM withdrawals. What is the total of the 8 charges?

The associative and commutative properties can help you complete multiplication problems with more than two integers.

MENTAL MATH

Always look to find compatible numbers—numbers that are easy to operate with mentally.

Example 2

Multiply: $-4 \cdot -3 \cdot -25$

Rewrite using the commutative property.

$(-4 \cdot -25) -3$

$= 100 \cdot -3 \qquad (-)(-) = (+)$

$= -300 \qquad (+)(-) = (-)$

If the product of two numbers is 1, each of the numbers is the **multiplicative inverse**, or **reciprocal**, of the other.

THE INVERSE PROPERTY OF MULTIPLICATION

The product of a number and its multiplicative inverse is 1.

$$\frac{a}{b} \cdot \frac{b}{a} = 1$$

Example 3

What is the multiplicative inverse of each number?

a. -3 **b.** $\dfrac{6}{5}$ **c.** $\dfrac{-4}{7}$

$\dfrac{1}{-3}$ $\dfrac{5}{6}$ $\dfrac{7}{-4}$

Try It

What is the multiplicative inverse of each number?

a. -8 **b.** $\dfrac{2}{5}$ **c.** $\dfrac{-8}{3}$

Division and multiplication are inverse operations. $30 \div -6 = -5$ because $-5 \cdot -6 = 30$. $-30 \div -6 = 5$ because $5 \cdot -6 = -30$. Dividing by a number is the same as multiplying by its multiplicative inverse.

$30 \div 6$ is the same as $30\left(\dfrac{1}{6}\right)$. $30 \div (-6)$ is the same as $30\left(\dfrac{1}{-6}\right)$.

The quotient of two integers is positive if the two integers have the same sign:	$(+) \div (+) = (+)$ $(-) \div (-) = (+)$
The quotient of two integers is **negative** if the two integers have **different signs**:	$(+) \div (-) = (-)$ $(-) \div (+) = (-)$

HINT

Some calculators have a reciprocal or inverse key, $\boxed{1/x}$. To find the reciprocal of $\dfrac{-4}{7}$, enter 4 $\boxed{+/-}$ $\boxed{\div}$ 7 $\boxed{=}$ $\boxed{1/x}$. The result will be -1.75. This is the same as $\dfrac{-7}{4}$.

Example 4

Yael lost $1200 on 400 shares of stock. How much did each share of stock change in value?

Since $1200 is a loss, the change per share can be written as $-1200 \div 400$. Since $1200 \div 400 = 3$, and a negative number divided by a positive number is negative, the change in value for each share was $-\$3$.

Check Your Understanding

1. Explain whether the following statement is true: $\dfrac{-3}{-4} = \dfrac{3}{4}$.

2. Suppose you have a product of four numbers. In all, three are positive and one is negative. What is the sign of the product?

2-4 Exercises and Applications

Practice and Apply

1. **Getting Started** Find the product of 13×-6.
   a. Multiply 13×6.
   b. Use the rules for multiplying integers, $(+) \times (-) = (-)$.

Multiply or divide.

2. $6 \cdot 8$

3. $-6 \cdot -8$

4. $-6 \cdot 8$

5. $6 \cdot -8$

6. $(-3)(-5)$

7. $24 \div -2$

8. $-24 \div -2$

9. $-24 \div 2$

10. $24 \div 2$

11. $-2(7)$

12. $\dfrac{-45}{9}$

13. $\dfrac{-46}{-23}$

14. $\dfrac{24}{-8}$

15. $\dfrac{0}{-9}$

16. $\dfrac{45}{5}$

17. $-7 \cdot 20$

18. $-6 \cdot 9 \cdot -5$

19. $-4 \cdot -85 \cdot 0$

20. $-1 \cdot -1 \cdot -1$

21. $3 \times -6 \div 2$

22. $-56 \div 7 \div -4$

23. $0 \div -11 \div -1$

24. $-9 \cdot -5 \div -15$

Number Sense Evaluate.

25. $|2 \times (-7)|$

26. $|15 \div (-3)|$

27. $|-4| \times |-7|$

28. $|-36| \div |-4|$

29. **Test Prep** Marta withdrew $8 a week for 6 weeks from her bank account. Which of the following shows how to find how much her balance changed?

   Ⓐ $-8 + 6$ Ⓑ $-8 - 6$ Ⓒ -8×6 Ⓓ $-8 \div 6$

30. **Measurement** Nancy's watch loses 8 minutes per day. How many minutes will her watch lose in 1 week?

31. Edwin invested in some pretty risky stock. After six months, he had lost $366. Approximately how much did he lose per month on this stock?

32. **Number Sense** Why is the mean of these numbers zero?

   $-1, -3, 3, 1, 2, -2$

33. Use your calculator to compute $-25 \times (-18) \div (-9) \times 48 \div (-24)$.

Santiago, Chile, Stock Exchange

34. Golf An eagle is 2 strokes under par. If you made eagles on 3 holes, how many strokes under par is this?

Problem Solving and Reasoning

35. Communicate Explain which properties could be used to rewrite the following expression so that it is easier to calculate: $4 \cdot -9 \cdot 25$

36. How is multiplying integers like multiplying whole numbers? How is it different? How is dividing integers like dividing whole numbers? How is it different?

37. Critical Thinking The temperature has been falling an average of 4° per hour. If the temperature at 12:00 A.M. is 10°F, what do you predict it will be at 6:00 A.M.?

38. **Test Prep** Which multiplication(s) is/are matched with the correct division?

Ⓐ $-16 \times \frac{1}{4}$ and $-16 \div -4$ Ⓑ $-16 \times \frac{-1}{4}$ and $-16 \div 4$

Ⓒ -16×4 and $-16 \div \frac{1}{4}$ Ⓓ -16×-4 and $-16 \div \frac{-1}{4}$

39. Communicate Teo has added a long list of numbers. There are many more negative numbers than positive numbers, but the sum is positive.

a. Do you know whether the mean is positive or negative? Why?

b. Do you know whether the median is positive or negative? Why?

Mixed Review

Find the mean and median of each data set. *[Lesson 1-2]*

40. 18.3, 21.4, 19.3, 8.7, 21.3, 17.4   **41.** 32, 67, 41, 53, 62, 31

42. A stereo manufacturer company surveys customers who have bought its products in the past. How useful will the data be in determining what features need to be added to its products to increase sales? Explain your answer. *[Lesson 1-5]*

Project Progress

When you make your time line, be sure that you have enough room for your range of dates. Subtract the earliest date from the latest date to see how many years your time line will represent.

Problem Solving

Understand
Plan
Solve
Look Back

Evaluating Expressions Using Integers

You'll Learn ...

■ to evaluate expressions involving integers, and to use the distributive property

... How It's Used

Integer expressions are evaluated when National Football League teams compile game data.

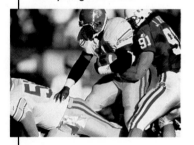

Vocabulary

order of operations

distributive property

▶ **Lesson Link** You have worked with expressions with one operation. In this lesson you will work with expressions that involve more than one operation. ◀

Explore Expressions

Call Your Operator

Materials: Scientific calculator

1. Using the digits for the year (for example, 1998) and any of the operations of $+$, $-$, $\times$, $\div$, write as many expressions as you can. For example,

$1 \times 9 \div 9 + 8 = 9$ as does $1 \div 9 \times 9 + 8$.

2. Compare your list with others in your group. Can you find expressions that have values equal to all of the numbers 0 to 10?

3. Enter $1 \cdot 9 + 9 \div 8$ into your calculator. What answer do you get? Explain what your calculator did.

4. Enter $(1 \cdot 9 + 9) \div 8$ into your calculator. Do you get the same answer as in Question 3? Explain what your calculator did.

5. Go back to your list of expressions using the digits from the date and $+$, $-$, $\times$, $\div$. Make a new list using the four operations and parentheses. Did you get other values for your expressions?

Learn Evaluating Expressions Using Integers

When simplifying expressions involving more than one operation, such as $-2 + 3 \times 4$, mathematicians have agreed on an order in which to perform operations so the expression always has the same value. If we need to change the order of operations, grouping symbols such as parentheses and the division bar allow us to do this.

ORDER OF OPERATIONS
Do any operations inside grouping symbols.
Do all multiplications and divisions, from left to right.
Do all additions and subtractions, from left to right.

Example 1

Use order of operations to evaluate $-2 + (6 + 4) \div (-2)$.

$-2 + (6 + 4) \div (-2)$

$= -2 + 10 \div (-2)$ Do any operations within the grouping symbols.

$= -2 + -5$ Do all divisions from left to right.

$= -7$ Do all additions from left to right.

Try It

Use order of operations to evaluate $5 + -30 \div (-6)$.

▶ **Technology Link**

Make up a simple example such as $1 + 2 \cdot 3$. If the calculator gives an answer of 7, it has an algebraic operating system. If it gives an answer of 9, it doesn't.

The **distributive property**, a very important mathematical property, makes use of parentheses.

$2(4 + 5) = 2 \cdot 4 + 2 \cdot 5$

The parentheses show that both the 4 *and* the 5 are multiplied by 2.

THE DISTRIBUTIVE PROPERTY OF MULTIPLICATION OVER ADDITION
In words: Multiplying a sum by a number is the same as multiplying each addend by the number, then adding the products.
In symbols: $a(b + c) = ab + ac$.

Example 2

Use the distributive property to evaluate the expression $-2(-3 - 4)$.

$-2(-3 - 4) = -2(-3 + -4)$ Subtraction is the same as adding the opposite.

$= (-2 \cdot -3) + (-2 \cdot -4)$ Use the distributive property.

$= 6 + 8$ Perform all multiplications from left to right.

$= 14$ Perform additions from right to left.

Try It

Use the distributive property to evaluate.

a. $-6(-4 + 8)$ **b.** $-8(100 - 1)$

Test Prep

Look for compatible numbers. To evaluate $7(3.1 + 2.9)$, it is quicker to add first. To evaluate $8(\frac{1}{8} + 1)$, it is quicker to multiply first.

WHAT DO YOU THINK?

Use the spreadsheet below to find the total change in inventory value.

	A	B	C	D	
1		**Change in**	**Value**	**Change**	
2	**Caps**	**Inventory**	**of Each**	**in Value**	
3	**Astros caps**	−12	$14	−$168	
4	**Rangers caps**	17	$14	$238	
5	**Total**	5	$14		

Ashley thinks ...

The value of the Astros caps went down, since −12(14) = −$168. The value of Rangers caps went up, since 17(14) = $238. Adding the values in column D, −168 + 238 = $70. The total change in inventory value is $70.

Seung thinks ...

The total change in cap inventory is −12 + 17, which is 5. The value of each cap is $14. Multiplying the numbers in row 5, the change in inventory value is 5(14) = $70.

What do you think?

If the value of a Rangers cap was $11, would both methods work?

Check | Your Understanding

1. Both Juanita and Julio worked the problem 2 + 3 · 4. Juanita got 20 and Julio got 14. Who is correct and why did they get different answers?

2. Is there a distributive property of multiplication over subtraction? Over multiplication? Over division? Explain using examples.

3. Show how the distributive property can help you find the product of 80 and 99 using mental math.

Practice and Apply

1. **Getting Started** Name the operation that should be done first in each expression.

   a. $21 - 2 \times 6$ **b.** $-15(80 + 30)$ **c.** $48 \div 3 \cdot 2$ **d.** $\dfrac{24 + 4}{-4}$

Evaluate each pair of expressions.

2. $15 - 5 + 9$
   $15 - (5 + 9)$

3. $27 - 15 \div 3$
   $27 - (15 \div 3)$

4. $-8 + 2(4 - 4)$
   $-8 + 2 \cdot 4 - 4$

5. $4(6 + -9)$
   $4 \cdot 6 + 4 \cdot (-9)$

6. $-2(4 - 5)$
   $-2 \cdot 4 + (-2) \cdot (-5)$

7. $18 \div -6 \cdot 3$
   $18 \div (-6 \cdot 3)$

8. Use the distributive property to write $5(-2 + 6)$ without parentheses.

Evaluate each expression two different ways.

9. $5(8 + 10)$ 10. $8\left(9 + \dfrac{1}{2}\right)$ 11. $-3(30 - 3)$ 12. $(100 - 2)8$

13. **Consumer** Sara has been saving her money to buy some video games. She has saved $39.24 so far, but she owes each of her twin brothers $5.65. If Sara gets her allowance of $8.50 and pays her brothers, how much money does she have?

Evaluate each expression.

14. $16 \div 4 \cdot (-2) + 6$ 15. $14 - (-8) + 6 \div (-3)$

16. $\dfrac{18 - 9}{9} + (-3)$ 17. $\dfrac{-3(9 + 2)}{-11} + (-2)$

18. **Test Prep** Which is *not* the use of the distributive property for $a(b + c)$?

    Ⓐ $ab - ac$ Ⓑ $ab + ac$ Ⓒ $a(b) + a(c)$ Ⓓ $(a)(b) + (a)(c)$

19. **Measurement** The temperatures for the past week were as follows: $-5°, -4°, -2°, 0°, 10°, 17°, -2°$. What was the mean temperature?

Operation Sense Copy each sentence below. Insert parentheses to make each sentence true.

20. $100 + 24 \div 3 + 1 = 31$ 21. $100 + 24 \div 3 + 1 = 106$

22. $-5 \times 3 + 3 \times 6 = -180$ 23. $-5 \times 3 + 3 \times 6 = -105$

24. Each week the student council has a popcorn and candy sale. The profits for the past month were: $25.00, −$7.25, $23.50, and $26.75.

a. Overall, how much did the student council make on its fund-raiser for the month?

b. If the money is to be divided equally between 3 different committees, how much does each committee get?

25. Science An inch of heavy, wet snow contains 0.2 inches of water, an inch of average snow contains 0.1 inches of water, and an inch of dry, powdery snow contains 0.06 inches of water. If 5 inches of each type of snow falls, how much water is contained in the snow?

Problem Solving and Reasoning

26. Choose a Strategy Carrie wants to bring snack food to the drama club meeting. She decides to buy 15 bagels at $0.50 each and 1 container of cream cheese for $1.50. How much will she spend?

27. Critical Thinking Using only the number 3, the operations $+, -, \times, \div$, and parentheses, write three different expressions that equal 1. You may use the number 3 more than once.

28. **Journal** Explain to a classmate how you would show that you want to add two numbers in an expression before you multiply.

29. Communicate Explain how you could use the distributive property to multiply each of the following mentally.

a. $36 \cdot 101$ **b.** $50 \cdot 99$ **c.** $49 \cdot 13$ **d.** $98 \cdot 42$

> **Problem Solving**
> ## STRATEGIES
> • Look for a Pattern
> • Make an Organized List
> • Make a Table
> • Guess and Check
> • Work Backward
> • Use Logical Reasoning
> • Draw a Diagram
> • Solve a Simpler Problem

Mixed Review

Sketch a box-and-whisker plot for each set of data. *[Lesson 1-3]*

30. 42, 51, 67, 83, 91, 51, 83, 72   **31.** 87, 93, 102, 93, 115, 84, 78, 91

Construct a frequency table for each histogram. *[Lesson 1-6]*

32.

33.

You will now connect your knowledge of integers, order of operations, and the distributive property to solve problems about money.

Money Makes the World Go Round

Jill, Jack, Jamie, and Jamal started a lawn-care business. They are a small company that specializes in a select number of tasks. The following spreadsheet lists each job, the charge per job, the expenses per job, the number of jobs done in the first month, and the total tips earned.

1. Copy the chart. Add a column F that shows the total amount made (or lost) on each type of job.

	A	B	C	D	E
1	Specific Job	Charge	Expenses	Number	Total
2		per Job	per Job	of Jobs	Tips
3				Done	Earned
4	Mow lawn	$10.00	$2.00	27	$67
5	Edge	$5.00	$3.00	24	$70
6	Weed gardens	$15.00	$1.00	45	$135
7	Plant new gardens	$50.00	$10.00	12	$147
8	Total Earnings				

2. How did you determine the amounts in column F? Write the expression you used.

3. Suppose the numbers in column C were negative? How would your expression change?

4. Find the total amount made (or lost) by the company. Enter this number in cell F 8.

5. If the partners divided the earnings evenly, how would you find each partner's earnings?

6. If the expenses for edging had been $8 per job, what would the total earnings for edging have been? Would it be a good idea to continue to offer this service? Explain your reasoning.

Section 2A Review

1. **a.** Which temperatures shown on the thermometer are positive?

   b. Which temperatures shown on the thermometer are negative?

   c. Name the pairs of opposites shown on the thermometer.

   d. Which temperature shown is farthest from 0?

   e. Which temperature shown is the coldest?

Use the distributive property to evaluate.

2. $15(100 - 2)$ 3. $-12(50 + 1)$ 4. $42(100 + 1)$ 5. $-13(100 + 2)$

Evaluate.

6. $|-2|$ 7. $|-3|$ 8. $|20|$ 9. $|27| - |36|$

10. $-65 + -35$ 11. $-4 \cdot -25$ 12. $-88 \div -22$ 13. $-6 - (-16)$

14. $\dfrac{56}{-8}$ 15. $75 + -75$ 16. $-36 - 36$ 17. $-100 \cdot 5$

18. $-1 \cdot -1 \cdot -1$ 19. $-1 + -1 + -1$ 20. $\dfrac{-1 + (-1)}{-2}$ 21. $29 - 4 \cdot 6$

22. $(29 - 4) \times 6$ 23. $-3 + \dfrac{3 \cdot 4}{6}$ 24. $4 - \dfrac{2(3 + 6)}{3}$

25. In November 1996, 1517 Italian *lira* could be exchanged for each U. S. dollar. Jane exchanged $50 for lira in the U. S. and an additional $400 in Italy. How many lira did she receive?

26. **Journal** Why must there be rules for order of operations for calculations?

Test Prep

When comparing integers with the same sign, think of their placement on a number line. The one that is the farthest to the left is the smaller integer.

27. Which list is sorted from least to greatest?

    Ⓐ $-1, -5, -8, -10$ Ⓑ $-10, -5, -8, -1$ Ⓒ $-10, -8, -5, -1$ Ⓓ None of these

28. Name two situations that would use positive and negative numbers.

Our Planet   Diverse Earth

Have you ever considered how different and diverse the world is? The earth contains an estimated 30 million species of insects and 260,000 species of plants. Although the world population is approximately 5.7 billion, there is only one human species. Yet how different that species can be. Over 3000 different languages are spoken in 191 different countries and 44 dependencies. There are countries with populations in the hundreds of millions and some with populations in the hundreds.

Think of how different the weather is across the earth. Winters in some countries rarely get above freezing, while the temperature on some deserts can rise to 180°F. There are hurricanes with winds of up to 210 mi/hr, tornadoes with even stronger winds, earthquakes that do billions of dollars of damage, and volcanoes whose lava can be as hot as 2012°F. There are also beautiful calm days, perfect for swimming, fishing, hiking, or any of the other forms of exercise and recreation.

1 Name some features of the earth that use large and small numbers.

2 What are some of the other diverse features of the earth?

You'll Learn ...

■ to plot pairs of integers on a coordinate grid

... How It's Used

Cartographers use a coordinate system based on latitudes and longitudes.

Vocabulary

latitude

longitude

coordinate system

x-axis

y-axis

origin

quadrant

ordered pair

x-coordinate

y-coordinate

▶ **Lesson Link** In Chapter 1, you learned how to make a scatterplot by plotting points. In this lesson, you will extend your knowledge to plotting points that involve negative numbers. ◀

To locate places on the earth, we use a system of imaginary lines called **latitude** and **longitude** . The lines that run east and west give the location with reference to the equator. They name the latitude. The lines that run north and south give the location with reference to an imaginary line running through Greenwich, England. They name the longitude. Any point on Earth can be located by its latitude and longitude.

Explore Coordinates

Finding Your Way

The following map shows the approximate latitudes and longitudes near where 0° latitude and 0° longitude intersect.

1. What are the approximate latitudes and longitudes of the following?

   a. Lagos   **b.** Namiba

   c. Ascension

2. The following are the approximate latitudes and longitudes of locations shown on the map. Name each location.

   a. Latitude of 13° N, longitude of 8° W

   b. Latitude of 4° S, longitude of 15° E

   c. Latitude of 16° S, longitude of 6° W

   d. Latitude of 14° N, longitude of 8° E

3. Explain how you found the places on the map.

Learn — Integers in the Coordinate System

Mapmakers use the system of latitude and longitude to show places on Earth. Mathematicians use a similar system of intersecting number lines to help locate points. Using these intersecting number lines, they create a *coordinate system*.

A **coordinate system** is formed by the intersection of a horizontal number line, the **x-axis**, and a vertical number line, the **y-axis**.

The lines intersect at the **origin**, $(0, 0)$.

The x-axis and the y-axis divide the coordinate grid into four **quadrants**. The axes are not in any quadrant.

Any point can be described by using an **ordered pair** (x, y).

The first coordinate, x, of an ordered pair (x, y), the **x-coordinate**, tells how far to move left or right from the origin along the x-axis.

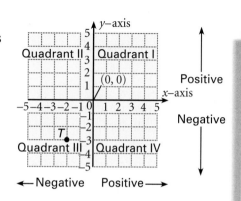

> ▶ **Language Link**
>
> The prefix *quad* means 4, as in quadrilateral (four sides), quadraphonic (4 channels), quadruplets (4 born at the same time), and quadruped (4-legged).

The second coordinate, y, of an ordered pair (x, y), the **y-coordinate**, tells how far to move down or up from the x-axis.

Point T is described by the ordered pair $(-2, -3)$.

Example 1

Plot the points $(-4, 3)$ and $(4, -3)$.

To plot the point $(-4, 3)$, start at the origin. Move 4 spaces to the *left* on the x-axis and 3 spaces *up* from the x-axis.

To plot the point $(4, -3)$, start at the origin. Move 4 spaces to the *right* on the x-axis and 3 spaces *down* from the x-axis.

Try It

Plot each point on a coordinate grid.

a. $(-1, -2)$ **b.** $(-5, 0)$ **c.** $(2, -3)$ **d.** $(-3, 2)$

Example 2

High and low tides are usually related to sea level. The points on the graph show the low and high tides, to the nearest foot, for several days. The *x*-coordinate represents low tide and the *y*-coordinate represents high tide. What are the coordinates of point *E*? Describe the low and high tides on that day.

To move from the origin, first move left 1 unit. Because we moved left, the *x*-coordinate is -1.

Then move up 2 units. Because we moved up, the *y*-coordinate is 2.

The point is $(-1, 2)$. The low tide was -1 foot (1 foot below sea level), and the high tide was 2 feet above sea level.

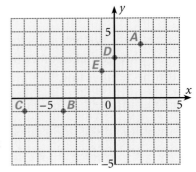

Try It

What are the coordinates of points *A*, *B*, *C*, and *D*? Describe the low and high tides on each day.

Notice the pattern in the signs of the *x*- and *y*-coordinates of all points in a quadrant. This can help you graph points or determine coordinates of an ordered pair on a graph.

Check | Your Understanding

1. Maps of the earth use a coordinate system of latitude and longitude. Does a globe use the same type of coordinate system? Explain.

2. How are the ordered pairs for points on an axis different from those in one of the four quadrants?

3. On a number line the origin is 0. Why is the origin $(0, 0)$ on a coordinate grid?

Practice and Apply

1. **Getting Started** To plot the point $(-2, -4)$;

   a. The -2 tells you to move 2 spaces along the _____ axis.

   b. Should you move right or left? Why?

   c. The -4 tells you to move 4 spaces from the _____ axis.

   d. Should you move up or down? Why?

Plot each point on a coordinate grid.

2. $(5, -2)$ 　　 3. $(-5, 0)$

4. $(-1, -2.5)$ 　　 5. $(3.5, -2.5)$

Find the coordinates of each point.

6. A 　　 7. B 　　 8. C

9. D 　　 10. E 　　 11. F

Name the points for each ordered pair.

12. $(4, 6)$ 　　 13. $(6, -3)$

14. $(0, -4)$ 　　 15. $(-5, -5)$

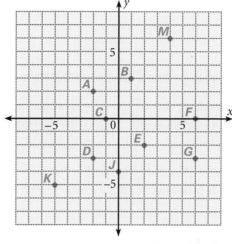

Geography Using the map, locate the approximate latitude and longitude coordinates of the following cities.

16. New York 　　 17. São Paulo

18. Nairobi 　　 19. Bombay

20. **Test Prep** Which city has latitude and longitude coordinates (26° N, 80° W)?

   Ⓐ Munich

   Ⓑ Chicago

   Ⓒ Buenos Aires

   Ⓓ Miami

21. Geometry Graph a triangle with vertices $(4, 6)$, $(1, 2)$, and $(4, 0)$. Graph another triangle with vertices $(-4, -6)$, $(-1, -2)$ and $(-4, 0)$. How are the triangles related? How are the coordinates of their vertices related?

Geometry Name the ordered pairs for the vertices of each figure. Name each figure.

22.

23.

Problem Solving and Reasoning

24. Critical Thinking Part of the square is missing. Describe how to graph and connect the appropriate points to complete it.

25. Communicate Without graphing, tell in which quadrant each point lies. Explain your choices.

    a. $(-160, 80)$ **b.** $(22.5, 45)$

    c. $(-416, -400)$ **d.** $\left(2, \dfrac{-1}{2}\right)$

Mixed Review

Sketch a bar graph to represent each set of data. *[Lesson 1-4]*

26.

Animal	Cat	Dog	Bird	Rat	Fish
Quantity	12	18	7	3	10

27.

Student	Abe	Ben	Chao	Deb	Ella
Height (in.)	43	52	46	47	58

28. The stalactites in an underwater cave are measured as follows: 47 in., 8 in., 26 in., $11\frac{1}{2}$ in., $30\frac{3}{4}$ in. What is the range in the lengths of the stalactites? *[Lesson 1-1]*

Find each absolute value. *[Lesson 2-1]*

29. $|-317|$ **30.** $|0|$ **31.** $|7 + 15|$

32. $|23 - 10|$

TECHNOLOGY

Using a Graphing Utility • Integers and Coordinates

Problem: In which quadrant is each of the following points located: (−3, −2), (−3, 2), (3, −2), and (3, 2)?

A graphing calculator's point-on command will help you find the answers.

① **Make sure your viewing window has a standard range.**

② **Starting from the home screen, access your calculator's point-on command.**

③ **Type in the x- and y-coordinates of the ordered pair (−3, −2). Press "enter." Make note of where the point is plotted.**

④ **Type in the x- and y-coordinates of each of the other pairs, pressing "enter" each time. Be sure to start from the home screen each time. Make note of where each point is plotted after you press "enter."**

Solution: (−3, −2) is in the third quadrant; (−3, 2), is in the second quadrant; (3, −2), is in the fourth quadrant; (3, 2) is in the first quadrant.

TRY IT

a. In which quadrant would (−2, 3) be located?

b. In which quadrant would (−4, −6) be located?

ON YOUR OWN

▶ Why does the viewing range have to be set properly when plotting points?

▶ How do you think the calculator plots points?

▶ If your calculator has a point-off command, what do you think it does?

Powers and Exponents

You'll Learn …

■ to change numbers from standard notation to exponential notation, and vice versa

… How It's Used

Astronomers use exponential notation to represent great distances.

Vocabulary

exponent

power

▶ **Lesson Link** You have studied multiplication for many years. In this lesson, you will learn shortcuts for multiplying the same number over and over. ◀

Explore Exponents

What Is Your Calculator Doing?

Materials: Scientific calculator

1. Find the $\boxed{x^2}$ key.

   a. Enter 4 and then press the $\boxed{x^2}$ key. What answer do you get? Enter 4 $\boxed{\times}$ 4 $\boxed{=}$. What answer do you get?

   b. Try a few more numbers. What does the $\boxed{x^2}$ do to any number that you enter?

2. Find the $\boxed{y^x}$ key or the $\boxed{\wedge}$ key.

   a. Enter 4 $\boxed{y^x}$ 3 $\boxed{=}$. What answer do you get? Enter 4 $\boxed{\times}$ 4 $\boxed{\times}$ 4 $\boxed{=}$. What answer do you get?

   b. Compare 2 $\boxed{y^x}$ 4 and 2 $\boxed{\times}$ 2 $\boxed{\times}$ 2 $\boxed{\times}$ 2. Compare 3 $\boxed{+/-}$ $\boxed{y^x}$ 4 and -3 $\boxed{\times}$ -3 $\boxed{\times}$ -3 $\boxed{\times}$ -3 $\boxed{=}$. What does the $\boxed{y^x}$ do to the numbers that you enter?

   c. Enter 3 $\boxed{+/-}$ $\boxed{y^x}$ 3 $\boxed{=}$. Enter 3 $\boxed{+/-}$ $\boxed{y^x}$ 4 $\boxed{=}$. Enter 3 $\boxed{+/-}$ $\boxed{y^x}$ 5 $\boxed{=}$. Enter 3 $\boxed{+/-}$ $\boxed{y^x}$ 6 $\boxed{=}$. Describe any patterns you see with odd exponents and even exponents.

Learn Powers and Exponents

Using an **exponent** is another way to show repeated multiplication.

Exponential Form	Expanded Form	Words	Value
base 3^5 exponent	$3 \times 3 \times 3 \times 3 \times 3$	Three to the fifth power	243

A **power** is a number that can be written as a product of equal factors.

32 is a power of 2.   32 is the fifth power of 2. $2^5 = 32$

Examples

1 The length of the Appalachian Trail is about 3^7 miles long.

Write 3^7 in standard form.

$$3^7 = 3 \times 3 \times 3 \times 3 \times 3 \times 3 \times 3 = 2187$$

The Appalachian Trail is about 2187 miles long.

2 Use a calculator to evaluate $(-4)^6$ and -4^6.

$(-4)^6$ is $-4 \times -4 \times -4 \times -4 \times -4 \times -4$. Enter 4 |+/−| |$y^x$| 6 |=| **4096**.

-4^6 is the opposite of $4 \times 4 \times 4 \times 4 \times 4 \times 4$. Enter 4 |$y^x$| 6 |=| |+/−| **−4096**.

Try It

Evaluate.

a. 5^4 **b.** 15^5 **c.** $(-2)^3$

> **HINT**
>
> Some calculators treat -4^6 as $(-4)^6$, others treat it as the opposite of 4^6. Check your calculator to see what it does.

We can now expand our order of operations to include exponents.

ORDER OF OPERATIONS

Do operations within parentheses or grouping symbols.
Do all exponents from left to right.
Do all multiplications and divisions from left to right.
Do all additions and subtractions from left to right.

Example 3

Evaluate $-2(9 - 6)^2 + 15$.

$-2(9 - 6)^2 + 15$

$-2(3)^2 + 15$ Do operations within parentheses or grouping symbols.

$-2(9) + 15$ Do all exponents from left to right.

$-18 + 15$ Do all multiplications and divisions from left to right.

-3 Do all additions and subtractions from left to right.

Try It

Evaluate.

a. $12 \div 3 \cdot 5 - 4^2$ **b.** $4(1 + 5)^2 \div 8$

c. Most computer fonts have $2^8 - 1$ different characters. Write this number in standard form. How many different characters are there?

WHAT DO YOU THINK?

Randy and Tanisha played a game where they would receive points based on the number of letters in words they could create by picking alphabet cards one at a time. A one-letter word would be worth 10 points, a two-letter word worth 100 points, a three letter word 1000 points and so on. They wondered how many points would be earned if players could not create a word with the cards they had during their turn.

Tanisha thinks ...

I'll make a chart and follow the pattern. Each time the exponent decreases by 1, the number is divided by 10. Looking at this pattern, I can see that the player would receive one point.

10^4	10,000	10,000
10^3	1,000	$10,000 \div 10$
10^2	100	$1,000 \div 10$
10^1	10	$100 \div 10$
10^0	?	?

Randy thinks ...

I'll use my scientific calculator.

I'll enter 10 $\boxed{y^x}$ 0.

The answer is 1.

What do you think?

What do you think the value of 4^0 is?

▶ **Technology Link**

Try entering different numbers to the zero power into your calculator. What do you get in each case?

Check | Your Understanding

1. If squaring a number always results in a positive number, explain why $-8^2 = -64$.

2. How is 3×6 different from 3^6?

3. Describe what happens when a nonzero number is raised to the zero power.

Practice and Apply

1. [Getting Started] Answer the questions to evaluate 8^4.

    a. What number is the base?

    b. What number is the exponent?

    c. How many times is 8 used as a factor?

    d. Multiply.

2. [Test Prep] What is the exponential form of $-2 \cdot -2 \cdot -2 \cdot -2$?

    Ⓐ -2^4 Ⓑ $(-2)^4$ Ⓒ 2^{-4} Ⓓ $(-2)^{-4}$

Geometry A shortcut to finding the area of a square rather than counting squares is to square the length of a side. Find each area.

3.   **4.**   **5.**   **6.**

Geometry A shortcut to finding the volume of a cube rather than counting cubes is to cube the length of a side. Find each volume.

7.   **8.**   **9.**   **10.**

11. Geography As the earth rotates each day, a person at the equator moves a distance of $2^2 \cdot 3 \cdot 5^2 \cdot 83$ miles around the earth, but a person at the arctic circle moves $2^2 \cdot 5 \cdot 17 \cdot 29$ miles. What are these distances in standard form?

Evaluate.

12. 7^2 **13.** $(-7)^2$ **14.** -7^2 **15.** 7^0

16. $(0)^4$ **17.** $(-1)^3$ **18.** $(-5)^0$ **19.** $(-2)^4$

20. -10^0 **21.** 1^3 **22.** $2(4-2)^3 \div 8$ **23.** $(7^2 + 11) - (5^2 + 35)$

24. $(2^4 + 3^2 + 7) \div 8$ **25.** $\dfrac{8^2 - 6(4)}{-2}$

PRACTICE 2-7

26. Patterns Fill in the chart. Describe any patterns that you see. Make a generalization if possible.

Number	Exponential Form	Number of Zeros in Number
1	10^0	0
10	10^1	1
100	10^2	?
1000	?	?
?	10^4	4

Problem Solving and Reasoning

27. Critical Thinking A square deck has an area of 121 square feet. What is the length of one side?

28. Choose a Strategy Each person has 2 parents. Each parent has 2 parents. Each grandparent has 2 parents. How many great-grandparents does a person have? Explain your answer.

Problem Solving

STRATEGIES

- Look for a Pattern
- Make an Organized List
- Make a Table
- Guess and Check
- Work Backward
- Use Logical Reasoning
- Draw a Diagram
- Solve a Simpler Problem

Critical Thinking Find each missing number.

29. $?^2 = 64$ **30.** $?^3 = -27$ **31.** $4^? = 64$ **32.** $16 = ?^2$ or $?^4$

33. Which do you think is greater, 2^6 or 6^2? Why? Use a calculator to see if your answer is correct.

Mixed Review

Identify each sampling as random or nonrandom. *[Lesson 1-5]*

34. From the population of Smith Junior High School students: Roberta asks the opinion of all the students in her social studies class.

35. From the population of voters in Orange County: Names are selected at random from the local telephone directory.

Add the following integers. *[Lesson 2-2]*

36. $43 + 52$ **37.** $-4 + 10$ **38.** $37 + (-26)$ **39.** $-31 + (-7)$

Scientific Notation Using Positive Exponents

▶ **Lesson Link** In Lesson 2-7, you worked with exponents. In this lesson, you will use exponents to write large numbers in a different form. ◀

Powers of 10 are very important when using this different notation for large numbers.

$10 = 10^1$, $100 = 10^2$, $1,000 = 10^3$, $10,000 = 10^4$, and so on.

Explore Scientific Notation

Is One a Lonely Number?

Look for patterns in the table below.

A		B	C
35	=	3.5×10	3.5×10^1
456	=	4.56×100	4.56×10^2
5,678	=	$5.678 \times$ _____?	$5.678 \times$ _____?
23,456	=	$2.3456 \times$ _____?	$2.3456 \times$ _____?
432,967	=	$4.32967 \times$ _____?	$4.32967 \times$ _____?
1,654,763	=	$1.654763 \times$ _____?	$1.654763 \times$ _____?

1. Complete column B using powers of 10 in standard notation.

2. Complete column C using powers of 10 in exponential notation.

3. What do you notice about all of the decimals in columns B and C?

4. How are the numbers of zeros in the powers of 10 in column B and the exponents in column C related to the whole numbers in column A?

5. How could you rewrite 11,854,623 to fit the pattern in columns B and C?

6. How could you rewrite 1,000,000,000 and 9,999,999,999 to fit the pattern in column C? What is the same about these two "rewrites?"

7. How could you rewrite 357,000,000 and 35,700,000 to fit the pattern in column C? What is the same about these two "rewrites?"

You'll Learn ...

■ to convert large numbers between standard notation and scientific notation

... How It's Used

Scientific notation makes it easier for geologists to describe features of the earth that involve large numbers.

Vocabulary

scientific notation

Problem Solving TIP

Make a place-value table for large numbers if you need it.

In describing features of the earth, scientists often use powers of 10 to express large numbers in **scientific notation** . In scientific notation, a number is written as a power of 10 times a number whose absolute value is less than 10 but greater than or equal to 1.

$$456{,}000{,}000 = 4.56 \times 10^8 \qquad -287 = -2.87 \times 10^2$$

To write a large number in scientific notation easily, move the decimal point to where you want it, count how many decimal places it moved, and write this as your power of 10. This works because moving the decimal left one place is the same as dividing by 10.

$2053 = 205.3 \times 10^1$ Move the decimal 1 place to the left.

    $= 20.53 \times 10^2$ Move the decimal another place to the left.

    $= 2.053 \times 10^3$ It is now in scientific notation.

Example 1

Mandarin, the principal language of China, is the world's most widely spoken language. It is estimated that 844 million people speak Mandarin as their primary language. Write this number in standard and scientific notation.

In standard notation, 844 million is written as 844,000,000.

In scientific notation, 844 million is written as 8.44×10^8.

Try It

Write the following numbers in standard and scientific notation.

a. English: 326 million people   **b.** German: 98 million people

Some numbers are too large for many calculators to display all of the digits. Some calculators automatically display such numbers in scientific notation.

Example 2

The earth is approximately 93 million miles from the sun. What is this distance in feet?

Enter 9.3 $\boxed{\times}$ 10 $\boxed{y^x}$ 7 $\boxed{=}$. The display will read 93000000. Press $\boxed{\times}$ 5280. The display shows *4.9104 11*.

The sun is about 4.9104×10^{11} feet from Earth.

Try It

The core temperature of the sun is estimated to be 15 million degrees Celsius. Find at least two ways to enter this number into your calculator.

Example 3

The following are calculator displays showing numbers in scientific notation. Write these numbers in standard notation.

a. *8.7 E 11*   **b.** *5.45 10*   **c.** *−4.5 15*

a. 8.7 E 11 means $8.7 \times 10^{11} = 8.7 \times 100,000,000,000$
= 870,000,000,000

b. 5.45 10 means $5.45 \times 10^{10} = 5.45 \times 10,000,000,000$
= 54,500,000,000

c. −4.5 15 means $-4.5 \times 10^{15} = -4.5 \times 1,000,000,000,000,000$
= −4,500,000,000,000,000

Try It

Write each calculator display in standard notation.

a. *9.6 E 10*   **b.** *−3.8 12*   **c.** *1.02 13*

Check   Your Understanding

1. Is there any number that cannot be represented in scientific notation?

2. Why is moving the decimal point left the same as dividing by a power of ten?

3. A number written in scientific notation has two factors. Describe each factor.

2-8 Exercises and Applications

Practice and Apply

1. **Getting Started** Use the following steps to write 28 million in scientific notation.

   a. Write 28 million in standard notation.

   b. How many places must the decimal point move to write the number as 2.8?

   c. Find the missing exponent: $28{,}000{,}000 = 2.8 \times 10^{?}$.

   d. Check your answer using your calculator.

2. **Test Prep** Which of the following numbers is in scientific notation?

   Ⓐ 68.954×10^{8} Ⓑ 0.956×10^{9} Ⓒ -11.00×10^{10} Ⓓ -3.458×10^{12}

Social Studies Write each of these 1994 approximate populations in scientific notation.

3. India: 936 million

4. Italy: 58 million

5. Germany: 81.1 million

6. Vatican City: 811

Social Studies Write each population in standard notation.

7. China: 1.20×10^{9}

8. U.S.: 2.6×10^{8}

9. Vietnam: 7.44×10^{7}

10. San Marino: 2.4×10^{4}

Write each calculator display in standard notation.

11. *9.14 E 9*   12. *3.006 12*   13. *1.8 07*   14. *−5.5 E 4*

15. **Number Sense** Without actually calculating, give the greater number in each pair. Explain.

   a. 3.4×10^{5} or 3.4×10^{4} **b.** 8.9×10^{5} or 3.95×10^{5}

   c. -4.6×10^{2} or 1.2×10^{2} **d.** 9.9×10^{7} or 1.1×10^{8}

16. Find at least two ways to enter 65.4 billion into your calculator.

17. **Science** The diameter of Earth is 1.28×10^{4} kilometers. The diameter of Jupiter is 1.43×10^{5} kilometers. How much larger is the diameter of Jupiter? Explain how you found your answer.

Problem Solving and Reasoning

18. **Communicate** Roger's family was trying to sell their house. The price listed in the real estate section of the paper was 105K (K = $1000).

   a. How much is their house selling for?

   b. Explain how this notation is similar to scientific notation. How is it different?

19. **Critical Thinking** A Russian cosmonaut spent 439 days in space, returning to the earth in March of 1995.

   a. How many hours did he spend in space? Write your answer in standard notation.

   b. How many minutes did he spend in space? Write this answer in scientific notation.

 Explain why the following are not examples of numbers in scientific notation.

20. 52.6×10^8 21. $3.71 + 10^9$ 22. 10×10^{12} 23. 0.43×10^9

Valeriy Polyakov, Russian cosmonaut

Mixed Review

For each stem-and-leaf diagram, construct the corresponding histogram. Assume the stems represent hundreds, and the leaves represent the tens digits. *[Lesson 1-6]*

24.

Stem	Leaf
0	77899
1	1233445567789
2	00344566789
3	1133457889

25.

Stem	Leaf
6	12244457788999
7	02245678
8	135579
9	03

Compute each of the following. *[Lesson 2-3]*

26. $-32 - (-8)$ 27. $-6 - 6$ 28. $23 - (-14)$ 29. $-32 - 42$

Project Progress

You should be able to use your knowledge of positive and negative numbers to divide your time line evenly, place events, and determine the amount of time that passed between significant events. Be prepared to answer questions about your time line!

Problem Solving

Understand
Plan
Solve
Look Back

Scientific Notation Using Negative Exponents

You'll Learn ...

■ to convert small numbers between standard notation and scientific notation

... How It's Used

Microbiologists work with very small numbers. Scientific notation makes this easier for them.

▶ **Lesson Link** In Lesson 2-8, you wrote large numbers in scientific notation using positive exponents. In this lesson you will learn to write very small numbers in scientific notation using negative exponents. ◀

Explore | Negative Exponents

Patterns Everywhere

The following fractions have been written as division problems, as division problems using exponents, and then as decimals.

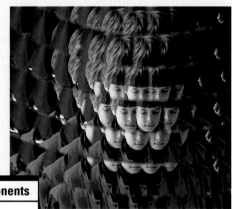

Number	Decimal Form	With Exponents
100	100.0	10^2
10	10.0	10^1
1	1.0	10^0
$\frac{1}{10}$	0.1	?
$\frac{1}{100}$	?	?

1. Continue the table until you reach $\frac{1}{100,000}$. Describe any patterns that you find.

2. How is each number related to the one above it?

3. As you move down the "Decimal Form" column, what happens to the decimal point?

4. As you move down the "With Exponents" column, what happens to the exponents?

5. Describe the relationship, if any, between the exponent and the location of the decimal point.

Learn Scientific Notation Using Negative Exponents

Negative exponents can be used to write very small numbers much as positive exponents were used to write very large numbers.

To write 0.00345 in scientific notation, move the decimal point to the right until there is only one nonzero digit to the left of the decimal point:

$0.00345 \rightarrow 0003.45$

Count the number of places you moved the decimal. This will be the exponent in the power of 10. Because you moved to the right, it will be negative, -3.

$0.00345 = 3.45 \times 10^{-3}$

HINT

Many calculators can be placed in scientific notation mode. In this mode, *all* numbers appear in scientific notation.

Example 1

The DNA in the chromosome of certain bacterium is very thin and is tightly packed inside the cell, twisted and coiled so that it is $\frac{1}{10000}$ cm long. Express this length in scientific notation.

Single human chromosome

Write 1 ten-thousandth as a decimal.

$\frac{1}{10000} = 0.0001$

0.0001

$00001. \times 10^{?}$

Move the decimal point 4 places to the *right* to get 1.0.

Since the decimal was moved 4 places, the exponent will be -4.

$\frac{1}{10000}$ cm $= 1.0 \times 10^{-4}$ cm.

Example 2

Write 52 millionths in scientific notation.

52 millionths $= 0.000052$ Write in decimal form.

$\qquad\qquad\quad = 5.2 \times 10^{-5}$ Move the decimal 5 places to the right.

Try It

a. Write 1 millionth in scientific notation.

b. Write 3 hundred-thousandths in scientific notation.

Examples

3 The shortest centipede measures approximately 7 hundredths cm long. Write this in standard and in scientific notation.

In standard notation, 7 hundredths is written as 0.07.

$$0.07 = 7 \times 0.01 = 7 \times 10^{-2}$$

In scientific notation, 7 hundredths is written as 7×10^{-2}.

4 A red blood cell is about 7 hundred-millionths of a cm in diameter. Enter this number into your calculator. There are several different ways to enter it.

a. Enter 7 $\boxed{\div}$ 100,000,000 $\boxed{=}$.
The display will read *0.00000007*.

b. Enter 7 $\boxed{\times}$ 10 $\boxed{y^x}$ 8 $\boxed{+/-}$ $\boxed{=}$.
The display will read *0.00000007*.

c. Some calculators have an $\boxed{EE}$ or $\boxed{E}$ key.
Enter 7 $\boxed{EE}$ 8 $\boxed{+/-}$. The display will read *7. −08*.

Try It

a. Some viruses are as small as 3 billionths of a cm. Write this number in standard and in scientific notation.

b. Enter 8 millionths into your calculator.

Some numbers are too small for many calculators to display all of the digits. The calculator either displays an error message or automatically displays the numbers in scientific notation.

Check | Your Understanding

1. How is writing a small number in scientific notation similar to writing a large number? How is it different?

2. Why is moving the decimal place to the left the same as multiplying by negative powers of ten? What other operation is the same as multiplying by a negative power of ten? Explain.

3. A small number written in scientific notation is written as two factors. Describe each factor.

2-9 Exercises and Applications

Practice and Apply

1. **Getting Started** Use the following steps to write 35 hundred-thousandths in scientific notation.

   a. Write 35 hundred-thousandths in standard notation.

   b. How many places must the decimal point move? In which direction?

   c. Find the missing exponent: $0.00035 = 3.5 \div 10^?$.

   d. Check your answer using a calculator.

2. Which of the following name the same number?

   a. 10^4 **b.** $\dfrac{1}{1000}$ **c.** $\dfrac{1}{10^4}$ **d.** 10^{-4}

3. **Test Prep** Which of the following numbers is greater than 1?

   Ⓐ 0.356   Ⓑ −2.9   Ⓒ 1.00007   Ⓓ 0.9999

Write each number in scientific notation.

4. Forty millionths   **5.** Four hundred fifty-five hundred-thousandths

Science The following are approximate lengths of very small organisms. Write each in scientific notation.

6. Water fleas: 0.0078 inches

7. *Euglena:* 254 thousandths mm

8. *Mycoplasma laidlawii:* 0.0000000254 inches

9. *Paramecium:* 0.00007 m

Paramecium

Measurement Write each amount in standard notation.

10. Strain of H39 bacteria: 1.0×10^{-16} m   **11.** A nanosecond: 10^{-9} second

12. Weight of smallest insectivore (insect-eating mammal): 5.2×10^{-2} kg

13. **Science** The human eye can revolve 0.0003 of an arc in 1 minute. Write this number in scientific notation.

Write each calculator display in standard notation.

14. *9.23 E −9*   **15.** *4.004 −8*

16. *2.5 −05*   **17.** *−2.1 E −4*

18. **Science** There are 3.5×10^4 species of mites, which are the largest and most diverse group of arachnids (8-legged insects). An adult spider mite is typically 3.8×10^{-2} in. long. Express each of these numbers in standard notation.

Red spider mite

19. **Number Sense** Without actually calculating, choose which number in each pair is greater. Explain your answers.

    a. 4.4×10^2 or 4.4×10^{-2}

    b. 1.9×10^{-3} or 1.95×10^{-3}

    c. -1.5×10^{-2} or 1.5×10^{-2}

    d. 9.8×10^{-7} or 1.8×10^{-8}

20. Find at least two ways to enter 2.3 millionths into your calculator.

21. The smallest hole ever drilled was 3.16×10^{-10} meters. Write this number in standard notation.

Problem Solving and Reasoning

22. **Communicate** Joan said that the number 45.545×10^{-5} is written in scientific notation. Do you agree or disagree? Explain.

23. **Critical Thinking** Arrange each of the following numbers from greatest to least. Explain your answer.

    a. 1.24×10^{-3} **b.** 2.24×10^{-2} **c.** 1.89×10^{-4} **d.** -2.6×10^{-2}

24. **Choose a Strategy** The width of a human hair is 7.9×10^{-3} inch. The width of a sheet of paper is approximately 3.0×10^{-3} inches. Which is wider and by how much? Explain how you got your answer.

25. **Journal** Explain how you would determine which is greater, 0.00056 or 5.1×10^{-4}.

Problem Solving

STRATEGIES

- Look for a Pattern
- Make an Organized List
- Make a Table
- Guess and Check
- Work Backward
- Use Logical Reasoning
- Draw a Diagram
- Solve a Simpler Problem

Mixed Review

Make a scatterplot for the data set. Decide whether there is an increasing trend, a decreasing trend, or no trend at all. *[Lesson 1-7]*

26. $(3, 9), (5, 4), (7, 3), (6, 4), (4, 6), (3, 4), (6, 8), (5, 2), (8, 6)$

Multiply or divide. *[Lesson 2-4]*

27. $12 \cdot (-4)$ 28. $(-4)(-10)$ 29. $-20 \cdot 3$ 30. $24 \cdot 4$

31. $-32 \div 8$ 32. $25 \div (-5)$ 33. $48 \div 8$ 34. $-100 \div (-10)$

Section 2B Connect

In this Connect, you will look at the diverse features of Earth and represent both the small and large numbers in scientific notation.

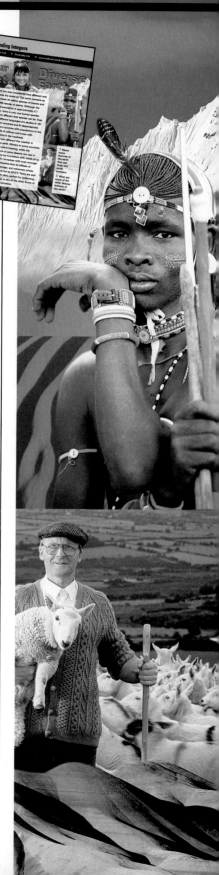

Our Diverse Planet Earth

Match each feature of Earth with its measurement.

1.	Largest female marine worm	**A.**	0.0128 oz
2.	Smallest male marine worm	**B.**	920,000,000°F
3.	Largest bird egg (ostrich)	**C.**	1×10^{-12} mm
4.	Smallest bird egg (hummingbird)	**D.**	39.3 in. long
5.	Diameter of a proton	**E.**	326,000,000 mi³
6.	Diameter of an electron	**F.**	2.8×10^{-10} °K
7.	Amount of water on the earth	**G.**	0.04 in. long
8.	Highest temperature in a lab setting	**H.**	1×10^{-15} mm
9.	Lowest temperature in a lab setting	**I.**	3.75 lb

10. Which numbers are written in standard notation? Which are in scientific notation?

11. If a number is in scientific notation, write it in standard notation.

12. If a number is in standard notation, write it in scientific notation.

13. What are the advantages of the two notations?

14. Sort the numbers from least to greatest.

15. If two measurements are written in scientific notation and use the same units, how can you tell which measurement is greater?

16. If two measurements are written in scientific notation but have different units, such as °F and oz, what comparisons can be made between the measurements?

Geography Using the map, locate the approximate latitude and longitude of each of these South American cities.

1. Santiago, Chile   **2.** Caracas, Venezuela

Plot each point. In what quadrant is each point?

3. $(2, -2)$ **4.** $(-3, 0)$ **5.** $(-4, 6)$ **6.** $(-2, -3)$

Find the area or volume of each of the following.

7.   **8.**

9. Journal Explain how -3^2 is different from $(-3)^2$.

Social Studies Write each of the approximate 1994 populations in either scientific notation or in standard form.

10. Tokyo: 27 million   **11.** Wyoming: 4.75×10^5

12. Science Thorium is toxic if 0.00000000000000024 g/m^3 are in the air. Write this number in scientific notation.

Write each of the following calculator displays in standard notation.

13. $4.14\ E\ 6$ **14.** $2.05\ -6$ **15.** $1.9\ -04$ **16.** $-5.2\ E\ 4$

17. Order the following numbers from smallest to largest.

    a. 1.56×10^{-3} **b.** 2.98×10^2 **c.** 9.96×10^3 **d.** -2.5×10^{10}

Test Prep

When asked to find the number that doesn't belong, first simplify each expression, then compare the results to find the one that is not the same.

18. Which of the following does not name the same number?

    Ⓐ 10^0 Ⓑ 1 Ⓒ $(-5)^0$ Ⓓ 10

Extend Key Ideas ● Patterns and Relationships

Sequences

A *sequence* is a set of numbers arranged in a certain order that can also be shown in a geometric pattern. The numbers in a sequence are called the *terms* of the sequence.

The sequence 1, 3, 6, 10, ..., is called the *triangular numbers*. The first term is 1, the second term is 3, the third term is 6, and so on. The rule for finding any term of the sequence is called the rule for the *n*th term.

1st term	2nd term	3rd term	4th term	*n*th term
1	3	6	10	$\dfrac{n(n+1)}{2}$

1 box   3 boxes   6 boxes   10 boxes

To find the fifth term, use $n = 5$, $\dfrac{n(n+1)}{2} = \dfrac{5(5+1)}{2} = 15.$

The fifth term in the sequence of triangular numbers is 15.

1. Find the sixth, seventh, and eighth terms of the sequence above.

2. The rule for the *n*th term of a sequence is $\dfrac{n(n-1)}{2}$. Give the first five terms of the sequence.

3. Give the rule for the *n*th term of the sequence of *square numbers* 1, 4, 9, 16, 25, 36. Use dots to draw the geometric pattern for the first five terms of the sequence.

4. Sequences can be used to predict patterns in everyday life. On Monday, the first day of a flu epidemic, three students in the eighth grade were absent. Each day, there was *n* times as many absences as the day before, until there were 48 on Friday. Find *n*. How many students were absent on Tuesday, Wednesday, and Thursday?

Chapter 2 Summary and Review

Graphic Organizer

Section 2A Operations Using Integers

Summary

- **Integers** are whole numbers and their opposites.

- The **absolute value** of a number is the distance it is from zero.

- When **adding integers with the same sign,** add the numbers and use the sign of the numbers. When adding **integers with different signs,** subtract the numbers and use the sign of the larger number. Subtracting is the same as adding the opposite.

- The product of two numbers with the same sign is positive. The product of two numbers with different signs is negative. Dividing by a number is the same as multiplying by its multiplicative inverse.

- When simplifying expressions involving more than one operation, follow the **order of operations.**

Review

1. Find $|-43|$.

2. Find $|-8| - 4$.

3. Add $82 + (-25)$.

4. Subtract $-67 - (-101)$.

5. Multiply $16 \times (-9)$.

6. Multiply $-29(-72)$.

7. Divide $-56 \div (-7)$.

8. Evaluate $-2(8 - 4)$.

9. Evaluate $\dfrac{3(18 - (-7))}{5}$.

10. The temperature was $-7°F$ and it went down $17°F$. What was the new temperature?

Section 2B Extending Integers

Summary

■ The **x-axis** and the **y-axis** intersect at the **origin**, and create a **coordinate system.** The two axes divide the system into four **quadrants,** and the location of any point can be described as an **ordered pair** (x, y).

■ A **power,** or **exponent,** is a number that indicates how many times the **base** should be multiplied by itself.

■ Very large and very small numbers written in **standard notation** can be expressed in **scientific notation** as a number between one and ten multiplied by a power of ten.

Review

11. Find the coordinates of each point.

   a. A **b.** B **c.** C

12. Give the coordinates of points A, B, and C.

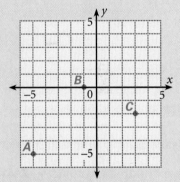

13. Write 4^6 in expanded form.

14. Write $7 \times 7 \times 7 \times 7$ in exponential form.

15. Evaluate 15^1.

16. Evaluate $(-3)^3$.

17. Write three hundred fifty thousand in scientific notation.

18. Write two ten-thousandths in scientific notation.

19. Write 7.25×10^{-5} in standard notation.

20. Write 3.78×10^5 in standard notation.

21. Write 77,600,000 in scientific notation.

22. Write 0.0000034 in scientific notation.

23. An amoeba, a one-celled animal, is approximately 9 millionths of a millimeter in diameter. Express its size in scientific notation.

24. At the Hot Springs in Arkansas, 950,000 gallons of spring water flow each day. Write this number in scientific notation.

Chapter 2 Assessment

Use <, >, or = to compare each number pair.

1. $5 \square -7$ **2.** $4 \square |-4|$ **3.** $|0| \square |-1|$ **4.** $|2| \square |-2|$

Add or subtract.

5. $3 + (-2)$ **6.** $-2 + 3$ **7.** $5 + (-7)$ **8.** $-7 + 5$

9. $25 + (-100)$ **10.** $-250 + 65$ **11.** $-250 + (-65)$ **12.** $8 - 27$

13. $-14 - 8$ **14.** $-6 - (-3)$ **15.** $-7 - (-17)$ **16.** $1 - (-8)$

17. $4 - 9 + (-3) - (-8) + 10$ **18.** $-12 - 16 - (-16) - (-12)$

19. The water level in the levee changed from 8 ft above sea level to 13 ft below sea level. How much did the water level rise or fall?

20. Find the coordinates of points A, B, and C.

Multiply or divide.

21. $4(-2)$ **22.** $-6(-5)$ **23.** -1.5×40 **24.** $-60 \div 3$

Evaluate.

25. $\dfrac{4(5 - (-10))}{5}$ **26.** $4 \cdot 5 - (-10) \div 5$ **27.** 9^3 **28.** -2^6

29. A *light year* is the distance light travels in one year. This is approximately 10^{13} kilometers. Write this number in standard notation.

Write each number in scientific notation.

30. two hundred thousand   **31.** 71,077,345   **32.** 0.0035

Write each number in standard notation.

33. 2.37×10^4 **34.** 1.7×10^0 **35.** 6.02×10^{-3}

Performance Task

Many calculators can be set so that numbers appear in *engineering* notation. Engineering notation is similar to scientific notation in that a number is shown as a multiplier and a power of ten. Each of the following is given in engineering notation. Write it in standard and scientific notation.

   a. *12.745 3*   **b.** *387.2257 6*   **c.** *−2.675 3*   **d.** *84 −3*

Multiple Choice

Choose the best answer.

1. What number is not represented in the stem-and leaf diagram below? *[Lesson 1-1]*

Stem	Leaf
7	3 5 9
6	0 2 2 5 7 8
5	1 7 8 8
4	3 6 6 9 9 9

Ⓐ 46   Ⓑ 65   Ⓒ 79   Ⓓ Not here

2. For which data set would the median be the mean of the two middle values? *[Lesson 1-2]*

Ⓐ 1, 3, 7, 10, 12, 16, 19, 20

Ⓑ 2, 6, 10, 13, 15

Ⓒ 8, 15, 20, 22, 27, 27, 29

Ⓓ Not here

3. Which frequency is incorrect? *[Lesson 1-6]*

Color	Tally	Frequency
Brown	ЖЖ ЖЖ IIII	14
Red	ЖЖ III	8
Yellow	ЖЖ ЖЖ ЖЖ ЖЖ II	17
Orange	ЖЖ ЖЖ II	12

Ⓐ Brown   Ⓑ Red

Ⓒ Yellow   Ⓓ Orange

4. Wind chill temperatures of less than $-25°$F are considered dangerous. Which is not less than $-25°$? *[Lesson 2-1]*

Ⓐ $-37°$ Ⓑ $-23°$ Ⓒ $-28°$ Ⓓ $-124°$

5. Which of the following is listed in order from least to greatest? *[Lesson 2-1]*

Ⓐ $-7, 5, 0, -5, 7$

Ⓑ $25, -14, 6, 14, 20$

Ⓒ $-13, -10, -2, 3, 5$

Ⓓ $-9, -6, 3, 0, 6$

6. Which is equivalent to subtracting -6? *[Lesson 2-2]*

Ⓐ Subtracting 6   Ⓑ Adding 6

Ⓒ Adding -6 Ⓓ Not here

7. To graph the point $(-3, 4)$, begin at the origin and: *[Lesson 2-6]*

Ⓐ Move right 3 units and up 4 units.

Ⓑ Move right 3 units and down 4 units.

Ⓒ Move left 3 units and up 4 units.

Ⓓ Move left 3 units and down 4 units.

8. Which expression means "multiply the sum of 5 squared and -9 by -2?" *[Lesson 2-7]*

Ⓐ $-2(5 + (-9))^2$ Ⓑ $-2 \cdot 5^2 + (-9)$

Ⓒ $-2(5^2 + (-9))$ Ⓓ $5^2(-9 + (-2))$

9. Which expression represents 7,500,000 in scientific notation? *[Lesson 2-8]*

Ⓐ 7.5×10^5 Ⓑ 7.5×10^6

Ⓒ 75×10^5 Ⓓ 75×10^6

10. This *Bacillus bacterium* is about 2.4×10^{-3} mm long. In standard notation, this is: *[Lesson 2-9]*

Ⓐ 0.0024 mm

Ⓑ 240 mm

Ⓒ 0.024 mm

Ⓓ Not here

Science

A rattlesnake gains a rattle every time it sheds its skin, about 3 times a year, plus it has about 5 additional rattles from babyhood. To find a rattlesnake's age, you could just count the rattles. Just don't get too close!

Arts & Literature

Samuel Butler (1600–1680) is remembered as a famous English poet and satirist. Butler was not a mathematician. However, from his poem, he should be:

> "And wisely tell
> what hour
> o'th'day
> The clock
> doth strike,
> by algebra."

Entertainment

A director must choose music for a movie carefully. Film is run at 24 frames per second. For music that is played at a speed of two beats per second

24 frames of film = 2 beats

48 frames of film = 4 beats.

Variables, Expressions, and Equations

Social Studies Link
www.mathsurf.com/8/ch3/social

Social Studies

Some mathematicians saw beyond their world, such as Hindu mathematician Brahmagupta. He wrote algebra formulas that helped him with astronomical calculations, such as determining the positions of planets.

KEY MATH IDEAS

Variables, formulas, **and** algebraic expressions **help with computations when two quantities are related mathematically.**

Equations **are statements that two expressions are equal.**

Many equations can be solved by using the Addition Property of Equality **and the** Multiplication Property of Equality**.**

People of the World

Grace Hopper, mathematician and U. S. Navy Admiral, codeveloped the Cobol programming language and contributed to the development of modern computers. In 1991, she received the National Medal of Technology.

CHAPTER PROJECT

Problem Solving

Understand
Plan
Solve
Look Back

In this project, you will research number patterns that exist in nature—flowers, sea animals, land animals, and so on—and express these patterns using variable expressions.

Problem Solving Focus

Finding Unnecessary Information

Real-life problem solving often involves lots of data. Some of the data is needed to find the answer, but usually not all of it. You need to understand which data will help you answer the question and which will not.

When solving a problem, you need to determine which information is needed to solve the problem, and which information can be ignored. Some of the problems below have unnecessary information. Some problems may not have unnecessary information. For each problem, state the information that you think is unnecessary.

1 Kivi plans to build a display cabinet for his collection of civil war miniature soldiers. It will have five shelves and will be 6 feet high. He has $35.00 to spend on materials and wants the shelves to be spaced evenly. How much space should he leave between each shelf?

2 The collection has over 500 pieces. On Kivi's birthday, his father buys him 4 metal soldiers and a horse for $45.00. His grandfather gives him $50.00 which Kivi uses to buy 4 identical soldiers. Should Kivi have money left over?

3 Kivi rents a booth at a collectors' fair. Visitors pay a $5.00 admission fee and $\frac{1}{4}$ of the profits go to booth renters. Last year's fair was three days and had 1,585 visitors. Expenses averaged $300 a day, and there were 45 booths. How much money did Kivi receive?

4 This year's fair will last 4 days. Kivi will display 250 of his rarest miniatures. If 35 collectors display, and the average attendance, expenses, and payment is the same as last year, what will Kivi's share be?

Where Did the Time Go?

On December 31, 1992, 97 people celebrated New Year's Eve in Shannon, Ireland. Shortly after midnight, they boarded a Concorde and flew to Bermuda, arriving at 11:21 P.M. the *previous day* so they could celebrate the New Year's arrival again.

Have you ever traveled to another city where the time is earlier than when you left home? This happens because the world is divided into 24 time zones. Time zones were established so that at approximately noon in any part of the world the sun will be directly overhead. If the whole world used the exact same time, it would be dark at noon in some places.

In the continental United States, there are four time zones: Eastern, Central, Mountain, and Pacific. Because of the rotation of the earth, it is earlier as you move westward. For example, when it is 10 A.M. in New York, it is only 7 A.M. in Los Angeles.

1 Airline schedules use local times. Discuss some advantages and disadvantages of this.

2 Discuss some situations where differences in time zones have led to confusion.

3 Look at a globe near the North and South Poles. What happens to the time zones there? What effect do you think this has?

3-1 Formulas and Variables

▶ Lesson Link You've probably seen mathematical sentences that involve letters, for example, $p = 2l + 2w$. Many of these are useful in everyday life. ◄

You'll Learn ...

■ how to use familiar formulas as an introduction to algebra

... How It's Used

Pilots of small planes use a formula based upon ground temperature to find how high they can fly before ice forms on the wings.

Vocabulary

formula

variable

substitute

constant

Explore | Formulas

Letter Fly!

Materials: Calculator (optional)

1. A flight attendant needs to count all the passengers on two planes so that snacks can be served. Each ● represents a passenger. How many snacks are needed?

2. Is there a method other than counting that the flight attendant could use to find the number of snacks needed for both planes?

3. How many small boxes are in each rectangle?

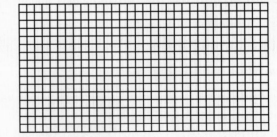

4. How is Question 3 similar to Question 1?

5. Try each of the following. Which are easy to compute? Which would take too long to compute without a shortcut method?

   a. Start with 3. Add 7 four times. What is the result?

   b. Start with −4. Add 3 six hundred times. What is the result?

   c. Start with 8. Add 12 six hundred times. What is the result?

6. Describe a shortcut method for finding the answers to Parts b and c in Question 5. Explain why it works.

Many real-world quantities are related mathematically. For example, *distance* equals *rate of speed* multiplied by *time*. In symbols this is $d = rt$.

Multiplication of r by t can be shown several ways:

$$rt \quad r \times t \quad r \cdot t \quad (r)(t)$$

A **formula** such as $d = rt$ states the relationship among unknown quantities represented by **variables** . Here the variables are d, r, and t. To use a formula, you need to **substitute** values for the variables. Some formulas include **constants** . For example, in the formula $p = 2l + 2w$, 2 is a constant. A constant is a number that does not vary.

Examples

1 A popular passenger plane for many years was the Douglas DC-3. It cruises at 160 mi/hr. At this speed how far would it fly in 2.5 hours?

$d = \quad r \cdot t$ Use the formula $d = rt$.

$d = 160 \cdot 2.5$ Substitute known values.

$d = 400$ Multiply to find the unknown value.

The Douglas DC-3 would travel 400 miles in 2.5 hours.

2 How long would it take each plane to fly from New York to Paris, a distance of about 3600 miles? Use the formula $t = \frac{d}{r}$.

Airspeeds

Make of plane:
Airbus 300 — 530 mi/hr
Boeing 747 — 600 mi/hr
Concorde — 1350 mi/hr

Speed (mi/hr): 0   500   1000   1500

Airbus 300

$t = \frac{d}{r} \rightarrow \frac{3600}{530} \approx 6.8$

Boeing 747

$t = \frac{3600}{600} = 6$

Concorde

$t = \frac{3600}{1350} \approx 2.7$

The Airbus would take about 6.8 hours, the Boeing 747, 6 hours, and the Concorde about 2.7 hours.

Test Prep

As you divide 3600 by larger numbers, the quotients get smaller.

Remember

The symbol $\approx$ means "is approximately equal to." **[Previous course]**

Example 3

Pilots sometimes use the temperature formula $T = G - 0.01h$, where G is the ground temperature and T is the temperature at an altitude of h meters. Both temperatures are in degrees Celsius. A pilot takes off when the ground temperature is 10°C and ascends to an altitude of 2000 meters. Is ice likely to form on the wings? Explain.

$T = G - 0.01h$	Use the given formula.
$T = 10 - 0.01(2000)$	Substitute known values.
$T = 10 \boxed{-} 0.01 \boxed{\times} 2000$	Use a calculator to evaluate.
$T = -10$	

The air temperature at 2000 meters is -10°C. Since 0°C is the freezing point of water, ice is likely to form on the wings at this altitude.

► Technology Link

If your calculator shows 19,980 instead of -10, it does not follow the order of operations you learned in Chapter 2! You will need to do the multiplication first.

Try It

a. It is approximately 300 miles from Havana, Cuba, to Miami, Florida. How long would it take each plane to make this trip?

Private plane	120 mi/hr
Bi-plane	215 mi/hr
Commercial plane	460 mi/hr

b. If the ground temperature is 20°C and a pilot ascends to an altitude of 2500 meters, is ice likely to form on the wings? Explain.

Study TIP

Make a list of useful formulas that you have used in this lesson and in other places. Keep the list in your notebook.

Check   Your Understanding

1. Explain the meaning of a variable in a formula.

2. Why are formulas useful?

3. Kaye used $d = t \cdot r$ rather $d = rt$. Does this formula give the same values for d? Why or why not?

4. The formula for the circumference of a circle is $C = 2\pi r$, where r is the radius of the circle and π is known to be 3.14159265…. Is π a constant or a variable? Why or why not?

Practice and Apply

Getting Started Decide if you would use $d = rt$, $r = \frac{d}{t}$, or $t = \frac{d}{r}$ to answer each question, where d, r, and t stand for *distance, rate of speed,* and *time*. Then answer the question.

1. A plane flies 600 miles in 3 hours. What is its speed?

2. How long would it take a helicopter to rise 6000 feet if it rises at 1500 feet per minute?

3. A motorcycle travels at an average speed of 55 miles per hour for 3 hours. How far does it travel?

4. A 3-toed sloth can run the 100-m dash in 22 minutes. How fast is this in m/min?

Solve each formula for the values given. The purpose of the formula is given.

5. $A = lw$ for $l = 95$ and $w = 37$ (*Area*, given *length* and *width*)

6. $P = 2l + 2w$ for $l = 5\frac{1}{2}$ and $w = 2\frac{1}{4}$ (*Perimeter*, given *length* and *width*)

7. $V = lwh$ for $l = 32$, $w = 14$, and $h = 7$ (*Volume*, given *length*, *width*, and *height*)

8. $C = 2\pi r$ for $r = 3.2$. Use 3.14 for π (*Circumference*, given the *radius*)

9. $F = 1.8C + 32$ for $C = 20$ (*Fahrenheit* temperature, given *Celsius* temperature)

10. $A = s^2$ for $s = 30$ (*Area* given *side length*)

11. $T = 0.04p$ for $p = \$24.75$ (*Tax* given *price*)

12. $C = np$ for $n = 24$ and $p = \$1.95$ (*Cost* given *number of items* and *price*)

13. History Charles Lindbergh was the first person to fly nonstop solo across the Atlantic. In 1927 he flew from New York to Paris, a distance of 3610 miles, in 33.5 hours. What was his average speed?

14. Meteorology One general principle is that if t is the time in seconds between a lightning flash and the following peal of thunder, then $d = \frac{1}{5}t$ gives your distance (d) from the lightning flash (in miles). If a person hears thunder 15 seconds after a flash, is the lightning more or less than 10,000 feet away? (1 mile = 5,280 ft)

15. Consumer A magazine article says to use the formula $S = 3F - 24$ to find your shoe size, where S is shoe size and F is the foot length in inches. Measure your own foot. Does the formula work for you?

16. **Journal** Describe a calculation you could not easily do without a formula. How does a formula make the calculation easier?

PRACTICE 3-1

17. **Test Prep** Which formula would give $T = 35$ if 7 is substituted for k?

    Ⓐ $T = \dfrac{k}{5}$ Ⓑ $k = T \times 5$ Ⓒ $T = 2k + 21$ Ⓓ $T = (k - 1)^2$

Problem Solving and Reasoning

Problem Solving
STRATEGIES

- Look for a Pattern
- Make an Organized List
- Make a Table
- Guess and Check
- Work Backward
- Use Logical Reasoning
- Draw a Diagram
- Solve a Simpler Problem

18. Choose a Strategy The longest parachute jump occurred in 1960 when Captain Joseph Kittinger jumped from a balloon at 102,200 feet. The entire jump took 825 seconds (13.75 minutes). If an object falls without air resistance, the distance it falls, in feet, is related to the time it falls, in seconds, by $d = 16t^2$. Estimate how long it would have taken an object to fall without air resistance from the same height as Kittinger's jump.

19. Communicate The graph shows the maximum recorded speed (without assistance from wind or gravity) for the three fastest birds.

Spinetailed swift

Magnificent frigate bird

Spur-winged goose

Maximum Airspeeds

Spinetailed swift 106 mi/hr
Magnificent frigate bird 95 mi/hr
Spur-winged goose 88 mi/hr

Type of bird

0 10 20 30 40 50 60 70 80 90 100 110
Speed (mi/hr)

a. Use $t = \dfrac{d}{r}$ to find how long it would take each to fly 500 miles. Round to the nearest hundredth.

b. Do you think these times are reasonable for these birds? Why or why not?

Mixed Review

Make a line plot for each set of data. *[Lesson 1-1]*

20. 8, 7, 11, 12, 10, 8, 12, 8, 11, 13   **21.** 89, 92, 85, 82, 84, 86, 92, 89, 85

22. A soft drink manufacturer conducts taste tests at a supermarket near the manufacturer's factory. Is this a good test to determine whether to change its soft drink formula? Why or why not? *[Lesson 1-8]*

Algebraic Expressions and Equations

▶ Lesson Link You have already learned how to apply the order of operations and the distributive property to operations with numbers. Now you can apply the same concepts to situations with variables. ◀

Explore | Algebraic Expressions

Runaway Runway

1. Airport runway A is 400 feet wide by 4000 feet long. What is its area?

2. Because some planes require longer runways, the airport plans to extend the runway by 1000 feet. What is the area of the added portion?

3. Add the area of the original runway and the area of the extension. What is the total area of the runway after it is extended? Can you find this area another way? Explain.

4. Suppose runway B will also be extended, but the length of the extension has not been determined. What is the area of the original runway? What is the area of the extension? Write the total area as the sum of the areas of the original runway and the extension.

5. Describe the area of the new runway B using the second method you used in Question 3. What is the length? What is the width? Write the area as the product of the length and width.

6. What do you know about the answers to Questions 4 and 5? Why is this true?

You'll Learn ...

■ how to apply algebraic expressions in a wide variety of situations

■ how to solve simple equations

... How It's Used

Physicians use algebraic expressions to determine safe and effective dosage levels of medicines.

Vocabulary

algebraic expression

evaluate

simplify

equation

solve

solution

Learn   Algebraic Expressions and Equations

An expression that involves variables, numbers, and operation symbols is called an **algebraic expression** . To **evaluate** an algebraic expression, substitute values for each variable and **simplify** by applying the order of operations.

Example 1

An airline estimates that each passenger with baggage weighs 224 pounds. A gallon of fuel weighs about 6 pounds. A Boeing 747 can carry 490 passengers and 47,000 gallons of fuel. Approximately how much added weight does the full plane carry?

$224p + 6g$ $224p + 6g$ represents the added weight.

$224(490) + 6(47,000)$ Substitute known values.

$= 109,760 + 282,000$ Evaluate using the order of operations.

$= 391,760$

A full Boeing 747 carries almost 400,000 pounds of added weight!

An **equation** states that two expressions are equal. $12 = 4 \times 3$ is an equation. Many equations with variables can be made to be true when the correct substitutions are made. Consider $12 = r \times 3$.

Replace r with 7.   Replace r with 4.

$12 = 7 \times 3$ $12 = 4 \times 3$

$12 = 21$ false for $r = 7$ $12 = 12$ true for $r = 4$

To **solve** an equation means to find the replacement that makes the sentence true. This replacement is called the **solution** .

Example 2

a. Solve $m + 2 = 5$.   **b.** Solve $3y = 60$.

You know $3 + 2$ is 5 and $3(20)$ is 60, so the solution to the first equation is $m = 3$, and $y = 20$ is the solution to the second.

Try It

Solve each equation.   **a.** $x + 10 = 30$ **b.** $3x = 24$

You can use a graphics calculator to evaluate expressions. The arrows represent the STO▸ key, and the results are shown on the right.

490→P
     490
47000→G
     47000
224P+6G
     391760

Remember

An expression does **not** have an = symbol, but an equation always does.

A landscaper has sketched a plan for a large rectangular garden with a flower bed and a rock garden. Write an expression for the area of the flower bed.

Emma thinks ...

I'll find the area of the entire garden and subtract the rock garden area.

The garden has an area of 30 times x ft^2.

The rock garden has an area of 30(5) ft^2.

So the flower bed area is 30x − 30(5) ft^2.

= 30x − 150 ft^2

Julio thinks ...

The flower bed has a length of 30 ft and a width of x − 5 ft. I'll multiply 30 by x − 5 and then write the area as a product.

30(x − 5) ft^2

x ft

5 ft

30 ft

What do you think?

Are Emma's and Julio's expressions equivalent? Why or why not?

Check Your Understanding

1. Why can't an algebraic expression be "solved?"

2. How can you evaluate an algebraic expression?

3. Write an expression equivalent to $10(12 + y)$.

4. Write an equation that's true, one that's false, and one that is true when you substitute correctly for a variable. Show the substitution.

Practice and Apply

1. **Getting Started** Follow the steps to evaluate the expression $25x + 40y$ for $x = 10$ and $y = 16$.

   a. Substitute the known values: $\quad 25 \cdot 10 + 40 \cdot$ _____

   b. Use the order of operations: $\quad = 250 +$ _____

   c. Simplify: $\quad\quad\quad\quad\quad\quad\quad = $ _____

Evaluate each expression. Remember that operations within parentheses should be done first.

2. $3x + 6y$ for $x = 50$ and $y = 20$

3. $12(x + 3)$ for $x = 25$

4. $12x + 36$ for $x = 2\frac{1}{2}$

5. $12 + 36x$ for $x = 2\frac{1}{2}$

6. $5 + 20y$ for $y = 2.5$

7. $(5 + 20)y$ for $y = 3.8$

8. $18(x + 3y)$ for $x = 10$ and $y = 12$

9. $(18x + 3) \cdot y$ for $x = 10$ and $y = 12$

Solve each equation.

10. $m - 3 = 5$

11. $t + 2 = 9$

12. $9y = 54$

13. $8x = 32$

14. $m = 5(-20)$

15. $r = -2(8 + 2)$

16. $m = 5(-2 + 1)$

17. $z = -\dfrac{45}{9}$

18. **Science** The expression for the mass of a piece of iron, in grams, is $7.9c$, where c is the number of cm^3 of iron. If there are 27 cm^3 of iron, what is its mass?

19. **Sports** When a tournament with n teams is held, the number of games needed for each team to play every other team is found using the expression $\frac{n \cdot (n - 1)}{2}$ where n is the number of teams. If there are 12 teams in a league, how many games are needed?

20. **Test Prep** Which expression always gives the same value as $3(x - 4)$?

    Ⓐ $3x + 4$ Ⓑ $3x - 4$ Ⓒ $3x - 12x$ Ⓓ $3x - 12$

21. **Chance** A coin is flipped r times. $h = \frac{1}{2}r$ represents the average number of times it would land heads up. What is the average number of times it would land heads up if the coin is flipped 25 times?

Problem Solving TIP

If you are not sure which algebraic expression is correct, pick a reasonable number and substitute it in each expression. Which result seems reasonable?

PRACTICE 3-2

22. Technology Complete the spreadsheet. Entries in column D are obtained by multiplying columns B and C.

	A	B	C	D
1	Fare Class	Number Sold	Ticket Price	Total of Sales
2	First Class	20	$220	
3	Business	17	$140	
4	Economy	81	$98	

Problem Solving and Reasoning

23. **Test Prep** Jill was on hold after making a call and had to listen to the same 30-second ad many times. Which expression would give the number of times she would hear the ad while waiting M minutes?

Ⓐ $30M$ Ⓑ $2M$ Ⓒ $\dfrac{M}{2}$ Ⓓ None of these

24. Critical Thinking Insert parentheses to make each expression equal 0.

a. $12 + 3 \cdot 5 - 75$ **b.** $12 - 3 \cdot 6 - 2$

25. Critical Thinking Alpha Air offers 1.0 frequent flyer mile for each mile traveled on Alpha Air (A), plus 0.5 mile for each mile traveled on Zeta Air (Z).

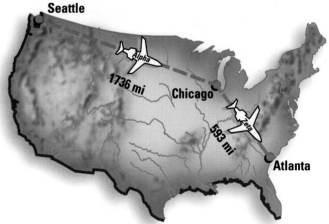

a. Write an expression for the miles earned on a one-way trip of A miles on Alpha Air and Z miles on Zeta Air. Then write an expression for the miles earned on a round-trip.

b. Alpha Airlines offers a free trip when a passenger earns 7500 frequent flyer miles. Mrs. Yager has already earned 3329 miles. If she flies from Seattle to Chicago to Atlanta and back, will she earn a free trip?

Mixed Review

Find the mean and median of each data set. *[Lesson 1-2]*

26. 8, 15, 17, 21, 34, 27, 31   **27.** 32.6, 42.8, 35.3, 42.8, 49.7

Find each absolute value. *[Lesson 2-1]*

28. $|732|$ **29.** $|78 - 78|$ **30.** $|-521|$ **31.** $|6 + 7|$

32. $|-1 - 3|$ **33.** $|-1 + 3|$ **34.** $|2 + (-2)|$ **35.** $|-2 + (-2)|$

3-3 Writing Algebraic Expressions

You'll Learn ...

■ how to translate verbal expressions into algebraic expressions

... How It's Used

Video game programmers must translate problems to computer commands and algebraic expressions precisely, or they won't get the results they want.

▶ **Lesson Link** You know that algebraic expressions and formulas can be used to represent real-life situations. When we translate words into mathematical symbols such as expressions and equations, we can use the expressions to help us solve problems. ◄

Explore | **Translating to Symbols**

Say What You Mean and Mean What You Say!

You are planning to leave today on vacation. You find a message written by your friend, who wrote it while listening to your answering machine. The friend is just learning English, and, unfortunately, used all capital letters and no punctuation. Here is the message:

YOUR FLIGHT DEPARTS CHICAGO AT 5 PM TOMORROW YOU WILL BE IN LONDON BY 8 AM IN THE MORNING YOU MUST CALL THE AIRLINE TO CONFIRM THIS CHANGE

1. When is the plane leaving, today or tomorrow?

2. When are you supposed to call the airline?

3. What can happen if words are translated to paper in a different way than they are intended?

4. If a teacher says, "Write the expression 3 times *x* plus 7," is there more than one way she could mean it?

5. The following headlines have actually appeared in newspapers. In each case, tell why the headline is unclear. Rewrite them to make them clearer.

   a. Local High School Dropouts Cut in Half

   b. Lansing Residents Can Drop Off Trees

   c. Dealers Will Hear Car Talk at Noon

   d. Squad Helps Dog Bite Victims

   e. Two Sisters Reunite After 18 Years at Checkout Counter

In the formula for distance, you could write *rate times time* instead of *rt*, but it is more convenient to use symbols. Often we choose letters such as *r* and *t* to remind us of the words they represent.

Example 1

A helicopter rises four times as fast as a hot-air balloon. Write an algebraic expression relating the rate of ascent of the helicopter to that of the balloon.

Let *b* equal the rate of ascent for the balloon.

Then 4*b* is the rate of ascent for the helicopter.

Example 2

Middle School Rave is selling its tapes by mail. Tapes cost $8.50 each, plus a $3.00 mailing charge per order. Write a formula for the total amount of any order. How much would Middle School Rave receive for an order of one tape? Of five tapes? Of ten tapes?

Total is $8.50 times the number of tapes, plus $3.00
$$T = 8.5 \times n + 3$$

For 1 Tape	For 5 Tapes	For 10 Tapes
$T = 8.5(1) + 3$	$T = 8.5(5) + 3$	$T = 8.5(10) + 3$
$T = 8.5 + 3$	$T = 42.5 + 3$	$T = 85 + 3$
$T = 11.5$	$T = 45.5$	$T = 88$

Remember

8.50 and 8.5 are the same number. **[Previous course]**

Middle School Rave would receive $11.50 for one tape, $45.50 for five tapes, and $88.00 for ten tapes.

Try It

a. An ostrich weighs about 100,000 times as much as a bee hummingbird. Write an expression relating the weight of the ostrich to the weight of the bee hummingbird.

b. A swim club charges a seasonal membership of $100 plus $2 each time a person swims. Write a formula for finding the total cost. Then find the cost for swimming 12, 20, and 48 times during the season.

▶ **Biology Link**

Even though the ostrich is the largest bird, it cannot fly.

When an airplane flies into a headwind, its speed is reduced. With a tailwind, the plane's speed is increased. Suppose a plane flies in still air at 300 mi/hr. Flying with a headwind of 10 mi/hr, the plane's speed with respect to the ground (the ground speed) is 290 mi/hr. With a tailwind of 10 mi/hr, its ground speed is 310 mi/hr.

Example 3

A plane flies in still air at 250 mi/hr. It flies into a headwind of unknown speed (w).

a. Write an expression for the plane's ground speed.

The ground speed, in mi/hr, is $250 - w$.

b. Suppose the plane flies for two hours into the steady headwind. Write an expression for the distance the plane travels.

Because the ground speed is $250 - w$ and the time is two hours, use $d = rt$ to multiply the ground speed by the time to find the distance.

$$d = \quad r \quad \times t$$

$$d = (250 - w)\, 2$$

$$= 500 - 2w \qquad \text{Use the distributive property to simplify.}$$

The distance flown with a headwind w is $500 - 2w$ miles.

Try It

If you stand on a moving airport walkway, you are carried along at 4.5 mi/hr. If you walk on it, your speed with respect to the ground is added to the walkway speed. Write an expression for your speed with respect to the ground if you walk on it at y mi/hr. Then write an expression for the distance you would travel on it in 0.05 hr.

Check | Your Understanding

1. When translating an English expression to an algebraic expression, how do you know what operations to use?

2. What situation might be translated into the expression $2c + 5$? Explain.

Practice and Apply

Getting Started Match each phrase on the left with an expression on the right, where *n* stands for a number.

1. 6 increased by a number   **a.** $\dfrac{n}{6}$

2. The quotient of a number and 6   **b.** $2n - 6$

3. A number decreased by 6   **c.** $6 + n$

4. Twice a number subtracted from 6   **d.** $6 - 2n$

5. 6 subtracted from twice a number   **e.** $n - 6$

6. Twice the sum of a number and 6   **f.** $2(n + 6)$

Write an expression for each situation.

7. The number of sides in *t* triangles   **8.** The number of inches in *f* feet

9. The number of yards in *i* inches   **10.** The number of seconds in *h* hours

11. To multiply a number by 9, first multiply by 10, and then subtract the original number. Write an expression or equation for this situation.

Write a formula for each situation. Then solve for two values and explain the solution in terms of the problem situation.

12. Science To change a Celsius temperature to Fahrenheit, multiply the number of Celsius degrees by 1.8, and then add 32.

13. Data To find the mean of three numbers, *a, b,* and *c,* add the numbers and divide by 3.

14. Geometry To find the approximate volume of a sphere in cm^3, multiply the cube of the radius by 4.19.

15. Give an example of an incorrect translation, and how using it could affect the solution to a problem.

Problem Solving and Reasoning

16. Math Reasoning If a plane travels *d* miles and fuel is consumed at *m* miles per gallon, then its total fuel consumption *g* is obtained by dividing *d* by *m.*

a. Write a formula to describe the situation.

b. A Concorde can have a fuel consumption rate as low as 0.2 miles per gallon. How many gallons of fuel would the Concorde use on a flight from Paris to New York, a distance of 3600 miles?

17. Critical Thinking Speeds of supersonic aircraft are usually given as a Mach number. The ground speed of a supersonic aircraft is the product of its Mach number and the speed of sound at the altitude of the plane.

a. Chuck Yeager was the first pilot to fly faster than the speed of sound in an airplane. In 1947 he flew at Mach 1.015 at an altitude of 42,000 ft where sound travels at 660 mi/hr. Find his speed in mi/hr.

b. The X-15 flew 4,535 mi/hr at Mach 6.72. What was the speed of sound when this speed was reached?

c. Can one plane fly faster at Mach 2.5 than another at Mach 2.6? If so, how? (Hint: The speed of sound in warm air at 0 ft is about 760 mi/hr.)

Lockheed F-117 Nighthawks

18. Choose a Strategy In 1935 Amelia Earhart became the first woman to fly nonstop solo from Hawaii to the mainland United States. The flight from Honolulu to Oakland, California (a distance of 2400 miles) took about 18.25 hours. Today's passenger jets routinely travel at 600 mi/hr. How much faster does a modern airline passenger travel per hour than Amelia Earhart did?

Problem Solving

STRATEGIES

- Look for a Pattern
- Make an Organized List
- Make a Table
- Guess and Check
- Work Backward
- Use Logical Reasoning
- Draw a Diagram
- Solve a Simpler Problem

Mixed Review

Sketch a box-and-whisker plot for each set of data. *[Lesson 1-3]*

19. 4, 7, 13, 6, 15, 4, 7, 12, 21, 3, 9   **20.** 23, 84, 53, 61, 43, 69, 64, 73

Add the following integers. *[Lesson 2-2]*

21. $-5 + 12$ **22.** $32 + (-40)$ **23.** $2 + (-3) + 5$ **24.** $-4 + 21 + (-5)$

25. $15 + (-15)$ **26.** $-17 + (-17)$ **27.** $-8 + (-9) + (-2)$ **28.** $4500 + (-201)$

Project Progress

Research some numerical facts about some things in nature. What happens to the numbers when you have a group of these things? Consider some patterns, formulas, or expressions that you can apply. Look for photos in magazines to help you make a visual presentation.

Problem Solving

Understand
Plan
Solve
Look Back

At the beginning of Section 3A, you saw that the world is divided into 24 time zones. There are four of these in the continental United States. Airlines, which always give flight information using local time, must keep in mind that when it is 6 P.M. in New York, it is 5 P.M. in Chicago, 4 P.M. in Denver, and 3 P.M. in Los Angeles. Formulas help us convert times from one designation to another.

Where Did the Time Go?

1. Suppose it is noon in your time zone. Name the local time in Los Angeles, Denver, Chicago, and New York.

2. Suppose you want to develop a general method for changing your local time to the time in other zones. Use x to represent the time in your zone. Then write an algebraic expression for the time in each of the other three time zones.

3. Assume you move three different times, each time to a new time zone in the United States. Write the three algebraic expressions for converting to each of the other zone times for your new home.

4. Greenwich mean time (GMT) is used by aviators. All times are expressed in relation to the time at Greenwich, England, which is in Zone 0. The 12 zones to the west are positive, and the 12 zones to the east are negative. Use variables to write formulas for converting standard time from each zone to Greenwich mean time.

To Convert from:	To GMT:
Zone 5 (location of New York)	Add 5 hours
Zone 8 (San Francisco)	Add 8 hours
Zone 10 (Honolulu)	Add 10 hours
Zone −1 (Rome)	Subtract 1 hour
Zone −3 (Moscow)	Subtract 3 hours
Zone −9 (Tokyo)	Subtract 9 hours

5. Use each formula to convert 3 A.M. and 10 P.M. in each city in the above table to Greenwich mean time.

6. Explain what you must do when your formula gives a number larger than 12; less than 0.

Section 3A Review

Evaluate each formula for the values given.

1. $t = \frac{d}{r}$ for $d = 150$ and $r = 3$

2. $P = 2l + 2w$ for $l = 55$ and $w = 25$

3. $A = s^2$ for $s = 13$

4. $T = 0.04p$ for $p = \$8.50$

5. A blimp has traveled 179 miles in 3.4 hours. Use $r = \frac{d}{t}$ to find its average speed.

6. One income tax formula is $t = 0.28i$, where i is income and t is the tax paid. What is the tax paid on an income of $12,150?

Evaluate each expression.

7. $10x + 20y$ for $x = 15$ and $y = 12$

8. $5 + 30y$ for $y = 2.5$

9. $12(x + 5)$ for $x = 3.8$

10. $(14x + 2) \cdot y$ for $x = 8$ and $y = 15$

11. $\dfrac{18(x - 2)}{3}$ for $x = 8$

12. $\dfrac{-8(y - 4)}{8}$ for $y = -4$

Solve each equation. Use number sense or guess and check.

13. $x - 5 = 7$

14. $8y = 64$

15. $y = -\dfrac{36}{4}$

16. $y = 8(-3)$

17. Once an African gray parrot is two weeks old and weighs about 120 g, it increases in weight about 85 g a week for the next few weeks. Write an expression and find the weight of a five-week-old parrot.

18. Write a problem situation that involves multiplying and adding. Translate it into an expression and evaluate the expression for a sample value of the variable.

Test Prep

To test if different expressions name the same quantity, you can substitute the same simple number in each expression. Try 0, for example.

19. Which expression is not equivalent to $4x$?

    Ⓐ $x + x + x + x$ Ⓑ $x + 3x$ Ⓒ $3x + 1$ Ⓓ $(3 + 1)x$

Watts the Use?

Suddenly, the lights go out, television and computer screens go dark, and you can't remember the last time you saw a flashlight. Without these rare power failures, we would certainly take electric energy for granted.

On November 9–10, 1965, the greatest power failure in history affected 30 million people and left an area of 80,000 square miles in darkness. In New York City, the power failed at 5:27 P.M. and was not restored for more than 13 hours. Can you imagine the resulting chaos—no elevators, no streetlamps, no computers, no television?

We forget that so many things are dependent on electricity. Electricity is a form of energy that can be changed into other forms of energy: heat to keep our homes warm, light for our lamps, sound energy in a stereo, and mechanical energy to turn motors in washing machines and dishwashers.

1 Name as many electrical appliances as you can that you use in your home or at school.

2 Which appliances do you think require the most electric energy to run for an hour?

3 Which appliances do you think require the most electric energy for the amount of time they are actually in use?

Solving Equations by Adding or Subtracting

You'll Learn ...

■ how to solve equations by undoing addition or subtraction

... How It's Used

Nutritionists use equations to determine individual dietary needs.

Vocabulary

Addition Property of Equality

equivalent equations

▶ **Lesson Link** You know that equations such as $x + 5 = 7$ and $x - 10 = 20$ can be solved by number sense or by using guess and check. Sometimes, however, it is more convenient to use other methods. ◄

Explore | Solving Equations

Does It Add Up?

1. Use guess and check to solve each equation.

   a. $x + 1 = 2$ b. $x + 2 = 3$

   c. $x + 3 = 4$ d. $x + 4 = 5$

2. Starting with Equation a, how could you get Equation b? Starting with Equation a, how could you get Equation c?

3. Describe the pattern for getting each new equation and write the next equation in the pattern. What is its solution?

4. What seems to be true about all the solutions for all the equations?

5. Use guess and check to solve each equation.

   a. $x - 1 = 3$ b. $x - 2 = 2$

   c. $x - 3 = 1$ d. $x - 4 = 0$

6. What seems to be the pattern for obtaining each new equation? What is the solution for each equation?

7. Write any conclusions you can make about Questions 1–6.

Learn | Solving Equations by Adding or Subtracting

In science class, you may have used a balance scale. For both pans of the scale to balance, the same total mass must be placed in each pan. If you add (or remove) a mass of 1 gram to one pan, you must add (or remove) the same mass on the other side.

When solving equations, you can use the same idea as in keeping a scale balanced. You can add or subtract the same number on each side of an equation. The equation is still true, and the solution is the same.

ADDITION PROPERTY OF EQUALITY

If $a = b$, then $a + c = b + c$.

To solve an equation, the goal is to find a value of the variable that makes the equation true. To do this, we try to isolate the variable on one side. For example, you know that 3 solves $x - 1 = 2$. To get from $x - 1 = 2$ to $x = 3$, add 1 to each side. Adding 1 undoes the subtraction of 1 from x. We say that $x - 1 = 2$ and $x = 3$ are **equivalent equations**.

DID YOU KNOW?

A good balance scale would be thrown out of balance if the ink from the period at the end of this sentence were added to one side ⊙←

Examples

1 Solve $x + 4 = 10$ to find the unknown mass.

$$x + 4 = 10$$

$$x + 4 + (-4) = 10 + (-4) \quad \text{Add } -4 \text{ to both sides.}$$

$$x + 0 = 6 \quad \text{Use the additive inverse property.}$$

$$x = 6 \quad \text{0 is the additive identity.}$$

Check: $x + 4 \stackrel{?}{=} 10$

$$6 + 4 \stackrel{?}{=} 10 \quad \text{Substitute for } x.$$

$$10 = 10 \checkmark \quad \text{The equation checks.}$$

The solution is 6, so the mass is 6 units.

Remember

The sum of a number and its additive inverse is 0. **[Page 68]**

```
←+———+———+→
 -4      0      4
```

2 A metal lightning rod placed on the roof of a building attracts lightning, steering its energy through a cable to a point 15 ft underground. If the building is 560 ft tall, how long is the cable?

Solve $560 = x - 15$.   Let x = the cable length

$$560 + 15 = x - 15 + 15 \quad \text{Add 15 to each side.}$$

$$575 = x + 0 \quad \text{Use the additive inverse property.}$$

$$575 = x \quad \text{0 is the additive identity.}$$

Check: $560 = 575 - 15$

$$560 = 560 \checkmark \quad \text{The equation checks.}$$

The cable is 575 ft long.

Example 3

The largest 24-hour drop in temperature recorded in the United States occurred in Billings, Montana. The temperature dropped 101° to −55°F. What had the temperature been before it began to drop?

Let x = the temperature before the drop. Choose a variable.

$$x - 101 = -55$$ Translate the given information into an equation.

$$x - 101 + 101 = -55 + 101$$ To isolate x, add 101 to each side.

$$x = 46$$

Check: $46 - 101 \overset{?}{=} -55$

$$-55 = -55 \checkmark$$

The temperature had been 46°F before it began to drop.

Try It

Solve each equation.

a. $x + 12 = 30$ **b.** $x - 16 = 5$

c. $540 = 35 + t$ **d.** $x + 45 = -100$

e. $x - 11 = -18$

f. The temperature rose 19° before dawn. The temperature at dawn was 7°F. What had the temperature been?

Check | Your Understanding

1. When Zia checked her solution in the equation $y - 16 = 7$, she got 7 = 7. Is 7 the solution? Why or why not?

2. When Gordy tried to solve $d - 10 = 5$, he subtracted 5 from both sides. Could he do that? Did it help him solve the problem?

3. In Example 1, the solution shows that you can solve the equation by adding −4 to both sides. This is equivalent to subtracting what number from each side? Why?

Practice and Apply

Getting Started For each balanced scale, what would you do to isolate the unknown weight on one side and still keep the scale balanced?

1.

2.

What is the next step in solving each equation?

3. $x - 5 = 10$ **4.** $x + 4 = 14$ **5.** $-1 = x - 6$ **6.** $7 = x + 4$

Solve each equation. Check your solution.

7. $y - 3 = 12$ **8.** $n + 5 = 11$ **9.** $c - 7 = 8$ **10.** $x + 20 = 32$

11. $m - 17 = 20$ **12.** $p + 35 = 20$ **13.** $a - 1.5 = 4.5$ **14.** $r + 3.8 = 6.2$

15. $r + 13 = 6$ **16.** $13 = m - 7$ **17.** $40 = a + 3$ **18.** $12 = m - 20$

19. $x + 2\frac{1}{2} = 10$ **20.** $x - 3\frac{3}{4} = 7$ **21.** $-1 = n - 33$ **22.** $8 = y + 25$

23. Electricity A three-way lightbulb has three different wattages available as you turn the switch three times in the same direction. The highest wattage is obtained by adding the two lower wattages. If the lowest wattage is 30 watts and the highest wattage is 100 watts, find the middle wattage.

24. Consumer Ordinary incandescent lightbulbs are cheaper, but they do not last as long as fluorescent bulbs. How much longer will a fluorescent bulb last than an incandescent bulb? Is your answer exact or approximate? Explain.

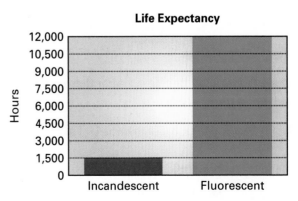

PRACTICE 3-4

25. Sports In bowling, a spare counts 10 points plus the number of pins on the next ball. In the scoresheet shown, the bowler has a score of 157 after a spare and an 8. What had the score been before the spare?

26. [**Test Prep**] Augustus Caesar died in the year 14 A.D. at approximately 76 years of age. Which is the best estimate of the year of his birth?

Ⓐ 90 B.C.   Ⓑ 60 B.C.

Ⓒ 60 A.D.   Ⓓ 90 A.D.

Problem Solving and Reasoning

27. Critical Thinking Choose the correct equation, then answer each question.

$500 + x = 5500$

$500 + 5500 = x$

$100 + x = 3000$

$100 + 3000 = x$

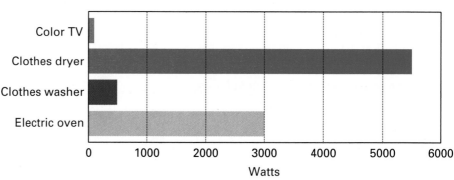

Watts Required

a. How many more watts does a clothes dryer require than a clothes washer?

b. How many more watts does an electric oven require than a color TV?

c. Can you think of any other equation to solve Questions a and b? Explain.

d. What question could be answered using $500 + 5500 = x$?

28. Choose a Strategy Bicycling burns off 6.0 calories per minute, but walking only burns off 3.5 calories per minute. How much longer would it take to burn off 1000 calories by walking than by bicycling?

> **Problem Solving**
> **STRATEGIES**
>
> • Look for a Pattern
> • Make an Organized List
> • Make a Table
> • Guess and Check
> • Work Backward
> • Use Logical Reasoning
> • Draw a Diagram
> • Solve a Simpler Problem

Mixed Review

Make a scatterplot. Decide whether there is an increasing trend, a decreasing trend, or no trend. *[Lesson 1-7]*

29. $(1, 9), (9, 1), (3, 8), (4, 6), (5, 4), (2, 9), (3, 7), (7, 3), (2, 8), (6, 5)$

Compute the following. *[Lesson 2-3]*

30. $45 - (-28)$ **31.** $6 + (-2) - (-7)$

32. $-3 - (-5) + 10$ **33.** $-9 + 8 - (-7)$

PROBLEM SOLVING 3-4

Solving Equations by Multiplying or Dividing

▶ Lesson Link A formula that you have used relating distance, rate of speed, and time is $d = rt$. When you know values for d and t, you can solve for r by using what you know about inverses. ◀

Algebra tiles can be used to model expressions and solve equations.

Key

$x + -1 = -2$

Any two opposite tiles on the same side of an equation can be removed. Remember that you can add the same quantity to both sides of an equation.

$(x + -x)$ $(1 + -1)$

You'll Learn ...

■ how to solve equations by undoing multiplication or division

... How It's Used

Electricians can determine how much current an appliance will use by solving equations.

Vocabulary

Multiplication Property of Equality

coefficient

Explore   Solving by Multiplying or Dividing

Lonely Tiles

Materials: Algebra tiles

1. What equation is shown by the tiles?

2. To "counteract" the negative tiles on the left in Question 1, how many positive tiles do you need? What tiles do you need to add to both sides? How many? What is the equation's solution?

3. What equation is shown by the tiles?

4. Rearrange the tiles on the right into three equal groups. For each x tile on the left, how many tiles on the right are there?

5. "Divide" each side by three by separating each side into three equal groups. Write the equation that helps you find the value of x. What is the value of x?

6. Model the equation $2x = -8$. How can you find the value of x?

Learn | Solving Equations by Multiplying or Dividing

A useful property for solving equations is the **Multiplication Property of Equality** . An equation stays true if you multiply or divide both sides by the same nonzero number.

MULTIPLICATION PROPERTY OF EQUALITY

If $a = b$, then $ac = bc$.

In $4x = 28$, the variable x is multiplied by 4. So 4 is called the **coefficient** of x. In $\frac{x}{4} = 5$, you could rewrite the equation as $\frac{1}{4}x = 5$. So the coefficient of x is $\frac{1}{4}$. Knowing the coefficient can help you isolate the variable.

Examples

1 Solve $4x = 28$.

$$\frac{4x}{4} = \frac{28}{4}$$ Divide both sides by the coefficient, 4, to undo multiplication by 4.

$$x = 7$$

Check: $4(7) \stackrel{?}{=} 28$

$28 = 28$ ✓

2 In China, $\frac{1}{3}$ of the population owns bicycles. There are about 400,000,000 people with bicycles in China. What is the population?

Let x stand for the population of China. Solve $\frac{1}{3}x = 400{,}000{,}000$.

$$\frac{1}{3}x = 400{,}000{,}000$$

$$3 \cdot \frac{1}{3}x = 3 \cdot 400{,}000{,}000$$ Multiply by 3, the reciprocal of $\frac{1}{3}$.

$$x = 1{,}200{,}000{,}000$$

The population of China is about 1,200,000,000.

Try It

Solve each equation.

a. $8x = 72$ **b.** $\frac{x}{6} = -30$ **c.** $14 = \frac{2}{3}k$

Each day the United States consumes about one out of every four barrels of oil that is produced worldwide. The United States recently consumed 17,000,000 barrels of oil a day. At that rate, how much oil is produced each day?

Enrique thinks ...

I'll let x stand for the number of barrels produced each day. Then $\frac{1}{4}x$ stands for the number of barrels used by the U.S.

$$\frac{1}{4}x = 17{,}000{,}000$$

Multiply both sides by 4, the reciprocal of $\frac{1}{4}$.

$$4 \cdot \frac{1}{4}x = 4 \cdot 17{,}000{,}000$$

About 68,000,000 barrels of oil are produced each day.

$$x = 68{,}000{,}000$$

Ashley thinks ...

To show $\frac{1}{4}$ of the whole amount, I'll divide x by 4.

$$\frac{x}{4} = 17{,}000{,}000$$

To undo division by 4, I can multiply by 4.

$$4 \cdot \frac{x}{4} = 4 \cdot 17{,}000{,}000$$

I'll use a calculator.

$$4 \;\boxed{\times}\; 17000000 \;\boxed{=}\; 68000000$$

About 68,000,000 barrels of oil are produced each day.

$$x = 68{,}000{,}000$$

What do you think?

Does one-fourth of the world live in the United States?

Check | Your Understanding

1. When solving equations such as $x - 2 = 40$ or $2x = 40$, how do you know which operation to use to isolate the variable?

2. When would a reciprocal help you solve an equation?

3. Give an example of a division equation that has a negative-number solution.

Practice and Apply

Getting Started What can you multiply or divide by to isolate the variable?

1. $10x = 60$

2. $\frac{1}{6}x = 3$

3. $\frac{n}{4} = 12$

4. $\frac{2}{3}x = 20$

5. In the equation $3x = 20$, what is the coefficient of x?

6. What is the reciprocal of 3? Of $\frac{1}{5}$? Of $\frac{3}{4}$?

Solve each equation.

7. $7y = 63$

8. $8x = -64$

9. $\frac{1}{2}x = 16$

10. $\frac{1}{4}x = -8$

11. $3y = 20.4$

12. $5y = -45.5$

13. $16y = 8$

14. $3a = 6$

15. $\frac{n}{6} = 15$

16. $\frac{x}{10} = 4$

17. $\frac{y}{5} = 0.2$

18. $\frac{z}{3} = -5$

19. $\frac{3}{4}x = 15$

20. $\frac{2}{3}y = 60$

21. $-8y = 124$

22. $-80y = 320$

23. $120x = 1500$

24. $-1.4y = 28$

25. $34h = 1.7$

26. $180y = 240$

27. **Test Prep** Watts of power (the amount of energy an appliance uses) are determined by multiplying the voltage by the current in amperes. An appliance uses 200 watts and the voltage is 120 volts. To find the current in amperes flowing through the circuit you would use:

Ⓐ $200 = 120a$

Ⓑ $120 = 200a$

Ⓒ $200 = \frac{120}{a}$

Ⓓ $120 = \frac{a}{200}$

28. **Music** A musical piece in 6/8 time means that there are six beats in a measure, and an eighth note represents one beat. If 96 eighth notes are played in 6/8 time, how many beats are played? How many measures?

29. **Energy** A gas heater for a swimming pool costs $2.40 per hour for the energy to run it. Suppose you want to keep this cost to about $100.00 a month. How long can you run the heater?

PRACTICE 3-5

30. Energy An appliance that uses 1000 watts of power for 1 hour uses 1 kilowatt-hour (1 kWh) of energy. (Note that *kilo* means 1000.) Most electric companies charge by the kilowatt-hour. An appliance that uses 200 watts for 5 hours also uses 1 kilowatt-hour of energy. Suppose a family uses 500 kWh in one month and they are charged $45. What is the cost per kWh?

Problem Solving and Reasoning

31. Communicate The bicycle is the most energy-efficient form of transportation (other than sailing). Biking burns only 35 energy calories per passenger mile against the automobile's 1860 calories. How many times as efficient as the automobile is the bicycle? Why do you think so few people use bicycles if they are so efficient?

32. Choose a Strategy The two train journeys in the world with the fastest average speeds are in France and Japan. The fastest is from Massey to St. Pierre, France. The second fastest is from Hiroshima to Kokuru, Japan.

Massey — St. Pierre
Speed = 152.6 mi/hr
Distance = 128.4 mi

Kokuru — Hiroshima
Speed = 143.2 mi/hr
Distance = 119.3 mi

Problem Solving

STRATEGIES

- Look for a Pattern
- Make an Organized List
- Make a Table
- Guess and Check
- Work Backward
- Use Logical Reasoning
- Draw a Diagram
- Solve a Simpler Problem

a. To the nearest minute, find the time it takes to travel from Massey to St. Pierre and from Hiroshima to Kokuru.

b. Which trip takes less time? By how much?

c. If you could travel from New York to San Francisco (about 2600 miles) at the same speed as the French train, how long would it take?

33. Journal Write a word problem that can be solved by using the equation $300 = 60x$. Show the solving process.

Mixed Review

What population would it make most sense to survey for each of the following products? *[Lesson 1-8]*

34. Children's bicycles   **35.** Answering machines   **36.** Surgical instruments

Multiply or divide. *[Lesson 2-4]*

37. $-18 \cdot 3$ **38.** $-3 \cdot 5 \cdot (-8)$ **39.** $\dfrac{-42}{7}$ **40.** $\dfrac{63}{-9}$

3-6 Solving Two-Step Equations

You'll Learn ...

■ how to solve equations by undoing operations in two steps

... How It's Used

In cutting heating costs, a consumer can use equations to determine how much insulation is needed.

▶ **Lesson Link**   You have already learned to solve equations such as $x + 7 = 20$ and $5x = 15$. By combining the methods you learned for solving such equations, you can solve equations such as $5x + 7 = 37$. To do this, you will use the order of operations in reverse. ◀

Explore   Two-Step Equations

It Could Be Your Undoing!

Materials: Algebra tiles

1. What equation is shown by the model?

2. Take three unit tiles from each side. What operation is represented by removing the three unit tiles from each side? What equation is represented after the tiles are removed?

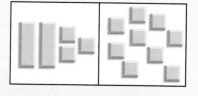

3. If you separate the remaining unit tiles into two equal groups, what operation is represented? How many unit tiles correspond to each x-tile?

4. What is the solution of the original equation?

Learn   Solving Two-Step Equations

When you evaluate an expression such as $5x + 3$ for $x = 2$, you substitute 2 for x and use the order of operations.

$$5(2) + 3 = 10 + 3 \quad \text{Step 1: Multiply first.}$$
$$= 13 \quad \text{Step 2: Then add.}$$

x, ÷ | Evaluating
      |_____→
         +, −

When you *solve* $5x + 3 = 13$, you *reverse* the process.

$$5x + 3 = 13$$
$$5x + 3 - 3 = 13 - 3 \quad \text{Step 1: Undo the addition.}$$
$$5x = 10 \quad \text{Step 2: Then undo the multiplication.}$$
$$x = 2$$

x, ÷ | Solving
      ↑_____
         +, −

Example 1

Solve $4y - 6 = 50$.

$$4y - 6 = 50$$

$4y - 6 + 6 = 50 + 6$ Add 6 to each side to undo the subtraction.

$4y = 56$ Use the property of additive inverses.

$\dfrac{4y}{4} = \dfrac{56}{4}$ Divide each side by 4 to undo the multiplication.

$y = 14$

Check: $4(14) - 6 \overset{?}{=} 50$

$56 - 6 \overset{?}{=} 50$

$50 = 50 \checkmark$ The solution checks.

Remember

$\frac{x}{2}$ and $\frac{1}{2}x$ mean the same thing.

Example 2

In the construction of a townhouse villa, 13 flat-plate solar collectors are installed on the rooftops, one for every two units and three for the clubhouse. How many units are in the villa?

Solve $\frac{x}{2} + 3 = 13$.

$\dfrac{x}{2} + 3 = 13$ Let $x =$ the number of townhouses.

$\dfrac{x}{2} + 3 - 3 = 13 - 3$ Subtract 3 from each side to undo the addition.

$\dfrac{x}{2} = 10$ Use the property of additive inverses.

$2 \cdot \dfrac{x}{2} = 2 \cdot 10$ Multiply both sides by 2 to undo the division.

$x = 20$

There are 20 townhouse units in the villa.

DID YOU KNOW?

Every 40 minutes the sun delivers as much energy to Earth's surface as all people on Earth use in a year.

Try It

Solve each equation.

a. $5x + 4 = 29$ **b.** $12x - 8 = 70$ **c.** $\dfrac{n}{3} - 4 = 6$ **d.** $\dfrac{k}{20} + 5 = 6.5$

Example 3

By installing more efficient bulbs that cost a total of $45, the Collins family can reduce their monthly cost of electricity by $3. Their power company also will give them $15 in rebates. For how many months can they light their home at this lower cost before the bulbs will pay for themselves?

Let x = number of months at the lower cost. When does the savings equal the cost of the bulbs?

Solve $3x + 15 = 45$.

$$3x + 15 = 45$$

$3x + 15 - 15 = 45 - 15$ Subtract 15 from each side.

$$3x = 30$$ Subtract.

$$\frac{3x}{3} = \frac{30}{3}$$ Divide each side by 3.

$$x = 10$$

At the lower cost, it will take ten months before the bulbs pay for themselves.

Try It

By installing more insulation and flow restrictors that cost $75, the Collins family can save $9 a month on water heating. They also receive $10 back from the water company. For how many months can they heat their water at this lower rate before the insulation and restrictors pay for themselves?

Check | Your Understanding

1. To solve $3x - 5 = 7$, you could divide both sides by 3 first. Is this the way you would solve it? Explain.

2. Explain why you would solve $2x + 3 = 9$ and $10000k + 5000 = 8712.5$ the same way.

3. Why are these types of equations called two-step?

Practice and Apply

Getting Started Give the first step you would use to solve each equation.

1. $3x - 5 = 13$ **2.** $4x + 6 = 18$ **3.** $\frac{x}{2} - 3 = 2$ **4.** $\frac{n}{4} + 5 = 7$

5. What number would you put in each _____ to solve $4x - 5 = 19$?

   a. $4x - 5 +$ _____ $= 19 +$ _____   **b.** $4x =$ _____   **c.** $x =$ _____

6. What number would you put in each _____ to solve $\frac{x}{5} + 6 = 11$?

   a. $\frac{x}{5} + 6 -$ _____ $= 11 - 6$ **b.** $\frac{x}{5} =$ _____   **c.** $x =$ _____

Solve each equation.

7. $3x - 6 = 15$ **8.** $4x + 3 = 25$ **9.** $2x - 3 = -5$ **10.** $-3 = 4x + 5$

11. $10x + 20 = 80$ **12.** $12x - 8 = 40$ **13.** $2x - 1.5 = 4.5$ **14.** $3x + 0.4 = 4$

15. $\frac{1}{2}x - 4 = 6$ **16.** $\frac{1}{3}x + 2 = 6$ **17.** $\frac{n}{6} - 3 = 4$ **18.** $7 = \frac{x}{5} + 1$

19. $\frac{2}{3}x + 3 = 9$ **20.** $5 = \frac{3}{4}y - 1$ **21.** $0.3x + 10 = 10$ **22.** $0.2x - 1 = 1$

23. Consumer Mrs. Hill paid an electric bill of $23 that included a $5 late fee. If electricity costs $0.10 per kWh, how many kilowatt-hours did she use?

24. Health A scuba diver at a depth of 200 ft rises at 6 ft per second to avoid overpressurization. How long does it take the diver to reach a depth of 40 ft?

25. Geography Jill walks 4 miles per hour from Memphis, TX to San Diego, TX. At Albany, TX, Jill has walked for 40 hr and has 350 miles to go. How many hours will she walk on the entire trip?

26. A recipe calls for 1 tsp of baking powder per 3 servings, plus 1 additional teaspoon. Cal used 6 tsp of baking powder. How many servings did he make?

27. **Test Prep** A health club charges $60 for joining plus dues of $20 a month. Another club charges a one-time lifetime fee of $1000. Which equation could you solve to find the number of months you would need to spend at the first club until you reach a cost of $1000? Let x equal the number of months.

   Ⓐ $20x - 60 = 1000$ Ⓑ $60x + 20 = 100$

   Ⓒ $20x + 60 = 1000$ Ⓓ $20x + 60x = 1000$

PRACTICE 3-6

28. How many shopping carts will fit completely into the carriage rack shown?

0.5 ft

|← 4.0 ft →|

|← 20 ft →|

29. Journal Write a word problem that could be solved by using the equation $200 = 10x + 50$.

30. A paging service charges $20.00 for activation plus $12.95 a month. Francine paid $123.60 for activation and service. How many months did this cover?

Problem Solving and Reasoning

31. Critical Thinking Peaches are dried at 675 watts at a specified time and then at 450 watts for 40 more hours. If a total of 19.35 kilowatt-hours are used in the process, for how many hours are the peaches dried at 675 watts? (One kilowatt-hour is equivalent to 1000 watts used for one hour.)

32. Math Reasoning The higher the R-value of an insulating material, the more effective it is as an insulator. An external wall of a house should have an R-value of 11 or greater. Suppose an exterior wall is covered with materials having an R-value of 2. How many inches of insulation with an R-value of 3.6 per inch will be needed to achieve a total R-value of 11?

33. Choose a Strategy Suppose you burn a 60-watt lightbulb 24 hours a day, 7 days a week for an entire year. If the cost per kilowatt-hour is 8¢, what is the cost per year? How much would you save by using a fluorescent 13-watt lamp for the same amount of time?

34. Communicate City taxi fare is $2.00 plus $1.50 a mile. If a person was charged $14.00 for a cab ride, how many miles was the ride? Public transportation for the same trip costs $1.25. Discuss the advantages and disadvantages of public transportation over using a cab.

> **Problem Solving**
> **STRATEGIES**
>
> • Look for a Pattern
> • Make an Organized List
> • Make a Table
> • Guess and Check
> • Work Backward
> • Use Logical Reasoning
> • Draw a Diagram
> • Solve a Simpler Problem

Mixed Review

Evaluate each expression. *[Lesson 2-5]*

35. $3 + 4 \cdot (-5)$ **36.** $-3(2 + 5)$ **37.** $-5 + \dfrac{3 - (-7)}{5}$ **38.** $\dfrac{-3 + 7}{2} - \dfrac{-5 + 9}{-4}$

Find each power. *[Lesson 2-7]*

39. $(-4)^2$ **40.** 3^5 **41.** 11^3 **42.** $(-2)^5$ **43.** $(-1)^{11}$

Solving Inequalities

▶ **Lesson Link**   You know that $3 = 2 + 1$ means the quantities on both sides of the equal sign are equal, and you can solve equations such as $x + 2 = 4$. You also know that $3 > 2$ means that "3 is greater than 2." Now you will see what to do when we replace the $=$ with $>$ in an equation. ◀

Recall that $<$ means "is less than" and $>$ means "is greater than." So $3 < 5$ means "3 is less than 5," and $5 > 3$ means "5 is greater than 3."

Explore   Inequalities

Don't Be Crude!

A barrel of crude oil contains 42 gallons. A barrel of crude can provide up to 42 gallons of gasoline. Suppose you are a refiner of crude oil and you make a record of the gasoline refined from a barrel.

1. Name one possible amount of gasoline in gallons that might be distilled from one barrel.

2. Compare your answer with several others. How many different answers were found?

3. Must each amount be a whole number of gallons? Would 25.50 gallons be reasonable? Is 12.25 gallons a possible amount?

4. Draw a number line. Mark a point to show the greatest amount of gasoline possible for one barrel. Mark another point to show the least amount possible.

5. On the same number line, graph as many points as you can to show possible amounts of gasoline from one barrel. How many points are there?

6. How do you think you could show all possible points on the graph?

You'll Learn ...

■ how to solve inequalities

... How It's Used

A homeowner can use an inequality to determine how many amperes an appliance will use before it overloads the circuit.

Vocabulary

inequality

Learn | Solving Inequalities

A sentence such as $x + 1 = 3$ has one solution. However, $x < 3$ has many solutions, for example, 2, 0, and -2.5. It is impossible to list all solutions, so we show them on a number line. Notice that 3 is not a solution, so we put an open circle at 3.

Two other symbols that we can use are $\leq$ (is less than or equal to) and $\geq$ (is greater than or equal to). Sentences that involve $<$, $>$, $\leq$, and $\geq$ are called **inequalities** .

The graphs for $x \leq 3$ and $x \geq 3$ are shown below. Notice that 3 is a solution, so we show a filled-in point at 3.

Test Prep

Pay close attention to the replacements allowed for the variable when you solve an inequality.

You can use your knowledge of solving equations to solve inequalities. Every inequality has a related equation that is formed by replacing the inequality symbol with an equal sign.

Example 1

Solve and graph $x - 5 > 3$.

You already know how to solve $x - 5 = 3$, the related equation for $x - 5 > 3$. First solve this related equation.

$$x - 3 = 5$$

$$x - 3 + 3 = 5 + 3 \quad \text{Add 3 to each side.}$$

$$x = 8$$

The solution of $x - 5 > 3$ will be the numbers less than 8 or greater than 8. Test a number less than 8 and one greater than 8 to see which is a solution.

Try 5. $\quad 5 - 3 \overset{?}{>} 5 \qquad$ Try 10. $\quad 10 - 3 \overset{?}{>} 5$

$\qquad\quad 2 > 5$ false $\qquad\qquad\qquad 7 > 5$ ✓ true

The numbers greater than 8 make up the solution set. To show the solution, draw an open circle at 8 with an arrow extending to the right.

Example 2

The Carter family will reduce heating costs by installing new storm windows and adding insulation. They have offered their daughter $10 for each storm window she installs, and they owe her $25 for spreading insulation in the attic. She wants to earn more than $200. How many storm windows must she install?

Solve $10x + 25 > 200$.

First solve the related equation, $10x + 25 = 200$.

$$10x + 25 = 200$$

$$10x + 25 - 25 = 200 - 25 \quad \text{Subtract 25 from each side.}$$

$$10x = 175$$

$$\frac{10x}{10} = \frac{175}{10} \quad \text{Divide both sides by 10.}$$

$$x = 17.5$$

Try a number less than 17.5 and another greater than 17.5.

Try 15. $10(15) + 25 \overset{?}{>} 200$ Try 20. $10(20) + 25 \overset{?}{>} 200$

        $150 + 25 \overset{?}{>} 200$ $200 + 25 \overset{?}{>} 200$

            $175 > 200$ false $225 > 200$ ✓   true

The numbers greater than 17.5 make up the solution set. Therefore, she must install 18 storm windows or more.

Try It

a. Graph $x < 4$.   **b.** Solve and graph $x + 4 \geq 9$.

Check | Your Understanding

1. Why might an inequality be needed instead of an equation? Give an example.

2. How can an inequality have more than one solution?

3. How do you know if the solution of the related equation is a solution of the inequality?

Practice and Apply

Getting Started | Match each situation with one of the following inequalities: $x > 20$, $x < 20$, $x \leq 20$, $x \geq 20$.

1. The maximum current is 20 amperes.

2. The minimum age is 20.

3. The time is more than 20 minutes.

4. The cost is less than $20.

5. **Test Prep** | Which inequality could you use to express allowable speeds if the maximum speed is 65 mi/hr?

   Ⓐ $x < 65$ Ⓑ $x > 65$ Ⓒ $x \leq 65$ Ⓓ $x \geq 65$

Write an inequality for each graph.

6.

```
<----+----+----+----+----●----+----+----+----> x
    -7   -6   -5   -4   -3   -2   -1    0    1
```

7.

```
<----+----+----+----◆----+----+----+----+----> x
     2    3    4    5    6    7    8    9   10
```

Determine whether 10 is a solution for each inequality.

8. $x \geq 10$ **9.** $x + 9 < 19$ **10.** $6x \leq 61$ **11.** $3x + 2 < 40$

Solve each inequality. Graph the solution.

12. $x - 5 < 2$ **13.** $x + 3 > 7$ **14.** $x + 7 \leq 10$ **15.** $x - 10 \geq 1$

16. $6m > 42$ **17.** $3y \leq 15$ **18.** $2v > 20$ **19.** $5p \geq 40$

20. $2w - 1 < 22$ **21.** $4z + 3 \geq 24$ **22.** $6k - 3\frac{1}{2} > 27$ **23.** $10n + 8 \leq 74\frac{2}{3}$

24. Consumer A homeowner installs a dishwasher on a circuit that can handle 20 amperes. If 11 amperes are used by other appliances, solve $d + 11 \leq 20$ to describe the number of amperes the dishwasher uses.

25. Geography A flood fringe may be defined as an area where the product of the depth of flood waters and the velocity of the water does not exceed 7. If flood waters reach a velocity of 14 ft/sec, how deep can they be for the region to remain a flood fringe?

26. Consumer The minimum recommended R-value for a home ceiling in one area is 19. Fiberglass sheets have an R-value of 3.33 per inch. What is the minimum number of sheets needed? Solve $3.33x \geq 19$.

Problem Solving and Reasoning

27. **Math Reasoning** It is estimated that a family can save up to two-thirds of their energy costs by converting from an electric clothes dryer to an energy-efficient gas dryer with electronic ignition. In four years, a family saves $320 by installing a gas dryer, approximately the cost of the new dryer. What is the amount they were spending per year on energy costs for an electric dryer?

28. **Critical Thinking** You can add the same number to both sides of an equation or multiply both sides by the same number, and the equation is still true. Can you always add the same positive or negative number to both sides of an inequality, or multiply both sides by the same number, and still get a true inequality? Explain.

29. **Communicate** For each inequality, describe a real-world situation that could be represented by the inequality.

    a. $x \geq 21$ **b.** $24x < 9.95$

30. **Choose a Strategy** You have made scores of 75 and 82 on your first two tests in Spanish. What scores can you get on your next test if you want an average of at least 80?

Mixed Review

31. Plot the following points on a coordinate grid. *[Lesson 2-6]*
    $(1, -1), (-3, 4), (0, -3), (5, 2), (4, 0), (-4, -3), (2, -4), (-3, -1)$

32. Which ordered pair(s) in Exercise 31 represent(s) points on the x-axis? Which represent points on the y-axis? *[Lesson 2-6]*

Write each number in standard notation. *[Lesson 2-8]*

33. 7.32×10^7 **34.** 6.3×10^2 **35.** 9.3734×10^{12} **36.** 8.64×10^6

Write each number in scientific notation. *[Lesson 2-8]*

37. $16,384$ **38.** 12^3 **39.** 144×10^2 **40.** 5 billion

Problem Solving

STRATEGIES

- Look for a Pattern
- Make an Organized List
- Make a Table
- Guess and Check
- Work Backward
- Use Logical Reasoning
- Draw a Diagram
- Solve a Simpler Problem

Project Progress

Explain some ways you might be able to use a pattern or equation to describe numerical facts about the natural things you are researching. For example, you might use a pattern or equation about a group of spiders to make a conclusion about each spider.

Problem Solving

Understand
Plan
Solve
Look Back

TECHNOLOGY

Using a Spreadsheet • Writing Formulas

Problem: Using the formula $F = 1.8C + 32$, a temperature expressed in degrees Celsius can be converted to degrees Fahrenheit. What Fahrenheit temperature would correspond to the following temperatures expressed in degrees Celsius: 0°, 10°, 20°, 50°, and 100°?

You can use a spreadsheet to generate these conversions quickly.

1 Enter the information into the spreadsheet as shown.

	A	B
1	Celsius	Fahrenheit
2	0	
3	10	
4	20	
5	50	
6	100	

2 In cell B2, enter the formula $=1.8*A2+32$.

	A	B
1	Celsius	Fahrenheit
2	0	= 1.8*A2 + 32
3	10	
4	20	
5	50	
6	100	

3 Highlight cells B2 through B6, and select the **Fill Down** command for your spreadsheet. The conversions will appear as shown:

	A	B
1	Celsius	Fahrenheit
2	0	32
3	10	50
4	20	68
5	50	122
6	100	212

Solution: The corresponding Fahrenheit temperatures are 32°, 50°, 68°, 122°, and 212°.

TRY IT

Use your spreadsheet to convert from Celsius to Fahrenheit: −5°, 5°, −17.8°, 273.15°, 450°, and 1000°.

ON YOUR OWN

▶ Use your spreadsheet and the formula $C = (F - 32)/1.8$ to convert these Fahrenheit temperatures to Celsius: 0°, 32°, 98.6°, 190°, 240°, 1500°. Use column C to convert the Fahrenheit temperatures back to Celsius.

Section 3B Connect

At the beginning of Section 3B, you learned that electric companies charge by the kilowatt-hour. In this Connect you will use your knowledge of solving equations and inequalities to learn more about how electric companies bill their customers.

Watts the Use?

One electric company charges its residential customers as follows:

MSM Gas and Electric

Date: 07/25/98

Electricity Rates

$0.1145 per kWh for up to 220 kWh

$0.1380 per kWh for kWh above 220 kWh

Gas Rates

1. Suppose your April bill is $19.10. How many kWh did you use?

2. Suppose your May bill is $25.19. How many kWh did you use?

3. Suppose your June bill is $30.02. How many kWh did you use?

4. What equation did you use for Question 3?

5. In July, the cost for up to 220 kWh will stay the same, but the cost for additional kWh will increase. The utility company assures customers that for 300 kWh, the electric cost should be no more than $35. What rates are possible? Is this reasonable?

6. Why might the rates change at 220 kWh?

7. Try to find an electric bill for your family or someone you know. See how the rate compares with that of the electric company mentioned above. Use the given rates in the bill above and determine how much the bill would be with these rates.

8. Discuss as many ways as you can think of to reduce electric and other energy costs. (Some of them have been mentioned in Section 3B.)

Section 3B Review

Solve each equation.

1. $a - 5 = 20$ **2.** $z + 3 = 27$ **3.** $x - 2.5 = 12.5$ **4.** $3x = -18$

5. $\frac{1}{3}x = 20$ **6.** $1.5x = 12$ **7.** $\frac{1}{2}x - 10 = 20$ **8.** $3x - 7 = 29$

9. Last month the Archer family paid an electric bill of $22.00. There is a basic service charge of $5.00 plus $0.09 per kilowatt-hour. Solve $0.09x + 5 = 22$ to find how many kilowatt-hours they used.

Solve and graph each inequality.

10. $x - 1 \leq 5$ **11.** $2x > 20$ **12.** $\frac{1}{2}x < 3$ **13.** $8x - 3 \geq 13$

14. An adult Panda bear and her cub eat up to 105 pounds of bamboo shoots per day. If the cub eats around 20 pounds of bamboo, how much does the mother eat? Solve $x + 20 \leq 105$.

Evaluate each expression for $x = 10$ and $y = 8$. *[Lesson 3-2]*

15. $6x + 3y$ **16.** $(6x + 3) \cdot y$

17. $6(x + y)$ **18.** $6x + 6y$

19. **Journal** Explain why an inequality is used in Exercise 14 rather than an equation.

Test Prep

Remember that words such as *maximum* and *minimum* often mean that either $\leq$ or $\geq$ is needed when translating words to an inequality.

20. Which inequality shows the allowable weights if the maximum weight is 2000 pounds?

Ⓐ $x < 2000$ Ⓑ $x > 2000$ Ⓒ $x \leq 2000$ Ⓓ $x \geq 2000$

21. The inequality $p \geq 40$ means that 40 is

Ⓐ Value of p Ⓑ Minimum value of p Ⓒ Maximum value of p Ⓓ None of these

REVIEW 3B

Compound Statements

A compound statement is formed by joining two statements. Statements joined by the word *and* are *conjunctions*. Statements joined by the word *or* are *disjunctions*. Knowing whether a compound statement is a conjunction or disjunction can help you decide whether it is true.

To vote, a person must be a U.S. citizen *and* at least 18 years old. To cash a check, banks require that you have a driver's license *or* a major credit card.

For a conjunction to be true, *both* statements must be true.

U.S. Citizen	At Least 18 Years Old	U.S. Citizen *and* at Least 18 Years Old
		True
True	True	False
True	False	False
False	True	False
False	False	

To be able to vote, both conditions must be true.

For a disjunction to be true, *only one* of the statements must be true.

To cash a check, at least one condition must be true.

Have a Driver's License	Have a Major Credit Card	Have a Driver's License *or* a Major Credit Card
		True
	True	True
True	False	True
True	True	False
False	False	
False		

Inequalities can be written as conjunctions and disjunctions.

6 is less than 10 *and* greater than 4. $6 < 10$ *and* $6 > 4$

5 is less than 4 *or* greater than 4. $5 < 4$ *or* $5 > 4$

$4 < x < 10$ is a special conjunction, meaning $4 < x$ and $x < 10$.

Determine whether each compound statement is a conjunction or a disjunction, and whether it is true or false.

1. A square has four sides and a triangle has three sides.

2. The product of 4 and 6 is 24 or the sum of 4 and 6 is 12.

3. $100 > 10 > 1$ **4.** $5 < 0$ or $-1 > 0$ **5.** $6 < 8$ and $0 > 1$

Chapter 3 Summary and Review

Graphic Organizer

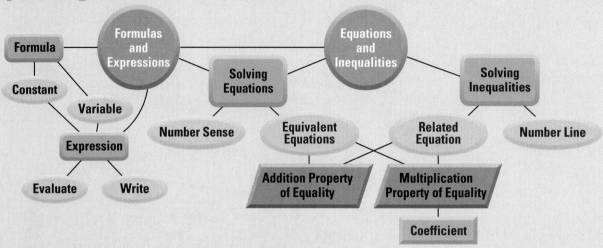

Section 3A Formulas and Expressions

Summary

- A **formula** states a real-world relationship involving unknown quantities represented by **variables** and known, unvarying numbers called **constants**. To use a formula, we **substitute** values for the variables.

- An expression that involves variables, numbers, and operation symbols is called an **algebraic expression**. To **evaluate** an algebraic expression, substitute values for each variable and **simplify** by applying the order of operations.

- An **equation** states that two expressions are equal. To **solve** an equation means to find the variable substitution values that make the equation true. These values are called the **solution**.

- Two expressions that always have the same value for the same substitutions are called **equivalent expressions**.

Review

1. Using d for miles traveled and f for gallons of fuel consumed, write a formula for miles traveled per gallon of fuel.

2. Write an algebraic expression for "$5.95 each, plus $3.00 shipping and handling."

3. Find the volume of a cube with 2.5 cm edges, using the formula $V = s^3$ where s is the length of one edge.

4. Simplify the expression $-5(w - 7)$.

5. Evaluate $2x - 6y$ for $x = 2$ and $y = 13$.

6. Solve the equation $1.3 + b = 517.9$.

7. Solve the equation $4p = 64$.

9. Are $x + 3$ and $2x$ equivalent expressions? Justify your answer.

8. Supersonic airplanes develop very high temperatures on their outer surfaces. The skin temperature S is given by the formula $S = (T + 460)(1 + \frac{M^2}{5}) - 460$, where T is the air temperature (°F) and M is the Mach number. Find the skin temperature of a plane flying at Mach 2 through 40°F air.

Section 3B Writing and Solving Equations and Inequalities

Summary

■ The **Addition Property of Equality** states that if $a = b$, then $a + c = b + c$. In other words, you can add or subtract the same number on each side of an equation and get an **equivalent equation**.

■ The **Multiplication Property of Equality** states that if $a = b$, then $ac = bc$. So you can multiply or divide both sides by the same nonzero number and get an equivalent equation.

■ When solving an equation, the goal is to isolate the variable on one side. To do this, undo the operations on the variable in reverse order, using the addition property to undo addition and subtraction, and the multiplication property to undo multiplication and division.

■ **Inequalities** are sentences involving $<$, $>$, $\leq$, or $\geq$. The solutions of an inequality are all the values that make the inequality true.

■ Solutions of inequalities are found by solving the corresponding equations and testing selected values. A number line is a convenient way to display all solutions at once.

Review

10. Solve $b - 32 = 59$.

11. Solve $49 + n = 83$.

12. Solve $w \div 4 = 1.17$.

13. Solve $1.98 = 24x$.

14. Solve $4 = \frac{k}{35}$.

15. The power (in watts) P put out by a voltage V through a resistance in ohms (R) is given by the formula $P = \frac{V^2}{R}$. Find the resistance when $V = 12$ volts and $P = 10$ watts.

16. Solve $35x - 8 = 167$.

17. Solve $82 - v > 44$.

18. Solve $9.1 \leq \frac{5z}{4}$.

19. Solve and graph $19h + 5 \geq 100$.

1. Use the formula $A = 2\pi rh$ to find A when $r = 3$ and $h = 5$. Use 3.14 for π.

2. Use the formula $F = \frac{9}{5}C + 32$ to find F when $C = 20$.

3. Evaluate $7x^2 + 1$ for $x = 3$; for $x = -3$.

4. In a diving contest, the number of points is the score times the degree of difficulty. Translate to an algebraic expression. Then find the number of points for a score of 27.45 and a degree of difficulty of 3.1.

5. Solve $46 = g + 20$.

6. Solve $19y = 57$.

7. Solve $35.20b + 101.86 = 379.94$.

8. The T Company estimates that a box of 24 herbal tea bags costs about $1.35 to produce, including $0.40 for packaging.

   a. How much does each individual tea bag cost to produce?

   b. If packaging costs remain the same, how much does it cost to produce a 60-bag box?

   c. A different-sized box costs $2.30 to produce. How many tea bags does it contain?

9. Solve $14 \leq 28v$.

10. Solve $70 + 8t > 14$. Graph the solution.

11. Mrs. Parks has a chandelier with four identical light bulbs surrounding a 100-watt center bulb. The maximum wattage of all of the bulbs is 400 watts. What is the allowable wattage of each of the surrounding bulbs?

Performance Task

In a small group, pick something for which you can write a simple formula. (Some possibilities: a person's height based on age, the top speed of a car based on engine horsepower, the cost of a sound system based on number of speakers.) Then, individually, write a formula that you think looks reasonable. Test it using a few variable values you think are realistic. How well does your formula work? How different were the formulas others in the group came up with? How accurately do you think your formula reflects the real-world relationship between your variables? Explain.

Performance Assessment

Choose one problem.

Going with the Flow

For a plane with airspeed v, the time t to travel east from Los Angeles to Dallas in still air would be given by the formula $t = \frac{1240}{v}$. However, an air current from west to east affects air travel times by making planes travel faster in one direction. How would the L.A.-to-Dallas formula need to be changed to account for the air flow, assuming the flow has a speed of 75 mi/hr? Explain your reasoning.

ATMMM!

Recently, a heavily-used automatic teller machine that was supposed to give $20 bills gave $100 bills instead. Its owner estimated that $85,000 was lost.

Determine the reasonableness of the owner's assertion. What formula could the owner use to determine the loss? What other information do you need?

Suppose you received $100 bills. Your new balance assumed you received $20 bills. How could you find this balance from your previous balance and the amount you actually received?

A SQUARE DEAL

Addition and subtraction "undo" each other. What operation "undoes" the squaring operation? Is there a problem in trying to undo the squaring operation? How would this problem be resolved in a real-life context? Explain your reasoning and give an example.

MARCH MADNESS

There are 64 teams in the NCAA Basketball Tournament, with 16 teams assigned to each region. These teams are "seeded" from strongest to weakest, and ranked 1 to 16. The teams begin play according to this method: 1 vs. 16, 8 vs. 9, 4 vs. 13, 5 vs. 12, 2 vs. 15, 7 vs. 10, 3 vs. 14, and 6 vs. 11. If the better team wins each game, the final round would have 1 vs. 2.

Is there a formula for each round that matches a team with the expected opponent? How would you match opponents for 32 teams?

People of the World

The concept of horizontal and vertical axes is an important part of Native American culture. The seven dimensions are the north, south, east, and west (horizontal), and the sky, earth, and human spirit (vertical). This is why 7 is considered a sacred number.

Arts & Literature

Leonardo da Vinci was not only an artist, but also a mathematician, a scientist, an inventor, an architect, and an engineer. His drawings in the late 1400s showing frictional forces were almost 200 years ahead of Isaac Newton.

Entertainment

Introduced in Sweden in 1918, the sport of orienteering emphasizes map-reading and direction-finding skills. Contestants use a map and compass to proceed from one point to another. The winner is the person who completes the course in the least amount of time.

and Inequalities

Social Studies Link
www.mathsurf.com/8/ch4/social

Science Link
www.mathsurf.com/8/ch4/science

Science

Bats can detect sound frequencies as high as 100,000 vibrations per second. Most people cannot detect frequencies above 20,000 vibrations per second.

Social Studies

Surveying is the technique of measuring to determine locations, forms, and boundaries of land. One of America's famous surveyors was Benjamin Banneker (1731–1806), an African American mathematician who helped survey the site on which our nation's capital was developed.

Benjamin Banneker

Black Heritage USA 15c

KEY MATH IDEAS

The slope of a line tells how steep it is. A line may also have positive slope or negative slope.

The x-intercept of a linear equation is the x value of the point where the line crosses the x-axis, and the y-intercept is the y value of the point where the line crosses the y-axis.

A linear inequality relates two variables using one of the signs $<$, $>$, $\leq$, or $\geq$.

If the graph of the solutions of a two-variable equation forms a straight line, the equation is a linear equation.

CHAPTER PROJECT

Problem Solving
Understand
Plan
Solve
Look Back

In this project, you will investigate costs of services that include a fixed initial charge plus a variable charge (for example, $8.50 plus $0.10 per minute). You might look at telephone rates, taxi rates, auto rental rates, or other services. You will investigate the patterns and graphs for the cost of such a service and use the pattern to help explain the related graph.

Problem Solving Focus

Write an algebraic expression for each situation.

1 Five years older than the Mustang

2 Three times as valuable as a 1965 Corvette

3 Thirty-eight horsepower less than that of a 1952 Olds Rocket Super 88

4 Twelve more classic car museums than last year

5 Twenty-five hundred dollars off the sticker price

6 One-tenth the number of parts stores

7 If Sally's Saturn is y years old, and Victor's Model A Ford is 60 years older, how old is Victor's car?

8 If a equals the speed in miles per hour, what is the speed in miles per minute?

9 If m equals the weight in ounces, what is the weight in pounds?

10 If a car travels 327.6 miles on g gallons of gasoline, what is the number of miles per gallon?

How Much Is That In Dog Years?

Have you ever heard that each year of a dog's life is equal to 7 years of a human's life? If so, did you ever wonder what it means, or whether it is actually true?

This "rule" may have developed from comparing the average life span of a dog to that of a human.

Humans live an average of 75 years. Dogs live an average of 12 years. If you multiply this number by 7, you find that humans should live an average of 84 years by this rule.

Each year of a dog's life certainly does not correspond to 7 years in a human's life. Many dogs are fully grown by a year. But there are few, if any, humans that are grown by age 7!

1 What factors, other than life expectancy, would you consider in selecting a pet?

2 Make a list of possible pets. If you want a pet today that would be alive when you turn 30 years old, which would you choose? (Don't forget, you'll have to take care of it too!)

3 Do you agree that the larger the animal, the longer it generally lives?

171

Understanding Two-Variable Relationships

You'll Learn ...

■ to describe patterns produced by relationships between two variables

... How It's Used

Genetic engineers use relationships among variables and DNA patterns to create new strands of life.

▶ **Lesson Link**   You have learned about solving equations with one variable. You will now explore equations that have two variables. ◀

Explore   **Two-Variable Relationships**

Those Are the Rules!

1. Draw the fifth figure in each left-to-right pattern.

4 sticks   **7 sticks**   **10 sticks**   **13 sticks**

3 sticks   **5 sticks**   **7 sticks**   **9 sticks**

4 sticks   **10 sticks**   **18 sticks**   **28 sticks**

2. For each pattern above, let n represent the figure number, and let s equal the number of sticks. Match each pattern with one of the following rules.

$$s = n(n + 3) \quad s = 3n + 1 \quad s = 2n + 1$$

Learn   **Understanding Two-Variable Relationships**

Many situations involve a relationship between two quantities whose values can vary. These relationships can be described by using words, tables of values, graphs, or equations. If you can describe a relationship by an equation, you can also describe it by a table.

Examples

1 Teresa has a dog-walking service. She charges $6 for each dog. If x is the number of dogs and y is the amount of dollars she earns, then $y = 6x$ shows the relationship between x and y. Make a table to show the amounts Teresa can earn walking dogs. (Assume 5 is the most she will walk.)

Let $x = 1$. $y = 6(1) = 6$.

Let $x = 2$. $y = 6(2) = 12$.

Let $x = 3$. $y = 6(3) = 18$.

Let $x = 4$. $y = 6(4) = 24$.

Let $x = 5$. $y = 6(5) = 30$.

x	$y = 6x$
1	6
2	12
3	18
4	24
5	30

From the table, you can see that she can earn $6 for walking 1 dog, $12 for walking 2, and so on. She can earn $30 for walking 5 dogs.

2 Great Dane puppies weigh about 4 pounds at birth. Their weight increases about a pound a week for the first 5 weeks. If a is the age in weeks and w is the weight in pounds, then $w = a + 4$ expresses the relationship between a and w. Make a table to show the approximate weight at the end of each week until a puppy is 5 weeks old.

Let $a = 0$. $w = 0 + 4 = 4$.

Let $a = 1$. $w = 1 + 4 = 5$.

Let $a = 2$. $w = 2 + 4 = 6$.

Let $a = 3$. $w = 3 + 4 = 7$.

Let $a = 4$. $w = 4 + 4 = 8$.

Let $a = 5$. $w = 5 + 4 = 9$.

a	$w = a + 4$
0	4
1	5
2	6
3	7
4	8
5	9

From the table, you can see that the puppy weighs about 4 pounds at birth, 5 pounds after 1 week, and so on until it is about 9 pounds after 5 weeks.

Try It

One airline allows up to 3 small dogs to ride in the passenger cabin. It charges $50 for each dog. If d is the number of dogs and A is the amount of fares collected, then $A = 50d$ expresses the relationship between d and A. Make a table to show the possible fares the airline could collect on one flight. Use 0, 1, 2, and 3 as values for d.

You can sometimes find the equation relating two variables by looking at a table of their values.

Example 3

A table giving mixtures of potting soil and sand for the bottom of an iguana cage is shown. Find a rule that relates the amount of sand (y) to the amount of potting soil (x). Use it to find the amount of sand you would need for 15 cups of potting soil.

Problem Solving TIP

The decimal pattern in the y column might give you a clue to the rule you are looking for.

x	y	
1	3.5	When 1 is substituted for x, $y = 3.5$.
2	7	When 2 is substituted for x, $y = 7$.
3	10.5	When 3 is substituted for x, $y = 10.5$.
4	14	When 4 is substituted for x, $y = 14$.
5	17.5	When 5 is substituted for x, $y = 17.5$.
6	21	When 6 is substituted for x, $y = 21$.
7	24.5	When 7 is substituted for x, $y = 24.5$.

▶ **Science Link**

Iguanas need to eat the same kind of green leafy vegetables as you do. They also can have an occasional snack of pizza or ice cream.

In each case $y = 3.5x$. Find the value of y when $x = 15$.

$y = 3.5(15)$ Substitute 15 for x.

$y = 52.5$ Multiply to solve for y.

The value of y when $x = 15$ is 52.5. For 15 cups of potting soil, you would need about 53 cups of sand.

Try It

Find the rule that relates x and y in this table. Then find y when $x = 50$.

x	1	2	3	4	5	6
y	30	60	90	120	150	180

Check   Your Understanding

1. How would you make a table for the equation $y = 7x$?

2. How would you make a table for the equation $y = x + 7$? How many solutions does the equation have?

3. A table shows that when $x = 2$, $y = 4$. Does this tell you that the rule relating x and y is $y = 2x$? Explain.

4-1 Exercises and Applications

Practice and Apply

1. **Getting Started** Follow the steps below to find the value of y when $x = 5$ in the equation $y = 12x$.

   a. Write the original equation: $y = 12x$

   b. Substitute 5 for x: $y = 12 \times$?

   c. Compute the value of y: $y = $?

Find the value of y when $x = 5$ in each of the following equations.

2. $y = 8x$ 3. $y = x + 3$ 4. $y = 40x$ 5. $y = x - 10$

Complete each table of values.

6.

x	0	1	2	3	4	5
$y = 20x$						

7.

x	0	1	2	3	4	5
$y = -6x$						

8.

x	0	1	2	3	4	5
$y = x + 6$						

9.

x	0	1	2	3	4	5
$y = x - 8$						

Make a table of values for each equation. Use 0, 1, 2, 3, 4, and 5 for x.

10. $y = 15x$ 11. $y = -10x$ 12. $y = x + 12$ 13. $y = x - 15$

Find the rule that relates x and y in each table. Then find y when $x = 20$.

14.

x	y
1	8
2	16
3	24
4	32
5	40

15.

x	y
1	−7
2	−14
3	−21
4	−28
5	−35

16.

x	y
1	10
2	11
3	12
4	13
5	14

17.

x	y
1	−2
2	−1
3	0
4	1
5	2

18. **Test Prep** The table below is represented by which of the lettered equations?

x	0	1	2	3	4
y	0	1	4	9	16

Ⓐ $y = x$ Ⓑ $y = 2x$ Ⓒ $y = x^2$ Ⓓ $y = 3x$

19. Government Each state has two senators and a varying number of representatives in the U.S. Congress. Make a table relating the total number in Congress to the number of representatives for a state.

20. Write a rule that relates the number of chairs to the number of tables.

21. Give examples of two different types of equations.

Problem Solving and Reasoning

22. Critical Thinking

Fig. 1   Fig. 2   Fig. 3

   a. Draw the next figure.

   b. What rule relates n, the figure number, to d, the number of dark tiles?

   c. What rules relates n to c, the number of light tiles?

   d. What rule relates n to t, the total number of tiles in each figure?

23. Math Reasoning

   a. Make a table using the four pairs of values represented on the graph.

   b. Write an equation that shows how the maximum number of goldfish is related to the number of gallons of water in an aquarium.

   c. Find two other pairs of values from the equation. Explain their meaning.

Maximum Number of Fish

Mixed Review

Evaluate each expression. *[Lesson 2-5]*

24. $2(3 + 7)(-5)$

25. $7(8 + 4) - 6(10 + 2)$

26. $\frac{1}{2}(8 + 4) + 17$

27. $8 + 5 - 3(1 + 11)^2$

Express each of the following in exponential form. *[Lesson 2-7]*

28. $3 \times 3 \times 3 \times 3 \times 3$

29. eight to the sixth power

Solutions of Two-Variable Equations

▶ **Lesson Link**   You have learned that equations sometimes have two variables and that such equations may have many solutions. You will now look at solutions and nonsolutions to two-variable equations. ◀

Explore   Solutions of Two-Variable Equations

Want a Polly or a Puppy?

The Dog and Parrot Emporium sells only parrots and puppies. Just for fun, the pet shop owner often takes inventory by counting the number of legs. Find all the different combinations of parrots and puppies that make a total of 24 legs.

1. Make a chart of the values using *x* for the number of parrots and *y* for the number of puppies. (Keep in mind the number of legs for each.) Write an expression for the number of legs using these variables.

2. If there are 24 legs in the Dog and Parrot Emporium, can the number of puppies or parrots ever be an odd number? Explain.

3. If there are 24 legs in the Dog and Parrot Emporium, can the number of parrots and puppies be the same? If so, how many of each would there be?

4. Write an equation that states that the number of parrot legs plus the number of puppy legs is 24. Use the variables from the chart.

5. For the pair (2, 7), which number is the *x*-coordinate and which is the *y*-coordinate? Is (2, 7) a solution of your equation? How do you know?

You'll Learn ...

■ to determine whether a pair of values is a solution of a two-variable equation

... How It's Used

Bakers are solving two-variable equations when they extend bread recipes to serve large numbers of people.

Problem Solving TIP

Make sure a mathematical solution makes sense in the context of a given problem.

Learn   Solutions of Two-Variable Equations

Remember

You graphed ordered pairs (x, y) in Chapter 2. **[Page 91]**

You substituted possible solutions in one-variable equations. If the result was a true statement, the substituted value was a solution. A similar process is used with two-variable equations. A solution of a two-variable equation is an ordered pair.

Example 1

Is the ordered pair (3, 13) a solution of the equation $y = 7 + 2x$?

$y = 7 + 2x$	Write the equation.
$13 = 7 + 2(3)$	Substitute 3 and 13 in the equation for x and y.
$13 = 7 + 6$	Multiply.
$13 = 13$	Add.

Because this is a true statement, (3, 13) is a solution of $y = 7 + 2x$.

Remember

Substitute known values for each variable. **[Page 123]**

You can find solutions to an equation by choosing a value for one variable and solving for the remaining variable.

Example 2

Find two solutions for the equation $2 - 0.5x = y$.

Let $x = 0$.	Select a value for one of the variables.
$2 - 0.5(0) = y$	Substitute the selected value for the variable.
$2 - 0 = y$	Multiply.
$2 = y$	Subtract. (0, 2) is one solution.
Let $x = 2$.	Select another value for one of the variables.
$2 - 0.5(2) = y$	Substitute the selected value for the variable.
$2 - 1 = y$	Multiply.
$1 = y$	Subtract. (2, 1) is another solution.

$(0, 2)$ and $(2, 1)$ are two solutions for $2 - 0.5x = y$.

Try It

a. Determine whether $(-1, 9)$ is a solution of $y = 7 + 2x$.

b. Find two other solutions for $2 - 0.5x = y$.

Example 3

Some people have box turtles as pets. If the turtle and start-up supplies cost $30 and food runs $10 per month, how much will it cost to obtain a box turtle and keep it for 3 months?

Let m = the number of months. Let c = total cost.   Define the variables.

$c = 30 + 10m$ Write an equation showing how the variables are related.

Let $m = 3$.   Select a value for the variable that fits the problem.

$c = 30 + 10(3)$ Substitute the value for the variable.

$c = 30 + 30$ Multiply.

$c = 60$ Add.

It would cost $60 to obtain a turtle and keep it for 3 months.

Try It

a. Refer to Example 3. How much would it cost to obtain a turtle and keep it for a year?

b. It costs about $55 to adopt a dog, and about $70 each month for food, supplies, vet, grooming, and training. How much does it cost to adopt and care for a dog for 2 years?

In some contexts, there are mathematical solutions that do not make sense. In Example 3, a solution of $c = 30 + 10m$ is $m = -3$ and $c = 0$. But owning a turtle for -3 months does not make sense. Also $m = 1000$ would not be reasonable for this situation because turtles only live about 40 years.

Check Your Understanding

1. How do you know whether an ordered pair is a solution of a two-variable equation?

2. The ordered pair $(3, 2)$ is a solution for a two-variable equation. Write an equation for which this ordered pair would be a solution.

3. Is a formula a two-variable equation? Explain.

4-2 Exercises and Applications

Practice and Apply

1. **Getting Started**

   a. Is 3 a solution of $12 = x + 9$?

   b. Is $(3, 12)$ a solution of $y = x + 9$?

   c. Is $(12, 3)$ a solution of $y = x + 9$?

2. **Test Prep** Which of these is **not** a solution of $y = 3x - 9$?

   Ⓐ $(2, -3)$ Ⓑ $(4, 3)$ Ⓒ $(-3, 0)$ Ⓓ $(-2, -15)$

Determine whether each ordered pair is a solution of the equation.

3. $y = x + 13$ **a.** $(10, 23)$ **b.** $(23, 10)$ **c.** $(2, 15)$

4. $y = x - 7$ **a.** $(8, 1)$ **b.** $(10, 3)$ **c.** $(3, -4)$

5. $y = \frac{1}{2}x + 3$ **a.** $(0, 0)$ **b.** $(5, 13)$ **c.** $(7, 6\frac{1}{2})$

6. $y = 0.25x$ **a.** $(0, 0.25)$ **b.** $(1, 4)$ **c.** $(4, 1)$

7. $3x - 1 = y$ **a.** $(0, 0)$ **b.** $(0, -1)$ **c.** $(\frac{1}{3}, 0)$

8. $2x = y$ **a.** $(2, 4)$ **b.** $(6, 12)$ **c.** $(100, 200)$

9. $x = y - 2$ **a.** $(0, 0)$ **b.** $(2, 2)$ **c.** $(0, 2)$

10. $4x = 4y - 8$ **a.** $(0, 0)$ **b.** $(2, 2)$ **c.** $(0, 2)$

Give two solutions for each equation.

11. $y = x + 2$ 12. $y = x - 8$ 13. $y = 2x + 3$ 14. $y = 3x - 2$

15. $5x + 2 = y$ 16. $x - 4 = y$ 17. $x + y = 9$ 18. $x - y = 5$

19. **Industry** The equation $y = 0.75t + 7.50$ represents the cost of a large pizza at Libonatti's, where t is the number of toppings. Make a table for the pizza parlor wall listing the number of toppings and the price.

20. **Cooking** A recipe calls for $\frac{1}{2}$ cup milk per serving, plus 2 cups. How many cups of milk are needed to make 12 servings?

21. **Mental Math** Choose multiples of 10 for x to quickly find three solutions of $y = 0.1x + 10$.

22. **Journal** Write a problem for which you might use the equation $y = 4x$.

Problem Solving and Reasoning

23. Math Reasoning

a. Use the graph to write an equation that relates x, the weight of the llama, to y, the weight of the cargo it can carry.

b. Use your equation to find how much cargo a 300 lb llama could carry.

c. How large would a llama have to be to carry 200 lb?

d. If the largest known llamas are about 400 lb, how would you explain the answer to Question c?

How Much Can a Llama Carry?

24. Communicate Angelica needs to buy one can of fish food that costs $3. While at a pet store she finds angelfish on sale for $1.50 apiece.

a. Let y equal the total amount Angelica will spend and let x equal the number of fish she will buy. Write an equation relating x and y.

b. How much will she spend if she buys fish food and 5 angelfish?

c. If Angelica buys food and spends $12, find the number of angelfish she buys.

d. Would a total cost of $6.50 for fish food and angelfish make sense? Explain your answer.

25. Communicate Describe the solutions of the equation $y = x$.

26. Critical Thinking Freda must decide whether to buy 2 oscars for $2.25 each that also cost $1.00 each to feed per month, or to buy 2 catfish for $8.00 each that feed on the bacteria at the bottom of the aquarium. If she plans to keep her aquarium for one year, which should she buy? Why?

Mixed Review

Evaluate. *[Lesson 2-5]*

27. $-15(-3) + 1$ **28.** $\dfrac{-15}{-3} + 1$ **29.** $-3^2 + (-3)^2$

Match each ordered pair with its point on the graph. *[Lesson 2-6]*

30. $(-2, 3)$

31. $(2, -3)$

32. $(-3, 2)$

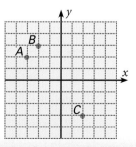

Graphing Two-Variable Relationships

Graphing Two-Variable Relationships

You'll Learn ...

■ to graph a two-variable relationship

... How It's Used

Designers often use such graphs to help make decisions.

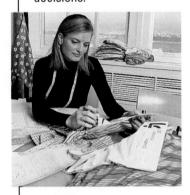

Vocabulary

linear equation

▶ **Lesson Link** You have learned how to write and find solutions for two-variable equations. In Chapter 2, you learned to graph points on a coordinate plane. Now you will learn to combine two-variable equations with graphing. ◀

Explore | Graphing Two-Variable Relationships

A Full House!

A pet shop has 12 kennels in which either 1 kitten or 1 puppy is displayed. The shop owner always keeps the kennels filled. But because pets are frequently sold, a puppy is sometimes replaced by a kitten or vice versa.

Materials: Graph paper

1. What equation represents the relationship between the number of dogs and cats that are displayed? Let c = the number of cats and let d = the number of dogs.

2. Name all the possible ordered pairs of the form (c, d) that satisfy the equation you wrote in Question 1. For example, one such ordered pair is $(11, 1)$, representing 11 cats and 1 dog.

3. On a sheet of graph paper, graph all the ordered pairs from Question 2. Graph c values on the horizontal axis and d values on the vertical axis.

4. What do you notice about the points you graphed in Question 3?

5. Suppose the number of kennels is increased and there are 8 kittens and 8 puppies. Graph the point $(8, 8)$. Does this ordered pair satisfy the equation you wrote in Question 1? What do you notice about the location of the point in relation to the points you graphed in Question 3?

Learn | Graphing Two-Variable Relationships

You know that a two-variable equation has solutions that are ordered pairs. If you graph the points that represent these ordered pairs and all the points lie on a straight line, the equation is called a **linear equation** .

Linear equations occur frequently in real-world situations. For example, at a pet show there is a basic entrance fee of $3 plus $1 for each event that is entered. If y is the total fee and x is the number of events entered, then $y = x + 3$ shows the relationship between x and y.

▶ **Language Link**

Notice that the root word of linear is *line.*

Examples

1 The line shown is the graph of the linear equation $y = x + 3$. Two points on the line are labeled A and B, and one point not on the line is labeled C. Which ordered pairs are solutions of the linear equation?

Test each ordered pair by substituting in the equation.

For A $(-3, 0)$ For B $(0, 3)$ For C $(3, 0)$

$y = x + 3$ $y = x + 3$ $y = x + 3$

$0 \stackrel{?}{=} -3 + 3$ $3 \stackrel{?}{=} 0 + 3$ $0 \stackrel{?}{=} 3 + 3$

$0 = 0$ ✓ $3 = 3$ ✓ $0 \neq 6$

The ordered pairs for A and B are solutions of the linear equation. The ordered pair for C, which does not lie on the line, is **not** a solution of the linear equation.

Try It

Use the graph above. Select two points on the line besides A and B and show that the ordered pairs for those points are solutions of $y = x + 3$. Then select a point that is **not** on the line, and show that its ordered pair is not a solution.

2 Graph the equation $y = 2x$.

Make a table of values. Graph the ordered pairs and connect the points with a line.

x	0	1	2	3
y	0	2	4	6

Notice that as the x values increase by 1 each time, the y values increase by 2. For any linear equation, as x values increase by an equal amount, corresponding y values will also increase (or decrease) by an equal amount.

▶ **Technology Link**

When using the same number many times, such as -3, store it in the memory of your calculator.

Try It

Graph the linear equation $y = -3x$.

WHAT DO YOU THINK?

A video club charges a membership fee of $3.00, plus $1.25 for each rental. So $y = 1.25x + 3$ shows the relationship between y, the total cost, and x, the number of video rentals. How much will it cost to rent a total of 15 videos?

Shauna thinks ...

I'll use a graphing calculator to graph $y = 1.25x + 3$. Then I'll find the value of y when $x = 15$.

$y = 21.75$ when x is 15, so it will cost $21.75 for 15 rentals.

Randy thinks ...

I'll substitute 15 for x in the equation $y = 1.25x + 3$, and then find the value of y.

$y = 1.25x + 3$

$y = 1.25(15) + 3$

$y = 18.75 + 3$. It will cost $21.75 for 15 rentals.

HINT

If you use a graphing calculator to graph a linear equation, you can press TRACE to find ordered pairs and points by using the left and right arrow keys.

What do **you** think?

Whose method do you think was faster? Explain.

Check Your Understanding

1. What does *linear* mean?

2. If an ordered pair for a point satisfies a linear equation, what do you know about the location of the point?

3. How would you graph the equation $y = x + 5$?

Practice and Apply

1. **Getting Started** To determine whether $(1, 2)$ is a solution of $y = 3x$, substitute _____ for x and _____ for y. If the ordered pair is a solution, the point $(1, 2)$ _____ (does/does not) lie on the graph of $y = 3x$.

   a. Graph only the points that satisfy $y = 3x$.

   $(-3, -9), (-1, 0), (2, 6), (0, 0), (1, 3), (4, 13), (0.5, 1.5), (\frac{1}{3}, 1)$

   b. Did the points that you graphed for $y = 3x$ fall on a straight line?

Graph each equation. Use 0, 1, 2, and 3 as x values.

2. $y = x - 2$ **3.** $y = -x$ **4.** $y = 3x$ **5.** $y = \frac{1}{2}x$

6. $y = 4x - 1$ **7.** $y = -x + 3$ **8.** $y = -2x + 2$ **9.** $y = -\frac{1}{2}x$

Graph the ordered pairs in each table. Connect the points to determine if the graphs are linear.

10.

x	y
−3	−4
0	−1
3	2
6	5

11.

x	y
0	−4
2	0
4	4
6	8

12.

x	y
−2	−4
−1	3
0	10
1	17

13.

x	y
2	12
4	6
6	4
8	3

14. **Test Prep** Which of the following is **not** a linear equation? (Plot at least three points to find out.)

   Ⓐ $y = x + 2$ Ⓑ $y = 4x$ Ⓒ $y = \frac{1}{x}$ Ⓓ $3y = x$

15. **Consumer** Jared has a coupon for $2.00 off any order. He decides to buy bulk cat food for Nemo that sells for $0.50 per pound. Use x for the number of pounds of cat food he will buy. Graph the price he will pay. What part of the graph does not make sense for the situation?

16. **Consumer** A pet supply store has a sale on doggie biscuits: Buy 3 boxes for $2 each and receive the 4th one free. Make a table showing the relationship between x and y where x is the number of boxes of biscuits being purchased and y is the total cost. Graph the ordered pairs from the table. Is the relationship linear?

17. **Geometry** When the length of a rectangle is 10 and the width varies, then the perimeter is related to the width.

x m

10 m

a. Make a table showing the relationship between y and x, where x is the width of the rectangle with length 10, and y is the perimeter. Use x values of 1, 2, 3, and 4.

b. Look at the changes in x values and y values. Is the relationship linear?

c. Graph the points from the table and connect them.

Problem Solving and Reasoning

18. **Critical Thinking** The number of times a cricket chirps per minute (n) is related to the temperature in degrees Fahrenheit (f). A cricket chirps 124 times per minute at 68°F, and 172 times per minute at 80°F. Assume the relationship is linear.

a. Make a table or graph to determine the temperature when a cricket chirps 140 times and 156 times. (Hint: Remember that in a linear relationship, equal changes in one variable cause equal changes in the other variable.)

b. For what values do you think this linear relationship holds? Why?

19. **Math Reasoning** Worms can be used to dispose of organic material in a compost pile. To determine the number of pounds of worms needed, multiply the number of pounds of scraps added to the pile per day by 2. You need 1 ft^3 of space for every pound of worms. Write and graph an equation that relates pounds of scraps per day to ft^3 needed.

Mixed Review

Find the opposite of each number. *[Lesson 2-1]*

20. 72   **21.** -360 **22.** $|-13|$ **23.** $|0.01|$

Write in scientific notation. *[Lessons 2-8 and 2-9]*

24. 28,430,000,000   **25.** 41.07×10^4 **26.** 0.0000625   **27.** 0.094

Project Progress

You may have discovered linear relationships in some of the services you have been researching. You can begin by making tables, developing equations, and sketching graphs to help you with information displays.

Problem Solving

Understand
Plan
Solve
Look Back

At the beginning of this section, you learned that some people use the rule that a "dog" year equals 7 human years. The rule would mean that a 14-year-old dog would correspond to a 98-year-old person.

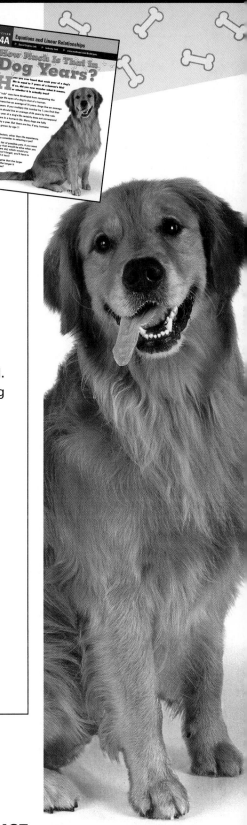

How Much Is That in Dog Years?

Are there patterns that relate human and dog years? Use what you have learned about patterns and linear relationships to answer the following questions.

1. Assume that a dog's "human age" is just the product of 7 and its actual age. What formula would describe the situation above? Is the formula linear?

2. The oldest dog on record was 29 years old. Using the formula, does this age correspond to the oldest human (121 years old)? Explain.

3. Most dogs are fully grown by the time they are a year and a half old. At what age are humans fully grown? Do the ages correspond, using the formula?

4. Dr. Diane Deads, D.V.M., has the following table on the wall in her waiting room:

Dog Age	1	2	3	4	5	6	7	8	9	10
Human Age	15	27	35	40	44	48	52	56	60	64

Graph this data on a grid. Is it linear? Is any part linear?

5. Would negative values be reasonable on this chart? Explain.

6. Could you describe or make a formula for all or part of this data?

7. Large breeds of dogs generally have short life spans; small breeds have longer life spans. Different breeds also have different developmental stages. How could you take this information into account in developing a conversion table or equation?

Section 4A Review

Find the value of _y_ for _x_ = 8 in each equation.

1. $y = 7x$ **2.** $y = \frac{1}{4}x$ **3.** $y = x - 5$ **4.** $y + x = 10$

Make a table of ordered pairs for each equation. Use 0, 1, 2, 3, and 4 as _x_ values.

5. $y = -3x$ **6.** $y = x + 10$ **7.** $y = 2.5x$ **8.** $y = 2x - 1$

Determine whether each ordered pair is a solution of the equation.

9. $y = x + 15$ **a.** $(15, 0)$ **b.** $(0, 15)$ **c.** $(14, 1)$

10. $y = 0.4x$ **a.** $(2, 0.8)$ **b.** $(0.8, 2)$ **c.** $(10, 4)$

Find a rule that relates _x_ and _y_. Then find the value of _y_ when _x_ = 60.

11.

x	0	1	2	3	4	5
y	0	4	8	12	16	20

12.

x	0	1	2	3	4	5
y	4	5	6	7	8	9

13. Graph $y = x + 4$.

14. An animal shelter allows the public to adopt any number of cats for a set fee of $10 plus $15 for each cat to cover the cost of shots.

a. Write an equation relating the cost, _y_, to _x_, the number of cats adopted. Then make a table of values showing the cost for adopting 1, 2, or 3 cats. Graph the ordered pairs and connect them with a line.

b. [Journal] Do the ordered pairs for all points on the line satisfy the equation? Do all these solutions make sense in this situation? Explain.

Test Prep

When you are asked to determine whether an ordered pair is a solution of an equation, remember that the _x_-coordinate appears first in each ordered pair.

15. Which of these ordered pairs is **not** a solution of $y = x - 10$?

ⓐ $(0, -10)$ ⓑ $(10, 0)$ ⓒ $(0, 10)$ ⓓ $(5, -5)$

Linear Equations and Inequalities

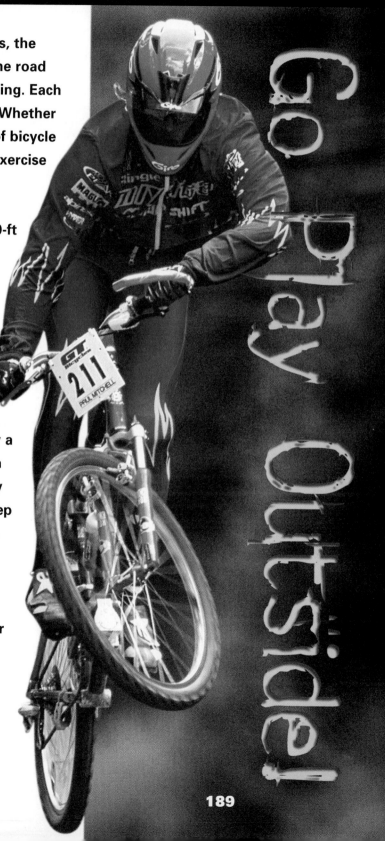

The rush of wind, the strain of muscles, the cadence matching your heart beat, the road speeding by below you. You must be cycling. Each year, millions take to the roads on bikes. Whether they are with their families or members of bicycle touring clubs, they pursue one goal—to exercise while enjoying the great outdoors.

For some, bicycling may provide the ultimate thrill, like riding down the 10,000-ft slope of Maui's volcano, Haleakala. Or there's the Tour de France, where it takes days to finish the entire course, covering almost 4,000 km.

Do you remember the first time you tried to ride a bike? Perhaps you used training wheels, or someone ran along, holding you up. The bike you learned on was probably a single-speed, built to be used primarily on flat surfaces. Other bicycles, with as many as 21 speeds, allow riders to navigate steep slopes with ease with a click of the finger.

1 Describe your first experience riding a bicycle.

2 Think of hills as slopes. Why is it harder to ride up hills than on flat surfaces?

3 How do gears make climbing a hill easier?

189

Understanding Slope

You'll Learn ...

■ to find the slope of a line

... How It's Used

Land use planners need to calculate slopes to make decisions about runoff.

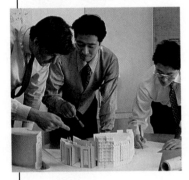

Vocabulary

slope

rise

run

positive slope

negative slope

▶ **Lesson Link** You have learned to graph equations with two variables, and to determine whether the graph is linear. Now you will learn ways that mathematicians describe these lines. ◀

Explore | Slope

The Ups and Downs of Graphing

Materials: Graph paper
Number cube
Coin (optional)

1. On a large sheet of graph paper, draw a coordinate plane with the origin at the center of the page. Label the *x*- and *y*-axes.

2. Flip a coin to see if you should move right (heads) or left (tails). Roll a number cube to determine the number of units you should move, for example, Right 5.

3. Flip the coin again to see if you should move up (heads) or down (tails). Roll the number cube again to determine the number of units you should move, for example, Up 2.

4. Using your results from steps 2 and 3, start at the origin and plot a point.

5. From your point, move the same number of spaces right or left as before, then move up or down as before. Plot a second point.

6. Move and plot several times. What geometric shape is formed by these points? Draw it.

7. Compare your results with those of your classmates.

Learn   Understanding Slope

Beginning skiers use slopes that are not as steep as those used by more advanced skiers. Some lines in the coordinate plane can also be considered "steeper" than others.

Mathematicians use a concept called **slope** to describe the steepness of a line. It relates the vertical change to the horizontal change. These are often called the **rise** and the **run** . When a line slants upward from left to right, it is said to have **positive slope** ; when it slants downward it has **negative slope** .

> ▶ **Language Link**
>
> When a variable is used for slope, it is usually the letter *m*. This comes from the French word *monter*, meaning "to climb."

For any line, the rise divided by the run is always the same. This is the slope of the line. A horizontal line has a slope of zero because it has zero rise. A vertical line is said to have no slope.

Example 1

Snow safety experts advise that avalanches are more likely to happen on a hill with a slope of between 0.5 and 1. Is an avalanche likely for Hotdog Hill?

$$\frac{\text{rise}}{\text{run}} = \frac{850}{1275}$$

Dividing to find the slope, 850 ÷ 1275 = 0.66666667. The slope is between 0.5 and 1, so an avalanche may be likely.

Try It

Determine the slope. Is an avalanche likely?

Example 2

Find the rise and run from point A to point B. Then find the slope of the line.

Because the line slants downward from left to right, we can say that the rise is negative.

The rise is -2 units. The run is 4 units.

The slope is $\frac{\text{rise}}{\text{run}} = \frac{-2}{4} = -\frac{1}{2}$.

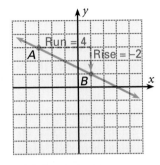

Try It

Determine the slope.

Example 3

Draw a line through the origin with a slope of $\frac{-3}{2}$.

Start at $(0, 0)$. Go 2 units right and 3 units down, the slope is negative. The slope is $\frac{-3}{2}$ or $-\frac{3}{2}$.

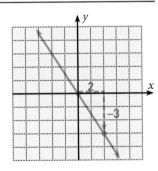

Try It

a. Draw a line through the origin with slope $\frac{2}{3}$.

b. Draw a line through $(1, 2)$ with slope -1.

Check   Your Understanding

1. Does a line have more than one slope? Explain.

2. How do you determine if a line has positive or negative slope?

3. How does a slope of $\frac{2}{3}$ compare with a slope of $\frac{4}{6}$? Why?

Practice and Apply

1. **Getting Started** To find the slope of a line through two points, you divide the _____ by the _____.

2. For the line at the right, the rise is _____, the run is _____, and the slope is _____.

Give the slope for each of these items.

3.

3 ft.
24 ft.

4.

4 ft.
6 ft.

5.

2 ft.
10 ft.

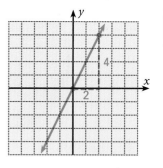

6. **Test Prep** A line having which slope would fall downward from left to right?

Ⓐ $\frac{1}{10}$ Ⓑ 10   Ⓒ -10 Ⓓ $\frac{9}{10}$

Find the slope of each line on the graph.

7. Line through A and B

8. Line through C and A

9. Line through D and E

10. Line through E and B

Draw a line through the origin with each of the given slopes.

11. $\frac{4}{5}$ 12. 2 13. $\frac{-1}{4}$ 14. -3

15. **Health** A wheelchair ramp is allowed a maximum of one inch of rise for every foot of run. Express this slope as a fraction. (Hint: Use the same units.)

16. Describe how slope and mountain-biking accidents are related.

Locations of Mountain-Biking Accidents

Uphill
15%

9%
Flat

76%
Downhill

17. Fine Arts This sculpture is at the Nasa Museum in Washington, D. C. What is the slope of the red line shown? Explain how you found it.

Problem Solving and Reasoning

18. Critical Thinking Patios, driveways, and streets are often designed so they have a slope of about $\frac{1}{48}$ toward their edges. Why would they be designed this way?

Problem Solving **TIP**

Draw a picture to show the effect of sloped edges.

19. a. Find the missing information for each ski run.

Ski Run	Total Rise	Total Run	Slope
Alpine Meadows	1800 ft	7200 ft	
Diamond Peak	1840 ft	3680 ft	
Bear Valley	1900 ft	4750 ft	
Donner Ski Ranch	750 ft	3000 ft	

b. Communicate Which ski areas would you recommend for advanced skiers? Explain.

20. Critical Thinking Architects use circular or winding stairs in buildings. What is the advantage of this kind of structure?

21. Critical Thinking How would you describe the calculation of the slope of a horizontal line? How would you describe the calculation of the slope of a vertical line?

Mixed Review

Add. *[Lesson 2-2]*

22. $12 + (-12)$ **23.** $-37 + (-4)$ **24.** $43 + 6 - 9$

Solve each formula. *[Lesson 3-1]*

25. $A = bh$, for $b = 7$ and $h = 9$ **26.** $P = 2l + 2w$, for $P = 42$ and $l = 8$

Patterns in Linear Equations and Graphs

► Lesson Link You know how to find the slope of a line by looking at its graph. You can also find the slope of a line by looking at its equation. ◄

Explore | Patterns in Linear Equations and Graphs

Materials: Graphing utility

Blizzard of a Graph!

On the ground there was 2 feet of snow. During the night, snow begins falling at 1 foot per hour in some areas, 2 feet per hour in others, and as much as 3 feet per hour in others.

If y is the amount of snow on the ground as it falls, and x is the number of hours it has been falling, then $y = x + 2$, $y = 2x + 2$, and $y = 3x + 2$ describe the relationship between snow on the ground and the number of hours it falls in the three locations.

1. Graph $y = x + 2$, $y = 2x + 2$, and $y = 3x + 2$ using a graphing utility. What do you notice about the steepness of the graphs? Do the graphs share any common points?

2. Graph $y = x + 2$, $y = x - 1$, and $y = x - 3$ using a graphing utility. What do you notice?

3. What is the relationship between the constant added to each x and the point where each graph crosses the y-axis?

4. Do you see any relationships between the coefficient of x and the slope of each line?

You'll Learn ...

■ to graph an equation and then find the slope and the intercepts

... How It's Used

Systems used by air-traffic controllers lock planes onto beams generated by linear equations so planes can land safely.

Vocabulary

x-intercept

y-intercept

parallel lines

Learn | **Patterns in Linear Equations and Graphs**

Remember

To make a table of ordered pairs, substitute different values for *x* and solve for *y*. **[Page 173]**

You already know that you can find the slope of a line by looking at the graph. You can also determine the **x-intercept** and **y-intercept** by looking at the graph. The *x*-intercept is the *x*-coordinate of the point where the line crosses the *x*-axis, and the *y*-intercept is the *y*-coordinate of the point where the line crosses the *y*-axis.

The slope and *y*-intercept often have meanings in real-world problems.

Example 1

A hockey player receives 2 minutes in the penalty box for each minor penalty. A player already has 4 minutes in minor penalties.

Graph $y = 2x + 4$, find the slope, and *y*-intercept. What are the meanings of the slope and *y*-intercept in the problem?

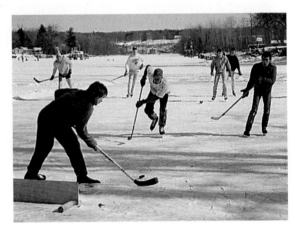

Make a table of ordered pairs by assigning values to *x* and then finding *y*. Graph the points and connect them with a line. You can choose any values for *x*. Try: −2, 0, and 2.

x	−2	0	2
y	0	4	8

Find the rise and run. Because rise = 4 and run = 2, the slope = $\frac{4}{2}$ or 2, and the line slants upward. The graph crosses the *y*-axis at 4, the *y*-intercept is 4. The slope matches the 2 minutes he receives for each additional minor penalty. The *y*-intercept means that if he receives no additional penalties, he will have 4 penalty minutes.

Although you can use negative numbers to make the graph, they do not make sense in this problem situation.

Examples

2 Graph $y = \frac{-3}{4}x - 3$. Find the slope, the x-intercept, and the y-intercept.

Make a table of ordered pairs using -4, 0, and 4 as x-values. Graph the points and connect them with a line.

x	−4	0	4
y	0	−3	−6

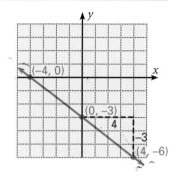

Find the rise and run. Because rise $= -3$ and run $= 4$, the slope $= \frac{-3}{4}$, and the line slants downward. The graph crosses the x-axis at -4 and the y-axis at -3. So the x-intercept is -4 and the y-intercept is -3.

Try It

Graph each equation. Find the slope, the x-intercept, and the y-intercept.

a. $y = 3x - 6$ **b.** $y = \frac{-1}{2}x + 4$

3 Graph $y = 2x - 1$ and $y = 2x + 3$ on the same grid. Then find the slope for each line.

Make a table of ordered pairs for each equation. Graph the points and connect them.

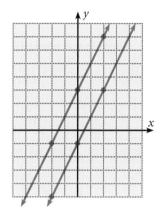

For $y = 2x - 1$

x	−2	0	2
y	−5	−1	3

For $y = 2x + 3$

x	−2	0	2
y	−1	3	7

For each graph, the rise is 4 and the run is 2. So the slope in each case is $\frac{4}{2}$ or 2.

> **Study TIP**
>
> Keep your study location free of things that distract you, but be sure to have a bottle of water to drink when you work.

Notice that the lines never intersect no matter how far they are extended. Such lines are called **parallel lines**. Parallel lines have the same slope.

Check Your Understanding

1. To graph a linear equation, how many points do you need to connect? Why is it a good idea to graph an additional point?

2. When you graph an equation such as $y = \frac{1}{4}x - 2$, can you assign any values to x? Would some values be easier to use than others? Explain.

PRACTICE 4-5

Practice and Apply

Getting Started

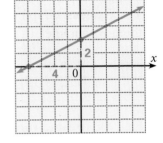

1. The rise is _____ and the run is _____. So the slope is _____.

2. The graph crosses the *x*-axis at $(-4, 0)$. So the *x*-intercept is _____.

3. The graph crosses the *y*-axis at $(0, 2)$. So the *y*-intercept is _____.

For each line, find the slope, the *x*-intercept, and the *y*-intercept.

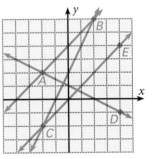

4. Line through *A* and *B*

5. Line through *C* and *B*

6. Line through *A* and *D*

7. Line through *C* and *E*

8. Which lines in Exercises 4–7 are parallel? Explain.

Graph each equation. Find the slope, the *x*-intercept, and the *y*-intercept.

9. $y = 2x - 6$

10. $y = x + 8$

11. $y = -x$

12. $y = \frac{1}{5}x$

13. $y = 5x + 2$

14. $y = -\frac{3}{4}x + 2$

15. $y = \frac{1}{2}x - 2$

16. $y = -7x$

17. **Test Prep** The slopes of two lines are given. Which represent parallel lines?

Ⓐ $\frac{6}{3}$ and $\frac{8}{4}$ Ⓑ $\frac{3}{6}$ and $\frac{6}{3}$ Ⓒ $\frac{3}{6}$ and $\frac{-3}{6}$ Ⓓ 4 and $\frac{1}{4}$

18. Peter has just learned how to ski and wants to start out on the beginner's hill. The $\frac{\text{rise}}{\text{run}}$ of the hills are $\frac{723 \text{ ft}}{4820 \text{ ft}}$, $\frac{819 \text{ ft}}{1820 \text{ ft}}$, and $\frac{778 \text{ ft}}{2593 \text{ ft}}$. Determine the slope of each hill. Which one is for beginners?

Problem Solving and Reasoning

19. Communicate Marty belongs to a swim club. With a membership fee of $20 per year, the members can swim any number of times for a reduced rate of $2 per swim. Make a graph to show the total cost for varying numbers of swims. Explain how to find a typical cost from the graph.

20. Critical Thinking

a. Is there a way to determine the slope and y-intercept of equations such as $y = 2x - 3$ and $y = -3x + 1$ just by looking at the equation? (Hint: You might use your answers to Exercises 9–16 to help you.)

b. The equation of a line is $y = \frac{2}{3}x + 6$. Predict the slope and the y-intercept without graphing.

c. Communicate Explain how you would change the equation $y = 2x - 3$ so the line will have a greater slope and a smaller y-intercept.

21. Choose a Strategy The formula $h = 450t + 1800$ gives the altitude of a mountain-climbing team t hours after they begin their climb, where h is the height above sea level in feet. At what altitude did they start their climb? How many feet are they climbing per hour?

22. Critical Thinking During winter break, Jerry can earn $12 for every 5 pairs of skis he waxes for the ski shop ($y = \frac{12}{5}x$) or he can earn $18 for every 7 snowboards he waxes ($y = \frac{18}{7}x$). Which job would earn Jerry more money? Explain.

23. Explain how you can determine the slope of a line by looking at its graph; by examining its equation.

> **Problem Solving**
> ## STRATEGIES
> - Look for a Pattern
> - Make an Organized List
> - Make a Table
> - Guess and Check
> - Work Backward
> - Use Logical Reasoning
> - Draw a Diagram
> - Solve a Simpler Problem

Mixed Review

Add or Subtract. *[Lesson 2-3]*

24. $40 - 50$ **25.** $-33 - 13$ **26.** $-42 - (-10)$ **27.** $-9 + 99$

28. A company gives an employee a pension based on the formula $P = \frac{sy}{60}$, where s is the employee's salary, and y is the number of years of employment. What is the pension for an employee with a salary of $40,000 and employed for 18 years? *[Lesson 3-1]*

Solve each equation. *[Lesson 3-2]*

29. $x = 23 + 17$ **30.** $x + 100 = 300$ **31.** $3x = 18$ **32.** $-x = 17$

T E C H N O L O G Y

Using a Graphing Calculator • Parallel Lines

Problem: Graph two lines that are parallel to the graph of $y = 2x + 1$.

You can use your graphing calculator to help graph lines quickly.

```
WINDOW FORMAT
Xmin = -5
Xmax = 5
Xscl = 1
Ymin = -5
Ymax = 5
Yscl = 1
```

```
Y1 = 2x+1
Y2 =
Y3 =
Y4 =
Y5 =
Y6 =
Y7 =
Y8 =
```

① Use the viewing window shown. Enter $2x + 1$ as Y1 and then graph it.

```
Y1 = 2x+1
Y2 = 2x+3
Y3 =
Y4 =
Y5 =
Y6 =
Y7 =
Y8 =
```

② Enter $2x + 3$ as Y2 and graph it along with Y1.

③ Enter $2x - 2$ as Y3 and graph it along with Y1 and Y2.

```
Y1 = 2x+1
Y2 = 2x+3
Y3 = 2x-2
Y4 =
Y5 =
Y6 =
Y7 =
Y8 =
```

Solution: The lines have the same slope as $y = 2x + 1$, so they are parallel.

TRY IT

a. Graph two lines that are parallel to the graph of $y = -2x + 3$.

b. Graph two lines that are parallel to the graph of $y = 1$.

ON YOUR OWN

▶ Your graphing calculator may let you make a table from these equations. Make a table for $y = -x + 2$ and a line parallel to it. Is there a value of x that has the same value of y for both equations?

X	Y1	Y2
0	1	3
1	3	5
2	5	7
3	7	9
4	9	11
5	11	13
6	13	15

X=0

▶ Try graphing two different lines that go through the point (0, 2). Are they parallel? How did you get them to go through the same point?

Pairs of Linear Equations

▶ **Lesson Link**   You have seen how to graph all the solutions of a single linear equation. Now you will learn how to find the solution of a pair of linear equations. ◄

Explore   Pairs of Linear Equations

Rocking the Boat

Materials: Spreadsheet software (optional)

1. The signs show the cost of renting a boat at two different locations. Copy and complete the table to find the total costs for various times. Extend the table if necessary. Use a spreadsheet program if one is available.

Vistas Boats
$3 + $2/hour

Ray's Rafting
$8 + $1/hour

Hours	Vistas Boats Cost	Ray's Rafting Cost
x	$2x + 3$	$x + 8$
1		
2		
3		
4		

2. Explain why $2x + 3$ is the cost of a boat rental at Vistas Boats, and $x + 8$ is the cost of a boat rental at Ray's Rafting.

3. Which rental arrangement is better if you plan to rent a boat for 1 hour? Why?

4. For what number of rental hours is the cost the same at either place?

5. After how many hours is it cheaper to rent a boat at Ray's Rafting?

6. Do you think that Ray's Rafting will always be cheaper for more than the number of hours you found in Question 5? Why or why not?

You'll Learn ...

■ to find a single solution of a pair of linear equations

... How It's Used

Firefighters use intersecting lines to pinpoint fire locations.

Vocabulary

system of linear equations

When two linear equations are considered together, they form a **system of linear equations** . An ordered pair that is a solution of both equations is called a *solution* of the system.

Example 1

► **History Link**

The Merry-Go-Round is the oldest amusement park ride still in use, first operated in 1799 in Salem, Mass., and still a favorite of the young and young at heart.

Wild World Carnival charges an admission of $10 plus $1 for each ride. Fantastic Fair charges an admission of $6 plus $2 for each ride.

a. Let x be the number of rides and let y be the total cost. Write an equation for the total cost at each park for admission plus x rides. Then make a table to show the cost for various numbers of rides.

b. Is there a number of rides for which the total cost is the same at each park? What ordered pair solves *both* equations that you wrote in Part a?

a. For Wild World Carnival, $y = x + 10$. For Fantastic Fair, $y = 2x + 6$.

Remember

The solution of a two-variable equation is an ordered pair, not a single number.
[Page 178]

Number of Rides	x	0	1	2	3	4	5	6
Wild World Carnival	$y = x + 10$	10	11	12	13	14	15	16
Fantastic Fair	$y = 2x + 6$	6	8	10	12	14	16	18

b. The cost is the same for 4 rides ($14). The ordered pair (4, 14) solves both equations. So (4, 14) is a solution of the system of equations $y = x + 10$ and $y = 2x + 6$.

Try It

a. Suppose Fantastic Fair raises its admission to $8 but still charges $2 a ride. For how many rides would the total cost be the same at both parks?

b. Suppose Fantastic Fair has free admission for a day, but still charges $2 per ride. For how many rides would the total cost be the same at both parks?

Another way to find the solution of a system of linear equations is to graph both equations and find a point that lies on both lines. Then determine the x and y values for that point.

Example 2

Glen needs to decide whether to purchase hang-gliding equipment. If he rents equipment, he will pay $75 for each flight. If he purchases equipment for $200, he will pay $25 for each flight. For what number of flights would each option cost the same?

Let x = number of flights. Let y = total cost.

$y = 75x$ This is the total cost if he rents equipment.

$y = 25x + 200$ This is the total cost if he buys equipment.

Find two or three solutions for each equation and graph each line. Find the point where the lines intersect.

x	$y = 75x$
0	0
2	150

x	$y = 25x + 200$
0	200
2	250

The lines intersect at (4, 300). Check the coordinates for x and y in both equations.

$y = 75x$	$y = 25x + 200$
$300 \stackrel{?}{=} 75(4)$	$300 \stackrel{?}{=} 25(4) + 200$
$300 = 300$ ✓	$300 = 300$ ✓

If Glen makes 4 flights, the total cost would be the same—$300.

Check Your Understanding

1. How do you know whether an ordered pair is a solution of a system of two equations?

2. How can you find the solution of a system of equations from a graph?

Test Prep

You may be able to find a solution of a system using number sense. If you see that Glen pays $50 more per flight if he rents, you might realize that he pays $200 more for 4 flights.

Practice and Apply

1. |Getting Started| Is the point (2, 1) a solution of both equations?

   a. Check to see whether (2, 1) solves $y = 2x - 3$.

   b. Check to see whether (2, 1) solves $y = \frac{-1}{2}x + 2$.

Solve each system of equations by graphing.

2. $y = -2x + 8$
   $y = -6x$

3. $y = -x$
   $y = 3x + 4$

4. $y = x - 1$
   $y = \frac{1}{3}x + 1$

5. $y = x + 3$
   $y = 4x + 3$

6. $y = -x + 4$
   $y = x$

7. $y = 4x - 15$
   $y = x + 3$

8. $y = 2x + 1$
   $y = -x + 4$

9. $y = x - 1$
   $y = x - 5$

10. Use the data in the table below.

Equipment to Rent	Rental Cost per Hour Regular Rates	Rental Cost per Hour with Card
Snowshoes	$2.00	$1.00
Skis	$5.00	$3.00

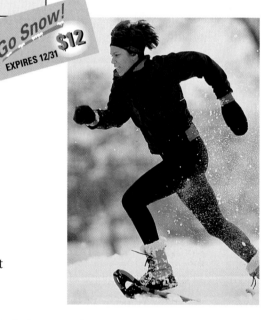

a. Make a table to show the total cost of renting skis and snowshoes for up to 7 hours—with and without the Go Snow card. Use the table to find the number of hours for which the cost is the same for both.

b. What system of equations represents the total cost for the two ski rental plans? Graph to determine the point where the lines for each equation intersect.

c. Communicate Suppose you have your own skis, and only need to rent snowshoes. For what number of hours would the total cost be the same with or without the card? Would you rather use a table or graph to determine the answer? Explain.

11. Science A cup weighing 3 oz is placed on one side of a balance scale. 6 tbsp of liquid weighing 0.5 oz per tbsp is poured into it. 6 tbsp of granules weighing 1 oz per tbsp is placed on the other side of the scale. Why is the scale balanced? Use a graph.

12. Number Sense Suppose one video plan is $2.50 per rental plus $5.00 membership, whereas another is $2.25 per rental plus $3.00 membership. Why is it easy to decide which is the less expensive plan without a table or graph?

Problem Solving and Reasoning

13. Communicate Margaret will probably get to ski five or six times this year. She can join the water-ski club for $25 a year. This will allow her to ski for $5 each time. She can also ski without joining for $10 each time. Should she join? Use a graph to support your answer.

14. Critical Thinking If two lines have the same slope and the same y-intercept, what point(s) would they have in common?

15. Choose a Strategy Which would be less expensive for 12 lifts, buying a weekend ski lift pass for $30.00 plus $1.50 per lift, or just paying $4.00 per lift?

16. **Journal** Write a problem that could be solved by graphing the system of equations $y = x + 5$ and $y = 2x$.

> **Problem Solving**
> ## STRATEGIES
> • Look for a Pattern
> • Make an Organized List
> • Make a Table
> • Guess and Check
> • Work Backward
> • Use Logical Reasoning
> • Draw a Diagram
> • Solve a Simpler Problem

Mixed Review

Multiply or divide. *[Lesson 2-4]*

17. $8 \times (-6)$ **18.** $\dfrac{-18}{-2}$ **19.** $10 \times 4 \div (-5)$ **20.** $6 \div 1 \times 4$

Write an expression for each of the following. *[Lesson 3-3]*

21. Sal is 4 years older than Daryn.   **22.** The number of inches in y yards

23. T. K. bought a shirt for $17 and several pairs of socks at $2 a pair.

Project Progress

You should be able to make some comparisons among some of the services you have been researching. Compare using graphs, tables, and equations. Be prepared to make some recommendations.

> **Problem Solving**
> Understand
> Plan
> Solve
> Look Back

Linear Inequalities

▶ **Lesson Link** In Chapter 3, you solved and graphed inequalities with one variable. Now that you can solve equations with two variables, you can see how inequalities with two variables are solved and graphed. ◀

You'll Learn …

■ to express two-variable inequalities graphically

… How It's Used

Water testers use inequalities to describe the levels of impurities permitted in drinking water samples.

Vocabulary

linear inequality

boundary line

Explore   Linear Inequalities

Which Side Are You On?

Materials: Graph paper and straightedge, or Graphing utility

Imagine yourself kayaking on a beautiful, tree-lined river. As you approach the rapids, you spot a rope supported by buoys dividing the river down the center, marked $y = x - 4$. You must immediately choose one side of the river.

1. Graph the equation $y = x - 4$, which represents the rope dividing the river.

2. Pick any point above the line that you graphed. Decide if the point you chose makes $y = x - 4$, $y > x - 4$, or $y < x - 4$ true. Support your conclusion.

3. Pick any point below the line. Decide if the point you chose makes $y = x - 4$, $y > x - 4$, or $y < x - 4$ true. Support your conclusion.

4. Suppose solutions for $y > x - 4$ indicate the challenging white water rapids and $y < x - 4$ indicates the more manageable side. Lightly shade the side you would choose, sketch your kayak on that side and label it appropriately, either $y > x - 4$ or $y < x - 4$.

Learn   Linear Inequalities

You know that to determine whether a value is a solution of a one-variable inequality, you can substitute and see if the inequality is true. You can do the same for an inequality with two variables.

Examples

1 Is (1, 5) a solution of $y > x + 2$?

$y > x + 2$ Write the inequality.

$5 \overset{?}{>} 1 + 2$ Substitute the ordered pair in the inequality.

$5 > 3$ ✓   Check to see if the resulting inequality is true.

The ordered pair (1, 5) is a solution of $y > x + 2$.

When you graph a one-variable inequality, such as $x > 3$, one boundary point ($x = 3$) separates the line into points that are solutions and points that are not.

Remember

You know how to graph inequalities on a number line. **[Page 156]**

When you graph a **linear inequality** , such as $y > x + 2$, a **boundary line** ($y = x + 2$) separates the coordinate plane into points that are solutions and points that are not.

The shaded region is the solution. Instead of an open circle, we can use a dashed line to show that the line is not part of the solution. (For $\geq$ and $\leq$, instead of a closed circle, use a *solid* line.)

2 Graph the inequality $y \leq 2x - 4$.

First, make a table of values for $y = 2x - 4$.

x	0	2	4
y	−4	0	4

Draw a solid line for $y = 2x - 4$. Choose any point not on the line to see if it is a solution of the inequality. (0, 0) is usually a convenient point. If it is a solution, all points on that side of the line are solutions. If it is not a solution, all points on the other side of the line are solutions.

$0 \leq 2(0) - 4$

$0 \leq -4$ is false. Shade the other side of the graph.

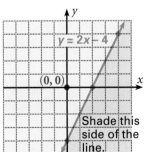

Some calculators let you test values in an inequality. They answer 1 for true, 0 for false. This screen shows that (5, 4) is a solution of $y \leq 2x - 4$.

Try It

Graph $y > x - 2$.

DID YOU KNOW?

To be eligible to be a San Diego lifeguard, you must run 50 m, swim 500 m, and run 50 m in ≤ a total of 10 min 30 sec.

Example 3

The number of lifeguards at Lake Waskobee must be at least $\frac{1}{20}$ of the number of swimmers in the lake. Graph the number of lifeguards needed. If there are 190 swimmers, up to how many lifeguards must there be?

Select the variables.

Let x = the number of swimmers.

Let y = the number of lifeguards.

$y \geq \frac{1}{20}x$ Write an inequality. "At least" means ≥.

Make a table. Use multiples of 20 for x.

x	20	40	60	80
y	1	2	3	4

There must be at least 10 lifeguards when there are 190 swimmers.

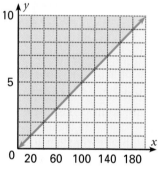

In the graph above, we shaded all the points above the line. However, in this context, not all points in the shaded region make sense. Since x and y represent people, only those points with coordinates that are whole numbers would be reasonable.

Try It

A school district mandates that there must be at least 1 teacher for every 25 students. Graph the inequality. How many teachers are needed for 264 students?

Check Your Understanding

1. How can you tell whether (3, 8) is a solution of $y < 3x + 2$?

2. How can you tell from a linear inequality whether to make the boundary line dashed or solid?

3. How do you know whether to shade above the line or below the line when graphing the solution of a linear inequality?

Practice and Apply

Getting Started Match each graph with the inequality it represents.
(Hint: Test (0, 0) in each inequality.)

1.   **2.**   **3.**   **4.**

Ⓐ $y \leq x + 1$ Ⓑ $y < x + 1$ Ⓒ $y > x + 1$ Ⓓ $y \geq x + 1$

Test whether each point is a solution of the inequality.

5. $y > 2x + 3$ **a.** $(0, 1)$ **b.** $(3, 9)$ **c.** $(-1, 0)$

6. $y \leq 2x + 3$ **a.** $(0, 1)$ **b.** $(3, 9)$ **c.** $(-1, 0)$

Graph each inequality.

7. $y \leq x + 2$ **8.** $y > 2x - 3$ **9.** $y \geq x + 5$ **10.** $y < -x$

11. $y < 0.5x - 1$ **12.** $y \geq x + 0.5$ **13.** $y > x$ **14.** $y \leq 5x$

15. The inequality $y < x$ represents all cases where there are more students than teachers. Which variable represents which group?

16. Write an inequality that states that there are at least as many skiers as skaters, where x represents the number of skiers.

17. **Health** Write an inequality for the statement: "The number of calories is at least 4 times the weight, in grams."

18. **Science** A raindrop in still air will fall as fast as 3 feet per second. Graph the distance it falls (y), in x seconds.

19. The Environment Club will have a party if the students collect at least 3.5 pounds of recyclable aluminum cans per student within a month. Graph the number of pounds (P) that must be collected by n students.

20. **Civics** Votes on proposals often require a two-thirds majority for the proposal to pass. The number of votes in favor must be at least twice the number opposed. Make a graph to show the number of votes required to pass a proposal. Use x as the number opposed, and y as the number in favor.

Problem Solving and Reasoning

21. **Communicate** Many communities allow no more than one-fourth of a store's window area to be covered by advertising. Is this storefront window within the law? How did you decide?

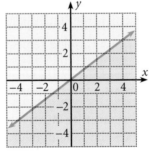

22. **Critical Thinking** Graph $y < x + 3$ and $y \geq 2x$ on the same set of axes. Notice that the grid is divided into four regions. Select a point in each region. Substitute the ordered pair for each point into both inequalities. Which region contains the point that solves both inequalities? What is true of all points in that region?

23. **Choose a Strategy** Films are rated by a panel of reviewers. For a film to be rated as a "must see," it must receive between 3 points and 4 points per reviewer. Graph the total points a "must see" film must have. Let x be the number of reviewers.

24. **Math Reasoning** What inequality would produce the graph at the right?

25. **Journal** Compare and contrast graphing a two-variable equation with graphing a two-variable inequality.

Problem Solving
STRATEGIES

- Look for a Pattern
- Make an Organized List
- Make a Table
- Guess and Check
- Work Backward
- Use Logical Reasoning
- Draw a Diagram
- Solve a Simpler Problem

Mixed Review

Express in exponential notation. *[Lesson 2-7]*

26. $2 \times 2 \times 2 \times 2$

27. 8×8

28. $7 \times 7 \times 7 \times 7 \times 7 \times 7$

29. 2 cubed

Solve each equation. *[Lesson 3-4]*

30. $13 = x + 10$

31. $x - 23 = 9$

32. $16 = x - 1$

33. $x + 8 = 11$

34. $2.4 = x + 1.8$

35. $x - 0.01 = 0.05$

36. $\frac{1}{2} = x - 2$

37. $x + 1\frac{7}{8} = 1\frac{3}{4}$

Section 4B Connect

At the beginning of Section 4B, we discussed bicycles and bicycling. We can use graphs and equations to look at bicycling situations.

Go Play Outside!

Materials: Graph paper or Graphing utility, Colored pencils

Sandy and her brother Mark will be having a bike race. Sandy averages 4 min/mi and Mark averages 6 min/mi. Sandy will give Mark a 5-minute head start.

1. Graph the line $y = 6x$ for Mark's ride and $y = 4x + 5$ for Sandy's. Label the axes appropriately.

2. Find the slope and y-intercept of each line. What do these represent?

3. Find the point where the lines intersect and label it. What does this point represent? What conclusions can you make?

4. Suppose Mark gets to choose how long the race will last, or how far it will go. Identify the part of the graph where Mark would win the race. What conditions should he choose?

5. Suppose Sandy gives Mark a $\frac{1}{2}$ *mile* head start. Use the fact that 4 min/mi is 15 mi/hr and 6 min/mi is 10 mi/hr to graph this situation a different way. Which head start is better for Sandy, 5 min or $\frac{1}{2}$ mi? Why?

Find the slope of each line. Then find the _x_-intercept and the _y_-intercept for each line.

1. Line through A and B

2. Line through C and B

3. Graph a line through the origin with a slope of $\frac{5}{6}$.

4. Graph $y = \frac{1}{2}x - 3$. Find the slope, _x_-intercept, and _y_-intercept.

5. Solve the following system of equations by graphing: $y = x - 1$ and $y = -2x + 5$.

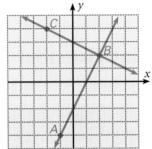

Graph each inequality.

6. $y \geq 2x - 5$ 7. $y < \frac{3}{5}x$

8. Mallory plans to go hot-air ballooning. She can ride with Balloons Are Us for $25 plus $5 per hour or with Up and Away for a flat rate of $10 per hour. Use either a table or a graph to find the number of hours for which the cost would be the same.

9. In a volleyball match between the teachers and the students, the teachers had to get more than double the score of the students to win. If x represents the students' score, write and graph an inequality that represents the score the teachers needed to win.

10. **Communicate** Suppose you try to solve a system of two linear equations by graphing. You find that the lines are parallel. What does this tell you about the solution?

11. **Journal** Describe how you know if an ordered pair is a solution of a two-variable equation or inequality.

Test Prep

When two answers are acceptable, choose the one that is best.

12. Which is a reasonable slope for an interstate highway exit ramp?

    Ⓐ -4 Ⓑ -2 Ⓒ -1 Ⓓ $-\frac{1}{12}$

Nonlinear Equations

When all the points on the graph of an equation lie on one line, the equation is linear. When the graph of an equation is a curve rather than a line, the equation is nonlinear. Compare the two graphs below.

y = x

y = x²

For $y = x$, the ordered pairs of the points shown are $(-2, -2)$, $(-1, -1)$, $(0, 0)$, $(1, 1)$, and $(2, 2)$.

Because all the points lie on one line, $y = x$ is a linear equation.

The following are some examples of linear equations:

$y = 2x$, $y = -x + 1$, $y = 5$, $y = 100x + 7$, $y = \frac{1}{7}x$

For $y = x^2$, the ordered pairs of the points shown are $(-2, 4)$, $(-1, 1)$, $(0, 0)$, $(1, 1)$, and $(2, 4)$.

Because all the points do not lie on one line, $y = x^2$ is a nonlinear equation.

The following are some examples of nonlinear equations:

$y = x^3$, $y = \frac{1}{x}$, $y = 1 - x^2$, $y = x^2 + x$

You might notice something about the variables that could tell you whether the graph of an equation will be linear.

You can always graph three or more points for an equation. If the points are not on a line, the equation is not linear.

Predict whether each of the following equations is linear or nonlinear. Explain how you decided.

1. $y = -2x + 8$

2. $y = x^2 + 1$

3. $y = 2x^2 + 3$

4. $y = 5x - 2$

5. $y = x - 2$

6. $y = x - 3^2$

7. $y = \frac{x}{2}$

8. $y = \frac{2}{x}$

Graphic Organizer

Section 4A   Equations and Linear Relationships

Summary

- Relationships between two quantities can be described using words, tables of values, graphs, or equations. If you can describe a relationship by an equation, you can also describe it by a table.

- You can sometimes find an equation relating two variables by looking at a table of the variables' values.

- The solutions of a two-variable equation are ordered pairs. An ordered pair is a solution if you can make a true statement by substituting the values of x and y into the equation.

- You can find a solution of an equation by choosing a value for one variable and solving for the remaining variable.

- You can graph the points that represent the solutions of a two-variable equation. If the points lie on a line, the equation is a **linear equation.**

Review

1. Find the value of y when $x = 3$ in the equation $y = -5x$.

2. Make a table of values for the equation $y = x + 4$. Use 0, 1, 2, 3, 4, and 5 for x.

3. Find the rule that relates x and y in the table. Then find y when $x = 23$.

x	1	2	3	4	5
y	−7	−14	−21	−28	−35

4. Determine whether each ordered pair is a solution of $y = 4x - 7$.

   a. $(7, 23)$ **b.** $(5, 13)$ **c.** $(1, 2)$

5. Give two solutions for the equation $y = -3x + 15$.

6. The XYZ CD Club charges $10 per CD plus $5 for shipping. Graph the price paid. Use x for the number of CDs purchased.

Section 4B   Linear Equations and Inequalities

Summary

- The **slope** of a line tells how steep it is. It relates the vertical change (**rise**) to the horizontal change (**run**). A line that slants upward from left to right has **positive slope,** and a line that slants downward has **negative slope.** **Parallel lines** have the same slope. They do not intersect.

- The **x-intercept** of a linear equation is the x value of the point where the line crosses the x-axis, and the **y-intercept** is the y value of the point where the line crosses the y-axis.

- A **system of linear equations** is two or more linear equations considered together. A **solution** of the system is an ordered pair that is a solution of both equations.

- A **linear inequality** relates two variables using one of the signs $<$, $>$, $\leq$, or $\geq$. An ordered pair is a solution of a linear inequality if you can make a true statement by substituting the values for x and y into the inequality.

- To graph a linear inequality, first graph the **boundary line** that separates the coordinate plane into points that are solutions and points that are not. Use a dashed line for inequalities with a $<$ or $>$ sign, and a solid line for ones with a $\leq$ or $\geq$ sign. Shade the region that contains the solutions.

Review

7. On a coordinate grid, draw a line through the origin with the given slope.

   a. 1 **b.** $\dfrac{-3}{2}$

9. Graph the equation $y = \frac{3}{5}x - 3$. Find the slope, the x-intercept, and the y-intercept.

10. Solve the system of equations by graphing.

   $y = \frac{1}{3}x - 2$ $y = -x + 2$

11. ProGym charges $50 plus $15 per month. FitGym charges $10 plus $20 per month. For what number of months is the cost the same?

8. For each line, find the slope, the x-intercept, and the y-intercept.

   a. Line through A and B

   b. Line through B and C

   c. Line through C and D

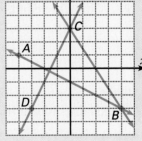

12. Graph each inequality.

   a. $y > \frac{2}{3}x - 3$ **b.** $y \leq -2x + 4$

Chapter 4 Assessment

1. Find the value of y when $x = 2$ in the equation $y = x + 7$.

2. Make a table of values for the equation $y = 3x$. Use 0, 1, 2, 3, 4, and 5 for x.

3. Find the rule that relates x and y in the table. Then find y when $x = 12$.

x	1	2	3	4	5
y	−5	−4	−3	−2	−1

4. Determine whether each ordered pair is a solution of $y = -2x + 4$.

   a. $(4, 12)$ b. $(7, -10)$ c. $(-3, 10)$

5. Give two solutions for the equation $-x + 4y = 21$.

6. Graph the equation $y = \frac{1}{3}x + 2$. Use 0, 1, 2, and 3 as x values.

7. Graph the ordered pairs in the table. Connect the points to determine if the graph is linear.

x	−4	−2	0	2	4
y	3	2	1	−1	−2

8. Rhoda has a bucket of gizmos. Each gizmo weighs 4 ounces, and the bucket (when empty) weighs 10 ounces. Graph the weight of the bucket of gizmos. Use x for the number of gizmos.

9. For each line, find the slope, the x-intercept, and the y-intercept.

   a. Line through U and V

   b. Line through W and X

   c. Line through X and Y

10. On a coordinate grid, draw a line through the origin with the given slopes.

    a. -5 b. $\frac{4}{3}$

11. Graph the equation $y = -\frac{3}{4}x - 3$. Find the slope, the x-intercept, and the y-intercept.

12. Solve the system of equations by graphing $y = 2x + 3$ and $y = -x - 3$.

13. Graph the equations $y = \frac{1}{3}x + 2$ and $x - 3y = 0$. Are these lines parallel? Explain.

14. Graph these inequalities.

    a. $y \geq x - 4$ b. $y < \frac{-2}{5}x + 1$

Performance Task

Make a table and graph of the following lines. Find the slope and y-intercept of each line. Which lines are parallel? What other observations can you make?

a. $y = x$ b. $y = x + 3$ c. $y = \frac{1}{4}x$ d. $y = \frac{1}{4}x + 3$ e. $y = \frac{-2}{3}x$ f. $y = \frac{-2}{3}x + 3$

Multiple Choice

Choose the best answer.

1. Consider the data 8, 9, 4, 7, 1, 9, 5, 6, 3, 5. Which of the following is equal to 5.5? *[Lesson 1-2]*

(A) Mean (B) Median

(C) Mode (D) Mean and median

2. Which of the following is not equal to 30? *[Lessons 2-2, 2-3, 2-4]*

(A) $41 + (-11)$ (B) $8 + 2 \times 11$

(C) $22 - (-8)$ (D) $2 + 3 \times 5$

3. A cubic foot of dry atmosphere normally contains about 0.000018 cubic feet of neon. Which of these represents 0.000018 in scientific notation? *[Lesson 2-9]*

(A) 1.8×10^{-4} (B) 0.18×10^{-4}

(C) 1.8×10^{5} (D) 1.8×10^{-5}

4. The table below is represented by which of the lettered equations? *[Lesson 4-1]*

x	0	1	2	3	4
y	0	2	4	6	8

(A) $y = x$ (B) $y = 2x$

(C) $y = x + 2$ (D) $y = x^2$

5. Which expression represents three times a number, subtracted from 12? *[Lesson 3-3]*

(A) $(12 - 3)n$ (B) $3n - 12$

(C) $12 - 3n$ (D) $n - 3 \cdot 12$

6. $x = 5$ is **not** a solution of which inequality? *[Lesson 3-7]*

(A) $6x \le 30$ (B) $4x > 20$

(C) $3x - 2 \ge 10$ (D) $2x + 3 < 15$

7. Solve $h + 17 = 32$ for h. *[Lesson 3-4]*

(A) 5 (B) 15 (C) 32 (D) 49

8. Solve $5y = 55$ for y. *[Lesson 3-5]*

(A) 1.1 (B) 5 (C) 11 (D) 275

9. Evaluate the formula $F = 1.8C + 32$ for $C = 35$. *[Lesson 3-1]*

(A) 95 (B) 97 (C) 99 (D) 102

10. Solve $3x - 6 = 21$ for x. *[Lesson 3-6]*

(A) 5 (B) 8 (C) 9 (D) 13

11. Which of the following is **not** a solution of the equation $3x + 2y = 10$? *[Lesson 4-2]*

(A) $(4, -1)$ (B) $(2, 2)$

(C) $(8, -2)$ (D) $(0, 5)$

12. Find the slope of the line through $(2, 3)$ and $(-1, 1)$. *[Lesson 4-4]*

(A) $\frac{2}{3}$ (B) $\frac{-2}{3}$ (C) $\frac{3}{2}$ (D) $\frac{-3}{2}$

13. Make a graph to determine which line is **not** parallel to the others. *[Lesson 4-5]*

(A) $y = 2x + 3$ (B) $x + 2y = 4$

(C) $y = 2x + 6$ (D) $2x - y = 4$

14. Find the solution of the system $y = 3x - 5$ and $y = -x + 7$. *[Lesson 4-6]*

(A) $(4, 3)$ (B) $(3, 5)$

(C) $(5, 10)$ (D) $(3, 4)$

15. Which inequality is graphed below? *[Lesson 4-7]*

(A) $y > x - 4$

(B) $y \le x - 4$

(C) $y < x - 4$

(D) $y \ge x - 4$

5 Ratio and Proportion

Entertainment Link
www.mathsurf.com/8/ch5/ent

Entertainment

In baseball, a player's batting average is the ratio of the number of hits to the number of official times at bat. A player's on-base average is the ratio of times on base to plate appearances. Walks and sacrifices are plate appearances but do not count as official times at bat.

Arts & Literature

Yaacov Agam's sculpture *Visual Welcome,* located next to the Tampa, Florida, Museum of Art, contains nine metal panels made from aircraft.

People of the World

An early monetary system in the Pacific Islands considered 10 coconuts to be equal in value to 1 string of white whale's teeth.

Social Studies

The dimensions of the Parthenon of ancient Greece form a golden rectangle. Rectangles with a length to width ratio of 1.618 are called golden rectangles because their shape is so pleasing to the eye.

KEY MATH IDEAS

A ratio is a comparison of two quantities.

A rate is a ratio in which quantities using different units are compared.

A unit rate is a comparison to 1 unit.

Equal ratios name the same amount.

A proportion is an equation stating that two ratios are equal.

A scale is the ratio of measurements in a drawing to measurements of an actual object.

Similar polygons have the same shape but not necessarily the same size. Their corresponding sides form proportions.

Science

Blood pressure is measured as a ratio, systolic pressure over diastolic pressure.

CHAPTER PROJECT

Problem Solving

Understand
Plan
Solve
Look Back

Design a large mural or wall painting with a positive message. You will be working on a small scale on paper or computer to design the mural. The project will culminate with the creation of the mural from the design voted the class favorite.

Problem Solving Focus

Identifying Missing Information

Evaluating information is an important problem solving skill. However, sometimes some of the necessary information is not given. It is important for you to be able to read the problem and understand if all the information needed to solve the problem is given.

For each problem, identify what additional information would be needed to solve the problem. Some of the problems are not missing information.

1 Ines buys a portable stereo on a time-payment schedule. She makes a down payment of $150 and agrees to pay $75 a month until she pays the full price. Write an equation that shows how long Ines needs to pay the full amount.

2 Ines makes a similar deal on a set of speakers. After a $75 down payment, she will pay $40 a month for 6 months. Write an equation showing how much the speakers will cost.

3 Ines likes to make tapes for her friends. A box of 3 blank cassette tapes costs $6.99 and a box of 10 costs $19.99. Write an equation to find the amount of money it will cost to buy 15 blank cassette tapes.

4 To help pay for her purchases, Ines sells her old stereo to her friend Max for $400. Max will pay part of Ines's payments on the stereo until he has paid off what he owes her. Write an equation showing the number of payments Max needs to make.

SHARING INFORMATION

Throughout time, people have learned to communicate in different ways. Drum beats, smoke signals, sign language—all of these have substituted for the spoken word.

Today, telecommunications are used. They allow people to communicate quickly and over great distances. *Tele* is Greek and means "far off; at a distance."

With the invention of the telegraph around 1837, the speed of communication was almost the speed of light (299,000 km/s, or 186,000 m/s). Alexander Graham Bell's invention of the telephone allowed the human voice, rather than Morse code, to be transmitted.

Radio, television, and the Internet resulted from the desire to make ideas and information known quickly around the world. As the new millennium begins, these telecommunications will probably be replaced by faster methods of communication.

1 Why is it important to be able to communicate quickly?

2 What forms of communication devices have you used?

3 What possible methods of communication do you see in the future?

221

Exploring and Estimating Ratios and Rates

Vocabulary

ratio

rate

unit rate

▶ **Lesson Link** In previous chapters, you learned to measure and calculate quantities. In this chapter you will learn to use math to compare quantities. ◀

Explore Comparisons

Incomparable!

Decide if each statement is very reasonable, unreasonable, or possibly reasonable. Justify your answers.

1. There are five computers per classroom.

2. There are 15 students for every 12 computers in the middle school.

3. There are twice as many fax machines in the main office as there are in the teacher's lounge.

4. The highest recorded speed for a Morse code message is 75 words per minute.

5. The cost for each minute of a cellular phone call is 28¢.

6. Make a comparison statement that you think is reasonable. Then make a comparison statement that you think is unreasonable. Explain your choices.

Learn Exploring and Estimating Ratios and Rates

In your everyday life, you are constantly comparing quantities. A **ratio** is a comparison of two quantities by division. A ratio can be written in three different ways. Because a ratio can usually be written as a fraction, it can be simplified. Suppose there are 15 computers in the math lab and 5 computers in your classroom. This can be written as follows:

$$\frac{15}{5}, \text{ or } \frac{3}{1} \qquad 3 \text{ to } 1 \qquad 3{:}1 \qquad \text{The ratio can be read as 3 to 1.}$$

89

Example 1

Write all of the ratios that can be made using the figure at the right.

1. Shaded area to total area:

 = 4:6 or 2:3

2. Total area to shaded area:

 = 6:4 or 3:2

3. Unshaded area to total area:

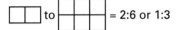 = 2:6 or 1:3

4. Total area to unshaded area:

 = 6:2 or 3:1

5. Shaded area to unshaded area:

 = 4:2 or 2:1

6. Unshaded area to shaded area:

 = 2:4 or 1:2

Example 2

The following graph shows the growth in the number of cellular phones since 1984.

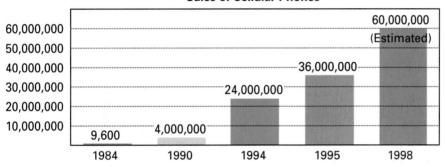

a. Estimate the ratio of the number of phones in 1990 to the number in 1994.

The number in 1990 is approximately 4 million and in 1994 is approximately 24 million. The estimated ratio is 4 to 24. Dividing, this is about 1 to 6.

b. Estimate the ratio of the number of phones in 1998 to the number in 1984.

The estimated number in 1998 is 60 million and in 1984 is about 10 thousand. The estimated ratio is $\frac{60,000,000}{10,000}$. Dividing, this is about 6000:1.

Try It

a. Write all of the ratios that can be made using this figure.

b. Estimate the ratio of the number of cellular phones in 1990 to the number in 1995.

A **rate** is a special case of a ratio in which quantities using different units are compared. Usually you will see the words *per, for,* or *each* when working with rates.

55 miles per hour   15 oranges for $2.00   28,800 bits per second

A **unit rate** is a comparison to 1 unit. For example, 55 miles per hour is a unit rate because it compares 55 miles to 1 hour.

Examples

▶ Biology Link

The germination rate is the number of seeds that develop or grow for each seed planted.

3 Of 240 seeds planted, 150 seeds germinated. What was the germination rate?

Find the unit rate by dividing.

$$\frac{150 \text{ seeds germinated}}{240 \text{ seeds planted}} = 0.625$$

The rate was 0.625 seeds germinated for each seed planted.

4 Approximately 500 billion telephone calls are made in the United States per year. Estimate the number of calls made per day.

$500 \div 365$ is about 1.5. Approximately 1.5 billion calls are made each day.

Try It

a. An airline's on-time rate is the number of on-time departures for each flight. What is the on-time rate for an airline with 872 on-time departures for 1060 flights?

b. If there are approximately 1.5 billion calls made per day in the United States, how many calls per hour are made?

M E N T A L   M A T H

You could also use compatible numbers and rounding when estimating ratios of quantities. Choose numbers that are easy to divide.

Check | Your Understanding

1. The ratio of the sizes of two groups is 7 to 2. Does this mean there are seven people in one group and 2 in the other? Is this possible?

2. Compare the terms *ratio, rate,* and *unit rate.* Explain how they differ.

3. Describe a rate that involves time and money.

4. What strategies help you estimate ratios and rates?

Practice and Apply

1. **Getting Started** Write each ratio.

    a. The number of triangles to the number of squares

    b. The number of shaded figures to the number of unshaded figures

    c. The number of polygons to the number of circles

2. Write each ratio or rate as a fraction.

    a. 45 to 1   **b.** 34:5   **c.** 70 words per min

3. Draw a picture to show each ratio.

    a. Triangles to squares 4:1   **b.** Triangles to circles 6:5

4. Write all of the ratios that can be made using each figure.

    a.   **b.**

5. A modem originally priced at $200 is on sale for $129. A faster modem priced at $350 is on sale for $249. Is the ratio of the sale price to the original price the same?

6. **Test Prep** Each of the following, except one, represents the same ratio. Which one does not belong?

    Ⓐ $\frac{1}{4}$ Ⓑ 4:1   Ⓒ 1 to 4   Ⓓ 1:4

7. **Estimation** The following display shows the relationship between the number of computers and students in 1995. Estimate each ratio.

    a. Number of students per computer in Montana to the number in Ohio

    b. Number of students per computer in Nevada to the number in Wyoming

    c. What is the largest ratio you can make from the data? The smallest?

States with Most Students per School Computer

Ohio	25.3
Rhode Island	21.6
Nevada	21.4

States with Fewest Students per School Computer

Wyoming	7.0
Alaska	7.6
Montana	7.9

8. **Chance** What is the chance of rolling a 3 if you roll one number cube?

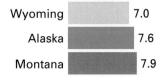

PRACTICE 5-1

Language Arts Write a ratio comparing the number of vowels to the number of consonants for each word.

9. Ratio   **10.** Rate   **11.** Percent   **12.** Compare   **13.** Fraction

14. Career In 1995, a survey asked 21.2 million American working mothers how they would spend an extra hour.

   a. Approximately _____ mothers would spend the hour with a child for every 1 who would spend it with a spouse.

   b. Approximately _____ mothers would spend the hour alone for every 1 who would spend it working.

Activity	Numbers of Working Mothers
with their child	9,680,000
alone	6,160,000
sleeping	3,300,000
with spouse	2,200,000
working	440,000

15. Computers A disk drive has 394.3 MB of memory stored and 105.7 MB of memory available. The capacity of the disk drive is the sum of the amount stored and the amount available. Estimate each ratio:

   a. Amount stored to capacity

   b. Capacity to amount available

   c. A 55 MB file is added to the amount stored. Will this affect all the ratios in Parts **a** and **b**? Explain your reasoning.

Problem Solving and Reasoning

16. Communicate When you write a ratio in fraction form, how do you decide which number to use as the denominator?

17. Journal Describe a situation that could be modeled by the ratio 5:2. Explain why this is not the same as modeling it by 2:5.

18. Critical Thinking The ratio of boys to girls in a class of 15 is 2 to 3. How many boys and girls would have to be added in order to have a class of 20 in the ratio of 1 to 1?

Mixed Review

Write each number in scientific notation. *[Lesson 2-9]*

19. 0.00694   **20.** 6 millionths   **21.** $\dfrac{1}{1,000,000,000}$

Solve each equation. *[Lesson 3-5]*

22. $4x = 32$ **23.** $\dfrac{x}{5} = 7$ **24.** $5 = \dfrac{1}{2}k$ **25.** $12 = -2x$

Proportions and Equal Ratios

▶ **Lesson Link** You have seen that ratios compare two quantities. In this lesson, you will see that a ratio can be compared with another ratio. ◀

Explore | Equal Ratios

More Stuffing, Please

Materials: Paper, Envelopes

A company wants to hire students to stuff envelopes neatly and quickly.

1. Determine your group's paper-folding rate (folding a sheet of paper into thirds so it can be stuffed into a legal-sized envelope) in sheets per minute.

2. Determine your envelope stuffing-and-closing rate (inserting a folded sheet and inserting the envelope's flap) in envelopes per minute.

3. Use your data to estimate/calculate the paper-folding and envelope-stuffing rates per hour, 4-hour shift, day, week, year, lifetime.

4. Suppose the company was very impressed with the entire class and hired everyone. How long would it take the class to fold, stuff, and insert the flap for 100,000 pieces of mail? (Could it be done in a year of math classes?)

You'll Learn ...

- to create and identify equal ratios and rates
- to express equal ratios and rates in tables
- to test for proportionality

... How It's Used

Judges often use ratios and proportions to determine degree of responsibility and to award damages.

Vocabulary

equal ratios

proportion

cross product

Learn | Proportions and Equal Ratios

Ratios that name the same amount are **equal ratios** . For example, $\frac{3}{6}$ and $\frac{2}{4}$ each represent one half. Here are two ways to find a ratio that is equal to a given ratio.

Multiply the numerator and denominator by the same nonzero number.

$$\frac{3}{1} \times \frac{6}{6} = \frac{18}{6}$$

Divide the numerator and denominator by the same nonzero number.

$$\frac{18}{6} \div \frac{6}{6} = \frac{3}{1}$$

Examples

1 Qiana paid $12 for 40 min of airtime on her monthly cellular phone bill. Complete the table to find rates equal to 12:40.

Cost ($)	3	?	12	?	48
Minutes	?	20	40	80	?

Remember

You can multiply or divide any number by 1 and not change the value of the number: $\frac{4}{4}$ is the same as 1. **[Previous course]**

Use division to find costs and number of minutes to the left of $\frac{12}{40}$ in the table.

$$\frac{12}{40} \div \frac{4}{4} = \frac{3}{10} \qquad \frac{12}{40} \div \frac{2}{2} = \frac{6}{20}$$

Use multiplication to find the values to the right of $\frac{12}{40}$ in the table.

$$\frac{12}{40} \times \frac{2}{2} = \frac{24}{80} \qquad \frac{12}{40} \times \frac{4}{4} = \frac{48}{160}$$

Cost ($)	3	6	12	24	48
Minutes	10	20	40	80	160

Each column of the table represents a rate equal to $12 for 40 min.

2 Paulo is running at a pace of 6 laps in 20 min. Estimate how long it would take him to run 20 laps.

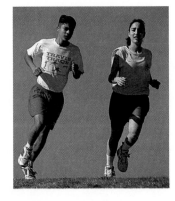

Build a table of equal rates.

Laps	6	12	18	24
Minutes	20	40	60	80

20 is between 18 and 24, but closer to 18. It will take him about 65 min to run 20 laps.

Try It

a. Donald paid $10 for 30 min of airtime on his monthly cellular phone bill. Complete the table to find rates equal to 10:30.

Cost ($)	1	?	10	?	50
Minutes	?	15	30	60	?

b. Twenty carnival tickets cost $5. Build a table of equal rates and use the table to estimate the cost of 45 tickets.

In an equal ratio table, any pairs of ratios form a **proportion**. A proportion is an equation stating that two ratios are equal. For example, $\frac{6}{20} = \frac{12}{40}$ is a proportion.

If the **cross products** of two ratios are equal, the ratios form a proportion. If the cross products are *not* equal, the ratios do *not* form a proportion, and the ratios are not equal.

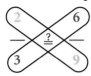

$2 \cdot 9 = 3 \cdot 6$ $18 = 18$

This is a proportion.

$2 \cdot 8 \neq 3 \cdot 4$ $16 \neq 12$

This is *not* a proportion.

Example 3

Do the ratios form a proportion?

a. $\frac{25}{120}$ and $\frac{35}{180}$

  Find the cross products.

$25 \cdot 180 \stackrel{?}{=} 120 \cdot 35$

$4500 \neq 4200$

not a proportion

b. $\frac{12}{75}$ and $\frac{8}{50}$

  Find the cross products.

$12 \cdot 50 \stackrel{?}{=} 75 \cdot 8$

$600 = 600$

a proportion

Try It

Do the ratios form a proportion?

a. $\frac{15}{35}$ and $\frac{2}{5}$ **b.** $\frac{15}{25}$ and $\frac{6}{10}$

Example 4

A 5 lb free weight costs \$2.35. A 12 lb free weight costs \$5.64. Are the prices proportional to their weights?

$\frac{2.35}{5} \stackrel{?}{=} \frac{5.64}{12}$ Write each rate.

$28.2 = 28.2$ The cross products are equal.

The prices are proportional to their weights.

HINT

Calculate one cross product, such as 2.35 ⊠ 12 = 28.2 and store the result. Calculate the other cross product and subtract your stored result. If the answer is 0, the rates are proportional.

Gabriella and Andre are looking at computer printers. The ads state that one prints 8 pages in 60 seconds, another prints 12 pages in 90 seconds. Are these rates equal?

Gabriella thinks ...

$\frac{8}{60} \stackrel{?}{=} \frac{12}{90}$.

I'll use cross products.

$8 \cdot 90 = 60 \cdot 12$.

They both equal 720. The ratios are proportional, so the rates are equal.

Andre thinks ...

$\frac{8}{60} \stackrel{?}{=} \frac{12}{90}$.

I can do this in my head.

12 is $1\frac{1}{2}$ times 8, and 90 is $1\frac{1}{2}$ times 60. The ratios are proportional, so the rates are equal.

MENTAL MATH

Usually if a problem can be done mentally, it is much quicker to do so. Always be on the lookout for numbers that are easy to compute mentally.

What do you think?

Suppose the second printer printed 16 pages in 100 seconds. How could you use Andre's method to see if the rates are equal?

Check | Your Understanding

1. How can you tell if two ratios are equal?

2. How can you create two ratios equal to a given ratio?

3. How can you use an equal ratio table if the numbers you are looking for are not in the table?

4. If two quantities always have a proportional relationship and one doubles, what happens to the other quantity? What if one is quartered?

5-2 Exercises and Applications

Practice and Apply

1. **Getting Started** Multiply or divide to find ratios equal to 4:12.

   a. $\frac{4 \times 3}{12 \times 3}$ **b.** $\frac{4 \times 6}{12 \times 6}$ **c.** $\frac{4 \div 4}{12 \div 4}$ **d.** $\frac{4 \div 2}{12 \div 2}$ **e.** $\frac{4 \times 2}{12 \times 2}$

Complete each table to create ratios equal to the given ratio.

2.

4	8	12	20	24
3				

3.

2				
11	22	33	44	55

4. **Test Prep** A ratio is equal to $\frac{4}{5}$. The denominator is 120. Which of these numbers is the numerator?

   Ⓐ 150   Ⓑ 96   Ⓒ 95   Ⓓ 6

5. **Test Prep** Which of these rates is the same as 5 oranges for $1.55?

   Ⓐ 4 oranges for $1.00   Ⓑ 3 oranges for $1.20

   Ⓒ 8 oranges for $2.48   Ⓓ 10 oranges for $15.50

Check each pair of ratios to see if a proportion is formed. Use = or ≠.

6. $\frac{2}{9} \square \frac{4}{16}$ 7. $\frac{3}{8} \square \frac{9}{24}$ 8. $\frac{5}{6} \square \frac{3}{4}$ 9. $\frac{16}{3} \square \frac{8}{2}$

10. $\frac{10}{4.5} \square \frac{20}{9}$ 11. $\frac{2.5}{10} \square \frac{7.5}{50}$ 12. $\frac{\frac{1}{2}}{8} \square \frac{1}{16}$ 13. $\frac{\frac{1}{3}}{10} \square \frac{30}{90}$

14. **Measurement** Fill in the following table of equal rates.

Ounces	32		96	128
Pounds		4	6	

15. **Estimation** The national budget average for public libraries is approximately $100 per 5 residents. A city has 240,000 residents and spends $1,000,000 on its library system. Is this figure about the same as the national average?

16. **Consumer** If phone calls are 30¢ per minute and are billed in 6 sec (0.1 min) increments, make an equal ratio table with at least six entries.

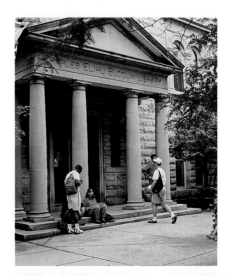

17. Industry Use cross products to test whether the data transfer times are equal for the following modems: 50 bits at 14,400 bits per second and 120 bits at 34,560 bits per second.

Problem Solving and Reasoning

18. Communication Write two ratios that are not equal. Explain why they are not equal.

19. [Journal] Describe two ways to tell whether two ratios form a proportion. Use numerical examples to illustrate.

20. Critical Thinking The following table shows operator service charges for various types of calls.

Operator Service Charges	
Customer-Dialed Calling Card Station	$2.50 per call
Operator-Dialed Station	$3.75 per call
Person To Person	$4.50 per call

a. If the charge for two calls was $7.50, what could the service have been? Why? What if there were 3 calls?

b. If the charge for one of these billing categories was $22.50, what could the service have been? Why?

21. Critical Thinking Like proportions, analogies are statements based on comparisons. An example of an analogy is: *1* is to *unicycle* as *2* is to *bicycle.* Select the word that best completes each analogy.

a. *4* is to *rectangle* as *3* is to tricycle/square/recreation/triangle.

b. *Book* is to *library* as photograph/painting/music/math is to *art museum.*

c. *Smoke* is to *fire* as steam/pollution/burn/coffee is to *boiling water.*

d. *Expression* is to *equation* as *ratio* is to graph/variable/numerator/proportion.

Mixed Review

Solve each formula for the values given. *[Lesson 3-1]*

22. $A = lw$ for $l = 17$ in. and $w = 4$ in.

23. $A = s^2$ for $s = 11$

24. $P = 2l + 2w$ for $l = 7$ and $w = 9$

25. $F = 1.8C + 32$ for $C = 14$

Solve each equation. *[Lesson 3-6]*

26. $\frac{x}{4} - 2 = 11$

27. $\frac{x}{9} + 4 = 10$

28. $11x - 2 = 97$

Relating Proportions and Graphs

▶ **Lesson Link**   You have learned that two equal ratios form a proportion. In this lesson, you will extend the idea of proportions to graphs. ◀

Explore   Proportions

Running Rectangles

Materials: Centimeter ruler, Standard paper

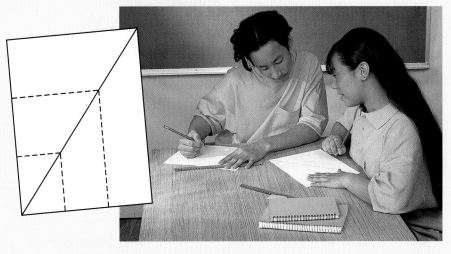

1. Take a sheet of paper measuring $8\frac{1}{2} \times 11$ inches and draw a diagonal. Randomly pick and label five points somewhere along the diagonal, being careful to spread the points out.

2. Construct the rectangles that have the selected diagonal point as the upper-right corner. Measure the length and width of each rectangle formed. Make a table of the data.

3. Make a scatterplot from the table.

4. Find the slope between several pairs of points. Describe any patterns that you find.

You'll Learn ...

■ to differentiate proportional and nonproportional relationships graphically

■ to link the constant of proportionality to slope

... How It's Used

Architects must use proportionality in designing building surfaces.

Vocabulary

constant of proportionality

Learn   Relating Proportions and Graphs

In an equal ratio table, you found that any two ratios form a proportion. Other relationships can also be discovered.

Example 1

The graph shows the time it takes to send copies through Tom's fax machine when it is set for faster draft-quality printing.

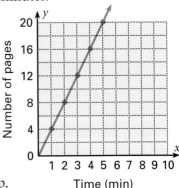

a. The rate is the number of pages divided by the number of minutes. What is the rate for each pair of numbers?

$\frac{6 \text{ pages}}{1 \text{ min}} = 6$; $\frac{12 \text{ pages}}{2 \text{ min}} = 6$. Similarly, $\frac{18}{3} = 6$; $\frac{24}{4} = 6$; and $\frac{30}{5} = 6$.

The rate is $6 \frac{\text{pages}}{\text{min}}$ for each pair.

b. Use the rate. How many pages could be sent in 8 min? In 20 min?

$6 \frac{\text{pages}}{\text{min}} \times 8 \text{ min} = 48 \text{ pages}$ $6 \frac{\text{pages}}{\text{min}} \times 20 \text{ min} = 120 \text{ pages}$

c. Write an equation describing the relationship.

$y = 6x$ describes the number of pages sent in x minutes.

Try It

The graph shows the time it takes to send copies through Tom's fax machine when it is set for best quality printing.

a. What is the rate for each pair of numbers?

b. How many pages could be sent in 10 min? In 20 min?

c. Write an equation describing the relationship.

If you look at x and y values in the graph for Example 1 you find that $\frac{y}{x}$ is the same for each pair of numbers.

$\frac{y}{x} = \frac{6}{1} = \frac{12}{2} = \cdots = 6$. Notice that $\frac{y}{x}$ or 6 is the slope of the line and that the line passes through the origin.

The value $\frac{y}{x}$ is called the **constant of proportionality** and is usually denoted by the variable k.

Example 2

The distance a car travels, y, in mi in x min is shown by the graph.

Remember

The slope of a line can be found by dividing the vertical change (rise) by the horizontal change (run). [Page 191]

a. Make a table of values for the graph. Find the value of k.

Time in Minutes (x)	60	120	180	240	300
Distance in Miles (y)	50	100	150	200	250

$k = \frac{y}{x} = \frac{5}{6}$ for each ratio.

b. Find the slope of any two points on the line. How are the slope and value of k related?

The slope is $\frac{\text{rise}}{\text{run}}$. Using $(60, 50)$ and $(180, 150)$, $\frac{\text{rise}}{\text{run}} = \frac{150 - 50}{180 - 60} = \frac{100}{120} = \frac{5}{6}$. The slope is $\frac{5}{6}$. The slope, which is the rate in mi/min $\left(\frac{5}{6}\right)$, is the same as the constant of proportionality, k.

Try It

The distance a canoe travels, y, in ft in x min is shown by the graph.

a. Make a table of values for the graph. Find the value of k.

b. Find the slope using coordinates of any two points on the line. How are the slope and value of k related?

Example 3

Graph each relationship, then connect the points with a line. Does either graph show a proportional relationship?

a.

x	2	3	4	6
y	4	6	8	12

b.

x	2	3	4	6
y	4	5	6	8

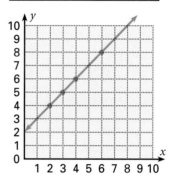

▶ **Literature Link**

There are other meanings for the word *proportion.* In Shakespeare's play *Henry IV,* the Archbishop of York describes Northumberland's power as having been "in the first proportion," meaning Northumberland had been very powerful.

In Table **a,** $k = \frac{4}{2} = \frac{6}{3} = \frac{8}{4} = \frac{12}{6} = 2$. Any two pairs of ratios form a proportion. The line connecting the points passes through the origin.

The graph shows a proportional relationship.

In Table **b,** there is no constant of proportionality, because $\frac{4}{2} \neq \frac{5}{3} \neq \frac{6}{4} \neq \frac{8}{6}$. The line connecting the points does not pass through the origin.

The graph does not show a proportional relationship.

Try It

Graph each relationship, then connect the points with a line. Does either graph show a proportional relationship?

a.

Calls (x)	0	3	6	9
Fee (y)	2	3	4	5

b.

Yards (x)	0	1	2	3
Feet (y)	0	3	6	9

Check | Your Understanding

1. How can scatterplots help you find equal ratios?

2. If two quantities are always proportional, what do you know about the slope when the quantities are graphed?

Practice and Apply

1. **Getting Started** For each equation, find one solution. Then find $\frac{y}{x}$.

   a. $y = 3x$ **b.** $y = 10x$ **c.** $y = 0.5x$

Is each table an equal ratio table? If so, find the value of k.

2.
x	2	4	6	8
y	3	5	7	9

3.
x	1	3	5	7
y	6	18	30	42

4.
x	20	30	40	50
y	2	3	4	5

5.
x	1	2	3	4
y	11	22	33	44

6. **Test Prep** If the value of k in $\frac{y}{x} = k$ is 45 and $x = 10$, what is the value of y?

   Ⓐ 4.5   Ⓑ 45   Ⓒ 450   Ⓓ 4500

7. If the value of k in $\frac{y}{x} = k$ is 50 and $y = 250$, what is the value of x?

8. **a.** Using any two points on the graph, calculate the slope of the line. (Note: This will *not* be the slope as it appears on the graph!)

   b. Make a table of values for the graph. Show that k, the ratio of each y to x, is equal to the slope.

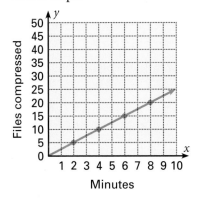

Files compressed vs. Minutes

9. This graph shows the price to item ratio of mouse pads. How many mouse pads could you buy for $7? Explain your reasoning.

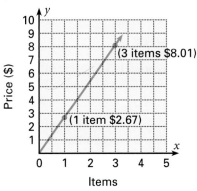

(3 items $8.01)
(1 item $2.67)
Price ($) vs. Items

10. **Measurement** Use a cm ruler to measure the width and height of each m. Graph the width on the *x*-axis and height on the *y*-axis. Are the ratios of width to height equal?

   m m m m

11. Career Tenika works part-time for a telecommunications company. Her weekly pay (p) is based on the number of hours (h) that she works. The graph shows this relationship.

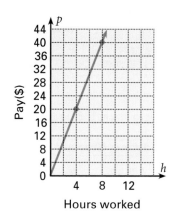

a. Calculate the slope using coordinates of any two points on the line. (Note: This will *not* be the slope as it appears on the graph.)

b. Make a table of values for the graph. Find the value of k.

c. Write a rate equation describing this relationship.

d. Use the equation to find the amount of pay Tenika would get for 17 hr of work.

Problem Solving and Reasoning

12. Communicate Does the graph show a proportional relationship? Explain.

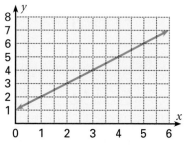

13. Critical Thinking Make a graph of downloading times to show that downloading a 900K file in 6 min is the same rate as downloading a 225K file in 1.5 min.

14. Critical Thinking This graph compares the rates of pay for two different positions at a computer company. What do the two points highlighted on the horizontal line represent? The two points highlighted on the vertical line?

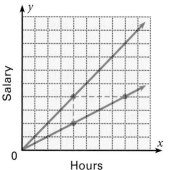

Mixed Review

Evaluate each expression. Let $p = 16$. *[Lesson 3-2]*

15. $3p + 21$ **16.** $\dfrac{p}{4} - 4$ **17.** $7(p + 9)$ **18.** $5 - 2p$

Determine whether 6 is a solution of each inequality. *[Lesson 3-7]*

19. $9x < 63$ **20.** $8x + 2 > 50$ **21.** $5x - 5 \le 25$ **22.** $4x \ge 12$

Project Progress

Work in small groups to brainstorm issues that are important in your life. On paper, create designs for a class mural that relay a positive message.

Problem Solving

Understand
Plan
Solve
Look Back

In this Connect you will use your knowledge of ratios, rates, and proportions to determine communication costs.

Sharing Information

Even with all the high technology forms of communication these days, people still find creative ways to communicate to people they care about. For instance, you may write notes to your friends and fold the notes in a unique way. Besides calling or writing, some creative ways to communicate are sending balloons, sending a telegram, or even sending a surprise fax.

Choose a few friends you would like to creatively say "hello" to. Choose a method to do this using the charts below. Calculate the cost for sending each "hello." You have $30 to spend and you must spend as much of it as you can.

1. Are the telegram rates proportional?

2. How much do you think a 75-word telegram would cost?

3. If the cost of 1 balloon goes up to $3.00, how much will 10 balloons cost? Why?

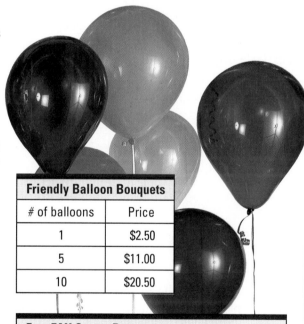

Friendly Balloon Bouquets

# of balloons	Price
1	$2.50
5	$11.00
10	$20.50

National Telegram Rates

# of Words	Price
1–15	$15.95
16–25	$22.95
26–35	$31.95
36–50	$41.95

Fast FAX Center Rates

	Send Price	Receive Price
First Page	$1.95	$2.35
Additional Pages	$0.65	$0.75

Write a ratio comparing the number of vowels to the number of consonants for each word.

1. Constant   **2.** Proportional   **3.** Rhythm   **4.** Queuing

Check each pair of ratios to see if a proportion is formed. Use = or ≠.

5. $\frac{2}{4} \square \frac{3}{8}$ **6.** $\frac{5}{6} \square \frac{2.5}{3}$ **7.** $\frac{12}{3} \square \frac{36}{6}$ **8.** $\frac{1.6}{8} \square \frac{8}{4}$

Complete each table to create ratios equal to the given ratio.

9.

4	8	12	20	24
9				

10.

			24	
12	24	36	48	54

11. Computers The bar graph shows the ways students at Hart Middle School use their computers at home.

a. What is the ratio of use for word processing to budgets?

b. Which two uses could be described by a ratio of 3 to 5?

c. Which two uses could be described by a ratio of 3.5 to 4.5?

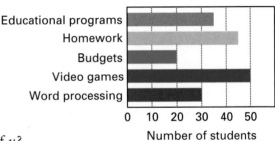

Use of Home Computers

12. If the value of k is 87 and $x = 10$, what is the value of y?

Test Prep

When comparing ratios, first write each ratio as a fraction, then use cross products to see if the ratios form a proportion.

13. Ms. Lehr's class found that the ratio of hours spent doing homework with a computer to the hours spent doing it without a computer was 2:5. Which of the following represents the actual number of hours?

Ⓐ 12 hours with a computer to 35 hours without

Ⓑ 10 hours with a computer to 20 hours without

Ⓒ 14 hours with a computer to 35 hours without

Ⓓ 20 hours with a computer to 70 hours without

REVIEW 5A

Problem Solving Using Proportions

The next time you sit in a movie theater enjoying movies like *Star Wars, Jaws,* and *Independence Day,* think about how these films are made. Huge space ships fly around, a massive shark eats people and ships, and the White House is blown to smithereens. How is it all done? Special effects.

Special effects may be visual or physical. Visual effects artists manipulate what you see with the aid of optical systems found in cameras and projectors. These artists also build models for miniature photography, a key aspect of visual effects; they skillfully photograph the models when it is not possible or practical to use the real thing.

Physical effects artists create the special effects used on the set or on location. They may build special mechanical devices to represent animals, as in *Free Willy.* They also plan and supervise the use of pyrotechnics, the controlled use of fires and explosions.

1 Name a few of your favorite special effects scenes. Do you think miniatures were built, special camera techniques were used, or the scenes were created by computer?

2 To build miniatures, special effects artists keep the dimensions in proportion to the actual object. What do you think this means?

how did they do that?

Solving Proportions

You'll Learn …

■ to use mental math and cross multiplication to solve proportions

… How It's Used

Technicians need to adjust the rates at which copiers operate.

▶ **Lesson Link** You have learned to determine if two ratios form a proportion. In this lesson, you will learn to find the values of any missing numbers in a proportion. ◀

Explore | Solving Proportions

Can You Squeeze Them In?

1. Estimate how many people could squeeze, standing, into a 32 ft² area (8 ft by 4 ft). How did you determine your estimate?

2. Use the above data to estimate the answers to the following questions.

   a. Can the entire school fit into this room?

   b. How many people could be squeezed into your school gym?

   c. Can the entire community/town/city fit into your school gym?

   d. How large an area would you need to fit everyone in your city or town?

   e. Could the entire U.S. population fit within your town?

3. Are there other considerations about the number of people that could fit in a given space?

Learn | Solving Proportions

In Lesson 5-2, you learned to determine if two ratios form a proportion by using equal ratios, mental math, and cross products. Sometimes you do not know all of the numbers in a proportion. You can use any of these methods to find the missing number. This is called *solving the proportion.*

Example 1

Leigh's copy machine can make 5 copies of the script in 2 min. She has 20 min to copy a revised script with changes for the cast. How many copies can she make in 20 min?

Define a variable: Let x = number of copies

Set up a proportion: $\dfrac{5 \text{ copies}}{2 \text{ min}} = \dfrac{x \text{ copies}}{20 \text{ min}}$

Use number sense to find x. Think: 2 min × 10 = 20 min, so 5 copies × 10 = 50 copies.

She can make 50 copies of the script.

You know that *if* the cross products of two ratios are equal, *then* the ratios form a proportion. The *converse* of this statement is also true:

If two ratios form a proportion, *then* their cross products are equal.

If $\dfrac{a}{b} = \dfrac{c}{d}$, then $ad = bc$.

The property above can help us find missing numbers in a proportion.

Example 2

India produces more feature-length films than any other country, an average of 1800 every two years. If it maintains this rate, how many films could it produce in 25 yr?

Let x = number of films   Define a variable.

$\dfrac{1800 \text{ films}}{2 \text{ yr}} = \dfrac{x \text{ films}}{25 \text{ yr}}$ Set up a proportion.

$1800 \cdot 25 = 2 \cdot x$ Write cross products.

$45{,}000 = 2x$ Multiply.

$\dfrac{45{,}000}{2} = \dfrac{2x}{2}$ Divide both sides by 2.

$22{,}500 = x$ Solve for x.

India would produce 22,500 films in 25 yr.

Try It

For 2 yr, the United States produced approximately 400 films. If it maintains this rate, how many films could be produced in 25 yr?

Solve the proportion $\frac{5}{6} = \frac{20}{x}$.

Mary thinks ...

I can see that 20 is just 5 multiplied by 4.

$$\frac{5}{6} \times \frac{4}{4} \rightarrow \frac{20}{x}$$

To find the value of x, I just need to multiply 6 by 4.

$$\frac{5}{6} \times \frac{4}{4} \rightarrow \frac{20}{24}$$

x is 24.

This means $\frac{5}{6} = \frac{20}{24}$. Because these are equal ratios, my answer checks.

Kele thinks ...

I can use cross products to solve the proportion.

$$\frac{5}{6} = \frac{20}{x}$$

$5 \cdot x = 6 \cdot 20$ These are the cross products.

$5x = 120$ Multiply.

$\frac{5x}{5} = \frac{120}{5}$ Divide both sides by 5.

$x = 24$

My answer is 24.

What do you think?

Which method would you have used? Would you use the same method to solve $\frac{5}{6} = \frac{21.5}{x}$?

Check | Your Understanding

1. Why does cross multiplication work for solving proportions?

2. Show why you might not need to use cross products to solve a proportion.

3. What strategies can you use to estimate proportional quantities?

5-4 Exercises and Applications

Practice and Apply

1. **Getting Started** Follow the steps to solve the proportion $\frac{x}{3} = \frac{7}{4}$.

   a. Write the cross products: $4 \cdot x = ?$ **b.** Multiply: $4x = ?$

   c. Divide both sides by 4: $\frac{4x}{4} = \frac{?}{4}$ **d.** Write your solution: $x = ?$

Write a proportion for each situation. Do not solve.

2. A camera filming a scene in miniature moves 2 ft in 0.5 sec. How far does the camera move in 3.5 sec?

3. How much should 12 cans of juice cost if 8 cans cost $2.50?

4. Kevin read 200 pages of a script in 6 hr. How long would it take him to read 500 pages?

Solve each proportion. Which method did you use? Why?

5. $\frac{3}{4} = \frac{x}{100}$ 6. $\frac{1.5}{6} = \frac{8}{x}$ 7. $\frac{1.5}{6} = \frac{3}{x}$ 8. $\frac{7}{8} = \frac{21}{x}$

Estimation Which is the best estimate for *x* in each proportion? Explain your choice.

9. $\frac{1.5}{67} = \frac{x}{185}$

   Ⓐ 3   Ⓑ 4   Ⓒ 7   Ⓓ 45

10. $\frac{6,756}{89} = \frac{42,000}{x}$

    Ⓐ 13   Ⓑ 130   Ⓒ 400   Ⓓ 540

11. $\frac{34.7}{x} = \frac{12.2}{14.1}$

    Ⓐ 5   Ⓑ 6   Ⓒ 30   Ⓓ 40

12. $\frac{4.8}{59} = \frac{x}{240}$

    Ⓐ 20   Ⓑ 2   Ⓒ 300   Ⓓ 30

Solve each proportion.

13. $\frac{2}{4} = \frac{k}{16}$ 14. $\frac{y}{4} = \frac{9}{10}$ 15. $\frac{17}{s} = \frac{102}{186}$ 16. $\frac{2}{7} = \frac{35}{h}$

17. $\frac{18}{8} = \frac{45}{w}$ 18. $\frac{9}{10} = \frac{d}{16}$ 19. $\frac{9}{p} = \frac{1.8}{1.6}$ 20. $\frac{a}{\frac{1}{2}} = \frac{16}{8}$

21. **Test Prep** Kareem's auto insurance costs $59.63 per month. What would be a good estimate for his yearly insurance cost?

    Ⓐ Less than $650   Ⓑ Between $650 and $700

    Ⓒ Between $700 and $750   Ⓓ Between $750 and $800

22. Science About 20 parts in 100 of the Dead Sea is salt. How much salt would be contained in 1 qt (32 oz) of Dead Sea water?

23. Chemistry Two samples containing only carbon and hydrogen are analyzed. If they have the same proportion of carbon and hydrogen, then they are probably the same substance. Do you think they are the same substance? Why?

Problem Solving TIP

It does not matter whether you compare carbon with hydrogen or each one with the total.

Sample Analysis

- Mass of hydrogen
- Mass of carbon

24. Gwilym Hughes of Wales has seen 22,188 films in his lifetime. If he has been watching films for 43 yr, estimate the number of films he could see in 80 yr.

Problem Solving and Reasoning

25. Critical Thinking This famous sculpture by Pablo Picasso is located in the city center plaza in Chicago. Before it was constructed in 1966, a maquette, or small model, was first created. The model's height is $41\frac{1}{4}$ in. and its width is 19 in. If the actual sculpture is 50 ft tall, how wide is it?

Algebra Solve each proportion.

26. $\dfrac{5}{x+1} = \dfrac{1}{3}$ **27.** $\dfrac{3}{2x} = \dfrac{1}{2}$ **28.** $\dfrac{x-1}{4} = \dfrac{7}{1}$ **29.** $\dfrac{3x}{4} = \dfrac{5}{2}$

30. Communicate If you know two of the four numbers in a proportion, can you find the other two? Why or why not?

31. Critical Thinking The lengths of the sides of a triangle are in a ratio of 6:5:3. The triangle's perimeter is 56 cm. What is the length of each side?

Mixed Review

Write each distance in scientific notation. *[Lesson 2-8]*

32. Sun to Mercury: 36,000,000 mi   **33.** Earth to the Moon: 238,840 mi

Find the value of y if x = 7. *[Lesson 4-1]*

34. $y = 4x$ **35.** $y = -6x$ **36.** $y = x + 5$ **37.** $y = x - 2$

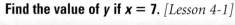

Using Unit Rates

▶ **Lesson Link** You know that rates are ratios that compare quantities that have different units and that unit rates compare to 1. Unit rates are especially useful in solving proportions. ◀

Explore   Unit Rates

What Is It for 1?

Materials: Calculator

A movie projector shows 192 frames of an old silent film in 12 seconds.

1. Complete the table.

Frames	16	32	64	144	192
Seconds					12

2. Write and solve a proportion to find how many frames can be shown in 1 second.

3. What does the reciprocal of your answer to **2** represent?

4. How can you use your answer to **2** to find how long it takes to show 48 frames? 80 frames? Any number of frames?

You'll Learn ...

■ to find unit rates and use rate formulas to solve proportion problems

... How It's Used

Camera operators must be able to use rate formulas to determine the speed of the film they need.

Learn   Using Unit Rates

Rates are ratios that compare quantities that have different units. Recall that a unit rate compares a quantity to 1 unit. Some examples of units rates are 55 miles per hour, 24 shots per roll of film, and $16.95 for each video.

Unit rates can be used to solve proportions and create rate formulas.

Example 1

A movie company has decided to shoot a film in Texarkana, Texas. Sandra is hired as a camera assistant for 12 weeks of filming. For the first 5 weeks she earns $620. At this rate, how much will she make for 12 weeks?

$$\frac{620}{5} = 124$$ Find the unit rate for 1 week. She makes $124 per week.

$$124 \times 12 = 1488$$ Multiply the unit rate by the number of weeks.

Sandra will earn $1488.

Try It

Matt is hired by the same company as a runner for the director. He makes $570 for the first 5 weeks. How much will he earn at the end of 12 weeks?

Example 2

A 16 oz jar of peanut butter costs $2.50. A 12 oz jar is on sale for $1.99. Which is the better buy?

Write the rate for the 16 oz jar as a unit rate per oz.

$$\frac{2.50}{16} = 0.15625$$ The unit rate is slightly less than $0.16 per oz.

Use the unit rate to find a rate formula. Let C = the cost of peanut butter and z = number of oz.

$C = 0.15625z$

Substitute 12 for z to see how much 12 oz would cost at this rate.

$0.15625 \boxed{\times} 12 \boxed{=}$ *1.875*

$C = 1.875$

12 oz would cost about $1.88. This is less than $1.99, so the 16 oz jar is a better buy.

Try It

Morph detergent costs $5.98 for 46 oz; A 75 oz box costs $8.99. Which is the better buy?

Example 3

The rate a movie camera runs is measured in frames per second (fps). The standard projection rate is 24 fps. Use the formula $F = 24s$.

a. How many frames can be filmed in 20 sec?

$F = 24s$ Write the rate equation.

$F = 24(20)$ Substitute 20 for s.

$F = 480$ Multiply.

480 frames could be shot in 20 sec.

b. How long would it take to film 1000 frames?

$F = 24s$

$1000 = 24s$ Substitute 1000 for F.

$41.67 = s$ Divide each side by 24 to solve for F.

It would take approximately 42 sec to film 1000 frames.

Try It

a. To produce slow motion, the camera rate must be higher than the projection rate. Suppose the camera rate is 48 fps.

Use the formula $F = 48s$. How many frames can be filmed in 60 sec? How long would it take to film 1200 frames?

b. A video camera records at 30 fps. This rate is used when editing video.

What formula would be used to determine the time it takes to record 9000 frames? How long would it take?

A camera rate higher than the projection rate creates slow motion; one lower than the projection rate creates fast motion.

Check Your Understanding

1. How can rates be converted to unit rates?

2. What proportion is equivalent to the rate formula $M = 15T$?

3. What operations help you solve rate formulas?

Practice and Apply

1. **Getting Started** If Lorene drove 45 mi in 1.5 hr, how far could she drive in 7 hr?

   a. Find the unit rate by dividing 45 by 1.5.

   b. Use the unit rate and $d = rt$ to find a rate formula where d = distance and t = time.

   c. Substitute 7 for t in the rate formula and solve for d.

Find the unit rate and create a rate formula.

2. $60 for 15 hr   3. 400 words in 10 min   4. 30 students for 3 computers

5. 330 mi in 6 hr   6. 800 m in 25 sec   7. $3 million for 75 days of filming

8. **Estimation** Fifty-nine F-117 jets cost 6 billion dollars to produce. Estimate the cost of one F-117.

9. **Consumer** A 7 lb whole boneless pork roast is advertised for $20.16.

   a. How much does the roast cost per pound?

   b. The ad reads, "You save 71¢ per pound." What was the original price per pound?

10. **Test Prep** Which of the following is a unit rate?

    Ⓐ 1 pizza for 3 students   Ⓑ 25 students in a classroom

    Ⓒ 200 mi in 5 hr   Ⓓ 27 wins out of 27 games

11. **Industry** The 365 special-effects scenes in *Star Wars* required 3838 separate components. What was the approximate average number of components per special-effects scene?

Consumer Which is the better buy?

12. A 2 lb box of pistachio nuts for $10.99 or a 5 lb box for $30.00

13. A 16 oz box of cereal for $3.49 or a 6 oz box of cereal for $1.25

Special effects scene from *Honey, I Shrunk the Kids.*

14. 15 collector cards for $2.75 or 80 for $13.00

15. $\frac{1}{4}$ lb of coffee for $2.00 or 1 lb for $8.50

16. 20 computer disks for $14.49 or 12 for $9.50

Problem Solving and Reasoning

17. **Communicate** The 102nd-floor observatory of the Empire State Building is at a height of 1250 ft. The 86th-floor observatory is at a height of 1050 ft. Are the floor heights roughly proportional? Explain.

18. **Critical Thinking** A loaf of bread costs $1.29 for 20 slices, a 40 oz jar of peanut butter costs $4.59, and a 22 oz jar of grape jelly costs $1.89. A sandwich uses two slices of bread, about 1.5 oz of peanut butter, and $\frac{3}{4}$ oz of jelly. Determine a reasonable estimate for the cost of a single peanut butter and jelly sandwich.

19. Give two examples of real-life situations that involve finding unit rates.

20. **Critical Thinking** For the movie *The Empire Strikes Back,* a camera that could film up to 96 fps was used to film special effects. How many more frames could this camera film in 20 sec than one at the standard rate of 24 fps?

21. **Critical Thinking** Jefferson County School District has approximately 10,000 students and a student-teacher ratio of 25:1.

   a. How many teachers are there?

   b. The school is required to lower the student-teacher ratio to 23:1. Explain how it might do this.

Mixed Review

Write in standard notation. *[Lesson 2-9]*

22. 1.0×10^{-6} **23.** 8.4×10^{-3} **24.** 21 hundred-millionths

Give two solution pairs for each equation. *[Lesson 4-2]*

25. $y = x + 5$ **26.** $2x + 7 = y$ **27.** $x - 6 = y$ **28.** $y = 3x - 1$

Project Progress

Examine the designs for the class mural and vote for your favorite design. Choose a scale to reproduce the design for the wall and plan the completion of the mural.

Problem Solving

Understand
Plan
Solve
Look Back

Problem Solving Using Rates and Proportions

You'll Learn ...

■ to solve problems with rates and proportions

... How It's Used

Nurses often have to use proportions when preparing intravenous solutions.

▶ **Lesson Link**   You have learned about unit rates and proportions. In this lesson, you will use these concepts to solve problems. ◀

Explore   Rates and Proportions

You Win!

Radio station YDLR, 98.3 FM, is having a giveaway. They will call a listener and say, "You are the YDLR winner! You have your choice: 98.3 pounds of pennies, nickels, dimes, quarters, or half-dollars."

You think you have a chance of being called. You want to get the most money you can, so you search the Internet and find the following information:

Coin	Penny	Nickel	Dime	Quarter	Half-dollar
Number in a pound	146	91	200	80	40

1. Are there one or more coin denominations you would rule out immediately? Why?

2. How much does each type of coin weigh? How did you decide?

3. What is the monetary value of a pound of each type of coin? Which coin denomination gives you the most money? How much is it?

4. Why is there more than one coin denomination in **3**?

5. Write a proportion relating weight and value.

DID YOU KNOW?

Pennies dated before 1981 weigh more than recently minted pennies.

Learn   Problem Solving Using Rates and Proportions

Problem solving skills are important in solving problems relating to rates and proportions. Often, it is best to break down a problem into several steps.

Example

► **Science Link**

When an explosion is filmed in close-up to make it look larger, the burst happens too quickly for it to appear believable when filmed at normal speed.

A small special-effects explosion that lasts only $\frac{1}{12}$ sec is filmed with a high-speed camera at a rate of 960 frames per second. When it is shown in the actual film, the scene must last for 5 sec so it appears to be much larger. How many frames are filmed? How many frames per second must be shown?

We have the length of the explosion and the speed at which it is filmed. We want to find the speed at which it must be shown to last 5 sec.

First find out how many frames are filmed. Then use the answer to find the projection rate.

$\frac{1}{12}$ sec • 960 fps = 80 frames filmed.

80 frames must be shown in 5 sec.

$\frac{80}{5} = 16$ Divide.

The rate of projection must be 16 fps.

Try It

A small special-effects bridge collapse that lasts only $\frac{1}{2}$ sec is filmed with a high-speed camera at a rate of 240 fps. When it is shown in the actual film, the scene must last for 4 sec. How many frames are filmed? How many fps must be shown?

Check | Your Understanding

1. Can you make a proportion from the Example?

2. Why would it make sense to break a problem into smaller steps?

Practice and Apply

1. **Getting Started** Shooting 15 sec at 24 fps is:

   a. _____ frames altogether;

   b. The same number of frames as _____ sec at 72 fps; and

   c. The same number of frames as 30 sec at _____ fps.

2. An animator makes 80 storyboards, or sketches, for a scene lasting $2\frac{1}{2}$ min. How many storyboards must be made for a 90 min, full-length animated film?

Problem Solving TIP

If you double both the minutes and the number of storyboards, you will have an equal ratio with whole numbers.

3. **Test Prep** Which circles have the same proportion shaded? (Choose all that apply.)

   Ⓐ   Ⓑ   Ⓒ 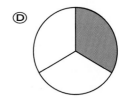   Ⓓ

4. In a movie, large sets are often created so that people appear to be smaller. If a 60 in. tall person appears next to a 96 in. high trash can, but the trash can appears to be 18 in. high in the film, how tall would the person appear to be?

5. **Industry** A television rating of 30 represents about 28.6 million homes. A television rating of 100 represents the total number of households with televisions.

   a. What is the total number of households with televisions?

   b. What does a rating of 1 represent?

6. **History** The Wheel of Life was patented by William Lincoln in 1867. A $2\frac{1}{2}$ ft long strip with 14 still photographs was placed inside the wheel and spun to create movement. How many photographs of this size would a 10 ft long strip have had?

7. **Patterns** Use the numbers 2, 4, 8, 16, 32. Write as many true proportions as you can that use these numbers (only use a number once in each proportion).

Problem Solving and Reasoning

8. **Communicate** *Proportional representation* gives political parties legislative representation in proportion to the ratio of their popular vote to the total number of votes. The parties in one small country received the following votes. There will be 100 legislators selected. How many Republicrat representatives should be selected? How did you decide?

Party	Votes
Republicrat	17,934
Demican	11,236
Preformed	9,120
Justiced	4,899
Total	43,189

9. **Math Reasoning** When you pedal a bicycle that has gears as shown, turning the pedal around once turns the rear wheel $\frac{52}{18}$ times. How far will the tire roll (turn) when you turn the pedal around once?

10. A worker honey bee collects enough nectar in its lifetime (about 2 months) to make $\frac{1}{10}$ pound of honey.

    a. How much would a colony of 20,000 worker bees collect in this time?

    b. How many 8-ounce ($\frac{1}{2}$ pound) jars of honey are produced?

81.7 in.

Chain wheel

Tire

Gear sprocket

18 teeth

52 teeth

Mixed Review

11. A cheetah can run 105 ft per sec. Use $d = rt$ to find how far it could run in 8 sec as it chases a wildebeest. *[Lesson 3-1]*

Graph each equation. Use 0, 1, 2, and 3 as *x* values. *[Lesson 4-3]*

12. $y = x + 2$ 13. $y = 4x$ 14. $y = 2x - 1$ 15. $y = -2x$

5-7 Scale, Scale Drawings, and Models

You'll Learn ...

■ to use scales and create scale drawings

... How It's Used

Special-effects artists often have to create scale models of buildings, people, and animals for their films.

Vocabulary

scale drawing

scale

similar polygons

▶ **Lesson Link** You have learned how to work with ratios and proportions. Now you will use these concepts to understand scale models and to make scale drawings. ◀

Explore | Scale

A Tangle of Rectangles

Materials: Graph paper or geoboard

1. Make a rectangle on your geoboard or graph paper. Measure the length and width.

2. Make a second larger rectangle that is the same shape but not the same size. Measure the length and width. Find the ratio of the lengths and the ratio of the widths of the two rectangles. What do you notice?

3. Make as many rectangles as you can that are the same shape but not the same size. Measure their lengths and widths. Find the ratios of the lengths and ratios of the widths of any two rectangles. What do you notice?

Learn | Scale, Scale Drawings, and Models

A **scale drawing** shows the shape of an object but not the actual size. A **scale** gives the ratio of the measurements in the drawing to the measurements of the actual object. The drawing length always comes first in the ratio.

The dimensions in the drawing are reduced or enlarged by the same ratio or scale. If the first value of the ratio is smaller, the scale drawing is a reduction; if it is larger, the scale drawing is an enlargement.

Scale is often used when looking at microscopic organisms.

Example 1

The largest bacteria that have been found by microbiologists are called *Epulopiscium* and are about 0.5 mm in length. A scale drawing will be made with a scale of 100 mm:1 mm. What should the length of the bacteria be in the drawing?

$$\frac{\text{scale}}{\text{actual}} \begin{array}{c} \rightarrow \\ \rightarrow \end{array} \frac{100 \text{ mm}}{1 \text{ mm}} = \frac{x \text{ mm}}{0.5 \text{ mm}} \begin{array}{c} \leftarrow \text{ scale} \\ \leftarrow \text{ actual} \end{array}$$

$100 \cdot 0.5 = 1 \cdot x$ Use cross products.

$\quad\quad 50 = x$ Multiply.

The length of the bacteria in the drawing is 50 mm.

A map is an example of a scale drawing.

Example 2

In the film *Independence Day,* the director chose the Bonneville Salt Flats of Utah to film many of the special effect scenes. The map is drawn to a scale of 1 in. = 40 mi.

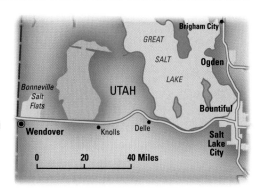

a. Approximately how far is it from the Salt Flats to Salt Lake City?

Measure the map length from the Salt Flats to Salt Lake City. It is about $2\frac{1}{4}$ in. Make a proportion of map lengths to actual lengths.

$$\frac{\text{map distance}}{\text{actual distance}} \begin{array}{c} \rightarrow \\ \rightarrow \end{array} \frac{1 \text{ in.}}{40 \text{ mi}} = \frac{2\frac{1}{4} \text{ in.}}{d \text{ mi}} \begin{array}{c} \leftarrow \text{ map distance} \\ \leftarrow \text{ actual distance} \end{array}$$

$1 \cdot d = 40 \cdot 2\frac{1}{4}$ Use cross products.

$\quad d = 90$ Multiply.

Salt Lake City is approximately 90 mi from the Salt Flats.

b. Which city is approximately 15 mi from the Salt Flats?

Wendover is close to the Salt Flats. It is approximately $\frac{3}{8}$ in. away. If 1 in. = 40 mi, then $\frac{3}{8}$ in. is $\frac{3}{8}(40) = 15$ mi. Wendover is approximately 15 mi away.

Scale drawings are often used in blueprints of buildings and models. When making a scale drawing, it is important to choose an appropriate scale.

Example 3

Suppose you want to construct a scale drawing of a model city that will measure 24 ft by 36 ft. Choose a scale that would allow you to draw it on a 12 in. by 16 in. sheet of paper.

If we use 1 in. = 2 ft, the scale drawing would be 12 in. by 18 in. and would not fit.

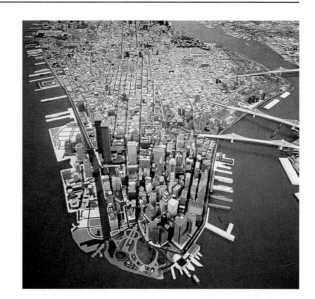

Try 1 in. = 3 ft.

$$\frac{\text{scale} \rightarrow}{\text{actual} \rightarrow}\frac{1 \text{ in.}}{3 \text{ ft}} = \frac{x \text{ in.}}{24 \text{ ft}}\frac{\leftarrow \text{ scale}}{\leftarrow \text{ actual}} \qquad 24 = 3x, \text{ so } 8 = x.$$

The width would be 8 in.

$$\frac{\text{scale} \rightarrow}{\text{actual} \rightarrow}\frac{1 \text{ in.}}{3 \text{ ft}} = \frac{x \text{ in.}}{36 \text{ ft}}\frac{\leftarrow \text{ scale}}{\leftarrow \text{ actual}} \qquad 36 = 3x, \text{ so } 12 = x.$$

The length would be 12 in.

For a scale of 1 in. = 3 ft, the dimensions would be 8 in. by 12 in. It would fit.

Try It

Suppose you want to construct a scale drawing of a house. The house measures 40 ft by 50 ft. Choose a scale that would allow you to draw it on a 6 in. by 9 in. sheet of paper.

Similar polygons have the same shape but may not have the same size. Their side lengths form proportions. These proportions can help you find a missing length in a pair of similar polygons.

$$\frac{3}{6} = \frac{4}{8} \qquad \frac{3}{6} = \frac{3.5}{7} \qquad \frac{3.5}{7} = \frac{4}{8}$$

Examples

4 Find the missing value in the pair of similar triangles.

Set up a proportion. $\frac{25}{30} = \frac{45}{n}$

Cross multiply. $25n = 1350$

Solve for n. $n = 54$

5 Leticia has an 8 in. by 10 in. photo that she will be reducing to fit into a small frame. The width of the reduced photo is $3\frac{1}{2}$ in. What is the height?

$$\frac{10 \text{ in.}}{x} = \frac{8 \text{ in.}}{3\frac{1}{2} \text{ in.}}$$

$10 \cdot 3\frac{1}{2} = 8x$ Cross multiply.

$35 = 8x$

$4\frac{3}{8} = x$ Divide.

The height of the reduced photo is $4\frac{3}{8}$ in.

10 in.

8 in.

x in.

$3\frac{1}{2}$ in.

Try It

Find the missing value in the pair of similar trapezoids.

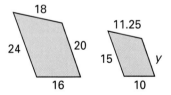

Check   Your Understanding

1. What is the advantage of using a scale drawing?

2. What happens to a scale drawing when the scale of 1 in. = 10 ft is changed to 1 in. = 40 ft? When it is changed to 1 in. = 2 ft?

3. How can the scale of a scale drawing or a map be used to help you find the actual size or distance?

4. How could you find the scale on a map that did not have a scale printed on it?

MENTAL MATH

Sometimes you can use mental math to multiply the scale by the approximate distance on the map.

Practice and Apply

1. **Getting Started** Fill in the blanks.

   a. A scale drawing has the same _____ but not necessarily the same _____ of the actual object.

   b. Similar polygons may be different in _____, but have the same _____.

Geography Use the map and a ruler. What is the approximate distance from

2. Seattle to New Orleans?

3. Miami to New York?

4. Which city is approximately 1200 mi from New Orleans?

5. If two cities are approximately $3\frac{1}{2}$ in. apart on the map, what is the actual distance between the two cities?

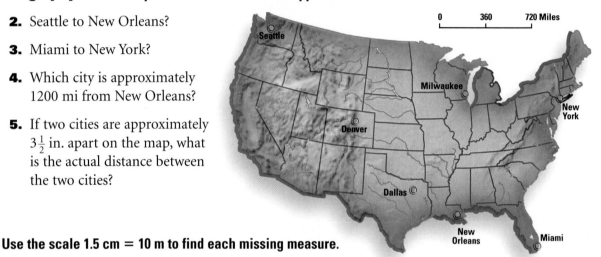

Use the scale 1.5 cm = 10 m to find each missing measure.

	Scale dimension	Actual dimension
6.	0.3 cm	?
7.	?	200 m
8.	4.5 cm	?
9.	?	89.5 m

10. Suppose you need to make a scale drawing of a 14 ft by 18 ft room on a 5 in. by 7 in. index card. What scale would you use?

11. **Science** An insect in a picture is $\frac{1}{4}$ in. long and is labeled "enlarged 8 times." What is the insect's actual length?

12. **Optics** On a pair of binoculars, 7 × 35 means an object appears to be enlarged 7 times, or an object 700 m away appears to be 100 m away (35 means only that the lens has a 35 mm diameter). If an object appears to be 75 m away, how far away is it actually?

13. In the movie *King Kong*, the scale $\frac{3}{4}$ in. = 1 ft was used. If the model was 18 in. tall, how tall was the "actual" Kong?

14. **Test Prep** Miles wants to make a scale drawing of the dinosaur *Brachiosaurus brancai*, which was 46 ft tall and approximately 73 ft long, on a sheet of paper that is $8\frac{1}{2}$ in. by 11 in. Which of the following scales could he use?

Ⓐ 1 in. = 8 ft   Ⓑ 1 in. = 5 ft

Ⓒ 1 in. = 3 ft   Ⓓ 1 in. = 2 ft

Geometry Find the missing measures in each pair of similar figures.

15.

16.

17.

18.

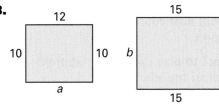

Problem Solving and Reasoning

19. **Journal** Why is it important that a road map be drawn to scale?

20. **Communicate** Explain how scale drawings and similar figures are alike.

21. **Critical Thinking** The average NBA player is approximately 6 ft 9 in. tall and the basket is 10 ft high. The average eighth grader is 5 ft 5 in. tall. How much should the basket be lowered for the eighth graders to make the ratio of player height to basket height the same?

22. **Critical Thinking** Two models of the same ship are constructed. One has a scale of 1:2400 and the other a scale of 1:3000. Which scale model is larger? Explain.

Mixed Review

Solve each equation. *[Lesson 3-2]*

23. $x + 7 = -9$ **24.** $2p = 88$ **25.** $5 = \frac{r}{9}$ **26.** $1 = h - 10$

Draw a line through the origin with each of the given slopes. *[Lesson 4-4]*

27. $\frac{2}{3}$ **28.** 3   **29.** $\frac{-1}{2}$ **30.** -2 **31.** 0

TECHNOLOGY

Using the Cabri Geometry Program • Scale Drawings

Problem: How does scaling a triangle using a scale factor of 2 affect the perimeter of the triangle?

① Use the **Triangle** tool to draw a triangle on the screen.

② Use the **Distance & Length** measurement tool. Click on a side of the triangle (not on a vertex) to find its perimeter.

③ Use the **Numerical Edit** tool to place the number 2 on the screen.

④ Use the **Point** tool to place a point in approximately the center of the triangle.

⑤ Now you are ready to scale the triangle. Use the **Dilation** tool. Click on the side of a triangle, on the point in the center, and then on the number 2. You will get a second triangle similar to the one shown.

⑥ Use the **Distance & Length** tool again to find the perimeter of the new triangle.

Solution: The perimeter of the scaled triangle is 2 times the perimeter of the original triangle.

TRY IT

Begin with a slightly larger triangle and use 0.5 as the scale factor. How does the perimeter of the new triangle compare to that of the original?

ON YOUR OWN

▶ Repeat the example above, but instead of using the **Distance & Length** tool, use the **Area** tool to find the area of each triangle. Divide the area of the scaled triangle by the area of the original. Is the area of the scaled triangle twice the area of the original?

▶ Repeat with different scale factors.

In this Connect you will use your knowledge of ratios, rates, proportions, and scale drawings to make a model for a special effect in a movie.

How Did They Do That?

Models of rooms on television shows are made before the actual set is created. Before the model is created, a scale drawing of the model is made. Suppose you are starring in your own television show, and the main set is a living room.

This scale drawing shows an incomplete floor plan of a living room. Use a ruler to measure the distances on the drawing to the nearest $\frac{1}{4}$ inch. The actual width of the room's model will be 4 ft and the actual width of the room on the set will be 16 ft.

1. Find the scale of the drawing to the model.

2. Models of the furniture must be created as well. What will the length of the couch be in the model?

3. Find the scale of the model to the actual set.

4. Find the length and width of a chair in your classroom. What size would the chair be for the scale drawing? For the model?

5. Since you will be the star of the show, what size will you be in the model? (use the same scale for height)

6. Complete the scale drawing by personalizing your set for the show.

Section 5B Review

Write and solve a proportion for each of the following situations.

1. How much should 10 bottles of juice cost if 6 cost $1.99?

2. Center Junior High had a win/loss ratio of 3:1. If it won 12 games, how many did it lose?

Solve each proportion. Which method did you use? Why?

3. $\dfrac{4}{5} = \dfrac{x}{100}$ **4.** $\dfrac{4.5}{8} = \dfrac{6}{x}$ **5.** $\dfrac{15}{3} = \dfrac{x}{8}$ **6.** $\dfrac{16}{s} = \dfrac{64}{72}$ **7.** $\dfrac{\frac{1}{2}}{7} = \dfrac{40}{h}$

Find the unit rate to create a rate formula for each of the following.

8. 27 students per 3 calculators   **9.** $\dfrac{\$450}{20 \text{ CDs}}$

Find the missing values for each pair of similar figures.

10.

11.

12.   When a scale drawing is an enlargement, will each measurement on the drawing be larger or smaller than the measurement on the actual object? Explain.

13. The gauge of a railroad track is the distance between the rails. The scale of a model Lionel train is 1 in. = 4 ft, and the distance between the rails is $1\frac{1}{4}$ in. What is the gauge of the actual railroad track?

Test Prep

When setting up a proportion to solve a problem, be careful to keep the units in each rate the same: $\frac{\text{mi}}{\text{hr}} = \frac{\text{mi}}{\text{hr}}$.

14. On their summer vacation, Vanessa's family drove 200 miles in 4 hours. Which proportion shows how long it would take them to drive 650 miles?

Ⓐ $\dfrac{200}{4} = \dfrac{650}{h}$ Ⓑ $\dfrac{650}{200} = \dfrac{4}{h}$ Ⓒ $\dfrac{650}{4} = \dfrac{200}{h}$ Ⓓ $\dfrac{4}{200} = \dfrac{650}{h}$

Fibonacci Sequence

The mathematician Fibonacci lived around 1200 A.D. He wrote a sequence of numbers that follows a certain pattern.

Each number in the Fibonacci sequence is the sum of the previous two numbers (for example, $2 + 3 = 5$, $3 + 5 = 8$). Starting the sequence with a pair of ones, the sequence continues as follows:

1, 1, 2, 3, 5, 8, 13, 21, 34, 55, 89, 144, 233, 377, 610, ...

Use a calculator to complete the table by dividing one number in the sequence by the preceding number. Round to five decimal places. Continue this process up to the fifteenth and fourteenth numbers in the sequence.

Ratio	Decimal
$\frac{1}{1}$	1
$\frac{2}{1}$	2
$\frac{3}{2}$	1.5
$\frac{5}{3}$	1.66667
$\frac{8}{5}$	

Examine the decimal equivalents of the Fibonacci ratios in this table. What happens?

The larger the two consecutive Fibonacci numbers, the closer the ratio of the two numbers will be to the golden ratio. The golden ratio is the ratio of the length to the width of a golden, or "perfect," rectangle; it is approximately 1.61828 to 1.

Use the golden ratio to set up a proportion to find the following:

a. The length of a golden rectangle with a width of 89 cm

b. The width of a golden rectangle with a length of 2.33 m

c. Examine your answers and refer to the table. What conclusions can you make?

265

Graphic Organizer

Section 5A Ratios, Rates, and Proportions

Summary

- A **ratio** is a comparison of two quantities.

- A **rate** is a ratio in which quantities using different units are compared. Usually you will see the words *per*, *for*, or *each* when working with rates.

- A **unit rate** is a comparison to 1 unit, such as 55 miles per hour.

- **Equal ratios** name the same amount. They may be obtained by multiplying or dividing the numerator and denominator by the same nonzero number.

- A **proportion** is an equation stating that two ratios are equal.

- Two ratios form a proportion if the **cross products** are equal.

Review

1. Write the ratio 3 to 7 as a fraction.

2. Draw a picture to show a ratio 2:5 of squares to triangles.

3. Write all the ratios that can be made using the figure at the right.

4. Ren types 300 words in 5 min and Stan types 440 words in 8 min. Use cross products to determine whether these rates are equal.

5. Is the table an equal ratio table? If so, find the value of k in $\frac{y}{x} = k$.

x	3	6	9	12	15
y	4	6	8	10	12

6. Complete the table to create ratios equal to the given ratio.

4		12			24
5	10		20	25	

Section 5B Problem Solving Using Proportions

Summary

- If two ratios form a proportion, then their cross products are equal.
  If $\frac{a}{b} = \frac{c}{d}$, then $ad = bc$.

- To solve a proportion is to find a missing number using equivalent ratios, mental math, or cross products.

- Unit rates can be used to solve proportions and create rate formulas.

- Many kinds of problems can be solved using unit rates and proportions.

- A **scale drawing** shows the actual shape of something but not the actual size. A **scale** gives the ratio of the measurements in the drawing to the measurements of the actual object. If the first number in the ratio is smaller, the scale drawing is a reduction; if it is larger, the scale drawing is an enlargement.

- Some examples of scale drawings are illustrations of microscopic organisms, maps, and blueprints of buildings.

- When making a scale drawing, it is important to choose an appropriate scale.

- **Similar polygons** have the same shape but may not have the same size. Their corresponding sides form proportions.

Review

7. Solve the proportion $\frac{90}{36} = \frac{x}{24}$.

8. Solve the proportion $\frac{21}{u} = \frac{39}{143}$.

9. Find the unit rate and create a rate formula for a rate of 6 gal in 2 hr.

10. Hoang's car travels 211 mi on 6 gal of gas. Estimate how far it would travel on 10 gal of gas.

11. The ratio of blue shoes to red shoes sold by Suzie's Shoe Store is 11:4. Last week the store sold 84 pairs of red shoes. About how many pairs of blue shoes were sold?

12. In May, City Video rented 2835 drama videos and 3402 comedy videos. In June, 4305 drama videos were rented. If the ratio of drama to comedy stayed the same, how many comedy videos were rented in June?

13. A scale drawing of a movie billboard is 3 in. tall and 7 in. across. If the scale is 2 in. = 5 ft, what are the dimensions of the actual billboard?

14. Find the missing measures in the pair of similar figures.

1. Write all the ratios that can be made using the figure at the right.

2. Write the ratio 13 to 81 as a fraction.

3. Draw a picture to show a ratio 4:3 of diamonds to hearts.

4. The bar graph shows the number of students in several classes at Wilson School. Estimate each ratio.

   a. Algebra students to woodworking students

   b. Woodworking students to home economics students

5. Kenny earned $94.25 for 13 hr of work. Amauri earned $137.75 for 19 hr of work. Use cross products to determine whether these rates of pay are equal.

6. Complete the table to create ratios equal to the given ratio.

3	6			21	30
5		20	25		

7. Solve each proportion.   **a.** $\frac{w}{27} = \frac{20}{45}$ **b.** $\frac{112}{32} = \frac{49}{p}$

8. Is the table an equal ratio table? If so, find the value of k.

9. If the value of k in $\frac{y}{x} = k$ is 12 and $x = 40$, what is the value of y?

x	4	8	16	24	28
y	5	10	20	30	35

10. Find the unit rate and create a rate formula for a rate of 110 mi in 2.5 hr.

11. Elton painted 12 paintings in 7 months. About how many paintings can he paint in 20 months?

12. A university has a male to female ratio of 8 to 5 among students. If 4250 women are attending this university, find the number of men attending and the total number of students.

13. In August, a salesman made 385 calls, of which 70 were successful. He had the same proportion of successful calls in September, when he made 56 successful calls. How many calls did he make in September?

14. A model spaceship with a scale of 3 in. = 80 ft is being built for a movie prop. The spaceship in the movie is 440 ft across. How large should the model be?

15. Find the missing measures in the pair of similar figures.

Performance Task

Find a reasonably simple illustration in a book or a magazine. Make a poster that is a scale drawing of the illustration using a scale of 6:1. Explain how you created your poster.

Performance Assessment

Choose one problem.

ARE STUDENTS PROPORTIONAL?

Measure the length of your forearm, x (the distance from your elbow to your wrist). Measure your height, y. Write the two measurements as an ordered pair. Do this for four other people in the class and graph the ordered pairs. What happens? What relationship exists between the two measurements? How can you tell if the students are proportional by looking at the graph?

Analogy is to Proportion as...

drive is to *car* as...
chicken is to *egg* as...
clock is to *time* as...
ear is to *hear* as...

An analogy is a comparison statement such as "*pencil* is to *write* as *brush* is to *paint*." Write some analogies of your own (you might want to start with the suggestions listed above). Then explain how analogies are related to proportions.

ITS NEW AND IMPROVED!

EXPRESSION YOURSELF

Many of the quantities in everyday life can be represented with mathematical expressions. For example, if your heart rate while exercising is 150 beats per minute and you exercise for m minutes, the expression that represents the number of times your heart beats would be $150m$. Write five expressions for quantities in your life that are related to other quantities. State what each variable represents.

Not Another Commercial!

During the prime time hours on some television networks, $2\frac{1}{2}$ minutes out of every 10 of program time are devoted to commercials. Write a ratio of commercial time to program time. The local television network charges companies as much as \$28,000 for 30 seconds to air a commercial during a popular TV show. At this rate, how much does the network make during the 30 minute program time?

6 Percent

→ **Cultural Link**
www.mathsurf.com/8/ch6/people

→ **Entertainment Link**
www.mathsurf.com/8/ch6/ent

People of the World

India will soon become the second country to reach the 1-billion mark in population. About 16% of the world's population live in India.

Entertainment

A favorite of scuba divers around the world, Australia's Great Barrier Reef extends 1250 miles, roughly the length of our Atlantic coastline from Maine to South Carolina.

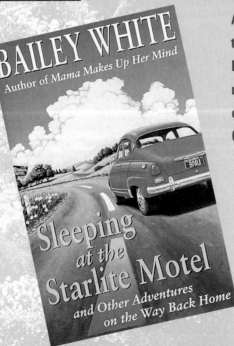

Arts & Literature

Of the books published in the United States, about 11% are fiction, 6% deal with medicine, and 2% are sports-related.

Science

Botanists have classified about 240,000 species of plants. However, 11 of these species provide 80% of the food for the world's population.

Social Studies

Norway has the dubious distinction of being the country with the highest rate of income tax—65%. Additional personal taxes make it possible for citizens to be charged in excess of 100%.

KEY MATH IDEAS

A percent is a ratio that compares a number to 100.

Compatible numbers can be used to help estimate percents.

The percent an amount increases is called the percent increase.

The percent an amount decreases is called the percent decrease.

Interest is money paid for the use of money. The amount of money deposited or borrowed is called the principal. There are two types of interest: simple interest and compound interest.

CHAPTER PROJECT

Problem Solving

Understand
Plan
Solve
Look Back

In this project, you will examine the time you spend on homework each day. Make a circle graph using a spreadsheet tool. You will write an analysis of your homework schedule and of any changes you may want to make to organize your time more efficiently.

Problem Solving Focus

Problem Solving

Understand
Plan
Solve
Look Back

Interpreting Math Phrases

In some problems, numerical information is given directly. At other times, numerical information is given as a ratio, such as "Write On sells pencils at three for forty-five cents." When developing a plan to solve a problem, you must be able to correctly interpret these ratio phrases and know when to use proportions.

For each problem, write down the answer and the arithmetic you used to get the answer. (For example, if you added 5 to 7 to get 12, write "5 + 7 = 12.")

1 Do It Write and Write On stationery stores have a sale. Write On sells pencils at three for forty-five cents. Do It Write sells them for two dollars and seventy-five cents a dozen. Jonah needs a dozen pencils. Which store charges more? How much more?

2 Do It Write sells stationery by the pound. Three pounds cost three dollars and eighty-five cents. Write On's price is one dollar and twenty cents a pound. Ben and Jo will share five pounds. Rounded to the nearest cent, which store has the better buy? How much less is it?

3 Write On matches the advertised prices of Do It Write and gives consumers half the difference in cash. Do It Write advertises Roll-Write ballpoint pens at six for two dollars and forty-cents. Write On's ad offers Roll-Write pens at one for fifty cents. Rob buys eight pens at Write On. Rounded to the nearest cent, how much cash does he get?

4 Write On sells magazines. *Sport!* costs two dollars and fifty cents a copy. Reg pays seventeen dollars and fifty cents a year for a monthly subscription. Rounded to the nearest cent, how much less per copy does Reg pay?

YOU ARE WHAT YOU EAT

What is your favorite food? What ingredients does it contain? Is it sweet or salty? Is it mostly vegetable, fruit, bread, meat, or something else? Is it healthy? Does it give you energy or slow you down? Does it have an ingredient to which you might be allergic? Before 1990, you could find answers to some of these questions, but not all of them.

Since the Nutrition Labeling and Education Act of 1990, fast-food restaurants have been required to provide nutritional information about the food they serve—hamburgers, French fries, milkshakes, and so on. Nutritional information is also required on items we buy at the grocery store. Every person needs certain amounts of nutrients each day based on his or her recommended caloric intake. The required amount of each nutrient is the daily value and is based on a 2000-calorie diet.

Reading labels on processed foods and learning about the nutritional benefits of foods can help you decide what foods you should eat to get the energy you need for your activities.

1 Describe your favorite food. Give as much information about its nutritional content as you can.

2 Why are labels on food products important?

Percents, Decimals, and Fractions

You'll Learn ...

■ to convert among fractions, decimals, and percents

... How It's Used

Advertisers use percents in many of the newspaper ads they create.

Vocabulary

percent

circle graph

▶ **Lesson Link** You have represented ratios as fractions and decimals. Now you will learn how to represent a ratio as a percent. ◀

Explore **Fractions, Decimals, and Percents**

Calculated Conversions

Materials: Calculator with [F⇄D] key

Use your calculator to convert fractions, decimals, and percents.

1. Enter 3 [÷] 4 [=] [F⇄D]. What is displayed? Press [F⇄D] again. What is displayed? Repeat for each fraction.

   a. $\frac{1}{100}$ **b.** $\frac{2}{5}$ **c.** $\frac{5}{4}$ **d.** $\frac{3}{3}$

2. Enter 0.3 [F⇄D]. What is displayed? Repeat for each decimal.

   a. 1.75   **b.** 0.85   **c.** 0.003   **d.** 2.25

3. Enter 25 [%]. What is displayed? Press [F⇄D]. What is displayed? Repeat for each percent.

   a. 30%   **b.** 45%   **c.** 3%   **d.** 99%

4. What patterns, if any, do you notice?

Learn **Percents, Decimals, and Fractions**

You find percents everywhere—40% off, 95% fat free, sales increase 10%. A **percent** is a ratio that compares a number to 100. *Percent* means "parts per hundred," "hundredths," or "out of every hundred."

We often see percents represented in a **circle graph**, sometimes called a pie chart.

Example 1

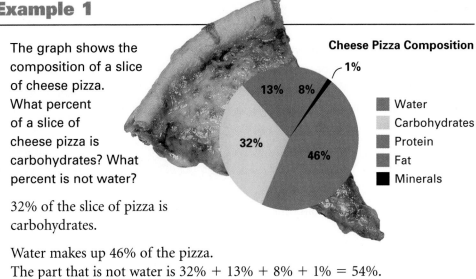

The graph shows the composition of a slice of cheese pizza. What percent of a slice of cheese pizza is carbohydrates? What percent is not water?

Cheese Pizza Composition

- Water
- Carbohydrates
- Protein
- Fat
- Minerals

1%
13% 8%
32%
46%

32% of the slice of pizza is carbohydrates.

Water makes up 46% of the pizza.
The part that is not water is 32% + 13% + 8% + 1% = 54%.

Often we need to find percents from fractions or decimals.

On the label shown, 18 of the 100 calories are from fat. 18 out of 100 can be expressed several ways:

Middle School Popcorn	
Calories:	100
Calories from Fat:	18

a. Decimal

0.18

b. Ratio

18 to 100

c. Fraction

$\frac{18}{100}$

d. Picture

Each of the expressions can also be represented as a percent.

$$\frac{18}{100} = 0.18 = 18\%$$

When rewriting a ratio as a decimal, as a fraction, or as a percent, it is helpful to think of "parts per hundred," or hundredths.

There are some percents that are used often. These are summarized in the table below. Notice that the fractions are in lowest terms.

Fraction	Percent	Fraction	Percent	Fraction	Percent	Fraction	Percent
$\frac{1}{4}$	25%	$\frac{1}{5}$	20%	$\frac{1}{6}$	$16\frac{2}{3}\%$	$\frac{1}{8}$	$12\frac{1}{2}\%$
$\frac{1}{2}$	50%	$\frac{2}{5}$	40%	$\frac{1}{3}$	$33\frac{1}{3}\%$	$\frac{3}{8}$	$37\frac{1}{2}\%$
$\frac{3}{4}$	75%	$\frac{3}{5}$	60%	$\frac{2}{3}$	$66\frac{2}{3}\%$	$\frac{5}{8}$	$62\frac{1}{2}\%$
1	100%	$\frac{4}{5}$	80%	$\frac{5}{6}$	$83\frac{1}{3}\%$	$\frac{7}{8}$	$87\frac{1}{2}\%$

MENTAL MATH

Because these percents are used so often, it would be wise to memorize the fractional relationships.

Example 2

A gram of fat contains more calories than a gram of protein or carbohydrates. Whole milk is 0.036 fat, however, 0.467 of its calories are from fat.

a. What percent of whole milk is fat?

Rewrite 0.036 as a fraction.

$0.036 = \dfrac{36}{1000}$ Write the decimal as a fraction.

$= \dfrac{36 \div 10}{1000 \div 10}$

$= \dfrac{3.6}{100}$ Divide numerator and denominator by 10.

$= 3.6\%$ Definition of percent.

3.6% of whole milk is fat.

b. What percent of whole milk calories are from fat?

Rewrite 0.467 as a fraction.

$0.467 = \dfrac{467}{1000}$ Write the decimal as a fraction.

$= \dfrac{467 \div 10}{1000 \div 10}$

$= \dfrac{46.7}{100}$ Divide numerator and denominator by 10.

$= 46.7\%$ Definition of percent.

46.7% of whole milk calories are from fat.

Another way to change a decimal to a percent is to move the decimal point two places to the right and add the percent sign:

$0.036 = 0.0\,3\,6 = 3.6\%$ $0.467 = 0.4\,6\,7 = 46.7\%$

Example 3

a. Rewrite $\frac{3}{5}$ as a percent.

Write $\frac{3}{5}$ as a fraction with a denominator of 100.

$\dfrac{3}{5} = \dfrac{3 \cdot 20}{5 \cdot 20} = \dfrac{60}{100} = 0.60 = 60\%$

b. Rewrite $\frac{5}{8}$ as a percent.

Because the denominator is not a factor of 100, divide numerator by denominator to change the fraction into decimal form.

$5 \div 8 = 0.625 = 62.5\%$

Try It

Rewrite each decimal or fraction as a percent.

a. 0.82   **b.** 0.125   **c.** $\dfrac{1}{2}$ **d.** $\dfrac{1}{8}$ **e.** $\dfrac{3}{500}$

You can also convert percents to decimals and fractions. Again, it may be helpful to think of "parts per hundred."

Example 4

Watermelon is 92% water and 6.9% carbohydrates.

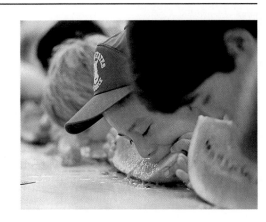

a. Rewrite 92% as a fraction and a decimal.

$92\% = \dfrac{92}{100}$ Write as a fraction with denominator 100.

$\dfrac{92}{100} = 0.92$ Write as a decimal.

b. Rewrite 6.9% as a fraction and a decimal.

$6.9\% = \dfrac{6.9}{100}$ Write as a fraction with denominator 100.

$\dfrac{6.9}{100} = \dfrac{6.9 \cdot 10}{100 \cdot 10} = \dfrac{69}{1000}$ Multiply numerator and denominator by 10 to eliminate the decimal.

$\dfrac{69}{1000} = 0.069$ Write as a decimal.

Another way to change a percent to a decimal is to delete the percent sign and move the decimal point two places to the left. For example:

$92\% = 0\,9\,2.\% = 0.92$

$6.9\% = 0\,0\,6.9\,\% = 0.069$

Try It

Rewrite each percent as a fraction and as a decimal.

a. 12%   **b.** 4.5%   **c.** 200%

HINT

Many scientific calculators have a percent key. Enter 6.9 %. The display reads 0.069.

Check | Your Understanding

1. How can fractions be changed to percents?

2. How can you tell if a decimal or a fraction will be renamed as a percent greater than 100? Less than 1?

3. Which is greater, 0.6 or 7%? Why?

6-1 Exercises and Applications

Practice and Apply

Getting Started For each figure below, write the fraction, decimal, and percent that describes how much of the figure is shaded.

1. a. Fraction = ?
   b. Decimal = ?
   c. Percent = ?

2. a. Fraction = ?
   b. Decimal = ?
   c. Percent = ?

3. Draw a diagram to show 75%.

4. Use the survey results shown in the circle graph.

   a. What percent of students say they eat out 3–5 times per week?

   b. What percent of students say they eat out no more than 5 times per week?

   c. What percent of students say they eat out at least once a week?

Times Students Eat Out Each Week

8%
13%
17%
25%
37%

- 0
- 1–2
- 3–5
- 6–8
- 9 or more

Write each fraction or decimal as a percent.

5. $\frac{4}{5}$ **6.** 0.18   **7.** $\frac{6}{5}$ **8.** 0.1667   **9.** 0.0035

Write each percent as a fraction in lowest terms and as a decimal.

10. 0.1%   **11.** 98%   **12.** 13.6%   **13.** 7.5%

14. 25%   **15.** 140%   **16.** 12.5%   **17.** 0.75%

18. **Test Prep** Which shows 345% expressed as a decimal?
   Ⓐ 34.5   Ⓑ 0.345   Ⓒ 3.45   Ⓓ 0.0345

19. **Chance** If there is about a 1% chance that eating a certain type of food would seriously harm you, would you eat it? Why or why not?

20. **Consumer** An orange-drink label reads "20% real fruit juice." What fractional part is real fruit juice?

21. Consumer Shoes you need are going on sale. Which sign would you like to see put up? Why?

| 20% off | 15% off | $\frac{1}{4}$% off | 0.5% off |

22. Number Sense The students at Adams Junior High conducted a survey of their favorite lunch foods. The chart displays the results. What percent of the students chose each food?

Favorite Food	Pizza	Chicken	Salad	Hamburger	Tacos	Other
Number of Students	51	10	38	19	30	2

 a. Pizza

 b. Anything but pizza

 c. Tacos

 d. Salad

23. Fine Arts To make the color light brown, you mix 7 parts red, 2 parts yellow, and 1 part blue. What percent of the light-brown coloring is red? Yellow? Blue?

Problem Solving and Reasoning

24. Journal Explain the differences between 500%, 50%, 5%, and 0.5%.

25. Communicate 90% means 90 out of 100. Explain how a student can score 90% on a test that has only 50 questions.

26. Communicate Explain how to rename a fraction with a denominator of 10 as a percent. Explain how to rename a fraction with a denominator of 1000 as a percent.

27. Math Reasoning A percentile is a point below which a given percent of data lie.

 a. What percentile is represented by the median? By the quartiles?

 b. Suppose there are 10,000 students taking a test in Alabama. What would it mean to score in the ninety-fifth percentile?

Mixed Review

28. Solve $x + 3 \leq 10$. Graph the solution on a number line. *[Lesson 3-7]*

29. Graph $y = -x - 1$. Find the slope, the x-intercept, and the y-intercept. *[Lesson 4-5]*

Solving Problems Using Percents

You'll Learn ...

■ to use proportions and equations to solve percent problems

... How It's Used

Consumers solve percent problems when shopping, making nutritional choices, and so on.

▶ **Lesson Link**   In Lesson 6-1, you learned to convert percents to fractions and decimals. Now you will learn different methods for solving percent problems. ◀

Explore   Percent

How Was Your Day?

How do you spend your day? How much time do you spend in school, sleeping, studying, eating, playing a sport, watching TV, and so on?

1. Make a list of your activities on a typical day. Write the amount of time spent on each activity.

2. Write a ratio that compares the amount of time spent on each activity to 24 hours.

3. Change each ratio to a percent.

4. Use a proportion to find the amount of time spent sleeping in a week; in a year.

5. What other method could you use to find the amount of time spent sleeping in one week?

Learn   Solving Problems Using Percents

A percent problem can be solved by substituting given information into the following proportion and then solving.

Percent problems can also be solved by writing an equation.

$$\frac{\text{part}}{\text{total}} = \frac{\text{percent}}{100}$$

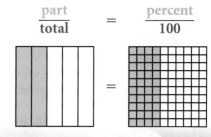

Example 1

It is recommended that people between the ages of 11–24 eat *1200* mg of dietary calcium each day. A cup of cooked spinach contains *276* mg of calcium, *23*% of the recommended daily allowance for calcium. Any one of these three numbers can be found using a proportion or an equation.

23% of 1200 is what number?

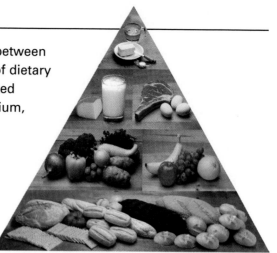

Proportion method: $\dfrac{\text{part}}{\text{total}} \rightarrow \dfrac{x}{1200} = \dfrac{23}{100} \leftarrow \dfrac{\text{percent}}{100}$ — Substitute in the proportion.

$$100x = 27600$$ — Use cross products.

$$x = 276$$ — Divide both sides of the equation by 100.

Remember

You solved proportions such as these using cross products.
[Page 243]

Equation method: 23% of 1200 is what number?

$\downarrow$ $\downarrow$ $\downarrow$ $\downarrow$ $\quad$ $\downarrow$

$$23\% \cdot 1200 = \quad x \quad \text{Write an equation.}$$

$$0.23 \cdot 1200 = \quad x \quad \text{Change 23\% to its decimal form.}$$

$$276 = \quad x \quad \text{Multiply.}$$

23% of 1200 is 276.

Example 2

What percent of 1200 is 276?

We'll use the proportion method:

$\dfrac{\text{part}}{\text{total}} \rightarrow \dfrac{276}{1200} = \dfrac{x}{100} \leftarrow \dfrac{\text{percent}}{100}$ — Substitute in the proportion.

$$27600 = 1200x \quad \text{Use cross products.}$$

$$23 = x \quad \text{Divide both sides by 1200.}$$

276 is 23% of 1200.

Example 3

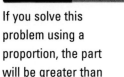

MENTAL MATH

When translating, think: 50% of 2 is 1. Replace each of these numbers with those from the problem, using a variable for the value you want to find.

276 is 23% of what number?

We'll use the equation method.

276 is 23% of what number?

$\downarrow$ $\downarrow$ $\downarrow$ $\downarrow$ $\downarrow$

$276 = 23\%$ · x Write an equation.

$276 = 0.23$ · x Change 23% to its decimal form.

$1200 =$ x Divide both sides by 0.23.

276 is 23% of 1200.

Try It

Solve each problem. Use the method of your choice.

a. 20 is what percent of 160?   **b.** 45% of 80 is what number?

c. 80% of what number is 72?

Equations and proportions can also be used to solve problems involving percents that are greater than 100 or less than 1.

Example 4

Problem Solving TIP

If you solve this problem using a proportion, the part will be greater than the total, because the percent is greater than 100.

President John F. Kennedy's oak rocking chair, valued before an auction at $5000, sold for 8850% of this amount. What was the selling price of the rocking chair?

We'll use the equation method.

8850% of 5000 is what number?

$\downarrow$ $\downarrow$ $\downarrow$ $\downarrow$ $\downarrow$

8850% · $5000 =$ x Write an equation.

88.5 · $5000 =$ x Change 8500% to its decimal form.

$442{,}500 \quad =$ x Multiply.

8850% of 5000 is 442,500. The rocking chair sold for $442,500.

Try It

A pesticide makes up 0.125% of a solution. How much solution is there if there are 4 ounces of pesticide in the solution?

In 1991, 8.3% of expenses in the U.S. went toward food. If a typical family spends about $300 per month on food, how much would you expect its monthly expenses to be?

Sarah thinks ...

I'll write the equation.

300   is   8.3%   of what number?
↓   ↓   ↓   ↓   ↓
300   =   0.083   ·   x

$$\frac{300}{0.083} = x$$

300 ÷ 0.083 = **3614.457831**

A family would spend about $3614 each month.

Daniel thinks ...

I can set up the proportion to find the missing number.

$$\frac{part}{total} \rightarrow \frac{300}{x} = \frac{8.3}{100} \leftarrow \frac{percent}{100}$$

30,000 = 8.3x   I'll use cross multiplication.

30000 ÷ 8.3 = **3614.457831**

A family would spend about $3614 each month.

What do you think?

Which method do you prefer? Why?

Check | Your Understanding

1. 40% of 30 is equal to 30% of 40. Why?

2. Explain two different ways to find 7% of a number.

3. Which is a greater percent, 348 out of 500 or 489 out of 1000? Why?

4. Explain why a proportion can be used to solve a percent problem.

Practice and Apply

1. **Getting Started** 40% of x is 12. Identify each number in the proportion.

$$\frac{\text{part}}{\text{total}} \rightarrow \frac{\Box}{\Box} = \frac{\Box}{\Box} \leftarrow \frac{\text{percent}}{100}$$

Solve.

2. What number is 20% of 75?

3. 16% of 25 is what number?

4. 5% of 180 is what number?

5. What number is $33\frac{1}{3}$% of 66?

6. What percent of 80 is 20?

7. What percent of 48 is 16?

8. 300 out of 1000 is what percent?

9. 70 is what percent of 35?

10. 22 is 50% of what number?

11. 75% of what number is 15?

12. 200% of what number is 16?

13. 1 is 80% of what number?

14. **Consumer** A bin contains 120 ears of white and yellow corn. Of these, 78 ears are yellow. What percent of the ears of corn are yellow? What percent are white?

15. Twenty percent of the eighth graders at Eisenhower Middle School—87 students—purchased a hot lunch ticket book. How many eighth graders are in the school?

16. **Health** The recommended daily allowance (RDA) of calcium is 1200 mg. Jim drank a glass of milk that had 30% of the RDA. How many milligrams of calcium did the glass of milk contain?

17. The following table summarizes the nationalities of 324 passengers on an international flight from Chicago to London.

Country	Canada	England	France	Mexico	Spain	Sweden	U. S.	Other
Percent	9%	32%	12%	6%	10%	5%	24%	2%

   a. How many passengers were from Sweden?

   b. How many passengers were from England?

   c. Approximately $\frac{1}{4}$ were from which country?

18. **Science** A bottle of saline nasal spray contains approximately 0.65% sodium chloride. If the bottle contains 44.3 mL of spray, how much sodium chloride is in the bottle?

19. Measurement What percent of a meter stick is 1 cm?

20. Social Studies The circle graph shows the predicted ethnic makeup of American students in 2050. The graph is based on 89 million students.

Predicted Student Makeup in 2050

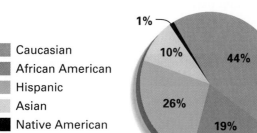

1%
10%
44%
26%
19%

Caucasian
African American
Hispanic
Asian
Native American

a. How many students will be Asian?

b. How many students will be African American?

c. Which population will be about 1 million?

21. Health *Major* minerals are those that make up over 0.01% of body weight; others are *trace* minerals. What *trace* mineral makes up the greatest amount of body weight?

Problem Solving and Reasoning

22. Communicate If 18 is 125% of a number, is the number greater than or less than 18? Why?

23. Critical Thinking What is 50% of 60% of a number?

24. **Test Prep** Add 20% of a number to the number itself. What percent of the result would you have to subtract to get the original number back?

Ⓐ $16\frac{2}{3}$% ⒷⒷ 20% Ⓒ 25% Ⓓ None of these

Minerals in Body of 70,000-g Male

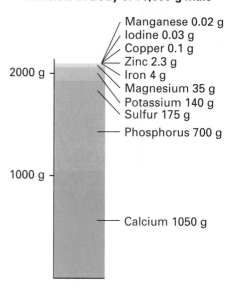

2000 g

Manganese 0.02 g
Iodine 0.03 g
Copper 0.1 g
Zinc 2.3 g
Iron 4 g
Magnesium 35 g
Potassium 140 g
Sulfur 175 g
Phosphorus 700 g

1000 g

Calcium 1050 g

Mixed Review

25. Write a formula to find the mean of four numbers—*a*, *b*, *c*, and *d*. Calculate for two sample values of the variables and explain the solution in terms of a situation. *[Lesson 3-3]*

Solve the system of equations by graphing. *[Lesson 4-6]*

26. $y = 2x - 5$
$y = -3x$

Estimating Percents

You'll Learn ...

■ to estimate percents of numbers, and what percent one number is of another

... How It's Used

Elected officials need to know roughly what percent of their constituents will support a bill.

▶ **Lesson Link** Often when using percents you do not need an exact answer. In this lesson you will learn how to estimate percents. ◀

Explore Estimating Percents

How Much Would You Tip?

OVERBOARD   by Chip Dunham

A tip is a gratuity for service. A restaurant bill comes to $14.78. In the United States, 15% of the bill is the common tip for foodservers, although 20% is not uncommon for excellent service.

1. a. Find 10% of the bill. How would you find 5% of the bill?

  b. How would you find 15% of the bill? 20% of the bill?

2. Estimate a reasonable tip for the following amounts. Explain.

  a. $23.78 with good service   **b.** $37.45 with great service

3. A couple leaves a tip of $8 after eating a $32 dinner. What percent did they tip? Was this reasonable? Why or why not?

4. Would doubling the tax be a reasonable tip? Why or why not?

5. When Jeff gets his bill, he usually uses division to calculate the tip. What are some ways he might do this? Why do they work?

▶ **Language Link**

The word *tip* may actually be an acronym for *To Insure Promptness.*

Learn Estimating Percents

When estimating percents, it is often helpful to use compatible numbers. To find what percent 16 is out of 30, think of the ratio as 16 out of 32 or as 15 out of 30. Both pairs of compatible numbers result in the same estimate, $\frac{1}{2}$, or 50%.

It may also be helpful to use fractions that are close to a given percent.

 $\frac{1}{4} = 25\%$ $\frac{1}{2} = 50\%$ $\frac{3}{4} = 75\%$ $\frac{1}{3} = 33\frac{1}{3}\%$

$\frac{2}{3} = 66\frac{2}{3}\%$ $\frac{1}{5} = 20\%$ $\frac{2}{5} = 40\%$ $\frac{3}{5} = 60\%$

$\frac{4}{5} = 80\%$ $\frac{1}{10} = 10\%$ $\frac{3}{10} = 30\%$ $\frac{7}{10} = 70\%$

Example 1

Estimate **24% of 81.**

24% is close to 25%, 81 is close to 80.   Choose compatible numbers.

$25\% = \frac{1}{4}$ Change percent to a fraction.

$\frac{1}{4} \cdot 80 = 20$ Find $\frac{1}{4}$ of 80.

24% of 81 is about 20.

Try It

a. Estimate 74.5% of 239.   **b.** Estimate 66% of 89.

MENTAL MATH

If you know fractions that are nearly equivalent, estimating is often easier.

Example 2

The label on a carton of orange juice states that one glass provides 11% of the RDA of potassium. If the RDA of potassium for an adult is 4000 mg, how many mg of potassium does one glass of orange juice contain?

11% is close to 10%, or $\frac{1}{10}$. $\frac{1}{10}$ of 4000 is 400.

One glass of orange juice contains about 400 mg of potassium.

Try It

A 340 mL serving of grapefruit juice only provides 1.8% of the RDA of potassium. If the RDA for a person is 4500 mg, how many mg are in this serving of grapefruit juice?

Problem Solving TIP

You can always adjust an estimate. You may feel that 450 mg is a better estimate.

Example 3

MENTAL MATH

Think: $\frac{1}{10}$ of what number is 23?

One day 23 students, or about 9% of all students who bought a hot lunch, chose fish. Estimate how many students bought a hot lunch.

9% is about 10%, or $\frac{1}{10}$.

So $23 = \frac{1}{10}x$.

$x = 10 \cdot 23$, so $x = 230$.

Approximately 230 students bought a hot lunch.

Check with your calculator: 9 % × 230 = **20.7**; 20.7 is close to 23.

Try It

a. An eighth-grade basketball team made 63 out of 190 shots. About what percent of the shots were made?

b. About 48% of the student body, or 125 students, are going on a field trip to NASA. About how large is the student body?

When finding the percent of a region, estimates are often used.

Example 4

Estimate the percent of the region that is shaded.

It is approximately 55%, because a little more than 50% is shaded.

Try It

Estimate the percent of the region that is shaded.

Check Your Understanding

1. What are some situations in which people commonly estimate percents?

2. Name two situations for which an estimate of a percent is acceptable. Name two situations for which the exact percent is necessary.

3. How can an estimate of 10% of a number help you to estimate 5% of the number? To estimate 15% of the number? Give examples.

Practice and Apply

1. ⟦Getting Started⟧ What fraction would you use to estimate each percent?

a. 34%   **b.** 19%   **c.** 0.9%   **d.** $9\frac{1}{2}\%$

Estimate each percent.

2. 76 out of 150   **3.** 23 out of 97   **4.** 33 out of 620   **5.** 62 out of 63

Estimate.

6. 38% of 608   **7.** 19% of 68   **8.** 75% of 159   **9.** 9% of 43.6

Estimate the percent that each shaded region represents.

10.   **11.**   **12.**   **13.**

Number Sense Use mental math. Replace each ☐ with >, <, or =.
Explain your answer.

14. 9% of 4238 ☐ 10% of 4238   **15.** 46% of 999 ☐ 46% of 666

16. $\frac{1}{2}\%$ of 4 ☐ $\frac{1}{2} \cdot 4$ **17.** 1% of 64 ☐ 2% of 46

18. **Geography** Estimate the areas. About what percent of the state of Texas could the state of New York cover?

19. **Health** Many toothpastes contain fluoride to help prevent tooth decay. Suppose a 181 g tube of toothpaste contains 0.15% fluoride. Estimate the number of grams of fluoride in this tube.

20. **Science** If 30 mg of vitamin C is 50% of the daily requirement, what is the daily requirement for vitamin C?

21. ⟦Test Prep⟧ The bill for last night's dinner was $28.93. What is a good estimate of a 15% tip?

Ⓐ $3.00   Ⓑ $4.50   Ⓒ $6.00   Ⓓ $43.00

PRACTICE 6-3

22. At Bonnabel Middle School, 372 students were asked to give the time of their school-night curfew. The results are shown in the circle graph. Use the graph to answer the following questions.

a. What time was the curfew of approximately $\frac{1}{3}$ of the students?

b. Approximately how many students had an 11 P.M. curfew?

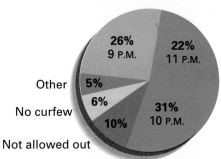

School-night Curfews

26% 9 P.M.
22% 11 P.M.
Other 5%
6%
No curfew 10%
31% 10 P.M.
Not allowed out

Problem Solving and Reasoning

23. Critical Thinking John's tennis coach discovered that when at least 85% of John's first serves are in bounds, John wins the match. In the present match, 73 out of 98 of John's first serves are in bounds. Will he win the match? Explain your reasoning.

24. Critical Thinking The average daily intake of calories is 2000. For a snack, Leandro had yogurt (250 calories) and a small bag of chips (160 calories). Approximately what percent of his total caloric intake did Leandro have?

25. **Journal** Which percents do you think are the easiest to use when estimating? Explain your choices.

26. Communicate Estimate each of the following. Explain how you found your estimate.

a. 148% of 97   **b.** 0.9% of 4230

Mixed Review

Solve each equation. Check your solution. *[Lesson 3-4]*

27. $y - 11 = 8$ **28.** $m + 3 = -1$ **29.** $p - 6 = -8$ **30.** $z + 150 = 72$

31. Graph $y < x - 3$ on a coordinate plane. *[Lesson 4-7]*

Project Progress

Make a chart of the classes in which you have homework and the days of the week. Record the time you spend on each subject each day. Change hr and min to a fraction and to a decimal. For example, 1 hr, 35 min, is $1\frac{35}{60}$ hr $= 1\frac{7}{12}$ hr ≈ 1.58 hr. At the end of the week, estimate what percent of total homework time you spent on each subject.

Problem Solving

Understand
Plan
Solve
Look Back

In this Section you will apply your knowledge of percents to understanding the nutrition facts on a food label.

You Are What You Eat

Examine this nutrition label from a frozen pizza. The serving size and number of servings are given on the label, but the serving size for one person may not be the serving size for another.

1. Decide on a different serving size. Is your serving size larger or smaller than the one shown here?

2. How many servings does the pizza contain now? Is your number of servings larger or smaller than the one shown here? How are the number of servings and the serving size related?

3. Use the original label to find what percent of the total fat is saturated fat.

4. By changing the serving size, what other items on the food label will change?

5. Make a new food label for the serving size you chose.

6. On the original label, total fat was listed as 11 g, or 17%. This means 17% of what number? What are the comparable numbers for your new label?

Nutrition Facts

Serving Size ⅙ pizza (139 g)
Servings Per Container: 6

Amount Per Serving
Calories 320   Calories from Fat 100

	% Daily Value*
Total Fat 11g	**17%**
Saturated Fat 6g	**30%**
Cholesterol 25mg	**8%**
Sodium 870mg	**36%**
Total Carbohydrate 39g	**13%**
Dietary Fiber 3g	**12%**
Sugars 6g	
Protein 3g	

Vitamin A	15%	•	Vitamin C	0%
Calcium	30%	•	Iron	6%

*Percent Daily Values are based on a 2,000 calorie diet. Your daily values may be higher or lower depending on your caloric needs:

	Calories	2,000	2,500
Total Fat	Less than	65g	80g
Sat. Fat	Less than	20g	25g Fat
Cholesterol	Less than	300mg	300mg
Sodium	Less than	2,400mg	2,400mg
Total Carbohydrate		300g	375g
Fiber		25g	30g

Calories per gram:
Fat 9 • Carbohydrate 4 • Protein 4

1. Write the fraction, decimal, and percent that describes how much of one figure is shaded.

a.   b.   c.   d.

Write each fraction, mixed number, or decimal as a percent.

2. $\frac{2}{5}$ **3.** 0.67   **4.** $1\frac{2}{3}$ **5.** 14.5   **6.** 0.0235

Write each percent as a decimal and as a fraction or mixed number in lowest terms.

7. 72%   **8.** 240%   **9.** 12.75%   **10.** 0.5%   **11.** 56%

Estimate.

12. 82 out of 412   **13.** 26 out of 98   **14.** 34% of 602   **15.** 21% of 61.2

16. What number is 40% of 68?   **17.** What percent of 55 is 11?

18. 78 is 50% of what number?   **19.** 10 is 80% of what number?

20. Number Sense Without evaluating, which expression is greater, 12% of 675 or 12% of 673? Why?

21. Social Studies In 1972, Richard Nixon received 47,170,179 votes out of 77,727,590 cast. Estimate the percent of votes Nixon received.

22. A hairspray label states that it contains 50% alcohol, 40% water, and 14% other ingredients. Is this reasonable? Explain.

Test Prep

Use compatible numbers to estimate percents.

23. In a tennis match, 53 of Cindy's 97 first serves were good. Which is the best estimate of the percent of first serves that were good?

Ⓐ 5%   Ⓑ $\frac{1}{2}$%   Ⓒ 20%   Ⓓ 50%

REVIEW 6A

The Price Is Right

As you look at advertisements in newspapers and magazines and on television, you see examples of how businesses use different techniques to attract customers. They offer sales—Presidents' Day sales, "back-to-school" sales, "going-out-of-business" sales, and so on. Discounts are sometimes given if you make bulk purchases. Many companies will give you "cents off" coupons to encourage you to buy their products instead of those of their competitors or to introduce their new products. Pricing techniques are often used to encourage you to buy their products. An item selling for $99.97, $99.98, or $99.99 is more appealing than one selling for $100.00. Many businesses offer you credit, which allows you to "buy now and pay later." Some companies' products always seem to be on sale, but are the sale prices actually a good buy?

1 Why would a company give a discount for bulk purchases?

2 How can a company afford to offer discounts and coupons for their products?

3 Why do you think a price of $99.99 is more appealing than a price of $100.00?

Percent Increase

You'll Learn ...

■ to find the percent increase of a number

■ to find the result or the original number given the percent increase

... How It's Used

A store manager must calculate the retail price of merchandise based on the wholesale cost and the percent markup.

Vocabulary

percent increase

▶ **Lesson Link**   You have learned about percents. Now you will learn to find the percent of increase. ◀

Explore   Percent Increase

Materials: Calculator

It's Taxing!

1. What is the percent of sales tax where you live? If your state does not have a sales tax, use 6.5%.

2. The price of a computer is $1999.99. How much sales tax will you pay on this price?

3. Add the amount of sales tax to the original price. Store the result in the memory of your calculator.

4. The amount of sales tax is what percent of the price of the computer?

5. Add 100% to the percent of sales tax. Now find this percent of the price of the computer. What does this number represent?

6. How does this number compare to the number you stored in your calculator? Why is this true?

Learn   Percent Increase

Stores buy merchandise at wholesale prices, but sell the merchandise at higher prices, called retail prices. The amount of increase between the wholesale and retail price of the merchandise may be used by the store owner to pay operating expenses and to make a profit. The difference between the retail price and the wholesale price is often represented as a percent, called the percent markup or **percent increase** .

Example 1

The Canoe and Trail Shop purchased sleeping bags at the wholesale price of $89.50 each and sold them at a retail price of $143.25 each. What was the percent increase?

To find the amount of increase, subtract the wholesale price from the retail price.

$143.25 - 89.50 = 53.75$	The increase was 53.75.
53.75 is what percent of 89.50?	Find the percent increase.
$53.75 = x \cdot 89.50$	Write an equation.
$\dfrac{53.75}{89.50} = x$	Divide.
$x = 0.6005587 \approx 0.60$	Round to the nearest hundredth.
$0.60 = 60\%$	Change the decimal to a percent.

The percent increase is about 60%.

Example 2

The sales tax rate of 9% in Orleans Parish in New Orleans is one of the highest in the nation. If Greg purchased a computer desk for $68.96, what was the total cost, including sales tax?

Method 1

Find the amount of tax on the purchase.

9% of $68.96 is the amount of tax.

$0.09 \boxed{\times} 68.96 \boxed{=}$ *6.2064*, or $6.21

Add the amount of tax to the cost of the desk.

$68.96 \boxed{+} 6.21 \boxed{=}$ *75.17*

The total cost of the desk is $75.17.

Method 2

First add the percent of tax to 100%.

$100\% + 9\% = 109\%$

Greg will pay 109% of the cost of the desk.

109% of 68.96 is the total cost.

$1.09 \boxed{\times} 68.96 \boxed{=}$ *75.1664* ≈ 75.17

The total cost of the desk is $75.17.

Try It

a. The Canoe and Trail Shop purchased four-person tents at the wholesale price of $115.25 each and sold them at $172.85 each. What was the percent increase?

b. In Jefferson Parish, the tax rate is 8.5%. Use both methods to find the total cost, including sales tax, of a computer desk priced at $72.93.

To find the final amount, you can multiply the original amount by the sum of 100% and the percent increase. So you can divide to find the original amount if you know the final amount.

Example 3

Because of a new subdivision, the enrollment at Lincoln Middle School increased to 495 students, about a 12% increase over last year's enrollment. What was last year's enrollment?

Final amount = original amount × (100% + percent increase).

There are about 12% more students this year than last year.

This means 495 is 100% + 12% = 112% of last year's enrollment.

495 is 112% of what number?

$$495 = 1.12 \cdot x \quad \text{Write an equation.}$$

$$\frac{495}{1.12} = \frac{1.12x}{1.12} \quad \text{Divide both sides by 1.12.}$$

$441.96 \approx x$

There were 442 students enrolled last year.

You can check your answer using a calculator.

$495 - 442 = 53$ more students.

See whether 53 is 12% of 442.

$53 \;\boxed{\div}\; 442 \;\boxed{=}\; 0.119909502$

0.1199 is very close to 12%.

Try It

The number of subscribers to the local newspaper is now 6200, which is an increase of 35% from last year. Approximately how many subscribers were there last year?

A fine for a parking ticket, if not paid on time, may increase 50% each month. How much would a person have to pay if an original fine of $100 is increased twice?

Lian thinks ...

I'll find the increase in the fine for the first month. $100 \times 0.5 = 50$

The late penalty is $50.

I need to add the increase to the original fine. I get $150. $100 + 50 = 150$

Now I need to find the increase the second time. I'll multiply 150 by 0.5. $150 \times 0.5 = 75$

I'll add this increase to 150. $150 + 75 = 225.$

The fine is now $225.

Andre thinks ...

I'll multiply the original fine by 1.5. This will give me the fine after one increase. $100 \times 1.5 = 150$

I'll multiply the new amount by 1.5 to get the fine after two increases. $150 \times 1.5 = 225$

The fine is now $225.

What do you think?

Why do they get the same answer?

Check   Your Understanding

1. Why can you find the final cost after a 40% increase by multiplying by 1.4?

2. What does a 100% increase mean? What are other ways to describe a 100% increase? What is meant by an increase of more than 100%?

3. Can 50% more than one number be less than 1% more than another number? Explain.

Practice and Apply

1. **Getting Started** The price of a CD before adding sales tax is $15.99. The sales tax rate is 7.5%. What is the total cost of the CD?

   a. To find the amount of sales tax, find 7.5% of $15.99.

   b. To find the total cost, add the amount of sales tax to the price of the CD.

   c. Or, to find the total cost, find 107.5% of $15.99.

Find the percent increase for each, then round to the nearest whole percent.

2. Old: 2551
New: 3000

3. Old: 45
New: 90

4. Old: 525
New: 600

5. Old: $23.65
New: $27.65

6. Old: $0.45
New: $1.00

7. Old: $4578
New: $5200

8. What is the wholesale price if the percent increase is 20% and the amount of increase is $18.60?

9. Find the total cost of a $659 TV with a price increase of 38%.

10. **Estimation** Describe some simple ways of finding a 50% increase.

11. **Consumer** The price of a theatre ticket has increased 40% over the last five years. If the cost of a ticket was $15 five years ago, what does it cost now?

12. **Fine Arts** After Rembrandt van Rijn had painted 50 self-portraits, he painted even more, increasing his total number of self-portraits by 24%. How many self-portraits did Rembrandt paint?

13. **Biology** Between 1960 and 1990, the average female became 3.1% taller. In 1960, the average female was about 157 cm tall. How tall was the average female in 1990?

14. **Test Prep** The cost of a computer before sales tax is added is $2353.00 and the cost after sales tax is added is $2494.18. Which of the following is the tax rate?

   Ⓐ 6%   Ⓑ 60%   Ⓒ 0.06%   Ⓓ 0.60%

15. In what month was the percent increase from 1996 to 1997 closest to 50%?

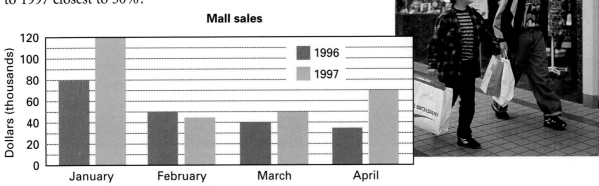

Mall sales

16. Consumer In 1994, sales of CDs, tapes, and LPs were $35.5 billion dollars. This was an increase of 16.5% from the year before. Approximately what were the 1993 sales?

17. Social Studies During 1994, the U.S. Secret Service confiscated more than $25 million in counterfeit bills. More than 160,000 counterfeit $10 bills were found. In 1993, 23,000 counterfeit $10 bills were found. What was the percent increase in counterfeit $10 bills found?

Problem Solving and Reasoning

18. Communicate Compare the two methods for finding total cost after sales tax is added. Which method do you prefer? Why?

19. Choose a Strategy Draw a figure that is 50% larger than this one.

20. Critical Thinking Suppose you make $20,000 a year and spend 25% of your salary on rent. If your salary increases 10% and your rent increases 5%, what percent of your salary will be spent on housing?

21. Critical Thinking A 12 oz drink has 10% fruit juice.

a. How many ounces are fruit juice?

b. A new, improved drink advertises "20% more fruit juice!" How much fruit juice is in the new drink?

c. What percent of the new, improved drink is fruit juice?

Problem Solving
STRATEGIES
• Look for a Pattern
• Make an Organized List
• Make a Table
• Guess and Check
• Work Backward
• Use Logical Reasoning
• Draw a Diagram
• Solve a Simpler Problem

Mixed Review

22. Make a table of values for $y = x^2 - x$. Use 0, 1, 2, 3, 4, and 5 for x. *[Lesson 4-1]*

23. Write all of the ratios that can be made using this figure. *[Lesson 5-1]*

Percent Decrease

▶ **Lesson Link** You have learned about percent increase. Now you will learn about percent decrease. ◀

You'll Learn ...

■ to find the percent decrease of a number

■ to find the result or the original number given the percent decrease

... How It's Used

Guitar amplifier manufacturers measure in percent the distortion decreases when various noise filtering systems are used.

Vocabulary

percent decrease

Explore | Percent Decrease

What Part of the Whole?

a. 0.6

b. $\dfrac{6}{10}$

c. $\dfrac{60}{100}$

1. Compare each unshaded amount to the whole. How can you use subtraction to find this amount?

2. Why can you use subtraction?

3. Write each percent as a subtraction from the whole.

   a. 95%   **b.** 2%   **c.** 50%

   d. $66\frac{2}{3}\%$ **e.** 37.5%

Learn | Percent Decrease

Store owners decrease the price of merchandise to promote business. This amount of decrease between the retail and sale price of merchandise makes goods more attractive to customers. The amount of decrease, or discount, is often represented as a percent, called the **percent decrease** or percent of discount.

Example 1

Enrique works at Music World. He receives a discount of 20% on all purchases. The retail price of a cassette tape is $7.99. What will Enrique pay with his discount?

► **Career Link**

As one of their fringe benefits, most retail employees receive a discount on purchases, usually ranging from 10% to 40% off the retail price.

Method 1

Find the amount of discount on the tape.

20% of $7.99 is the amount of discount.

0.2 ☒ 7.99 ▣ *1.598* ≈ $1.60

Subtract the amount of discount from the cost of the tape.

7.99 ⊟ 1.60 ▣ *6.39.*

The tape will cost $6.39.

Method 2

First subtract the percent of discount from 100%.

100% − 20% = 80%

Enrique will pay 80% of the cost of the tape.

80% of $7.99 is the discounted price.

0.8 ☒ 7.99 ▣ *6.392* ≈ 6.39

The tape will cost $6.39.

Try It

The retail price of a package of 3.5-inch floppy disks is $12.87. Laura has a 5%-off coupon. What will Laura have to pay for the disks?

Example 2

The sale price for a pair of jeans is $29.95. The original price was $40.00. What is the approximate percent of discount?

40 − 29.95 = 10.05   Find the amount of discount.

10.05 is what percent of 40?   Find the percent of discount.

10.05 = $x \cdot 40$ Write an equation.

10.05 ⊡ 40 ▣ x Divide both sides by 40.

$x = $ *0.25125* ≈ 0.25 = 25%

The percent of discount is 25%.

Try It

Jeans were reduced from $30.99 to $24.99 at the annual "back-to-school" sale. What was the approximate percent of discount?

If you know the discount and the final price, you can find the original price.

Example 3

A store advertised a sale of 12.5% off all sporting goods. The sale price of a soccer ball was $69.97. What was the original price?

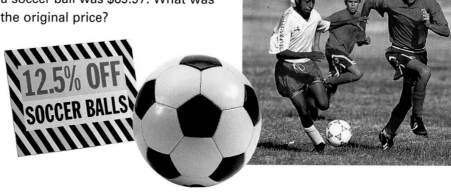

sale price = original price × (100% − percent of discount)

sale price = original price × (1.00 − 0.125)   Change the percents to decimals.

69.97 = x(1.00 − 0.125)   Write an equation.

69.97 = x(0.875)   Subtract.

69.97 ÷ 0.875 = x Divide both sides by 0.875.

79.96571 = x

The original price was $79.97.

Try It

A 13-inch color TV is on sale for $269.96. If the sale price reflects a 3.5% discount, what was the original price of the TV?

Check Your Understanding

1. Why can you find a 30% discount by multiplying by 70%?

2. Why is it possible to have a 150% increase, but not a 150% decrease?

3. Lee found the percent decrease from 120 to 100 using the following method: The percent increase from 100 to 120 is 20%. So the percent decrease from 120 to 100 is 20%. Is this true? Explain.

Practice and Apply

1. **Getting Started** What percent of the original price would you pay for each of the following?

a. 22% off   **b.** 30% off   **c.** 20% off   **d.** 40% off

Find the percent decrease for each, then round to the nearest whole percent.

2. Old: 436
New: 278

3. Old: 98
New: 90

4. Old: 225
New: 200

5. Old: $33.65
New: $27.65

6. Old: $1.05
New: $1.00

7. Old: $4598
New: $4200

8. What is the original price of a sweater if the percent of discount is 20% and the sale price is $28.40?

9. How much money will you save on a pair of shoes priced at $25.50 if they are going on sale for 7.5% off?

10. Find the percent of discount on a pair of roller skates that regularly sell for $47.50 and are now $39.99.

11. **Health** The number of reported cases of tetanus in 1994 was 94% fewer than the 486 cases reported in 1950. How many cases were reported in 1994?

12. **Consumer** The price of a jet printer in 1990 was $899. In 1996, the price of the same type of printer had dropped to $327. What is the percent decrease in price?

13. **History** The price of a scientific calculator has dropped an average of 75% in the last ten years. If a calculator sold for $125 ten years ago, what would it sell for now?

14. **Test Prep** Zoe noticed a sale brochure that advertised a radio originally priced at $59.95 on sale for $49.95. Which of the following is approximately the percent of discount?

Ⓐ 83%   Ⓑ 20%   Ⓒ 17%   Ⓓ 120%

PRACTICE 6-5

Problem Solving and Reasoning

15. Critical Thinking Carol works at a floral shop. She receives a discount of 10% on all purchases. This week, the shop is having a 5%-off sale. Carol gets both discounts. If she buys a $15 flower arrangement, which option will give her the best price?

Ⓐ Take 10% off and then 5% off that discounted amount.

Ⓑ Take 5% off and then 10% off that discounted amount.

Ⓒ Take 15% off.

16. Communicate Is a 25% discount on a $40 item the same as a 40% discount on a $25 item? Explain.

17. **Journal** Compare the two methods for determining the price of an item with a discount in Example 1. Which method do you prefer? Why?

18. Choose a Strategy Ellen needs to raise the price of a $10 item and lower the price of a $15 item so they are equal. But she can only enter percent increases and percent decreases in the pricing computer. Give an example of how she can do this.

19. Communicate A sign read "Buy a dozen, get 15% off your order." You need 10 CDs for gifts. They are priced at $7.88 each.

a. How much would 10 CDs cost? How much would 12 CDs cost?

b. How many CDs would you buy? Explain.

> **Problem Solving**
> ## STRATEGIES
> • Look for a Pattern
> • Make an Organized List
> • Make a Table
> • Guess and Check
> • Work Backward
> • Use Logical Reasoning
> • Draw a Diagram
> • Solve a Simpler Problem

Mixed Review

20. Determine whether each ordered pair is a solution of $y = -9 - 2x$. *[Lesson 4-2]*

a. $(-4, -17)$ **b.** $(11, -31)$ **c.** $(0, 9)$

Use = or ≠ for each pair of ratios. *[Lesson 5-2]*

21. $\frac{10}{16} \square \frac{5}{8}$ **22.** $\frac{12}{20} \square \frac{36}{54}$ **23.** $\frac{1}{0.25} \square \frac{3}{0.75}$ **24.** $\frac{2}{1.5} \square \frac{3}{2.5}$

> ### Project Progress
>
> Find the percent increase/decrease from day-to-day on your homework chart. Determine which homework days are the heaviest and lightest for you. Why do you think these are your heaviest/lightest days?

> **Problem Solving**
> Understand
> Plan
> Solve
> Look Back

Applications of Percent Change

▶ **Lesson Link** You have been working with percents in many forms. Now you will learn how percents can be used, combined, and applied. ◀

Explore Combining Percents

How Did I Get Here?

Discuss the following situations. In which situations do you get the original amount back?

1. Judy's Boutique increased the whole-sale price of jewelry by 50%. Then the boutique had a 50%-off sale.

2. Bellas cut its prices by 50%. At the end of the sales promotion, the manager entered a code in the store's computer to increase prices 50%.

3. Michael received a 25% hourly raise, but his work hours were cut by 20%.

4. A company cut its workforce by 50%. New owners increased it by 100%.

You'll Learn …

■ to use and apply percent increase and decrease

■ to calculate simple and compound interest

… How It's Used

Alan Greenspan, Chairman of the Board of Governors of the Federal Reserve System, sets the prime interest rate, the lowest rate one bank can charge another when lending money. Every new bank loan is affected when the prime rate is changed.

Learn Applications of Percent Change

Consumers often need to combine the percent increase and decrease.

Example 1

An airline announced a 15% increase in airfares. But Brenda's company offers employees a 15% discount. How much will Brenda pay for a ticket that cost $179 before the 15% increase?

179 ⊠ 1.15 ⊟ **205.85**   Original price × (100% + 15%).

205.85 ⊠ 0.85 ⊟ **174.9725** ≈ $174.97   Increased price × (100% − 15%).

Brenda will pay $174.97 for her ticket.

Vocabulary

interest

principal

simple interest

compound interest

Example 2

Tickets for the Boyz II Men concert are $35 each, plus a service charge. A 20% discount is offered for tickets purchased two weeks in advance. Compare the price of a ticket under the following conditions.

► History Link

In 1850, tickets to hear Jenny Maria Lind sing in the concert "Swedish Nightingale" sold for as much as $653.

a. 20% discount is applied *before* a 10% service charge:

$35 \times 0.80 = 28$ First apply the 20% discount.

$28 \times 1.10 = 30.8$ Then apply the 10% service charge.

20% discount is applied *after* a 10% service charge:

$35 \times 1.10 = 38.50$ First apply the 10% service charge.

$38.50 \times 0.80 = 30.80$ Then apply the 20% discount.

The price of the ticket is the same, $30.80.

b. 20% discount is applied *before* a $5 service charge is added:

$35 \times 0.80 = 28$ First apply the 20% discount.

$28 + 5 = 33$ Then add the $5 service charge.

20% discount is applied *after* a $5 service charge is added:

$35 + 5 = 40$ First add the $5 service charge.

$40 \times 0.80 = 32$ Then apply the 20% discount.

The ticket is $33 if the discount is applied before the service charge is added, $32 if it is applied after the service charge is added.

Problem Solving TIP

You'll only pay 80% ($4) of the $5 service charge if the discount is applied afterward.

Try It

a. In July, Mrs. Silverman paid $85.13 for electricity. Her August bill was 20% more than her July bill. The weather cooled, and her September bill was 20% less than her August bill. What did she pay for electricity in September?

b. Tickets for the Whitney Houston concert are $40 each, plus a service charge. What is the price of a ticket if a 20% discount is applied...

i. before a 20% service charge is applied?

ii. before a $10 service charge is added?

Sometimes, if something has increased or decreased, you want to know what percent increase or decrease it will take to get back to the original number.

Example 3

In Harry Truman's State of the Union speech of 1946, he noted that factory payrolls had dropped 40% less than two years after World War I ended. If factory payrolls had dropped to $2.325 billion, what had they been? What percent increase would have returned payrolls to their old levels?

If payrolls dropped 40%, they reached 60% of their old level. Find the old level.

$0.60x = 2.325$ Write an equation.

$x = \dfrac{2.325}{0.60}$ Divide both sides by 0.60.

$x = 2.325 \boxed{\div} 0.60 \boxed{=}$ **3.875**   The old level was 3.875 billion.

Payrolls dropped $3.875 - 2.325 = 1.550$ billion. To find the percent increase needed to return payrolls to their old level, find what percent of 2.325 is 1.550.

$x \cdot 2.325 = 1.550$ Write an equation.

$x = \dfrac{1.550}{2.325}$ Divide both sides by 2.325.

$x = 1.550 \boxed{\div} 2.325 \boxed{=}$ **0.6667**

$0.6667 = 66\frac{2}{3}\%$ Change the decimal to a percent.

It would have taken a $66\frac{2}{3}\%$ increase to return payrolls to their old level.

Check: Payrolls dropped to $2.325 billion. If they increased by $66\frac{2}{3}\%$, would they return to $3.875 billion?

$2.325 \boxed{\times} 0.67 \boxed{=}$ **1.55775**   Round $66\frac{2}{3}\%$ to 0.67.

$1.55775 + 2.325 = 3.88275$ Because we rounded, the number is not exact, but it is close to 3.875.

Try It

Tara's expenses increased 25% to $1450 last year. What percent decrease would return expenses to their old levels?

Problem Solving TIP

Solve a simpler problem to find the percent increase that will reverse a certain percent decrease. For example, if payrolls had dropped 40% from $100 to $60, it still takes a $66\frac{2}{3}\%$ increase to return payrolls to their old level.

► History Link

In ancient Greece and Sumeria, the words for interest were the same as the words for calves. When a loan of cows was repaid, the cows were returned with interest—their calves.

Interest is money paid for the use of money. When you deposit money into a savings account, someone else will use your money, so you earn interest. When you borrow money from a bank, you use someone's money, so you pay interest. The amount of money deposited or borrowed is called the **principal**.

When a person receives a loan, interest is charged so that the lender is compensated for not having the money. One way to do this is to charge **simple interest**.

To calculate simple interest, use the following formula.

$I = p \times r \times t$ I = interest, p = principal, r = interest rate, t = time

Example 4

Celia borrowed $800 for 2 years at 15% simple interest. How much interest will she pay? What will her total payment be?

$I = p \times r \times t$ I = interest, p = principal, r = interest rate, t = time in years

$I = 800(0.15)(2) = 240$

The simple interest is $240. She will pay $800 + 240 = \$1040$.

When you get a loan from a bank or a credit card, you actually pay interest on your interest! This is called **compound interest**.

Example 5

Suppose Chandler borrowed $800 for 2 years at 15% interest compounded annually. How much will he owe?

After the first year, he will owe $800(1.15) = \$920$.   1.15 is 100% + 15%

After the second year, he will owe $920(1.15) = \$1058$. Notice that this is $18 more than Celia owed paying simple interest.

DID YOU KNOW?

How often interest compounds is not as important as the rate. 10% annual interest compounded every second for a year is about the same as 10.5% simple interest.

Check   Your Understanding

1. Explain why the item described is not free.

2. Some people compute the tip they leave on the amount of the bill before taxes. Others compute it on the amount after taxes. Who leaves a larger tip?

3. Does a 40% decrease cancel a 40% increase? Why or why not?

Practice and Apply

1. **Getting Started** The original price of a skateboard was $60. To find a 50% increase followed by a $33\frac{1}{3}\%$ increase, answer each question.

   a. What percent do you multiply $60 by to find the new price after the 50% increase?

   b. What is the new price?

   c. What price do you use to find the $33\frac{1}{3}\%$ increase? What percent do you multiply by to find the new price?

   d. What is the price after the $33\frac{1}{3}\%$ increase?

Start with 100. Find each result (+ means increase, − means decrease).

2. +50% followed by +50%

3. −50% followed by −50%

4. +50% followed by −50%

5. −50% followed by +50%

6. +25% followed by −20%

7. −50% followed by +100%

8. −80% followed by +400%

9. +100% followed by −99%

10. **Social Studies** Franklin Roosevelt received 22,825,016 votes in 1932. In 1936, 1940, and 1944, his vote total increased 21.6%, decreased 1.7%, then decreased 6.1% About how many votes did he receive in 1944?

11. **Consumer** During the summer months, prices at a popular resort are 25% higher than during nonsummer months. However, travel club members receive a 20% discount. How much would a room that costs $49.94 during nonsummer months cost a travel club member during the summer?

12. **Consumer** A particular type of carpeting costs $14.95 a square yard plus 10% for installation. How much would you pay per square yard for carpeting and installation during a 20%-off sale? The discount applies to both the carpeting and the installation.

Find the simple interest for each.

13. Savings Account
    Principal: $675
    Rate: 6%
    Time: 3 years

14. Loan
    Principal: $1675
    Rate: 15%
    Time: 4 years

15. Checking Account
    Principal: $2675
    Rate: 7.5%
    Time: 6 months

16. Consumer Cindy earned $74.70 at 9% simple interest on her savings account in 2 years. What was her principal?

17. Sales dropped 20% to $7 million last year. What percent increase would return sales to their level before the drop?

18. [**Test Prep**] Mike deposited $300 and earned $12 in simple interest on his savings account for 6 months. Which of the following equations would you use to find the yearly interest rate on the savings account?

Ⓐ $12 = 300 \cdot 6 \cdot x$ Ⓑ $300 = 12 \cdot 0.5 \cdot x$
Ⓒ $12 = 300 \cdot 0.5 \cdot x$ Ⓓ $300 = 12 \cdot 6 \cdot x$

19. A school district had to cut the number of employees by 10%.

a. If a school district had 1500 employees before the cut, how many employees would it have after the cut?

b. By what percent would the district have to increase the number of employees to get back to the original number of employees?

20. Consumer A used-car dealer bought a car for $1200. To make a profit, the dealer calculated a sticker price that was 20% higher. Eventually the dealer sold the car for 30% less than the sticker price. Did the dealer make money on the car?

21. Music Doubling the 220 Hz frequency of middle C results in high C. In a chromatic scale, each note increases the frequency by about 5.95%. How many notes would it take to reach high C from middle C? (Hint: Use a calculator.)

Problem Solving and Reasoning

22. Math Reasoning Raul found a discount travel agency that offered a 28% discount on the $225 price of a white-water rafting trip down the Colorado River. However, the agency also charges a 10% service fee. Is it better for Raul if the travel agency subtracts the discount and then adds the service fee or if the agency adds the service fee and then subtracts the discount?

23. Critical Thinking A store has increased its wholesale prices 60%. What is the greatest percent of discount it can offer during a sale without selling its products below cost?

24. Communicate Which is better for the customer, computing discounts successively or combining the discounts and then computing? Explain.

Mixed Review

Solve each equation. *[Lesson 3-5]*

25. $2y = 38$ **26.** $\frac{x}{7} = 5$ **27.** $39 = -13a$ **28.** $\frac{2b}{5} = -4$ **29.** $-9p = 3$

Solve each proportion. *[Lesson 5-4]*

30. $\frac{7}{8} = \frac{x}{64}$ **31.** $\frac{2.1}{5.8} = \frac{6.3}{x}$ **32.** $\frac{15}{x} = \frac{150}{80}$ **33.** $\frac{a}{0.2} = \frac{1}{2}$

TECHNOLOGY

Using a Graphing Calculator • Compound Interest

Problem: Which investment strategy will cause your $100 investment to double in the least time: if you earn 6% simple interest or if you earn 4.5% interest compounded monthly?

You can use a graphing calculator to graphically compare simple and compound interest to solve this problem.

1 Let *x* represent years. Enter Y1=100(1+.06X), Y2=100(1+.045/12)^(12X), and Y3=200.

2 Graph all three functions, using a Range of Xmin=0, Xmax=30, Xscl=5, Ymin=100, Ymax=225, and Yscl=10.

3 Find the point where Y1 intersects Y3 and the point where Y2 intersects Y3.

TRY IT

a. Which investment strategy will cause your $100 investment to double in the least time: if you earn 5% simple interest or if you earn 3.5% interest compounded monthly?

b. Which investment strategy will cause your $100 investment to double in the least time: if you earn 4% simple interest or if you earn 2.75% interest compounded daily (use 365 instead of 12)?

Solution: It will take $16\frac{2}{3}$ years to double your investment using the 6% simple interest. It will take about 15.4 years for the investment to double with 4.5% interest compounded monthly.

ON YOUR OWN

▶ How does a graphing calculator help you "see" the solution?

▶ Why do you think Y3 was entered as 200?

▶ Why do you think the compound interest graph curves up from left to right?

TECHNOLOGY

Using a Spreadsheet • Compound Interest

Problem: Which investment strategy will cause your $100 investment to increase the most in 4 years: if you earn 4% interest compounded annually or if you earn 3.75% interest compounded monthly?

A spreadsheet can help you find the answer to this problem.

① Enter the following information in your spreadsheet as shown.

	A	B	C	D	E	F
1	Year	Amount	Annual Rate	Month	Amount	Monthly Rate
2	0	100		0	100	

② Enter the following formulas.
In cell C2, enter =.04.
In cell F2, enter =.0375/12.
In cell A3, enter =A2+1.
In cell B3, enter =B2+B2*C$2.
In cell D3, enter =D2+1.
In cell E3, enter =E2+E2*F$2.

	A	B	C	D	E	F
1	Year	Amount	Annual Rate	Month	Amount	Monthly Rate
2	0	100	0.04	0	100	0.003125
3	1	104		1	100.3125	

③ Select cells A3 to F50 and use the **Fill Down** command.

	A	B	C	D	E	F
1	Year	Amount	Annual Rate	Month	Amount	Monthly Rate
2	0	100	0.04	0	100	0.003125
3	1	104		1	100.3125	
4	2	108.16		2	100.6259	
5	3	112.4864		3	100.9404	
6	4	116.9858		4	101.2558	
50	48	657.0528		48	116.1562	

Solution: $100 at 4% interest compounded annually is $116.99; $100 at 3.75% interest compounded monthly is only $116.16.

TRY IT

Which investment strategy will cause your $100 investment to increase the most in 4 years: if you earn 5% interest compounded annually or if you earn 5% interest compounded quarterly (4 times a year)?

ON YOUR OWN

▶ Which is easier, computing compound interest by calculator or by using a spreadsheet? Explain.

▶ Why must you divide the interest rate by the number of compounding periods?

▶ Why do you have to enter formulas by using the "=" symbol?

In this Section you will connect your knowledge of percents to a situation involving increasing net worth.

The Price Is Right

Materials: Spreadsheet software (optional)

You own a T-shirt company. Your company starts the year with a net worth of $10,000.

1. Place these events in order so that you have the highest net worth at the end of the year.

   a. An increase in sales raises your net worth by 10%.

   b. You must pay $2,000 to repair equipment.

   c. A problem with the shirt manufacturer causes you to lose $5,000.

   d. You collected $15,000 in payments owed.

   e. A decrease in sales causes your net worth to decrease by 10%.

2. Describe the strategy you used.

3. What is your company's net worth at the end?

4. What would the company's net worth have been if the events had occurred in reverse order?

Find the percent increase or decrease. Round to the nearest percent.

1. Old: 4000
   New: 3000

2. Old: 68
   New: 90

3. Old: 990
   New: 990

4. Old: $45.62
   New: $32.75

5. Old: $0.75
   New: $1.00

6. Old: $4250
   New: $5000

7. What is the wholesale price of a tape player if the percent increase is 60% and the amount of increase is $65.98?

8. The percent discount is 40%. The amount of discount is $32.75. What is the original price?

9. The cost of a computer is $3562. The cost before taxes is $3298. What is the tax rate?

10. Find the sales tax on a purchase of $125.53 if the tax rate is 7.5%.

11. Find the sale price of a $63 dress at a 30%-off sale.

Test Prep

Tests always include the most common incorrect answers. Be sure you calculate your percent decrease from the *original* amount.

12. The price of a graphing calculator has dropped from $125.00 to $87.50. Which of the following is the percent decrease?

    Ⓐ 30%　Ⓑ 43%　Ⓒ 70%　Ⓓ 143%

13. NuVideo has 20%-off ticket price sale. Brian was about to buy an XK VCR with a $239.50 ticket price, but decided on a model that was 25% more than the XK's sale price. How much did he pay?

14. Sales dropped 40% to $5 million last year. What percent increase would return sales to their original level?

15. Find the simple interest paid on a loan of $2000 at 15% for 2 years.

16. **Journal** Write and solve a problem involving sales tax in which the final price is given.

17. **Critical Thinking** The price of an answering machine is reduced 15%. The sales tax is 8%. Is the final cost equal to the original price less 7%? Explain.

18. **Critical Thinking** Nellie gets a discount of 10% on all purchases. This week, her shop is having a 15%-off sale. Nellie gets both discounts. If she buys a VCR, which will give her the best price?

    Ⓐ 10% off then 15% off　　Ⓑ 15% off then 10%　　Ⓒ Take 25% off.　　Ⓓ Any of these.

Credit Card Purchases

Yolanda realized when she opened her morning mail that one item would forever change her life. The envelope contained an application for a credit card, which she hurriedly filled out and returned. Soon she received her card and information that she had a credit limit of $1500. It also stated that she would have to pay 18% interest at 1.5% per month on any balance not paid in 30 days.

It didn't take Yolanda long to buy things with her card until she charged to her limit—$1500. Then she realized that she had to pay it off, so she decided not to use the card anymore. The company that issued the card told her that she could make a minimum payment of $20 each month. That's what Yolanda decided to do. That way, she thought she would eventually pay off the entire balance and still have money to spend. But would she?

1. She made her first payment. At 1.5% monthly interest, how much interest was charged for the first month?

2. What was her balance after the first month?

3. She made her second $20 payment. How much interest was charged the second month? What was her balance after the second month?

4. Approximately how long will it take Yolanda to pay off her credit card debt by continuing to make $20 payments?

5. Suppose her payment each month had been $22.17. What would her balance have been after 1 month? After 2 months?

6. What advice would you give Yolanda?

Graphic Organizer

Understanding percents

Write

Percent

Fraction — Decimal

Solve

Equation

Proportion

% < 1, % > 100, 1% –100%

Using Estimates

Compatible numbers

Fractions

Increase

Decrease

Combine

Problem Solving with Percents

Interest

Simple

Compound

Section 6A Understanding Percents

Summary

- A **percent** is a ratio that compares a number to 100. *Percent* means "parts per hundred," "hundredths," or "out of every hundred."

- You often see percents represented in a **circle graph** or pie chart.

- You can rewrite a ratio as a decimal, as a fraction, or as a percent.

- Percent problems can be solved by using a proportion or writing an equation.

- When estimating percents, it is often helpful to use compatible numbers or to use fractions that are close to a given percent.

Review

1. Write the fraction, decimal, and percent that tell how much of the figure is shaded.

2. Use the information in the circle graph.

   a. What percent of the students in the Garden Club are freshmen?

   b. What percent of the students in the Garden Club are sophomores?

   c. What percent of the students in the Garden Club are juniors or seniors?

3. What number is 35% of 460?

4. 18 is 24% of what number?

Students in the Garden Club

28%

16%

32%

24%

- Freshmen
- Sophomores
- Juniors
- Seniors

5. Of the passengers on an international flight, 36% were American. If there were 81 American passengers, how many passengers were on the plane all together?

6. Estimate the percent of the figure that is shaded.

7. Estimate the percent: 69 out of 710.

8. Estimate 26% of 157.

Section 6B Problem Solving with Percents

Summary

- The difference between the retail price and the wholesale price can be represented as the percent markup or **percent increase**.

- To find the percent increase, subtract the wholesale price from the retail price and divide the difference by the wholesale price.

- Store owners sometimes decrease the price of merchandise. The amount of decrease, or discount, can be represented as the **percent decrease**.

- To find the percent decrease, subtract the sale price from the retail price and divide the difference by the original retail price.

- **Interest** is money paid for the use of money. The amount of money deposited or borrowed is called the **principal**. You can calculate the **simple interest** by using the formula $I = p \times r \times t$, where I = interest, p = principal, r = interest rate, and t = time.

Review

9. Jenny's buys a box of cereal for $2.15 and sells it for $2.95. What is the percent increase?

10. Lupe bought a model airplane priced at $49.95. What was the tax rate if she had to pay $53.20 with tax?

11. Find the total cost of a $21 toaster with a price increase of 16%.

12. A compact disc player normally sells for $260. Find its price during a 15%-off sale.

13. Find the percent decrease of a stock that went from $55 to $14.

14. Makzan earned $540 in simple interest on his savings account in 3 years. If the interest rate was 7.5%, what was his principal?

15. The Jackson family purchased a home for $120,000. Later they sold it at an increase of 24%, but their real estate agent took 6% of the selling price. What amount did the Jacksons receive when they sold the house?

16. A used-car dealer bought a station wagon for $3500 and tried to sell it for a sticker price that was 30% higher. Eventually he sold it and broke even (no profit or loss). What was the percent discount from the sticker price?

Chapter 6 Assessment

1. Use the information in the circle graph.

   a. What percent of the animals at Barney's Pet Store are dogs?

   b. What percent of the animals at Barney's are not dogs or cats?

   c. There are 58 animals at Barney's. How many are cats?

Animals at Barney's Pets

- Dogs
- Cats
- Fish
- Birds
- Other

12% 7% 41% 31% 9%

2. Write the fraction, decimal, and percent that tells how much of the figure is shaded.

3. A serving of tom kha soup contains 18 g of fat, which is 90% of the maximum recommended daily value. What is the maximum recommended daily value for fat?

4. Write 62% as a fraction in lowest terms and as a decimal.

5. **a.** What percent of 64 is 40?

   b. 15% of what number is 57?

6. Estimate the percent: 119 out of 600.

7. Estimate 32% of 3120.

8. Estimate the percent of the shaded region.

9. Find the percent increase or decrease for each and specify whether it is an increase or decrease.

   a. Old 642; new 890   **b.** Old 385; new 246

10. Jimbo's Market sells mushrooms for the retail price of $2.19 per lb after a 24% increase. What was the wholesale price?

11. Find the cost of a $220 computer tape drive with a price increase of 14%.

12. A dress normally sells for $180. Find its price during an 18%-off sale.

13. A $2100 computer is now $1750. Find the percent of discount.

14. During a 16%-off sale, Reggie bought a television that was originally priced at $425. He also had to pay 8% sales tax. How much did he pay for the television set, including tax?

15. Lou bought a roll-top desk for $265 and tried to sell it for an asking price that was 42% higher. Eventually he sold it for the same price as the purchase price. What was the percent discount from the asking price?

16. Randi opened a savings account with $850. If the account earned 5% simple interest, what was the balance in the account after 3 years?

Performance Task

Draw pictures to represent 0%, 10%, 20%, 30%, 40%, 50%, 60%, 70%, 80%, 90%, and 100%. Be creative! How would you draw a picture to represent 150%?

Multiple Choice

Choose the best answer.

1. Which of the following is equal to 10?
[Lessons 2-2, 2-3, 2-4]

Ⓐ $12 - (-2)$ Ⓑ $20 - 2 \times 5$

Ⓒ $8 + (-2)$ Ⓓ $1 + 4 \times 2$

2. Which of the following represents 43,200,000 in scientific notation?
[Lesson 2-9]

Ⓐ 4.32×10^7 Ⓑ 4.32×10^8

Ⓒ 43.2×10^6 Ⓓ 0.432×10^8

3. Solve $8x + 6 = 102$. *[Lesson 3-6]*

Ⓐ $x = 10.5$ Ⓑ $x = 12$

Ⓒ $x = 13.5$ Ⓓ $x = 15$

4. $x = 12$ is a solution of which inequality?
[Lesson 3-7]

Ⓐ $-3x + 7 < -30$ Ⓑ $2x - 5 > 20$

Ⓒ $-2x + 4 > -20$ Ⓓ $3x - 5 > 30$

5. Which of the following is **not** a solution of the equation $5x - 3y = 4$? *[Lesson 4-2]*

Ⓐ $(-1, -3)$ Ⓑ $(2, 2)$

Ⓒ $(5, 6)$ Ⓓ $(8, 12)$

6. Find the slope of the line through $(3, -2)$ and $(1, 4)$. *[Lesson 4-4]*

Ⓐ 3 Ⓑ -3 Ⓒ $-\frac{3}{5}$ Ⓓ $-\frac{1}{3}$

7. Is the table below an equal ratio table? If so, find k. *[Lesson 5-3]*

x	2	4	6	10
y	3	6	9	15

Ⓐ $\frac{2}{3}$ Ⓑ $\frac{3}{2}$ Ⓒ $\frac{15}{2}$

Ⓓ Not an equal ratio table

8. Solve the proportion for t: $\frac{20}{35} = \frac{16}{t}$.
[Lesson 5-4]

Ⓐ 21 Ⓑ 25 Ⓒ 28 Ⓓ 43.75

9. Which of the following is **not** a unit rate?
[Lesson 5-5]

Ⓐ 1 CD for $14 Ⓑ 65 mi/hr

Ⓒ $9 for 1 hr Ⓓ 42 g in 1 serving

10. Which is the largest scale listed below that can be used to make a scale drawing of a 35 in. $\times$ 42 in. painting on an 8.5 in. $\times$ 11 in. sheet of paper? *[Lesson 5-7]*

Ⓐ 1:3 Ⓑ 1:4 Ⓒ 1:5 Ⓓ 1:6

11. Which percent tells how much of the figure is shaded? *[Lesson 6-1]*

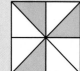

Ⓐ 25% Ⓑ 30%

Ⓒ 37.5% Ⓓ 40%

12. 70 is 35% of what number? *[Lesson 6-2]*

Ⓐ 24.5 Ⓑ 50 Ⓒ 140 Ⓓ 200

13. Estimate 78% of 7684. *[Lesson 6-3]*

Ⓐ 5000 Ⓑ 5500 Ⓒ 6000 Ⓓ 6500

14. A customer in a restaurant left $18.25 on the table for a $16.00 dinner. If there was no tax, what percent did the customer tip?
[Lesson 6-4]

Ⓐ 12% Ⓑ 14% Ⓒ 16% Ⓓ 18%

15. A store in the mall is discounting shirts 24% this week. How much will you pay for a shirt that is regularly $29.99? *[Lesson 6-5]*

Ⓐ $7.20 Ⓑ $22.79 Ⓒ $25.79 Ⓓ $37.19

16. Monique earned $504 simple interest in 4 years. If the interest rate was 6%, what was her principal? *[Lesson 6-6]*

Ⓐ $2100 Ⓑ $2500 Ⓒ $3200 Ⓓ $8400

Cultural Link
www.mathsurf.com/8/ch7/people

Arts & Literature Link
www.mathsurf.com/8/ch7/arts

People of the World

Babatunde Olatunji, a master drummer originally from Nigeria, refers to repeating decimals when describing recurring patterns in drum rhythms.

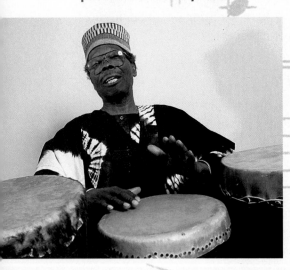

Entertainment

In the 500s B.C., Pythagoras concluded that musical tones that combine to give pleasing harmonies have small arithmetic ratios to one another, such as 1:1, 2:1, 3:2, and 4:3.

Arts & Literature

Within the beauty of poetry, stanzas of poems often fit a framework of numbers of syllables and lines. The Japanese Haiku consists of 17 syllables in a 5 - 7 - 5 pattern.
Kono michi ya
Yuku hito nashi ni
Aki no kure

and Irrational Numbers

Social Studies Link
www.mathsurf.com/8/ch7/social

Social Studies

In 1917, the British Secret Service deciphered a numerical telegram from the German foreign minister, Arthur Zimmerman, to his minister in Mexico. It communicated that if the U.S. entered the war, then Mexico would join Germany and reclaim Texas, New Mexico, and Arizona. It is now a historical document called the *Zimmerman telegram*.

KEY MATH IDEAS

Greatest common multiples (GCM) and least common factors (LCF) are used when working with fractions.

If a number can be written as a terminating decimal or a repeating decimal then it is a rational number.

The square root of a number can be positive or negative.

The Pythagorean theorem is a formula that can be used for all right triangles.

Science

In a sunflower center, the number of clockwise-curving spirals and the number of counterclockwise-curving spirals are two consecutive numbers in the Fibonacci sequence, such as 34 and 21 or 89 and 55.

CHAPTER PROJECT

Problem Solving

Understand
Plan
Solve
Look Back

In this project, you will choose a stock from the newspaper to "adopt" and report your investment strategies. Start with $500 to invest. Buy any stock. Record and monitor the progress of your investment (for example, cost per share, number of shares purchased, daily gains and losses). Write a summary of your investment and give advice to future investors.

Problem Solving Focus

For each problem, identify the additional information needed to solve the problem. Some of the problems are not missing any information.

Identifying Missing Information

Evaluating information is important to solving a problem. When you plan, you need to recognize when necessary information is not given in the problem.

1 Approximately 516,000 high school students play inter-scholastic basketball. About 148,000 are seniors. Estimate the percent of high school interscholastic basketball players who are seniors.

2 There are about 4,000 college basketball scholarships available for these 148,000 seniors to fill. Estimate the percent of college basketball players who receive scholarships.

3 Fewer than 3 in 100, or 2.5%, of seniors who play college basketball go on to play professionally. How does that figure compare with the percent of college seniors who go on to play professional football?

4 The average professional basketball player has a career span of three to four years. However, many superstars like Michael Jordan play for many more years than the average player. What percent of professional basketball players play more than the average number of years?

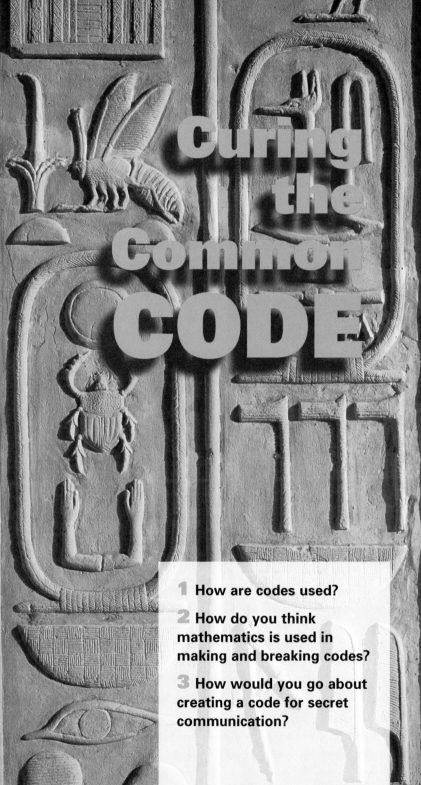

Curing the Common CODE

Smoke signals, Morse code, Braille, binary code, area codes, zip codes, bar codes—codes can be found everywhere. They've been used throughout history for various purposes.

A *Vigenère tableau* was based on shifted alphabets and could be compared to reading a coordinate grid. Using the key *LAMP* the message "code" is deciphered:

Encoded Message: NOPP
Key: LAMP
Decoded Message: CODE

In 1835, Morse code was developed by ex-painter Samuel Morse and Alfred Vail. The first telegraph message, using short electric pulses called dots and dashes, followed a few years later.

During World War II, the Germans used a code generated by a machine called "Enigma" to communicate the strategic positions of their U-boats (submarines). Without the Germans' knowledge, the Allies broke Enigma's code and escaped the destruction once caused by the German U-boats.

1 How are codes used?

2 How do you think mathematics is used in making and breaking codes?

3 How would you go about creating a code for secret communication?

323

7-1 Divisibility Patterns and Prime Factorization

You'll Learn ...

■ to use rules for determining whether a number is divisible by another number

... How It's Used

Egyptologists use divisibility to decipher patterns used in hieroglyphics.

Vocabulary

prime number

composite number

divisible

multiple

factor

prime factor

Fundamental Theorem of Arithmetic

prime factorization

▶ **Lesson Link** You have used patterns to solve problems. Now you will use patterns to determine whether a number divides without a remainder. ◀

A **prime number** is an integer larger than 1 that is only divisible by itself and 1.

Prime numbers: 2, 3, 5, 7, 11, ...

A **composite number** is a positive integer that is not prime. It has factors other than 1 and itself.

Composite numbers: 4, 6, 8, 9, 10, ...

Explore   Primes and Composites

The Chart Is Smart

Materials: Hundred chart

1. Circle 2 and cross out all the other multiples of 2.

2. Circle the next number that has not been crossed out and cross out all of its multiples.

3. Continue this process until all numbers except 1 are either circled or crossed out.

4. Did you use any shortcuts in this process? Describe.

5. Are the circled numbers prime numbers or composite numbers? How do you know?

1	2	3	4	5	6	7	8	9	10
11	12	13	14	15	16	17	18	19	20
21	22	23	24	25	26	27	28	29	30
31	32	33	34	35	36	37	38	39	40
41	42	43	44	45	46	47	48	49	50
51	52	53	54	55	56	57	58	59	60
61	62	63	64	65	66	67	68	69	70
71	72	73	74	75	76	77	78	79	80
81	82	83	84	85	86	87	88	89	90
91	92	93	94	95	96	97	98	99	100

Learn   Divisibility Patterns and Prime Factorization

We say that 15 is **divisible** by 5 because 15 divided by 5 has no remainder.

We say that 15 is a **multiple** of 5 because 15 is divisible by 5.

We say that 5 is a **factor** of 15 because 15 is divisible by 5.

$200 \div 4 = 50$ 4 and 50 are *factors* of 200.

$4 \times 50 = 200$ 200 is a *multiple* of 4 and 50.

Divisibility rules can tell if a given number is divisible by another number.

	Divisibility Rule
2	The ones digit is a *2, 4, 6, 8,* or *0.*
3	The sum of the number's digits is divisible by *3.*
4	As a number, the last two digits are divisible by *4.*
5	The number ends in *5* or *0.*
6	The number is divisible by *2* and *3.*
8	As a number, the last three digits are divisible by *8.*
9	The sum of the number's digits is divisible by *9.*
10	The ones digit is *0.*

Remember

Even numbers are all divisible by 2. [Previous course]

Example 1

Enemy X always end their secret messages with a number divisible by 3 and 5, and not 8. A suspicious message ending with 5385 was found. State the divisibility rules that satisfy 5385 to find out if it's from Enemy X.

► **Career Link**

A cryptanalyst's job is to encipher and decipher codes.

Divisible by 2, 4, 6, 8, or 10?   5385 is odd so it's not divisible by an even number.

No, because it is not even.   Eliminate the even numbers.

By 5? Yes, because it ends with 5.   Test for divisibility by an odd number.

By 3? Yes, because 5 + 3 + 8 + 5 = 21 is divisible by 3.

By 9? No, because 5 + 3 + 8 + 5 = 21 is not divisible by 9.

5385 is divisible by 3 and 5, and not 8, so the message is from Enemy X.

Try It

Is each number divisible by 2, 3, 4, 5, 6, 8, 9, or 10?

a. 38   **b.** 240   **c.** 236   **d.** 345

A **prime factor** of a number is a factor that is a prime number. For example:

List all factors of 36 and identify the primes.   1, 2, 3, 4, 6, 9, 12, 18, 36

2 and 3 are the prime factors of 36.

FUNDAMENTAL THEOREM OF ARITHMETIC

All integers greater than 1 are prime or can be written as a unique product of prime numbers.

Prime factorization is the result of writing a number as a product of prime numbers. The prime factorization of a number can be found using a factor tree.

Prime factorization is written in standard form using exponents, with factors in increasing order.

$24 = 2 \times 2 \times 2 \times 3 = 2^3 \times 3$

$2^3 \times 3$ is the prime factorization of 24.

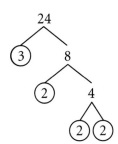

Example 2

Use a factor tree to find the prime factorization of 140.

Draw branches for 140.

Circle 2 because it's prime.

Circle 7 because it's prime.

Circle 2 because it's prime.

Factor 140.

Factor 70 because it's composite.

Factor 10 because it's composite.

Circle 5 because it's prime.

$140 = 2 \times 7 \times 2 \times 5$ Write 140 as a product of the prime numbers.

$140 = 2^2 \times 5 \times 7$ Write in standard form.

$2^2 \times 5 \times 7$ is the prime factorization of 140.

Example 3

The message to the right provides the address for a secret party. You were informed to find the prime factorization for the address.

Secret Party

When? **3:30 p.m.**
Where? **Oak St.**
(you know what to do with the time)

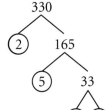

Draw a factor tree for 330.

Write the prime factorization in standard form.

$330 = 2 \times 3 \times 5 \times 11$

The address could be 23511 Oak Street.

Try It

Use a factor tree to find the prime factorization of each number.

a. 54   **b.** 132   **c.** 236   **d.** 354

WHAT DO YOU THINK?

What is the prime factorization of 138?

Steve thinks ...

138 is obviously even because it ends with 8.

69 is divisible by 3 because $6 + 9 = 15$ is divisible by 3.

Hmm. ... The divisibility tests don't work for 23, so 23 is prime.

I'm done because 2, 3, and 23 are all prime.

The prime factorization for 138 is $2 \times 3 \times 23$.

Tanisha thinks ...

I can use a factor tree to find the prime factorization.

I've circled all the prime numbers.

The ends of all the branches are circled, so I'm done.

Well, $2 \times 3 \times 23$ is the prime factorization for 138.

What do you think?

1. What is the difference between Steve's and Tanisha's methods?

2. Why did both Steve and Tanisha stop when they found out 2, 3, and 23 are all prime?

3. How would you find the prime factorization for a number?

Check Your Understanding

1. Which divisibility rules are similar? Explain.

2. How many prime numbers are there? Explain.

3. Describe how factor trees are related to the Fundamental Theorem of Arithmetic.

Practice and Apply

Getting Started State whether each number is prime or composite.

1. 17 **2.** 28 **3.** 49 **4.** 42 **5.** 31

Determine whether each given number is divisible by 2, 3, 4, 5, 6, 8, 9, or 10.

6. 45 **7.** 63 **8.** 79 **9.** 86 **10.** 102

11. 261 **12.** 636 **13.** 5354 **14.** 8004 **15.** 4672

List all of the factors for each number and identify the prime factors.

16. 70 **17.** 88 **18.** 96 **19.** 100 **20.** 138

Use a factor tree to determine the prime factorization of each number.
Express your answer using exponents.

21. 54 **22.** 80 **23.** 128 **24.** 156 **25.** 220

26. 333 **27.** 375 **28.** 480 **29.** 505 **30.** 1238

31. **Test Prep** Which of the following is the prime factorization of 42?

Ⓐ 6×7 Ⓑ 2×21 Ⓒ 23×7 Ⓓ $2 \times 3 \times 7$

32. **Industry** A software company identifies its CD-ROMs with serial numbers. They use a six-digit code where the first five digits are divisible by the last digit. Are the following serial numbers from an imitation CD-ROM?

a. 34569-3   **b.** 88888-6

Algebra The equations below involve prime factorization.
Solve for the variable in each equation.

33. $n = 3^4$ **34.** $k = 2^3 \times 7$

35. $w = 2 \times 5^4$ **36.** $g = 3 \times 5 \times 17$

37. **Science** The Kamchatka Brown Bear lives in Russia. The male weighs up to 360 kilograms. Use a factor tree to find the prime factorization of 360. Express your answer using exponents.

38. **Science** Every 17 years, cicadas emerge from dormancy in the Northeast and Midwest. This happened in Maryland in 1996. In what years will the next three outbreaks occur?

39. An eighth-grade class took care of 102 guppies and 136 mollies in the classroom aquarium. Each student took home an equal number of guppies and mollies. What is the greatest number of students there can be in the class?

40. **Logic** Solve this puzzle: "The number is greater than 500 and less than 550. The number is odd and is a multiple of 9 and the ones digit is 1. What is the number?"

41. **History** Marin Mersenne (1588–1648), a French mathematician, invented the Mersenne number $2^n - 1$. You can find Mersenne numbers by substituting integers for n. Prime numbers found using this formula are called Mersenne primes. Find two Mersenne primes.

Problem Solving and Reasoning

42. **Communicate** If you scramble the digits in a number that is divisible by 3, the number is still divisible by three. Does this work for numbers divisible by 2? By 4? By 5? By 8? By 9? Explain.

43. **Math Reasoning** A number is divisible by 12 if it is divisible by both 3 and 4. Find three multiples of 12 and explain why those numbers are divisible by 12 according to this rule.

44. [Journal] Devise a divisibility rule for 25. Show examples and explain why your rule works.

45. [Test Prep] The divisibility rule for 11 is this: Calculate the sum of every other digit. Calculate the sum of the other digits. Take the difference of the two sums. If the result is a multiple of 11, then the original number is a multiple of 11. Which of the following is a multiple of 11?

Ⓐ 3577   Ⓑ 4818   Ⓒ 7575   Ⓓ 111

Mixed Review

Find the slope of each line, given the coordinates A (0, 0), B (6, 3), C (−4, 5), D (−1, −2). *[Lesson 4-4]*

46. Line through A and B   47. Line through A and C

48. Line through C and D   49. Line through B and D

50. It takes a video editor 10 hours to edit 8 minutes of video. At this rate, how long would it take to edit 30 minutes of video? *[Lesson 5-6]*

Greatest Common Factors (GCF)

You'll Learn ...

■ to find the GCF of two or more numbers

... How It's Used

When carpenters and other craftspeople use fractions, they need the GCF.

Vocabulary

common factor

greatest common factor (GCF)

▶ **Lesson Link**   You have used divisibility rules to find prime factors of numbers. Now you will use these skills to find common factors between numbers. ◀

When two numbers have matching factors, they are called **common factors** .

Factors of 12 are 1, 2, 3, 4, 6, 12.   Factors of 16 are 1, 2, 4, 8, 16.

Common factors of 12 and 16 are 1, 2, and 4.

Explore   **Greatest Common Factor**

Birthday Connections

1. Write the month and the date of your birthday. Use a number for the month: January = 1, February = 2, and so on. Find the product of the month and date.

2. Find the prime factorization for this number.

3. List the factors that are common to every group member.

4. Multiply the common factors together.

5. Divide each of your group member's original products by this product. What happens?

Learn   **Greatest Common Factors (GCF)**

The **greatest common factor (GCF)** is the largest number of two or more numbers that is a common factor.

You can make a list of the common factors to find the GCF.

Factors of 12 are 1, 2, 3, 4, 6, 12.   Factors of 16 are 1, 2, 4, 8, 16.

The common factors are 1, 2, 4.

The greatest common factor of 12 and 16 is 4.

Example 1

Find the GCF of 36 and 48.

1, 2, 3, 4, 6, 9, 12, 18, 36   List all the factors of 36.

1, 2, 3, 4, 6, 8, 12, 16, 24, 48   List all the factors of 48.

1, 2, 3, 4, 6, 12   List the common factors.

The GCF of 36 and 48 is 12.

Making a list to find the GCF for larger numbers can be impractical.

The GCF can also be found using prime factorization.

The GCF is found by multiplying together the smallest power of each common prime factor.

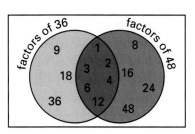

Example 2

Use prime factorization to find the GCF of 378 and 180.

Draw a factor tree for each number.

Write each prime factorization.

$378 = 3 \times 3 \times 2 \times 3 \times 7 = 2 \times 3^3 \times 7$

$180 = 2 \times 3 \times 3 \times 2 \times 5 = 2^2 \times 3^2 \times 5$

Identify the common prime factors.

2 and 3^2 are the smallest power of each common prime factor.

$2 \times 3^2 = 18$ Multiply the smallest power of each prime factor.

The GCF of 378 and 180 is 18.

Try It

Use prime factorization to find the GCF of each pair of numbers.

a. 72 and 138   **b.** 49 and 21   **c.** 276 and 136

You would use the same procedure of multiplying the smallest power of each common prime factor to find the GCF of more than two numbers.

Example 3

A juice company has a contest with twist-off caps. Each winner must provide the nine-digit code on the bottle. The winner is legitimate if the GCF of the code numbers is 28. Is 140-308-420 a winner?

Find the GCF of 140, 308, and 420.   Find the prime factorization for each number.

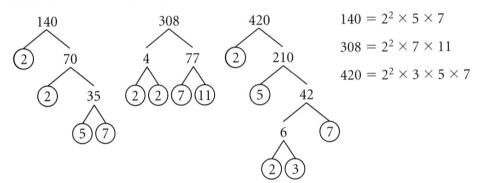

$140 = 2^2 \times 5 \times 7$

$308 = 2^2 \times 7 \times 11$

$420 = 2^2 \times 3 \times 5 \times 7$

$2^2 \times 7 = 28$ It's a winner because the GCF is 28.

Problem Solving **TIP**

If you're used to working with only two numbers and you're asked to work with three, the same technique will be effective.

The GCF is used when writing a fraction in lowest terms.

Example 4

Write $\frac{36}{42}$ in lowest terms.

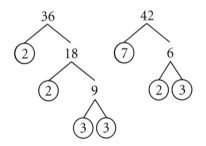

$36 = 2^2 \times 3^2$ and $42 = 2 \times 3 \times 7$

$2 \times 3 = 6$ is the GCF of 36 and 42.

$\frac{36 \div 6}{42 \div 6} = \frac{6}{7}$ is written in lowest terms.

Try It

a. Find the GCF of 455, 230, and 160.   **b.** Write $\frac{9}{12}$ in lowest terms.

Check | Your Understanding

1. Explain how you would find the GCF of three numbers.

2. Explain how the GCF is used when writing a fraction in lowest terms.

Practice and Apply

1. **Getting Started** Use the following steps to find the GCF of 27 and 45:
   a. List all the factors of 27.   **b.** List all the factors of 45.
   c. List the common factors.   **d.** Identify the greatest common factor.

Find the GCF of each group of numbers.

2. 12, 40   **3.** 8, 12   **4.** 9, 15   **5.** 28, 35   **6.** 6, 8, 14

7. 27, 63   **8.** 15, 90   **9.** 30, 60   **10.** 75, 100   **11.** 32, 56, 72

Use prime factorization to find the GCF of each group of numbers.

12. 75, 135   **13.** 56, 132   **14.** 33, 110   **15.** 70, 14   **16.** 34, 102

17. 20, 25, 50   **18.** 17, 31, 37   **19.** 24, 48, 60   **20.** 35, 45, 63   **21.** 18, 26, 72

Write each fraction in lowest terms.

22. $\dfrac{6}{8}$ **23.** $\dfrac{10}{25}$ **24.** $\dfrac{4}{12}$ **25.** $\dfrac{9}{36}$ **26.** $\dfrac{30}{40}$

27. $\dfrac{45}{50}$ **28.** $\dfrac{24}{36}$ **29.** $\dfrac{34}{51}$ **30.** $\dfrac{250}{300}$ **31.** $\dfrac{66}{121}$

32. Find a pair of numbers that has a GCF of 42.

33. **Geography** An airline is having a contest: If your three-digit area code and 20 have a GCF ≥ 4, you can enter the drawing for round-trip tickets to anywhere in the United States. Which area codes in Texas qualify?

34. The following message is based on a code that uses ordered pairs. If the GCF = 1 the pair stands for A. If the GCF = 2 the pair stands for B. The pattern continues until the GCF = 26 = Z. Decipher this message: (9, 6) (16, 24) (15, 10) (6, 39) (22, 121)!

35. **Algebra** Two numbers have a greatest common factor of $x(x^2 + 2x + 1)$. Substitute $x = 2$ to find the greatest common factor. Write the greatest common factor using prime factorization.

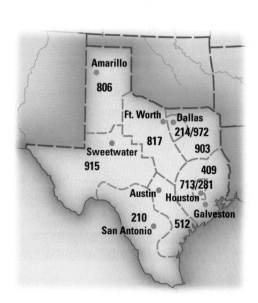

36. Science Dr. Pascal studies the effects of light sources on house plants. The number of plants in each class are 24, 30, 36, and 42. He wants to subdivide the classes into groups of the same size for the research project. What is the largest group size that will work in all four classes?

37. **Test Prep** Which pair of numbers does not have 4 as a common factor?

Ⓐ 12, 14   Ⓑ 24, 36   Ⓒ 40, 60   Ⓓ 36, 44

38. The first two numbers in Lucia's lock combination are 12 and 16 and the last number in her combination is the GCF of 12 and 16. What is Lucia's combination?

Problem Solving and Reasoning

39. Critical Thinking Two numbers that have a GCF of 1 are said to be *relatively prime.* The numbers may be prime or composite. Find three pairs of relative primes.

40. Choose a Strategy I am a number less than 100. I am relatively prime with 99. If I am paired with 100, I am our GCF. If I am paired with 25, 25 is the GCF and not me. What number am I?

41. Communicate Select two prime numbers. What is their GCF? Will any pair of prime numbers have the same GCF? Explain.

42. Geometry Draw a rectangle that has sides with lengths that have a GCF of 5, and that has a perimeter that is a multiple of 4.

> **Problem Solving**
> ## STRATEGIES
>
> • Look for a Pattern
> • Make an Organized List
> • Make a Table
> • Guess and Check
> • Work Backward
> • Use Logical Reasoning
> • Draw a Diagram
> • Solve a Simpler Problem

Mixed Review

Graph each equation. Find the slope, the *x*-intercept, and the *y*-intercept for each of the following. *[Lesson 4-5]*

43. $y = 2x - 4$ **44.** $y = x - 9$ **45.** $y = -3x + 8$ **46.** $y = \frac{1}{3}x + 6$ **47.** $y = -7x$

48. An eye in a photograph is 13.5 cm long and is labeled "enlarged 9 times." What is the actual length of the eye? *[Lesson 5-7]*

Project Progress

Think about how you use your knowledge of factors, multiples, and divisibility to decide how many shares of a stock to buy.

> **Problem Solving**
>
> Understand
> Plan
> Solve
> Look Back

Least Common Multiples (LCM)

▶ Lesson Link You applied your knowledge of factors to finding the greatest common factor. Now you will apply your knowledge of multiples to find the least common multiple. ◀

When two numbers have some multiples that are the same, these multiples are called **common multiples** .

Multiples of 3 are 3, 6, 9, 12, 15, 18, 21, 24, …

Multiples of 4 are 4, 8, 12, 16, 20, 24, 28, …

Common multiples of 3 and 4 are 12, 24, …

You'll Learn …

■ to find the LCM of two or more numbers

… How It's Used

Architects and others who use rational numbers need the LCM when performing operations such as addition and subtraction.

Vocabulary

common multiple

least common multiple (LCM)

Explore Common Multiples

Numbers Zip Something in Common

Everyone must remember numbers: phone numbers, zip codes, area codes, birthdates, ages, addresses, and so on.

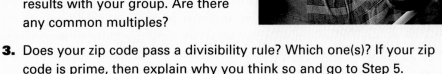

1. What numbers do your group members have in common?

2. Find the first four multiples of your street address. Compare your results with your group. Are there any common multiples?

3. Does your zip code pass a divisibility rule? Which one(s)? If your zip code is prime, then explain why you think so and go to Step 5.

4. Name a number that is a factor of your zip code. Find a number that is a multiple of that factor and that is closest to your zip code, but is not your zip code.

5. Find two multiples of your zip code. Discuss how you did it.

Learn Least Common Multiples (LCM)

The **least common multiple (LCM)** is the smallest non-zero common multiple.

You can make a list of the common multiples to find the LCM.

Example 1

Paul makes $3 an hour for watering his parents' garden and $7 an hour for mowing the lawn. Find the least common multiple of 3 and 7.

3, 6, 9, 12, 15, 18, 21, 24, 27, 30, 33, 36, 39, 42, 45, …   List multiples of 3.

7, 14, 21, 28, 35, 42, 49, 56, 63, 70, 77, 84, 91, 98, 105, …   List multiples of 7.

21, 42, …   List the common multiples.

The least common multiple is 21.
Identify the least common multiple.

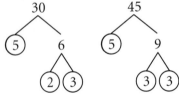

Making a list to find the LCM for larger numbers can be impractical.

The LCM can also be found using prime factorization.

The LCM is found by multiplying the highest power of each prime factor.

Example 2

Use prime factorization to find the LCM of 30 and 45.

Draw a factor tree for each number.

Circle all of the prime factors.

$30 = 2 \times 3 \times 5$ Find the prime factorization for each number.

$45 = 3^2 \times 5$

$2, 3^2,$ and 5 Identify the highest power of each prime factor.

$2 \times 3^2 \times 5 = 2 \times 9 \times 5 = 90$ Multiply.

The LCM of 30 and 45 is 90.

Try It

Use prime factorization to find the LCM of the following pairs of numbers.

a. 6 and 5   **b.** 49 and 21   **c.** 276 and 136

You would use the same procedure to find the LCM of more than two numbers.

Example 3

Cara bought an answering machine with a feature to check messages when she's not at home, but Cara needs a code. For the code, she wants to use the LCM of the numbers in her birthday 6/24/86. What's Cara's code?

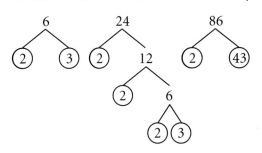

Find the prime factorization.

$$6 = 2 \times 3$$

$$24 = 2^3 \times 3$$

$$86 = 2 \times 43$$

$$2^3 \times 3 \times 43 = 1032 \quad \text{Multiply.}$$

Cara's answering machine code is 1032.

The least common denominator (LCD) is a least common multiple (LCM).

Example 4

Write $\frac{1}{6}$ and $\frac{5}{8}$ using their LCD.

You need to find the LCM of 6 and 8.

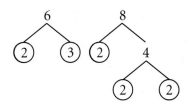

Determine the prime factorization.

$$6 = 2 \times 3$$

$$8 = 2^3$$

$$2^3 \times 3 = 8 \times 3 = 24 \quad \text{Multiply.}$$

$$\frac{1 \times 4}{6 \times 4} = \frac{4}{24} \qquad \frac{5 \times 3}{8 \times 3} = \frac{15}{24}$$

$$\frac{1}{6} = \frac{4}{24} \text{ and } \frac{5}{8} = \frac{15}{24}$$

Try It

Write each pair of fractions using its LCD.

a. $\frac{2}{7}$ and $\frac{2}{3}$ **b.** $\frac{7}{12}$ and $\frac{5}{16}$

Study TIP

Make connections with what you learn to remember it better, such as "fractions" and "LCM."

Check | Your Understanding

1. Explain how you would find the LCM of three numbers.

2. Explain how the LCM is used to find the LCD.

Practice and Apply

1. **Getting Started** Use the following steps to find the LCM of 8 and 12.
   - **a.** List the first ten multiples of 8.
   - **b.** List the first ten multiples of 12.
   - **c.** List the common multiples.
   - **d.** Identify the least common multiple.

Find the LCM for each pair of numbers.

2. 12, 20   3. 8, 20   4. 4, 25   5. 15, 20   6. 25, 50

7. 36, 48   8. 10, 80   9. 60, 30   10. 42, 12   11. 7, 12

Use prime factorization to find the LCM for each group of numbers.

12. 14, 52   13. 22, 8   14. 13, 11   15. 24, 62   16. 47, 32

17. 3, 4, 15   18. 6, 8, 36   19. 14, 56, 125   20. 12, 20, 42   21. 24, 13, 11

22. **Science** Suppose Earth and Mars were aligned with the sun. Earth completes its orbit in 365 days and Mars completes its orbit in 687 days (orbits rounded to the nearest Earth day). When do both planets return to these same positions in their orbits?

Rewrite each group of fractions with the LCD.

23. $\frac{2}{3}$ and $\frac{1}{6}$ 24. $\frac{3}{5}$ and $\frac{2}{15}$ 25. $\frac{3}{8}$ and $\frac{3}{4}$

26. $\frac{1}{2}$ and $\frac{1}{8}$ 27. $\frac{5}{9}$ and $\frac{5}{12}$ 28. $\frac{8}{15}$ and $\frac{7}{30}$

29. $\frac{3}{4}, \frac{2}{3}$, and $\frac{7}{10}$ 30. $\frac{1}{8}, \frac{4}{7}$, and $\frac{7}{12}$ 31. $\frac{1}{9}, \frac{4}{14}$, and $\frac{5}{12}$ 32. $\frac{4}{11}, \frac{5}{7}$, and $\frac{7}{12}$

33. **Industry** A city recycling program picks up different plastics on different days. Use the codes for plastic containers shown at the right to determine when it picks up all plastics on one day.

34. **Algebra** Two numbers have a least common multiple of $k^3 + 4k$. Substitute $k = 2$ to find the least common multiple. Write the least common multiple using prime factorization.

35. ▮ **Test Prep** ▮ Mia sees a movie every 4 weeks, takes piano lessons every week, visits her cousins every 9 weeks, and meets with her book club every 3 weeks. When will Mia do all four of these things in the same week?

Ⓐ Every 36 weeks   Ⓑ Every 12 weeks

Ⓒ Every 27 weeks   Ⓓ None of the above

> **Problem Solving TIP**
>
> When events occur at regular intervals, use the LCM to find out when they all occur at once.

Problem Solving and Reasoning

36. Choose a Strategy In order to break a code, you need to identify all the pairs of numbers that have an LCM of 40. Find two of these pairs of numbers.

37. Critical Thinking Instead of using prime factorization, how would you determine the LCM of two numbers that do not have any factors in common?

38. Geometry Determine the measurements and draw a rectangle such that the width and length are divisible by 2 and have an LCM of 30.

39. Communicate Since the year 1401, homophonic substitutions have been found in codes. These codes use several numbers to represent one letter. For example, A = 1, 8, 15; B = 2, 9, 16; and so on. Decode this message and describe how you could use multiples to develop a code similar to this one.

> **Problem Solving STRATEGIES**
>
> • Look for a Pattern
> • Make an Organized List
> • Make a Table
> • Guess and Check
> • Work Backward
> • Use Logical Reasoning
> • Draw a Diagram
> • Solve a Simpler Problem

8,15,22; 5,12,19; 12,19,26; 16,23,30

14,21,28; 15,22,29; 23,30,37

Mixed Review

Solve each system of equations by graphing. *[Lesson 4-6]*

40. $y = 5x - 3$
$y = -3x$

41. $y = -x + 5$
$y = -2x + 2$

42. $y = \frac{3}{4}x + 2$
$y = -x - 5$

43. $y = -\frac{1}{4}x$
$y = -\frac{1}{2}x + 1$

Express each number as a percent. *[Lesson 6-1]*

44. 3.7   **45.** 1.76   **46.** 2.02   **47.** 0.005   **48.** 2.004

49. 3.2   **50.** 2.064   **51.** 0.003   **52.** $1\frac{1}{2}$ **53.** $6\frac{2}{5}$

54. $\frac{1}{320}$ **55.** $2\frac{3}{4}$ **56.** $6\frac{1}{3}$ **57.** $\frac{1}{500}$ **58.** $4\frac{4}{6}$

TECHNOLOGY

Using a Spreadsheet • GCF and LCM

Problem: What is the product of GCF (12, 18) and LCM (12, 18)?

A spreadsheet can help answer this question.

① Label your spreadsheet columns as shown.

③ Enter their GCF and LCM in columns C and D, respectively.

	A	B	C	D	E	F
1	Number A	Number B	GCF	LCM	A*B	C*D
2	12	18	6	36	=A2*B2	=C2*D2
3						
4						
5						
6						

② Enter 12 and 18 in columns A and B.

④ In cell E2, enter the formula "= A2*B2". In cell F2, enter "= C2*D2".

Solution: GCF (12, 18) $\times$ LCM (12, 18) = 12 $\times$ 18 = 216.

TRY IT

a. Find the GCF and the LCM of 84 and 244. What is the product of the GCF and the LCM?

b. Repeat the process for 24 and 36.

ON YOUR OWN

▶ How does a spreadsheet help compute LCM $\times$ GCF?

▶ Describe how a spreadsheet can show $\frac{12 \times 18}{\text{LCM (12, 18)}} =$ GCF (12, 18).

▶ Describe how a spreadsheet can show a relationship between the LCM and the GCF of three numbers.

Section 7A Connect

You've used prime and composite numbers to find the LCM and GCF. Now use primes and composites to make a code based on the bar graph below.

Curing the Common Code

By looking at the bar graph, you can determine the letters that occur most and least often in English.

Use the bar graph and the directions below to create a code.

It will work best when you use a number only once.

1. Identify all letters with a frequency less than or equal to 20 ($F \le 20$). Represent each of them with a prime number.

2. Identify all letters with a frequency greater than 20 and less than or equal to 50 ($20 < F \le 50$). Represent each of them with a number divisible by 6.

3. Identify all letters with a frequency greater than 50 ($F > 50$). Invent a method to represent each of these letters.

4. Create a way to determine the end of a message.

5. Write a message with your code. (This is called encoding.)

6. Exchange messages with a group member and decode them.

7. Discuss how you could make another code.

Section 7A Review

Use divisibility rules. State whether the given number is divisible by 2, 3, 4, 5, 6, 8, 9, or 10. Indicate when the number is prime.

1. 342 **2.** 622 **3.** 1280 **4.** 618 **5.** 93,509,188

Find the prime factorization of each number.

6. 48 **7.** 475 **8.** 120 **9.** 144 **10.** 3750

Find the GCF and the LCM of each group of numbers.

11. 4, 9 **12.** 12, 15 **13.** 15, 24 **14.** 24, 60, 120

Write each fraction in lowest terms.

15. $\frac{9}{15}$ **16.** $\frac{21}{56}$ **17.** $\frac{15}{35}$ **18.** $\frac{64}{80}$ **19.** $\frac{24}{36}$

Find the LCD for each group of fractions.

20. $\frac{4}{5}$ and $\frac{2}{3}$ **21.** $\frac{1}{4}$ and $\frac{5}{12}$ **22.** $\frac{1}{3}$ and $\frac{7}{9}$ **23.** $\frac{5}{8}$ and $\frac{11}{12}$ **24.** $\frac{2}{5}, \frac{9}{10}$, and $\frac{3}{4}$

25. If the first part of this credit card number is not divisible by the last digit, the credit card is a fake. Is the credit card number fake? Describe how to determine this.

26. Communicate Do you think the GCF of an odd and an even number can ever be even? Explain your answer.

Test Prep

Some multiple-choice questions include unnecessary information. You need to read them carefully to determine the useful information.

27. Suppose Cara stayed at school every Monday until 4:30 P.M. for the spirit squad, every other Wednesday until 5:00 P.M. to meet with the math club, and every third Thursday until 4:45 P.M. to study. How often would she stay late at school for three days in the same week ?

Ⓐ Every sixth week Ⓑ Every week

Ⓒ Every second week Ⓓ Every fourth week

Rational Numbers

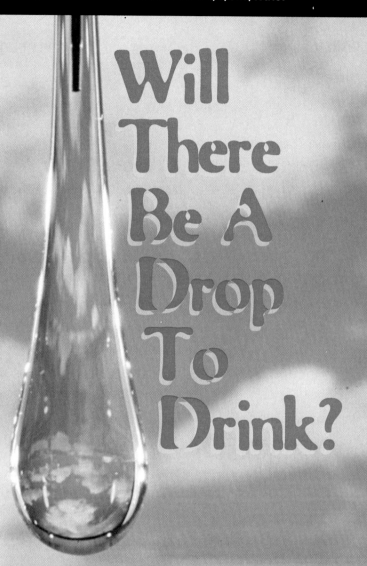

Will There Be A Drop To Drink?

"Water, water everywhere, and all the boards did shrink. Water, water everywhere, nor any drop to drink."

—Samuel Taylor Coleridge,
The Rime of the Ancient Mariner
(1772–1834)

When the poet wrote these lines, he was talking about sailors adrift in a sea of salt water.

Although about $\frac{37}{50}$ of Earth's surface is water, only about 3% of all Earth's water is fresh water. Approximately $\frac{4}{5}$ of all Earth's fresh water is locked in glacial ice. Of the remaining fresh water, only about 5% is available as surface water in streams and lakes. Most fresh water is underground.

As the human population increases, more fresh water is needed to grow food and for people to drink. Like the sailors in Coleridge's poem, we may be surrounded by water but lacking in fresh water to drink.

1 What is meant by "surface water"?

2 What do you think most of the surface fresh water is used for?

3 Do you think there was more freshwater in the poet Coleridge's lifetime? Explain.

343

Defining Rational Numbers

You'll Learn ...

■ to compare and order rational numbers

... How It's Used

Quiltmakers use rational numbers every day in order to make precise measurements and to fit patterns together.

Vocabulary

rational numbers

terminating decimal

repeating decimal

▶ **Lesson Link**   You have seen how the LCM and GCF are used when working with fractions. Now you will apply these rational numbers. ◀

Explore | Fractions

Crease Please

Materials: 2 sheets of paper per student

1. Fold one sheet of paper in half three times. Unfold and label each crease $\frac{1}{8}, \frac{2}{8}, \frac{3}{8}, \frac{4}{8}, \frac{5}{8}, \frac{6}{8}, \frac{7}{8}, \frac{8}{8}$.

2. Fold a different sheet of paper into thirds twice.

3. Label each crease from left to right, using $\frac{1}{9}, \frac{2}{9}, \frac{3}{9}, \frac{4}{9}, \frac{5}{9}, \frac{6}{9}, \frac{7}{9}, \frac{8}{9}, \frac{9}{9}$.

4. On each sheet of paper, write all fractions in lowest terms.

5. Use the folded paper to find which number in each pair is greater.

   a. $\frac{1}{8}, \frac{1}{9}$ **b.** $\frac{7}{8}, \frac{8}{9}$ **c.** $\frac{1}{4}, \frac{2}{9}$ **d.** $\frac{3}{8}, \frac{1}{3}$ **e.** $\frac{1}{2}, \frac{5}{9}$

6. Compare answers with your group. How would you determine the greater number without the creased papers?

7. Discuss how you would use the LCM to compare the numbers.

Learn | Defining Rational Numbers

Rational numbers are numbers that can be written as a ratio of two integers, and the denominator is not zero. Integers, fractions, and many decimals are rational numbers.

Integers	Fractions	Decimals
$-17 = \frac{-17}{1}$ and $4 = \frac{4}{1}$	$\frac{3}{2}$ and $-4\frac{3}{5} = \frac{-23}{5}$	$-0.75 = \frac{-3}{4}$ and $6.7 = \frac{67}{10}$

Example 1

Compare $\frac{5}{9}$ and $\frac{7}{12}$.

$$\frac{5}{9} \;\square\; \frac{7}{12}$$

$\frac{20}{36} < \frac{21}{36}$ Write the fractions with a common denominator and compare the numerators.

$\frac{5}{9} < \frac{7}{12}$ Write the original fractions.

Example 2

Water has different freezing points at different altitudes. List the freezing points in increasing order.

Altitude (ft)	−1100	1030	0 (sea level)	−1120	1200
Freezing Point (°C)	−1.1	1.03	0	−1.12	1.2

$$-1.1 \qquad 1.03 \quad 0 \qquad -1.12 \quad 1.2$$
$$\downarrow \qquad\quad \downarrow \qquad \downarrow \qquad\quad \downarrow \qquad \downarrow$$

$-1.10 \qquad 1.03 \quad 0.00 \quad -1.12 \quad 1.20$ Write with same number of decimal places.

$-1.12 \quad -1.10 \quad 0.00 \qquad 1.03 \quad 1.20$ Write the numbers in increasing order.

A **terminating decimal** has a fixed number of digits.

$$\frac{5}{8} = 0.625$$

A **repeating decimal** has a repeating digit or repeating group of digits.

$$\frac{1}{3} = 0.\overline{333} = 0.\overline{3}$$

$$\frac{5}{7} = 0.714285714\ldots = 0.\overline{714285}$$

The bar indicates the repeating digits.

Both terminating decimals and repeating decimals are rational numbers.

Example 3

Write each fraction as a decimal. State whether it's terminating or repeating.

a. $\frac{7}{25}$ **b.** $\frac{4}{9}$

a. Enter 7 ÷ 25 = to get **0.28**

$\frac{7}{25} = 0.28$ is a terminating decimal.

b. Enter 4 ÷ 9 = to get **0.44444444**

$\frac{4}{9} = 0.\overline{4}$ is a repeating decimal.   Put a bar over the 4 to show it repeats.

Try It

Write each fraction as a decimal. State whether it's terminating or repeating.

a. $\frac{5}{6}$ **b.** $\frac{1}{8}$ **c.** $\frac{3}{4}$

▶ **History Link**

The *Atocha* sank off the Florida Keys during a hurricane. More than 300 years later, in the 1970s, treasures worth $400 million were recovered.

Example 4

About 0.019 of the people on the Spanish ship *Atocha* survived the devastating wreck of September 4, 1622.

What fraction of the people aboard the *Atocha* survived?

The *Treasure Salvors'* crew searched for 15 years to finally discover the *Atocha's* treasure.

0.019   Read 0.019 as 19 thousandths.

$0.019 = \frac{19}{1000}$ Write as a fraction.

$\frac{19}{1000}$ of the people aboard the *Atocha* survived.

Try It

Write each decimal as a fraction or mixed number.

a. 0.15 **b.** 2.6 **c.** 0.046

Example 5

Write $0.\overline{15}$ as a fraction in lowest terms.

Let $n = 0.\overline{15}$	Let a variable equal the repeating decimal.
$100 \times n = 100 \times 0.\overline{15}$	Multiply by 10^2 because 2 digits repeat.
$100n - n = 15.\overline{15} - n$	Subtract n.
$99n = 15.\overline{15} - 0.\overline{15}$	Substitute. Recall that $n = 0.\overline{15}$
$\dfrac{99n}{99} = \dfrac{15}{99}$	Divide by 99 to solve for n.
$n = \dfrac{15}{99} = \dfrac{5}{33}$	Write fraction in lowest terms.

Try It

Write each fraction in lowest terms.   **a.** $2.\overline{13}$ **b.** $0.\overline{24}$

Remember

$n = 1n = 1 \times n$

[Page 146]

To compare two noninteger numbers, write both as decimals or as fractions with common denominators.

Example 6

Harry watched Old Faithful shoot steaming water into the air reaching a height of 42.2 meters. Sure enough, being faithful to its name, about 76 minutes later Fred saw it display its burst of beauty, this time at a height of $42\frac{1}{3}$ meters. Compare these two heights. Who saw the geyser shoot higher?

Compare 42.2 and $42\frac{1}{3}$.   Write the fraction as a decimal.

Compare 42.2 and 42.33.   Compare decimals.

The geyser shot higher when Fred was watching.

Try It

a. Compare -4.3 and $-4\frac{1}{3}$.   **b.** Compare 2.07 and $2\frac{1}{7}$.

Check Your Understanding

1. How can you tell if a fraction will be a terminating or repeating decimal?

2. Explain how to write $0.\overline{33}$ as a fraction.

7-4 Exercises and Applications

Practice and Apply

1. **Getting Started** Compare and order $\frac{-2}{3}, \frac{5}{6}, 0, \frac{-4}{7}, \frac{9}{10}, \frac{-1}{5}$, and $\frac{1}{6}$.
   a. Find the LCD (use the LCM).
   b. Write all fractions with the LCD.
   c. List in order from least to greatest.

Replace each ☐ with >, <, or = to compare each pair of numbers.

2. 3.04 ☐ 3.005
3. -0.8 ☐ -0.0789
4. -0.28 ☐ -0.2
5. 0.009 ☐ 0.01

6. $-\frac{3}{5}$ ☐ 0.51
7. $\frac{7}{12}$ ☐ $\frac{1}{2}$
8. -4.03 ☐ $\frac{-32}{8}$
9. $\frac{5}{8}$ ☐ $\frac{3}{4}$

Write each fraction as a decimal and state whether it is repeating or terminating.

10. $\frac{1}{5}$
11. $\frac{11}{25}$
12. $\frac{4}{33}$
13. $\frac{2}{7}$
14. $\frac{-4}{9}$

Write each decimal as a fraction or mixed number in lowest terms.

15. 0.45
16. -0.3003
17. 4.56
18. $0.\overline{21}$
19. $2.\overline{3}$

Compare each group of numbers and order them on a number line.

20. $-\frac{3}{4}, -\frac{1}{3}, -\frac{5}{9}, 0, -1$
21. $-0.\overline{12}, 0.8\overline{3}, 1, -\frac{3}{5}$
22. $6\frac{2}{3}, 6.7, 6.\overline{23}$

23. **Science** Marine mammals, like the porpoise and the sea cow, get oxygen by breathing air, not from the water through gills, as fish do. A sea cow can stay underwater for $\frac{9}{30}$ hour. A porpoise can be underwater for $\frac{1}{4}$ hour. Which marine mammal can stay underwater longer?

porpoise

sea cow

24. The largest species of beaked whales is Baird's beaked whale, also called the giant bottlenose whale. The female can grow to be as long as 12.8 m. Express this length as a mixed number in lowest terms.

25. Ana spent 2.4 hours on her homework, while Lance spent $2\frac{1}{4}$ hours on his. Who spent more time on homework?

348 *Chapter 7 • Number Sense, Rational Numbers, and Irrational Numbers*

26. Change the percents given in the graph to fractions and arrange them in order from greatest to least.

27. History The Greek mathematician Archimedes approximated π to be between $3\frac{10}{71}$ and $3\frac{1}{7}$. Write each as a decimal.

28. `Test Prep` Which is listed from least to greatest?

Ⓐ $-3, -3\frac{2}{3}, -3.7$　　Ⓑ $\frac{1}{2}, \frac{1}{3}, \frac{1}{4}$

Ⓒ $-0.875, -\frac{4}{5}, 0$　　Ⓓ $0.\overline{6}, 0.1\overline{6}, \frac{1}{6}$

29. Science Because a camel's hump stores fat and not water, a camel can lose up to 37.5% of its body weight. What fraction of the camel's weight is this?

How Kids Wake Up

Other methods 19%
Parents call to them 43%
Use an alarm 22%
Wake themselves up 16%

Problem Solving and Reasoning

30. Communicate Explain how to find a number between $\frac{2}{5}$ and 0.42.

Number Sense Find a number that is between each pair.

31. $\frac{1}{4}$ and $\frac{1}{5}$　　**32.** $0.\overline{12}$ and $0.\overline{13}$　　**33.** $\frac{-7}{8}$ and $\frac{-7}{9}$

34. `Journal` The decimal conversions of $\frac{1}{7}, \frac{2}{7}, \frac{3}{7}, \frac{4}{7}, \frac{5}{7},$ and $\frac{6}{7}$ display a very interesting pattern. Convert the fractions and describe the pattern.

Mixed Review

Write an algebraic expression for each situation. *[Lesson 3-3]*

35. 12 increased by a number　　**36.** 8 subtracted from twice a number

37. Number of inches in k yards　　**38.** The number of sides in s squares

Solve each percent problem. *[Lesson 6-2]*

39. What is 75% of 200?　　**40.** What is 10% of 50?

41. 50% of what number is 20?　　**42.** 6 is 60% of what number?

Project Progress

As you keep track of your gains and losses, find places to use negative numbers. Consider whether or not your calculations would be more efficient if all your numbers were written as decimals or all as fractions.

Problem Solving

Understand
Plan
Solve
Look Back

Add and Subtract Rational Numbers

You'll Learn ...

■ to add and subtract rational numbers

... How It's Used

Telephone repair people add and subtract integers, fractions, and decimals when they make adjustments during a repair after a storm.

▶ **Lesson Link** You have learned about the types of rational numbers. Now you will add and subtract rational numbers. ◀

Explore | **Rational Numbers**

Hydro ≈ Water

Arctic Ocean

Hudson Bay

Atlantic Ocean

Mediterranean Sea

Gulf of Mexico

Pacific Ocean

Red Sea

Indian Ocean

Parts of salt per 1000 parts ocean water
32 or less   34   36   38 or more
33   35   37

Oceans have different amounts of salt and salinity in them. A hydrologist might study the map to understand the varied salinity of the oceans. The "saltiest" oceans are shown in purple.

1. What is the salinity of the Hudson Bay? The Mediterranean Sea? The Red Sea?

2. Name the body of water with the highest salinity; the lowest salinity. Express the salinity of each as a fraction.

3. What would the salinity be if you made a mixture of 30% water with $\frac{32}{1000}$ salinity and 70% water with $\frac{37}{1000}$ salinity?

4. The average salinity of the ocean is $\frac{34.5 \text{ parts salt}}{1000 \text{ parts ocean water}}$. With your group, discuss how hydrologists would arrive at this number.

5. Discuss some reasons for the variation of salinity in the oceans.

Adding and subtracting decimals is similar to adding and subtracting integers. Align the decimal points.

Example 1

Subtract 32.74 − 12.678.

$$
\begin{array}{r}
32.740 \\
-12.678 \\
\hline
20.062
\end{array}
$$

Align decimal points and write with the same number of decimal places.

Subtract.

Try It

Add or subtract each of the following.

a. 84.6 + 27.03   **b.** 55 − 18.25

c. 309.1 − (−217.95)   **d.** −0.66 + 4.4

Study TIP

You will usually make fewer mistakes if you don't skip steps.

Use a common denominator to add and subtract fractions with unlike denominators.

Example 2

The Osage orange tree produces large spherical fruits, which vary from $3\frac{2}{3}$ inches to $5\frac{1}{12}$ inches in diameter. What is the range in size of the fruit?

Subtract $5\frac{1}{12} - 3\frac{2}{3}$.

Write fractions with a common denominator.

$$
\begin{aligned}
5\frac{1}{12} &= \;\; 5\frac{1}{12} = \;\; 4\frac{13}{12} \quad \text{Rename } 5\frac{1}{12}. \\
-3\frac{2}{3} &= -3\frac{8}{12} = -3\frac{8}{12} \\
\hline
& \qquad\qquad\qquad 1\frac{5}{12} \quad \text{Subtract.}
\end{aligned}
$$

The range in diameter is $1\frac{5}{12}$ inches.

The fruit of the Osage orange tree is not edible. It is named after the Osage Indians who used its yellow wood for bows and wagon wheels.

▶ **Science Link**

Plants such as the orange tree use their fruits to disperse their seeds.

Calculating with positive and negative fractions is similar to calculating with positive and negative integers.

Example 3

Find $4\frac{5}{8} - \left(-3\frac{3}{5}\right)$.

$4\frac{5}{8} - \left(-3\frac{3}{5}\right) = 4\frac{25}{40} - \left(-3\frac{24}{40}\right)$ Write fractions with a common denominator.

$4\frac{25}{40} + 3\frac{24}{40} = 7\frac{49}{40} = 8\frac{9}{40}$ Add the opposite of $-3\frac{24}{40}$ and rename the result.

Try It

Add or subtract.   **a.** $5\frac{3}{5} - 3\frac{2}{20}$ **b.** $7\frac{1}{6} + \left(-1\frac{1}{3}\right)$

Example 4

Problem Solving TIP

Here's a good thing to know when you see fraction coefficients:
$\frac{3}{7}x = \frac{3x}{7}$.

Jan and Hillary jog $6\frac{1}{5}$ miles from their house to the park daily. If they take a water break after $2\frac{1}{3}$ miles, how much farther do they have to jog to get to the park?

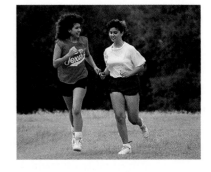

Solve the equation $n + 2\frac{1}{3} = 6\frac{1}{5}$.

$$n + 2\frac{1}{3} = 6\frac{1}{5}$$

$$n + 2\frac{1}{3} + \left(-2\frac{1}{3}\right) = 6\frac{1}{5} + \left(-2\frac{1}{3}\right)$$ Add $-2\frac{1}{3}$ to both sides.

$$n + 0 = 6\frac{3}{15} + \left(-2\frac{5}{15}\right)$$ Simplify and rewrite fractions.

$$n = 5\frac{18}{15} + \left(-2\frac{5}{15}\right) = 3\frac{13}{15}$$ Rewrite $6\frac{3}{15}$ as $5\frac{18}{15}$ and subtract.

They have to jog $3\frac{13}{15}$ miles more to get to the park.

Try It

Find n for each of the following.   **a.** $n + \frac{3}{4} = -4\frac{1}{2}$ **b.** $n - 10\frac{5}{8} = 3\frac{7}{12}$

Check   Your Understanding

1. Why do you use the LCD when you add and subtract fractions?

2. How is adding negative fractions similar to adding negative integers?

Practice and Apply

1. **Getting Started** Add $\frac{4}{5} + \frac{5}{6}$.

   a. Write each fraction using the LCD.

   b. Add the numerators and write the result over the LCD.

   c. Write in lowest terms.

Add or subtract each of the following. Write each answer in lowest terms.

2. $0.3124 + 0.214$ 3. $-127.123 - 33.59$ 4. $45.34567 + 28.13$ 5. $124.16 - (-39.98)$

6. $\frac{2}{3} + \frac{4}{3}$ 7. $\frac{12}{20} - \frac{17}{20}$ 8. $\frac{3}{9} - \left(-\frac{3}{9}\right)$ 9. $\frac{-4}{5} + \frac{4}{6}$ 10. $\frac{9}{10} - \frac{3}{12}$

11. $7\frac{3}{5} + 2\frac{4}{5}$ 12. $8\frac{2}{3} - \left(-5\frac{1}{3}\right)$ 13. $7\frac{1}{7} - 2\frac{4}{7}$ 14. $9\frac{1}{6} - 3\frac{5}{6}$ 15. $-12\frac{4}{5} - 1\frac{11}{12}$

Solve each equation.

16. $n = \frac{3}{4} + \frac{7}{12}$ 17. $2\frac{1}{2} - n = 4$ 18. $n + \left(-\frac{2}{7}\right) = \frac{4}{5}$ 19. $n - 12 = -\frac{6}{8}$

20. **Geography** The United States, Russia, China, and India use about 0.45 of the world's daily consumed fresh water. What fraction of fresh water is consumed by other countries?

21. Venus orbits the sun at an average of 21.75 miles per second, while Earth orbits the sun at an average of 18.46 miles per second. How much faster is the orbital speed of Venus?

22. Alexandro weighed a bag of jelly beans at the candy store and the scale read 0.65 pounds. He added on a bag of sour candies and the scale then read 1.13 pounds. How much do the sour candies weigh?

23. **Science** Use the circle graph to determine what fraction of Earth's surface is fresh water. About $\frac{71}{100}$ of Earth's surface is salt water, and about $\frac{6}{25}$ is land.

24. **Social Studies** If $\frac{7}{25}$ of the households in the United States have three or more television sets, what fraction of households have fewer than three television sets?

Salt water $\frac{71}{100}$

Land $\frac{6}{25}$

Freshwater

25. **Test Prep** Which of these is equivalent to $8\frac{8}{15}$?

Ⓐ $8\frac{4}{7}$ Ⓑ $7\frac{23}{15}$ Ⓒ $7\frac{15}{23}$ Ⓓ $7\frac{15}{8}$

Problem Solving and Reasoning

26. Health A set of quadruplets were born in Great Britain on April 10, 1988, weighing $2\frac{9}{16}$ lb, $2\frac{1}{8}$ lb, $2\frac{1}{4}$ lb, and $2\frac{5}{16}$ lb. What was the average weight of the babies?

27. **Journal** Write a paragraph to explain why having the same number of decimal places is similar to having fractions with common denominators.

28. Communicate Write a word problem that would require subtracting fractions with unlike denominators and that has $\frac{1}{3}$ as an answer. Explain how you decided on the numbers used in your word problem.

29. Algebra Ana's stock rose $\frac{3}{4}$ of a point Wednesday, rose $\frac{3}{8}$ of a point Thursday, and fell $1\frac{1}{4}$ points Friday. Write an algebraic expression for the situation and find the overall change in her stock for these three days.

30. Math Reasoning A wetland is a location other than a river, lake, or open ocean in which the soil is saturated with water. In 1900, 39.4% of Florida was wetlands. In 1990, 30.6% of Florida was wetlands. What fraction of wetlands was lost from 1900 to 1990?

Mixed Review

Solve each equation. *[Lesson 3-4]*

31. $x - 10 = 7$ **32.** $4 + y = 14$

33. $-10 - k = 44$ **34.** $9 + p = -17$

35. $-r + 2.4 = 7.3$ **36.** $j = 88 - 2$

37. $n + (-2.9) = -5.1$ **38.** $64 - t = 38$

Find the percent of increase in each situation. Round to the nearest whole percent. *[Lesson 6-4]*

39. A pair of in-line skates wholesales for $150.00 and retails for $215.00.

40. There were 16 jazz band members and now there are 20.

Multiply and Divide Rational Numbers

▶ **Lesson Link** You have learned how to add and subtract rational numbers, and now you will learn how to multiply and divide rational numbers. ◀

Explore | Multiplication and Division

Hauling H$_2$O

Materials: Calculator

The bottled-water company delivers water in two sizes: 5-gallon bottles that sell for $8.00 and 3-gallon bottles that sell for $5.50.

Your delivery truck carries 195 bottles on a delivery-truck route, $66.\overline{66}\%$ of which are 5-gallon bottles.

1. How many 5-gallon bottles are on your truck before delivery? How many 3-gallon bottles?

2. What is the total value of bottled water on a full delivery truck?

3. Compare your answers with your group and discuss how you used $66.\overline{66}\%$.

4. The company is having a special promotion: If you buy four bottles you get the fifth bottle free. If during the year you use 24 three-gallon bottles, how much money would you save with this special deal?

5. If you use 24 three-gallon bottles a year, how many total gallons of water is this? How many 5-gallon bottles would this be?

6. Which would be more economical for you, buying 3-gallon bottles or 5-gallon bottles? Why?

You'll Learn ...

■ to multiply and divide rational numbers

... How It's Used

Caterers, who are responsible for covering their expenses, use rational numbers to ensure they make a profit.

Learn   Multiply and Divide Rational Numbers

To multiply decimals, first multiply as with integers. Then count the total number of decimal places in the factors. Show this total number of decimal places in the product.

Example 1

The average American household of 2.5 people uses 5230.4 gallons of water a month. The cost per gallon is $0.0025. Determine the average monthly bill for water usage.

Multiply 5230.4 × 0.0025.

$$
\begin{array}{r}
5230.4 \quad \leftarrow \text{1 decimal place} \\
\times 0.0025 \quad \leftarrow \text{4 decimal places} \\
\hline
261520 \\
+1046080 \\
\hline
13.07600 \quad \leftarrow \text{5 decimal places}
\end{array}
$$

The average monthly bill is $13.076, or $13.08.

Try It

Multiply each.

a. -24×0.15 **b.** -7.99×-7.03

Example 2

Divide -16.92 by 0.3.

$$0.3\overline{)-16.92}$$

$$3\overline{)-169.2}$$ Multiply the divisor by a power of 10 to make it a whole number. Multiply the dividend by the same power of 10.

$$\begin{array}{r} -56.4 \\ 3\overline{)-169.2} \end{array}$$ Divide. Put the point and negative sign in the quotient.

Try It

Divide each.

a. $3.36 \div 1.5$ **b.** $-60 \div 0.88$

To multiply with mixed numbers, first rewrite them as improper fractions.
Multiply numerators; then multiply denominators.

Example 3

A four-person household uses about $242\frac{1}{2}$ gallons of water daily. About $\frac{3}{50}$ of daily water comes from the bathroom sink. How many gallons of water is this?

Write $242\frac{1}{2}$ as an improper fraction and multiply.

$$\frac{3}{50} \times 242\frac{1}{2} = \frac{3}{50} \times \frac{485}{2} = \frac{1455}{100}$$

Write $\frac{1455}{100}$ as a mixed number in lowest terms.

$$\frac{1455}{100} = 14\frac{55}{100} = 14\frac{11}{20}$$

$14\frac{11}{20}$ gallons of water comes from the bathroom sink daily.

Try It

Multiply.   **a.** $8\frac{3}{4} \times \frac{-5}{12}$ **b.** $6 \times 3\frac{2}{3}$

Dividing by a mixed number is the same as multiplying by its reciprocal.
The product of a number and its reciprocal is 1.

$\frac{3}{4}$ and $\frac{4}{3}$ are reciprocals because $\frac{3}{4} \times \frac{4}{3} = 1$.

Test Prep

Stay smart! Review what you've learned earlier in the school year; you never know when you'll need it.

Example 4

Divide $2\frac{5}{6} \div \frac{1}{3}$.

$2\frac{5}{6} \div \frac{1}{3} = \frac{17}{6} \div \frac{1}{3}$ Write $2\frac{5}{6}$ as an improper fraction.

$\frac{17}{6} \times \frac{3}{1} = \frac{17 \times 3}{6 \times 1} = \frac{51}{6}$ Change divisor to its reciprocal and multiply.

$8\frac{3}{6} = 8\frac{1}{2}$ Write as a mixed number in lowest terms.

Try It

Divide.   **a.** $-2\frac{1}{2} \div \frac{-5}{8}$ **b.** $\frac{9}{10} \div \frac{1}{5}$

WHAT DO YOU THINK?

Randy and Mary are putting $3\frac{3}{4}$ liters of pasta sauce into 1.5-liter jars. How many 1.5-liter jars do they need?

Randy thinks ...

First, I'll write everything as a fraction. $3\frac{3}{4} = \frac{15}{4}$. Also,

$1.5 = \frac{3}{2}$. I think of fractions as "minidivision expressions."

$\frac{15}{4} \div \frac{3}{2} = (15 \div 4) \div (3 \div 2)$

I'll use my calculator. $($ 15 $\div$ 4 $)$ $\div$ $($ 3 $\div$ 2 $)$ $=$ 2.5

Since there is no such thing as 2.5 jars, we need 3 jars.

Mary thinks ...

I need to rewrite $3\frac{3}{4}$ as an improper fraction. $\qquad 3\frac{3}{4} = \frac{15}{4}$

I'll convert the decimal to a fraction. $\qquad 1.5 = \frac{15}{10} = \frac{15 \div 5}{10 \div 5} = \frac{3}{2}$

Now I'll set up my division $\qquad \frac{15}{4} \div \frac{3}{2} = \frac{15}{4} \times \frac{2}{3} = \frac{15 \times 2}{4 \times 3} = \frac{30}{12}$
expression and divide.

$\frac{30}{12} = 2\frac{1}{2}$. We'll need to round $2\frac{1}{2}$ jars to 3 jars.

What do you think?

1. Explain the meaning of Randy's phrase "minidivision equations."

2. Describe another way of dividing $3\frac{3}{4} \div \frac{3}{2}$.

Check Your Understanding

1. Explain how to multiply and divide with mixed numbers.

2. Describe how to determine the reciprocal of a number.

7-6 Exercises and Applications

Practice and Apply

1. **Getting Started** Divide $3\frac{1}{4} \div \frac{1}{6}$.
   a. Rewrite the mixed number as an improper fraction.
   b. Multiply by the reciprocal of the divisor.

Multiply or divide each of the following. Write each answer in lowest terms.

2. -1.23×0.5

3. 0.009×0.8

4. 2.46×0.26

5. $4\overline{)0.128}$

6. $-3.2\overline{)-2.976}$

7. $\frac{1}{5} \times \frac{5}{9}$

8. $\frac{7}{8} \times \frac{2}{3}$

9. $3 \times -\frac{7}{9}$

10. $\frac{3}{5} \times \frac{8}{9}$

11. $\frac{1}{2} \times \frac{1}{3}$

12. $-7\frac{6}{7} \times -11$

13. $\frac{13}{23} \times 2\frac{4}{5}$

14. $\frac{3}{6} \div \frac{-1}{2}$

15. $\frac{4}{8} \div \frac{7}{9}$

16. $4 \div \frac{2}{3}$

17. $\frac{4}{7} \div \frac{4}{9}$

18. $8 \div \frac{1}{4}$

19. $30 \div \frac{1}{5}$

20. $-3\frac{1}{2} \div \frac{3}{4}$

21. $\frac{1}{6} \div 3\frac{4}{5}$

22. **Science** The oceans cover about 7.5 million square miles of Earth's surface. If $\frac{3}{25}$ of the oceans are capped with glacial ice, what is the approximate area of the glaciers on our planet?

23. **Geography** The Antarctic ice sheet covers an area $1\frac{1}{2}$ times the area of the 48 contiguous states, which is 3,016,345 square miles. What is the area of the Antarctic ice sheet?

24. The Dall's porpoise is one of the fastest swimmers in the species. It can travel up to 50 kilometers per hour. At this speed, how far would this porpoise travel in $\frac{3}{4}$ hour?

25. **Algebra** Some cacti can store 100 gallons of water over a 4-month rainy season. Write an expression with fractions that states the average amount of water stored each rainy month.

26. The eighth-grade class budgeted $1420 for the graduation dinner. Each person's dinner will cost $6.75. What is the greatest number of people that can attend the dinner?

27. **Test Prep** Choose the expression that results in the product with the greatest absolute value.

Ⓐ $3 \times \frac{1}{2}$ Ⓑ $3 \times \frac{1}{3}$ Ⓒ $3 \times \frac{1}{4}$ Ⓓ $3 \times \frac{1}{5}$

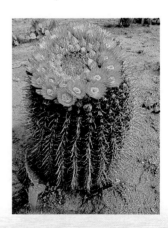

Problem Solving and Reasoning

28. Communicate Some say that the average ratio of inches of snow to inches of water is 10 to 1. If the snow is equivalent to $2\frac{7}{8}$ inches of water, how many inches of snow are there? Explain your reasoning.

29. Math Reasoning Will the following calculator key strokes correctly evaluate $\frac{1}{2} \div \frac{3}{4}$? 1 ÷ 2 ÷ 3 ÷ 4 =. Explain your reasoning.

30. Critical Thinking The Great Lakes hold approximately 5439 cubic miles of water. The table shows the fraction of water volume in each lake.

  a. Which lake is the largest?   **b.** Smallest?

  c. What is the approximate volume of each lake?

Great Lake	Superior	Michigan	Huron	Erie	Ontario
Volume Part	$\frac{53}{100}$	$\frac{11}{50}$	$\frac{4}{25}$	$\frac{1}{50}$	$\frac{7}{100}$

31. Choose a Strategy The product of two positive numbers is greater than one. Can both of these numbers be less than one? Describe your strategy and how you used it.

32. Math Reasoning Multiplication of integers satisfies the *closure property* because if you multiply any two integers the product will be an integer. Does multiplication of even numbers satisfy the closure property? Multiplication of odd numbers? If not, give an example.

Problem Solving
STRATEGIES

- Look for a Pattern
- Make an Organized List
- Make a Table
- Guess and Check
- Work Backward
- Use Logical Reasoning
- Draw a Diagram
- Solve a Simpler Problem

Mixed Review

Solve each equation. *[Lesson 3-5]*

33. $9x = 81$ **34.** $\frac{x}{4} = 16$ **35.** $-x = 44$ **36.** $18x = 3$

37. $-5x = 205$ **38.** $20x = -140$ **39.** $x \div 7 = 3$ **40.** $4 \cdot x = 88$

Find the percent of decrease. Round to the nearest whole percent. *[Lesson 6-5]*

41. Price of a video game that was $54.00 and marked down to $36.00

42. If there were 120 apples in the basket and 30 were eaten

43. Price of a skateboard that was $26.00 before sale of $5.00 off

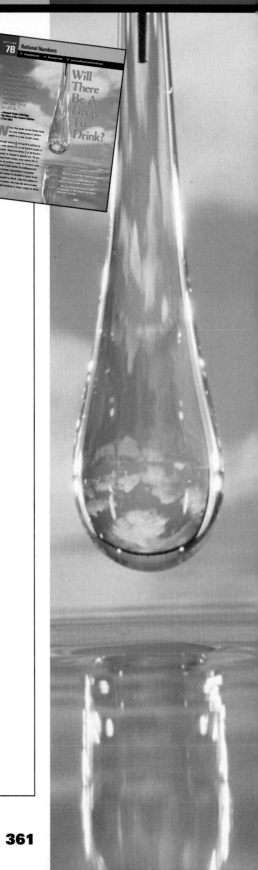

You have learned how to work with rational numbers. Now you will apply what you have learned to understand how water is used by the world.

Will There Be a Drop to Drink?

Materials: Calculator

Some of the most beautiful cities in the world are located near water. The oceans cover at least 70% of Earth's surface.

We've all heard, "Don't leave the water running!!" Why? It must be an important resource.

Use your calculator to compare data about water usage. You will compare how much water is used for industrial, agricultural, and household purposes.

1. The United States gets $\frac{37}{50}$ of its freshwater from surface sources and the other part from underground sources. What part of our freshwater comes from underground?

2. Use the table below to discuss how the former Soviet Union, United States, and China use water. How does each country use its freshwater resources? What fractional part is used for household consumption?

	Industry	Agriculture	Household
Former Soviet Union	$\frac{9}{20}$	$\frac{51}{100}$	?
United States	$\frac{29}{50}$	$\frac{17}{50}$	?
China	$\frac{1}{20}$	$\frac{93}{100}$	?

3. On a worldwide basis water uses are allocated as follows: $\frac{1}{10}$ for domestic use, $\frac{1}{10}$ for industrial use, and $\frac{4}{5}$ for agricultural use. Does this allocation account for all of the world's water usage?

4. Discuss how the world uses water compared to the three countries mentioned above.

Section 7B Review

Compare each group of numbers and order them on a number line.

1. $-1.07, 1.05, -1$
2. $\dfrac{-2}{3}, \dfrac{2}{6}, \dfrac{-1}{3}$
3. $1\dfrac{1}{2}, 1\dfrac{3}{5}, -1\dfrac{2}{3}$
4. $1.5, -\dfrac{3}{4}, 1\dfrac{3}{4}$

Write each fraction as a decimal and determine whether it's terminating or repeating.

5. $\dfrac{3}{4}$
6. $-\dfrac{5}{6}$
7. $11\dfrac{5}{7}$
8. $-\dfrac{3}{9}$
9. $4\dfrac{7}{10}$

Write each decimal as a fraction or mixed number.

10. -2.34
11. 3.005
12. -0.451
13. $0.\overline{364}$
14. $2.\overline{11}$

Calculate.

15. $0.3 + 7.12$
16. $8 - 0.00725$
17. $3.4 \times (-0.039)$
18. $100.46 \div 0.32$

19. $\dfrac{1}{6} + \left(-\dfrac{1}{8}\right)$
20. $8\dfrac{1}{2} + 2\dfrac{3}{4}$
21. $3 - 1\dfrac{3}{8}$
22. $\dfrac{2}{3} - \left(-\dfrac{5}{7}\right)$

23. $\dfrac{4}{9} \times \dfrac{-3}{8}$
24. $3\dfrac{1}{4} \times \dfrac{6}{7}$
25. $5 \div \dfrac{1}{3}$
26. $-4\dfrac{1}{5} \div -2\dfrac{2}{3}$

Solve.

27. $\dfrac{2}{3} = \dfrac{4}{5} + x$
28. $\dfrac{-3}{4} = -\dfrac{-1}{3} - x$
29. $\dfrac{6}{7} + \dfrac{-3}{7} = x$

30. A number is divided by -6, multiplied by $\frac{3}{4}$, and added to $6\frac{1}{2}$. The result is 18.5. What is the number? Explain how you solved this problem.

Test Prep

When taking multiple choice tests, express fractions in lowest terms.

31. Tina swam four laps in $3\frac{3}{10}$ minutes. The swim-team record for the distance is $2\frac{9}{10}$ minutes. How far is Tina from matching the team record?

Ⓐ $\dfrac{1}{10}$ minute   Ⓑ $\dfrac{1}{5}$ minute   Ⓒ $\dfrac{3}{10}$ minute   Ⓓ None of these

Irrational Numbers

HOME SWEET HOME

Around the world, people live in a variety of dwellings. Whether the residence is an adobe hut on the plains, a tent in the desert, a high-rise apartment in a big city, or a house in the suburbs, it is called home. Each of these homes is based on an architect's or builder's plan. Building homes involves using numbers such as integers, decimals, or fractions.

People have different homes due to climate, culture, or landscape. In places without trees, you may find a home built of stone or mud. In the forest, you'd be able to find a log cabin. In the southwest United States, the Anasazi people carved their homes into the rock of a mountainside.

1 What are some other types of homes you can think of?

2 What can influence whether or not a home is built of brick?

3 How do you think the need for shelter influences mathematics?

7-7 Perfect Squares and Square Roots

You'll Learn ...

■ to take square roots and identify perfect squares

... How It's Used

Mechanical engineers use square roots to design bridges.

Vocabulary

square root

radical sign

perfect square

▶ **Lesson Link** You have learned about exponents and powers. Now you will learn about square roots and perfect squares. ◀

Explore | Perfect Squares

Drawing Square Conclusions

Materials: Geometry software, Calculator

1. Draw a square. Use the measurement tool to determine the area and the length of a side.

2. Make a table to record each measurement. Your table will be used to record the side length and area of six different squares.

3. Draw squares with areas 1, 4, 9, 16, 25, and 36 square units. Use the measurement tool to verify each area and determine the side length. Record the measurements in your table.

4. Plot the data on a coordinate grid. Use the area as the *x*-coordinate and the side length as the *y*-coordinate. Connect the points and determine whether the graph is a curved or straight line.

5. Draw a square with an area of 21 and determine the length of a side.

6. Discuss how the squares with areas 1, 4, 9, 16, 25, and 36 differ from the square with area 21.

Learn | Perfect Squares and Square Roots

The **square root** of a number N is the number that when multiplied by itself gives the number N. The symbol for the square root is the **radical sign**.

You have seen the exponent ^{2} used as $5^2 = 5 \times 5 = 25$.

The inverse of x^2 is $\sqrt{x}$ used as $\sqrt{25} = 5$ because $5 \times 5 = 25$.

A **perfect square** is a number with an integer square root such as 9, 16, and 25.

Example 1

Use the square root key $\boxed{\sqrt{x}}$ on your calculator to determine whether each of the numbers is a perfect square.

a. 222   **b.** 169   **c.** 351.56

Enter 222 $\boxed{\sqrt{x}}$ *14.89966443*   222 is not a perfect square.

Enter 169 $\boxed{\sqrt{x}}$ *13*   169 is a perfect square.

Enter 351.56 $\boxed{\sqrt{x}}$ *18.74993333*   351.56 is not a perfect square.

Try It

Use your calculator to determine whether each number is a perfect square.

a. 729   **b.** 864   **c.** 1444   **d.** 1064.15

HINT

A calculator finds square roots quickly, but the display may not show all of the digits.

You can use the square root to find the side length of a square if you only know the area.

Example 2

Ed pours a foundation with an area of 144 ft² for a square shed. How many feet of lumber does Ed need to frame one side of this foundation? To frame the entire foundation?

144 ft²

▶ **Industry Link**

Foundations can be made by pouring cement into a frame. Some cements have sand in them.

Enter 144 $\boxed{\sqrt{x}}$ *12*

Enter 4 $\boxed{\times}$ 12 $\boxed{=}$ *48*

Ed needs 12 feet of lumber to frame one side and 48 feet total.

Try It

Evaluate:

a. $2 \times \sqrt{36}$ **b.** $3 \times \sqrt{49}$ **c.** $5 \times \sqrt{100}$ **d.** $7 \times \sqrt{169}$

You can estimate the square root of a number that is not a perfect square by using the nearest perfect squares.

Example 3

State the two consecutive integers that $\sqrt{7}$ is between. Determine $\sqrt{7}$.

The perfect square numbers nearest to 7 are 4 and 9.

$\sqrt{4} < \sqrt{7} < \sqrt{9}$ because $4 < 7 < 9$.

$2 < \sqrt{7} < 3$, so $\sqrt{7}$ is between 2 and 3.

The side of the red square is between 2 and 3.

Enter 7 $\boxed{\sqrt{x}}$ *2.645751311*   So $\sqrt{7} \approx 2.65$.

Try It

State the two consecutive integers that the square root is between. Use your calculator to find each square root to the nearest tenth.

a. $\sqrt{10}$ **b.** $\sqrt{21}$ **c.** $\sqrt{30}$ **d.** $\sqrt{80}$

To find the square root of a fraction, find the square root of the numerator and the denominator.

Example 4

Find $\sqrt{\dfrac{64}{49}}$.

$\sqrt{\dfrac{64}{49}} = \dfrac{\sqrt{64}}{\sqrt{49}}$ Rewrite as two square roots.

$= \dfrac{8}{7} = 1\dfrac{1}{7}$ Take the square roots. Write in lowest terms.

Try It

Find each of the square roots.

a. $\sqrt{\dfrac{25}{64}}$ **b.** $\sqrt{\dfrac{100}{625}}$ **c.** $\sqrt{\dfrac{121}{324}}$ **d.** $\sqrt{\dfrac{36}{225}}$

Check   Your Understanding

1. Describe how taking a square root is similar to finding the side of a square.

2. Will the square of any integer be a perfect square? Explain.

Practice and Apply

1. **Getting Started** Find the square root of $\sqrt{\dfrac{9}{144}}$.
   a. Write the square roots of the numerator and the denominator.
   b. Take each square root.
   c. Write the fraction in lowest terms.

State whether or not each number is a perfect square.

2. 130   3. 49   4. 289   5. 1000   6. 225

Find the two consecutive integers that each is between.

7. $\sqrt{34}$ 8. $\sqrt{52}$ 9. $\sqrt{70}$ 10. $\sqrt{110}$ 11. $\sqrt{27}$

Determine each square root and write in lowest terms.

12. $\sqrt{\dfrac{64}{121}}$ 13. $\sqrt{\dfrac{36}{16}}$ 14. $\sqrt{\dfrac{169}{144}}$ 15. $\sqrt{\dfrac{81}{225}}$ 16. $\sqrt{\dfrac{1}{9}}$

17. **Social Studies** The Great Pyramid of Khufu has a square base that covers about 53,000 m². About how long is each side of the base?

18. **Patterns** List the first ten perfect squares. How do the numbers in the list increase? Describe the pattern.

19. Architects can design homes using a computer application. According to the floorplans, the living room of a new house being built is 85 square feet. State two consecutive integers that $\sqrt{85}$ is between.

20. Angela built a square dog house that is 33 in. long on each side for her new beagle puppy. What is the area of the floor for the puppy to sleep on?

21. The area of the square window above the door on Dmitri's house in Santorini, Greece, is 144 in². How long is one side of the window?

22. **Algebra** Write a formula for finding the length of the side of a square with area x.

23. **Science** The formula $t = \frac{\sqrt{d}}{4}$ shows how to find the time (t), in seconds, that it takes a falling object to free-fall a given distance (d), in feet. Find the falling time for a skydiver to fall 900 feet before opening the parachute.

900 ft

24. **Test Prep** Which is the length of a side of a square with an area of 324 in^2?

Ⓐ 162 in.　　Ⓑ 18 in.　　Ⓒ 81 in.　　Ⓓ 104,976 in.

Problem Solving and Reasoning

25. **Measurement** The Daryma family of Mongolia live in a round tent called a *yurt* that has a floor area of 64π ft^2. What is the radius of their tent? (Area of a circle $= \pi r^2$)

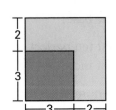

26. **Journal** Explain how you would estimate $\sqrt{12}$ using perfect squares.

27. **Number Sense** A method for finding perfect squares involves multiplying four consecutive whole numbers and adding 1 to their product. For instance, $(4 \cdot 5 \cdot 6 \cdot 7) + 1 = 841$ and $\sqrt{841} = 29$. Find five perfect squares using this method.

28. **Choose a Strategy** Find the area of the yellow portion in the diagram. Could the area be rearranged into another perfect square? Draw a diagram to support your answer.

29. **Communicate** If you multiply a perfect square by a perfect square, is the answer a perfect square? Support your answer with an example.

Problem Solving

STRATEGIES

• Look for a Pattern
• Make an Organized List
• Make a Table
• Guess and Check
• Work Backward
• Use Logical Reasoning
• Draw a Diagram
• Solve a Simpler Problem

Mixed Review

Plot each point on a coordinate grid. *[Lesson 2-6]*

30. $(4, 7)$　　31. $(-6, 0)$　　32. $(5.5, 2.5)$

33. $(-3, -3)$　　34. $(0, 1)$　　35. $(9, -6)$

Write each rate or ratio as a fraction. *[Lesson 5-1]*

36. 9 to 5　　37. 11:66　　38. 45 miles per hour

39. Number of feet in a yard　　40. Number of minutes in an hour

Square Roots and Irrational Numbers

▶ **Lesson Link**   You have learned about perfect squares and square roots. You will now learn about other square roots and other types of numbers. ◀

Explore   Irrational Numbers

Is That Rational?

Materials: Graph paper, Calculator

Recall that a rational number is a ratio such as $\frac{a}{b}$, where a and b are both integers.

1. Draw a square that is closest to 10 square units on graph paper.

2. Draw the next larger square.

3. Find the length of a side of each square.

4. Try to find a rational number $\frac{a}{b}$ so that $\left(\frac{a}{b}\right)^2 = 10$. Use a calculator. List the numbers you tried and the square of each number.

5. Did you find a rational number that has a square of 10? If not, what is the closest rational number you found?

9 sq. units   16 sq. units

Vocabulary

principal square root

negative square root

irrational number

real numbers

Learn   Square Roots and Irrational Numbers

You know that $\sqrt{9} = 3$ because $3^2 = 9$. You also know that $(-3)^2 = 9$, so it must be true that $\sqrt{9}$ is also -3.

The positive square root is called the **principal square root** . The negative square root is the **negative square root** .

Principal Square Root $(\sqrt{})$	Negative Square Root $(-\sqrt{})$	Both Square Roots $(\pm\sqrt{})$
$\sqrt{9} = 3$	$-\sqrt{9} = -3$	$\pm\sqrt{9} = \pm 3$

-9 does not have a square root because $-9 = (-3)(3)$.

It is important to know that $-\sqrt{9} \neq \sqrt{-9}$.

Both square roots of a number have the same absolute value.

► **History Link**

On September 16, 1620, 35 pilgrims left England on the *Mayflower*.

Example 1

In the 1600s, when pilgrims first settled in New England, their houses were very plain. Here is a square floor plan with an area of 900 ft². What is the length of one side of this structure?

Find $\sqrt{900}$.

$\pm\sqrt{900} = \pm 30$

-30 does not work because length cannot be a negative value.

The length of the structure is 30 feet.

Borning room | Kitchen | Pantry | Saltbox Floor Plan

Keeping room | Parlor | 30 ft

Entry

A number that cannot be expressed as a repeating or terminating decimal is an **irrational number** .

An integer that is not a perfect square has an irrational square root.

Together, the rational and irrational numbers make up the **real numbers** .

Example 2

Use your calculator to determine whether each square root is rational or irrational.

a. $-\sqrt{723}$ **b.** $\sqrt{256}$

Enter 723 $\boxed{\sqrt{x}}$ $\boxed{+/-}$. -26.88865932 $-\sqrt{723}$ is irrational.

Enter 256 $\boxed{\sqrt{x}}$. 16 $\sqrt{256}$ is rational.

Try It

Use your calculator to determine whether or not the following are irrational. If it is rational, then find the square root.

a. $\sqrt{167}$ **b.** $-\sqrt{900}$ **c.** $\pm\sqrt{5476}$ **d.** $\sqrt{59841}$

Determine $\sqrt{10{,}816}$.

Enrique thinks ...

Let's see ... maybe 10,816 can be factored into perfect squares.

It can! $10{,}816 = 169 \times 64$. So, $\sqrt{10{,}816} = \sqrt{169 \times 64}$.

$$= \sqrt{169} \times \sqrt{64}$$
$$= 13 \times 8 = 104.$$

I'll use my calculator to check. $104 \;\boxed{x^2}\; 10{,}816$. $\sqrt{10{,}816} = 104$

Sarah thinks ...

I'll just use my calculator.

I'll enter $10{,}816 \;\boxed{\sqrt{x}}\; 104$.

$\sqrt{10{,}816} = 104$

What do you think?

1. Describe how Enrique used the fact that 10,816 could be factored into perfect squares.

2. Sarah and Enrique both used their calculators. How did they use their calculators differently to get the same answer?

3. Enrique used the property $\sqrt{a \times b} = \sqrt{a} \times \sqrt{b}$. Give an example that shows that the property does not work for addition: $\sqrt{a + b} \neq \sqrt{a} + \sqrt{b}$.

> **Problem Solving TIP**
>
> If you're guessing whether a property works, you should check your answer. (For example, $\sqrt{169 \times 64} = \sqrt{169} \times \sqrt{64}$).

Check | Your Understanding

1. Explain the difference between the principal and negative square roots.

2. Explain the difference between $-\sqrt{9}$ and $\sqrt{-9}$. What does your calculator show when you enter $9 \;\boxed{+/-}\; \boxed{\sqrt{x}}$?

7-8 Exercises and Applications

Practice and Apply

1. **Getting Started** Use your calculator to determine whether $\sqrt{95}$ is rational or irrational.

   a. Enter 95 $\boxed{\sqrt{x}}$.

   b. Determine if this is rational or irrational.

Identify each number as rational or irrational.

2. $\sqrt{4}$ 3. $\sqrt{17}$ 4. $\sqrt{20}$ 5. $\sqrt{200}$ 6. $0.12\overline{3}$

7. $0.202002000\ldots$ 8. $\sqrt{\dfrac{9}{25}}$ 9. π 10. $\sqrt{3}$ 11. $0.\overline{3}$

Use a calculator to find each square root and round to the nearest thousandth.

12. $\sqrt{2}$ 13. $\sqrt{15}$ 14. $\sqrt{29}$ 15. $\sqrt{99}$ 16. $\sqrt{147}$

17. $\sqrt{252}$ 18. $\sqrt{1000}$ 19. $\sqrt{2000}$ 20. $\sqrt{1600}$ 21. $\sqrt{456}$

Geometry Find the side length of each of the squares with the given area.

22. 45 in^2 23. 30 in^2 24. 36 cm^2 25. 42.25 m^2

26. **History** The term *radical* is taken from the Arabic word *jidr,* meaning "plant-root." In Arabic math texts, a square number was thought of as growing out of a root number. For example, 49 grows out of 7, the jidr. What would the jidr be of 196?

27. **Geography** The Shikushi family in Japan has a square home with four square rooms measuring 121 ft^2 each. Removable, sliding paper screens separate the rooms. In the summer, they remove the screens to allow breezes to go through and the house becomes one large room. What would the dimensions of this large room be?

Cabbage seed splitting open

28. **Science** You can find the number of seconds that it takes a pendulum to swing back and forth. First, find the square root of the pendulum's length in meters, then double it. How long will it take a pendulum that is 1.2 meters long to swing back and forth?

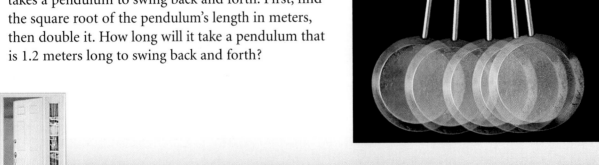

29. **Test Prep** In Italy, the Pellegrini family lives in a five-room house that has a floor area of 1292 ft². If the house has a square base, what would be the length of a wall?

Ⓐ 35.94 ft   Ⓑ 40.94 ft

Ⓒ 12.92 ft   Ⓓ 84.94 ft

1292 ft²

Problem Solving and Reasoning

30. **Journal** Is the square root of 2000 twice the square root of 1000? Explain.

31. **Critical Thinking** List the first ten perfect squares and their factors. Examine the number of factors for each. What conclusions can you draw about the number of factors of perfect squares?

32. **Estimation** Using the formula $d = \sqrt{1.5h}$, where d = distance, in miles, to the horizon and h = the height, in feet, of the viewer's eyes above the ground, you can find how far you can see to the horizon. If Sandy climbed a live oak tree so that her eyes were 32 feet above the ground, how far ahead could she see?

h=height

d=distance to horizon

33. **Communicate** The restaurant at the top of the Eiffel Tower in Paris is 980 feet high. Use the formula in Exercise 32 to determine how far the diners can see. If the Eiffel Tower was twice as high, could they see twice as far? Explain.

Mixed Review

Find the value of *y* when *x* = 8 for each of the following. *[Lesson 4-1]*

34. $y = x - 2$ **35.** $4x + 7 = y$ **36.** $2x = 6 + y$ **37.** $y = x + 9$

Make a table of five pairs of coordinates for each equation. Use 0, 1, 2, 3, 4, and 5 for *x*. *[Lesson 4-1]*

38. $y = x + 5$ **39.** $y = x - 3$ **40.** $y = 2x + 1$ **41.** $x = y + 4$

42. Which of the tables is an equivalent ratio table? *[Lesson 5-2]*

x	2	4	6	8
y	3	5	7	9

x	3	6	9	12
y	9	18	27	36

The Pythagorean Theorem

You'll Learn ...

■ to use the Pythagorean theorem with right triangles

... How It's Used

Bricklayers use the Pythagorean theorem to build straight walls.

Vocabulary

Pythagorean theorem

▶ **Lesson Link** You have learned about squares and square roots and will now apply what you have learned to solving problems about right triangles. ◀

Explore | **Pythagorean Theorem**

Squeeze in the Squares (²s)

Materials: Graph paper, Scissors, Markers (three different colors)

1. Use the procedures in Parts 2 and 3 for each set of squares.

a. 3 by 3	**b.** 3 by 3	**c.** 5 by 5	**d.** 6 by 6
4 by 4	8 by 8	12 by 12	8 by 8
5 by 5	10 by 10	13 by 13	10 by 10

2. Draw a set of three squares on graph paper. Shade each square with a different color and cut each one out.

3. Without overlapping, can you cover the largest square with the two smaller squares? You can cut along the graph lines of each square.

4. Does the area of the largest square equal the sum of the areas of the two smaller squares for **a**? For **b**? For **c**? For **d**?

5. Can you make a right triangle using the sides of each of the sets of squares you worked with above?

6. What relationship do you notice between the sets of squares?

Learn | **The Pythagorean Theorem**

The **Pythagorean theorem** states that, for every right triangle, the sum of the squares of each leg is equal to the square of the hypotenuse.

The equation for the Pythagorean theorem is $a^2 + b^2 = c^2$, a and b for the lengths of the legs and c for the hypotenuse.

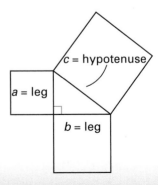

c = hypotenuse

a = leg

b = leg

Example 1

Find the missing length of the right triangle shown.

$12^2 + 5^2 = c^2$ Apply the Pythagorean theorem.

$169 = c^2$ Apply exponents. Add.

$\sqrt{169} = \sqrt{c^2}$ Take square root of both sides.

$13 = c$

The hypotenuse is 13 cm.

Try It

Find the missing length.

a.

b.

Example 2

A *tukul* is a traditional Ethiopian grass house. The length of the roof is 10 ft and the height of the roof is 6 ft. Find the distance from the wall to the center of the room.

$a^2 + 6^2 = 10^2$ Apply Pythagorean theorem.

$a^2 + 36 = 100$ Apply exponents.

$a^2 = 64$ Subtract 36 from both sides.

$\sqrt{a^2} = \sqrt{64}$ Take square root of both sides.

$a = 8$

The distance between the wall and the center of the *tukul* is 8 ft.

Try It

Find the missing length.

a.

b.

Sometimes the sides of a right triangle are not rational numbers.

Test Prep

Read questions carefully and determine the necessary information to solve the question.

Example 3

The second story of an Austrian chalet is triangular. The floor is 18 ft across. The center of the floor to the highest point on the ceiling is 12 ft. Find the length of the slanted roof.

$$18 \div 2 = 9$$ Find the length of the base of the triangle.

$$9^2 + 12^2 = c^2$$ Apply Pythagorean theorem.

$$225 = c^2$$ Apply exponents. Add.

$$\sqrt{225} = \sqrt{c^2}$$ Take square root of both sides.

$$15 = c$$

The length of the roof is approximately 15 ft.

Example 4

What is the length of the hypotenuse?

$$(\sqrt{3})^2 + (\sqrt{3})^2 = c^2$$ Apply Pythagorean theorem.

$$3 + 3 = c^2$$ Apply exponents.

$$6 = c^2$$ Add.

$$\sqrt{6} = \sqrt{c^2}$$ Take square root of both sides.

$$\sqrt{6} = c$$

The hypotenuse is $\sqrt{6}$ units.

Try It

Find the missing length.

a.

12 in.   13 in.

b.
$\sqrt{6}$ m c 8 m

Check | Your Understanding

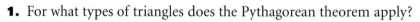

1. For what types of triangles does the Pythagorean theorem apply?

2. Explain how square roots are used with the Pythagorean theorem.

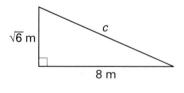

Practice and Apply

1. **Getting Started** Find the missing length of the triangle shown.

   a. Apply the Pythagorean theorem.

   b. Apply exponents and simplify.

   c. Take the square root of both sides.

Find the length of the missing side for each right triangle.

2.

3.

4.

5. **Geometry** A flag shop is constructing flags for the Solomon Islands. If the rectangular flags are to be 4 ft by 6 ft, what would the length of the yellow stripe be?

6. **Social Studies** If the flags being made for Jamaica are the same size as the Solomon Island flags, what length of yellow fabric is necessary for each Jamaican flag?

Solomon Islands

Jamaica

7. **Science** Sunset Crater, a volcano in Arizona, has an altitude of 1200 ft. If you stand at the base of the slope—which is 2000 ft from the peak—how far are you standing from the pipe?

8. **Estimation** Paul has a 12 ft ladder to use to fix the leaking roof of his garage. If the base of the ladder is placed at least 4 ft from the garage to make climbing safe, is the ladder long enough for Paul to reach the 10 ft garage roof?

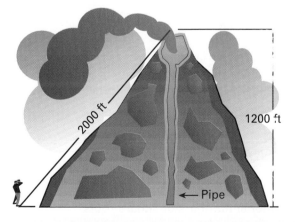

9. **Test Prep** The Comanche Indians cure buffalo hides and stretch them over a wooden framework to build tepees. If the radius of a tepee is 15 ft and the hides are extended 25 ft up on the slanted sides, how high will the center of the tepee be?

Ⓐ 200 ft   Ⓑ 29 ft   Ⓒ 20 ft   Ⓓ 4.5 ft

Problem Solving and Reasoning

Math Reasoning If the lengths of the sides of a triangle satisfy $a^2 + b^2 = c^2$, the triangle is a right triangle. The longest side is c, the hypotenuse. Does the set of side lengths make a right triangle?

10. 4, 5, 7   **11.** 7, 24, 25   **12.** 20, 21, 29   **13.** 5, 12, 13

14. Communicate The ancient Egyptians used ropes tied with knots to form a 3-4-5 triangle to help them with right angles when building the pyramids. Explain how this system would work.

15. Measurement A square courtyard with a diagonal walkway has an area of 81 square feet.

   a. Find the length of the sides of the courtyard.

   b. Find the length of the walkway.

16. Patterns Use the Pythagorean theorem to find the length of the hypotenuse in right triangles when the legs are integer values of equal length. When do you get an integer length for the hypotenuse?

Mixed Review

Give two solution pairs for each of these equations. *[Lesson 4-2]*

17. $x = 2y$ **18.** $y = x + 4$ **19.** $3x = 5y$ **20.** $y = 3x + 2$

Solve each proportion. *[Lesson 5-4]*

21. $\dfrac{2}{3} = \dfrac{44}{x}$ **22.** $\dfrac{9}{x} = \dfrac{27{,}000}{36{,}000}$ **23.** $\dfrac{x}{5} = \dfrac{20}{100}$

24. If a cookie recipe calls for 3 cups of sugar to make 4 dozen cookies, how many cups of sugar are needed to make 10 dozen cookies?

Project Progress

Look back at your results from the investment period. Look for any use of irrational numbers or square roots.

Problem Solving

Understand
Plan
Solve
Look Back

Section 7C Connect

You have learned to use the Pythagorean theorem for right triangles. You will now use the Pythagorean theorem to design parts of a house.

Home Sweet Home

Materials: Calculator

Some people prefer to build or fix up their own house. Measurements and calculations are crucial if you want windows to close, doors to open, stable walls, and straight floors. The Pythagorean theorem can be used for many aspects of building a house.

1. A foundation can keep the wooden frame of a house from rotting after years of rain, wind, and snow. Compare the two foundations shown by determining the depth of each.

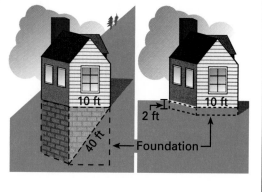

2. The frame of a house is like your body's skeleton. Corner bracing can add strength to a house frame. How long is the entire length of bracing?

3. How long is a part of the bracing that is between two 10-ft-tall wood planks? Explain how you got your answer.

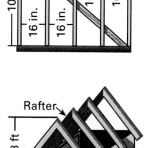

4. Rafters are the parallel beams that support a roof. What is the total length of wood used in the rafters of this roof?

5. Draw a sketch of a house that you would build for yourself and describe how you would use the Pythagorean theorem.

Section 7C Review

Use your calculator to determine whether each is a perfect square.

1. 1000   **2.** 3025   **3.** 686   **4.** 3222   **5.** 1296

Determine each square root and write in lowest terms.

6. $\sqrt{1296}$ **7.** $\sqrt{68}$ **8.** $\sqrt{\dfrac{49}{81}}$ **9.** $\sqrt{\dfrac{100}{625}}$ **10.** $\sqrt{\dfrac{144}{36}}$

11. $-\sqrt{36}$ **12.** $-\sqrt{1764}$ **13.** $\pm\sqrt{12.25}$ **14.** $\pm\sqrt{4096}$ **15.** $-\sqrt{\dfrac{36}{4}}$

Identify each number as rational or irrational.

16. $\sqrt{376}$ **17.** $\sqrt{1296}$ **18.** $0.\overline{62}$ **19.** $\dfrac{7}{9}$ **20.** $-\sqrt{\dfrac{4}{9}}$

Find the side length of a square with the given area.

21. 32 in^2 **22.** 12 ft^2 **23.** 441 cm^2 **24.** 34 m^2 **25.** 4.25 ft^2

Find the missing side length of each right triangle.

26.

27.

28.

29. Explain why you think it is easier for craftspeople (for example, carpenters or mechanics) to use rational numbers in their work.

Test Prep

On a multiple-choice test you will often see a familiar formula to apply and you will have to know what the variables represent.

30. The formula $a^2 + b^2 = c^2$ satisfies all right triangles, where c is the hypotenuse. Which of the following triangles is a right triangle?

Ⓐ

Ⓑ

Ⓒ
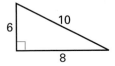

380   Chapter 7 • Number Sense, Rational Numbers, and Irrational Numbers

Modular Arithmetic

People keep track of time using months, days of the week, hours, and so on. In mathematics, modular arithmetic can be used to show these ways of counting. If today is Monday, then 7 days later it's Monday again. Days of the week use modulo 7 because there are seven days in a week.

	Sat.	Sun.	Mon.	Tues.	Wed.	Thurs.	Fri.
Day							
Day (Modulo 7)	1	2	3	4	5	6	0

If we apply the modulo 7 table above to a calendar for January 2011, you'll see how multiples of seven are always Fridays.

If you divide a date by 7 and there is a remainder of 1, then it's a Saturday.

Remainder 2 is a Sunday = 2 (modulo 7).

Remainder 3 is a Monday = 3 (modulo 7).

Remainder 4 is a Tuesday = 4 (modulo 7).

JANUARY 2011

S	M	T	W	T	F	S
						1
2	3	4	5	6	7	8
9	10	11	12	13	14	15
16	17	18	19	20	21	22
23	24	25	26	27	28	29
30	31					

February 2011 has a total of 28 days and February 1 is on a Tuesday. You can determine which day is February 28 by using modulo 7 and letting Tuesday = 1 (modulo 7). $28 \div 7 = 4$ with 0 remainder. So, the last day of February is on a Monday.

	Tues.	Wed.	Thurs.	Fri.	Sat.	Sun.	Mon.
Day							
Day (Modulo 7)	1	2	3	4	5	6	0

1. Use modular arithmetic to find what day February 14 falls on in 2011.

2. In 2011, March 1 is on a Tuesday; the month ends March 31. Make a modulo 7 table for March.

Use modular arithmetic to find the day of the week for the following dates.

3. March 9

4. March 22

5. March 31

Graphic Organizer

Section 7A Number Theory

Summary

- A **prime number** is an integer greater than 1 that is only divisible by itself and 1. A **composite number** is an integer that is not prime.

- An integer is a **multiple** of a number if it is **divisible** by that number—that is, if it can be divided without a remainder. A number is divisible by each of its **factors**.

- The **Fundamental Theorem of Arithmetic** states that all integers greater than 1 can be written using **prime factorization**.

- A **common factor** of two numbers is a factor of both numbers. The largest of these is the **greatest common factor (GCF)**.

- A **common multiple** of two numbers is a multiple of both numbers. The smallest common multiple is the **least common multiple (LCM)**.

Review

1. Is 162 divisible by 2, 3, 4, 5, 6, 8, 9, or 10?

2. Determine the prime factorization of 924.

3. Find the GCF of 39 and 45.

4. Write $\frac{84}{112}$ in lowest terms.

5. Find the LCM of 15 and 25.

6. Find the LCD of $\frac{3}{15}$ and $\frac{2}{20}$.

Section 7B Rational Numbers

Summary

- A **rational number** is a number that can be written as a ratio of two integers. Integers, fractions, terminating decimals, and repeating decimals are rational numbers.

- A **terminating decimal** has a fixed number of digits. A **repeating decimal** has a repeating digit or repeating group of digits.

- Add and subtract fractions by writing them with a common denominator.

- Use the **reciprocal** and multiply when you divide by a fraction.

Review

7. Write $\frac{3}{16}$ as a decimal and determine whether it is repeating or terminating.

8. Replace ☐ with $>$, $<$, or $=$ to compare 3.806 ☐ 3.8059.

9. Write 0.12 as a fraction in lowest terms.

10. Add $5.84 + 12.638$.

11. Subtract $7\frac{8}{9} - 2\frac{5}{6}$.

12. Divide $2\frac{3}{8} \div 3\frac{1}{3}$.

Section 7C Irrational Numbers

Summary

- A **square root** of a number (N) gives N when multiplied by itself. The positive square root is the **principal square root** and its opposite is the **negative square root**.

- A **perfect square** is a number with an integer square root.

- A number that cannot be expressed as a repeating or terminating decimal is an **irrational number**. The rational and irrational numbers make up the **real numbers**.

- The **Pythagorean theorem** states that in a right triangle, the sum of the squares of the legs is equal to the square of the hypotenuse.

Review

13. State whether or not 92 is a perfect square.

14. Find the square root of $\frac{25}{36}$.

15. Find the two consecutive integers that $\sqrt{54}$ is between.

16. What is the side length of a square with area 32 cm²?

17. Find $\pm\sqrt{529}$.

18. Find $-\sqrt{729}$.

1. Determine whether 615 is divisible by 2, 3, 4, 5, 6, 8, 9, or 10.

Determine the prime factorization of each number.

2. 315   **3.** 266   **4.** 372   **5.** 213

6. Find the GCF of 24 and 64.   **7.** Find the GCF of 180 and 428.

Write each fraction in lowest terms.

8. $\dfrac{54}{126}$ **9.** $\dfrac{322}{330}$ **10.** $\dfrac{63}{141}$ **11.** $\dfrac{75}{180}$

12. Find the LCM of 36 and 32.   **13.** Find the LCM of 84 and 63.

14. Loaves of Breads bakery has free samples of blueberry muffins every 5 days, whole-wheat bread every 8 days, and sourdough rolls every 6 days. How often does the bakery give free samples of all three breads on the same day?

15. Determine whether $\dfrac{7}{11}$ is repeating or terminating as a decimal.

16. Replace $\square$ with $>$, $<$, or $=$ to compare 3.14159 $\square$ $\dfrac{22}{7}$.

17. Write $0.\overline{15}$ as a fraction in lowest terms.

18. Subtract $10.6724 - 3.87$.

19. Calculate and express each as a mixed number in lowest terms.

    a. $6\dfrac{3}{4} + 12\dfrac{7}{18}$ **b.** $3\dfrac{5}{7} \times 7\dfrac{2}{13}$

20. State whether 150 is a perfect square.

21. Find the two closest perfect squares for 89.

22. Estimate the square root of 150.

23. Use a calculator to find $\sqrt{67}$ and round to the nearest thousandth.

24. Find $\sqrt{\dfrac{49}{81}}$.   **25.** Find $\sqrt{8} \times \sqrt{18}$.

26. Decide whether side lengths 8, 15, and 17 would make a right triangle.

27. Find the length of the missing side for the right triangle.

Performance Task

Make a poster that you could use to explain how to write a repeating decimal such as $2.\overline{7}$ as a fraction.

Performance Assessment

Choose one problem.

School Dances

Damon, a disc jockey, charges $275 for two hours and $400 for 3 hours. At school dances he charges $2 for each song requested, half of which goes toward the school's library fund. If at the spring dance, 75 songs are requested, how much will go toward the library fund? How much does Damon make per hour for a 3-hour dance? How much do you think he should charge for a dance that lasts $2\frac{1}{2}$ hours?

One Earth, One Chance

The Sierra Club used 0.074 of its donations toward outdoor activities, 0.096 toward fundraising, and 0.234 toward public education. People who donate to the Sierra Club can offer $15, $25, $35, $50, or $100. Calculate how much of each donation goes toward outdoor activities, fundraising, and public education. Create a display to show your results.

Telephone Dilemma

Joel's telephone is 6 ft away from the telephone jack on the same wall. The telephone jack is 8 in. above the floor. The telephone is mounted 2 ft above the floor. Will a 10 ft cord connect Joel's telephone to the telephone jack on the wall? Show your work and draw a diagram of Joel's telephone dilemma.

An Alternative Spud Topper

One serving of cottage cheese is 110 grams. Cottage cheese is $\frac{2}{55}$ carbohydrates, $\frac{1}{44}$ fat, and $\frac{1}{8}$ protein. How many grams of carbohydrates, fat, and protein are in one serving of cottage cheese?

8 Geometry and Measurement

Entertainment Link
www.mathsurf.com/8/ch8/ent

Entertainment

Dating back to 1851, the America's Cup is the oldest international trophy sport. In 1995, the first all-woman crew competed in the America's Cup in their yacht, America[3].

Science

In 1791, the Paris Academy of Sciences defined the meter as $\frac{1}{10,000,000}$ of the distance from the North Pole to the equator.

Arts & Literature

The largest painting in the world measures 72,437 ft² and is made of brightly colored squares and a smiley face. Compare that to a football field, which is only 45,000 ft².

People of the World

The Maori people of New Zealand used a *mattang,* an instrument made of sticks, to read the parallel patterns of ocean waves. They could locate nearby islands by feeling the motion of water around their boat.

Social Studies

Four colors are all you need in order to have a map without neighboring countries of the same color.

KEY MATH IDEAS

There are many quantities that can be measured. For example, length, area, volume, mass, capacity, weight, time, and so on.

The metric system and U.S. customary system are two commonly used measurement systems in the United States.

The measure of lines and angles determine how a polygon is classified.

CHAPTER PROJECT

Problem Solving

Understand
Plan
Solve
Look Back

In this project, research and report on an ancient culture, its system of measurement, and how it used lines, angles, and polygons in its civilization. You will report the units used to measure quantities such as length, area, money, time, capacity, weight, and so on. Report how the culture converted units of measurement and how they constructed angles and other geometric shapes.

Problem Solving Focus

Problem Solving

Understand
Plan
Solve
Look Back

Solving Problems

There is often more than one way to solve a problem. You should use the strategy that works best for you. Trying different strategies can help you decide which one suits your problem-solving style.

The following problem has already been solved using three different methods.

Three friends buy fresh corn at an outdoor market. Amani buys twice as much corn as Brad. Brad buys three more ears of corn than Chris. All together, Amani, Brad, and Chris buy 17 ears of corn. How much corn does each of them buy?

You know:

- There are 17 ears of corn,
- Amani has twice as many as Brad,
- Brad can't have more than eight ears of corn,
- Chris has three less than Brad.

Guess and Check	Draw a diagram	Logical Reasoning
Guess: 6 ears for Brad. B = 6 A = 6 × 2 = 12 C = 6 − 3 = 3 **Check:** 6 + 12 + 3 = 21 Too big. **Guess:** 5 ears for Brad. B = 5 A = 5 × 2 = 10 C = 5 − 3 = 2 **Check:** 5 + 2 + 10 = 17 It works.	Let ❑ = ears Chris buys. C = ❑ B = ❑ + 3 A = (❑ + 3) + (❑ + 3) You have four ❑'s and three 3's. You have four ❑'s and 9. 17 − 9 = 8 The four ❑'s stand for 8 ears of corn. 8 ÷ 4 = 2 Each ❑ = 2.	■ No one can have more than 17. ■ Amani must have the most. ■ Chris must have the least. ■ The other amounts are based on Brad's amount. So find Brad's amount first. B = 5 A = 5 × 2 = 10 C = 5 − 3 = 2

Solve the following problem. You may use one of the above methods or a method of your own.

1 Four friends work out at a health club. Mark uses the treadmill three times as long as Joan. Allison uses it half as long as David. David uses it 15 minutes longer than Mark. All together, they use the treadmill for 2.5 hours. How long is each person on the machine?

Measurement

Where am I? Where am I going? How do I get there? If you aren't certain about a location, you can look on a map. It hasn't always been this way.

In the past, people marked trails with stones and noted landmarks such as trees and streams. But snow and rain could interfere with this system. Stars were used for navigation, but that only worked on clear nights.

In 1978, the U.S. Department of Defense said, "We've got to have a system that really works." So since then the government has worked on something called the Global Positioning System, or GPS. There are 24 satellites orbiting the earth connected to a computer system. In a way, you could think of the satellites as "human-made stars." GPS is accurate enough to give positions, anywhere in the world, within the width of your street, 24 hours a day.

This means that everyone will have the ability to know exactly where they are, all the time. Finally, one of humankind's basic needs will be fulfilled.

1 GPS is widely used by backpackers and sailors. What other uses can you think of for GPS?

2 GPS allows every square meter of the earth's surface to have a unique address, similar to a coordinate plane. How do you think GPS might change what we know to be a phone book?

Units of Measurement

You'll Learn ...

■ to choose an appropriate unit of measurement

... How It's Used

Mask-makers use units of measurement when they mix materials to make glues or varnishes that hold the masks together.

Vocabulary

U.S. customary units

metric system

▶ **Lesson Link** You've seen how numbers are used in measurement. In this lesson, you'll learn more about the units used in measurement. ◀

Explore | **Using Units**

Study Your Desk?

Materials: Unsharpened pencils, Paper, 2 optional length units

1. Lay a line of pencils across a desk. How many pencils did you use? Estimate using $\frac{1}{2}$, $\frac{1}{4}$, 0.5, or 0.25 if appropriate.

2. Measure the length of the desk with two other objects or units. Record and compare the measurements.

3. Cover the desks with sheets of paper without overlapping. How many sheets of paper did you use? This is the area of the desk in sheets of paper. What other objects or units would be appropriate for measuring the area of the desk?

4. Discuss the difference between units of length and units of area.

Learn | **Units of Measurement**

U.S. customary units use the inch, foot, and mile as units of length. The **metric system** uses the centimeter, meter, and kilometer as units of length.

Metric System		U.S. Customary Units	
centimeter (cm)	millimeter (mm) = 0.1 cm	inch (in.)	foot (ft) = 12 in.
	meter (m) = 100 cm		yard (yd) = 3 ft
	kilometer (km) = 1000 m		mile (mi) = 5280 ft

In each system of measurement you can change the units by using a ratio.

To convert from feet to inches, use the ratio $\frac{12 \text{ in.}}{1 \text{ ft}}$.

To convert from inches to feet, use the ratio $\frac{1 \text{ ft}}{12 \text{ in.}}$.

Example 1

GPS satellites orbit about 11,000 mi above the earth's surface. Convert this altitude to ft.

To convert from mi to ft, use the ratio $\frac{5,280 \text{ ft}}{1 \text{ mi}}$.

$$\frac{11,000 \text{ mi}}{1} \times \frac{5,280 \text{ ft}}{\text{mi}} = \frac{11,000 \text{ mi} \times 5,280 \text{ ft}}{1 \text{ mi}}$$

$$= \frac{11,000 \times 5,280 \text{ ft}}{1} = \frac{58,080,000 \text{ ft}}{1}$$

The satellites are about 58 million ft above the earth.

To change units within the metric system, use powers of ten.

To convert from meters to centimeters, use the ratio $\frac{100 \text{ cm}}{1 \text{ m}}$.

To convert from centimeters to meters, use the ratio $\frac{1 \text{ m}}{100 \text{ cm}}$.

Example 2

The radius of the earth is 6,371,000 m. Convert the earth's radius to km.

To convert from m to km, use the ratio $\frac{1 \text{ km}}{1,000 \text{ m}}$.

$$\frac{6,371,000 \text{ m}}{1} \times \frac{1 \text{ km}}{1,000 \text{ m}} = \frac{6,371,000 \text{ m} \times 1 \text{ km}}{1,000 \text{ m}}$$

$$= \frac{6,371,000 \text{ km}}{1,000} = 6,371 \text{ km is the earth's radius.}$$

▶ **Science Link**

The radius of the earth is the distance from its center to any point on its surface. The radius of the earth is not the same to every point on the earth's surface.

Try It

Convert each unit of length.

a. 32 km to m   **b.** 10,365 ft to mi

Measurements don't just involve length. You can take measurements of area, volume, weight, time, mass, capacity, and other quantities.

The table below shows some common units of measurement. Notice that both customary and metric units are given for capacity.

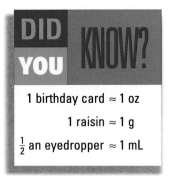

Measurement	Units		
Weight	**Ounce** (oz)	**Pound** (lb) = 16 oz	**Ton** (T) = 2000 lb
Time	**Second** (sec)	**Minute** (min) = 60 sec	**Hour** (hr) = 60 min
Mass	**Gram** (g)	**Kilogram** (kg) = 1000 g	
Capacity	Metric: U.S. Customary:	**Milliliter** (mL) **Pint** (pt) = 2 cups	**Liter** (L) = 1000 mL **Quart** (qt) = 2 pt

Units of measurement are usually expressed according to the size of the object. For example, tons are more appropriate units than ounces to indicate a car's weight. Minutes are more appropriate units than seconds to express the time it takes to cook a hard-boiled egg.

Example 3

Determine an appropriate unit for measuring each.

a. Weight of a pencil   oz is a small unit of weight.

b. Time it takes to take one step   sec is a small unit of time.

c. Mass of a watermelon   kg is a large unit of mass.

d. Capacity of a soda can   mL is a small unit of capacity.

Try It

Determine appropriate units for measuring each.

a. Capacity of an olive jar   **b.** Time it takes to brush your teeth

c. Weight of a boat   **d.** Mass of a car

Units of length, area, and volume can often be distinguished by the use of exponents.

	Length	Area	Volume
Metric	mm, cm, m, …	mm^2, cm^2, m^2, …	mm^3, cm^3, m^3, …
U.S. Customary	in., ft, yd, …	$in.^2$, ft^2, yd^2, …	$in.^3$, ft^3, yd^3, …

Area is expressed using square units, such as ft^2 (square feet). Volume is expressed using cubic units, such as m^3 (cubic meters).

Example 4

Determine an appropriate unit for measuring each.

a. Distance between two cities   mi, because it is a unit of length.

b. Area of a fingernail mm^2, because it is a unit of area.

c. Volume of a stick of butter in^3, because it is a unit of volume.

d. Capacity of a carton of milk   qt, because it is a unit of capacity.

Try It

Determine an appropriate unit for measuring each.

a. Area of a classroom   **b.** Volume of a sugar cube

c. Mass of a compact disc   **d.** Distance between state borders

Sometimes it is necessary to change units twice in order to convert to the desired unit.

Example 5

Originally, sailors who used GPS were always within 18.63 mi of the reported position. What is this distance in yd?

First, convert mi to ft. Then convert ft to yd.

$$\left(\frac{18.63 \text{ mi}}{1} \times \frac{5,280 \text{ ft}}{1 \text{ mi}}\right) \times \frac{1 \text{ yd}}{3 \text{ ft}} =$$

$$\left(\frac{18.63 \cancel{\text{ mi}} \times 5,280 \text{ ft}}{1 \cancel{\text{ mi}}}\right) \times \frac{1 \text{ yd}}{3 \text{ ft}} =$$

$$(98,366.4 \text{ ft}) \times \frac{1 \text{ yd}}{3 \text{ ft}} =$$

$$\frac{98,366.4 \cancel{\text{ ft}} \times 1 \text{ yd}}{3 \cancel{\text{ ft}}} = 32,788.8 \text{ yd}$$

▶ **Industry Link**

The U.S. Coast Guard started a $14 million program to improve the precision of the civilian's GPS to be within 65 ft of the reported position.

Check Your Understanding

1. Why do you get two different numbers when you measure the same thing using different units—for example, 550 cm and 5.5 m?

2. How do you know what units are appropriate for a length measurement? For area? For time?

Practice and Apply

1. **Getting Started** The highest point in the world is Mount Everest, at 29,028 ft. Express this altitude in miles.

    a. Write the ratio of miles to feet with ft in the denominator.

    b. Multiply the ratio by 29,028 ft.

What U.S. customary unit would you use for each measurement?

2. The volume of earth removed during an archaeological dig

3. The distance traveled in one day by a flock of geese

4. The area of a sail on a sailboat

What metric unit would you use for each measurement?

5. A single dose of cough syrup

6. The distance from the top of a diving board to the water surface

7. The mass of your backpack containing your books

Convert each measurement.

8. 7.8 m to cm   9. 2500 L to mL   10. 2.5 hr to min

11. 64 oz to lb   12. 5 ft 4 in. to in.   13. 10 pt to qt

14. **Geography** The area of the United States is 3,615,200 mi^2 and Canada is 3,850,000 mi^2. Which country has a larger area and by how many square miles?

15. **Science** For a geology experiment, a group of students measure the mass of a piece of copper. Their results were 15.64 g, 15.69 g, 15.67 g, 0.01566 kg, and 0.01564 kg. What is the average of the students' measurements?

16. The stopwatch on the right shows the 1995 Boston Marathon record set by Cosmas N'Deti of Kenya in hours, minutes, and seconds. How much time is this in seconds?

17. **Test Prep** Which of these would be an appropriate unit for the area of a rose petal?

Ⓐ cm^2 Ⓑ ft^2 Ⓒ mm^3 Ⓓ in^3

Problem Solving and Reasoning

18. **Critical Thinking** Mont Blanc, the highest peak in the Alps, is 4,807 m above sea level. A climber on Mont Blanc is 88 m from the top. What is her altitude in meters? In kilometers?

19. **Journal** The *cubit* is an ancient unit of measurement defined as the distance from a king's elbow to the tip of his middle finger, about 18 in. What is the problem with this definition? Why do you think standardized measurement units were developed?

20. **Communicate** How would you use proportions to change inches to yards? Give an example.

21. **Measurement** What customary unit would be most appropriate for measuring the area of the GPS display used in agriculture.

22. **Math Reasoning** The Grand Canyon, in Arizona, is 277 miles long. What is this length in yards? Inches? Compare the numerical values of the three measurements. Describe the relationship between these numerical values and the units of measurement associated with them.

Mixed Review

State whether each number is prime or composite. *[Lesson 7-1]*

23. 27   **24.** 91   **25.** 37   **26.** 63

27. 49   **28.** 72   **29.** 1755   **30.** 363

Find the GCF of each pair of numbers. *[Lesson 7-2]*

31. 14, 42   **32.** 16, 64   **33.** 17, 71   **34.** 33, 90

35. 21, 66   **36.** 13, 169   **37.** 82, 16   **38.** 9, 261

Significant Digits and Precision

You'll Learn ...

■ to identify more precise measurements

... How It's Used

Farmers use precise measurements when they analyze the quality of their soil.

Vocabulary

precision

significant digits

▶ **Lesson Link** Now you'll apply what you know about units of measurement to calculate with measurements using significant digits. ◀

Explore Precision

How Close Can You Get?
Materials: Meter stick

1. Measure the distance from the floor to the top of your desk. Record the length to the nearest 1 m, nearest 0.5 m, nearest 1 cm, nearest 0.5 cm, and nearest 1 mm.

2. Compare your measurements with those of others in the group. Did you all get the same numbers? Why or why not?

3. Calculate the height of two desks atop one another using each measurement. (Hint: Multiply by 2.) Do the same for five desks.

4. Which heights are the most exact? Discuss your reasoning.

5. With your group, invent a technique of determining the most accurate measurement from a group of measurements.

Learn Significant Digits and Precision

The **precision** of a measurement is determined by the unit of measure. The smaller the unit of measure, the more precise the measurement.

Example 1

Determine the more precise height of the national Capitol dome, 287 ft or 96 yd?

Choose the measurement with smaller units.

The foot (ft) is smaller than the yard (yd).

287 ft is the more precise measurement.

287 ft

96 yd

When you compare measurements with the same unit, the more precise measurement can be determined by the decimal places.

Example 2

Using GPS, a geologist finds the distance between two mountain peaks. Which measurement is most precise, 1068 m, 1067.52 m, or 1067.5 m?

Choose the measurement to the smallest decimal place.

1067.52 m is the most precise measurement.

Try It

For each pair of measurements, determine the more precise measurement.

a. 0.5 mi, 2638 ft   **b.** 2 m, 197.5 cm   **c.** 36 in., 35.75 in.

The digits that represent the actual measurement are **significant digits**. The last significant digit in a measurement is an estimated digit.

The paper clip is 2.85 cm long.

└─ Estimated digit

When you read a measurement, there are rules for determining the number of significant digits.

1. All nonzero digits (1–9) are significant.

2. Zeros between nonzero digits are significant.

3. Zeros to the right of a decimal point and to the right of a nonzero digit are significant.

4. Zeros to the right of a decimal point and to the left of a nonzero digit are not significant.

Example 3

Determine the number of significant digits in each measurement.

a. 420.040 m

4, 2, and 4 are significant.   Apply Rule 1.

All zeros are significant.   Apply Rules 2, 3, and 4.

6 significant digits.

b. 0.00420 m

4 and 2 are significant.

The last zero is significant.

3 significant digits.

Try It

Determine the number of significant digits in each measurement.

a. 0.0050 m   **b.** 3.05607 kg   **c.** 3000 mi   **d.** 11.050 in.

Adding and subtracting measurements require that the answer be as precise as the least precise value of the two measurements.

Example 4

▶ **Science Link**

An *ornithologist* is someone who studies birds.

To study the toucan, an ornithologist trekked to 6540.75 ft altitude in South America. The ornithologist wants to be at 9455 ft to observe the flocks of toucans. How much higher in altitude does the ornithologist have to go?

The answer will be given to the ones place.

9455.

$-$ 6540.75   Subtract.

2914.25 $\approx$ 2914

The ornithologist has to climb 2914 ft.

Multiplying and dividing measurements require that the answer have as many significant digits as the value in the operation with the least number of significant digits.

Example 5

Remember

To round a number, look at the decimal place to the right.

If the digit to the right is $\leq$ 4, then round down.

If the digit to the right is $\geq$ 5, then round up.

[Previous course]

A rectangular sandbox is built with the lengths 4.75 ft and 3.125 ft. Use significant digits to express the area of the sandbox.

The answer will have 3 significant digits.

Enter: 4.75 $\boxed{\times}$ 3.125 $\boxed{=}$ *14.84375*

The area of the sandbox is 14.8 ft^2.

Try It

Calculate and give the number of significant digits in each answer.

a. 11.4 g + 2.65 g   **b.** 32.06 mL $-$ 22.3 mL

c. 2.3 in. $\times$ 20.3 in.   **d.** 32.5 m $\div$ 1.5

Check | Your Understanding

1. Describe how precision is affected by the unit of measurement used.

2. How do significant digits affect the calculation of measurements?

8-2 Exercises and Applications

Practice and Apply

1. **Getting Started** Determine the number of significant digits in 407.050.

   a. Count the number of nonzero digits.

   b. Count the number of significant zeros.

   c. Add the total number of significant digits from **a** and **b**.

Determine the number of significant digits in each measurement.

2. 0.074 m   3. 0.0056 km   4. 57.048 mi   5. 11.050 in.

Determine which measurement is more precise.

6. 1 yd, 37 in.   7. 235 cm, 230 cm   8. 18 in., $17\frac{11}{16}$ in.   9. 0.3 L, 0.25 L

10. **Science** A measurement of 0.088 m is converted to cm. How many significant digits does the measurement have before conversion? How many after?

11. **Industry** A jet pilot completes a test flight which, according to the on-board GPS-based clock, lasts 2.75 hr. Another test flight on the next day lasts 0.55 hr. Using significant digits, how much total flight time did the pilot log for the two days?

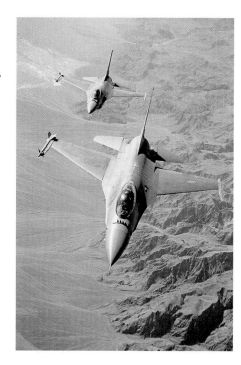

Calculate and give each answer with the correct number of significant digits.

12. 8.4 g + 5.20 g   13. 45 mi − 0.9 mi

14. 9.79 cm × 9.5 cm   15. 32.8 m × 1.5 m

16. **Test Prep** Determine the most precise measurement.

   Ⓐ 89 ft   Ⓑ 89.0 ft   Ⓒ 90 ft   Ⓓ 88.999 ft

17. **Algebra** The formula for converting temperatures from Fahrenheit to Celsius is $C = \frac{5}{9}(F - 32)$. The normal daily low temperature in Everglades National Park is 56°F. What is this temperature in °C, using significant digits.

18. **Measurement** One leg of a right triangle is measured at 1.38 cm, the other at 0.67 cm. What is the length of the hypotenuse? Use significant digits.

Problem Solving and Reasoning

19. **Math Reasoning** An Olympic marathon covers 42.2 km of distance through the streets of the host city, followed by a 400 m lap around the main stadium. What is the total distance of the race, in meters? Use significant digits.

20. **Communicate** The hypotenuse of a right triangle with two equal sides measures 4.04 ft. Find the length of each leg, using significant digits. How could you use an algebraic equation to solve this? Explain.

21. **Journal** The following are the points for the women's gymnastics gold, silver, and bronze medal winners in the 1996 Olympics: 39.255, 39.075, 39.067. How many significant digits are there? Why do you think it is important to be this precise?

22. **Operation Sense** An all-terrain vehicle's GPS indicates that it has traveled 76.34 mi in 2.18 hr. Using significant digits, what is the vehicle's average speed?

Mixed Review

Find the LCM for each pair of numbers. *[Lesson 7-3]*

23. 3, 7   **24.** 10, 40   **25.** 5, 11   **26.** 36, 48

27. 8, 26   **28.** 480, 160   **29.** 12, 10   **30.** 27, 36

Order each group of numbers on a number line. *[Lesson 7-4]*

31. $-\frac{4}{5}, -0.33, 2.2, \frac{1}{2}$ **32.** $-0.\overline{3}, 0, \frac{1}{3}, 0.25$ **33.** $1, -\frac{1}{5}, 0.\overline{12}, -0.1$

Write each as a fraction or mixed number in lowest terms. *[Lesson 7-4]*

34. 0.85   **35.** 2.17   **36.** $0.\overline{6}$ **37.** 0.5   **38.** -8.012

Project Progress

Choose an ancient civilization, then research what units of measurement it used. Investigate units that measured such quantities as time, money, length, area, volume, and weight.

Problem Solving

Understand
Plan
Solve
Look Back

Position

▶ **Lesson Link**   You've learned units for describing distance, mass, and other measurements. Now you'll learn how position and orientation are described. ◀

Explore | Position

Can the Guide Guide?

1. Use the map of Paris to name three landmarks southeast of Place de la Concorde, where the guillotine was during the French Revolution.

2. How far is the Eiffel Tower from the Hôtel des Invalides, which contains Napoleon's tomb?

3. Have one person in the group secretly write down the names of three landmarks on the map. This person will be the "guide" and will conduct a tour from the Arc de Triomphe.

4. The guide must lead the group to the three secret landmarks, in order, by giving only verbal directions. The guide can use information such as direction, distance, and street names.

5. The other members in the group try to identify each of the landmarks after the guide has given the directions. If the tour group cannot determine a landmark based on the guide's directions, then the guide must provide new directions to that landmark.

6. What are some ways that people describe where things are in your town? Your state? The country? The world?

You'll Learn ...

■ to locate places using map coordinates and latitude and longitude

... How It's Used

Police officers can locate places on a map quickly so they can arrive at an emergency promptly.

Vocabulary

absolute position

relative position

You use a grid to identify the location of places on a map. It is similar to a mathematical coordinate grid because it has horizontal and vertical coordinates.

Example 1

Use the map to answer the following.

a. What university is located in J-4?

b. Give the map coordinates of Memorial Park.

a. Find J on the vertical axis and 4 on the horizontal axis. Rice University is in J-4.

b. Memorial Park is in I-3 and I-4.

Absolute position of a location is given as coordinates, whereas the **relative position** of a location is given in relationship to another place.

Example 2

Use the map to answer the following.

a. Give the position of Hart Plaza relative to John F. Kennedy Square.

b. Give the absolute position of Hart Plaza using the map coordinates.

a. Hart Plaza is three blocks southeast of John F. Kennedy Square.

b. Hart Plaza is between G-4 and H-4.

Try It

Use the map to answer the following.

a. Give the position of the zoo relative to the Kickapoo River.

b. Give the absolute position of Bradley Park using the map coordinates.

World maps usually show positions using lines of latitude and longitude. Both of these measurements use degrees as their units.

Remember

Latitude and longitude are the imaginary lines we use to locate places on the earth. Latitude lines run east and west. Longitude lines run north and south.

[Page 90]

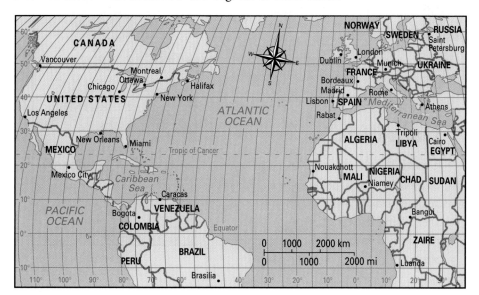

Example 3

Use the map above to answer the following to the nearest 5°.

a. What country occupies 55° N, 65° W?

Find 55° north of the equator.

Find 65° west of 0° longitude.

Canada occupies 55° N, 65° W.

b. Give the latitude and longitude of Bordeaux, France.

Identify the longitude.

Identify the latitude.

Bordeaux is 45° N, 0°.

▶ **Geography Link**

The *prime meridian* is 0° longitude and runs through Greenwich, England.

Example 4

A sailing crew uses GPS to navigate the oceans. Its GPS receiver reports its position as 10° S, 30° W. What country is nearest to the crew?

Find 10° S, 30° W.

Brazil is the closest country.

Try It

Use the map above to answer the following to the nearest 5°.

a. What country occupies 0°, 55° W?

b. Give the latitude and longitude of New Orleans, Louisiana.

WHAT DO YOU THINK?

Use the map to give the position of Dallas relative to Omaha.

Shauna thinks ...

It looks like the map scale is 250 miles to a half inch. I'll measure the distance between Dallas and Omaha in inches. Then I'll multiply that by $\frac{500 \text{ mi}}{\text{in.}}$ and round my answer to the nearest tens place.

$$1\frac{1}{8} \text{ in.} \times \frac{500 \text{ mi}}{\text{in.}} = \frac{9}{8} \text{ in.} \times \frac{500 \text{ mi}}{\text{in.}} = 562.5 \text{ mi}$$

Dallas is about 560 mi south of Omaha.

Kele thinks ...

The map scale shows that 2° latitude is about 140 mi. Dallas and Omaha are about 8° latitude apart.

I'll multiply. $8 \times \frac{140}{2} = 560 \text{ mi}$

Dallas is almost 560 mi south of Omaha.

Problem Solving TIP

Be prepared! Look for ways to apply what you already know to new situations.

What do you think?

1. How did Shauna use a ratio to answer the question?

2. Explain how Shauna and Kele used estimation.

Check | Your Understanding

1. How is a map grid different from a coordinate grid?

2. Describe how latitude and longitude are similar to the *x*- and *y*-axes.

Practice and Apply

1. **Getting Started** Give the map coordinates of the International Peace Garden.

2. What hospital is located in 9D?

3. What airport is located in 9E?

4. What is the position of Pioneer Valley Hospital relative to Salt Lake City Municipal Airport No. 2?

5. **History** Founded in 1847, Salt Lake City built its streets in a perfect grid. What is the position of the Valley Fair Mall relative to West Ridge Golf Course?

6. **Geography** What is the absolute position of Katmandu using latitude and longitude?

7. **Geography** How many degrees of latitude are between Thimphu and Dhaka? How many degrees of longitude?

8. **Logic** The tropic of Cancer is at $23\frac{1}{2}°$ N latitude. The tropic of Capricorn is the same distance south of 0° latitude. At what latitude is the tropic of Capricorn?

9. **Science** Geologists think that the Himalayan mountains were formed when India collided with Asia almost 100 million years ago. The highest point in the world is located at 28.0° N, 86.6° E. What is its name?

10. **Test Prep** How many degrees latitude is it from Jacksonville, Florida, to Key West?

    Ⓐ 6°   Ⓑ 1°   Ⓒ 3°   Ⓓ 12°

11. How many miles are between Jacksonville, Florida, and Key West?

12. How many kilometers are between Cape Canaveral and Tallahassee?

13. How many miles are between Tampa and Miami?

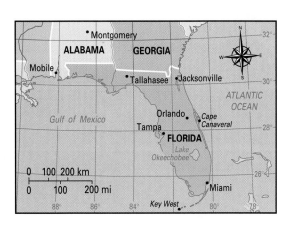

PRACTICE 8-3

Problem Solving and Reasoning

14. Critical Thinking Name a lake and a city in Mexico that are approximately on the same latitude and 375 miles away from each other.

15. ![Journal] What kind of measuring device would you invent to measure distances and directions while traveling? How precise should it be? Make a sketch of it and describe how it would work.

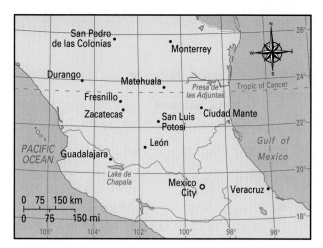

16. Communicate The west coast of Cuba is at 85° W and the east coast of Cuba is at 74° W. If at that latitude, a 5° change in longitude represents about 300 mi, how far is it from coast to coast? Explain your answer.

17. Math Reasoning There is 111 km between each degree longitude at the equator. The distance between longitudes changes as you travel toward the polar regions. Describe how this distance changes and explain why it changes.

18. Algebra Describe the relative position of $(-3, 5)$ with respect to the origin $(0, 0)$ on a coordinate grid.

19. Math Reasoning Kachina hiked 1 mile east, turned right, and walked $\frac{3}{4}$ mile. After a lunch break, she walked in the same direction 1.25 miles, turned left, and continued her hike. What direction is Kachina facing?

20. Math Reasoning A backpacker uses her GPS receiver to find out how much farther she needs to travel. The red dot on the GPS receiver screen shows where she is. The blue dot shows her destination. How far is that point from her current position?

Mixed Review

Find each unit rate. *[Lesson 5-5]*

21. 220 mi in 4 hr   **22.** 18 birds in 9 nests   **23.** $48 for 8 hr

24. $3.99 for 3 lb   **25.** 32 children in 14 homes   **26.** $100 for 10 CDs

Add or subtract. *[Lesson 7-5]*

27. $1.024 + 2.091$ **28.** $0.041 - 0.144$ **29.** $42.1 + 98.156$

30. $\frac{4}{5} + 1\frac{1}{2}$ **31.** $5\frac{1}{3} - 2\frac{2}{3}$ **32.** $9\frac{1}{4} + 2\frac{9}{10}$

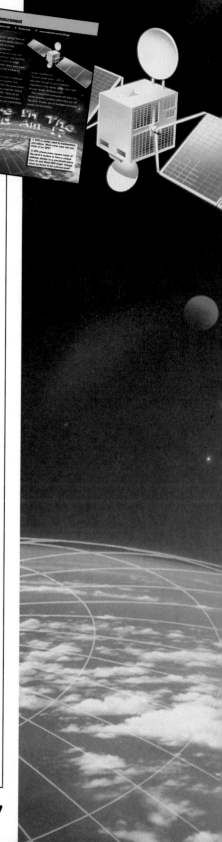

You've learned about precision and have converted units of measurement. Now you'll use this knowledge to learn more about GPS.

Where in the World Am I?

The Navstar GPS is controlled by the U.S. military at Falcon Air Force Base in Colorado. In 1995, there were 24 satellites orbiting the earth to enable people all over the world to navigate.

There are two types of Global Positioning Systems. The Precise Positioning Service (PPS) is only for the U.S. Department of Defense. The Standard Positioning Service (SPS) is for the general public.

The PPS is encoded and needs a decoder to be used. The SPS is not encoded and is used by fishing boats, cars, airplanes, and backpackers.

Types of GPS		
GPS-Determined Measurements	**PPS Precision**	**SPS Precision**
Distance in any direction N, S, E, or W	Within 17.8 m	Within 100 m
Altitude	Within 27.7 m	Within 156 m
Time (1,000,000,000 ns = 1 sec)	Within 100 ns	Within 340 ns

1. Which GPS service is more precise? Discuss your reasoning.

2. Why would there be two levels of precision for GPS service?

3. One GPS satellite has an orbit approximately 93,305 mi long and completes the orbit in 12 hr. How fast does a GPS satellite travel?

4. Suppose a ship is 200 km east of Boston. If a GPS satellite is 17,500 km directly above Boston, what is the distance between the GPS satellite and the ship? Use the Pythagorean theorem.

5. Some say that a GPS receiver in a backpack could someday help guide blind people. Discuss some other possible applications for GPS.

What metric unit would you use for each measurement?

1. The amount of water in an aquarium

2. The lenth of the diagonal of a television screen

3. The area of your hand

Convert each measurement.

4. 0.79 ft to yd   **5.** 245 min to hr   **6.** 500 mL to L

7. 2500 L to mL   **8.** 1.48 km to m   **9.** $1\frac{3}{4}$ lb to oz

Determine the number of significant digits in each measurement.

10. 409 g   **11.** 0.006 mm   **12.** 2300 lb   **13.** 0.0510 mL   **14.** 72.0 in^2

Determine which measurement is more precise.

15. 0.5 gal, 1.89 L   **16.** 6.2 cm, 6.20 cm   **17.** 3499 in., 3500 in.   **18.** 201 cm, 2 m

Calculate and give each answer with the correct number of significant digits.

19. 8.4 g + 5.20 g   **20.** 45 mi − 0.9 mi   **21.** 9.79 cm × 9.5 cm   **22.** 32.8 m × 2.4 m

23. If 22° N, 76° E is in India, what country is 39° N, 90° E in?

24. **Journal** A distance is measured as 6.35 km and recorded as 6350 m. Could someone think there are four significant digits in this measurement? Explain.

Test Prep

When you convert units of measurement on a multiple choice test, the possible answers can have the same number of significant digits. Make sure your answer has the decimal point in the proper place.

25. An eyelash is 11.3 mm long. How many cm is this?

   Ⓐ 1130 cm   Ⓑ 113 cm   Ⓒ 1.13 cm   Ⓓ 0.0013 cm

Bzzzt... Beeometry

Look around you. Look out the window. What shapes do you see? Circles? Rectangles? Triangles? Nature contains many shapes, some rare and some very common. One shape that appears over and over is the hexagon, which has six sides.

Why are hexagons so common? For one thing, hexagon-shaped surfaces don't break easily. Perhaps that is why the wax combs inside a beehive are hexagons. The cells in a comb are used for raising young bees and for storing honey. They are built with almost mathematical accuracy, to provide the maximum strength and storage space with the minimum use of materials. Bees construct these structures entirely by instinct. Various plant cells are also hexagonal-shaped.

The star shape also appears in nature frequently. You have probably seen a picture of a starfish. You may find other star shapes in nature in star fruits, in the cross section of an orange, and in the petals of some flowers.

1 Try to draw a section of a honeycomb with pentagons, or five-sided shapes. What happens?

2 Make a list of things in nature that you know exhibit geometric shapes.

409

8-4 Lines and Angles

You'll Learn ...

■ to draw, measure, and identify angles

... How It's Used

Lighting technicians know how to set a dramatic mood by staging lights at various angles.

Vocabulary

angle

vertex

line

line segment

endpoints

ray

straight angle

right angle

acute angle

obtuse angle

complementary

supplementary

congruent

angle bisector

 ► Lesson Link You have learned how to use various units of measurement. Now you will learn about lines and angles. ◄

An **angle** is formed when two lines (or line segments, or rays) meet at one point, called the **vertex** . Angles are usually measured in degrees.

There are 360° in a complete circle.

Explore | Angles

The Angle in Creases

Materials: Sheet of wax paper, Compass, Scissors

1. Use your compass to draw the largest circle possible on the sheet of wax paper. Cut out the circle.

2. Fold the circle in half by lining up the edge of your circle. Fold the circle in half again.

3. Fold the circle in half two more times.

4. Each time you folded the circle, you made an angle. What part of the circle was located at the vertex of each angle?

5. The full circle shows 360°. When you fold the full circle in half, you make a 180° angle. What is the resulting angle measure if you fold this in half?

6. What is the number pattern that results each time an angle is folded in half? Write an algebraic equation for this.

7. If each quarter of the circle is 90°, what is the angle measure of three-quarters of a circle? How did you arrive at your answer?

8. On your circle, label as many creases as you can with the appropriate angle measure.

9. Use your circle as a measuring tool to approximate the measure of angles you can find in your classroom.

In geometry, a straight **line** extends infinitely in both directions. A line that includes points A and B is written as $\overleftrightarrow{AB}$.

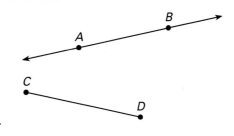

A **line segment** is part of a straight line that includes its endpoints. A line segment with **endpoints** C and D is written as $\overline{CD}$.

$\overline{CD}$ measures $1\frac{1}{4}$ in. and is written as $m\overline{CD} = 1\frac{1}{4}$ in.

A **ray** has one endpoint and extends infinitely in only one direction. A ray with endpoint M that includes another point, N, is written as $\overrightarrow{MN}$.

You will often see an angle drawn as two rays that meet at one point.

An angle is measured with a protractor. The angle shown is written as $\angle ABC$, where B is the vertex and A and C are on opposite sides of the angle.

$\angle ABC$ measures $43°$ and is written as $m\angle ABC = 43°$.

Example 1

Molybdenite is a mineral used to strengthen metal alloys. Use a protractor to measure the angle in the specimen shown.

The angle is $115°$.

DID YOU KNOW?

Molybdenite can be found in California, Colorado, and Washington.

Try It

Use a protractor to measure each angle.

a.

b.

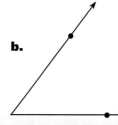

Some angles can be classified as one of four types, depending on their measurements.

If $m\angle ABC = 180°$, then $\angle ABC$ is a **straight angle** .

If $m\angle ABC = 90°$, then $\angle ABC$ is a **right angle** .

If $0° < m\angle ABC < 90°$, then $\angle ABC$ is an **acute angle** .

If $90° < m\angle ABC < 180°$, then $\angle ABC$ is an **obtuse angle** .

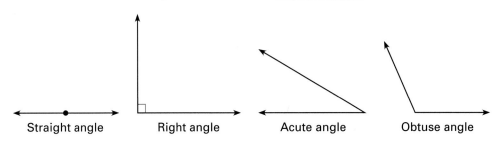

| Straight angle | Right angle | Acute angle | Obtuse angle |

Example 2

Classify the angle found in honeycomb.

$m\angle RST$ in the honeycomb is $> 90°$.

$\angle RST$ is obtuse.

Try It

Classify the angle found in bee wings.

Two angles with measures that have a sum of 90° are **complementary** angles.

$\angle ABD$ is a right angle, so

$\angle ABC$ is the complement of $\angle CBD$.

Two angles with measures that have a sum of 180° are **supplementary** angles.

$\angle GHJ$ is a straight angle, so

$\angle GHI$ is the supplement of $\angle IHJ$.

Example 3

Find the measure of the complement of ∠DBE.

$90° − 38.5° = 51.5°$

The complement of ∠DBE is 51.5°.

Example 4

Find the measure of the supplement of ∠XYZ.

$180° − 94° = 86°$

The supplement of ∠XYZ is 86°.

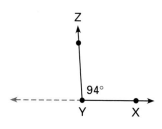

Try It

Find each angle measure.

a. Supplement of 132.7°   **b.** Complement of 18°

In geometry, two figures are **congruent** if they have the same shape and size.

An **angle bisector** divides an angle into two congruent angles. $\overrightarrow{KW}$ is the angle bisector of ∠PKB.

∠PKW ≅ ∠WKB states that the two angles are congruent.

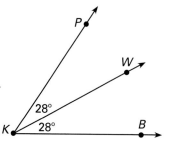

Example 5

Is $\overrightarrow{ST}$ an angle bisector?

Measure both angles with your protractor.

$m∠RST = 45°$ and $m∠TSU = 45°$

∠RST ≅ ∠TSU, so $\overrightarrow{ST}$ is an angle bisector.

Study TIP

When possible, invent formulas to help you understand math definitions. For example, $C = 90°$ − angle.

Check Your Understanding

1. Do all acute angles have possible complements? Explain.

2. Describe how to find a supplementary angle; a complementary angle.

8-4 Exercises and Applications

Practice and Apply

1. **Getting Started** State whether ∠*FDE* and ∠*BAC* are congruent.

   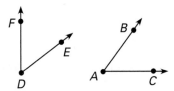

   a. Measure ∠*FDE*. Measure ∠*BAC*.

   b. Are the measures equal?

Classify each angle measurement as right, straight, obtuse, or acute.

2. 112°   **3.** 28°   **4.** 90°   **5.** 60°   **6.** 179.5°

7. 6°   **8.** 45°   **9.** 180°   **10.** 90.5°   **11.** 140°

Find the measure of the complement of each angle measure.

12. 45°   **13.** 22°   **14.** 85°   **15.** 9.1°   **16.** 17.6°

Find the measure of the supplement of each angle measure.

17. 120°   **18.** 39°   **19.** 90°   **20.** 175°   **21.** 60°

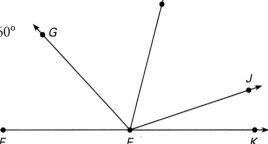

Use a protractor to measure each angle.

22. ∠*HEK*   **23.** ∠*GEK*   **24.** ∠*FEG*

25. ∠*JEF*   **26.** ∠*FEK*   **27.** ∠*HEF*

Identify each as a ray, line, or line segment and draw each.

28. $\overline{RS}$ **29.** $\overrightarrow{TV}$ **30.** $\overleftrightarrow{ST}$ **31.** $\overrightarrow{RV}$

32. Science Gypsum, a mineral found in North America, is shown at the right. What kind of angles do you see?

33. **Test Prep** Two sides of a square meet to form what kind of angle?

   Ⓐ Acute   Ⓑ Obtuse   Ⓒ Right   Ⓓ Straight

34. What is the measure of the two resulting angles after a 120° angle is bisected?

35. What is the measure of the two resulting angles after a 314° angle is bisected?

36. History Measure the obtuse angle above the entrance to Saint Peter's Basilica, constructed during the 1500s in Rome.

Problem Solving and Reasoning

37. Math Reasoning Pilots often use the numbers on a clock face to indicate angles. "Twelve o'clock" means "dead ahead." Suppose one pilot radios another, "Bogies at two o'clock!" At what angle have enemy planes been spotted?

38. Journal In Al Held's 1992 acrylic painting *Ima Ima II* how many acute angles can you find? How many obtuse angles? How many right angles? How do you think the kinds of angles in the painting affect the mood the painting creates?

39. Communicate Explain how to construct two line segments, one 6 cm and the other 3.5 cm long, meeting to form a 30° angle.

40. Math Reasoning A wheel has six equally spaced spokes that form six congruent angles. If each of these angles is to be bisected, what will the angle measure be between spokes?

Geometry In the figure at the right, $m\angle ACB = 140°$.

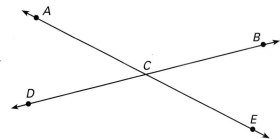

41. Algebra Two angles are supplementary. One angle measures x degrees, the other y degrees. Write an equation expressing that these angles are supplementary, and solve this equation for y. Find y if $x = 71°$.

42. What is $m\angle ACD$? What is $m\angle BCE$?

43. How are $\angle ACD$ and $\angle BCE$ related?

Mixed Review

Solve each rate and proportion. *[Lesson 5-6]*

44. $0.60 each cup = _____ for 8 cups

45. 60 mi/hr = _____ mi in 4 hr

46. _____ ft per sec = 36 ft in 9 sec

47. $24 for 3 hr = _____ per hr

Add or subtract, writing each answer in lowest terms. *[Lesson 7-5]*

48. $\frac{3}{5} + \frac{1}{4}$ **49.** $5\frac{2}{3} - 2\frac{2}{3}$ **50.** $6.902 + 0.53$ **51.** $36.17 - 8.66$

8-5 Parallel and Perpendicular Lines

You'll Learn ...

■ to recognize and construct parallel and perpendicular lines

... How It's Used

Weavers create parallel and perpendicular designs on their looms.

Vocabulary

parallel

perpendicular

perpendicular bisector

transversal

interior angle

exterior angle

alternate angle

corresponding angle

vertical angle

▶ **Lesson Link** You have learned about several types of angles. Now you will apply this knowledge to identify more types of angles. ◀

Lines in a plane that never intersect are **parallel** .
$\overleftrightarrow{AB}$ and $\overleftrightarrow{CD}$ are parallel. This is written as $\overleftrightarrow{AB} \parallel \overleftrightarrow{CD}$.

Lines that form a right angle are **perpendicular** .
$\overline{QR}$ is perpendicular to $\overleftrightarrow{AB}$, written as $\overline{QR} \perp \overleftrightarrow{AB}$.

$\overline{QR}$ is perpendicular to $\overleftrightarrow{CD}$, written as $\overline{QR} \perp \overleftrightarrow{CD}$.

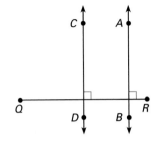

A **perpendicular bisector** is perpendicular to a line segment so that the line segment is divided into two congruent parts. For example, $\overleftrightarrow{CD}$ is a perpendicular bisector of $\overline{QR}$.

Explore | Transversals

Crisscross

Materials: Geometry software

1. Draw two parallel lines. Now draw a third line crossing the parallel lines at a slant. Label the eight angles in your diagram.

2. Measure the angles in your diagram until you find two that are congruent. State that the angles are congruent using the ≅ symbol.

3. Complete measuring all the angles in your diagram. How many different angle measures did you find?

4. Identify as many congruent pairs of angles as you can.

5. Identify as many supplementary pairs of angles as you can.

6. Are there any complementary angles?

7. Rotate the third line until it forms right angles with the parallel lines. How many right angles are there in total?

8. Draw a line segment so one of the other lines is a perpendicular bisector.

9. Discuss what you noticed about the angles in your figure.

Learn | Parallel and Perpendicular Lines

A line that crosses two or more other lines is a **transversal** . A transversal of two separate lines forms eight angles.

The four angles between the two lines are **interior angles** .

Angles *3, 4, 5,* and *6* are interior angles.

The four angles outside the two lines are **exterior angles** .

Angles *1, 2, 7,* and *8* are exterior angles.

Alternate angles are on opposite sides of the transversal. They are both interior or both exterior.

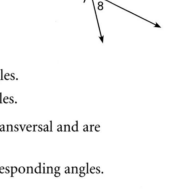

Alternate angles are congruent if the transversal crosses two parallel lines.

Angles *1* and *8,* and *2* and *7* are alternate exterior angles.

Angles *3* and *6,* and *4* and *5* are alternate interior angles.

Corresponding angles are on the same side of the transversal and are congruent when the transversal crosses parallel lines.

Angles *1* and *5, 2* and *6, 3* and *7,* and *4* and *8* are corresponding angles.

Example 1

In the diagram, $\overleftrightarrow{ST} \parallel \overleftrightarrow{VW}$. Identify both pairs of alternate interior angles.

First identify all interior angles.

$\angle SAN, \angle TAN, \angle VBM,$ and $\angle WBM$

Match the interior angles that are on opposite sides of the transversal $\overleftrightarrow{MN}$.

$\angle SAN$ and $\angle WBM$ are alternate interior angles.

$\angle TAN$ and $\angle VBM$ are alternate interior angles.

> ► **Science Link**
>
> Many birds migrate each year by flying to a warmer climate.

Try It

In the diagram, $\overleftrightarrow{DE} \parallel \overleftrightarrow{FG}$. Identify both pairs of alternate exterior angles.

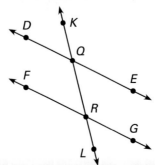

Example 2

In the diagram, $\overleftrightarrow{AC} \parallel \overleftrightarrow{DF}$.

Find $m\angle DYE$.

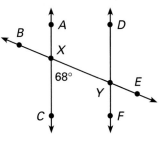

$\angle AXE$ and $\angle CXE$ are supplementary angles.

$m\angle AXE = 180° - m\angle CXE = 180° - 68° = 112°$

$\angle AXE$ and $\angle DYE$ are corresponding angles so $\angle AXE \cong \angle DYE$.

$m\angle DYE = 112°$

When two lines intersect they form two pairs of **vertical angles**. Vertical angles are congruent.

Angles 1 and 3, and 2 and 4 are vertical angles.

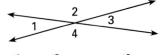

$m\angle 1 = m\angle 3 \qquad m\angle 2 = m\angle 4$

Example 3

Use the diagram to determine $m\angle 2$.

Identify the angle vertical to $\angle 2$.

$\angle 2$ and $\angle 4$ are vertical angles, so $m\angle 2 = 158°$.

$m\angle 2 = 158°$

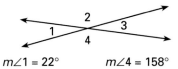

$m\angle 1 = 22° \qquad m\angle 4 = 158°$

Try It

In the diagram, $\overline{PQ} \parallel \overline{RS}$. Find each angle measure.

a. $m\angle 4$ **b.** $m\angle 6$ **c.** $m\angle 5$

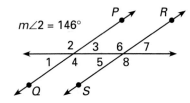

$m\angle 2 = 146°$

Check | Your Understanding

1. Describe a situation in which alternate interior angles formed by a transversal are not congruent.

2. What does the definition of *parallel* tell you about the distance between parallel lines?

3. Suppose a transversal is perpendicular to two parallel lines. What are the angle measures for all interior and exterior angles? Explain.

8-5 Exercises and Applications

Practice and Apply

1. **Getting Started** $\overleftrightarrow{XT} \parallel \overleftrightarrow{BW}$. Find the measures of all angles in the diagram.

   a. Identify all angles with a measure of 60°.

   b. Identify all angles with a measure of 120°.

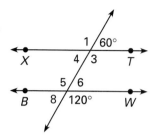

In the figure shown at right, $\overleftrightarrow{EF} \parallel \overleftrightarrow{GH}$. Use the figure for Exercises 2–10.

2. Name all alternate interior angles.

3. Name all alternate exterior angles.

4. Name two pairs of corresponding angles.

5. Name two pairs of vertical angles.

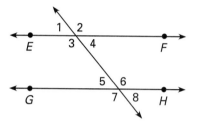

If $m\angle 6 = 130°$, find each angle measure.

6. $m\angle 5$ **7.** $m\angle 7$ **8.** $m\angle 3$ **9.** $m\angle 2$ **10.** $m\angle 1$

In the figure on the right, $\overleftrightarrow{ST} \parallel \overleftrightarrow{UV}$. Use the figure to find the measure of each angle.

11. $m\angle 4$ **12.** $m\angle 1$

13. What kind of angles are $\angle 2$ and $\angle 8$?

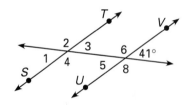

14. **Test Prep** How many angles are formed when a transversal crosses three parallel lines?

   Ⓐ 8   Ⓑ 6   Ⓒ 12   Ⓓ 16

15. **Science** Movement along a fault usually causes earthquakes. What is the angle of the fault plane to the layers in the side of the hill?

Complete each statement to make it true.

16. _____ lines intersect at a 90° angle.

17. _____ lines never intersect.

18. A _____ intersects a line segment at 90° and divides it into two equal lengths.

19. Vertical angles are always _____.

20. Geography In midtown Manhattan, almost all streets are either parallel or perpendicular—except for Broadway. What kind of angles are formed at the intersection of Broadway and 7th Avenue?

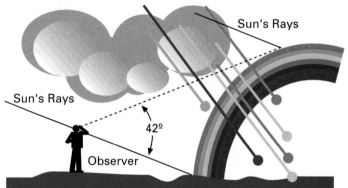

Problem Solving and Reasoning

21. **Journal** When you see a rainbow, the sun is behind you and the rain is in front of you. The points in the red arc of a rainbow form a 42° angle with the sun's rays. Use words such as *parallel, transversal,* and *alternate interior angles* to describe what is happening in the diagram.

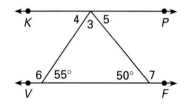

Sun's Rays

Sun's Rays

42°

Observer

22. Communicate If two lines are both perpendicular to the same line, what is the relationship between those two lines? Explain.

23. Measurement $\overleftrightarrow{KP} \parallel \overleftrightarrow{VF}$. Find the measure of each numbered angle.

24. Geometry $\overleftrightarrow{KP} \parallel \overleftrightarrow{VF}$. Find the sum of the angles of the triangle. How does this sum relate to a straight angle?

Mixed Review

Solve each proportion. *[Lesson 5-7]*

25. $\dfrac{1 \text{ in.}}{40 \text{ ft}} = \dfrac{x \text{ in.}}{160 \text{ ft}}$ **26.** $\dfrac{1 \text{ in.}}{x \text{ mi}} = \dfrac{3 \text{ in.}}{36 \text{ mi}}$ **27.** $\dfrac{2 \text{ cm}}{1 \text{ km}} = \dfrac{10 \text{ cm}}{x \text{ km}}$

Multiply or divide, then write each answer in lowest terms. *[Lesson 7-6]*

28. $\dfrac{1}{2} \times \left(-\dfrac{4}{9}\right)$ **29.** $\dfrac{7}{8} \div \dfrac{8}{9}$ **30.** 5.072×1.54 **31.** $5.2\overline{)9.256}$

Project Progress

As you learn more about a culture, find out how it charted the stars and planets. A culture's knowledge of astronomy can be related to its knowledge of geometry.

Problem Solving

Understand
Plan
Solve
Look Back

Polygons

▶ **Lesson Link** You've learned about line segments and angles. Now you're ready to learn about shapes made from them. ◀

A **polygon** is a closed figure formed by three or more points joined by line segments (sides). A **vertex** of a polygon is a point at which two sides intersect.

Explore Polygons

Getting in Shape

Materials: Geoboard™, Rubber bands

1. Wrap a rubber band around any three pegs on the Geoboard™ to outline a polygon with three sides.

2. How many unique three-sided polygons can you outline?

3. How many vertices does a three-sided polygon have?

4. How many unique four-sided polygons can you outline?

5. How many vertices does a four-sided polygon have?

6. How many unique five-sided polygons can you outline? How many six-sided polygons?

7. How many vertices do five- and six-sided polygons have?

8. Discuss the relationship between number of sides and number of vertices a polygon has.

Learn Polygons

A polygon is classified by the number of sides it has.

Number of Sides	3	4	5	6	7	8
Polygon	Triangle	Quadrilateral	Pentagon	Hexagon	Heptagon	Octagon
Example						

You'll Learn ...

■ to classify polygons

... How It's Used

People who make stained glass use polygons in their designs.

Vocabulary

polygon
vertex
triangle
quadrilateral
pentagon
hexagon
heptagon
octagon
Venn diagram
equilateral triangle
isosceles triangle
scalene triangle
parallelogram
rectangle
rhombus
square
trapezoid
diagonal
regular polygon
convex polygon
concave polygon

A **Venn diagram** shows a relationship by visually grouping things into sets.

Three important types of triangles are shown in the Venn diagram to the right.

An **equilateral triangle** has three congruent sides.

An **isosceles triangle** has at least two congruent sides.

A **scalene triangle** has no congruent sides. All sides have different lengths.

A triangle has the same number of congruent sides as it has congruent angles.

The sum of a triangle's angle measures always equals 180°.

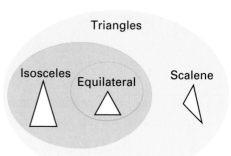

Triangles

Isosceles Equilateral Scalene

▶ **Science Link**

Humpback whales belong to the order of Cetacea. Members of Cetacea are mammals that live in the ocean.

Example 1

An isosceles triangle can be seen in the shape of the tail on a humpback whale. What is the length of $\overline{FG}$?

$m\overline{FG} = m\overline{DF}$ because $\triangle DFG$ is isosceles.

$m\overline{FG} = 6.6$ ft

Example 2

In the scalene triangle shown, find the missing angle measure.

$32° + 76° + x = 180°$ Write an equation.

$108° + x = 180°$ Add.

$x = 72°$ Subtract 108° from both sides.

32°   76°

Try It

$\triangle ABC$ is equilateral.

a. Determine the length of $\overline{BC}$.

b. Determine the length of $\overline{AC}$.

c. Determine all angle measures of triangle ABC.

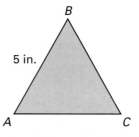

B

5 in.

A   C

A Venn diagram can show the types of quadrilaterals.

A **parallelogram** is a quadrilateral with two pairs of parallel sides.

A **rectangle** is a quadrilateral with four right angles.

A **rhombus** is a parallelogram with four equal sides.

A **square** is a rectangle with four equal sides.

A **trapezoid** is a quadrilateral with exactly one pair of parallel sides.

The Venn diagram shows that a rectangle is a type of parallelogram.

Study TIP

Make a Venn diagram whenever you study vocabulary. You will see how the meanings relate to each other.

Example 3

Determine $m\angle ABC$ in parallelogram $ABCD$.

A parallelogram has two pairs of parallel sides, so $\overline{AB} \parallel \overline{CD}$ and $\overline{AD} \parallel \overline{BC}$.

$\angle ADC \cong \angle BCK \cong \angle PBR \cong \angle ABC$
They are all corresponding or vertical angles.

$m\angle ADC = m\angle ABC = 56°$

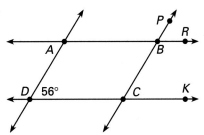

A **diagonal** of a polygon connects two vertices that do not share a side.

Example 4

In the trapezoid:

$\angle ADC \cong \angle BCD$ and $\angle DAB \cong \angle CBA$.

Measure $\angle ACD$ and $\angle BDC$ formed by the diagonals, $\overline{AC}$ and $\overline{BD}$.

$m\angle ACD = 54°$ and $m\angle BDC = 54°$

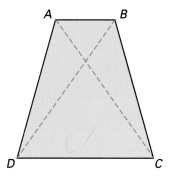

Try It

a. Determine $m\angle RST$ in parallelogram $QRST$.

b. Determine $m\angle TQR$ in parallelogram $QRST$.

c. Identify the diagonal line segment.

All sides and all angles are congruent on a **regular polygon**.

Equilateral Triangle	Square	Regular Pentagon	Regular Hexagon	Regular Heptagon	Regular Octagon

All diagonals of a **convex polygon** are on the inside of the figure.

At least one diagonal of a **concave polygon** is outside the figure.

Example 5

Describe and classify each figure. Be as specific as possible.

Heptagon, seven sides   How many sides?

Irregular   Regular or not?

Concave   Concave or convex?

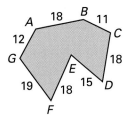

The sum of angle measures in a polygon with k sides always equals $180°(k - 2)$.

Example 6

Find the sum of the angles in a pentagon.

A pentagon has five sides. Substitute $k = 5$ in $180°(k - 2)$.

$180°(3) = 540°$. The sum of the angles is 540°.

Try It

Describe and classify the figure on the right. Be as specific as possible.

Check | Your Understanding

1. What polygons, besides parallelograms, have parallel sides? Explain.

2. Do all regular hexagons have the same measurements? Explain.

Practice and Apply

1. **Getting Started** Find the measure of the missing angle.
   a. Add 61° + 23°.
   b. Subtract the sum from 180°.

Identify the polygon outlined in each photograph. Be as specific as possible.

2.
3.
4.
5.

Decide whether each statement is true or false.

6. All squares are parallelograms.
7. Some trapezoids are parallelograms.
8. All rectangles are squares.
9. An isosceles triangle can have three equal sides.

Find the measure of the missing angle.

10. 67° 74°
11. 57° 52°
12. 50° 40°
13. 59° 60°

Determine the sum of all angles in each polygon.

14. Quadrilateral
15. Hexagon
16. Heptagon
17. Octagon

18. **Test Prep** Which figure can have only one right angle?
   Ⓐ Parallelogram   Ⓑ Square   Ⓒ Trapezoid   Ⓓ Right triangle

19. **Career** A lapidary, a craftsperson who cuts and polishes precious stones, cuts along the flat side of a crystal. What shapes appear on each of the crystal faces?

   a.
   Amythest

   b.
   Garnet

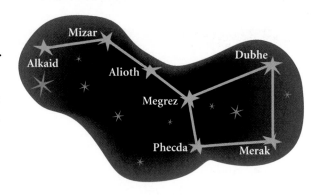

20. **Science** Name the stars of the Big Dipper that form the vertices of a polygon. Name the polygon.

21. **Algebra** In astronomy, constellations are often identified by connecting stars with imaginary line segments. How many stars are required to make a polygon with n sides?

Problem Solving and Reasoning

22. **Journal** Use the vocabulary from this lesson to describe what the orange and starfruit have in common and how they are different. Compare each fruit to a polygon and identify where the sides and vertices are.

23. **Critical Thinking** Recall that a concave polygon has at least one diagonal outside the figure. Try to draw a concave triangle, concave quadrilateral, concave pentagon, concave hexagon, and so on. Distinguish between polygons with an odd number of sides and an even number of sides. What conclusion can you make based on your drawings?

24. **Algebra** Use the $(k - 2)180°$ formula and the distributive property to find each of the angle measurements in the regular nonagon (nine-sided polygon) shown.

25. **Choose a Strategy** Draw an isosceles triangle with side lengths of 4 in. and 7 in. Determine the length of the third side. Is this the only possible isosceles triangle that has the side lengths 4 in. and 7 in? Explain.

Problem Solving

STRATEGIES

- Look for a Pattern
- Make an Organized List
- Make a Table
- Guess and Check
- Work Backward
- Use Logical Reasoning
- Draw a Diagram
- Solve a Simpler Problem

Mixed Review

Graph each equation. Use 0, 1, 2, and 3 as *x* values. *[Lesson 4-3]*

26. $y = x - 1$ 27. $y = 2x$ 28. $y = \frac{1}{3}x$ 29. $y = 3x - 3$

Find each square root and write in lowest terms. *[Lesson 7-7]*

30. $\sqrt{36}$ 31. $\sqrt{49}$ 32. $\sqrt{100}$ 33. $\sqrt{169}$

34. $\sqrt{\frac{16}{64}}$ 35. $\sqrt{\frac{144}{9}}$ 36. $\sqrt{\frac{49}{36}}$ 37. $\sqrt{\frac{9}{121}}$

3-D Views

▶ Lesson Link In Lesson 8–6, you learned about two-dimensional shapes. Now you will learn how to visualize three-dimensional shapes. ◀

You'll Learn ...

■ to represent three-dimensional shapes in a drawing

... How It's Used

Sculptors use preliminary sketches to plan the designs of their 3-D sculptures.

Explore 3-D Views

Centimeter Cubist

Materials: 10 multilink cubes

You are an artist who makes sculptures from cubes. Before creating the sculptures, you draw preliminary sketches. Sketch your idea by creating: (1) three views: front, right, and top; or (2) one base plan.

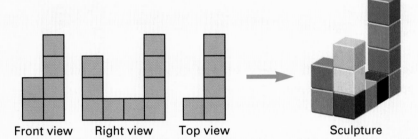

Front view   Right view   Top view   Sculpture

The illustrations show the two ways of sketching an idea for a sculpture and the resulting piece.

1. Draw a base plan for a different sculpture. The numbers in your squares should have a sum of 10.

2. Using your base plan, draw the three views of your planned sculpture.

Base plan   Sculpture

3. Build your sculpture based on your sketches.

4. Build a group member's sculpture based on his or her sketches.

5. Did he or she build your sculpture correctly? Did you build his or hers correctly?

6. If you were going to create a 20-foot-tall sculpture, why would you sketch your ideas instead of immediately building it?

7. Discuss some other ways of planning 3-D objects by using drawings.

When you visualize a 3-D object, it is helpful to make a sketch. For shapes built from cubes, you can draw a base plan to show the height of several stacks of cubes. You can also represent a 3-D object by drawing the right, front, and top views.

Example 1

Draw a base plan of the 3-D object shown.

Front   Right side

There are two columns that are 3 cubes tall.

There are two columns that are 2 cubes tall.

There is one column that is 1 cube tall.

Right side   Front

Drawing the right view, front view, and top view of a 3-D object shows how the object appears from different views.

Example 2

Draw the right, front, and top views of the 3-D object shown.

The front has two stacks of 3 cubes.

The right has one stack of 3 cubes.

There are four stacks that use only 1 cube.

Right view   Front view   Top view

Try It

Use the drawing on the right for the following.

a. Draw a base plan.

b. Draw the right view.

c. Draw the front view.

d. Draw the top view.

Front   Right side

A net shows the surface of a 3-D figure as if it were unfolded.

Draw a net for the galena crystal shown at right.

Andre thinks ...

I'll "unfold" the crystal like a pizza box.

Emma thinks ...

I'll leave all the small sides connected.

What do you think?

1. Can you make a net for any rectangular box? Explain.

2. Is there only one possible net for a rectangular box? Explain.

Check Your Understanding

1. What would result if you had to build something from only a front view and top view?

2. What would result if you had to build something from a base plan without numbers?

Practice and Apply

1. **Getting Started** Draw a base plan using the illustration shown.

a. Draw the top view.

b. Count the number of cubes in each column and label each square in the view.

2. Draw the right, front, and top views for the 3-D object shown.

3. Draw a base plan for the cube tower shown.

4. This chair design is called the Kubus Chair. Draw a base plan for it.

5. **Science** Amethyst, the February birthstone, is a purple type of quartz crystal. The crystal shown is rectangular. Draw a net for a rectangular prism.

6. **Test Prep** Which net would make the solid shown?

Ⓐ

Ⓑ

Ⓒ

Ⓓ

History Shown is a photograph of Ft. McHenry in Baltimore, Maryland, where Francis Scott Key wrote "The Star-Spangled Banner" during the War of 1812.

7. Draw a top view of Ft. McHenry.

8. What general shape does this remind you of?

Problem Solving and Reasoning

9. Critical Thinking Which net matches the 3-D figure?

Ⓐ

Ⓑ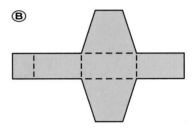

10. Patterns Construct a solid shape by gluing or taping together a copy of the net shown. What do you get?

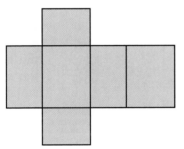

11. Math Reasoning Gems can be cut in different ways. The picture shows the top view of one type of faceted cut. Sketch how you think the right and front views look.

12. Communicate A ziggurat is a type of pyramid with terraces. The photo at the right shows Chichén Itzá, the Mayan ziggurat. Describe how you would draw a net for this shape?

Mixed Review

Draw a line through the origin with the given slope.
[Lesson 4-4]

13. $\frac{5}{8}$ **14.** 3   **15.** -1 **16.** $-\frac{1}{2}$

Identify each number as rational or irrational. *[Lesson 7-8]*

17. $\sqrt{10}$ **18.** $0.\overline{6}$ **19.** $\sqrt{19}$ **20.** $\sqrt{225}$ **21.** 0.2323

TECHNOLOGY

Using Geometry Software • Drawing Side and Top Views

> **Problem:** **Construct the top and side views of a square nut.**
>
> You can use dynamic geometry software to help with this exercise.

1 Use the **Regular Polygon** tool to construct a square. Use the **Measure** menu to find the length of each side and the measure of each angle.

3 Use the **Circle** tool to draw a circle inside the square. The circle will have the same center as the square. Hide the diagonal line segments and you'll have the top view of your square nut.

2 Use the **Segment** tool to draw two diagonals between opposite pairs of vertices. This shows the center of the square.

4 Draw a rectangle with length the same as a side of the square. This is the side view of the square nut.

> **Solution:** Length measurements may vary.

ON YOUR OWN

TRY IT

What would the top and side views of a hexagonal nut look like?

▶ How do you think the geometry software calculates the lengths of the sides of your construction?

▶ Is it easier to construct these views using geometry software or by hand? Explain.

▶ How do you think an architect's design program can help you construct these views?

Section 8B Connect

In this section, you'll have a chance to apply your creativity to what you've learned about flat and three-dimensional shapes.

Bzzzt... Beeometry

Materials: Paper, Scissors, Tape

Draw six congruent squares on a sheet of paper, in order to construct a net for a "geometry cube."

You will design the net with drawings and labels from Exercises 1–6.

1. On one square, draw a line, line segment, or a ray.

2. On another square, draw any angle and label its measure.

3. On another square, draw parallel or perpendicular lines.

4. On another square, draw parallel lines with a transversal and label all angle measurements.

5. On another square, draw any polygon and include its classification.

6. On the last square, write "roll again."

7. How many pairs of parallel lines are on your net?

8. How many pairs of perpendicular lines are on your net?

9. How many acute angles are on your net? Obtuse angles?

10. How many right angles are on your net?

11. Classify all of the polygons on your net.

12. Cut out your net and use tape to make a "geometry cube."

13. All the group members will roll their cubes. If a cube lands on "roll again," then that player must roll the cube again.

14. When all cubes say other than "roll again," each player must create a drawing that uses each figure shown on the cubes.

Section 8B Review

Use the illustration to classify each angle as right, straight, obtuse, or acute.

1. ∠ABD **2.** ∠DBF **3.** ∠FBC

4. ∠EBF **5.** ∠ABE **6.** ∠ABC

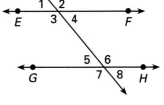

7. Find the angle measure complementary to 57.5°.

8. Find the angle measure supplementary to 108°.

$\overleftrightarrow{EF} \parallel \overleftrightarrow{GH}$. If $m\angle 3 = 130°$, find each angle measure.

9. $m\angle 2$ **10.** $m\angle 7$ **11.** $m\angle 6$ **12.** $m\angle 8$

Match each pair of angles with the angle classification.

13. ∠6 and ∠7 **A.** Alternate interior angles

14. ∠5 and ∠4 **B.** Alternate exterior angles

15. ∠1 and ∠8 **C.** Corresponding angles

16. ∠3 and ∠7 **D.** Vertical angles

Identify the polygon in each photograph. Be as specific as possible.

17.   **18.**   **19.**   **20.**

21. Journal State the difference between a top view and a base view of a 3-D figure.

Test Prep

On a multiple choice test, you need to know the difference between a line and a line segment. Both may appear in the answer choices of a single question.

22. $\overrightarrow{CD}$ is Ⓐ A line. Ⓑ A line segment. Ⓒ An angle. Ⓓ A ray.

Extend Key Ideas ▸ Algebra

Slopes of Parallel and Perpendicular Lines

Slope is the ratio of the change in y-coordinates to the change in x-coordinates.

On the first graph notice that $\overleftrightarrow{AB} \parallel \overleftrightarrow{CD}$. If you determine the slopes of $\overleftrightarrow{AB}$ and $\overleftrightarrow{CD}$, you will find they are equal.

$\text{slope} = \frac{\text{rise}}{\text{run}}$ slope of $\overleftrightarrow{AB} = \frac{-3}{-6} = \frac{1}{2}$

slope of $\overleftrightarrow{CD} = \frac{-3}{-6} = \frac{1}{2}$

$\overleftrightarrow{AB}$ and $\overleftrightarrow{CD}$ have the same slope and are parallel.

So ...
- If lines have equal slope, lines are parallel.
- If lines are parallel, lines have equal slope.

On the second graph notice that $\overleftrightarrow{EF} \perp \overleftrightarrow{GH}$. If you determine the slopes of $\overleftrightarrow{EF}$ and $\overleftrightarrow{GH}$, you will find that the product of their slopes is -1.

$\text{slope} = \frac{\text{rise}}{\text{run}}$ slope of $\overleftrightarrow{EF} = \frac{-9}{6} = \frac{-3}{2}$

slope of $\overleftrightarrow{GH} = \frac{6}{9} = \frac{2}{3}$

The product of the slopes is $\frac{-3}{2} \times \frac{2}{3} = \frac{-3 \times 2}{2 \times 3} = \frac{-6}{6} = -1$. So ...

- If the product of the slopes $= -1$, lines are perpendicular.
- If lines are perpendicular, the product of the slopes $= -1$.

Find the slope to determine whether the lines are $\parallel$ or $\perp$.

1. Determine whether $\overleftrightarrow{AB}$ and $\overleftrightarrow{CD}$ are $\parallel$ or $\perp$.
   a. Plot the points $A(-4, 5)$, $B(3, 7)$, $C(-5, -2)$, and $D(2, 0)$.
   b. Draw lines $\overleftrightarrow{AB}$ and $\overleftrightarrow{CD}$.
   c. Find the slopes of $\overleftrightarrow{AB}$ and $\overleftrightarrow{CD}$.
   d. Are they $\parallel$ or $\perp$?

2. Determine whether $\overleftrightarrow{EF}$ and $\overleftrightarrow{GH}$ are $\parallel$ or $\perp$.
   a. Plot the points $E(-4, 7)$, $F(3, 0)$, $G(-4, -2)$, and $H(6, 8)$.
   b. Draw lines $\overleftrightarrow{EF}$ and $\overleftrightarrow{GH}$.
   c. Find the slopes of $\overleftrightarrow{EF}$ and $\overleftrightarrow{GH}$.
   d. Are they $\parallel$ or $\perp$?

435

Chapter 8 Summary and Review

Graphic Organizer

Section 8A Measurement

Summary

- **U.S. customary units** use the inch, foot, and mile as units of length; ounce, pound, and ton for weight; and pint and quart for capacity.

- The **metric system** uses the centimeter, meter, and kilometer as units of length; gram and kilogram for mass; and milliliter and liter for capacity.

- The units and number of decimal places determine the **precision** of a measurement. The **significant digits** represent the actual measurement. Significant digits are used when calculating with measurements.

- **Absolute position** is given as coordinates. **Relative position** is given in relationship to another place.

- World maps usually show position using **latitude** (degrees north or south of the equator) and **longitude** (degrees east or west of the prime meridian).

Review

1. What metric unit would you use for the capacity of a car's gas tank?

2. Convert 12 lb to oz.

3. Determine which measurement is more precise: 438 ft or 137 yd.

4. Calculate 8.45 cm × 4.267 cm. Write your answer using the correct number of significant digits.

5. To the nearest degree, determine the latitude and longitude of Columbus, Ohio.

6. What is the position of Springfield, Illinois relative to Madison, Wisconsin?

Section 8B   Elements of Geometry

Summary

- An **angle** is formed when two lines meet at one point, called the **vertex**.

- A **line** extends infinitely in both directions. A **line segment** is part of a line with two **endpoints**. A **ray** has only one endpoint.

- An angle can be classified as **acute, right, obtuse,** or **straight. Complementary** angles have a sum of 90°. **Supplementary** angles have a sum of 180°.

- **Parallel** lines (∥) never intersect. **Perpendicular** lines (⊥) form 90° angles.

- A line crossing two other lines is a **transversal**. Together they form **interior angles** and **exterior angles**.

- A **polygon** is formed by three or more segments meeting at **vertices**. On a **regular polygon,** all sides and all vertex angles are congruent.

- A regular triangle is called **equilateral**. An **isosceles triangle** has at least two congruent sides, and a **scalene triangle** has none.

- A **quadrilateral** has four sides. Quadrilaterals include **rectangles, rhombuses, squares, parallelograms,** and **trapezoids**.

Review

7. Find the complementary angle and the supplementary angle of 38°.

9. In the figure shown, which

  a. Segments are ∥ ?

  b. Segments are ⊥ ?

  c. Angle is a supplement to ∠A?

8. Draw a base plan for the cube tower.

10. Classify 150° as a right, straight, obtuse, or acute angle.

11. Find the sum of the angles of a pentagon.

Chapter 8 Assessment

1. What metric unit would you use for the length of your school?

2. Convert 17 ft 3 in. to inches.   3. Is 25.8 lb or 98.4 oz more precise?

4. Calculate 8.29 gal + 25.9 gal using significant digits.

5. How many degrees of latitude are between Calgary and Victoria? How many degrees of longitude?

6. What is the position of Regina relative to Winnipeg?

7. Classify 100° as a right, straight, obtuse, or acute angle.

8. Find the complementary angle and the supplementary angle of 54°.

9. In the figure, name a pair of
   a. Alternate interior angles.
   b. Vertical angles.
   c. Corresponding angles.

10. Name all angles that are supplementary with ∠2. ($\overleftrightarrow{AB} \parallel \overleftrightarrow{CD}$)

11. Determine whether or not each polygon appears to be regular. Tell whether or not it is convex.

a.   b.   c.

12. Classify the shape of this polygon by the number of sides. Then find the sum of the angles.

13. Shown are front and base plans for a 3-D object. Sketch the right plan.

2	3
1	

Base plan   Front view

14. Draw a net for the figure shown. (Each face is an equilateral triangle.)

Performance Task

Construct each figure using paper, scissors, and tape. Then unfold each one to find a net.

a.   b.   c.

Multiple Choice

Choose the best answer.

1. Evaluate $(2 + 5)^2 - 8$. *[Lesson 2-7]*
   - Ⓐ 19 Ⓑ 21 Ⓒ 41 Ⓓ 57

2. Solve $5x + 13 = -22$. *[Lesson 3-6]*
   - Ⓐ $x = -9$ Ⓑ $x = -7$
   - Ⓒ $x = -5$ Ⓓ $x = -2$

3. Find the solution of the system $y = 4x - 8$ and $y = -2x + 16$. *[Lesson 4-6]*
   - Ⓐ $(4, 8)$ Ⓑ $(3, 10)$ Ⓒ $(8, 4)$ Ⓓ $(5, 12)$

4. Solve the proportion for x: $\frac{x}{160} = \frac{45}{96}$. *[Lesson 5-4]*
   - Ⓐ 27 Ⓑ 36 Ⓒ 75 Ⓓ $341.\overline{3}$

5. Find 32% of 625. *[Lesson 6-4]*
   - Ⓐ 216 Ⓑ 200
   - Ⓒ 1953.125 Ⓓ 20,000

6. Which is divisible by 9? *[Lesson 7-1]*
   - Ⓐ 438,633 Ⓑ 482,963
   - Ⓒ 748,164 Ⓓ 914,286

7. Find the LCM of 42 and 90. *[Lesson 7-3]*
   - Ⓐ 6 Ⓑ 66 Ⓒ 210 Ⓓ 630

8. Subtract $\frac{11}{12} - \frac{5}{18}$. *[Lesson 7-5]*
   - Ⓐ $\frac{23}{36}$ Ⓑ $\frac{33}{10}$ Ⓒ $\frac{46}{72}$ Ⓓ $\frac{43}{36}$

9. Find the missing side length. *[Lesson 7-9]*
   - Ⓐ 17 Ⓑ 161
   - Ⓒ $\sqrt{161}$ Ⓓ 289

10. Which of the following is an irrational number? *[Lesson 7-8]*
    - Ⓐ 3 Ⓑ $\frac{1}{3}$ Ⓒ $\sqrt{221}$ Ⓓ $\sqrt{289}$

11. Which unit is best for the height of a building? *[Lesson 8-1]*
    - Ⓐ Kilogram Ⓑ Centimeter
    - Ⓒ Liter Ⓓ Meter

12. Calculate 8.23 ft × 7.8 ft and give the answer with the correct number of significant digits. *[Lesson 8-2]*
    - Ⓐ 64 ft^2 Ⓑ 64.2 ft^2
    - Ⓒ 64.19 ft^2 Ⓓ 64.194 ft^2

13. Classify $\angle CAE$. *[Lesson 8-4]*
    - Ⓐ Obtuse
    - Ⓑ Straight
    - Ⓒ Acute
    - Ⓓ Right

14. If $\overleftrightarrow{AB}$ and $\overleftrightarrow{CD}$ are parallel, which of the following best describes the pair $\angle 1$ and $\angle 2$? *[Lesson 8-5]*
    - Ⓐ Complementary
    - Ⓑ Congruent
    - Ⓒ Supplementary
    - Ⓓ Vertical

15. Which is **not** a parallelogram? *[Lesson 8-6]*
    - Ⓐ Rectangle Ⓑ Rhombus
    - Ⓒ Square Ⓓ Trapezoid

16. All sides and angles are congruent on a *[Lesson 8-6]*
    - Ⓐ regular polygon
    - Ⓑ concave polygon
    - Ⓒ triangle
    - Ⓓ straight angle

Area and Volume

▶ Arts & Literature Link
www.mathsurf.com/8/ch9/arts

▶ Entertainment Link
www.mathsurf.com/8/ch9/ent

Arts & Literature

The cubism art movement was largely attributed to European artists Pablo Picasso and George Braque.

Entertainment

Yokohama City, Japan, is the home of the world's largest Ferris Wheel, which boasts a diameter of 328 feet.

People of the World

Indian mathematician, Srinivasa Ramanujan (1887–1920), developed a formula for calculating a decimal approximation for π. Sixty-seven years after his death, computers, using a formula very similar to his, calculated the value of π to more than 100 million decimal places.

Science

The circumference of Earth is 24,830 miles. Using a unit of measure called *stadia,* Eratosthenes (276–195 B.C.) estimated the circumference of Earth to be about 24,811 miles, based on the distance between two Egyptian cities.

Social Studies

The perimeter of the base of the Great Pyramid of Khufu in Egypt, divided by twice its height, results in the value 3.14, remarkably close to the value of π.

KEY MATH IDEAS

Perimeter **and** area **are measurements of a two-dimensional figure.**

Surface area **and** volume **are measurements of a three-dimensional figure.**

Prisms, cylinders, pyramids, **and** cones **are all three-dimensional figures.**

Both two-dimensional and three-dimensional figures can be dilated using a scale factor.

CHAPTER PROJECT

Problem Solving

Understand
Plan
Solve
Look Back

In this project, you will design and make the most efficient package for an item of your choice. You'll first measure the item and record the dimensions. You will also write a summary of how you decided on your package.

Problem Solving Focus

Checking for a Reasonable Answer

When you look back to check your answer to a problem, it is important to evaluate whether rounding is reasonable. Deciding whether to round up or down often depends upon common sense and what you are asked to solve.

Each of the problems below gives the answer, but the answer may not be accurate enough for the situation. State if each answer is "close enough," "too low," or "too high," and explain why.

1 After graduation, the Whitman Middle School invites the graduates and their guests to a celebration banquet. Long tables are set up in the gymnasium for the banquet. Each table holds 25 people. If 1539 people attend the banquet, how many tables are there? **Answer: 61**

2 The printing company delivers the yearbooks in boxes that contain 48 books each. There are 538 graduates. If each one gets a book, how many boxes will be delivered? **Answer: 11**

3 Each graduate receives a souvenir pin with the name of the school and the year of their graduation. The pins are packed in boxes of a dozen, and cost $28.00 a box. Individual pins cost $3.00. How many boxes should the school buy? **Answer: 44 plus 10 individual pins**

4 The day before graduation, the school takes all the graduates to an amusement park. They are taken to the park in buses that each hold 24 people. An adult chaperone will ride on each bus. How many buses should the school request? **Answer: 22**

The Great Stage

Radio City Music Hall opened on December 27, 1932, as the first building of Rockefeller Center in New York City. S. L. "Roxy" Rothafel conceived the building and was determined to make Radio City the world's biggest theatrical environment in his time. Rothafel designed the interior of the music hall to feature a golden arch and ceiling that gives the appearance of a huge sunset.

Virtually everything about Radio City is big and impressive. The stage itself is still one of the largest and best equipped theatrical stages in the world. The stage measures 144 feet wide by 60 feet deep. It features a revolving turntable, 43 feet in diameter, and three stage elevators, each 70 feet long. Each elevator is capable of being lowered 27 feet into the basement or raised 13 feet above the level of the stage. In fact, the elevator system—and the hydraulics that run it— became the design prototype for the elevators in U.S. aircraft carriers during World War II.

1 What mathematical measurements might the original architects and engineers have used to design Radio City Music Hall?

2 What mathematical measurements of the great stage might set designers for a production company want to know? How might these be used?

3 How might mathematics be used in producing a 45-minute stage show?

443

9-1

Perimeter and Area of Polygons

You'll Learn ...

■ to find the area and perimeter of polygons

... How It's Used

Landscapers use perimeter and area to determine the amount of materials needed for a garden.

Vocabulary

perimeter

area

▶ **Lesson Link**   You've looked at units of measurement and many kinds of polygons. Now you'll determine perimeter and area of polygons. ◀

The **perimeter** (*p*) is the distance around a figure.

The perimeter of the figure to the right is 35 centimeters.

Explore | Perimeter

Side by Side

Materials: Geometry software

1. Use your geometry software to draw regular polygons with 3, 4, 5, and 6 sides. Make two different polygons for each number of sides.

2. On paper, make a table with the following headings: Number of Sides, Regular Polygon, Side Length, and Perimeter.

Number of Sides	Regular Polygon	Side Length	Perimeter

3. For each regular polygon, measure the length of a side and the perimeter. Use these measurements to complete the table.

4. Look for a pattern in the data from your table. In a regular polygon, what is the relationship between the number of sides, the side length, and the perimeter? State the rule for this relationship.

5. Test your rule to see if it works with regular polygons that have more than 6 sides.

Learn | Perimeter and Area of Polygons

You can calculate the perimeter of any figure by adding all the side lengths.

You can calculate the perimeter of rectangles and squares using a formula.

The perimeter of a rectangle is two times the base (b) plus two times the height (h).

$$p = 2b + 2h = 2(b + h)$$

The perimeter of a square is four times the length of a side (s).

$$p = 4s$$

Example 1

A large theater will have an orchestra pit, where a full orchestra will play the music for a musical or opera. What is the perimeter of the orchestra pit shown?

Add all side lengths.

$$10 + 40 + 10 + 13 + 65 + 13 = 151 \text{ ft}$$

The perimeter of the orchestra pit is 151 ft.

Examples

2 Use a formula to find the perimeter of the rectangle.

$$p = 2(b + h)$$

$$p = 2\left(8\frac{1}{4} + 5\frac{3}{4}\right) = 2 \cdot (14) = 28$$

The perimeter is 28 in.

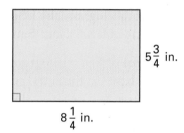

$5\frac{3}{4}$ in.

$8\frac{1}{4}$ in.

3 Find the perimeter of the L-shaped figure.

First, find x. $x = 15 - 3$

$$x = 12$$

$$p = 3 + 4 + x + 3 + 15 + 7$$

$$p = 3 + 4 + 12 + 3 + 15 + 7 = 44$$

The perimeter is 44 m.

Try It

a. Use a formula to find the perimeter of the square.

0.53 in.

b. Find the perimeter of the L-shaped figure.

The **area** (A) of a polygon is the number of square units contained in that polygon. You can calculate the area of rectangles and squares using a formula.

The area of a rectangle is the base (b) times the height (h). $A = b \cdot h$

The area of a square is the length of a side (s) squared. $A = s^2$

Example 4

The New York State Theater has scenery-storage areas in each wing. Each is 40 ft by 35 ft. What is the area of one of these storage areas?

$A = b \cdot h$

$A = 40 \cdot 35$ Substitute and solve.

$A = 1400 \text{ ft}^2$

You can use the formula for the area of a rectangle to find the area of other polygons.

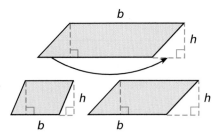

In a parallelogram, the height (h) is the perpendicular distance between the bases (b).

The area of a parallelogram is the length of the base (b) times the height (h): $A = b \cdot h$.

Example 5

Find the area of the parallelogram.

$A = b \cdot h$

$A = 13.5 \cdot 7.5$ Substitute and solve.

$A = 101.25 \text{ cm}^2$

Try It

Find the area of each polygon.

a.

b.

The height of a triangle is the perpendicular distance between the base and the opposite vertex.

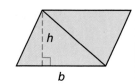

The area of a triangle is $A = \frac{1}{2}b \cdot h$.

The area of a triangle is $\frac{1}{2}$ the area of a rectangle or parallelogram.

Example 6

Find the area of the triangle.

$A = \frac{1}{2}b \cdot h$

$A = \frac{1}{2} \cdot 5\frac{1}{4} \cdot 3\frac{1}{2} = \frac{1}{2} \cdot \frac{21}{4} \cdot \frac{7}{2}$ Substitute and solve.

$A = \frac{147}{16} = 9\frac{3}{16}$ ft^2

The area of a trapezoid is $A = \frac{1}{2}h(b_1 + b_2)$.

Example 7

Find the area of the trapezoid.

$A = \frac{1}{2}h(b_1 + b_2)$

$A = \frac{1}{2} \cdot 12(10 + 15)$ Substitute and solve.

$A = \frac{1}{2} \cdot 12 \cdot 25 = 150$ cm^2

Try It

Find the area of each polygon.

a.
17.5 mm
12 mm

b.
16 in.
20 in.
23 in.

Check   Your Understanding

1. Describe the difference between the perimeter and the area of a polygon.

2. Which formula would you use to find the area of a rhombus?

Practice and Apply

1. ⬛ **Getting Started** ⬛ Find the area of the triangle.

a. Use the formula $A = \frac{1}{2}b \cdot h$.

b. Solve.

4 cm
5.5 cm

Find the perimeter and area of each polygon.

2.

$h = 16$ in.
$b = 21$ in.

3.

6.25 cm

4.

427 in.   449 in.
318 in.
602 in.

5.

2 m
4 m
8 m   2 m
4 m
4 m

6.
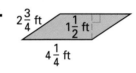
$2\frac{3}{4}$ ft $1\frac{1}{2}$ ft
$4\frac{1}{4}$ ft

7.

6 cm   7.2 cm
5 cm
8 cm

8.

4.65 cm
5 cm
3.5 cm   4.1 cm
10.2 cm

9.

16.1 m
16.1 m   14.75   16.1 m
16.1 m

10.

4.8 cm
12.4 cm

11.

4.5 cm
5.25 cm   5.25 cm
5.25 cm

12.

$5\frac{1}{4}$ ft
$3\frac{3}{4}$ ft $4\frac{1}{2}$ ft
$5\frac{1}{4}$ ft

13.
$3\frac{1}{3}$ ft
$3\frac{1}{3}$ ft

14. Science A halogen floor light is designed to give maximum light in a triangular shape. What is the area of maximum light for this bulb?

15. Career A set designer wants to make a parlor room 16 ft by 24 ft.

a. How much tape does he need to mark out the room on the stage?

b. How much carpet does he need to cover the whole floor?

Stage light
17 ft
15 ft
18 ft
Stage

PRACTICE 9-1

16. ▨ Test Prep ▨ Niambi is carpeting the floor of her room, which is 9 ft by 13 ft. How much carpet will she have to buy to cover the entire floor?

Ⓐ 22 ft   Ⓑ 117 ft²   Ⓒ 44 ft²   Ⓓ 484 ft

Use the figure to the right for Exercises 17–19.

17. What is the value of *y*? What is the value of *x*?

18. Find the areas of the square, the rectangle, and the triangle. Find the total area.

19. Find the perimeter of the figure.

Problem Solving and Reasoning

Algebra Find the missing dimension in each figure.

20.

10.8 cm
$A = 63.72$ cm²   *h*

21.

15 ft *b*
$A = 555$ ft²

22.

s
s
$A = 21.16$ m²

23. a. The figure to the right is a regular pentagon. Find the perimeter.

b. Communicate How could you find the area of the pentagon? Explain.

3.25 cm
4 cm
4 cm   4 cm
4 cm   4 cm

24. Critical Thinking Draw a polygon made by connecting a trapezoid, a triangle, and a parallelogram. Label the bases and heights. Find the perimeter and the total area of your figure.

25. Choose a Strategy A stage crew wants to design a room that is 48 m².

a. List four pairs of possible dimensions.

b. Which of your dimensions has the smallest perimeter? The largest?

> ## Problem Solving
> ### STRATEGIES
> • Look for a Pattern
> • Make an Organized List
> • Make a Table
> • Guess and Check
> • Work Backward
> • Use Logical Reasoning
> • Draw a Diagram
> • Solve a Simpler Problem

Mixed Review

Write each fraction or decimal as a percent. *[Lesson 6-1]*

26. $\frac{3}{4}$ **27.** 0.09   **28.** $\frac{9}{5}$ **29.** 1.42   **30.** 0.0038

Use the Pythagorean theorem ($c^2 = a^2 + b^2$) to decide whether each set of lengths would make a right triangle. *[Lesson 7-9]*

31. 2, 3, 5   **32.** 3, 4, 5   **33.** 6, 8, 10   **34.** 5, 7, 11

Scale and Area

▶ **Lesson Link**   You know how to find perimeter and area of some polygons. Now you'll see how scaling a polygon affects the perimeter and area. ◀

Explore   Scaling a Rectangle

Expanding Dimensions

Materials: Dynamic geometry software

1. Draw three small rectangles. Measure the base, height, perimeter, and area of each rectangle.

2. Record your measurements in three tables, each with four columns.

3. Drag one base of each rectangle until you double the height. Record the new dimensions in your table.

Base	Height	Perimeter	Area

4. Drag one height of each rectangle until you double the base. Record the new perimeter and area. How do the perimeter and area measurements of each rectangle compare?

5. Discuss any conclusions regarding what you found about doubling the dimensions, perimeter, and area.

Learn   Scale and Area

A **dilation** is a proportional reduction or enlargement of a figure. The ratio of the original and new dimensions is called the **scale factor**.

$$\frac{10}{4} = 2.5 \qquad \frac{5}{2} = 2.5$$

The scale factor is 2.5 for the dilation.

You can use the scale factor to find the dimensions of the dilated figure. The blue triangle is dilated by a scale factor of $\frac{2}{3}$.

$$h = \frac{2}{3} \cdot 4 = 2.\overline{6} \text{ cm} \qquad b = \frac{2}{3} \cdot 3 = 2 \text{ cm}$$

Examples

1 A theater-in-the-round is where the stage is in the middle of the audience. A model of this stage will be made by reducing it by a scale factor of $\frac{1}{10}$. Find the area and perimeter of the model's main stage.

First, find the base and height.

$$b = \frac{1}{10} \cdot 9 = \frac{9}{10} \qquad h = \frac{1}{10} \cdot 6 = \frac{6}{10} = \frac{3}{5}$$

$$p = 2\left(\frac{9}{10}\right) + 2\left(\frac{3}{5}\right) = \frac{9}{5} + \frac{6}{5} = \frac{15}{5} = 3 \qquad \text{Find the perimeter.}$$

$$A = \left(\frac{9}{10}\right) \cdot \left(\frac{3}{5}\right) = \frac{27}{50} \qquad \text{Find the area.}$$

The model will show the main stage with $p = 3$ units and $A = \frac{27}{50}$ units^2.

2 The rectangle shown will be dilated by a scale factor of 5.25. Find the resulting perimeter and area.

First, find the base and height.

$$b = 5.25 \cdot 7 = 36.75 \text{ in.} \qquad h = 5.25 \cdot 4 = 21 \text{ in.}$$

$$p = 2(36.75) + 2(21) = 115.5 \text{ in.} \qquad \text{Find the perimeter.}$$

$$A = (36.75) \cdot (21) = 771.75 \text{ in}^2. \qquad \text{Find the area.}$$

Try It

Determine the scale factor used to dilate the blue rectangle.

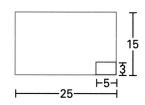

Example 3

Use a spreadsheet to observe the effect on the perimeter and area if a 3 in. by 5 in. rectangle is dilated by a scale factor of 3.

Find *b* and *h* for each dilated rectangle.

Use $p = 2(b + h)$ and
$A = b \cdot h$

The perimeter increases by a factor of 3.

The area increases by 3^2, or 9 times.

	A	B	C	D
	Base	Height	Perimeter	Area
1				
2	5	3	16	15
3	15	9	48	135
4	45	27	144	1215
5	135	81	432	10935

A pattern of dilated rectangles emerges with scale factors 1, 2, and 3.

Scale Factor	Perimeter	Area
1	$1 \cdot 15 = 15$	$1^2 \cdot 15 = 15$
2	$2 \cdot 15 = 30$	$2^2 \cdot 15 = 60$
3	$3 \cdot 15 = 45$	$3^2 \cdot 15 = 135$

Scale Factor	p	A
1	$1 \cdot p$	$1^2 \cdot A$
2	$2 \cdot p$	$2^2 \cdot A$
3	$3 \cdot p$	$3^2 \cdot A$

This pattern can be used for any polygon.

You can use this fact to find the new perimeter or area of any dilation.

For a dilation with scale factor *x*,

1. The new perimeter is $x \cdot p$, and

2. The new area is $x^2 \cdot A$.

▶ **Fine Arts Link**

A *thrust stage* allows some of the audience to view part of a performance from the side.

Example 4

A community theater wants to enlarge its thrust stage by a scale factor of 1.25. What will the new area of the thrust stage be?

$A = (1.25)^2 \cdot (13 \cdot 8)$

$= (1.5625) \cdot (104) = 162.5 \text{ ft}^2$

The new area will be 162.5 ft^2.

13 ft

8 ft

Try It

Find the new area and perimeter of a 4 m by 5 m rectangle that is dilated by a scale factor of $1\frac{3}{4}$.

An 8 cm by 6 cm rectangle is dilated by a scale factor of $\frac{1}{2}$. Find the perimeter and area of the new rectangle.

6 cm

8 cm

Seung thinks ...

First, I'll find the perimeter and area of the original rectangle.

$$p = 2(8 + 6) = 28 \text{ cm} \qquad A = 6 \cdot 8 = 48 \text{ cm}^2$$

Then, I'll multiply by the scale factor to find the new perimeter and multiply by the square of the scale factor to find the area.

$$p = \frac{1}{2} \cdot 28 = 14 \text{ cm}$$

$$A = \left(\frac{1}{2}\right)^2 \cdot 48 = \frac{1}{4} \cdot 48 = 12 \text{ cm}^2$$

Sarah thinks ...

I'm going to find the new base and height. Then I'll calculate the perimeter and area.

New base: $\frac{1}{2} \cdot 8 = 4 \text{ cm}$ New height: $\frac{1}{2} \cdot 6 = 3 \text{ cm}$

$$p = 2(b + h) = 2 \cdot (4 + 3) = 14 \text{ cm}$$

$$A = b \cdot h = 4 \cdot 3 = 12 \text{ cm}^2$$

What do you think?

1. Why doesn't Sarah multiply by $\frac{1}{4}$ when she calculates the new area?

2. In what circumstances might you choose Sarah's method? Seung's?

Check   Your Understanding

1. What is a dilation?

2. What happens when you dilate a figure by a scale factor less than 1? Greater than 1? Equal to 1?

Practice and Apply

1. **Getting Started** Find the area of the triangle when it is dilated by a scale factor of 4.

   a. Multiply each dimension by the scale factor 4.

   b. Use the formula $A = \frac{1}{2}b \cdot h$, using the new dimensions.

Find the perimeter and area of each polygon after the given dilation.

2. Scale factor = 3

3. Scale factor = 4.8

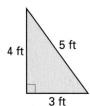

4. Scale factor = 0.5

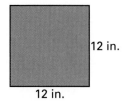

5. Scale factor = 1.5

6. Scale factor = $\frac{1}{10}$

7. Scale factor = 0.25

Fine Arts A Shakespearean theater group wants to buy material for its new rectangular stage. On the model, the stage is 40 cm by 100 cm. The scale factor reads 25.

8. What is the minimum length of a string of lights around the perimeter of the stage?

9. The group wants to cover the stage with special flooring. What is the area that will need to be covered?

10. **Science** The rectangular cells of an onion are viewed under a microscope that enlarges each cell by the scale factor 360. If each plant cell appears to be 6 cm, what is the size of the specimen?

11. **Test Prep** Determine the scale factor of a dilation of the red figure to the blue figure.

Ⓐ 2.5　　Ⓑ 2　　Ⓒ $\frac{1}{2}$　　Ⓓ 6.25

5 cm
2 cm
4 cm
10 cm

Problem Solving and Reasoning

Number Sense Decide whether the scale factor will produce a dilation that is an enlargement or a reduction.

12. Scale factor $= \frac{3}{4}$　　**13.** Scale factor = 4.5　　**14.** Scale factor = 0.01

15. Math Reasoning Using the right triangle as shown, what is the effect on the perimeter and area if you double only one of the two dimensions?

16. Communicate Create a rectangle and describe the effects on the perimeter and area if you double only one of its dimensions.

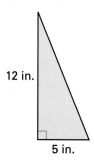

12 in.

5 in.

The background curtains on the stage of a theater are 1250 ft². The production company wants to make a model of the stage using a scale factor of $\frac{1}{25}$.

17. Measurement Find the area of the curtains in the model.

18. Patterns What is a possible set of dimensions for the curtains in the stage model?

19. Journal Write an explanation of how to find the perimeter and area of a polygon after a dilation by scale factor $= k$.

Mixed Review

Solve each. *[Lesson 6-2]*

20. What number is 15% of 90?　　**21.** 40% of 200 is what number?

22. What percent of 39 is 13?　　**23.** 100 is 25% of what number?

Convert each unit. *[Lesson 8-1]*

24. 3 hr to min　　**25.** 150 cm to m　　**26.** 42 kg to g　　**27.** 196 in. to ft

PROBLEM SOLVING 9-2

Project Progress

Identify the shapes that your item exhibits, such as squares, circles, triangles, or pentagons. Measure the perimeter and area of the sides of your chosen item.

Problem Solving

Understand
Plan
Solve
Look Back

9-3 | Circles

▶ **Lesson Link** You've seen how to measure the distance around a polygon and its area. Now you'll do the same for circles. ◀

The distance around a circle is the **circumference** (C).

The **center** of a circle is a point that is the same distance from all points on the circle.

A **radius** (r) of a circle is the segment or distance from the center of the circle to any point on the circle.

You'll Learn ...

■ to find the area and circumference of circles

... How It's Used

Set builders often work with the measurements of circular objects for the stage.

Vocabulary

circumference

center

radius

diameter

π (pi)

inscribed

circumscribed

Explore | A Circle's Ratio

Circle Search

Materials: Dynamic geometry software

1. Draw a circle. Draw a line segment from the circle to its center to show the radius.

2. Measure the radius (r), circumference (C), and area (A) of the circle. Make a table to record the data. Leave space for a total of nine columns in your table.

3. Drag the circle until it is about $\frac{1}{2}$ of its original area. Record the results in your table. Drag the circle again, but double the original area.

4. Drag the circle until it has about $\frac{1}{2}$ of its original circumference. Record the results in your table. Drag the circle again, but double the original circumference.

5. Label the last two columns of your table $\frac{C}{2r}$ and $\frac{A}{r^2}$. Calculate these ratios and record them in your table. How do these two ratios compare?

6. From the data in your table, discuss any relationships between the radius, circumference, and area of a circle.

Area	$\frac{1}{2}$ Area	2 Area	$\frac{C}{2r}$	$\frac{A}{r^2}$

The **diameter** of a circle is the segment or distance of the segment that passes through the center and has both endpoints on the circle.

$2r = d$
$r \qquad r$

Example 1

Find the diameter of a circle with radius $2\frac{3}{4}$ in.

$$d = 2r = 2\left(2\frac{3}{4}\right)$$

$$d = \frac{2}{1} \cdot \frac{11}{4} = \frac{22}{4} = 5\frac{1}{2} \text{ in.}$$

The diameter is $5\frac{1}{2}$ in.

$2\frac{3}{4}$ in.

For every circle, the ratio of the circumference to the diameter is represented by the Greek letter **π (pi)**. In calculations, $\pi \approx 3.14$ is often used.

$\dfrac{C}{d} = \pi$ \qquad Solve the ratio to find the circumference formula.

$C = \pi d = \pi(2r)$ \quad $d = 2r$.

$C = 2\pi r$ \qquad The formula for circumference is $C = 2\pi r$.

Example 2

Radio City Music Hall, where the Rockettes perform, features a revolving turntable 43 ft in diameter. Find the circumference of Radio City Music Hall's turntable.

$C = 2\pi r = \pi d$

$C \approx (3.14) \cdot 43 = 135.02 \text{ ft}$

The circumference is ≈ 135 ft.

Remember

$\approx$ means "approximately equal to." **[Previous course]**

Try It

a. Find the radius of a circle with diameter 3.46 m.

b. Find the circumference of a circle with diameter 3.46 m.

3.46 m

$$\frac{A}{r^2} = \pi \qquad \text{π is also the ratio of the area of a circle to the radius squared.}$$

$$A = \pi r^2 \qquad \text{The formula for the area of a circle is $A = \pi r^2$.}$$

▶ History Link

In the 1800s, Major Culberson reported a Blackfoot tepee made of 40 skins that would fit 100 people.

Example 3

In the mid-1800s, the Blackfoot people used 6 buffalo skins to build tepees that had 10 ft diameter floors. What is the floor area of a tepee this size?

First, find the radius. $5 \text{ ft} = r$

$A = \pi r^2$

$A = \pi(5)^2 = 25\pi \text{ ft}^2$

$ \approx (25 \cdot 3.14) \text{ ft}^2$

$A \approx 78.5 \text{ ft}^2$

10 ft

A polygon inside a circle with all its vertices on the circumference is **inscribed** in the circle.

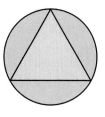

A polygon outside a circle with one point of each side on the circle is **circumscribed** about the circle.

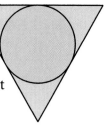

Example 4

Determine whether the pentagon circumscribes or inscribes the circle.

The pentagon is inside the circle and all the vertices are on the circumference. The pentagon is inscribed in the circle.

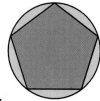

Try It

a. Find the area of a circle with $r = 4$ cm.

b. Does the square circumscribe the circle?

Check | Your Understanding

1. How are perimeter and circumference alike? How are they different?

2. What are the two ratios that equal π?

9-3 Exercises and Applications

Practice and Apply

1. $\boxed{\textbf{Getting Started}}$ Find the area of the circle shown. Use $\pi = 3.14$.

    a. Find the radius.   **b.** Find the area.

8 cm

Sketch each figure.

2. Square inscribed in a circle   **3.** Pentagon circumscribed about a circle

Find the circumference of each circle. Use $\pi = 3.14$.

4.

2 in.

5.

4.5 m

6.

$d = \frac{1}{3}$ ft

7.

$d = 10$ mi

Find the area of each circle. Use $\pi = 3.14$.

8.

15 mm

9.

$3\frac{1}{4}$ ft

10.

$d = 2.65$ cm

11.

$d = 3.1$ km

12. Science The earth's circumference is approximately 25,000 mi. Find the approximate diameter of the earth.

25,000 mi

14. Algebra A circle has an area of 42 cm². Write an equation and solve for r, the radius.

13. Career A costume designer is making costumes for an Elizabethan play. An actress's neck has a 14 in. circumference. The ruff (collar) will be made from a circle with a 6.2 in. radius. How much lace is needed to accent the circumference of the ruff?

Queen Elizabeth I of England (1533–1603)

15. Geography In the U.S. Midwest some farmers use a circular irrigation method. Suppose the length of an irrigation arm is 500 ft. What is the area of the irrigated circle?

16. [Test Prep] A circle has a radius of 4.5 m. Which is the best approximation for the area of this circle?

   Ⓐ 20.25 m²   Ⓑ 20.25π m²

   Ⓒ 63.6 m²   Ⓓ 63.6π m²

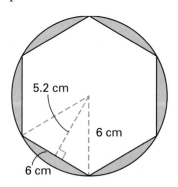

Problem Solving and Reasoning

17. Communicate A theater owner wants to design a Greek style semicircular stage with a radius of 30 ft. Explain how to find the perimeter and area of the stage. Include an illustration.

18. Number Sense Investigate what happens to the perimeter and area of a circle when you double the radius. Give an example and write about your conclusions.

19. [Journal] TV and FM radio signals have a line-of-sight range, which means mountains can interfere. A radio tower has a broadcast range with a 23 mi radius. How much area does the broadcast cover?

Theater of Dionysos in Athens, Greece

20. Math Reasoning A regular pentagon, hexagon, and octagon circumscribe a circle with a radius of 5 in. Which polygon has an area measurement closest to the area of the circle. Explain.

21. Geometry A hexagon is inscribed in the circle.

   a. Find the area of the triangle.

   b. Find the area of the hexagon.

   c. Find the area of the circle.

   d. Find the area of the shaded region.

5.2 cm

6 cm

6 cm

Mixed Review

Estimate each percent. [Lesson 6-3]

22. 34 out of 198   **23.** 67 out of 97   **24.** 49 out of 76   **25.** 2 out of 19

Give the number of significant digits in each number. [Lesson 8-2]

26. 104.96   **27.** 5.0401   **28.** 0.0006   **29.** 105   **30.** 20.40

Surface Area of Prisms and Cylinders

▶ **Lesson Link**   You know how to find the area of flat figures, such as polygons and circles. Now you'll learn about the surface area of 3-D figures. ◀

A **polyhedron** is a 3-D figure that is composed of polygons. Each polygon surface is called a **face**.

The **edge** of a polyhedron is where two faces meet.

A **vertex** of a polyhedron is the intersection of three or more faces.

The **surface area** (SA) of a polyhedron is the sum of the areas of all the faces.

Three Polyhedrons

Five faces:
4 triangles
1 square

Six faces:
6 rectangles

Ten faces:
2 octagons
8 rectangles

You'll Learn ...
■ to find surface area of prisms and cylinders

... How It's Used

Interior designers use surface area to figure the amount of material to cover solid objects.

Vocabulary
polyhedron
face
edge
vertex
surface area
prism
base
cylinder

Explore   **Prisms**

Surfing the Surface

Materials: Four sheets of 8.5 in. by 11 in. paper, Tape, Scissors

1. Find the area of one sheet of paper.

2. Make 3-D figures using one sheet of paper for each.

Figure a: Roll paper so opposite edges can be taped together.

Figure b: Fold paper into equal thirds and tape edges together.

Figure c: Fold paper into equal fourths and tape edges together.

Figure 2a

Figure 2b

Figure 2c

3. Is the surface area of each of these figures greater than, less than, or equal to the area of the original sheet of paper? Explain.

4. What shapes are needed to complete the surface of each figure? Draw these shapes and calculate their areas. Tape them onto the appropriate figures.

5. Rank the three solids in total surface area from least to greatest. Justify your ranking.

A **prism** is a polyhedron that has two congruent faces that are parallel polygons. Each parallel, congruent face is called a **base**.

A net helps you find the surface area because it shows all faces as flat polygons.

5 in.

3 in.
3 in.
3 in.
5 in.
3 in.
3 in.
3 in.

Example 1

Find the surface area of the rectangular prism.

First, sketch a net; then find the area of each face. There are three different rectangular faces.

Two faces are 30 cm by 24 cm.

$A = b \cdot h = 30 \cdot 24 = 720 \text{ cm}^2$

Two faces are 30 cm by 5 cm.

$A = b \cdot h = 30 \cdot 5 = 150 \text{ cm}^2$

Two faces are 24 cm by 5 cm.

$A = b \cdot h = 24 \cdot 5 = 120 \text{ cm}^2$

The surface area of the rectangular prism is

$SA = 2(720 + 150 + 120) = 1980 \text{ cm}^2.$

5 cm
24 cm
30 cm

30 cm
24 cm
5 cm

Try It

Find the surface area of a rectangular prism that is 1 in. by 2 in. by 3 in.

1 in.
2 in.
3 in.

Example 2

A 24 in. wide ramp from a stage to the audience floor needs to be built. The stage is 6 in. above the audience floor. The ramp will extend 8 in. away from the stage. What is the surface area of the ramp?

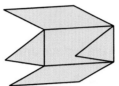

Find the area of each face.

Each triangle has $b = 8$ in. and $h = 6$ in.

$$A = \frac{1}{2}(b \cdot h) = \frac{1}{2}(8 \cdot 6) = \frac{1}{2}(48) = 24 \text{ in}^2$$

One face is 6 in. by 24 in. with $A = 144$ in².

One face is 8 in. by 24 in. with $A = 192$ in².

One face is 10 in. by 24 in. with $A = 240$ in².

The surface area is

$$SA = 2(24) + 144 + 192 + 240 = 624 \text{ in}^2.$$

A **cylinder** is a 3-D figure with two congruent circles for bases.

Notice the base of the rectangle is the circumference of a circle. The height of the rectangle is the height of the cylinder.

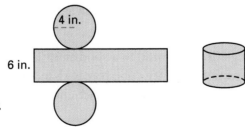

Try It

a. Find the area of each circle of the cylinder.

b. Find the area of the cylinder's side.

c. Find the surface area of the cylinder.

Check | Your Understanding

1. How many length measurements do you need to find the surface area of a prism? A cylinder? Draw a diagram to explain.

2. How many faces would a pentagonal prism have? A hexagonal prism?

Practice and Apply

1. **Getting Started** Find the surface area of the rectangular prism.

   a. Draw the net for the prism. Label the dimensions for each face.

   b. Find the area of each face.

   c. Find the sum of the areas.

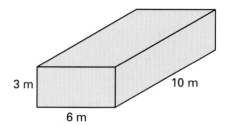

3 m   10 m

6 m

Sketch a net for each, then find the surface area.

2.

5.4 m

6.5 m   1.8 m

3.

4.3 in.   5 in.

5 in.

5 in.   12 in.

4.

3.5 cm

7.2 cm

5.

$2\frac{1}{2}$ ft

$2\frac{1}{2}$ ft

$2\frac{1}{2}$ ft

6.

9 m

12 m

7.

5 yd

$2\frac{1}{4}$ yd $6\frac{1}{2}$ yd

8. **Literature** A decorative platform is being constructed for a performance of *Hansel and Gretel*. Which shape would have the greater surface area, a cube 4 ft on each side or a rectangular prism that is 8 ft by 4 ft by 2 ft?

9. **Science** Water changes from a liquid to a solid at 32°F, the freezing point. Each section in an ice cube tray is $1\frac{1}{2}$ in. by 1 in. by 1 in. How much surface area does an ice cube from this tray have?

10. **Test Prep** A can has a diameter of 8 cm and a height of 15 cm. Find the area of paper for a label to cover the curved side.

    Ⓐ 3014.4 cm²   Ⓑ 120 cm²

    Ⓒ 188.4 cm²   Ⓓ 376.8 cm²

8 cm

15 cm

15 cm

11. What is the surface area of a box that is 12 in. by $7\frac{1}{2}$ in. by 4 in?

12. The box for a videotape is 19 cm tall, 10.5 cm long, and 2.5 cm wide. It is open on one of the long and narrow sides so that the tape can be put in. What is the surface area of the box?

Problem Solving and Reasoning

13. Geometry Find the surface area of the hexagonal prism.

14. Number Sense Find the surface area of a cylinder with 3 m height and 1 m radius. Also, find the surface area of a cylinder with 1 m height and 3 m radius. How does the formula πr^2 affect these results?

15. Choose a Strategy A cereal company is making a jumbo-size box by doubling the dimensions of its midsize box which is 12 in. by 8 in. by 2 in. How much more cardboard will be needed to make the jumbo size?

Problem Solving

STRATEGIES

- Look for a Pattern
- Make an Organized List
- Make a Table
- Guess and Check
- Work Backward
- Use Logical Reasoning
- Draw a Diagram
- Solve a Simpler Problem

Math Reasoning Determine a shortcut formula for finding the surface area.

16. A cube   **17.** A rectangular prism

18. **Journal** Invent a possible surface-area problem that a set designer for a movie or play might have to solve.

19. The diameter of cylinder A is half that of cylinder B. Both have the same height.

a. Communicate Predict which will have the greater total surface area, one of cylinder B or two of cylinder A? Explain.

b. Critical Thinking Which do you think would hold more, one of cylinder B or two of cylinder A? Why?

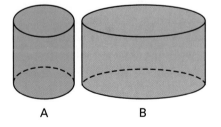

A   B

Mixed Review

Find the percent increase for each. *[Lesson 6-4]*

20. Old: 1420
New: 1562

21. Old: 12.9
New: 25.8

22. Old: $9.88
New: $14.82

Classify each angle as right, straight, obtuse, or acute. *[Lesson 8-4]*

23. 130°   **24.** 45°   **25.** 90°   **26.** 180°   **27.** 25°

9-5 Surface Area of Pyramids and Cones

You'll Learn ...

■ to find the surface area of pyramids and cones

... How It's Used

Model builders know how to make polyhedrons such as pyramids and cones.

Vocabulary

pyramid

height

slant height

▶ Lesson Link You've worked with polyhedrons called prisms; now you'll work with polyhedrons called pyramids. ◀

A **pyramid** is a polyhedron with one base—all the other faces are triangles. The shape of the base is used to name the pyramid.

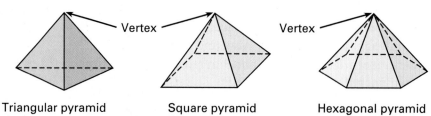

Triangular pyramid · Square pyramid · Hexagonal pyramid

Explore | Surface Area of a Pyramid

Build Your Own Pyramid

Materials: 2 sheets of 8.5 in. by 11 in. paper, Scissors, Tape, Ruler

1. Cut an 8.5 by 8.5 in. square from your sheet of paper.

2. Fold the square along each of the two diagonals, one at a time.

3. Cut out one of the V-shaped sections. Tape the cut edges together to make the pyramid.

4. Cut and attach a shape to fit on the uncovered face. Determine the surface area of your pyramid.

Step #2 · Step #3

Learn | Surface Area of Pyramids and Cones

The **height** of a pyramid is the perpendicular distance from the base to the opposite vertex.

The **slant height** is the perpendicular distance from the edge of the base to the opposite vertex.

Height · Slant height

You can find the surface area of a pyramid by looking at its net.

For a square pyramid, notice that the slant height is the height of a triangular face. The base of each triangular face is a side of the square.

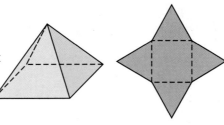

Example 1

In a play such as *Joseph and the Technicolor Dream Coat,* which has a scene in Egypt, a square pyramid might be part of the set.

A square pyramid for a stage could have a height of 3 ft and a base area of 64 ft².

Find the surface area of this pyramid.

The pyramid base is a square with area 64 ft².

The pyramid has four triangular faces.

$$A = \frac{1}{2}b \cdot h = \frac{1}{2}(8 \cdot 5) = 20 \text{ ft}^2$$

The surface area of the pyramid is

$$A = 64 + 4(20) = 144 \text{ ft}^2.$$

Try It

a. What kind of pyramid is shown?

b. What is the height of the pyramid?

c. Use the Pythagorean theorem ($c^2 = a^2 + b^2$) to find the slant height of the pyramid.

d. What is the area of the triangular face?

e. What is the surface area of the pyramid?

Remember

The Pythagorean theorem ($c^2 = a^2 + b^2$) can be used to determine the length of a side in a right triangle: *a* and *b* are legs and *c* is the hypotenuse.

[Page 374]

A triangular pyramid has four triangular faces. Only one of them is the base of the pyramid. The slant height of the pyramid is the height of a triangular face that is not the base.

Example 2

The triangular pyramid has an equilateral triangle base and three other faces. What is the surface area of this pyramid?

First, find the area of the base.

Use the Pythagorean theorem to find h.

$$a^2 + b^2 = c^2$$

$$h^2 + 6^2 = 12^2$$

$$h^2 = 12^2 - 6^2$$

$$h^2 = 108$$

$$h \approx 10.4 \text{ m}$$

So $A = \frac{1}{2}bh$

$$A \approx \frac{1}{2}(12)(10.4) \quad \text{Substitute.}$$

$$A \approx 62.4 \text{ m}^2$$

Find the area of one of the **three** congruent triangles.

$$A = \frac{1}{2}b \cdot h$$

$$A = \frac{1}{2}(12 \cdot 12) = 72 \text{ m}^2$$

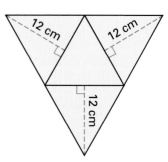

The surface area of the triangular pyramid is

$$SA \approx 62.4 + 3(72) = 278.4 \text{ m}^2.$$

Try It

a. What is the slant height of the pyramid?

b. Use the Pythagorean theorem ($a^2 + b^2 = c^2$) to find the height of the triangular base.

c. What is the area of a triangular face?

d. What is the surface area of the pyramid?

A **circular cone** is a 3-D figure with a circular base and one vertex.

To find the surface area of a cone, you find the area of the base and the area of the curved surface.

The area of the curved surface is $A = \frac{1}{2}Cs$.

The area of the base is $A = \pi r^2$.

The surface area of a cone is $SA = \left(\frac{1}{2}Cs\right) + \pi r^2$.

s = slant height

Example 3

Denise needs to make a model of a cinder cone volcano for a school play. The cone should be 4 ft tall, the base 4 ft in diameter, and the slant height about 4.48 ft. She needs to know the surface area of the cone in order to buy wire mesh to make the frame. What is the surface area of this cone?

Area of curved surface $= \frac{1}{2}Cs$

$A = \frac{1}{2}(2\pi \cdot 2)4.48 \approx 28.13 \text{ ft}^2$

Area of base $= \pi r^2$

$A = \pi(2)^2 \approx 12.56 \text{ ft}^2$

$SA \approx 28.13 + 12.56$ Take the sum to find the surface area.

$\approx 40.69 \text{ ft}^2$

Denise needs approximately 40.69 ft² of wire mesh.

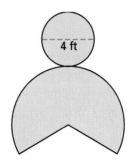

4 ft

Check   Your Understanding

1. What is the difference between the slant height and the height of a pyramid or cone?

2. How can you tell by looking at a net whether the solid is a prism, a pyramid, a cone, or a cylinder?

Practice and Apply

1. [Getting Started] Find the surface area of the triangular pyramid with the net shown.

   a. How many faces does the pyramid have?

   b. What is the area of the pyramid's base?

   c. What is the area of each of the other faces?

   d. Take the sum of the areas of the faces and the base to determine the surface area of the pyramid.

For each figure, find   **a. The slant height.**   **b. The surface area.**

2.

3.

4.

5. An amusement park wants a square pyramid in its Ancient Wonders theme area. The pyramid is to be 8 ft high and have a 12 ft wide square base. What is the surface area of the pyramid that will be built?

6. A triangular pyramid has an equilateral triangle with side length of 4 ft for a base. The height of the pyramid is 3.2 ft and the slant height is approximately 3.4 ft. What is the approximate surface area of this pyramid?

7. [Test Prep] Which do you need to find the area of the base of a cone?

   Ⓐ π   Ⓑ Radius

   Ⓒ Slant height   Ⓓ A and B

8. Fine Arts In a staged version of *Sleeping Beauty*, the princess wears a cone-shaped headpiece 18 in. tall. It is constructed of cardboard and wrapped with velvet fabric. How much fabric is needed to cover the cone if the actress's head has a 22 in. circumference?

Shakespeare's *Richard III*, 1949

9. **Social Studies** Sioux tepees are cone-shaped. If the diameter of a tepee is 18 ft and the height is 12 ft, how much buffalo hide is needed to cover the outside surface?

10. **Algebra** A square pyramid has a total surface area of 176 yd^2. If the slant height is 7 yd and the area of the base is 64 yd^2, then what is the height of the pyramid? Round your answer to the nearest hundredth place.

Problem Solving and Reasoning

11. **Communicate** Your classmate is confused about the difference between the height of a pyramid and the slant height. Describe the difference between the two.

For Exercises 12 and 13, refer to the square pyramid and cone of the same height, with the diameter of the cone's base equal to the side of the square base of the pyramid.

12. **Math Reasoning** Which is greater, the perimeter of the square base or the circumference of the circular base?

13. **Critical Thinking** Which do you think has the greater surface area? Explain.

14. What would happen to the surface area of a pyramid if you double its height? Give an example and explain.

15. **Number Sense** How many faces does a hexagonal pyramid have? Octagonal pyramid? Describe the number pattern.

Mixed Review

Find the slope, *x*-intercept, and *y*-intercept for each equation. *[Lesson 4-5]*

16. $y = 2x - 1$ 17. $y = x + 3$ 18. $y = \frac{1}{2}x + 2$ 19. $y = -2x$

20. $y = -x + 1$ 21. $y = 3x + 0$ 22. $y = -0.5x - 2$ 23. $y = 4x - 5$

$\overleftrightarrow{AB} \parallel \overleftrightarrow{CD}$. **Use the diagram on the right to answer the questions.** *[Lesson 8-5]*

24. Find the measures of all angles in the diagram.

25. Identify all interior angles.

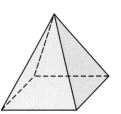

TECHNOLOGY

Using Geometry Software • Measuring Polygons

Problem: Construct a triangle. What are its perimeter and area?

You can use geometry software to answer this question.

1 Choose the Polygon Tool. Click on three different vertex points for your triangle.

2 When you return to your first point and click, your triangle will be complete.

3 Use the length tool to calculate the perimeter of the triangle.

Perimeter of this triangle

4 Use the area tool to calculate the area of the triangle.

22.70 cm   Area of this triangle

Solution: The answers may vary.

TRY IT

a. Construct another triangle. What are its perimeter and area?

b. Construct a quadrilateral. What are its perimeter and area?

ON YOUR OWN

▶ How do you think geometry software calculates the perimeter of a polygon?

▶ Is it easier to find the area of a polygon using geometry software rather than a formula? Explain.

▶ Describe what would happen to the area of your triangle if you moved one of the vertices.

Section 9A Connect

In the beginning of Section 9A, you learned about a historical American theater hall. Now you will design a stage set for a play.

The Great Stage

Materials: Drawing paper, Ruler, Compass, Drawing pens

You and your group are in charge of designing a stage set for a school play.

The producer wants an archway that looks like a palace entrance. The archway must have a semicircular (half-circle) top and cylindrical columns for support.

You must also design rectangular steps up to a doorway in the arch.

You must decide the quantity of various materials you will use to make this archway. Do this by using what you know about area, perimeter, and surface area.

1. Each person in the group draws a sketch of each part of the design: each column, the semicircle, and the stairs. Each drawing should show the actual dimensions of the props and the drawing scale.

2. Calculate the material needed to cover the surface area of all the props.

3. Decide on the materials you would use to cover these props; for example, paint, fabric, paper, tile, and so on.

4. Make a list of the amount of materials you'll need to cover the props.

5. Decide on a layout of the stage and draw a top view of this stage plan including the props you have just designed.

6. Draw the front view of your stage plan. Identify a story line that would be appropriate for your design.

Fill in the appropriate vocabulary term for each sentence.

1. The distance around a polygon is the _____.

2. The _____ of a circle is π times the diameter.

3. A _____ has two parallel polygons that are the same size and shape.

4. A reduction of a geometric figure by a scale factor is a _____.

5. **Journal** Explain the difference between a prism and a pyramid and the difference between a cylinder and a cone.

Find the perimeter/circumference and area for each figure.

6.

6 m

7.

$9\frac{1}{2}$ in.
$6\frac{1}{2}$ in. $7\frac{1}{2}$ in.

8.

8 cm
8 cm 7 cm 8 cm
15.73 cm

9.

$3\frac{1}{4}$ ft   5 ft
3 ft
$5\frac{1}{4}$ ft

10.

121 mm   121 mm
54 mm

11.

16 ft
8 ft
5 ft
6 ft
11 ft   8 ft

Find the surface area of each figure.

12.

5 cm
3 cm 7 cm

13.

61 m
40 m   40 m

14.

20 in.
25 in.

15.

18 cm   16 cm

Test Prep

When using formulas on a test, always use pencil and paper to substitute and solve for a missing value.

16. The diameter of a bicycle wheel is 18 in. What is its circumference?

Ⓐ 21.52 in.   Ⓑ 28.52 in.   Ⓒ 56.52 in.   Ⓓ 85.52 in.

REVIEW 9A

The Big Deliveries

The year was 1907 and business in the United States was flourishing. Few people had telephones or cars, so how were messages and packages delivered? Jim Casey, an enterprising 19-year-old from Seattle, had an idea. He borrowed $100, started the American Messenger Company, and hired other teenagers to work for him.

Jim's company did very well because of his old-fashioned values: customer courtesy, reliability, round-the-clock service, and low rates. Jim had an idea that no one else had thought of — consolidated delivery. Packages to be delivered to one neighborhood were put into a single delivery vehicle. This saved time and money.

During the 1930s Jim's company changed its name to United Parcel Service or UPS. This company now delivers over 12 million documents and packages around the world.

1 What mathematics might a package-delivery company use to keep delivery going accurately and on time?

2 Why might delivery companies set limits on overall dimensions and weight of packages?

9-6 Volume of Rectangular Prisms

You'll Learn ...

■ to determine the volume of rectangular prisms

... How It's Used

Volume tells you how much space a package occupies and how much it might weigh. Weight and space are important factors for a delivery company.

Vocabulary

volume

▶ **Lesson Link** You've learned how to find the surface area of rectangular prisms. Now you'll find the volume of rectangular prisms. ◀

The **volume** is the number of cubic units in a solid.

The volume of this solid is 1 cm³.

1 cm

1 cm   1 cm

Explore | **Filling a Rectangular Prism**

Fill It Up!

Materials: Centimeter cubes, 8.5 in. by 11 in. paper, Tape, Centimeter ruler

1. Make two different rectangular prisms (without bases) by folding two 8.5 in. by 11 in. sheets of paper into equal fourths: one using the longer side and one using the shorter side. Tape the edges to form the prism.

   11 in.

   $8\frac{1}{2}$ in.

2. Make a layer of unit cubes to cover the base of each rectangular prism.

   a. How tall is a single layer of cubes?

   b. How many cubes cover each base?

3. For each prism, how many cubes are needed to make two layers? Three layers? Four layers? Make a table to record your data.

4. **a.** How tall is each rectangular prism (in centimeters)?

   b. How many layers are needed to fill each prism?

5. How many cubes would fill each prism?

Learn | **Volume of Rectangular Prisms**

The volume of a prism is found by multiplying the area of the base (B) by the prism height (h).

$V = B \cdot h$

B

h

476 *Chapter 9 • Area and Volume*

The area of the base of a polyhedron is shown by B. The length of the base of a polygon is shown by b.

Example 1

A next-day delivery service delivers a package with dimensions 12 in. by 7 in. by 30 in. What is the volume of the package?

First, draw the prism and label the dimensions.

Find the area of the rectangular base.

$B = 12 \cdot 30 = 360 \text{ in}^2$

$V = B \cdot h$

$V = 360 \cdot 7$

$V = 2520 \text{ in}^3$

The volume is 2520 in³.

7 in.

30 in.   12 in.

Example 2

Find the height of a rectangular prism with volume 72 cm³ and base dimensions 6 cm by 3 cm.

First, find the area of the rectangular base.

$B = 6 \times 3 = 18 \text{ cm}^2$

Then use the volume formula to solve.

3 cm   6 cm

$V = B \cdot h$

$72 = 18 \cdot h$

$4 = h$

The prism has a height of 4 cm.

Try It

Find the volume of each figure.

a.

4.2 cm

9.8 cm   5 cm

b.

$6\frac{1}{2}$ in.

$6\frac{1}{2}$ in. $6\frac{1}{2}$ in.

You can find the volume of some irregularly-shaped solids by breaking the figure into rectangular prisms.

▶ **History Link**

In 1720, it took the postal service three days to deliver a parcel from Philadelphia to New York (almost 100 miles).

Example 3

Speedy Delivery, Inc., charges by volume for irregularly-shaped packages. If it charges $170.63 for a package with the dimensions shown, how much do they charge per in³?

This solid is composed of two rectangular prisms.

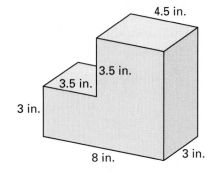

Find the volume of each rectangular prism.

Find the volume of the bottom prism, V_{bottom}.

$V_{bottom} = (8)(3)(3)$

$V_{bottom} = 72 \text{ in}^3$

Find the volume of the top prism, V_{top}.

$V_{top} = (4.5)(3.5)(3)$

$V_{top} = 47.25 \text{ in}^3$

Find the total volume: $V_{bottom} + V_{top}$.

$V_{bottom} + V_{top} = 72 + 47.25 = 119.25 \text{ in}^3$

$\dfrac{170.63}{119.25} \approx \$1.43 \text{ per in}^3$

Try It

Find the volume of the figure shown.

Check Your Understanding

1. Would the volume of a package change if you measured it in cubic centimeters instead of cubic inches? Explain.

2. Describe the difference between the surface area and volume of a rectangular prism.

3. In formulas for area and volume, describe the difference between b and B. Give examples of how b and B are used.

Practice and Apply

1. **Getting Started** Find the volume of the rectangular prism.
   a. Multiply the length and width to determine the area of the base.
   b. Multiply the area of the base by the height.

Find the volume of each figure.

2.
   7 in.
   20 in.
   3 in.

3.
   6.5 m   12 m
   8.5 m

4.
   15 cm
   15 cm
   15 cm

5.
   3 yd
   $5\frac{1}{4}$ yd
   $6\frac{1}{3}$ yd

6.
   9.4 cm
   9.4 cm
   9.4 cm

7.
   $2\frac{1}{2}$ ft
   4 ft
   $1\frac{1}{2}$ ft
   $3\frac{1}{4}$ ft

Problem Solving TIP

Drawing a diagram is helpful when solving volume problems. Remember to label the dimensions.

Sketch each figure, then find its volume.

8. A box of granola cereal that measures 23 cm by 8 cm by 35 cm

9. A fly-casting pool in the park that is 30 ft wide, 40 ft long, and 5 ft deep

10. **Test Prep** A cube-shaped storage container measures $1\frac{1}{2}$ ft on each side. What is the volume of 6 such containers?

    Ⓐ $3\frac{3}{8}$ ft³   Ⓑ $20\frac{1}{4}$ ft³   Ⓒ $4\frac{1}{2}$ ft³   Ⓓ None of these

11. **Geography** Falan paid $38.40 to ship a package by air from Washington, D.C., to his family in Bombay, India. The package was 18 in. by 24 in. by 20 in. What did he pay per cubic in?

12. **Number Sense** A box has base dimensions of 32 ft by 16 ft and its volume is 6144 ft³. What is the height of this box?

13. **Algebra** The formula for the volume of a sphere is $\frac{4}{3}\pi r^3$ where r is the radius of the sphere. What is the volume of a sphere where $r = 3$ cm?

PRACTICE 9-6

14. Science The concrete in bridges expands in the hot sun. To prevent the road from buckling, engineers build gaps, called expansion joints, between segments of the road. What is the total volume of an expansion joint that is 25 ft by 1 ft by 4 in?

Problem Solving and Reasoning

15. Algebra Draw a cube with a side length of 5 cm. Find its volume. Write a formula for finding the volume of a cube.

16. Communicate Which formula do you prefer to use in finding the volume of a rectangular prism: $V = B \cdot h$ or $V = l \cdot w \cdot h$? Explain.

Patterns The chart at the right has been started to list all the possible sets of whole-number dimensions that make a rectangular prism with a volume of 36 ft³.

L	W	H	V
1	2	18	36
			36
			36

17. Copy and complete the chart.

18. Find the surface area of each prism.

19. Which set of dimensions has the greatest surface area? The least?

20. Critical Thinking An airline reserves some of its cargo space for shipping packages but limits the size of packages. A corrugated box is 48 in. by 18 in. by 36 in. Redesign the box so that it has the same volume but less surface area.

21. Math Reasoning A rectangular box has dimensions of 18 in. by 6 in. by 6 in. A large coffee table book has dimensions of 18 in. by 9 in. by 4 in. Find the volume of each and determine whether the book will fit in the box. Explain.

22. Estimation Seth can't fit everything in his 5040 in³ suitcase. Use the photograph to estimate the volume of clothes he's trying to pack.

Mixed Review

Check to see if the point is a solution of both equations. *[Lesson 4-6]*

23. Point $(2, -3)$

$y = x - 5$

$y = 2x - 7$

24. Point $(1, 3)$

$y = 2x + 1$

$y = 4x - 1$

25. Point $(-4, 1)$

$y = 3x + 13$

$y = -x - 5$

Find the sum of the angle measures for each polygon. *[Lesson 8-6]*

26. Triangle   **27.** Octagon   **28.** Pentagon   **29.** Square

Scale and Volume

▶ **Lesson Link**   Now that you know about volume of a rectangular prism, you'll see how volume is affected when dimensions are scaled up or down. ◀

Explore   Scaling a Rectangular Prism

Which Dimension?

Materials: Spreadsheet software

Examine the effect on the volume of a rectangular box if you multiply one of its dimensions by a scale factor.

	A	B	C	D	E
1	Scale Factor	Length	Width	Height	Volume
2	1	4	3	2	?
3	2	8	3	2	?
4	3	12	3	2	?

3 in.   2 in.
4 in.

... How It's Used

Package design involves the scaling of boxes up or down to see the effect on volume, which in turn affects weight and cost of shipping.

1. Use a spreadsheet to make a table similar to the one shown. Apply scale factors 1 through 5 to the length of the box. Find each volume.

2. How do the new volumes compare to the original volume?

3. Predict the volume of the box if the length is scaled by a factor of 6.

4. Make another table, but this time hold the length constant and apply the scale factor to the width. How do the resulting volumes compare to those in the first table?

5. Make a third table, this time applying the scale factor to height only. How do the resulting volumes compare to the two previous tables?

6. Make a conclusion about scaling one dimension of a rectangular box.

Learn   Scale and Volume

The volume of a rectangular prism is affected when its length measurements are scaled. The change of volume depends on whether one, two, or three dimensions are scaled.

When one dimension of a rectangular prism is scaled, multiply the original volume by the scale factor to find the volume of the scaled prism.

When two dimensions of a rectangular prism are scaled, multiply the original volume by the square of the scale factor to find the volume of the scaled prism.

Example 1

A delivery service charges 1¢ per in³ for foam filler to package fragile items. Suppose a breakable parcel that was originally in a 6 in. by 4 in. by 4 in. box needed to be put in a larger box. Determine the ratio of the volume of the larger box to the volume of the original box.

The volume of the original box is 96 in³.

a. How much is the foam filler if one 4 in. dimension is tripled?

The box is 6 in. by 12 in. by 4 in.

The volume of foam filler is
$V = 6 \cdot 12 \cdot 4$
$V = 288$ in³.

The cost of foam filler for a 6 in. by 12 in. by 4 in. box is $2.88.

Since $288 \div 96 = 3$, the volume of the larger box is 3 times greater than the original box.

b. How much is the foam filler if both 4 in. dimensions are tripled?

The box is 6 in. by 12 in. by 12 in.

The volume of foam filler is
$V = 6 \cdot 12 \cdot 12$
$V = 864$ in³.

The cost of foam filler for a 6 in. by 12 in. by 12 in. box is $8.64.

Since $864 \div 96 = 9$, the volume of the larger box is 9 times greater than the original box.

Try It

a. Find the volume of a 3 in. by 5 in. by 8 in. rectangular box.

b. Find the volume of the same box after one dimension has been increased by a scale factor of 4.

c. Find the volume of the same box after two dimensions have been increased by a scale factor of 4.

8 in.

3 in. 5 in.

A dilation of a three-dimensional figure changes all three dimensions by the scale factor. The blue rectangular prism is a dilation of the red rectangular prism.

You can find the scale factor by using the ratio of any two corresponding dimensions.

$$\frac{4}{2} = 2 \qquad \frac{6}{3} = 2 \qquad \frac{8}{4} = 2$$

The scale factor of the dilation is 2.

The volume of the red prism is 24 cm³. So, $24 \cdot 2^3 = 24 \cdot 8 = 192$, since the scale factor is 2. The volume of the blue prism is 192 cm³.

When a prism is dilated, the volume is multiplied by the cube of the scale factor.

Example 2

A rectangular prism is 7 cm by 6 cm by 12 cm. Find the volume of the prism after a dilation by a scale factor of 22.

The original volume

$V = 7 \cdot 6 \cdot 12$

$V = 504 \text{ cm}^3$

The volume of the dilation

$V = (22)^3 \cdot 504$

$V = 5{,}366{,}592 \text{ cm}^3$

▶ **Science Link**

The pupil is in the iris of the eye. In dim light, the iris dilates to let more light into the eye.

Try It

A rectangular prism has a volume of 43 ft³. Find the volume after the dilation.

a. Scale factor $= 5$ **b.** Scale factor $= \dfrac{1}{2}$

The pattern will work for the dilation of any prism with volume V.

Scale Factor	Volume of Dilated Prism
1	$1^3 \cdot V$
2	$2^3 \cdot V$
3	$3^3 \cdot V$
…	…
n	$n^3 \cdot V$

WHAT DO YOU THINK?

A 5 cm by 3 cm by 2 cm rectangular prism is dilated by a scale factor of 6. Find the volume of the dilated prism.

3 cm
2 cm   5 cm

Steve thinks ...

Scale each dimension by 6.

5 cm becomes $6 \cdot 5 = 30$ cm.

3 cm becomes $6 \cdot 3 = 18$ cm.

2 cm becomes $6 \cdot 2 = 12$ cm.

The volume of a dilated prism is

$V = 30 \cdot 18 \cdot 12 = 6480$ cm^3.

Gabriella thinks ...

Find the original volume.

$V = 5 \cdot 3 \cdot 2 = 30$ cm^3.

Multiply the original volume by 6^3.

The new prism's volume is

$V = 6^3 \cdot 30 = 6480$ cm^3.

What do you think?

1. Describe how Steve solved the problem.

2. Why are both Steve's and Gabriella's answers given in cm^3?

Check | Your Understanding

1. If you want to scale two dimensions of a rectangular prism, does it matter which pair of dimensions you scale? Explain.

2. What happens to the volume of a rectangular prism when you dilate it by a scale factor greater than 1? Less than 1?

Practice and Apply

1. **Getting Started** Find the volume of a rectangular prism of 360 ft^3 after a dilation of $\frac{1}{2}$.
   a. Find $\left(\frac{1}{2}\right)^3$.
   b. Multiply this by 360 to find the new volume.

Find the volume of each prism after scaling one dimension by the indicated scale factor.

2. Scale factor = 8

8 cm
11 cm
5 cm

3. Scale factor = $\frac{1}{3}$

24 in.
18 in.
36 in.

4. Scale factor = 0.5

2 m
6 m
4 m

Find the volume of each figure after the dilation.

5. Scale factor = 3

8 in.
7 in.
4 in.

6. Scale factor = 0.8

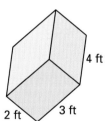

4 ft
2 ft
3 ft

7. Scale factor = 2

1.2 m
1.2 m
1.2 m
1.2 m

8. **Science** Alkaline earth metals are found in many sea shells. A researcher ships some abalone shells to the lab. The delivery company charges $1.25 per cubic ft for next-day delivery. What will a $1\frac{3}{4}$ ft × $1\frac{1}{2}$ ft × 2 ft package cost for next-day service?

9. **Test Prep** What is the scale factor between a cubic box that exactly fits a $3\frac{1}{2}$ in. diameter softball and one that exactly fits a 9 in. diameter basketball?

   Ⓐ 3　　Ⓑ $31\frac{1}{2}$　　Ⓒ $\frac{7}{18}$　　Ⓓ $2\frac{4}{7}$

10. Measurement Find the volume of the figure to the right after a dilation of 2.5.

11. Number Sense Find the volume of the figure to the right after a dilation with a scale factor of 10. Do the same for a dilation with a scale factor of $\frac{1}{10}$. Find the ratio of these volumes.

12. Algebra Write a volume formula for a box with $V = 214$ cm³ after

    a. One dimension is scaled by *s*.   **b.** Two dimensions are scaled by *s*.

    c. Three dimensions are scaled by *s*.

14 cm
8 cm
5 cm
9 cm
5 cm
5 cm

Problem Solving and Reasoning

13. You have a package 24 in. by 18 in. by 12 in. to ship. E-Z Shipping charges by volume $0.002 per in³, whereas Speedy Shipping charges by surface area $0.005 per in².

    a. Which company is cheaper for this package?

    b. Communicate Will this be true for all shapes of packages? Explain.

14. Patterns A manufacturing company wants you to design a box with 4 times the volume of its standard 12 in. × 6 in. × 4 in. box. Find as many whole-number solutions as you can.

15. Choose a Strategy Sally wants to make a scale model of a long hut 45 ft by 25 ft by 10 ft for a social studies project.

    a. Choose a scale factor for her. Why did you select it?

    b. Find the surface area of the model hut.

    c. Find the volume of the model hut.

Problem Solving
STRATEGIES
- Look for a Pattern
- Make an Organized List
- Make a Table
- Guess and Check
- Work Backward
- Use Logical Reasoning
- Draw a Diagram
- Solve a Simpler Problem

Mixed Review

Test whether each point is a solution of the inequality. *[Lesson 4-7]*

16. $y > 2x - 5$ **a.** $(2, -3)$ **b.** $(4, 5)$ **c.** $(1, -2)$

17. $y \leq 3x + 1$ **a.** $(2, 7)$ **b.** $(-2, -6)$ **c.** $(4, -13)$

18. How many cubes are needed to build a tower with this base plan? *[Lesson 8-7]*

19. How many of the cubes can be seen from a front view of the tower? *[Lesson 8-7]*

20. How many cubes can be seen from a side view of the tower? *[Lesson 8-7]*

4	5	4
3	4	3
2	3	2
1	2	1

Side

Volume of Prisms and Cylinders

▶ Lesson Link You've learned how to find the volume of rectangular prisms. Now you'll find the volume of other prisms and cylinders. ◀

You'll Learn ...

■ to find the volume of prisms and cylinders

... How It's Used

Packages come in shapes of prisms and cylinders. The volume of these packages determine space needed for shipping.

Explore Volume of a Cylinder

Volume in the Round

Materials: 2 sheets of 8.5 in. by 11 in. paper, Tape, Centimeter cubes, Centimeter ruler

1. Make two different cylinders, each from a sheet of paper. Roll one along the longer side and the other along the shorter side. Tape the sides together for each one.

2. Make a layer of unit cubes to cover the circular base of each cylinder.

   a. Estimate the number of cubes needed to cover each base.

   b. Calculate the area of each base by measuring the radius and then using $A = \pi r^2$ (use cm^2). Compare this result with your estimate.

3. a. Using cm, how tall is a single layer of cubes?

   b. For each cylinder, how many cubes are needed for two layers? Three layers? Four layers?

4. a. Using cm, how tall is each cylinder?

   b. Estimate how many layers of cubes are needed to completely fill each cylinder. Describe how you made the estimate.

$8\frac{1}{2}$ in.

11 in.

5. How many cubes will completely fill each cylinder? Discuss why you think the numbers differ.

Learn Volume of Prisms and Cylinders

The volume of prisms and cylinders can be found by taking the product of the base area (B) and the height (h). $V = B \cdot h$

For a triangular prism, the area of the base $B = \frac{1}{2}(b \cdot h)$. You may recognize this as the formula for the area of a triangle.

B = *area of a prism base* and b = *length of a triangular base*.

Also, there are two heights to consider—the height of the triangle and the height of the prism. Both of them are represented by the variable h.

Example 1

Posters can be sent through the mail in boxes that are triangular prisms. Find the volume of the triangular box.

First, find the area of the triangular base (B).

$$B = \frac{1}{2}(b \cdot h)$$

$$B = \frac{1}{2}(6 \cdot 5\frac{1}{4}) = 15\frac{3}{4} \text{ in}^2$$

Use B to find the volume.

$$V = B \cdot h$$

$$V = 15\frac{3}{4} \cdot 38\frac{1}{4}$$

$$V = 15.75 \cdot 38.25$$

$$V = 602.4375 \text{ in}^3$$

The volume is 602.4375 in³.

Try It

a. What is the height of the triangular base.

b. What is the area of the triangular base.

c. What is the volume of the prism.

For a cylinder, the area of the base $B = \pi r^2$, where $r = $ radius. The volume of a cylinder then is $V = Bh = (\pi r^2)h$.

Example 2

Find the volume of the cylinder.

First, find the area of the base (B).

$$B = \pi \cdot r^2$$

$$B = \pi \cdot (2)^2 \approx 12.56 \text{ m}^2$$

Use B to find the volume.

$$V = B \cdot h$$

$$V \approx 12.56 \cdot 4.5$$

$$V \approx 56.52 \text{ m}^3$$

The volume is 56.52 m³.

Try It

Find the volume of each cylinder.

a.

b.

Check | Your Understanding

1. A stack of 40 nickels is $2\frac{1}{2}$ in. tall. The diameter of a nickel is $\frac{13}{16}$ in. Describe how you would find the volume of the stack of nickels.

2. Describe the similarities and differences between finding the volume of a prism and a cylinder.

3. Explain how to find the volume of a prism or cylinder with a height of zero.

4. Based on what you know about finding the volume of a triangular prism, describe how you would find the volume of a hexagonal prism.

Practice and Apply

1. **Getting Started** A cylinder has a diameter of 5 m and a height of 6 m.

   a. Sketch the cylinder and label the radius and height.

   b. Use the formula $A = \pi r^2$ to find the area of the base (use 3.14 for π).

   c. Multiply by the height to find the volume.

Find the volume of each solid, using 3.14 for π.

2.
   2 ft
   6 ft
   10 ft

3.
   9 cm
   3 cm

4.
   $9\frac{1}{2}$ in.
   12 in.   16 in.

5.
   6 cm
   20 cm

6.
   2.4 m
   3 m
   4 m

7.
   14.4 cm
   8 cm

8. **Industry** A photographic-supply company is designing a package to hold a tripod. The base of the package is an isosceles triangle with a base of 15 in. and a height of 20 in. The length of the package is 22 in. What is the volume of this package?

   20 in.
   22 in.
   15 in.

9. **Science** A *hotbed* is a bed of soil that is enclosed in glass. The heat trapped under the glass is useful for raising seedlings. A hotbed forms the shape of a triangular prism that is 1.2 m long. The triangular base has a height of 0.3 m and a base length of 0.5 m. What is the volume of this hothouse?

PRACTICE 9-8

10. **Test Prep** A grain silo shaped like a cylinder is 30 ft tall and 8 ft in diameter. To the nearest hundred ft³, how many cubic ft of grain can the silo hold?

Ⓐ 75,400 ft³   Ⓑ 82,400 ft³   Ⓒ 1,500 ft³   Ⓓ 7,500 ft³

Problem Solving and Reasoning

Operation Sense Find the volume of the shaded region in each figure.

11.

24 in.
3 in.
7 in.

12.

2 cm
6 cm
3 cm
12 cm
16 cm

13. Geometry A hotel in Detroit is shaped like a cylinder with a diameter of 35 m and a height of 230 m.

a. To the nearest m³, what is the volume of the building?

b. The curved surface is covered with glass. How much glass is there on the surface of the hotel?

14. **Journal** A classmate is confused about the difference between the height of the triangle in the base of a triangular prism and the height of the prism. Write an explanation with an illustration to help clarify the two heights.

15. Communicate The base areas of a triangular, rectangular, and hexagonal prism are equal. Which prism do you think has the greatest volume? The least? Explain.

Mixed Review

Find the coordinates of each point. *[Lesson 2-6]*

16. *A*   **17.** *B*

18. *C*   **19.** *D*

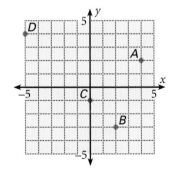

Complete each table of values. *[Lesson 4-1]*

20.

x	0	1	2	3	4	5
y = x + 7						

21.

x	0	1	2	3	4	5
y = −3x						

9-9 Volume of Pyramids and Cones

You'll Learn ...

■ to find the volume of pyramids and cones

... How It's Used

A CAD operator creates drawings and 3-D models of motorcycles, cars, airplanes, and other things that require detailed engineering and design.

▶ **Lesson Link** You've found the volume of prisms and cylinders. Now you'll use that knowledge to find the volume of pyramids and cones. ◀

Explore   Cone to Cylinder

Cups and Cones

Materials: Scissors, Tape, Centimeter ruler, 2 sheets of 11 in. by 17 in. paper, Compass, Centimeter cubes

1. Use a compass to draw a circle with a 12.7 cm radius. Use a ruler to draw a radius on your circle. Cut out the circle.

2. Cut along the radius line that you drew.

3. Pull one edge of the cut radius until you produce a cone with a 15.2 cm diameter circular base. Use tape to keep this cone in place.

4. Measure the height of the cone.

5. Cut out a rectangle that will make a cylinder with the same height as the cone. The cylinder should also have the same diameter as the cone's base.

6. Calculate the volume of the cylinder by measuring the dimensions.

7. Estimate the volume of the cone by filling it with centimeter cubes. Record the estimate.

8. Place the cone inside the cylinder so that both of their circular bases are on the tabletop. Estimate the volume between the cylinder and the cone by filling the space with centimeter cubes. Record the estimate.

9. Discuss the relationship between the volume of the cylinder and the volume of the cone.

Chapter 9 • Area and Volume

Learn | Volume of Pyramids and Cones

The volume of a cone is $\frac{1}{3}$ the volume of a cylinder.

$V_{cone} = \frac{1}{3}(B \cdot h)$ where B is the area of the base and h is the height.

Example 1

Find the volume of the cone.

First, find the area of the circular base (B).

$B = \pi \cdot r^2$

$B = \pi \cdot 6^2 \approx 113.04 \text{ cm}^2$

Use B to find the volume.

$V = \frac{1}{3}(B \cdot h)$

$V \approx \frac{1}{3}(113.04) \cdot 8$

$V \approx 301.44 \text{ cm}^3$

The volume is about 301.44 cm³.

Try It

Find the volume of the cone.

The formula used to find B, the area of a figure's base, will depend on the shape of the base.

Finding the area of the square base will be different than finding the area of a triangular base.

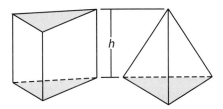

The volume of a pyramid is related to the volume of its related prism.

For a prism with volume $V = B \cdot h$, the related pyramid has volume $V = \frac{1}{3}(B \cdot h)$.

Example 2

Find the volume of the pyramid.

Let h_t = *height of the triangle.*

$$V = \frac{1}{3}B \cdot h$$

$$V = \frac{1}{3}\left(\frac{1}{2}b \cdot h_t\right) \cdot h$$

$$V = \frac{1}{3}\left(\frac{1}{2}(5 \cdot 12)\right) \cdot 15$$

$$V = \frac{1}{3}(30) \cdot 15 = 150 \text{ in}^3$$
The volume of the pyramid is 150 in³.

15 in.

12 in.

5 in.

Example 3

Find the volume of the pyramid.

$$V = \frac{1}{3}B \cdot h$$

$$V = \frac{1}{3}(9^2) \cdot h$$

$$V = \frac{1}{3}(81) \cdot 25$$

$$V = \frac{1}{3}(81) \cdot 25 = 675 \text{ cm}^3$$
The volume of the pyramid is 675 cm³.

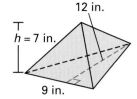

25 cm

9 cm   9 cm

Try It

Find the volume of each pyramid.

a.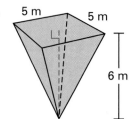

5 m   5 m

6 m

b.

12 in.

$h = 7$ in.

9 in.

Check | Your Understanding

1. How are the volumes of pyramids and cones similar?

2. Given a cone that has a height of 18 cm and a circular base with a diameter of 8 cm, describe the cylinder that has 3 times the volume of that cone.

3. As the height of a pyramid increases does the slant height increase? Explain.

Practice and Apply

1. [Getting Started] Find the volume of the pyramid.

    a. Find the area of the base.

    b. Multiply the base area by the height and divide by 3 to find the volume.

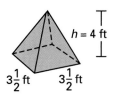

$h = 4$ ft

$3\frac{1}{2}$ ft $3\frac{1}{2}$ ft

Find the volume of each solid. Use 3.14 for π.

2.

$h = 8$ in.

12 in.   12 in.

3.

$h = 6$ cm

9 cm —4 cm

4. $h = 8$ m

├—— 12 m ——┤

5. $h = 7$ ft

4 ft

12 ft

6. 36 mm

├—40 mm—┤

7. 10 cm

├— 6 cm —┤

8. Geography The Great Pyramid of Khufu in ancient Egypt was a square pyramid 147 m high, with each side of the base 230 m. To the nearest m³, how much limestone rock made up the pyramid?

9. Algebra A cone with height of 25 mm is 3685 mm³. What is the radius of the base?

10. Number Sense Two square pyramids are each 10 inches tall. One pyramid has a 25 in² base and the other has a 64 in² base. Which pyramid has the greater volume?

11. Science The funnel at the right is used to put coolant, a mixture of antifreeze and water, in the radiator of a car. What is the maximum volume of coolant that the funnel can hold?

├—14.5 cm—┤

12 cm

12. [Test Prep] An ice-cream company sells a prepackaged sugar cone with a 6 cm diameter with ice cream, fudge, and nuts filled to the top of the cone. To the nearest cm, what is the volume of this cone if it is 14 cm tall?

   Ⓐ 301 cm³   Ⓑ 151 cm³   Ⓒ 603 cm³   Ⓓ 132 cm³

11 cm

1.5 cm

Problem Solving and Reasoning

13. Math Reasoning Which solid has a greater volume, the pyramid or cone?

14. Communicate Suppose you know the dimensions of a cone but have forgotten the formula for the volume of a cone. Describe a way you could find the volume.

15. Algebra Write an equation and use the Pythagorean theorem to find the height of a cone that has a slant height of 15 in. and a radius of 9 in.

16. Critical Thinking A dinnerware factory packs its dinnerware in a pyramid-shaped box.

a. How much cardboard is saved by using a pyramid design over a square-based prism design?

b. How much volume is saved?

17. Choose a Strategy A manufacturer of cone-shaped hats wants to ship each hat in a cylinder with the same diameter and height. How much packing filler is needed for each cylinder to completely fill the package?

Problem Solving STRATEGIES

- Look for a Pattern
- Make an Organized List
- Make a Table
- Guess and Check
- Work Backward
- Use Logical Reasoning
- Draw a Diagram
- Solve a Simpler Problem

Mixed Review

Evaluate. *[Lesson 2-7]*

18. -5^2　　**19.** 4^3　　**20.** $(-2)^5$　　**21.** 8^2　　**22.** -6^0

Determine if each ordered pair is a solution of the equation. *[Lesson 4-2]*

23. $y = 4x$　　**a.** $(2, 8)$　　**b.** $(4, -16)$

24. $x = y + 1$　　**a.** $(7, 6)$　　**b.** $(3, 2)$

25. $y = 3x - 2$　　**a.** $(1, 1)$　　**b.** $(2, -4)$

Project Progress

You should know the volume of your chosen item. Be able to describe the relationship between the dimensions of your package and the dimensions of your item. Also, look back on how you decided on the final package.

Problem Solving

Understand
Plan
Solve
Look Back

Section 9B Connect

In the beginning of Section 9B, you learned how some teenagers started what is today one of the largest package-delivery companies in the world. Now you will use your knowledge of volume to solve packaging problems involved in operating a business of your own.

The Dig on Deliveries

Materials: Calculator

You and your friends have a part-time job buying used stereo-sound components and shipping them to a relative in another state who refurbishes and resells them.

The boxing, foam packing, and shipping costs come out of your pay of $25 per component. You have the three components to ship (see photos). Your local post office has the box sizes shown in the lower right chart to use for shipping.

Woofer-tube

Sub-woofer

Band-pass enclosure

1. Determine the volume, to the nearest in^3, of each sound component.

2. Choose the box size to ship each component. (You may ship more than one component per box.) Determine the volume of foam packing needed for each box.

3. The foam packing material is $0.99 per ft^3. If a delivery company charges $0.002 per in^3 for shipping, what is the total cost of boxing, packing, and shipping for the three components? How much profit did you make?

2 in. x 10 in. x 13 in.	$1.75
10 in. x 12 in. x 15 in.	$2.25
10 in. x 14 in. x 20 in.	$2.50
12 in. x 16 in. x 24 in.	$3.25
16 in. x 20 in. x 24 in.	$3.50

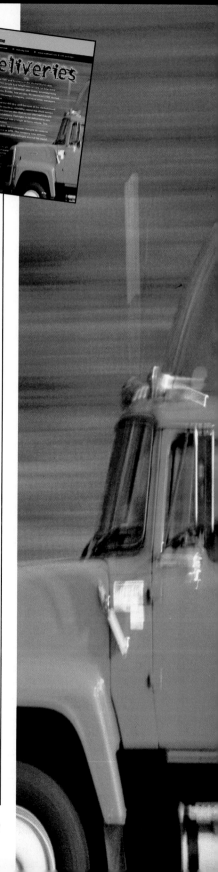

Section 9B Review

Find the volume of each solid. Use 3.14 for π.

1.
2 in.   17 in.
$16\frac{1}{2}$ in.

2.
$\frac{1}{2}$ in.   12 in.
1 in.

3.
3.2 cm
6 cm

4.
7.3 m
7.3 m
7.3 m

5. $h = 12$ m
18 m   18 m

6. $4\frac{1}{2}$ ft
2 ft
3 ft

7.
14 in.
10 in.   4 in.

8. $3\frac{1}{2}$ in.
6 in.

9. 10.5 cm
17.5 cm

Find the volume for each after the given dilation.

10. Scale factor = 10
2 ft
3 ft $6\frac{1}{2}$ ft

11. Scale factor = $\frac{1}{3}$
9 in.
9 in.
9 in.

12. Which has the greater volume: a can 16 cm in diameter and 24 cm high or a box 16 cm by 12 cm by 24 cm?

13. A model-rocket club uses the design to the right to see which student can get the most distance from a launch. What is the volume of the rocket?

3 in.
15 in.
2 in.

Be careful with cylinder and cone formulas that include *r* for radius. The given dimensions may include a value for the diameter instead. Never use a value for the diameter in these formulas.

14. To the nearest 10 cubic cm, what is the volume of a cylinder with a diameter of 10 cm and a height of 14 cm?

ⓐ 440 cm³   ⓑ 4400 cm³   ⓒ 1100 cm³   ⓓ 7700 cm³

Comparing Areas of Map Projections

A map shows the earth's surface on a plane. If the earth were flat, it would be easy to represent its surface on a flat sheet of paper. But the earth is a sphere, and a spherical surface is not easily flattened.

A **map projection** is an attempt to represent a spherical surface as a flat surface.

Use the facts that Greenland has an area of 840,050 mi² and Canada has an area of 3,851,809 mi² to compare the following two representations of the earth.

The **cylindrical projection** was originally ideal for navigation and is still used today. The lines of longitude and latitude appear as straight lines that intersect at right angles. The North and South Poles are greatly exaggerated.

The **conic projection** usually shows latitude lines as parts of circles, and longitude lines radiate from the North or South Pole.

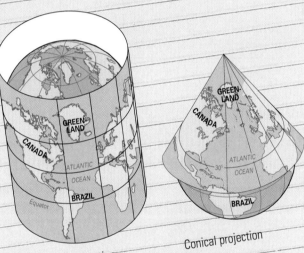

Cylindrical projection

Conical projection

Try It

1. Look up *map projection* in an encyclopedia or atlas. Why is the cylindrical projection most accurate for areas located on the equator?

2. Imagine that you are a sailor navigating from the coast of Brazil to Greenland. Describe an advantage of using the cylindrical projection.

3. Compare the cylindrical and conic projections to a globe. If you wanted to compare the areas of the seven continents, which projection would you use? Why?

4. Describe how the areas of Greenland and Canada compare on each of the above projections.

Chapter 9 Summary and Review

Graphic Organizer

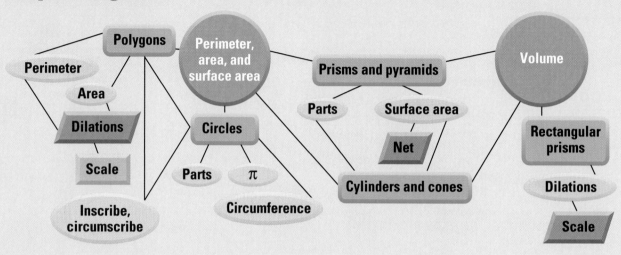

Section 9A Perimeter, Area, and Surface Area

Summary

- The **perimeter** (p) is the distance around a figure.

- The **area** (A) of a polygon is the number of square units it contains. Area of a rectangle $= bh$, area of a square $= s^2$, and area of a triangle $= \frac{1}{2}bh$.

- The distance around a circle is the **circumference**. The **radius** is the distance from the **center** to any point on the circle. The **diameter** $= 2r$. π **(pi)** is used to calculate the area of a circle.

- A **polyhedron** is a 3-D figure composed of polygonal **faces** that meet at **edges**. A **vertex** of a polyhedron is the intersection of three or more faces. **Prisms, cylinders, pyramids,** and **cones** are polyhedrons.

- The **surface area** (SA) of a polyhedron is the sum of the areas of all the faces. A net can be helpful in finding the surface area of a polyhedron.

Review

1. Find the perimeter and area of each polygon.

a.
7 cm
6 cm
4 cm

b.
2 in.
4 in.
5 in.
5 in.

2. Find the perimeter and area of

a. The polygon in Exercise 1a after a dilation of a scale factor of 3.

b. The polygon in Exercise 1b after a dilation of a scale factor of $\frac{2}{5}$.

3. For the circle shown, find the circumference and the area.

8.3 cm

4. One of the rings in a three-ring circus has a circumference of 141.3 ft. Find the diameter of the ring.

5. Find the surface area of each figure.

a.

7 ft

5 ft

b.

12 cm

15 cm

25 cm

6. Find the slant height and the surface area.

a.

12 in.

10 in.

10 in.

b.

20 m

15 m

Section 9B   Volume

Summary

■ The **volume** of a solid measures the space it occupies.

■ Volume (V) of a prism or cylinder $= B \cdot h$, and volume (V) of a pyramid or cone $= \frac{1}{3}B \cdot h$ where $B =$ area of the figure's base.

■ In a dilation with a scale factor of x, the volume of the solid is multiplied by x^3.

Review

7. Find the volume of each solid.

a.

5 cm

5 cm   5 cm

b.

25 ft

14 ft   21 ft

8. Find the volume of each solid.

a.

3 in.

$6\frac{1}{2}$ in.

b.

15 cm

7 cm   11 cm

9. a. Sketch a triangular prism with height 4 cm where the triangle has a base 10 cm and height 6 cm. Then find its volume.

b. Sketch a cone with diameter 8 in. and height 5 in. Then find its volume.

10. a. Find the volume of the solid in Exercise 7a after scaling two dimensions by a scale factor of $\frac{1}{5}$.

b. Find the surface area and volume of the solid in Exercise 7b after a dilation of a scale factor of 7.

11. Find the volume of a triangular prism where $B = 3$ m^2 and

a. $h = 4.5$ m

b. $h = 9$ m

12. Find the volume of a cylinder where $B = 12$ ft^2 and

a. $h = 2$ ft

b. $h = \frac{1}{2}$ ft

1. Refer to the parallelogram shown below.

  a. Find the perimeter and area.

  b. Find the perimeter and area after a dilation of a scale factor of 4.

2. Refer to the triangle shown below.

  a. Find the perimeter and area.

  b. Find the perimeter and area after a dilation of a scale factor of $\frac{3}{4}$.

3. Find the diameter, area, and circumference of the circle at the right.

4. Which shows **a.** a square circumscribed about a circle. **b.**

5. Refer to the rectangular prism shown below.

  a. Sketch a net of the prism.

  b. Find the surface area of the prism.

6. Refer to the cylinder shown below.

  a. Find the surface area of the cylinder.

  b. Find the volume of the cylinder.

7. Refer to the pyramid shown below. Find the slant height and surface area of the pyramid.

8. A disposable paper cup has the shape of a cone with diameter 5 cm and height 6 cm. How much water does the cup hold?

9. A simplified drawing of Monique's house is shown at the right.

  a. What is the volume of the house?

  b. Monique plans to paint her house. How much surface area will she cover? (Do not include the roof or the floor.)

Performance Task

Make a chart showing a drawing of every kind of 3-D figure you have learned. Label each figure with its name. Show formulas for surface area and volume of each figure.

Performance Assessment

Choose one problem.

THINK GLOBALLY, ACT LOCALLY

Find your home location on a globe of the earth. Determine the latitude and longitude of your home. Then draw a map showing the region that is within 5° latitude north or south, and within 5° longitude east or west of your home. Use the scale of the globe to determine the perimeter and area of this region.

BUILDING A CUBE THE HARD WAY

Make three copies of the net shown at the right on pieces of stiff paper. The sides shown with tick marks are all the same length. Make the patterns as large as you can, but all the same size. Cut out each net. Fold and tape each one to make three figures. Put the three figures together to make a cube. How does this three-dimensional puzzle relate to the formula for the volume of a pyramid?

Roll-to-Roll CARPETING

Dena bought a 10 ft by 8 ft piece of lime green carpet that is 1 in. thick. When the carpet is rolled up it forms a cylinder 10 ft long and $1\frac{1}{2}$ ft in diameter. What is the volume of this roll of carpet and about how many layers of carpet are there in the cylinder?

How Much Is Money?

You'll need a quarter, dime, nickel, and penny. Find the area of the circular base of each coin. Now find the height of each coin. Use this information to find the volume of each coin. Compare the ratios of coin value to volume.

10 Algebra: Functions

► Entertainment Link
www.mathsurf.com/8/ch10/ent

► Science Link
www.mathsurf.com/8/ch10/science

Entertainment

Jugglers now use mathematics to describe *siteswaps*—how high a pin goes and in which hand it is caught.

Science

Jupiter's four largest moons—Callisto, Io, Europa, and Ganymede—were discovered by Galileo in the year 1609.

Arts & Literature

The graph of the frequencies of the 12-step chromatic scale forms an exponential curve. High C has double the frequency of middle C.

and Relationships

Social Studies Link
www.mathsurf.com/8/ch10/social

People of the World

Astronomer Annie Jump Cannon (1863–1941) published a catalog listing more than 1000 stars according to their color spectra. It took ten volumes to contain the catalog.

Social Studies

The shape of the flag of the United States was determined in 1959 by executive order of President Dwight Eisenhower. Federal standards require that the ratio of its width to its length must be 1:1.9.

KEY MATH IDEAS

A function is a relationship that gives one output value for each input value.

The input is the independent variable and the output is the dependent variable.

The graph of a linear function is a line.

The graph of a quadratic function is nonlinear; it is a curve called a parabola.

An expression such as $2x^4 - 3x + 2$ is a polynomial.

Like terms have the same variable raised to the same exponent.

CHAPTER PROJECT

Problem Solving

Understand
Plan
Solve
Look Back

Find a situation you would like to model with an equation or function; for example, the height of a baseball over time as it leaves the bat, the thickness of a book given the number of pages, the value of a doll given its age. As you learn about the various models in this chapter, decide which is the best for your situation. Try to find a way to use the model for the situation you chose.

Problem Solving Focus

Checking for a Reasonable Answer

When you look back, it is important to check your answer to a problem to make sure that it is reasonable. Sometimes you may find that your answer is mathematically correct, but makes no sense in the real world.

Read each problem and its answer. Show why each is mathematically correct. Then explain whether the answer is reasonable or not.

1 Lois and Jack have the same birthday, but Jack is 15 years older than Lois. The sum of their ages is 9. How old is each one of them?
Answer: Jack is 12, Lois is −3

2 Tyra bought Jack a tie and Lois a bracelet. The bracelet was on sale, but was $39 more than Jack's tie. The bill totaled $25. How much was each gift?
Answer: Bracelet $32, tie −$7

3 There is a snowstorm on the day of their birthday party. When the guests arrive, the temperature is 12°F. By the time they leave, the storm causes a temperature drop of 18°F. What is the temperature then? **Answer: −6°F**

4 Jack makes hot soup for his guests. He empties 3 cans of soup concentrate into a pot, adds 3 cans of milk and warms the soup. He pours an 8 oz cup of soup for Lois, leaving 40 oz of soup in the pot. How much does a can hold? **Answer: 8 oz**

5 The entire party lasted two hours. If they spent 40 minutes making and eating soup, 20 minutes opening gifts, 45 minutes looking at pictures, and 25 minutes playing in the snow, how much time was left for eating cake?
Answer: −10 minutes

A World in Motion

Motion, the act or process of changing position, surrounds us in our daily lives. Earth rotates on its axis and around the sun. When we fly kites, the wind, which is air in motion, makes our kites soar into the sky or fall to the ground. Periodic motion can be seen in the pendulum of a grandfather clock as it swings and repeats its movement regularly and exactly. We observe and experience motion in our own movements as well as in those of others, such as in a handshake, the blink of an eyelid, a walk around the block.

The graceful movements of a dancer, a football quarterback running for a touchdown, a child running in the park— each is an example of motion. Imagine a bird flying to its nest, a dog running to greet its owner, a cat licking its paws. Motion occurs each time we move or observe movement.

1 Name three examples of motion in your everyday life.

2 What do you think is meant by slow motion? Motion picture? Range of motion?

3 When you are sitting still in class, is motion occurring? Explain.

10-1 Functions

You'll Learn ...

■ to recognize a function and to find the input and output values of a function

... How It's Used

Computer graphics artists use functions to add effects such as shading to their artwork.

Vocabulary

function

▶ **Lesson Link** In previous lessons, you looked at many different relationships between numbers. In this lesson, you will look at one of these relationships in which one number depends on another number. ◀

If you put whole carrots into a food processor and use the "slice" blade, you know that the result will always be sliced carrots. The result depends on the vegetable you put in and the type of blade used.

A machine that performs a duty can be used to represent relationships in mathematics. We *input* a value, apply a *rule*, and get an *output* value.

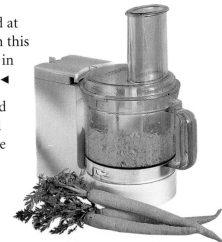

Explore Functions

What's My Rule?

| Input 4 | What's my rule? | Output 4 |

1. Here is a "rule" machine. Find as many rules as possible that will give you the output value for the given input value.

2. When the input is 4, what output does each rule give?

3. Compare your output values for an input value of 4 to another person's output values. Try to guess the rules the other person used.

4. If you used the same rule, is it possible to get two different output values if you both use 6 as the input value?

Learn Functions

When each input value for a rule results in exactly one output value, this special relationship is called a *function*. A **function** is a relationship in which an output value depends on an input value, and gives only one output for each input. Two different input values can have the same output value, but two different output values cannot have the same input value.

Example 1

Ashley's salary as a dance instructor depends on the number of hours she works. If she is paid $7 an hour, what is her salary for 8 hours? 15 hours? 25 hours? If her salary was $133, how many hours did she work? Is her salary a function of the hours she works?

	Rule: Multiply by 7	
Input		**Output**
8	8×7	56
15	15×7	105
25	25×7	175

For 8 hours, her salary is $56. For 15 hours, her salary is $105. For 25 hours, her salary is $175.

To reverse multiplying by 7, you can divide by 7: $133 \div 7 = 19$. She worked 19 hours for $133.

Yes, her salary is a function of her hours worked. For each number of hours (input), there is only one value for her salary (output).

Try It

Denika is Ashley's assistant. She earns $5.50 an hour. How much does she make for 20 hours? Is her salary a function of her hours worked? If she earned $55.00, how many hours did she work?

MENTAL MATH

Only SIDO rules out a function (Same Input, Different Output). These situations are okay for functions: Same input, same output; Different input, same output.

Example 2

Is the cost a function of the number of items? Explain.

Input (items)	4	9	1	8	4
Output (cost)	$2.00	$4.00	$0.50	$4.00	$3.00

4 items may cost $2, or 4 items may cost $3 (for the input 4, there is more than one output). So cost is not a function of the number of items.

Try It

Is the price a function of the number of Buddy Biscuits? Explain.

Buy 4, and the 5th one is free!

Biscuits	1	2	3	4	5
Price	$0.75	$1.50	$2.25	$3.00	$3.00

Example 3

Country western line dancing had a rise in popularity in 1996. The number of dancers in each row is related to the length of the dance floor. Examine the table below. Is the relationship a function? If so, what's the rule? Explain.

Floor Length (ft) Input	Dancers per Row Output
12	4
15	5
24	8
39	13

If you divide each input value by 3, you get the output value.

$12 \div 3 = 4$
$15 \div 3 = 5$
$24 \div 3 = 8$
$39 \div 3 = 13$

There is only one output value for each input value, so the relationship is a function. The rule is "Divide the input value by 3 to get the output value."

Try It

Is the relationship a function? If so, what is the rule? Explain your answer.

a.

Input	2	5	0	6	4
Output	4	25	0	36	16

b.

Input	1	2	3	2	1
Output	10	20	30	40	50

Check Your Understanding

1. What is special about a function? Give an example of a relationship that *is* a function. Give an example of a relationship that *is not* a function.

2. The $\boxed{x^2}$ key on a calculator squares the number that you input. Is this a function? Explain.

3. Why is the rule "Round a number to the nearest 10" a function, but the rule "Round a number" is not?

Practice and Apply

1. **Getting Started** Answer each question for the given function machine.

   a. What number is the input value?

   b. What number is the output value?

   c. What is the rule?

   d. If you input 6, what is the output?

   | 4 | Multiply by 3 and subtract 4 | 8 |

For the function machine shown, find the output value for each input value.

2. Input of 4   3. Input of −1

4. Input of 10   5. Input of 0

   | Input | Multiply by 4 and add 1.75 | Output |

For the function machine shown, find the input value for each output value.

6. Output of 1   7. Output of 4

8. Output of 9   9. Output of −4

   | Input | Divide by 4 | Output |

What is a possible rule for the input and output shown in each table?

10.

Input	Output
−1	−2
0	0
1	2
2	4

11.

Input	Output
5	9
7	13
9	17
11	21

12.

Input	Output
7	0
6	0
5	0
4	0

13. **Test Prep** Which situation does **not** describe a function?

   Ⓐ Distance traveled given the rate of speed.

   Ⓑ Distance traveled given the time it takes.

   Ⓒ Distance traveled given the age of the commander.

   Ⓓ They are all functions.

14. **Geometry** Is the area of a circle a function of its diameter?

15. An average person skiing cross country at 6 mi/hr burns about 13.5 calories per min.

  a. Write a rule for how many calories would be burned by skiing 6 mi/hr. Use the rule to find the number of calories burned in 15 min; 20 min; 30 min; 45 min.

  b. To burn 300 calories, approximately how long must Donna ski?

  c. Does the number of calories burned depend on the number of minutes spent skiing? Does the relationship describe a function? Explain.

16. **Chemistry** There are three different forms, or *isotopes*, in which hydrogen atoms occur. Is the number of neutrons a function of the number of protons?

	Protons	Neutrons
Hydrogen-1 (protium)	1	0
Hydrogen-2 (deuterium)	1	1
Hydrogen-3 (tritium)	1	2

Problem Solving and Reasoning

17. **Communicate** A flare is launched straight up from the ground. The table shows the relationship of the height above the ground with respect to time. Is the relationship a function? Explain.

Time (sec)	0	1	2	3	4	5
Height (m)	0	20	30	30	20	0

18. If you are given the output of a function, would there be only one input?

Critical Thinking Guess my rule.

19.

If You Say ...	−2	−1	1	2
I Say ...	2	1	1	2

20.

If You Say ...	3	5	6	10
I Say ...	8	24	35	99

Mixed Review

Find the percent decrease for each. *[Lesson 6-5]*

21. From 100 to 77   **22.** From 1000 to 977   **23.** From 0.3 to 0.21   **24.** From 1000 to 10

25. Draw a net for the number cube shown. (Note that numbers on opposite faces add up to 7.) *[Lesson 8-7]*

Linear Functions

▶ Lesson Link You have learned about special relationships called functions. In this lesson, you will represent functions in different ways. ◀

Explore Linear Functions

Materials: Graphing utility

Is It Possible?

1. Using a graphing utility, press [Y=] and enter the equation Y=1.5X−1. Press [GRAPH] to graph the equation. Use one of the [ZOOM] key options to get an integer window.

2. Press [TRACE]. What point is shown?

3. Move along the line by pressing the left and right arrow keys. What happens to the value of *x*? Is it possible to find two points on the graph with the same *x*-coordinate but with different *y*-coordinates?

4. Graph another linear equation. Use the trace feature again. Can you find two different *y* values for the same *x*-coordinate on this graph?

Learn Linear Functions

You have used function machines to enter an input, perform a function, and receive an output. The value of the output depended on the value of the input.

Input *x*	Add 4	Output *y*

If we let *x* represent the input and *y* the output, this relationship can be represented by the function rule $x + 4 = y$ or $y = x + 4$. The output (*y*) depends on the input (*x*).

When the value of *y* depends on the value of *x*, *y* is a function of *x* and is called the **dependent variable** ; *x* is called the **independent variable** .

In graphing, we use the horizontal axis (*x*-axis) for the independent variable and the vertical axis (*y*-axis) for the dependent variable.

You'll Learn ...

■ to represent functions using tables, graphs, and equations

... How It's Used

A printer uses linear functions to determine costs of large print jobs.

Vocabulary

dependent variable

independent variable

linear function

▶ **Math Link**

The equation $y = 3x + 2$ is a statement that the expressions y and $3x + 2$ are equal. The function $y = 3x + 2$ means the value of y is given by the rule $3x + 2$.

Examples

1 Graph the equation $y = 3x + 2$. Does it describe a function? Is it linear?

Make a table of input and output values.

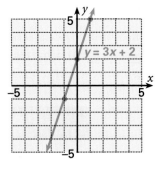

Input	Function Rule	Output
x	$3x + 2$	y
-1	$3(-1) + 2$	-1
0	$3(0) + 2$	2
1	$3(1) + 2$	5

The equation is a function, because each input (x) value has a single output (y) value. It is a **linear function** because the graph is a line.

2 The swim team is sponsoring a swim-a-thon to raise money. Paula's pledges totaled $3 for each lap completed.

a. Write and graph the rule that relates the money pledged to the number of laps completed. If after fifteen minutes, Paula had raised $27, how many laps did she complete?

Let $y =$ the money pledged and $x =$ number of laps completed; the rule is then $y = 3x$.

Locate the output, or dependent value, 27 on the y-axis. Find the approximate corresponding x value: $x = 9$ laps.

b. Does the rule describe a function? Explain.

The rule describes a function because for each input value there is only one output value.

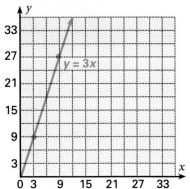

Try It

a. Graph $y = -2x$. Does it describe a linear function? Explain.

b. The Spanish club is selling T-shirts as a fund-raiser. The T-shirts sell for $4 each. Write and graph the rule that relates the money earned to the number of T-shirts sold. If after one day James had collected $36, how many T-shirts did he sell? Does the rule describe a function? Explain.

In the weightless conditions aboard a space station, the height of a pushed pencil can be modeled by a linear function of the time since it was released. A pencil pushed downward from a height of 120 cm drops 2.5 cm per second. Make a set of output values for the function $y = -2.5x + 120$.

Tanisha thinks ...

I can find output values by using the tables in a calculator. If I enter $-2.5x$ ➕ 120 as the function Y_1 and look at the table formed, I can find the output values.

The output values are 120, 117.5, 115, 112.5, and so on.

Daniel thinks ...

I noticed that 120 is the y-intercept. I can just subtract 2.5 for each increase of 1 in the x values.

x	0	1	2	3	4	5
y	120	117.5	115	112.5	110	107.5

$-2.5 \quad -2.5 \quad -2.5 \quad -2.5 \quad -2.5$

What do 🟊 you 🟊 think?

What method would you use if you wanted to know how long it would take for the pencil to hit the floor? Why?

Check | Your Understanding

1. How can you use the graph of a function to find the input value for a given output value?

2. How can you tell from a table if a relationship is a function?

3. Is the graph $y = \frac{1}{2}x - 5$ the graph of a linear function? Explain.

PRACTICE 10-2

Practice and Apply

1. | Getting Started | Given the function rule $y = x + 3$,

   a. What is the dependent variable?

   b. What is the independent variable?

   c. Find the output values for the following input values: $x = -5$, $x = 0$, $x = 5$.

Given the following function rules, complete the table of values.

2. $y = 2x - 6$

Input (x)	Output (y)
−1	
0	
1	
2	
3	

3. $y = -x + 10$

Input (x)	Output (y)
−1	
0	
1	
2	
3	

4. $y = 3x - 5$

Input (x)	Output (y)
−1	
0	
1	
2	
3	

5. | Test Prep | Which number is the input value for $y = 1.5x - 4$, if the output value is 2?

   Ⓐ −1   Ⓑ 4   Ⓒ 1   Ⓓ $1\frac{1}{3}$

Graph each linear equation. Does the equation describe a function?

6. $y = -x + 8$ **7.** $y = 2x - 1$ **8.** $y = 3$ **9.** $x = 3$

10. Consumer Some airlines offer in-flight phones. The total cost to use the in-flight phone on one airline is $8 + $2 per min.

   a. Find a rule and make a table of values for the cost of 6 different call lengths.

   b. Is this relationship a function?

   c. Is the total cost dependent on the number of minutes used?

11. Science The distance the fastest marine animal, a killer whale, can travel is a function of the time traveled. The killer whale travels approximately 34.5 mi/hr.

   a. Write an equation to show the relationship between distance and time.

   b. Use your equation to find how far the whale can travel in 2 hr, 6 hr, and 10 hr.

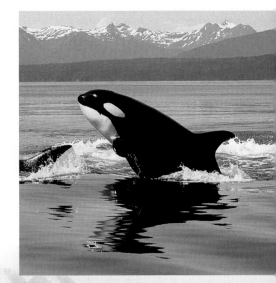

Does each table of values represent a function? Explain your answer.

12.

Input (x)	Output (y)
−1	1
0	0
1	1
2	1
3	1

13.

Input (x)	Output (y)
−2	8
−1	4
0	0
−1	−4
−2	−8

14.

Input (x)	Output (y)
0	0
100	10
100	−10
400	20
400	−20

15. Jenny is placing an ad in the newspaper classifieds to sell her snowboard. The cost of the ad is $18 plus $6.50 for each line.

a. Write an equation that relates the cost (c) of an ad in the classifieds to the number of lines (n) in the ad.

b. Make a graph relating these values.

c. Is the cost of the ad a function of the number of lines it has?

Problem Solving and Reasoning

16. Critical Thinking Isaac wondered if airlines base ticket prices on the distance flown. He found the approximate mileage between some cities and round-trip fares.

a. Is ticket price a function of distance? Explain.

b. What other things might affect the cost of a ticket?

Cities	Distance (mi)	Price ($)
Chicago-Baltimore	675	298
Denver-Los Angeles	1050	445
Jacksonville-Charleston	675	189
Knoxville-Buffalo	675	442
Milwaukee-Boston	1050	895
Tampa-Pittsburgh	1050	189

17. Journal Give an example of a function in your everyday life. Explain why it is a function and define the dependent and independent variables.

Mixed Review

18. Start with 1000. What is the result of a 27% decrease followed by a 30% increase? *[Lesson 6-6]*

Find the perimeter and area of each polygon. *[Lesson 9-1]*

19. An equilateral triangle with sides 4 in. long

20. A 2 m by 6 m rectangle

21. A parallelogram with base 23 cm and height 10 cm

10-3 Quadratic Functions

You'll Learn ...

■ to represent quadratic functions as graphs, tables, and equations

... How It's Used

Projectile motion, the motion in a launched fireworks display, can be modeled using quadratic equations.

Vocabulary

nonlinear function

quadratic function

parabola

▶ **Lesson Link**   You have studied linear functions. In this lesson, you will extend many of the ideas that you learned about linear functions to another type of function. ◄

Explore | Quadratic Functions

Materials: Graphing calculator

Ups and Downs

1. Graph $y = x^2$ using the standard graphing calculator screen. Is this graph a function? Explain.

2. Where is the value of y increasing? Where is it decreasing?

3. Trace along the graph (or evaluate) to find y when x is 4. Then trace along the graph to find y when x is -4.

4. Trace along the graph to find a negative value for y. How does the function equation help to explain your findings?

5. Change the function to $y = x^2 - 4$ and graph. Does this change your answer to Question 4? Explain.

Learn | Quadratic Functions

You have already learned about linear functions; in this lesson you will look at a **nonlinear function** called a **quadratic function** . A quadratic function is a function in which the highest power of x is 2. The following are examples of quadratic functions.

$$y = x^2 \qquad y = -x^2 \qquad y = 2x^2 \qquad y = 4x^2 - 6 \qquad y = x^2 + 2x + 1$$

The graph of a linear function is a straight line; this is because equal changes in x result in equal changes in the value of y. Recall that the change in y divided by the change in x is the slope.

The graph of a quadratic function is a ∪ or upside-down ∪-shaped curve, called a **parabola** .

For quadratic functions, equal changes in x do not result in equal changes in the value of y.

Look at the graph of the quadratic function representing the height of a ball thrown into the air. As x increases by 1, y changes by different amounts.

Height (ft)

Time (sec)

Examples

1 Make a table and graph for $y = 2x^2 + 4$. Use both positive and negative values for x. What happens to the y value as the x value increases?

x	y
−2	12
−1	6
0	4
1	6
2	12

$y = 2x^2 + 4$

As the values of x increase, the values of y decrease until $x = 0$; then they begin to increase again.

2 Graph each function. How are the graphs alike? How are they different?

a. $y = x^2$ and $y = -x^2$ **b.** $y = x^2$ and $y = x^2 + 3$

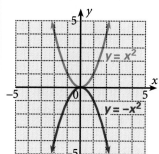

$y = x^2$

$y = -x^2$

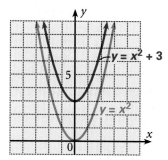

$y = x^2 + 3$

$y = x^2$

a. Both graphs are parabolas. $(0, 0)$ is part of both graphs. They are both symmetric about the y-axis.

The graph of x^2 opens upward, whereas the graph of $-x^2$ opens downward.

b. Both graphs are parabolas, open upward, and are symmetric about the y-axis.

The y-intercept of the graph of x^2 is $y = 0$, whereas the y-intercept of the graph of $x^2 + 3$ is $y = 3$.

Try It

a. Make a table and graph for $y = 2x^2 - 4$.

b. Graph $y = x^2$ and $y = 2x^2$. How are the graphs alike? How are they different?

Sometimes when we are working real-world problems, some values do not make sense in the problem. The part of a graph that solves a problem may not look like a whole parabola.

Example 3

A pilot drops supplies to scientists working at an Antarctic Substation. Ignoring air resistance, if the drop is made from 800 ft, the function $h = -16t^2 + 800$, where t is time in sec and h is height in ft, will model the situation. Make a table and a graph using $t = 0$ to 8 sec. Could you use negative values for t or h? Why was the graph not a complete parabola?

Time (sec)	Height (ft)
0	800
1	784
2	736
3	656
4	544
5	400
6	224
7	16
8	−224
9	−496

You could use negative values for t and h to see the entire graph, but it would not make sense in the problem to use negative values for time or height. Because the negative values were not used, the graph was not a parabola.

Try It

A pilot drops food to a village from a height of 500 ft. Ignoring air resistance, the function $h = -16t^2 + 500$, where t is time in sec and h is height in ft, will model the situation. Make a table and a graph using $t = 0$ to 6 sec.

Check | Your Understanding

1. How does a quadratic function differ from a linear function?

2. How does multiplying x^2 by -1 affect the graph of a quadratic function?

3. Compare the graphs of $y = x^2 - 2$ and $y = x - 2$. How are they alike? How are they different?

4. When can you ignore negative values of x? Why?

Practice and Apply

Getting Started Which are graphs of linear functions? Which are graphs of quadratic functions? Which are neither?

1.

2.

3.
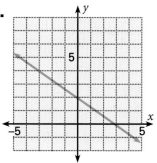

Graph each set of functions and describe the similarities and differences within the set of graphs.

4. $y = x^2$, $y = x^2 + 3$, and $y = x^2 - 3$

5. $y = x^2$, $y = 2x^2$, $y = 4x^2$, and $y = 8x^2$

6. $y = x^2$ and $y = -x^2$

7. $y = 2x^2$ and $y = -2x^2$

Match each graph with the function that describes it.

8.

9.

10.

11.

12.

13.
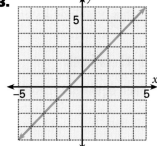

ⓐ $y = x^2 + 1$ ⓑ $y = x + 1$ ⓒ $y = x^2 - 3$

ⓓ $y = -x^2 + 2$ ⓔ $y = x + 3$ ⓕ $y = -x^2$

14. Science A toy rocket was launched into the air. The function $h = 50t - 5t^2$ models this situation, where h = height in m and t = time in sec.

a. When is the rocket 105 m in the air? Explain.

b. What happens at 10 sec?

15. [**Test Prep**] The area of a square can be modeled by a quadratic function. Which is the function rule for the area of a square?

Ⓐ $y = 4x$ Ⓑ $y = x \cdot x \cdot x \cdot x$

Ⓒ $y = x^2$ Ⓓ $y = 4x^2$

16. Geometry The formula $d = \frac{n^2 - 3n}{2}$ gives the number of diagonals (d) for a polygon with n sides.

a. How many diagonals does a square have?

b. How many diagonals does a hexagon have?

c. How many diagonals does an octagon have?

Problem Solving and Reasoning

17. Communicate Ossie dropped a pebble into a canyon. He heard it hit the ground 5 sec later. The function $h = -16t^2$ will model this situation. Time (t) is in sec, height (h) is in ft. Graph the function. If the pebble hits the ground in 5 sec, how deep is the canyon? Why is the value negative?

18. Critical Thinking Answer each question about the functions.

i. $y = 4x^2$ **ii.** $y = -4x^2$

iii. $y = x^2 + 2$ **iv.** $y = 2 - x^2$

a. Which graph(s) will open upward? How do you know?

b. Which graphs pass through the point $(0, 0)$? How do you know?

c. Which graphs are symmetric about the y-axis?

19. |Journal| How can you tell the shape of a parabola from its function rule?

Mixed Review

Solve each equation. *[Lesson 3-2]*

20. $x + 5 = 12$ **21.** $y - 10 = 17$ **22.** $\frac{1}{3}p = 4$

23. Find the perimeter of a triangle with side lengths of 9 cm, 8 cm, and 5 cm after it is dilated by a scale factor of 3. *[Lesson 9-2]*

Other Functions

▶ **Lesson Link** In the last lesson, you looked at one type of nonlinear function, a quadratic function. In this lesson, you will look at other types of nonlinear functions. ◀

You'll Learn ...

■ to graph and evaluate other types of functions

... How It's Used

The rate that carbon 14 decays is an exponential function that helps paleontologists determine the age of a fossil.

Explore | **Other Functions**

Which Is Which?

Which graph do you think is appropriate for each situation? Explain your reasoning.

a.   b.   c.

d.   e.

Vocabulary

exponential function

step function

1. The temperature of a cup of cocoa that cools quickly at first, then more and more slowly as it reaches room temperature.

2. The size of a bacteria colony doubles every hour.

3. The length of the side of a square increases as the enclosed area increases linearly.

4. The output value is the input value rounded to the nearest integer.

5. The distance of a train from the station as it approaches the station and then passes the station.

Learn | Other Functions

In all linear and quadratic functions, a variable was raised to an exponent.

In many nonlinear functions, the exponent will be a variable. These nonlinear functions, such as $y = 2^x$, are called **exponential functions**.

Examples

1 Graph the function $y = 0.5^x$ for $x \geq 0$. What is the value of y when x is 2? What is x when y is 0.125?

You can use a graphing utility.

Trace to 2 on the x-axis and find the corresponding value of y, $y = 0.25$. Then trace until you find $y = 0.125$. The corresponding value of x is 3.

2 A colony of bacteria is being grown in a laboratory. The lab technicians begin with a single bacterium. Every hour, the number of bacteria doubles. How long will it take the colony to number 1000?

You can find the answer from a table or a graph.

Hours (x)	0	1	2	3	4	5	6	7	8	9	10
Number (y)	1	2	4	8	16	32	64	128	256	512	1024

The function $y = 2^x$ can be used to model this situation. Using a graphing utility, trace to find x when y is approximately 1000.

The colony will number 1000 in approximately 10 hr.

Try It

a. Graph the function $y = 0.9^x$. What is the approximate value of y when x is 4? What is the value of x when y is approximately 0.8?

b. Suppose the number of bacteria triples every hour. The function $y = 3^x$ can be used to model this situation. How long will it take the colony to number 5000?

Functions can also be made up of pieces or steps. In a **step function**, different rules may be applied to different input values. The graph of a step function is not connected.

Example 3

Wind speeds are usually given to the nearest 10 mi/hr. Graph the function that rounds a number to the nearest 10.

Numbers ending in 5 or more round up. Make a table.

x	3	5	8	14	15	18	20	24	25	34
y	0	10	10	10	20	20	20	20	30	30

The value of y is 10 for any value of $x \geq 5$ but less than 15, so this part of the graph is a flat segment.

Because 14.99 rounds to 10, whereas 15 rounds to 20, we use an open circle at (15, 10) to show that the point is not included.

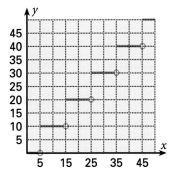

Try It

Graph the function that rounds a number to the nearest 100.

Check | Your Understanding

1. Explain the difference between the functions $y = x^2$ and $y = 2^x$.

2. How are the graphs of $y = 2^x$ and $y = 0.5^x$ alike? How are they different?

3. How can you tell from the equation that a function is exponential?

Practice and Apply

Getting Started Match each function to its graph.

1. $y = 2x$ **2.** $y = x^2$ **3.** $y = 2^x$ **4.** $y = $ round down to the whole number

Ⓐ

Ⓑ

Ⓒ

Ⓓ

Graph each function.

5. $y = 1.5^x$ **6.** $y = 1.5x$ **7.** $y = 4x$ **8.** $y = 4^x$

9. Suppose the population of butterflies on an island doubles in size each year. If there are 1,000 butterflies now, in how many years will there be 1,000,000 butterflies? Show how this is modeled by $y = 1,000 \cdot 2^x$.

10. John bought a new bank. The first day, he put two pennies in it. Each day he doubled the number of pennies he put in. The equation $y = 2^x$ models this situation.

a. Graph the equation.

b. On what day did John add $0.64?

c. What was the first day John added more than $2.00 to the bank?

11. Consumer Ready Rent-All rental charges for a VCR are as follows.

Rental Time	Rental Fee
1 day or portion thereof	$10.00
Over 1 day, up to 3 days	$20.00
Over 3 days up to 5 days	$35.00

a. Graph the function.

b. What kind of function is this?

Identify each function as linear, quadratic, exponential, or step.

12. $y = 0.6^x$ **13.** $y = 0.6x^2$ **14.** $y =$ round to nearest ten   **15.** $y = 6x$

16. **Test Prep**   The equation $y = x^2 - 5$ describes which type of function?

   Ⓐ Linear   Ⓑ Quadratic   Ⓒ Exponential   Ⓓ Step

17. Tabitha's mom started a savings account to help pay for her college education. She deposited $1000 and is receiving 7% interest compounded annually on her money. The function $A = 1000(1.07)^t$ will show the balance (A) after t years.

   a. How much money is in the account after 5 years?

   b. Approximately how many years will it take to have a balance of $2000?

18. **Chance** What are the chances that a 90% free-throw shooter will make the next 10 free throws in a row? Graph 0.9^x and find y when x is 10.

Problem Solving and Reasoning

19. **Choose a Strategy** As the value of x increases, what happens to each value?

   a. $2x$ **b.** x^2 **c.** 2^x **d.** 0.2^x

20. **Journal** Give an example of a step function you might see in your everyday life. Why is it a step function?

Communicate Without graphing, describe each graph.

21. $y = 5^x$ **22.** $y = \left(\dfrac{1}{2}\right)^x$

> **Problem Solving**
>
> ### STRATEGIES
>
> • Look for a Pattern
> • Make an Organized List
> • Make a Table
> • Guess and Check
> • Work Backward
> • Use Logical Reasoning
> • Draw a Diagram
> • Solve a Simpler Problem

Mixed Review

Write an expression for each situation. *[Lesson 3-3]*

23. Twice a number, subtracted from 10   **24.** Three times a number, plus 3

Find the circumference and area of a circle with each given radius. *[Lesson 9-3]*

25. $r = 6$ m   **26.** $r = 18$ mm   **27.** $r = 2.9$ m   **28.** $r = 87$ cm

Project Progress

Sketch and label a graph for the situation you chose. Compare your sketch to the graphs of the function models you have seen. Rule out any that do not work.

> **Problem Solving**
>
> Understand
> Plan
> Solve
> Look Back

Using a Graphing Calculator • Graphing Functions

Problem: The distance from Kansas City, Missouri, to Denver, Colorado, is 600 mi. How long will it take to make the trip at different rates of speed?

1 Remember that $t = \frac{d}{r}$. Time depends on the rate of speed, so use X as the rate of speed. Use the viewing window shown and enter 600/X as Y1.

2 Press GRAPH. Then press TRACE and the left and right arrow keys to find solutions.

3 If your calculator can make a table, you can use it to display solutions.

Solution: At 20 mi/hr, it would take 30 hr; at 55 mi/hr, it would take 10.9 hr.

Why does an x-value of 0 produce an error?

TRY IT

A $10,000 prize will be split evenly among the winners. How much will each person receive if there are different numbers of prizewinners? Graph the solutions.

ON YOUR OWN

▶ Change the range for the original problem to include negative numbers for x and y. Describe the shape of the graph. Trace to the left of 0. What are some other solutions? Do these make sense in the problem situation?

Section 10A Connect

In this Connect, you will combine your knowledge of the different types of functions.

The World in Motion

Materials: Graphing utility

Kirt estimated that as a pelican swooped down toward the water, it was about 20 ft high, then 12, then 8, then 5, then 3. Then it stayed very close to the water as it flew. He used his graphing utility and found several possible function models for its height over time based upon the initial height.

He started with time at 0 sec.

a. $y = -4x + 20$ **b.** $y = x^2 - 8x + 20$ **c.** $y = 20(0.6)^x$

1. Graph each function.

2. Which are good models for the height of the pelican? Which are not? Which do you feel is the best model? Why?

3. Do you think a step function would be a good model? Why or why not?

4. Suppose the pelican flew down to the water and immediately back up again. How would your answer to Question 2 change?

For the function machine shown, find each missing value.

1. Input −1 output ___
2. Input ___ output −8
3. Input 4 output ___
4. Input ___ output −6
5. Input 3 output ___
6. Input ___ output 100

Input	Multiply by 2 and subtract 8	Output

Test Prep

Use inverse operations to find the input value of a function.

7. Which is the input value for $y = 5x$ if the output value is −30?
   Ⓐ −150   Ⓑ 6   Ⓒ −6   Ⓓ 5

Sketch an example of a graph for each type of function.

8. Linear   9. Quadratic   10. Exponential   11. Step

12. If y is a function of x, name the dependent variable and the independent variable.

Is y a function of x? Explain.

13.

x	−1	0	1	2	3
y	1	0	1	2	3

14.

x	−2	−1	0	−1	−2
y	8	4	0	−4	−8

15. Graph $y = x$, $y = x^2$, and $y = 4^x$. Describe the similarities and differences.

16. **Geology** Antarctic glaciers flow approximately 0.0005 km/hr. Write an equation to show the relationship between distance and time. Find how far a glacier travels in a week.

17. **Science** The height of a penny dropped into a well is modeled by the function $h = -16t^2$, where time (t) is in sec and height (h) is in ft.
    a. Make a table of values and graph the function, using $t = 1$ to 8 sec.
    b. If the penny hits bottom in 4 sec, how deep is the well? Why is the value of h negative?

18. A bank offers a 6% annual-interest savings account. The function $A = 1000(1.06)^t$ gives the balance (A) after t years. If $1000 is invested, how much money is in the account after 5 years? Approximately how many years will it take to have a balance of $2000?

WHICH CAME FIRST?

When we think of animals living today that are direct descendants of dinosaurs, we probably think of alligators, lizards, komodo dragons, or rhinoceroses. But we probably don't think of birds.

The earliest bird fossil found was that of Archaeopteryx, a bird that lived about 140 million years ago. It had wings with both feathers and claws, teeth, and a dinosaur-like tail. It could barely fly, and may even have climbed trees.

Today's birds are also varied in shape and form. From the ostrich, to the penguin, to the burrowing owl, to the peacock, nature has given birds colors and abilities of which we can only dream.

1 What do you think distinguishes birds from other classes of vertebrates?

2 How much longer have birds been on Earth than humans?

3 Samuel Butler said that a chicken is just an egg's way of making more eggs. Do you agree?

531

10-5 Polynomials

You'll Learn ...

■ to evaluate polynomials

... How It's Used

Computer programmers use polynomials to program 3-D graphics for video games.

Vocabulary

polynomial

term

monomial

binomial

trinomial

degree

▶ **Lesson Link** You have learned about linear functions and several nonlinear functions. Now you will learn about another type of nonlinear function. ◀

Explore Polynomials

Let's Box!

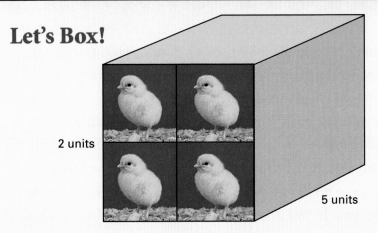

2 units

5 units

2 units

1. Find the area of each square end of the box pictured above.

2. Find the area of the rectangular faces.

3. Find the surface area of the box by adding the areas of all the faces.

4. If the square ends had side length x units, write an expression that would give the surface area of the box.

5. How does the surface area change as the length of the side of the square changes? Explain your answer.

▶ **Language Link**

Poly- means many or too many.

Learn Polynomials

A **polynomial** is an algebraic expression that is the sum of one or more parts, called **terms** . Each term is a signed number, a variable, or a number multiplied by a variable or variables. The variables can have whole-number exponents.

Polynomial: $-2x^3 - 4x^2 + 3x + 1$

Terms: $-2x^3$ $-4x^2$ $3x$ 1

Some polynomials have special names.

monomial: x, $2x^3$, -2 **Monomials** have one term.

binomial: $x + 1$, $2x^3 - 7x$ **Binomials** have two terms.

trinomial: $x + 3x^2 - 4x^3$, $x^2 - 4x + 3$ **Trinomials** have three terms.

The **degree** of a polynomial with one variable is the value of the largest exponent of the variable that appears in any term.

$2x^3, 2x^3 - 7$, and $-4x^3 + 3x^2 + x$ have degree 3

$x^2 - 4x + 3$ has degree 2

x and $x + 4$ each have degree 1

-2 has degree 0

Polynomials are usually written with the term that has the highest degree first, the next highest second, and so on. This is called writing a polynomial in descending order.

$x^4 + 3x - 2x^6 + 5$ written in descending order is $-2x^6 + x^4 + 3x + 5$.

Examples

1 Write the polynomial $x^5 + 2x - 6x^3 + 2x^2$ in descending order. What is the degree of the polynomial?

$x^5 - 6x^3 + 2x^2 + 2x$ The term with the highest degree is x^5, then $-6x^3$, then $2x^2$, and finally $2x$.

Because the largest exponent is 5, the degree of the polynomial is 5.

2 The height of a sagging highwire x m from the end can be modeled by the polynomial $15 + 0.00025x^3 - 0.375x - 0.005x^2 + 0.000004x^4$. Write this polynomial in descending order. What is the degree of the polynomial?

$0.000004x^4 + 0.00025x^3 - 0.005x^2 - 0.375x + 15$ The exponents are in order.

Since the largest exponent is 4, the degree of the polynomial is 4.

Try It

Write the trinomial $x + 2 - 4x^2$ in descending order. What is the degree of the polynomial?

Polynomials can be evaluated by replacing the variables with the given numbers and using the order of operations to simplify the expression.

Examples

3 Evaluate $x^3 + x^2 - x + 3$ for $x = -4$.

$(-4)^3 + (-4)^2 - (-4) + 3$ Substitute -4 for x in the polynomial.

$= -64 + 16 + 4 + 3$ Simplify powers, then add or subtract.

$= -41$

4 The volume of a cube can be represented by the function $V = s^3$, where V = volume and s = the length of a side. Find the volume of a cube with each given side length.

a. 3 in.   **b.** 1.5 in.   **c.** 2 cm

Substitute the given side length into the equation $V = s^3$.

a. $V = (3)^3 = 27$. The volume of the cube is 27 in³.

b. $V = (1.5)^3 = 3.375$. The volume of the cube is 3.375 in³.

c. $V = (2)^3 = 8$. The volume of the cube is 8 cm³.

Try It

a. Evaluate $x^3 - x^2 + x + 5$ for $x = 0$ and $x = -3$.

b. The volume of a hemispheric birdbath is a function of the length of its radius and can be represented by the function $V = \frac{2}{3}\pi r^3$, where V = volume and r = the length of the radius. Find the volume of a birdbath with each given radius length. Use $\pi = 3.14$.

i. 1 ft   **ii.** 4 ft   **iii.** 2.25 m

Check | Your Understanding

1. What do the prefixes *mono-*, *bi-*, *tri-*, and *poly-* mean?

2. How do you determine the degree of a polynomial?

3. Are the polynomials $3x^2 - 2 + x - x^3$ and $x - 2 - x^3 + 3x^2$ the same? How do you know?

Your graphing utility can help you evaluate polynomials.

Study TIP

Understanding common prefixes and suffixes can help you learn the meanings of unfamiliar words.

Practice and Apply

1. **Getting Started** State the number of terms in each polynomial expression.

   a. $-2x^2 + 3x + 1$ **b.** $4x$ **c.** $-2x^3 + 6$

Identify each expression as a monomial, binomial, or trinomial.

2. $0.75y$ **3.** $a + 3 - 4a^2$ **4.** $2b^5$ **5.** $x + 12$ **6.** $3x^3 + 2x^2 + 9$

Write each polynomial expression in descending order, then find the degree of each polynomial.

7. $4 + 2x$ **8.** $2x + 4x^2 - 3$ **9.** $x^2 - x^3 - x^4$ **10.** $2x + 4x^3 + 1$

Evaluate each polynomial for $x = -3$.

11. $3x + 6$ **12.** $x^2 + 3x - 3$ **13.** $3x^2 - 4x + 12$ **14.** $x^3 - 3$

Evaluate each polynomial for $g = 2$ and for $g = 10$.

15. $g - g^2 + g^3$ **16.** $g^2 - 9g$ **17.** $5 - g$ **18.** $25g^2 - 4$

19. **Geometry** The surface area of a cylinder with a height of 12 in. is given by $2\pi r^2 + 24\pi r$. Find the surface area of a cylinder with a radius, r, of 2 in.

20. **Language Arts** The words *monomial, binomial, trinomial,* and *polynomial* use the prefixes *mono-, bi-, tri-,* and *poly-*. Find some other words that use these prefixes and give their meanings.

21. **Test Prep** Which of the following is the degree of the polynomial $5 + 3x^4 - 2x^5 + x^8$?

   Ⓐ 18   Ⓑ 8   Ⓒ 5   Ⓓ 4

22. **Patterns** Evaluate each polynomial in the table for $x = 0, 1, 2,$ and 3. Describe the pattern that is formed.

	$x = 0$	$x = 1$	$x = 2$	$x = 3$
$x + 1$				
$x^2 + 2x + 1$				
$x^3 + 3x^2 + 3x + 1$				
$x^4 + 4x^3 + 6x^2 + 4x + 1$				

23. **Geometry** At Epcot Center in Orlando, Florida, the Spaceship Earth is built in the shape of a sphere with a diameter of approximately 165 ft. Use $\pi = 3.14$ to answer each question.

   a. Use the formula $S = 4\pi r^2$, where S = surface area and r = radius, to find the approximate surface area.

   b. Using the formula $V = \frac{4}{3}\pi r^3$, where V = volume and r = radius, find the approximate volume.

24. **Science** Niels Bohr's model of the atom shows that electrons rotate around the nucleus in a series of orbits called *shells*. $2x^2$ represents the number of electrons in each shell, where $x = 1$ in the first shell, $x = 2$ in the second shell, and so on. How many electrons could be orbiting the nucleus in the fourth shell of an atom?

Problem Solving and Reasoning

25. **Critical Thinking** The Birdseed Box uses boxes that are the same length, width, and height. Write an expression that will give the total volume of any number of boxes.

26. **Journal** Give some examples of expressions that are polynomials. Give some examples of expressions that are not polynomials and explain why they are not.

27. **Math Reasoning** The differences between terms of this sequence form a pattern.

   sequence: 0   1   3   6   10   15

   differences: 1   2   3   4   5

   Evaluate $\frac{2n^3 + 3n^2 + n}{6}$ for $n = 0$, 1, 2, 3, and 4 to create a sequence. Describe the pattern in the differences.

Mixed Review

Solve each equation. *[Lesson 3-4]*

28. $x + 20 = 55$ **29.** $88 = x - 17$ **30.** $x + 4\frac{1}{2} = 5\frac{1}{2}$ **31.** $x - 40 = 140$

Find how much fabric is needed to cover each object. *[Lesson 9-4]*

32. The cover of a photo album that is 10 in. by 13 in. by 3 in.

33. A gift box that is 28 cm by 28 cm by 16 cm and its lid that is 28 cm by 28 cm by 2 cm

Adding Polynomials

▶ Lesson Link   In the last lesson, you were introduced to polynomials. In this lesson, you will learn to add polynomials. ◀

Explore   Adding Polynomials

Family Reunion

Materials: Algebra tiles

1. What expression is modeled by the tiles?

2. What expression is modeled by the tiles?

3. Model the two sets of tiles above with your tiles. Combine the two sets. Remove any zero pairs. What expression remains?

4. Model $x^2 + 4x - 3$ with algebra tiles. Model $4x - 2x^2 + 1$ with more algebra tiles. Combine the two sets and remove any zero pairs. What expression remains?

5. When you combine algebra tiles, do you combine x^2 tiles with x tiles? x tiles with unit tiles? How can you apply this to adding expressions?

You'll Learn ...

■ to add polynomials

... How It's Used

Many irregularly-shaped pieces were used to renovate the Statue of Liberty.

Sometimes you will have to add polynomials in order to find the area of irregular figures.

Vocabulary

like terms

simplified

Learn   Adding Polynomials

Recall from the last lesson that polynomials contain terms. **Like terms** are terms that have the same variable raised to the same exponent.

For the polynomial $3x^2 + 4x^3 - 6x + 2 - 8x^3 - 2x^2$, $3x^2$ and $-2x^2$ are like terms because both contain the variable x raised to the second power; $4x^3$ and $-8x^3$ are like terms because both contain the variable x raised to the third power. Like terms can be combined using the distributive property.

$$3x^2 + -2x^2 = (3 + -2)x^2 = 1x^2 \qquad 4x^3 + -8x^3 = (4 + -8)x^3 = -4x^3$$

A polynomial is **simplified** when it contains no like terms.

Examples

1 Simplify each expression.

a. $1 + 4x + 3x^2 - 5x$ **b.** $3w^2 + (-6w) + 4w^2 - 2w$

a. $3x^2 + 4x - 5x + 1$ List the terms in descending order.

   $= 3x^2 + (4 - 5)x + 1$ Group like terms.

   $= 3x^2 + -1x + 1$ Combine like terms.

   $= 3x^2 - x + 1$ $-1x = -x$.

b. $3w^2 + 4w^2 + (-6w) - 2w$ List the terms in descending order.

   $= (3 + 4)w^2 + (-6 - 2)w$ Group like terms.

   $= 7w^2 + (-8)w$ Combine like terms.

   $= 7w^2 - 8w$

2 Add the polynomials $2x^2 - 4x - 8$, $-x^2 + 2$, and $x - 3$.

$(2x^2 - 4x - 8) + (-x^2 + 2) + (x - 3)$

$= 2x^2 - 4x - 8 + -x^2 + 2 + x - 3$ Write without parentheses.

$= (2x^2 - x^2) + (-4x + x) + (-8 + 2 - 3)$ Group like terms.

$= x^2 + (-3x) + (-9)$ Combine like terms to simplify.

$= x^2 - 3x - 9$

Polynomials can also be added vertically in columns. If there is a term missing in one of the polynomials, it can be replaced by 0 as a placeholder.

x^2	x	constant	
$2x^2$	$-4x$	-8	Arrange terms in descending order.
$-1x^2$	$+0x$	$+2$	Group like terms by aligning them vertically.
$+0x^2$	$+x$	-3	
$1x^2$	$+(-3x)$	$+(-9)$	$= x^2 - 3x - 9$ Combine like terms and simplify.

Try It

Simplify each expression.

a. $5x^2 + 12x + 2x^2 - 5x + 1$

b. $-6n^2 - 3n + 2n + (-5)n^2 - 9$

c. Add $5x^2 + 2x - 4$, $5x - 2x^2$, and $x - 6$.

Example 3

Find an expression for the floor area of the chicken coop. If x is 20 ft, what is the area?

To find the floor area, add the polynomials.

$(x^2 + 7x + 6) + (x^2 - 4)$

$(x^2 + x^2) + 7x + (6 - 4)$ Group like terms.

$2x^2 + 7x + 2$ Combine like terms.

or

$(x^2 + 7x + 6)$ Arrange terms in descending order.

$+ (x^2 + 0x - 4)$ Group like terms by aligning them vertically.

$2x^2 + 7x + 2$ Combine like terms.

When x is 20:

$2(20)^2 + 7(20) + 2$

$= 2(400) + 140 + 2$

$= 942$

The chicken coop has an area of 942 ft^2.

Try It

Find an expression for the area of the total region. What is the area when $x = 10$?

$x^2 - 4x - 5$ $x^2 + 5x - 6$

Check | Your Understanding

1. Give an example of like terms and of terms that are not alike. Explain.

2. Can the sum of two binomials be a trinomial? Explain.

3. When you write a polynomial in descending order, what in the expression is descending?

PRACTICE 10-6

Practice and Apply

1. **Getting Started** Fill in the blanks.

   To simplify the polynomial $4p + 3p^2 - p + 5p^2$, write the polynomial in _____ order. Then combine _____ by using the _____ property.

Simplify each, if possible. If the expression cannot be simplified, write "already simplified." Write answers in descending order.

2. $2x^2 - 4x + 8x^3 + x$ 3. $4y^2 + 2y$ 4. $4p - 3$

5. $2m^2 - 8m + 5m + 5m^2$ 6. $5b^2 - 4b + 2b^3 + (-3)b$ 7. $5a - 4a + 3a + 6$

Find each polynomial sum. Write the answers in simplest form.

8. $(2m - 6m^2) + (-2m^2 - 2m + 1)$ 9. $(2x) + (-2x^2 - 2x + 1)$

10. $(-y^3 + 3y) + (4y^2 + 3y - 1)$

11. $\begin{array}{r} 5x^2 + 6x + 2 \\ + \ 8x^2 - 2x - 9 \\ \hline \end{array}$ 12. $\begin{array}{r} 5z^2 + 3z - 1 \\ + \quad\ -3z + 1 \\ \hline \end{array}$ 13. $\begin{array}{r} x^2 + 3x - 6 \\ + \ 3x^2 - 4x + 15 \\ \hline \end{array}$

14. **Measurement** The volume of a tennis ball can is approximately 620 cm³. A tennis ball has a diameter of approximately 6.68 cm.

    a. Use the formula for the volume of a sphere, $V = \frac{4}{3}\pi r^3$, to find the approximate volume of a tennis ball. Use $\pi = 3.14$.

    b. How many tennis balls do you think will fit into one can? Explain your reasoning.

15. **Test Prep** Which of the following pairs of terms are like terms?

    Ⓐ x^2 and $3x^2$ Ⓑ x^3 and $3x$ Ⓒ $7x$ and 7 Ⓓ x^2 and y^2

16. **Consumer** Carpet is sold for $9.95 per square yd. To find the area of her family room, Marjorie used the formula $A = x^2 + 2x$, where A = area in yd² and x = length of the room = 3 yd. How much did it cost Marjorie to carpet her family room?

17. A zoo built an aviary for its exotic birds. The total volume includes the flight space, x^3, an exercise room, $5x^2$, a private loft, $4x^2$, and a nesting box, $7x$. Write the polynomial that represents the total volume of the aviary, then simplify it. Evaluate the polynomial for $x = 6$ ft.

18. If you know the cube of a counting number x, x^3, you can find the cube of the next counting number by adding $3x^2 + 3x + 1$. The cube of 5 is 125. Show how you can add polynomials and evaluate to find 6^3.

Geometry Find the total area of each figure.

19.
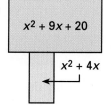

$x^2 + 9x + 20$

$x^2 + 4x$

20.

x^2

$12x^2 - 4x$

x^2

21.
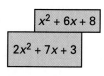

$x^2 + 6x + 8$

$2x^2 + 7x + 3$

22.

x^2

$16x^2$

Problem Solving and Reasoning

23. Critical Thinking Write an expression that contains four terms and simplifies to $2x$.

24. [Journal] Is simplifying an equation the same as solving it? Explain.

25. Communicate Jennifer simplified the expression $4x + 3x$ to $7x^2$. Was she correct? Explain your reasoning.

26. Choose a Strategy Find the missing term.

$(3x^2 - 6x) + (\underline{\hspace{1cm}} - 2x^2) = x^2 - 8x$

27. Critical Thinking When asked to simplify $x^2 + x^2$, four students got the following answers. Who is correct? What do you think each of the students did to get their answer?

a. Willard's answer is x^4.   **b.** Bryant's answer is $2x^4$.

c. Katie's answer is $2x^2$.   **d.** Matt's answer is x^2.

> **Problem Solving**
> ## STRATEGIES
> • Look for a Pattern
> • Make an Organized List
> • Make a Table
> • Guess and Check
> • Work Backward
> • Use Logical Reasoning
> • Draw a Diagram
> • Solve a Simpler Problem

Mixed Review

Solve each equation. *[Lesson 3-5]*

28. $14x = 84$ **29.** $27 = \frac{3}{4}x$ **30.** $\frac{x}{5} = -60$ **31.** $7.1x = 63.9$

Find each surface area. *[Lesson 9-5]*

32.

10 cm

6 cm

33.

9.5 cm

1.5 cm

10-7 Subtracting Polynomials

You'll Learn ...

■ to subtract polynomials

... How It's Used

A carpenter subtracts polynomials when calculating the amount of material needed to construct the walls if space is left for doors and windows.

▶ **Lesson Link** In the last lesson, you learned to add polynomials. In this lesson, you will learn to subtract polynomials. ◀

Explore Subtracting Polynomials

The Buddy System

Materials: Algebra tiles

1. What expression is modeled?

2. What would remain if you subtracted or removed 1 x^2 tile and 1 negative x tile?

3. What would remain if you added 1 negative x^2 tile and 1 positive x tile to the original expression? Remember to remove zero pairs.

4. Compare the results from Steps 2 and 3. Why did this happen?

5. What would remain if you added 1 negative x^2 tile, 3 positive x tiles, and 1 negative unit tile to the original expression? Explain.

Learn Subtracting Polynomials

Recall from previous work with algebra tiles that the following are additive inverses and make up zero pairs.

$$x^2 + (-x^2) = 0 \qquad -x + x = 0 \qquad 1 + -1 = 0$$

In Chapter 2, you learned that the opposite of a number is called its additive inverse. When you add a number to its additive inverse, you get zero. The additive inverse of 3 is -3; of x^3, $-x^3$; of $-5x^2$, $5x^2$. You also learned that subtraction of integers is the same as adding the opposite.

$a - b$ is the same as $a + (-b)$.

542 *Chapter 10 • Algebra: Functions and Relationships*

Examples

1 Find the additive inverse of the polynomial $x^2 + 4x - 8$.

$-(x^2 + 4x - 8)$ Take the opposite of the polynomial.

$= -(x^2 + 4x + -8)$ Change subtraction to adding the opposite.

$= -x^2 + -4x + 8$ Take the opposite of each term in the polynomial.

$= -x^2 - 4x + 8$

When you subtract polynomials, add the opposite or additive inverse.

2 Subtract $(6x^3 + 2x^2 - 5) - (x^3 - 3x^2 + 7)$.

$(6x^3 + 2x^2 - 5) + -(x^3 - 3x^2 + 7)$ Add the opposite of the second polynomial.

$= (6x^3 + 2x^2 + -5) + -(x^3 + -3x^2 + 7)$ Change subtracting to adding the opposite.

$= (6x^3 + 2x^2 + -5) + (-x^3 + 3x^2 + -7)$ Find the opposite of all terms in the parentheses.

$= (6 + -1)x^3 + (2 + 3)x^2 + (-5 + -7)$ Group like terms.

$= 5x^3 + 5x^2 + -12$ Combine like terms.

$= 5x^3 + 5x^2 - 12$

As with addition, subtraction can be done vertically.

$(6x^3 + 2x^2 - 5) + -(x^3 - 3x^2 + 7)$ Add the opposite of the second polynomial.

$= (6x^3 + 2x^2 + -5) + -(x^3 + -3x^2 + 7)$ Change subtracting to adding the opposite.

$= (6x^3 + 2x^2 + -5) + (-x^3 + 3x^2 + -7)$ Find the opposite of all terms in the parentheses.

$$
\begin{array}{r}
(6x^3 + 2x^2 + -5) \\
+\ (-x^3 + 3x^2 + -7) \\
\hline
5x^3 + 5x^2 + -12
\end{array}
$$
Group like terms by aligning them vertically.

Combine like terms.

$= 5x^3 + 5x^2 - 12$

Remember

You can use the distributive property of multiplication to remove parentheses when simplifying polynomials.
[Page 83]

MENTAL MATH

Many steps in subtracting polynomials can be done mentally.

Try It

a. Find the additive inverse of $-2x^3 + 1$.

b. Subtract $(4x^3 + 6x^2 - 2x) - (2x^3 - 8x + 5)$.

Examples

3 At For the Birds, the annual revenue from selling a macaw cage at a price (p) is given by $-4p^2 - 100p + 4,200$. The cost is $-1,300p + 60,000$. Profit is revenue minus cost. What is the profit function for selling the cages? What is the profit when cages are sold for $150? For $200?

$$\text{Revenue} \qquad - \qquad \text{Cost}$$

$$-4p^2 - 100p + 4,200 - (-1,300p + 60,000)$$

$= -4p^2 - 100p + 4,200 + 1,300p - 60,000$ Change subtracting to adding the opposite.

$= -4p^2 + (-100 + 1,300)p + (4,200 - 60,000)$ Group like terms.

$= -4p^2 + 1,200p - 55,800$ Combine like terms.

The profit function is $-4p^2 + 1,200p - 55,800$. Evaluate.

$$-4p^2 + 1,200p - 55,800 \qquad\qquad -4p^2 + 1,200p - 55,800$$

$$= -4(150)^2 + 1,200(150) - 55,800 \qquad = -4(200)^2 + 1,200(200) - 55,800$$

$$= -90,000 + 180,000 - 55,800 \qquad\qquad = -160,000 + 240,000 - 55,800$$

$$= 34,200 \qquad\qquad\qquad\qquad\qquad = 24,200$$

The annual profit is $34,200 when cages are priced at $150; $24,200 when they are priced at $200.

4 Find the unknown side length.

Add the known lengths of the sides.

$(x^2 + 4) + (2x^2 - 4x) + (3x + 1) + (2x - 3)$

$= 3x^2 + x + 2$

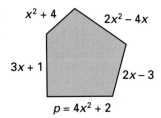

Subtract from the given perimeter.

$(4x^2 + 2) - (3x^2 + x + 2) = x^2 - x$

The length of the unknown side is $x^2 - x$.

Try It

a. The annual revenue from selling parakeets at a price p is given by $-70p^2 - 25p + 200$. The cost is $-1520p + 500$. What is the profit function for selling the parakeets? What is the profit when parakeets are sold for $10?

b. The perimeter is $7x^2 + 3x + 8$. Find the unknown side length.

WHAT DO YOU THINK?

How much higher does a clay disk propelled upwards with an initial velocity of 100 ft/sec go, over time, than one propelled at 70 ft/sec from a platform 25 ft high? Subtract $-16t^2 + 70t + 25$ from $-16t^2 + 100t$ to find out.

Ashley thinks ...

I'll write the polynomials vertically, like a regular subtraction problem.

$$\begin{array}{r} -16t^2 + 100t \\ -\ (-16t^2 + 70t + 25) \end{array} = \begin{array}{r} -16t^2 + 100t \\ +\ 16t^2 - 70t - 25 \end{array}$$

Now I can combine like terms. $\longrightarrow$ $30t - 25$

My answer is $30t - 25$. It is 5 ft higher after 1 sec, 35 ft after 2 sec, and so on.

Kele thinks ...

I'll do the subtraction horizontally.

$$(-16t^2 + 100t) - (-16t^2 + 70t + 25)$$

I'll add the opposite of the second polynomial.

$$-16t^2 + 100t + -(-16t^2 + 70t + 25)$$

$$-16t^2 + 100t + (16t^2 - 70t - 25)$$

I'll group like terms.

$$(-16 + 16)t^2 + (100 - 70)t + (-25)$$

I'll combine like terms. $0t^2\ \ +\ \ 30t\ \ -\ \ 25$

My answer is also $30t - 25.$

What do you think?

Is the disk with the greater initial velocity always higher?

Check | Your Understanding

1. How are addition and subtraction of polynomials related?

2. How do you find the additive inverse of a polynomial expression?

3. Add a polynomial expression and its inverse. Explain your result.

Practice and Apply

1. **Getting Started** Write the additive inverse of each monomial.

   a. $-x^3$ **b.** $4x^2$ **c.** $2x$ **d.** $-7x^5$ **e.** 27

Find the additive inverse of each polynomial.

2. $3x^3 - 5x^2 + (-x) + 2$ 3. $x^4 - 2$ 4. $4x^2 - 12x + 9$

5. $3x^3 - (-2x)$ 6. $-4x^3 + 7x^2 + 13x - 2$ 7. $-x^5 + 2x + 9x^3 - 3$

Subtract Write your answers in simplest form.

8. $(5x^2 + 6x + 2) - (8x^2 - 2x - 9)$ 9. $(2x) - (-2x^2 - 2x + 1)$

10. $(-y^3 + 3y) - (4y^2 + 3y - 1)$ 11. $(2m - 6m^2) - (-2m^2 - 2m + 1)$

12. $\begin{aligned}&(3m^2 + 3m - 5)\\ -\;&(3m^2 + 3m - 5)\end{aligned}$ 13. $\begin{aligned}&(4v^3 - 3v^2 + 1)\\ -\;&(2v^3 + 5v^2 - 6v + 2)\end{aligned}$

14. $\begin{aligned}&(5g^2 + 4g - 7)\\ -\;&(2g^2 + 3g - 5)\end{aligned}$ 15. $\begin{aligned}&(5a^3 - 4a^2 + 2a + 3)\\ -\;&(4a^3 + 2a^2 + 6)\end{aligned}$

Geometry Find an expression for the area not covered by the bird.

16.

$x^2 - 2x$

$A = 5x^2 + 9x - 20$

17.

$x^2 - 2x - 1$

$A = 12x^2 - 4x$

18.

$x^2 + 10$

$A = 4x^2 + 8x + 1$

19.

$2x^2 + 4x + 3$

$A = 14x^2 + 8x + 6$

20. **Test Prep** Which of the following polynomials is the additive inverse of the polynomial $2x^2 - 4x + 7$?

         Ⓐ $-2x^2 - 4x + 7$ Ⓑ $2x^2 + 4x + 7$

         Ⓒ $-2x^2 + 4x + -7$ Ⓓ $-2x^2 - 4x - 7$

Geometry Find the missing side length, based on the perimeter of each figure.

21.
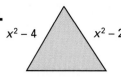
$x^2 + 2x$
$x^2 + 2x + 5$
$p = 3x^2 + 4x + 10$

22.
$x^2 - 4$ $x^2 - 2$
$3x + 2$
$p = 3x^2 - 10$

23.
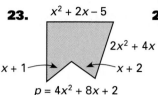
$x^2 + 2x - 5$
$2x^2 + 4x$
$x + 1$ $x + 2$
$p = 4x^2 + 8x + 2$

24.
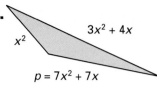
$3x^2 + 4x$
x^2
$p = 7x^2 + 7x$

25. Physics How much higher does a disc propelled upwards with an initial velocity of 40 m/sec go, over time, than one propelled at 30 m/sec from a platform 8 m high? Subtract $-5t^2 + 30t + 8$ from $-5t^2 + 40t$.

Problem Solving and Reasoning

26. Critical Thinking Find two monomials with a difference of $4x^3$.

27. Communicate Josie simplified the expression $4x - 3x$ and got an answer of 1. Was she correct? Explain your reasoning.

28. Critical Thinking What would you subtract from $8x^2$ to get $-18x^2$?

29. [Journal] What conclusion can you make about two polynomials with a difference of zero? Explain your answer.

30. Critical Thinking Find the missing term.

$(-2x^2 - 4x) - (\underline{} - 3x^2) = x^2 - 8x$

31. A *matrix* is a rectangular array of numbers. It can be used to add or subtract polynomials. The first two rows show the aligned coefficients of $x^3 - x^2 + 2x - 4$ and $2x^3 - 3x^2 + 5$. The third row shows the sum of each pair of corresponding coefficients. Use a matrix to subtract $x^5 - 3x^2 + 2$ from $3x^5 + 2x^4 - 2x + 3$.

$$\begin{array}{cccc} x^3 & x^2 & x^1 & x^0 \end{array}$$
$$\begin{bmatrix} 1 & -1 & 2 & -4 \\ 2 & -3 & 0 & 5 \\ 3 & -4 & 2 & 1 \end{bmatrix}$$

Mixed Review

32. A heron weighing 2 kg eats 340 g of food daily. What percent of its weight does it eat daily? *[Lesson 6-2]*

Determine the prime factorization of each. *[Lesson 7-1]*

33. 90   **34.** 256   **35.** 87   **36.** 101   **37.** 375

Find the volume of each. *[Lesson 9-6]*

38.

7.25 in.
7.25 in.
7.25 in.

39.

3.8 m
10.2 m   6 m

Multiplying Polynomials and Monomials

You'll Learn ...

■ to multiply polynomials and monomials

... How It's Used

Astrophysicists often multiply numbers in scientific notation.

▶ Lesson Link In the last two lessons, you added and subtracted polynomials. In this lesson, you will learn to multiply polynomials and monomials. ◀

Explore   Multiplying Polynomials and Monomials

It's Powerful!

Compound microscopes use two or more lenses to expand the size of an image. Understanding how to multiply powers will give you an idea of how much an image can be expanded when lenses are used together.

1. Multiply 2^3 by 2^4. What is the product?

2. Is the result a power of 2? Write the result as a power of 2.

3. How does the product appear to relate to the exponents in 2^3 and 2^4?

4. Test your conjecture on the product of 3^2 and 3^4.

5. Suppose you multiply 2^3 and 100^4. Would you be able to relate the product to the exponents in the same way? Explain.

Remember

Exponential form is a base with an exponent that tells how many times the base is used as a multiplier. **[Page 97]**

Learn   Multiplying Polynomials and Monomials

Recall that 5^2 is the same as $5 \cdot 5$, and 5^4 is the same as $5 \cdot 5 \cdot 5 \cdot 5$.

To multiply $5^2 \cdot 5^4$, think $(5 \cdot 5)(5 \cdot 5 \cdot 5 \cdot 5)$. This is 5^6.

When you multiply two powers with the same base, add their exponents.

MULTIPLYING POWERS WITH LIKE BASES

In words: When multiplying powers with like bases, add their exponents.

In symbols: $a^m \cdot a^n = a^{m+n}$ **Example:** $x^4 \cdot x^5 = x^{4+5} = x^9$

Example 1

a. Multiply $6^7 \times 6^8$.

$6^7 \times 6^8 = 6^{7+8} = 6^{15}$

b. Multiply 2×2^5. (Note that 2 is 2^1.)

$2^1 \times 2^5 = 2^{1+5} = 2^6$

The methods for multiplying numerical bases, such as 6 and 2 above, can help you multiply monomials.

Example 2

a. Multiply x by x^4.

x is x^1.

$x^1 \cdot x^4 = (x)(x \cdot x \cdot x \cdot x) = x^{1+4} = x^5$

b. Multiply $2x^2(3x^3)$.

$2x^2 \cdot 3x^3 = 2 \cdot 3(x \cdot x)(x \cdot x \cdot x) = 6x^{2+3} = 6x^5$

Try It

Multiply.

a. $5^2 \times 5^4$ **b.** $8^3 \times 8^0$ **c.** $x^5(x^3)$ **d.** $4x^3 \cdot -8x^3$

Because you can multiply a monomial times a monomial, the distributive property can help you multiply a monomial times a polynomial.

Example 3

a. Multiply $5x^2$ by $2x^3 + 6$.

$5x^2(2x^3 + 6) = 5x^2 \cdot 2x^3 + 5x^2 \cdot 6$ Use the distributive property.

$= 10x^{3+2} + 30x^2$ Multiply monomials.

$= 10x^5 + 30x^2$ Simplify.

b. Multiply $-5x^4$ by $3x + 5 - 2x^3$.

$-5x^4(3x + 5 - 2x^3)$

$= -5x^4 \cdot 3x + -5x^4 \cdot 5 + -5x^4 \cdot -2x^3$ Use the distributive property.

$= -15x^{4+1} + -25x^4 + 10x^{4+3}$ Multiply monomials.

$= -15x^5 - 25x^4 + 10x^7$ Simplify.

Try It

a. Multiply $-2x^2$ by $5x^4 + 6x$.   **b.** Multiply $2x^2$ by $3x^2 + 5x - 1$.

In Chapter 2, you studied scientific notation. The rules for multiplying powers can help you multiply two numbers written in scientific notation.

Examples

4 The smaller the bird, the faster it needs to flap its wings to stay airborne. A hummingbird flaps its wings 1.5×10^3 times per min. How many times would it flap its wings if it could stay airborne for a year (5.256×10^5 min)?

$(1.5 \times 10^3)(5.256 \times 10^5)$

$= (1.5 \cdot 5.256) \times (10^3 \cdot 10^5)$ Group numbers and bases together.

$= 7.884 \qquad \times \qquad 10^8$ Multiply the numbers, add the exponents.

A hummingbird would flap its wings 7.884×10^8 times, or approximately 800 million times in a year.

5 A light year, the distance light travels in a year, is 5.87×10^{12} miles. A parsec is 3.26×10^0 light years. Multiply to find how many miles are in a parsec. Write the answer in scientific notation.

$(5.87 \times 10^{12}) \times (3.26 \times 10^0)$

$= (5.87 \cdot 3.26) \times (10^{12} \cdot 10^0)$ Group numbers and bases together.

$\approx 19.1 \times 10^{12}$ Multiply. Add exponents.

$\approx 1.91 \times 10^{13}$ Rewrite in scientific notation.

There are about 1.91×10^{13} miles in a parsec.

Try It

a. Multiply 7×10^4 by 5×10^6. Write the answer in scientific notation.

b. In 1995, the estimated population of the U. S. was 2.6×10^8. Each person's share of the national debt is about $\$1.9 \times 10^4$. What is the national debt?

Check | Your Understanding

1. Explain how to multiply two powers with the same base.

2. Why can't you simplify the product of w^3 and x^2?

3. When multiplying $-2x^3$ by a polynomial, how do you know what the sign of each term will be?

Practice and Apply

1. **Getting Started** Use these steps to multiply x^4 by x^3.
   a. Write x^4 as the product of factors. _____ · _____ · _____ · _____.
   b. Write x^3 as the product of factors. _____ · _____ · _____.
   c. Count the total number of x factors. _____.
   d. $x^4 \cdot x^3 =$ _____.

Multiply.

2. $7^2 \cdot 7^7$ 3. $4^1 \cdot 4^6$ 4. $c^3 \cdot c^6$ 5. $2r^2 \cdot 3r^4$ 6. $(-4r^3)(5r^2)$

7. $(-3d^6)(8d^4)$ 8. $(-s^2)(-s^2)$ 9. $(4f^6)(5f^9)$ 10. $8y^2 \cdot y^0$

11. $9b^3 \cdot \frac{1}{3}b^2$ 12. $4y^2(-3y^5 - 6)$ 13. $-6t(1 - t^2)$ 14. $-2s^7(s^2 + 2s - 1)$

15. $5g^4(3g^3 - 2g^2 + 5g + 8)$ 16. $-\frac{1}{2}a^2(10a - 8)$ 17. $m(2m + 4)$

18. **Test Prep** Which monomial is the product of $-5x^3 \cdot -5x^3$?
   Ⓐ $-10x^3$ Ⓑ $25x^3$ Ⓒ $25x^6$ Ⓓ $-10x^6$

Multiply each of the following. Write your answers in scientific notation.

19. $(3.2 \times 10^4) \cdot (3.1 \times 10^5)$ 20. $(1.3 \times 10^2) \cdot (2.7 \times 10^6)$ 21. $(5.1 \times 10^3) \cdot (1.6 \times 10^3)$

22. Find an expression for the area of each region and the total area of the figure. Simplify if possible.

$2x$

$3x + 1$ $5x - 2$ 4 $4x + 5x + 3$

23. **Journal** Why do you add exponents when you multiply powers with the same base?

24. Find the volume of the bird house.

25. If each person's share of the national debt is 1.9×10^4 dollars, how much of the debt are the people in the following states responsible for?
   a. Florida: population 1.3×10^7
   b. Oklahoma: population 3.1×10^6
   c. Wyoming: population 4.5×10^5
   d. California: population 3.1×10^7

$2x + 2$

$2x$

$2x$

$2x$

PRACTICE 10-8

26. Geometry Multiply to find an expression for the volume of the box. Simplify if possible.

27. Math Reasoning What is $(3^2)^3$? (Think of it as $3^2 \cdot 3^2 \cdot 3^2$.) What is the expanded product $(a^2)^3$?

28. Critical Thinking Find an expression for the surface area of the figure at the right.

29. Communicate When you multiplied powers with like bases, you added exponents.

a. What do you think you would do when dividing powers with like bases?

b. Try your conjecture on $\dfrac{2^3}{2^2}$

Mixed Review

Find the GCF of each set of numbers. [Lesson 7-2]

30. 40, 56   **31.** 125, 175   **32.** 18, 48   **33.** 63, 15, 126

Find the volume of each after the dilation. [Lesson 9-7]

34. Scale factor $= 0.5$ **35.** Scale factor $= 4$ **36.** Scale factor $= \dfrac{1}{3}$

25 cm   18 cm   10 cm

2.4 m   2.4 m   2.4 m

1 in.   12 in.   9 in.

Project Progress

Decide on a model. (You might also try graphing some polynomial functions, such as $y = x^3$, before you decide.) Explain how the model you chose fits or does not fit your situation.

Problem Solving

Understand
Plan
Solve
Look Back

Section 10B Connect

In this Connect, you will link your knowledge of polynomials.

Which Came First?

Materials: Centimeter cubes

Stacked boxes of eggs are to be marked "fragile." Suppose all visible sides are marked. How many boxes will be marked on 1 side? On 2 sides? Use cubes to simulate the exercise.

1. Build a 2 by 2 by 2 cube. How many small cubes did you use? If all the visible faces are marked, how many cubes will have 3 marked faces? 2 marked faces? 1 marked face? 0 marked faces? Copy the table and complete the column for the 2 by 2 by 2 cube.

2. Build a 3 by 3 by 3 cube. Complete the column for this cube. Then build a 4 by 4 by 4 cube, and so on, to finish the table. Describe any patterns you see in the table.

	Dimensions			
	$2 \times 2 \times 2$	$3 \times 3 \times 3$	$4 \times 4 \times 4$	$5 \times 5 \times 5$
Number of boxes				
Number with 3 Sides Marked				
Number with 2 Sides Marked				
Number with 1 Side Marked				
Number with 0 Sides Marked				

3. For an $n \times n \times n$ cube of boxes, how many boxes are there? If all visible faces of the $n \times n \times n$ cube are marked, match the number of boxes to the correct expression.

   a. The total number of boxes   **i.** 8

   b. The number with 3 marked sides   **ii.** $12(n - 2)$

   c. The number with 2 marked sides   **iii.** n^3

   d. The number with 1 marked side   **iv.** $(n - 2)^3$

   e. The number with 0 marked sides   **v.** $6(n - 2)^2$

4. In a 20 by 20 by 20 cube, how many boxes would be unmarked?

Identify each polynomial expression as a monomial, binomial, trinomial, or none of these. Explain your choice.

1. $4x^2 + x$ **2.** $4x + x^5 + 2$ **3.** $-2x^3$ **4.** $x^3 + x^2 - x + 3$

Find the degree of each polynomial expression. Write the polynomial expression in descending order.

5. $-6 + 8x$ **6.** $2x^3 + 3x^2 - 9$ **7.** $x^2 - x - x^5$ **8.** $28x$ **9.** $x^7 - 3$

Simplify each if possible. If the expression cannot be simplified, write "already simplified." Write your answer in descending order.

10. $-6x^2 - 3x + 8x^3 + 2x$

11. $8x^2 + 8x$

12. $-6y^3 + 4y + -3y^3 - 5y$

13. $8x - 2x + 4x + 5$

14. $(2x^2 - 5x + 2) + (-4x^2 - 3x)$

15. $(2x) - (-2x^2 - 2x + 1)$

16. $(5x^2 + 3x + 1)$
     $+ (3x^2 + 4x - 5)$

17. $(5p^2 + 3p - 7)$
     $- (4p^2 + 5p + 2)$

18. $a(a^7)$ **19.** $x^2 \cdot x^4$ **20.** $3y(y^2 + 2y - 4)$ **21.** $4x^2 \cdot -5x^8$

22. $-2m^2(2m - 6)$ **23.** $(y + 3)y$ **24.** $x^5 \cdot y^5$ **25.** $x^3(x^2 + 5)x$

26. The function $h = -5(t^2 - 5t + 10)$ can be used to find the approximate height of a launched flare in t sec. Write this function another way.

Test Prep

When asked to multiply numbers in scientific notation, remember to group numbers together and bases together, then add exponents.

27. Which is the product of 1.2×10^6 and 4.1×10^8?

    Ⓐ $5.3 \cdot 10^{14}$ Ⓑ $4.92 \cdot 10^2$

    Ⓒ $4.92 \cdot 10^{14}$ Ⓓ $4.92 \cdot 10^{48}$

28. Multiply to find the expression for each area. Add; Simplify if possible.

$2x$ $3x + 1$ $4x - 2$ 3 $10x + 3$

Extend Key Ideas ▷ Algebra

Variation

When a situation can be modeled by a linear function, where y divided by x is constant, y varies directly with x. This is called **direct variation.** If one quantity is doubled, the other is doubled. For example:

Stamps (x)	1	2	3	4	5
Price (y)	0.32	0.64	0.96	1.28	1.60

$\frac{y}{x} = 0.32$. The price varies directly with the number of stamps.

But if the *product* of x and y is constant, the variables are *inversely* related. If one quantity is doubled, the other is halved. This is **inverse variation.** For example:

Gallons Used (x)	1	2	3	4	5
Miles per Gallon (y)	120	60	40	30	24

The product of x and y is 120.

Are the quantities in each of the following directly related or inversely related?

1. Your cost for a field trip depends on the number of students who sign up.

2. The number of snacks needed for the swim team depends on the number of swimmers.

3. The time it takes to read *Don Quixote* depends on the number of pages you read each day.

4. In the 1500s, when Michelangelo was commissioned to paint the ceiling of the Sistine Chapel, he spent 216 weeks lying on his back, only inches away from the vast panorama. How many artists would have been needed in order to complete the painting of the ceiling in 18 weeks? In 4 weeks?

Graphic Organizer

Section 10A Functions

Summary

■ A **function** is a relationship that gives one output value for each input value. Two different output values cannot have the same input value.

■ In a function, the input is the **independent variable** and the output is the **dependent variable**. To graph a function, use the x-axis for the independent variable and the y-axis for the dependent variable.

■ A function is a **linear function** if its graph is a line. A **quadratic function** is a **nonlinear function** in which the value of x is squared. Its graph is a ∪ or upside-down ∪-shaped **parabola**. In an **exponential function**, the exponent is a variable. A **step function** has a graph that is not connected.

Review

1. For the function machine shown,
  a. Find the output value for an input of -3.
  b. Find the input value for an output of 24.

In	Multiply by 6	Out

2. What is a possible rule for the input and output shown in the table?

Input	2	4	6	8
Output	7	13	19	25

3. Graph the equation $y = 3x - 2$. Does the equation describe a linear function?

4. Graph the functions $y = 2x^2$ and $y = 2x^2 - 4$ and explain their differences.

5. A ball was thrown. Its height (h, in ft) after t sec is given by $h = 64t - 16t^2$. Graph the function. How high did the ball go?

6. A plumber charges $25 for every half hour or portion thereof. Graph this function.

Summary

- A **term** (or **monomial**) is a signed number, a variable, or a number multiplied by a variable or variables. The variables can have whole-number exponents.

- A **polynomial** is a sum of one or more terms. A **binomial** is a polynomial with two terms and a **trinomial** is a polynomial with three terms. The **degree** of a polynomial with one variable is the largest exponent in a term.

- A polynomial is written in descending order if the terms are written in order from the highest-degree term to the lowest-degree term.

- Polynomials can be evaluated by replacing the variables with the given numbers and using the order of operations rules to simplify the expression.

- **Like terms** are terms that have the same variable raised to the same exponent. A polynomial is **simplified** when it contains no like terms.

- Add polynomials by combining like terms. You can use the distributive property or add the polynomials vertically. Subtract a polynomial by adding its opposite, or additive inverse. You can find the additive inverse of a polynomial by changing the sign of each term.

- When multiplying powers with like bases, add their exponents: $a^m \cdot a^n = a^{m+n}$. This rule can be used to multiply monomials or numbers in scientific notation.

- Use the distributive property to multiply a monomial times a polynomial.

Review

7. Write $3x - 4x^3 + 5 - 7x^2$ in descending order. Find the degree of the polynomial.

8. a. Evaluate $x^3 - 4x + 3$ for $x = 3$.

   b. Evaluate $2x^2 + 7x - 3$ for $x = -5$.

9. Simplify.

$2x - 5x^2 + 4 - 5x + 10 + 5x^3$

10. Add.

$(p^2 - 5p + 7) + (3p^2 + 5p - 8)$

11. Find the total area.

12. The perimeter is $2x^3 - 6x + 8$. Find the missing side length.

13. Find the additive inverse of the polynomial $-6x^3 + 9x^2 + 2x - 15$.

14. Subtract $(4g^2 + 7) - (3g^2 - 8g + 4)$. Write the answer in lowest terms.

15. Find the area of a rectangle with a width of $3x^2$ and a length of $2x - 5$.

16. Multiply $(2.3 \times 10^5) \cdot (1.8 \times 10^9)$ and write the answer in scientific notation.

17. Multiply $-3u^3(5u^2 - 7u + 4)$.

1. For the function machine shown,

   a. Find the output value for an input of 12.

   b. Find the input value for an output of 31.

In	Subtract 15	Out

2. What is a possible rule for the input and output shown in the table?

Input	5	7	9	11
Output	−11	−15	−19	−23

3. For the function rule $y = 4x - 7$, complete the table of values.

x	−1	0	1	2	3
y					

4. Is the area of a house (in ft^2) a function of the number of rooms in the house? Explain.

5. Graph the function $y = 1.25x$.

6. Graph each pair of functions and describe the similarities and differences.

   a. $y = x^2 - 3$ and $y = 3 - x^2$

   b. $y = -4x^2$ and $y = -x^2$

7. A call costs 15¢ for the first min, 10¢ for each additional min. The time is rounded to the next whole number before the charge is calculated. Graph the price as a function of time.

8. Graph the equation $y = -x + 4$. Does the equation describe a linear function?

9. Evaluate $2x^3 - 3x - 8$ for $x = 5$.

10. Write the polynomial $2x - 3x^4 + 1 + 7x^6$ in descending order and give its degree.

11. Find the additive inverse of the polynomial $-6x^2 + 12x - 5$.

Simplify, if possible. Write your answer in descending order.

12. $7 + 3x - 5x^3 + 6x$

13. $(5z^2 - 4) + (-3z^2 + 2z - 5)$

14. $(5r^3 - 2r + 5) - (7r^2 + 3r - 2)$

15. $7p^2 \cdot 3p^5$

16. $x(3x^3 - 4x^2 + 7x)$

17. $8u^5(5u^3 + 4u^2 - 3u - 2)$

18. Multiply $(4.8 \times 10^7) \cdot (1.2 \times 10^{10})$. Write your answer in scientific notation.

Find the area of each shaded region.

19.

$2x^2 - 5x - 2$

   $A = 5x^2 + 3x - 4$

20.

   $2x^2 - 8x + 7$

Performance Task

A flare is shot upwards at 40 m/sec. The height after t sec is given by $h = 40t - 5t^2$. Sketch a graph of this function. Label your graph to show when the flare is rising, when it is falling, and when it hits the ground.

Multiple Choice

Choose the best answer.

1. Which pair of ratios does **not** form a proportion? *[Lesson 5-2]*

Ⓐ $\frac{88}{121} \stackrel{?}{=} \frac{48}{66}$ Ⓑ $\frac{81}{36} \stackrel{?}{=} \frac{54}{24}$

Ⓒ $\frac{15}{35} \stackrel{?}{=} \frac{24}{56}$ Ⓓ $\frac{28}{40} \stackrel{?}{=} \frac{55}{75}$

2. 64 is 8% of which number? *[Lesson 6-2]*

Ⓐ 5.12   Ⓑ 12.5   Ⓒ 80   Ⓓ 800

3. Find the quotient $\frac{5}{7} \div \frac{3}{14}$. Write the answer in lowest terms. *[Lesson 7-6]*

Ⓐ $\frac{70}{21}$ Ⓑ $\frac{13}{14}$ Ⓒ $\frac{10}{3}$ Ⓓ $\frac{15}{98}$

4. How many sides does a pentagon have? *[Lesson 8-6]*

Ⓐ 4   Ⓑ 5   Ⓒ 6   Ⓓ 7

5. For the pyramid shown, which of the following is equal to 384? *[Lessons 9-5, 9-7]*

Ⓐ Slant height

Ⓑ Surface area

Ⓒ Volume

Ⓓ Both B and C

6. A circle has a diameter of 7 in. Find the approximate area of the circle. *[Lesson 9-3]*

Ⓐ 38.5 in²   Ⓑ 44.0 in²

Ⓒ 22.0 in²   Ⓓ 153.9 in²

7. Find the volume of a 6 ft by 4 ft by 5 ft rectangular prism. *[Lesson 9-6]*

Ⓐ 15 ft³   Ⓑ 120 ft³

Ⓒ 40 ft³   Ⓓ 20 ft³

8. What is a possible rule for the input and output shown in the table? *[Lesson 10-1]*

Input	6	7	8	9
Output	14	17	20	23

Ⓐ $y = x + 8$ Ⓑ $y = \frac{1}{3}(x + 4)$

Ⓒ $y = 3x - 4$ Ⓓ $y = x - 8$

9. Which function is shown in the graph below? *[Lessons 10-2, 10-3, 10-4]*

Ⓐ $y = 2x$

Ⓑ $y = x^2$

Ⓒ $y = 2^x$

Ⓓ $y = 3^x$

10. Which of the following is a polynomial of degree 2? *[Lesson 10-5]*

Ⓐ $5x + 3$ Ⓑ $2x^3 + 7x - 4$

Ⓒ $3x^2$ Ⓓ $7x^3 - 6x + 2$

11. Which of the following shows $(3x^2 + 7x - 3) + (8x^2 + 5)$ in simplest form? *[Lesson 10-6]*

Ⓐ $11x^2 + 7x + 2$

Ⓑ $8x^2 + 3x^2 + 7x + 2$

Ⓒ $-5x^2 + 7x - 8$

Ⓓ $11x^2 + 7x - 8$

12. Find the additive inverse of $4x^3 + 2x - 5$. *[Lesson 10-7]*

Ⓐ $4x^3 - 2x + 5$ Ⓑ $-4x^3 - 2x + 5$

Ⓒ $-4x^3 + 2x - 5$ Ⓓ $-4x^3 - 2x - 5$

13. Find the product of $2x^3 \cdot 5x^4$. *[Lesson 10-8]*

Ⓐ $7x^{12}$ Ⓑ $7x^7$ Ⓒ $10x^{12}$ Ⓓ $10x^7$

Similarity, Congruence, and

Entertainment

A knowledge of angles and reflections is essential to successful billiard players, as they must frequently bank their shots to avoid moving their opponents' ball.

Arts & Literature

The works of Dutch artist M. C. Escher (1898–1972) consist almost entirely of interlocking, infinitely repeating designs called tessellations, which are based on translations, rotations, and reflections.

Circle Limit III by M. C. Escher.
©1996 Cordon Art-Baarn-Holland.
All rights reserved.

People of the World

Despite having asthma, Jackie Joyner-Kersee achieved world records in the heptathalon. Great athletes like her often do weight lifting training which can strengthen muscles symmetrically.

Transformations

Science Link
www.mathsurf.com/8/ch11/sci

Science

A periscope uses reflections in two mirrors, enabling the viewer to see above the line of sight. The mirrors are parallel to each other and at a 45° angle to the horizon line.

KEY MATH IDEAS

Two figures are similar if they have the same shape but not necessarily the same size. Two figures are congruent if they have the same shape and size.

For an angle in a right triangle with measure x, the trigonometric ratios sin, cos, and tan can be used to find the length of a side.

A line of symmetry divides a figure into two identical halves.

A tessellation is a pattern of repeated figures that covers a plane.

Social Studies

The Japanese have long perfected the art of paper folding, called *origami,* which is a striking application of the many properties of reflections.

CHAPTER PROJECT

Problem Solving

Understand
Plan
Solve
Look Back

In this project, using a 3 in. by 5 in. card, you will make a hypsometer—a device for measuring tall objects. You will use it to measure the height of a building. After you have made the hypsometer, align it with the top and bottom of the building. Determine the distance between you and the building and you'll be able to find the height of the building. Explain how this works after you've tried it.

Problem Solving Focus

Checking the Rules of the Problem

After you have solved a problem, look back to make sure you followed the rules of the problem. If you followed all the rules, then your answer is probably correct.

Each problem below has three answers. State which of the three answers is correct, and which rule the other two answers didn't follow.

1 At the Winthrop Fair, there is an apple-bobbing contest. Each contestant has two minutes to bob for apples. The one who gets the most wins. Mary, Colin, LuAnn, and Jamie enter. Mary comes up with twice as many apples as Colin. Between them, Colin and LuAnn get two fewer than Mary. Jamie gets half as many as LuAnn. All together, the four bobbers get 15 apples. How many did each get?

Answer #1	Answer #2	Answer #3
M = 8	M = 8	M = 8
C = 6	C = 2	C = 4
L = 6	L = 2	L = 2
J = 3	J = 1	J = 1

2 Jamie met Marsha, Albert, and Seena at the fair. They all went over to the ticket booth, where they bought tickets to use on all of the rides at the fair. Jamie bought 3 times as many tickets as Marsha, but he gave $\frac{1}{3}$ of them to his little brother. Albert bought half as many tickets as Jamie. Seena bought 5 more tickets than Marsha. Marsha bought 6 fewer tickets than Albert. All together, they bought 83 tickets. How many did each person buy?

Answer #1	Answer #2	Answer #3
J = 24	J = 36	J = 18
M = 8	M = 12	M = 6
A = 12	A = 18	A = 12
S = 13	S = 17	S = 11

building is part art, part science. Engineers use science (including math!) to make sure that bridges can support the weight of the vehicles and pedestrians using them. Architects working with engineers use their artistic instincts and training to create bridges that are not only strong but pleasing to the eye.

Both strength and attractiveness are usually enhanced by a property called symmetry, which in the case of bridges means that one side is the mirror image of the other. When a symmetric bridge is made up of numerous triangles (as many bridges are), the triangles come in pairs: Each triangle on one side of a bridge has an identical twin on the other—another triangle congruent to the first one, as a mathematician would say. Later in this chapter, you will be learning more about symmetry. First, though, you will learn about congruency as well as similarity, different ways in which two triangles (and other shapes) can be alike.

Un·a·bridged

1 Why might a bridge with matching triangles on each side be stronger than one where the triangles on each side are different?

2 Why might a bridge with matching triangles on each side be better than one that doesn't?

Similar Figures

▶ **Lesson Link**
You've seen the results of scaling a rectangle. Now you'll see how angle and side measurements correspond on scale drawings. ◀

You'll Learn ...

■ to identify similar figures

... How It's Used

Sign makers use similar figures as repetitive design elements in their work.

Vocabulary

similar

corresponding angles

corresponding sides

similarity ratio

Explore **Similar Polygons**

The Size Factor

Materials: Dynamic geometry software, $8\frac{1}{2}$ in. by 11 in. paper

1. With the geometry software, draw a polygon with 3, 4, or 5 sides.

2. On paper, make a table with as many columns as the polygon has sides. Label the first column "side 1," the second, "side 2," and so on.

3. Measure each side of the polygon using the measure tool, and record your measurements in your table. Use the dilate tool to shrink or enlarge your polygon. Notice that the side measurements change.

4. Record the new measurements in the appropriate columns.

5. In each column, find the ratio between the old and new measurements. What do you notice? Why do you think you got these results?

6. Use the dilate tool again and record a third set of measurements. Find the ratios between the second and third measurements for each table column. What do you notice?

7. Do you think the dilation changed the angle measurements?

Learn **Similar Figures**

Two figures are **similar** if they have the same shape but not necessarily the same size.

$\triangle ABC \sim \triangle XYZ$ means $\triangle ABC$ is similar to $\triangle XYZ$.

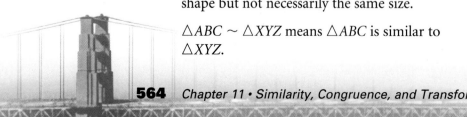

In similar figures, corresponding angles are congruent.

∠*MLO* and ∠*SRU* are corresponding angles.

In similar figures, pairs of **corresponding sides** have equal length ratios.

$\overline{TU}$ and $\overline{NO}$ are corresponding sides.

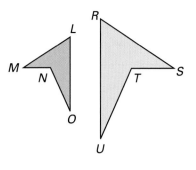

When viewing two similar figures, we see that one is a scale drawing of the other.

The ratio between corresponding side lengths of similar figures is the **similarity ratio** . The similarity ratio of similar figures can be compared to the scale factor of scale drawings.

Example 1

A cantilever bridge has two cantilevers that extend from both sides of a waterway. These two cantilevers meet at the middle of the waterway.

△*QSR* ~ △*DEF*. Find the similarity ratio of the two figures.

$\overline{QR}$ and $\overline{DF}$ are corresponding sides.   Identify corresponding sides.

$$\frac{m\overline{QR}}{m\overline{DF}} = \frac{85\ \text{ft}}{100\ \text{ft}} = \frac{17}{20}$$ Take the ratio of their lengths.

The similarity ratio of △*QSR* and △*DEF* is $\frac{17}{20}$.

Example 2

The hexagons are similar. Find *m*∠*XST*.

∠*FAB* and ∠*XST* are corresponding angles.

So *m*∠*XST* = 137°.

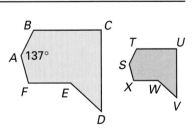

Try It

PQRS ~ *BCDE*

a. Find the similarity ratio of figure *PQRS* to figure *BCDE*.

b. Find the measure of ∠*PQR*.

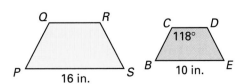

If pairs of corresponding angles are congruent, the triangles are similar.

Example 3

Determine whether $\triangle ABC$ and $\triangle DEF$ are similar.

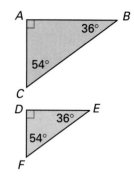

$\angle CAB \cong \angle FDE$

$\angle ACB \cong \angle DFE$

$\angle ABC \cong \angle DEF$

All corresponding angles are congruent.

$\triangle ABC \sim \triangle DEF$

Example 4

Are the figures similar?

$\frac{1}{3}$ and $\frac{3}{5}$ are ratios for two pairs of corresponding sides.

$\frac{1}{3} \neq \frac{3}{5}$. The figures are not similar.

Try It

Are the figures similar?

a.

b.

Check | Your Understanding

1. If the ratio between all corresponding sides of two figures is 1, are the figures similar? Explain.

2. Are any two regular pentagons similar? Explain.

Practice and Apply

1. **Getting Started** Decide whether the triangles are similar.

a. Write a proportion for the corresponding sides.

b. Determine if the cross products are equal.

Decide whether each pair of figures is similar.

2.

3.

4. The two trapezoids are similar.

a. Find x.

b. Find the measure of $\angle 1$.

5. **Industry** The main span of New York's Brooklyn Bridge is 1595 ft long. On a blueprint for the bridge, the span measures 31.9 in. What is the scale factor of the blueprint?

6. **Measurement** The two jeans pockets are similar. Find x, the length of the top of the smaller pocket.

7. **Test Prep** Given that triangles ABC and DEF are similar, what is the length of side $\overline{BC}$ on $\triangle ABC$?

Ⓐ 28 mi   Ⓑ 35 mi

Ⓒ 14 mi   Ⓓ 42 mi

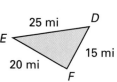

8. Quadrilateral I was shrunk and flipped to make quadrilateral II. Find the similarity ratio of I to II.

9. Algebra Write an algebraic expression that represents the area of the dilation of a square with an area of 64 unit^2, where the scale factor is x.

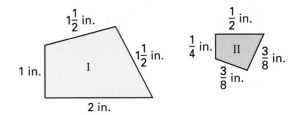

Problem Solving and Reasoning

10. **Journal** Are all squares similar? Are all rectangles similar? Which polygons do you think will always be similar?

11. Communicate The photo shows how the cables that support the roadway are directly connected to the towers. A fan pattern is shown by the cables connecting several points of the roadway to several points on the tower. Describe why the triangles formed by the cables on one side of a tower are not similar.

12. Technology Using geometry software, draw a polygon and dilate it by a scale factor of 2. Then measure the area of each polygon using the area tool. Calculate the ratio of the two areas. What is the area ratio for a scale factor of 3?

13. Math Reasoning Draw a conclusion about dilating figures using a scale factor less than 1 versus using a scale factor greater than 1. Give an example to support your conclusion.

Mixed Review

List all factors for each number and identify the prime factors. *[Lesson 7-1]*

14. 45   **15.** 66   **16.** 81   **17.** 48   **18.** 100

For the rule "add 5," find the output value for each input value. *[Lesson 10-1]*

19. 7   **20.** 5.5   **21.** 0.01   **22.** $\frac{3}{4}$ **23.** −22

Congruent Figures

▶ **Lesson Link**   You know how to identify similar polygons. Now you'll work with polygons with the same size and shape. ◄

Explore   Congruent Polygons

Congratulations! They're Twins!

Materials: Paper, Ruler, Protractor, Compass

1. On a sheet of paper, draw a polygon with 6, 7, or 8 sides. Do this so no one can see your work.

2. With your group, take turns describing your figure as the others try to draw an identical figure. You can use length and angle measurements to describe your figure.

3. When describing your figure, what did you say to make it easier for those who are drawing? What units of measurement did you use?

4. When taking your turn to draw, what did you find most helpful?

You'll Learn ...

■ to identify congruent figures

... How It's Used

The art of jewelry-making exhibits the use of congruent shapes.

Vocabulary

congruent polygons

Learn   Congruent Figures

Congruent polygons have the same shape and size.

To indicate congruence, write $ABCD \cong NMLK$.

Congruent

Congruent

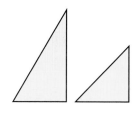

Not congruent

Corresponding angles of congruent figures are congruent.

   $\angle DCB \cong \angle KLM$ in the congruent parallelograms.

Corresponding sides of congruent figures are congruent.

   $\overline{AD} \cong \overline{NK}$ in the congruent parallelograms.

You can determine whether two figures are congruent by matching a tracing or comparing measurements.

Example 1

Problem Solving TIP

Similar figures and congruent figures don't always have to be your usual polygons.

Determine whether the two figures are congruent.

Trace Figure A.

Put the tracing of Figure A over Figure B.

Try to match Figure A and Figure B.

Figure A ≅ Figure B.

Example 2

Determine whether $\triangle ABC \cong \triangle DEF$.

First, measure $\angle DEF$, $\angle EFD$, and $\angle FDE$.

$$m\angle DEF = 90° = m\angle ABC$$

$$m\angle EFD = 20° \neq m\angle BCA$$

$$m\angle FDE = 70° \neq m\angle CAB$$

Measure $\overline{EF}$, $\overline{DF}$, and $\overline{DE}$.

$$m\,\overline{EF} = 37 \text{ mm} \neq m\,\overline{BC}$$

$$m\,\overline{DF} = 40 \text{ mm} \neq m\,\overline{AC}$$

$$m\,\overline{DE} = 13 \text{ mm} \neq m\,\overline{AB}$$

All corresponding parts are not congruent.
$\triangle ABC$ and $\triangle DEF$ are not congruent.

Try It

Determine whether the squares are congruent.

Example 3

Determine whether the two hexagons are congruent.

They both have the same angle and side length measures, but the measurements do not occur in the same order. The hexagons are not congruent.

If two figures are congruent and you know the measurements of one, you can find the measurements of the other figure.

Example 4

Trapezoids *ABCD* and *EFGH* are congruent. Find the length of $\overline{FG}$.

$\overline{FG}$ corresponds to $\overline{BC}$.

$m\overline{BC} = 50$ ft $m\overline{FG} = 50$ ft

Try It

The two pentagons are congruent.

a. What side corresponds to $\overline{ST}$?

b. Find the length of $\overline{FG}$.

c. Find $m\angle HIJ$.

Check Your Understanding

1. Are any two regular hexagons congruent? Are they similar? Explain.

2. If all the angles of an octagon are congruent to the angles of another octagon, are the octagons congruent? Explain.

Practice and Apply

1. [Getting Started] Determine whether the parallelo-grams are congruent.

   a. Measure the corresponding sides.

   b. Measure the corresponding angles.

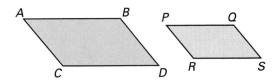

The two pentagons are congruent.

2. Find $m\angle STP$.

3. Find $m\overline{XY}$.

Determine whether each pair of figures is congruent.

4.

1.5 cm   1.8 cm   3.0 cm   2.1 cm   3.6 cm   4.2 cm

5.

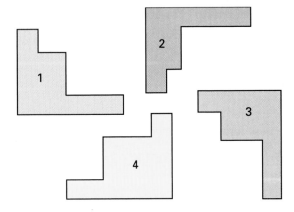

6. [Test Prep] Two of the figures shown are congruent. Which are they?

  Ⓐ 2 and 4   Ⓑ 1 and 3

  Ⓒ 1 and 2   Ⓓ 3 and 4

7. Algebra In the figure, the polygons are congruent. Find the value of x.

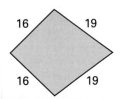

3y   2x   16   19   16   19

8. Algebra In the figure, the polygons are congruent. Find the value of x.

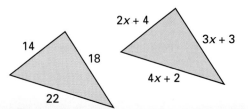

14   18   22   2x + 4   3x + 3   4x + 2

PRACTICE 11-2

9. Geometry Construct a polygon congruent to the one shown, and describe how you did it. Label the vertices and the corresponding sides.

Problem Solving and Reasoning

10. Communicate The photograph shows the Forth Rail Bridge, a cantilever bridge in Scotland. Terry thinks that the highlighted triangles on the bridge are not congruent because they don't appear to be the same size in the photo. Explain the error in Terry's reasoning.

11. Technology With geometry software, construct a triangle congruent to the one shown. Measure the length of each side. Then move the vertices around until all side measures match those in the figure. (You may not be able to match them exactly; just do your best.) Now measure the angles inside the triangle, rounding to the nearest degree. How did the corresponding angles compare?

12. Math Reasoning If you are checking two triangles for congruency, do you need to measure every side and every angle? If not, how many measurements do you need?

13. Journal What steps would you perform to construct a copy of this regular octagon? Is there more than one way to do it?

Mixed Review

Find the GCF for each pair of numbers. *[Lesson 7-2]*

14. 13, 52   **15.** 16, 24   **16.** 28, 49   **17.** 20, 50   **18.** 15, 40

Decide whether each equation describes a function. *[Lesson 10-2]*

19. $y = 2$ **20.** $y = 3x + 2$ **21.** $y = -4x$ **22.** $y = |x + 1|$

Triangle Congruence

You'll Learn ...

■ to identify congruent triangles

... How It's Used

A percussionist can have a set of triangles. If the triangles are not congruent, then they will produce different pitches.

Vocabulary

Side-Side-Side

Side-Angle-Side

Angle-Side-Angle

Side-Angle-Angle

▶ **Lesson Link** Now that you've learned about congruent figures, you're ready to take a closer look at triangles and ways of showing their congruence. ◀

Explore | Congruent Triangles

Stone Bridges

Below is an illustration of a stone bridge with the wooden framework used to build it. The people who built the bridge set up the wooden framework to support the stones as the bridge was built.

Because the sketch is not drawn to scale, you only know the measurements shown. You will determine whether triangles that appear to be congruent are congruent.

1. With triangles 1 and 2, all corresponding sides are congruent. Are the triangles congruent? Explain.

2. With triangles 3 and 4, all corresponding angles are congruent. Are the triangles congruent? Explain.

3. With the measurements given for triangles 5 and 6, do you know if they are congruent? Explain.

4. With the measurements given for triangles 7 and 8, do you know if they are congruent? Explain.

5. Discuss the minimum information necessary to determine whether or not two triangles are congruent.

You don't need every measurement to know that two triangles are congruent. Small marks are used to signify that corresponding parts are congruent.

Side-Side-Side

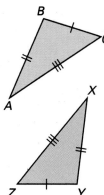

$\overline{AB} \cong \overline{XY}$
$\overline{BC} \cong \overline{YZ}$
$\overline{CA} \cong \overline{ZX}$

Side-Angle-Side

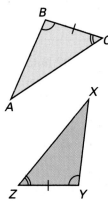

$\overline{AB} \cong \overline{XY}$
$\angle ABC \cong \angle XYZ$
$\overline{BC} \cong \overline{YZ}$

Angle-Side-Angle

$\angle ABC \cong \angle XYZ$
$\overline{BC} \cong \overline{YZ}$
$\angle BCA \cong \angle YZX$

Side-Angle-Angle

$\overline{BC} \cong \overline{YZ}$
$\angle BCA \cong \angle YZX$
$\angle CAB \cong \angle ZXY$

Example 1

Are the triangles congruent? If so, state the rule that justifies your answer.

Yes, because of the Side-Side-Side rule.

Try It

Bascule bridges, as seen along the Chicago River, open upward to let ships pass. Suppose the dimensions are as labeled.

Are the two triangles congruent? If so, state the rule that justifies your answer.

Example 2

Are the triangles congruent? If so, state the rule that justifies your answer.

Yes, because of the Side-Angle-Side rule.

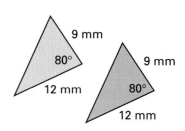

Example 3

Are the triangles congruent? If so, state the rule that justifies your answer.

No. The length measurements "2 m" do not appear on corresponding sides.

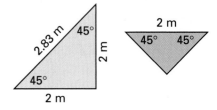

Try It

Suspension bridges, such as the Golden Gate Bridge in San Francisco, are used to span long distances.

► History Link

Completed on May 28, 1938, the Golden Gate Bridge in California spans 6450 ft. That's more than a mile!

Are the two triangles shown in this bridge congruent? If so, state the rule that justifies your answer.

Check | Your Understanding

1. Why isn't there an Angle-Angle-Angle rule? Explain.

2. Suppose you know that four parts of a triangle are congruent to four corresponding parts of another triangle. Is this enough information to know that the triangles are congruent? Explain.

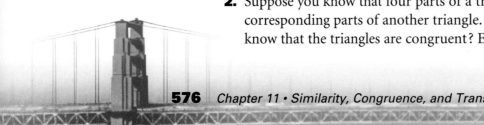

Practice and Apply

1. ▢ **Getting Started** △GHI ≅ △SQR and $\overline{HI}$ corresponds to $\overline{QR}$.

   a. $\overline{HG}$ corresponds to _____.

   b. $\overline{IG}$ corresponds to _____.

   c. ∠H corresponds to _____.

   d. ∠I corresponds to _____.

   e. ∠G corresponds to _____.

2. For each pair, what rule tells you that the two triangles are congruent?

   a.

   b.

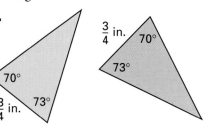

State whether each pair of triangles has congruence; if it does, give the rule that justifies your answer.

3.

4.

5.

6.

7.

8.

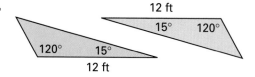

9. For each rule, draw a pair of triangles that satisfy it.

   a. Side-Side-Side   **b.** Angle-Side-Angle   **c.** Side-Angle-Side

10. **Test Prep** How far is it from Cauchy Square to the Weierstrasse?

Ⓐ 0.20 km

Ⓑ 0.17 km

Ⓒ 0.10 km

Ⓓ Insufficient information

11. **Career** A surveyor at this native-plant preservation area concludes that the fences on the right and left sides of the land are the same length. State the rule used to determine this.

Problem Solving and Reasoning

12. **Communicate** Refer to the two triangles and find $m\overline{EF}$ if you can; if not, explain why not.

13. **Math Reasoning** The three angles of one triangle are congruent to the three angles of a second triangle. Are the triangles congruent? Explain.

14. **Critical Thinking** Truss bridges are built over canyons and rivers. The parts of the trusses are arranged in the form of triangles, as in the portion shown. Make a similar shape out of line segments. Then, taking as few measurements as possible (including at least one angle), finish your truss by adding a left half that is the mirror image of the right. What is the minimum number of measurements you need?

Mixed Review

Find the LCM for each pair of numbers. *[Lesson 7-3]*

15. 6, 20   **16.** 35, 40   **17.** 2, 10   **18.** 5, 12   **19.** 4, 15

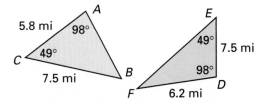

Graph each function and decide whether it is linear or quadratic. *[Lesson 10-3]*

20. $y = x^2 + 1$ **21.** $y = 4x$ **22.** $y = -x^2$ **23.** $y = (-x)^2$

Trigonometry

▶ Lesson Link You've seen various ways of finding missing side lengths of triangles. Now you'll learn another way. ◀

The longest side of a right triangle is the hypotenuse. You can refer to the two other sides in relationship to an acute angle.

The side next to ∠1 is the **adjacent leg**. The side across from ∠1 is the **opposite leg**.

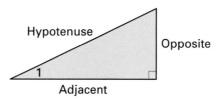

You'll Learn ...

■ to use ratios in order to find missing side lengths of a right triangle

... How It's Used

Navigators continuously calculate to determine the distance between their ship and their destination.

Explore | Trigonometric Ratios

Finding the Right Ratio

Materials: Dynamic geometry software, $8\frac{1}{2}$ in. by 11 in. paper

1. With the software, draw three similar right triangles. In each triangle, label one acute angle 1, 2, and 3.

2. On a sheet of paper, make a table with six columns labeled "angle," "opposite," "adjacent," "hypotenuse," " $\frac{\text{opposite}}{\text{hypotenuse}}$," and " $\frac{\text{adjacent}}{\text{hypotenuse}}$."

3. Record the measures of ∠1, ∠2, and ∠3 in the "angle" column.

4. Use the measure tool to find the length of each side of all three triangles and record your measurements in the table.

5. Use the measurements from Steps 3 and 4 to calculate and record the ratios for the remaining columns. Do you notice a pattern? Explain.

Vocabulary

adjacent leg

opposite leg

trigonometric ratios

sine

cosine

tangent

Learn | Trigonometry

As you have already learned, when triangles have two pairs of congruent angles and a corresponding pair of congruent sides, the triangles are congruent.

Now you will learn how to find the other sides of right triangles.

Example 1

Use the right triangle shown to answer each.

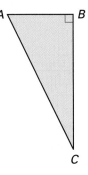

a. Name the hypotenuse. Answer: $\overline{AC}$

b. Name the leg opposite $\angle CAB$. Answer: $\overline{BC}$

c. Name the leg adjacent to $\angle CAB$. Answer: $\overline{AB}$

Try It

a. Name the hypotenuse.

b. Name the leg opposite $\angle MKL$.

c. Name the leg adjacent to $\angle MKL$.

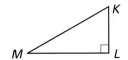

For any right triangle, the lengths of the hypotenuse, an adjacent leg, and an opposite leg may be compared by using three common **trigonometric ratios**.

TRIGONOMETRIC RATIOS

Sine

The sine of x is

$\sin(x) = \frac{\text{opposite}}{\text{hypotenuse}}$

Cosine

The cosine of x is

$\cos(x) = \frac{\text{adjacent}}{\text{hypotenuse}}$

Tangent

The tangent of x is

$\tan(x) = \frac{\text{opposite}}{\text{adjacent}}$

Example 2

For the triangle shown, evaluate the trigonometric ratios for $\angle CAB$.

$\sin \angle CAB = \dfrac{\text{opposite}}{\text{hypotenuse}} = \dfrac{3}{5} = 0.6$

$\cos \angle CAB = \dfrac{\text{adjacent}}{\text{hypotenuse}} = \dfrac{4}{5} = 0.8$

$\tan \angle CAB = \dfrac{\text{opposite}}{\text{adjacent}} = \dfrac{3}{4} = 0.75$

$\sin \angle CAB = 0.6 \qquad \cos \angle CAB = 0.8 \qquad \tan \angle CAB = 0.75$

Try It

Use the triangle in Example 2 to answer each question.

a. What is the sine ratio of $\angle ACB$?

b. What is the tangent ratio of $\angle ACB$?

Example 3

Use a calculator to find the cosine of $\angle BAC$.

Be sure that your calculator is set on degrees.

Enter 37 [cos].

The display reads **0.79863551**

$\cos 37° \approx 0.8$

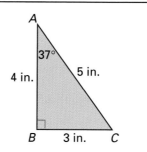

Using trigonometric ratios, we can find the unknown side lengths of a right triangle using one acute angle and one known side length.

Example 4

How high above ground level is the end of this drawbridge?

You're looking for the opposite leg and you know the hypotenuse, so use the sine ratio.

$\sin 45° = \dfrac{l}{150}$ Use a calculator.

$0.7071 \approx \dfrac{l}{150}$ Solve.

$106.066 \approx l$

The end of the drawbridge is about 106 ft high.

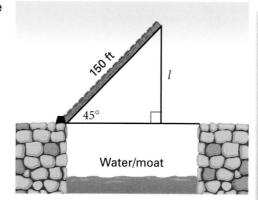

▶ **History Link**

In medieval times, a moat was dug around a castle and a lowered drawbridge was the only way into the castle.

Try It

a. Find the length of y on the right triangle.

b. Find the length of the hypotenuse.

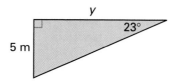

Check   Your Understanding

1. If you know the sine of one angle in a right triangle, what two sides do you know the ratio for? Explain.

2. What happens when you use your calculator to find the sine, cosine, and tangent of 90°?

3. How can the sine ratio for a given angle be the same no matter how big the triangle?

Practice and Apply

1. | **Getting Started** | Find the length of side $\overline{PQ}$ on the triangle shown.

    a. Is $\overline{QR}$ opposite or adjacent to $\angle QPR$?

    b. Is $\overline{PQ}$ opposite or adjacent to $\angle QPR$?

    c. Which ratio, sine, cosine, or tangent, compares the side opposite to the side adjacent?

    d. Use the ratio from 1c above to find the length of $\overline{PQ}$.

Use the lengths of the sides to write and evaluate the sine, cosine, and tangent ratios for each of the labeled angles.

2.

3.

4.

5. The top of a building forms a 68° angle with a point 250 m away from the building's base, as shown. How high is the building?

6. The head of this origami dinosaur forms a right triangle. For this triangle, what is the ratio of the length of the leg adjacent to the 35° angle and the length of the hypotenuse?

7. Find the length represented by x.

8. Find the length represented by k.

9. | **Test Prep** | Which represents the cosine of an angle in a right triangle?

    Ⓐ $\dfrac{\text{opposite}}{\text{adjacent}}$ Ⓑ $\dfrac{\text{adjacent}}{\text{hypotenuse}}$ Ⓒ $\dfrac{\text{hypotenuse}}{\text{opposite}}$ Ⓓ None of these

10. Science A model rocket travels straight up from its launch pad. At a point, there is a 55° angle. Determine the distance between the nose of the rocket and the launch pad.

55°
100 ft

Problem Solving and Reasoning

11. Critical Thinking The New River Gorge Bridge in West Virginia has the world's longest single steel span, arching 876 ft above the river. The bridge forms a 30° angle with the side of the gorge. How long is the bridge?

876 ft

30°

12. Communicate Suppose two right triangles have a pair of congruent acute angles. Are the triangles similar? Are they congruent? Explain.

13. Geometry Construct a right triangle with a 60° angle. Then measure all three sides. Use your calculator to find the sine, cosine, and tangent of 60°.

14. Choose a Strategy A right triangle has a 15° angle and the adjacent side is 6 ft. A classmate calculates that the length of the opposite leg is 1.6 ft and the hypotenuse is 7 ft. Check your classmate's calculations and make corrections if necessary.

Mixed Review

Write each as a fraction or mixed number in lowest terms. *[Lesson 7-4]*

15. 2.02　　**16.** 0.05　　**17.** 4.24　　**18.** 1.33　　**19.** 9.9

Identify each function as linear, quadratic, exponential, or step. *[Lesson 10-4]*

20. $y = 0.5x^2$　　**21.** $y = 0.5^x$　　**22.** $y = 5$　　**23.** $y = 5x$

Problem Solving
STRATEGIES

- Look for a Pattern
- Make an Organized List
- Make a Table
- Guess and Check
- Work Backward
- Use Logical Reasoning
- Draw a Diagram
- Solve a Simpler Problem

Project Progress

Stand the 3 in. by 5 in. card on the 3 in. side. Cut a slit the width of one ruler above the bottom of the card. Fold the longer flap vertically so it makes a right angle. Along the crease of the flap, mark $\frac{1}{2}$ in. lengths. Tape the ruler-width part of the card onto a ruler.

Problem Solving

Understand
Plan
Solve
Look Back

Indirect Measurement

You'll Learn ...

■ to apply your knowledge of geometry and trigonometric ratios

... How It's Used

Paleontologists use indirect measurement to figure out what the size of a living dinosaur was based on bone measurements.

▶ **Lesson Link**   You've seen how to find the side lengths of right triangles using trigonometric ratios. Now you'll apply these ratios to real-world situations. ◀

Explore   **Indirect Measurement**

It's Not What You Know, It's Where You Know It

Materials: Dynamic geometry software, $8\frac{1}{2}$ in. by 11 in. paper

1. Draw two parallel lines. Draw two transversals that are perpendicular to each other.

2. Label all intersection points.

3. On paper, make a table with three columns. Label the columns "part," "measurement," and "reason."

4. In the first column of your table, list all sides and all angles of both triangles that appear in your drawing.

5. Measure all angles and all side lengths of these two triangles. Enter the results in the second column of your table.

6. Find as many other side and angle measurements as you can and enter them in your table's second column. For each measurement, use the third column of your table to briefly state how you got the measurement.

7. Discuss the results with your group. How many angle measurements could you find? How many side measurements?

8. What was listed most frequently in the third column of your table?

Learn   **Indirect Measurement**

Sometimes a length can't be measured with a ruler. Often you can find the measurement indirectly.

When solving a problem with similar triangles, you can use the similarity ratio.

Example 1

Part of a bridge roadway is 150 m long. On its scale model, the corresponding length is 2 m. On the same model, a cable from the roadway to the top of a tower is almost 2.17 m. How long is the actual cable?

2.17 m

2 m

The triangles on the bridge and model are similar.

$\frac{150}{2} = 75$ Use a ratio to find the scale factor.

$75 \cdot 2.17 = 162.75$ m

The cable is almost 163 m long.

Example 2

Megan, who is 5 ft tall, stands in the shadow of a redwood tree. Megan is 388 ft from the tree and her shadow is 7 ft long. If the tip of Megan's shadow and the tree's shadow are at the same point on the ground, how tall is the tree?

5 ft

x

7 ft   388 ft

The diagram shows the similar triangles.

$7 + 388 = 395$ ft   Find the length of the tree's shadow.

$\frac{x}{395} = \frac{5}{7}$ Set up a proportion and solve.

$x \approx 282$

The tree is approximately 282 ft tall.

> ▶ **Literature Link**
>
> Author John Steinbeck referred to redwood trees as "ambassadors from another time."
>
>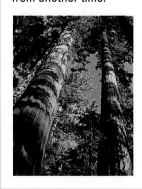

Try It

Find the length of the base of the larger triangle. The triangles are similar.

2.5 cm

5.0 cm

1.0 cm

Example 3

$\triangle TSR \sim \triangle TUV$. Find the length of $\overline{RT}$.

Identify the corresponding sides.

$\overline{UV}$ corresponds to $\overline{SR}$.

$\overline{VT}$ corresponds to $\overline{RT}$.

$\dfrac{x}{56} = \dfrac{15}{52.5}$ Set up a proportion and solve.

$x = 16$

The length of $\overline{RT}$ is 16 mm.

Try It

In the figure, the triangles are similar.

Find x.

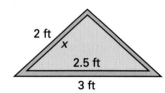

When you solve a problem with right triangles, you can use trigonometric ratios.

Example 4

A person on a boat sees a seagull perched on a bridge 22° above the horizon. The boat is 800 ft from the bridge. How far is the seagull from the passenger?

The passenger's line of vision forms a hypotenuse.

The adjacent side is 800 ft with respect to the 22° angle.

$\cos 22° = \dfrac{800}{h}$ Use the cosine to set up a proportion.

$0.927 \approx \dfrac{800}{h}$ Use a calculator to find cos 22°.

$0.927 \cdot h \approx 800$ Solve.

$h \approx 863$

The distance is about 863 ft.

Find the height of the larger triangle.

45°

15 ft

|15 ft|

75 ft

h

WHAT DO YOU THINK ?

Mary thinks ...

The vertical line is 15 ft tall and is 15 ft from the 45° angle. Using similar triangles, I find that the height is $\frac{1125}{15}$ ft or 75 ft.

Enrique thinks ...

I used the tangent of 45° and my calculator: $\tan(45°) = 1$.

Solving the proportion $1 = \frac{h}{75}$, I find that the height must be 75 ft.

What do you think?

1. Determine a similar situation in which only Mary's method would work to solve the problem.

2. Determine a similar situation in which only Enrique's method would work to solve the problem.

3. Is there another way to find the answer? Explain.

Check   Your Understanding

1. Suppose a real-world problem requires the height of some object that can't be measured directly. Which method is easier to use, similarity ratios or trigonometry? Explain.

2. What do we mean by indirect measurement?

Practice and Apply

1. **Getting Started** Find the length of $\overline{EG}$.
   a. Determine the length of $\overline{GF}$.
   b. Set up and solve a proportion using the given lengths of the similar triangles.

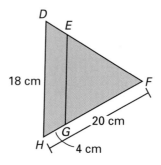

18 cm

20 cm

4 cm

2. Find the length of side $\overline{BC}$.

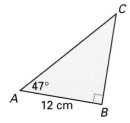

47°
12 cm

3. Find the length of side $\overline{UV}$.

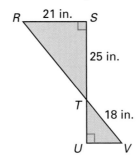

21 in.

25 in.

18 in.

4. Find the length of side $\overline{LM}$.

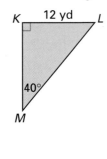

12 yd

40°

5. **Test Prep** On the two triangles shown, $\triangle CBD \sim \triangle CAE$. If $\overline{CD}$ measures 5 cm, what does $\overline{CE}$ measure?

Ⓐ 7.6 cm   Ⓑ 7.3 cm   Ⓒ 7.1 cm   Ⓓ 7.9 cm

7 cm

11 cm

6. **Marine Navigation** A ship near shore measures the compass heading to a lighthouse as 50° east of north. It also measures the compass heading to an oil refinery as 90° east of north. The refinery is known to be 4 mi directly south of the lighthouse. How far is the ship from the lighthouse? From the refinery? (Start by applying your knowledge of parallel lines and alternate interior angles.)

4 mi

50°

Problem Solving and Reasoning

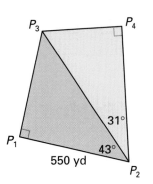

7. **Algebra** A surveying team plots two points, P_1 and P_2, 550 yd apart. It then plots two more points, P_3 and P_4, and measures four angles, as shown. How far apart are P_3 and P_4?

8. **Patterns** The points $A(1, 1)$; $B(4, 1)$; and $C(4, 5)$ form a triangle when connected. Compare the slope of $\overline{AC}$ to the tangent of $\angle CAB$.

Communicate Use the diagram of the house to answer these questions.

9. Suppose you know that $\angle A$ measures $22°$. How can you find s?

10. Suppose instead of $m\angle A$, you know that $d = 20$ ft. Explain how you could find s.

11. How many similar triangles are identified? Describe where they are.

12. **Estimation** The rope between a parasailer and the boat is 600 ft long and forms a $30°$ angle with the water. About how far above the water is the parasailer?

13. **Number Sense** Suppose you use a trigonometric ratio to find a length measurement on a bridge. Why will your measurement be only an approximation?

14. **Math Reasoning** Draw a right triangle with a $45°$ angle. Find the cos $45°$ and sin $45°$ and use your drawing to explain their relationship.

Mixed Review

Add or subtract. Write each answer in lowest terms. *[Lesson 7-5]*

15. $0.219 - 0.043$

16. $128.6 + 204.7$

17. $\dfrac{5}{8} - \dfrac{3}{16}$

18. $3\dfrac{7}{8} + 4\dfrac{6}{8}$

Write each polynomial expression in descending order and find its degree.
[Lesson 10-5]

19. $2x + 5 - 3x^2$

20. $x^4 + 4x - 2x^2$

21. $3x - x^2 - x^3 - 3$

22. $x^5 + x^{10}$

T E C H N O L O G Y

Using a Search Engine • Searching the World Wide Web

Problem: Search for documents related to music, then search for documents about music and not opera. What is the difference between the number of documents found in each search?

Search engines have different ways to search. For example, typing "music NOT opera" or "music–opera" are just two possible ways to search for music except for opera. Learn how your favorite search engine works so you can answer the question.

① **After you've learned what you need to know about a search engine, search for music. Record the number of matching documents found.**

Search! found **1362470** documents
about: **music**.
Documents **1–10** sorted by **confidence**

65% **Music**

② **Search for music except for opera using the appropriate keystrokes. Record the number of matching documents.**

Search! found **1277440** documents
about: **music NOT opera**.
Documents **1–10** sorted by **confidence**

57% **Music NOT Opera**

Solution: The music except for opera search had 85,030 less documents than the music search.

ON YOUR OWN

TRY IT

a. What would you type if you're looking for information about boats that don't have sails?

b. If you wanted information about all mammals except for whales, what would you type in your search?

▶ Describe how *not* affects a search. Why does the number of matching documents decrease?

▶ Search engines usually use commands that act like the words *or, and,* and *not.* Give three examples of a search each using one of these words.

Section 11A Connect

At the beginning of Section 11A, you saw that geometry is used in the design and construction of bridges. Now you'll construct a model of your own bridge design using what you know about geometry.

Un-a-bridged

Materials: Toothpicks, Scissors, Tape, Ruler

Before bridges are built in the real world, scale models are made using proportions. You can build a model bridge out of toothpicks.

Your group is a team of people hired to design and build a bridge.

Warren Truss

Pratt Truss

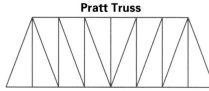

1. Decide on a bridge design that includes congruent and similar triangles. Choose from the two designs shown, or make your own.

2. Determine the toothpick measurements for the model bridge. Use your ruler, scissors, and tape to construct the necessary lengths.

3. When you are finished constructing your model bridge, count the pairs of similar triangles. How many pairs can you find? How do you know that these are similar pairs? Do the same for congruent triangles.

4. How many pairs of congruent triangles can you find? How do you know that they are congruent?

5. How many right triangles are used in your bridge? Are they all congruent to each other? How do you know?

6. Push gently on your bridge. Can it support a load? Would the result have been different if you had based your bridge on parallelograms instead of triangles? Explain.

7. Is there a place on your bridge where both sides are mirror images of each other? If so, where is it and what would your bridge be like without this feature?

1. The trapezoids are similar. Find the length represented by *x*.

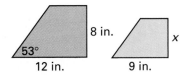

8 in.
53°
12 in.
x
9 in.

2. Measure to determine if the two pentagons are congruent.

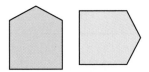

State whether each pair is congruent and the rule that justifies your answer.

3.

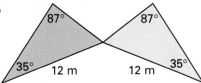

87° 87°
35° 12 m 12 m 35°

4.

51° 51°
7.5 cm 7.5 cm

5. A lens casts a 3 in. image of a tree onto a sheet of paper. The image is 5 in. from the lens, and the lens is 10 ft from the tree. Find the object's size.

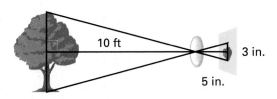

10 ft
3 in.
5 in.

6. **Journal** Suppose you're given the hypotenuse length of a right triangle and the measure of one of the acute angles. How would you use this information to prove congruence to another triangle by the Angle-Side-Angle method?

7. A tornado watcher spots the top of a funnel cloud 14° above the horizon as the funnel crosses a lake 2.5 mi away. How high is the top of the funnel to the nearest 10 ft?

Test Prep

On a multiple choice test, be careful not to confuse similar figures and congruent figures. Also, when finding a missing part of similar triangles, check to make sure the proportion is set up correctly.

8. $\triangle ABC \sim \triangle DEF$. What is the length of $\overline{EF}$?

   Ⓐ 3.75 in.   Ⓑ 1 in.

   Ⓒ 4.4 in.   Ⓓ 5.4 in.

A
16 in.
B 6 in. *C*
E 10 in. *D*
F

REVIEW 11A

Transformations

Doing What Comes Naturally

"He's a born comedian." "She was born to be in the Olympics." When people say things like that, they mean that you were born with certain abilities.

The use of geometric shapes and patterns in centuries-old Native American art is an example of talents with which the artisan seemed to be born. We can be fairly certain he or she never studied geometry as you are doing.

Native American artisans have found that a repeating pattern is especially fitting when the work already involves repetition. The repetition involved in the work includes adding rows of colored threads to a woven blanket or sewing rows of beads to a decorative vest. A repeating design usually consists of repetitions of the same basic shape. The differences between shapes—their location and orientation—are related to transformations of the shapes.

1 What shapes do you see in this Native American design?

2 Choose a shape of your own and draw a design by repeating your shape.

593

11-6 Transformations and Congruence

You'll Learn ...

■ to move all the points of a figure and still have a congruent shape

... How It's Used

Transformations are the basis for patterns in art and architectural design.

Vocabulary

transformation

reflection

rotation

center of rotation

angle of rotation

translation

▶ **Lesson Link** You've seen many types of polygons. Now you will explore what happens when polygons are flipped or moved. ◀

A **transformation** is an operation that affects all points of a figure, such as a slide, flip, or turn.

You've seen your reflection in a mirror or in water. In math, a **reflection** is a transformation that flips a figure over a line.

A reflection is congruent to the original figure.

Reflection

Explore | Reflections

Time to Reflect
Materials: Dynamic geometry software

1. Display the x- and y-axes and draw a rectangle in the first quadrant.

2. Use the reflection tool to reflect the rectangle with respect to the y-axis.

3. Find the coordinates of each vertex of both rectangles. Identify corresponding vertices.

4. Is there a pattern between the x-coordinates of the corresponding corners? The y-coordinates?

5. Draw a polygon, reflect it with respect to the x-axis, and find the pattern between the coordinates of corresponding vertices. What can you conclude about reflections with respect to the y-axis? The x-axis?

Learn | Transformations and Congruence

A **rotation** is a transformation that turns a figure about a point called a **center of rotation**. The **angle of rotation** is the angle of the turn. A rotated image of a figure is congruent to the original figure.

The transformation of a figure is labeled using prime notation for the corresponding vertices. For example, A corresponds to A'.

594 *Chapter 11 • Similarity, Congruence, and Transformations*

Example 1

The origin is the center of rotation. Rotate trapezoid *ABCD* clockwise 90° and 270° and give the vertex coordinates for each.

Use $\overline{CD}$ as a guide to rotate the trapezoid. $D(0, 0)$ is the center of rotation.

$A'B'C'D'$ is the result of the 90° rotation.

$A'(2, -1)$　　$B'(2, -3)$　　$C'(0, -4)$　　$D'(0, 0)$

$A''B''C''D''$ is the result of the 270° rotation.

$A''(-2, 1)$　　$B''(-2, 3)$　　$C''(0, 4)$　　$D''(0, 0)$

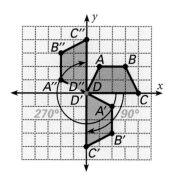

Try It

This pattern is from the Native American baskets of British Columbia. Rotate the figure clockwise 180° and 360°. Use the origin as the center of rotation and find the vertex coordinates.

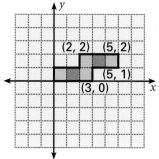

▶ **History Link**

The swamps and forests of British Columbia, Canada, were a great resource for many regional tribes known for their basket weaving.

A transformation that slides all points of a figure the same distance in the same direction is called a **translation**. All *x*- and *y*-coordinates of a translated figure change by adding or subtracting. A translated image of a figure is congruent to its original figure.

Example 2

The vertices of a triangle are $A(2, 5)$, $B(4, 2)$, and $C(0, 2)$.

Give the vertices of $\triangle ABC$ translated to the right 4 units and up 2.

On the *x*-axis, "right" is a positive direction, so add 4 to each *x*-coordinate.

On the *y*-axis, "up" is a positive direction, so **add 2** to each *y*-coordinate.

Locate points *A*, *B*, *C* and draw $\triangle ABC$.

$$
\begin{array}{ccc}
\triangle ABC & (x + 4, y + 2) & \triangle A'B'C' \\
\downarrow & \downarrow & \downarrow \\
A(2, 5) \rightarrow & (2 + 4, 5 + 2) \rightarrow & A'(6, 7) \\
B(4, 2) \rightarrow & (4 + 4, 2 + 2) \rightarrow & B'(8, 4) \\
C(0, 2) \rightarrow & (0 + 4, 2 + 2) \rightarrow & C'(4, 4)
\end{array}
$$

Label corresponding vertices A', B', and C'.

The coordinates of $\triangle A'B'C'$ are $A'(6, 7)$, $B'(8, 4)$, and $C'(4, 4)$.

A reflection across the *x*-axis changes the sign of each *y*-coordinate.

A reflection across the *y*-axis changes the sign of each *x*-coordinate.

Example 3

△*ABC* has coordinates *A*(3, 5), *B*(6, 1), and *C*(1, 2). Reflect △*ABC* across the *x*-axis and determine the coordinates of △*A'B'C'*.

Each *y*-coordinate changes because the reflection is across the *x*-axis.

Plot the vertices of △*A'B'C'* and draw the triangle.

△*ABC y*-coordinates are positive.

So △*A'B'C' y*-coordinates are negative.

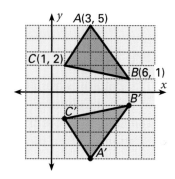

△*ABC*		(*x*, −*y*)		△*A'B'C'*
↓		↓		↓
A(3, 5)	→	(3, −5)	→	*A'*(3, −5)
B(6, 1)	→	(6, −1)	→	*B'*(6, −1)
C(1, 2)	→	(1, −2)	→	*C'*(1, −2)

Example 4

Reflect Figure *STUV* across the *y*-axis and determine the coordinates of *S'T'U'V'*. The sign of each *x*-coordinate changes because the reflection is across the *y*-axis.

Plot and draw *S'T'U'V'*.

S'T'U'V' x-coordinates are positive.

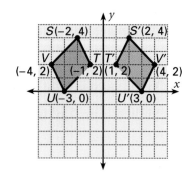

$S(-2, 4) \rightarrow S'(2, 4)$

$T(-1, 2) \rightarrow T'(1, 2)$

$U(-3, 0) \rightarrow U'(3, 0)$

$V(-4, 2) \rightarrow V'(4, 2)$

Try It

This pattern can be found in ancient Pueblo pottery. Determine the vertex coordinates of *A* and *B* after each reflection.

a. Reflect Figure *A* across the *x*-axis.

b. Reflect Figure *B* across the *y*-axis.

Rotate the figure clockwise 180° using the vertex of the right angle as the center of rotation.

Shauna thinks ...

I'll use the vertical side as a reference. If that line swings around 180°, the fan will look like this.

Julio thinks ...

Let's see. I can use either the horizontal or vertical side as a reference.

I'll use the horizontal side. After rotating 180°, that side will be oriented horizontally.

What do you think?

1. Explain why Julio said he could use either the horizontal or vertical side as a reference for his rotation.

2. Explain why Shauna and Julio got the same result.

Check | Your Understanding

1. Describe how a figure's coordinates change after the figure is translated to the left on a coordinate grid.

2. Describe how a figure's coordinates change after the figure is reflected across the y-axis.

Practice and Apply

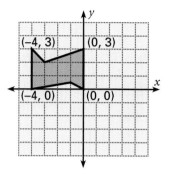

1. **Getting Started** Rotate the blue image clockwise 90°. What are the new coordinates? Use the origin as the center of rotation.

   a. Turn the figure to the right so the vertex on the origin stays there.

   b. Plot the new vertex coordinates.

   c. Identify the new vertex coordinates.

2. What transformation of the blue T-shirt gives the yellow T-shirt?

3. What transformation of the pink shoe gives the yellow shoe?

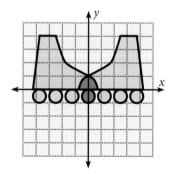

4. **Geometry** Find the coordinates of points A and B on the trapezoid that has been translated 1.5 units left and 4.5 units up.

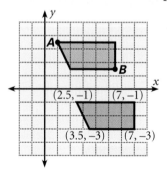

5. Across which axis was the figure reflected?

6. **Social Studies** The Yurok people of northern California wove intricate baskets using plants such as sourgrass. On the basket, what transformations do the parallelograms and triangles exhibit?

7. **Test Prep** Some of these happy faces are transformations of each other. Which two are translations of each other?

Ⓐ 2 and 3   Ⓑ 3 and 7   Ⓒ 2 and 7   Ⓓ 4 and 6

Problem Solving and Reasoning

8. Algebra The blue rhombus has been reflected across the y-axis. Give a general rule for changing coordinates (x, y) of the blue rhombus into corresponding coordinates on the green one.

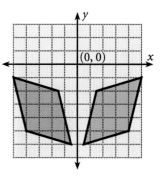

Critical Thinking What transformations, if any, will turn each collection of shapes into a math word you've recently learned? (Turning the book and using a mirror may help you decide.)

9. ROTATE   **10.** REFLECT   **11.** TRANSLATE

12. **Journal** Describe how two different transformations can result in the same image and provide an example.

13. Math Reasoning Is there a transformation that changes a parallelogram into a trapezoid? Explain.

14. Communicate Explain the difference between reflections and rotations. Provide a sketch as an example.

Mixed Review

Multiply or divide. Write each answer in lowest terms. *[Lesson 7-6]*

15. 26.9×14.2 **16.** 0.081×-0.9 **17.** $\frac{4}{7} \times \frac{4}{9}$ **18.** $12 \times \frac{5}{6}$

19. $2.04 \div 3$ **20.** $44 \div \frac{1}{4}$ **21.** $9\frac{1}{3} \div \frac{3}{28}$ **22.** $-4.5 \div -2.25$

Add. Simplify if possible. *[Lesson 10-6]*

23. $(2x^2 + 4x + 5) + (x^3 + 5x^2 - 4x - 7)$ **24.** $(8p^5 - p^2) + (2p^5 + 4p^3 + 11)$

You'll Learn ...

■ to transform a figure and have a shape that is similar to but not congruent to the original

... How It's Used

Photo developers create similar figures when creating enlargements.

▶ **Lesson Link**   You've seen how transformations result in congruent figures. Now you'll use a transformation that results in a figure that is similar to but not congruent to the original. ◀

Explore | Dilations

This Is Getting Expansive

Materials: Graph paper, Ruler

This design is adapted from Sioux art. It represents six directions: east (red), west (yellow), north (blue), south (black), up, and down.

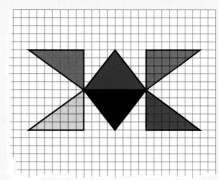

1. Copy this figure onto graph paper.

2. On another piece of graph paper, draw a scale drawing of this design using a scale factor of 2.

3. Is each of the six triangles of the dilated design congruent to its corresponding triangle of the original design? Is it similar? Explain.

Learn | Transformations and Similarity

The coordinates of a dilation on the coordinate plane can be determined by multiplying every coordinate by the scale factor.

Example 1

Use a scale factor of 2 to dilate △ABC. Give the vertex coordinates of the dilation.

$$
\begin{array}{ccccc}
\triangle ABC & & (2 \cdot x, 2 \cdot y) & & \triangle A'B'C' \\
\downarrow & & \downarrow & & \downarrow \\
A(2, 1) & \rightarrow & (2 \cdot 2, 2 \cdot 1) & \rightarrow & A'(4, 2) \\
B(2, 4) & \rightarrow & (2 \cdot 2, 2 \cdot 4) & \rightarrow & B'(4, 8) \\
C(4, 3) & \rightarrow & (2 \cdot 4, 2 \cdot 3) & \rightarrow & C'(8, 6)
\end{array}
$$

A scale factor greater than 1 causes an enlargement, whereas a positive nonzero scale factor less than 1 causes a reduction.

▶ **Language Link**

The prefix *non-* means "not."

So "*x* is a nonzero number" means $x \neq 0$.

Example 2

Use a scale factor of $\frac{1}{3}$ to dilate Figure *KLMN*. Give the coordinates of the vertices that correspond to *KLMN*.

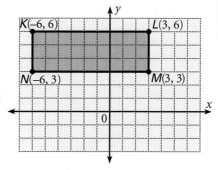

Find the new vertex coordinates, then plot the dilated figure.

$$KLMN \qquad \left(\frac{1}{3} \cdot x, \frac{1}{3} \cdot y\right) \qquad K'L'M'N'$$

$$\downarrow \qquad\qquad \downarrow \qquad\qquad \downarrow$$

$$K(-6, 6) \rightarrow \left(\frac{1}{3} \cdot -6, \frac{1}{3} \cdot 6\right) \rightarrow K'(-2, 2)$$

$$L(3, 6) \;\;\rightarrow \left(\frac{1}{3} \cdot 3, \frac{1}{3} \cdot 6\right) \;\;\rightarrow L'(1, 2)$$

$$M(3, 3) \;\;\rightarrow \left(\frac{1}{3} \cdot 3, \frac{1}{3} \cdot 3\right) \;\;\rightarrow M'(1, 1)$$

$$N(-6, 3) \rightarrow \left(\frac{1}{3} \cdot -6, \frac{1}{3} \cdot 3\right) \rightarrow N'(-2, 1)$$

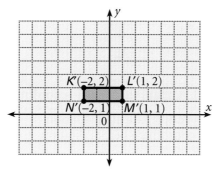

Try It

Find the new vertex coordinates after each dilation.

a. Use a scale factor of 2.5.

b. Use a scale factor of $\frac{2}{3}$.

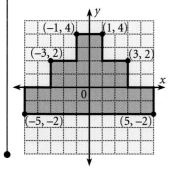

Example 3

The point *A'*(4, 12) is on a polygon that has been dilated by a scale factor of 4. What are the coordinates of the corresponding point *A*?

$(4 \div 4, 12 \div 4) \rightarrow A(1, 3)$ Divide *A'* coordinates by 4.

If you have a figure and its dilation and you know the coordinates of corresponding vertices, then you can find the scale factor of the dilation.

▶ **Geography Link**

Native American tribes of the Northwest are known for using animal designs in wood carvings. They also used animal names for geometric designs, such as "snake track" or "grasshopper."

Example 4

The design shown here is one of many from Northwest American tribes that are based on diagonal lines.

Find the scale factor of the dilation by comparing corresponding vertices.

Compare the x- or y-coordinates of $A(-3, 3)$ and $A'(-1, 1)$.

$$\frac{\text{coordinate after dilation}}{\text{coordinate before dilation}} = \frac{-1}{-3} = \frac{1}{3}$$

The scale factor of the dilation is $\frac{1}{3}$.

Try It

a. Find the scale factor of the dilation of Figure A to Figure B.

b. Find the scale factor of the dilation of Figure B to Figure A.

Check | Your Understanding

1. Before drawing a dilation, how can you tell whether it will be an enlargement or a reduction?

2. If Figure X is a dilation of Figure Y, can Y also be a dilation of X? Explain.

3. What happens to the coordinates of a figure after a dilation of a scale factor of 1?

Practice and Apply

1. **Getting Started** Which two figures are dilations of each other?

2. Trapezoid 2 is a dilation of trapezoid 1. Classify the dilation as a reduction or an enlargement, and find the scale factor.

3. The smaller hand is a dilation of the larger hand. Classify the dilation as a reduction or an enlargement, and find the scale factor.

4. **a.** Use a scale factor of $\frac{1}{3}$ to dilate pentagon *ABCDE*. Find the coordinates of the vertices of the dilation.

   b. Graph pentagon $A'B'C'D'E'$.

5. **Test Prep** Which of the following properties does *not* remain the same after a dilation?

   Ⓐ Angle measure   Ⓑ Side length

   Ⓒ Orientation   Ⓓ Shape

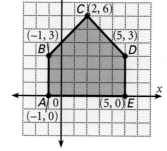

6. Complete the sentence: Two figures with the same shape but different sizes are _____ but not _____.

7. An image on a photo can be considered a dilation of the figure on a negative. A typical negative is $1\frac{1}{4}$ in. by $\frac{7}{8}$ in. What is the scale factor if the photo is 6 in. by 4.2 in?

8. A figure on a coordinate grid includes the points $K(-3, 5)$; $L(2, 0)$; and $M(4, 2)$. What are the coordinates of the corresponding points after a dilation of:

   a. 3   **b.** 0.6   **c.** $\frac{1}{4}$ **d.** 2.5

9. Draw an enlargement of this Native American symbol for "lizard" with a scale factor of $2\frac{1}{2}$.

10. Draw a reduction of this figure using a scale factor of 0.5.

Problem Solving and Reasoning

Measurement Reduce $\triangle ABC$ by a scale factor of $\frac{3}{4}$.

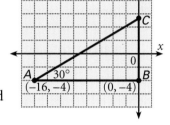

11. How long is side $\overline{A'B'}$?   **12.** What are the coordinates of vertex A'?

13. a. Technology Using geometry software with x- and y-axes showing, draw a polygon that crosses at least one axis. Dilate the figure by a scale factor of 2 and use $(0, 0)$ as the center. Display all vertex coordinates and divide the corresponding x-coordinates. What do you find?

b. Communicate Is this ratio what you would have expected? Explain.

Critical Thinking Use the figure to answer Exercises 14 and 15.

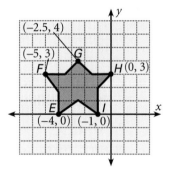

14. Reflect the figure across the y-axis and give the new coordinates.

15. Use a scale factor of 2 to enlarge the reflection. What are the new vertex coordinates? Graph the enlargement.

Mixed Review

Determine each square root and write in lowest terms. *[Lesson 7-7]*

16. $\sqrt{\dfrac{36}{49}}$ **17.** $\sqrt{\dfrac{4}{9}}$ **18.** $\sqrt{\dfrac{121}{16}}$ **19.** $\sqrt{\dfrac{64}{81}}$ **20.** $\sqrt{\dfrac{169}{144}}$

Write the additive inverse of each polynomial. *[Lesson 10-7]*

21. $-2x^3 + 4x^2 - 2x + 5$ **22.** $4x^4 - (x^2 + 8)$ **23.** $x^2 - (-5x - 2)$

Project Progress

What object will you measure and how far away from it will you be?

Problem Solving

Understand
Plan
Solve
Look Back

Symmetry

▶ **Lesson Link**   You've seen how transformations affect figures. Now you'll see how transformations can show whether a figure has symmetry. ◀

A figure has **symmetry** if it coincides with itself after a transformation.

A figure has **line symmetry** if there is a **line of symmetry** that divides the figure into two identical halves. Line symmetry is based on the reflection.

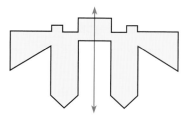

You'll Learn ...

■ to recognize several types of symmetry

... How It's Used

Luthiers, people who make and repair string instruments, use concepts of symmetry to craft instruments that allow the strings to vibrate properly.

Explore   **Line Symmetry**

The Splittin' Image

Materials: $8\frac{1}{2}$ in. by 11 in. paper, Scissors

1. Fold a sheet of paper in half. At a point on one side of the fold, draw a curved line that starts and finishes on the fold.

2. With the paper folded, cut along the line you drew. Compare each side of the fold and describe what happened after you cut the shape. What is the line of symmetry?

3. Fold a fresh sheet of paper in half, then fold it in half again. Draw a curved line that begins on one fold and ends on the other. Cut along the line. How many lines of symmetry does it have?

Vocabulary

symmetry

line symmetry

line of symmetry

rotational symmetry

point symmetry

Learn   **Symmetry**

Example 1

Which line is a line of symmetry?

$\overleftrightarrow{AR}$, because it separates mirror images.

Example 2

How many lines of symmetry does the figure have?

Find every line that produces a mirror image.

The figure has three lines of symmetry.

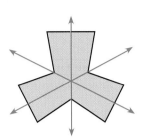

A figure has **rotational symmetry** if it can be rotated onto itself after a rotation of less than 360°.

 120°

▶ **Fine Arts Link**

Pottery samples from the various Southwest Native American tribes appear very similar, except to an expert, who will look closely at the decorations to determine the artisans.

Example 3

Does the painted design of an ancient Pueblo bowl have rotational symmetry? If so, after how many degrees of rotation does the pattern rotate onto itself?

Rotate the design to see if the pattern coincides.

Try 90° clockwise.

A 90° rotation works!

The Pueblo design has rotational symmetry because the pattern coincides after a 90° rotation.

The design also coincides after a 180° or 270° rotation.

90°

Try It

a. How many lines of symmetry does the figure have?

b. Does the figure have rotational symmetry? If so, after how many degrees of rotation does it rotate onto itself?

A figure has **point symmetry**, a specific type of rotational symmetry, when it rotates onto itself after a rotation of exactly 180°.

Example 4

Does this central piece of a Navajo sand painting have point symmetry?

Rotate the figure 180°.

Yes, the sand painting design has point symmetry.

Example 5

What kinds of symmetry does the figure have?

It has two lines of symmetry.
Check for line symmetry.

It has rotational symmetry for 180°.
Check for rotational symmetry.

It has point symmetry also.

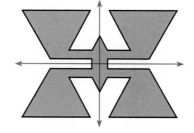

Try It

What kinds of symmetry does this hurricane symbol have?

▶ **Science Link**

According to the Beaufort scale of wind effects, a hurricane is in action when the wind speed is 73 mi/hr or more. The Beaufort number for a hurricane is 12.

Check | Your Understanding

1. Describe the relationship between a figure with a line of symmetry and a reflection.

2. How many lines of symmetry does a circle have? Explain.

3. If a figure has rotational symmetry, is it guaranteed to have point symmetry? Explain.

Practice and Apply

1. **Getting Started** In each of the following, which lines are *not* lines of symmetry?

a.

b.

c.

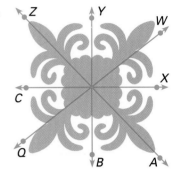

2. **History** Mound builders built large monuments made of earth between 1000 B.C. and A.D. 700. Artifacts of their life and culture have been found within these mounds. What kinds of symmetry are in this prehistoric plate pattern found in Tennessee? Sketch the plate and identify any lines of symmetry and rotation points.

Ohio Serpent Mound, Adena culture

3. **Test Prep** Which rotation will give the same result as a rotation 90° clockwise?

Ⓐ 90° counterclockwise   Ⓑ 180° counterclockwise

Ⓒ 270° counterclockwise   Ⓓ 360° counterclockwise

4. How many degrees does it take for a regular octagon to rotate onto itself?

5. How many degrees does it take for an equilateral triangle to rotate onto itself?

6. a. How many degrees could you rotate this Alaskan star pattern around its center to produce an identical figure?

b. Does the pattern have rotational symmetry?

7. Science There are 400 species of the passion flower, some of which bear fruit. How many lines of symmetry does this passion flower have?

Copy each letter and draw any and all lines of symmetry.

8. A **9. E** **10. W** **11. Z**

12. The word "TOOT" has a vertical line of symmetry. Find at least three other words that have a vertical line of symmetry.

Problem Solving and Reasoning

This deer pattern appears on a woven bag used by the Winnebago tribe for storing dried food.

13. Patterns Are there similar figures? Congruent figures? Explain.

14. Communicate What kind of symmetry, if any, does the overall pattern have? Explain.

15. Math Reasoning How could you transform a deer in the upper row to create one in the bottom row?

16. You can think of point symmetry as a reflection across a point instead of a line. Explain how a reflection across a point works and then compare it to a 180° rotation.

17. Choose a Strategy Draw a figure with four lines of symmetry.

Mixed Review

Identify each of these numbers as rational or irrational. *[Lesson 7-8]*

18. $\sqrt{5}$ **19.** $\sqrt{22}$ **20.** $0.\overline{45}$ **21.** $\dfrac{\sqrt{36}}{6}$ **22.** 0.343443444

Find each product. Write your answers in scientific notation. *[Lesson 10-8]*

23. $(8.6 \times 10^4) \cdot (6.7 \times 10^9)$ **24.** $(3.0 \times 10^6) \cdot (2.9 \times 10^3)$

25. $(1.1 \times 10^2) \cdot (4.9 \times 10^5)$ **26.** $(3.2 \times 10^5) \cdot (1.3 \times 10^2)$

Problem Solving
STRATEGIES

• Look for a Pattern
• Make an Organized List
• Make a Table
• Guess and Check
• Work Backward
• Use Logical Reasoning
• Draw a Diagram
• Solve a Simpler Problem

Covering the Plane

You'll Learn ...

■ to create endless patterns using transformations

... How It's Used

Fabric designers make one pattern that, when trans-lated, creates a continuous pattern that can be printed on many yards of fabric.

Vocabulary

tessellation

▶ **Lesson Link** You'll use what you know about transformations that produce congruent figures to cover flat surfaces in interesting and attractive patterns. ◀

Explore Tessellations

Seeing Double, Triple, Quadruple ...

Materials: Graph paper, Power polygons

1. Trace the outline of one shape onto graph paper. Trace more outlines of that shape to make a pattern without gaps or overlaps.

2. Use another polygon to make another pattern without gaps or overlaps.

3. When did you use translations? Rotations?

4. Describe how the properties of each shape affected your use of translations or rotations.

5. Use both shapes together to draw another pattern without gaps or overlaps.

Learn Covering the Plane

A **tessellation** is a repeating pattern of figures that covers a plane (flat surface) without gaps or overlaps.

Example 1

Is the woven thunderbird design from the Winnebago tribe a tessellation?

No, because there are gaps between the thunderbird shapes.

Example 2

Is the design made by M. C. Escher, the artist, a tessellation?

Yes, because there are no gaps or overlaps.

Many tessellations are made by rotating, reflecting, or translating one shape again and again.

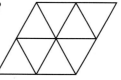

Symmetry Drawing E20 by M. C. Escher.
©1996 Cordon Art-Baarn-Holland.
All rights reserved.

Example 3

What transformation is used to make this tessel-lation of an octagon?

Translations are used.

Some tessellations use more than one transformation.

Example 4

Does this tessellation display any of the transformations?

a. Translations   **b.** Rotations   **c.** Reflections

Check for each transformation.

Translations are shown.   Rotations are shown.   Reflections are shown.

Try It

Does this tessellation display any of the transformations?

a. Translations

b. Rotations

c. Reflections

Drawing by Ryan Evans from *Tessellation Winners: Original Student Art*, The Second Contest (Palo Alto, CA: Dale Seymour Publications, 1994). Copyright © 1994 by Dale Seymour Publications.

Triangles and quadrilaterals tessellate, but many shapes don't. To find out whether a shape tessellates, you have to experiment. For example,

Some irregular pentagons do; Regular pentagons don't.

When a shape is tessellated, you can find the total area of the tessellation by multiplying the area of a single shape by the number of shapes used.

Example 5

A bathroom wall is 6 ft by 10 ft = 60 ft². The tiles used to cover the wall are squares with $\frac{1}{2}$ ft side lengths. How many tiles are needed to cover the bathroom wall?

$\left(\frac{1}{2}\right)^2 = \frac{1}{4}$ ft²   Find the area of one tile.

$60 \div \frac{1}{4} = x$ Divide by $\frac{1}{4}$.

$60 \cdot 4 = 240$ Multiply by the reciprocal of $\frac{1}{4}$.

About 240 tiles are needed to cover the bathroom wall.

Try It

A 24 inch by 60 inch counter will be covered by square tiles with 4-inch side lengths. How many tiles are needed? Tiles can be cut to fit if necessary.

Check   Your Understanding

1. Can any shape create a tessellation? Explain.

2. If you know the area of a shape used to tessellate a surface and the number of shapes used, can you always calculate the area of the tessellation? Explain.

3. If someone gives you two different shapes and asks whether or not they can form a tessellation, describe what steps you would take to answer their question.

4. Can you use more than one transformation to create a tessellation? Explain and provide an example.

Practice and Apply

1. **Getting Started** State whether each pattern will tessellate.

   a.   **b.**   **c.**

2. Use eight translations of the figure to produce a tessellation.

3. **a.** Which regular polygons tessellate?

   b. Explain why regular pentagons do not tessellate.

4. **Test Prep** Which transformation would have to be used for the tessellation shown?

   Ⓐ Translation   Ⓑ Rotation

   Ⓒ Reflection   Ⓓ Dilation

   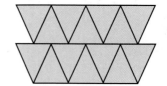

5. **History** Tiles on floors or ceilings often form tessellations. The Alhambra in Spain, built around 1300, is an elaborate example of Islamic architecture. How many square tiles with 6 in. sides would it take to cover a wall with an area of 1000 ft²?

6. **a.** Name and draw a polygon that will tessellate.

   b. Name and draw a polygon that will not tessellate.

   c. Name and draw two polygons that can tessellate together.

7. Name the figures used in each tessellation.

   a.   **b.**   **c.**

Social Studies A tribe from British Columbia called these designs the mouth and the fish net.

Mouth

Fish Net

8. What polygons are used?

9. Can the patterns be produced using
   a. Only translations?   b. Only rotations?
   c. Only reflections?   d. A combination?

Problem Solving and Reasoning

10. This pattern is created using a rhombus and a parallelogram. Can this tessellation be created using only reflections and translations? Explain.

11. **Communicate** A flooring contractor has 175 tiles that are 6 in. by 6 in. for covering a kitchen floor that is 15 ft by 10 ft. Does he have enough tiles? Explain.

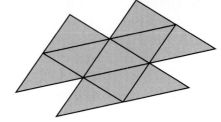

12. **Patterns** You can tessellate any triangle or quadrilateral using 180° rotations around the midpoints of the sides. This pattern starts with an obtuse triangle. Do the same thing with an acute triangle and a trapezoid and sketch the result for each.

13. **Math Reasoning** Find five letters of the alphabet that tessellate. (*Hint:* You can draw the letters.)

Mixed Review

Find the missing side length for each right triangle. [*Lesson 7-9*]

14.
5 ft, 9 ft, c

15.
24 in., a, 18 in.

16.
b, 10 m, 6 m

Solve each proportion. [*Lesson 5-4*]

17. $\frac{4}{5} = \frac{x}{100}$ 18. $\frac{2.5}{20} = \frac{7.5}{x}$ 19. $\frac{6}{7} = \frac{21}{x}$ 20. $\frac{4.3}{8.6} = \frac{x}{50}$

Section 11B Connect

At the beginning of Section 11B, you saw how Native American arts and crafts repeat shapes to make patterns. You'll design your own pattern by using various transformations.

Doing What Comes Naturally

The Pueblo people of the American Southwest are known for their pottery. Pottery made by the Zuni, Laguna, and Acoma tribes display many patterns, including geometric designs and natural shapes such as birds and lizards.

Symmetry and transformations are frequently used in the paintings on their pottery.

1. Look at the photo and notice the symmetry. Discuss the types of symmetry you see. Is there a type of symmetry that every piece has?

2. Now discuss the types of transformations you see and how often they appear. Point out tessellations if you see any.

3. With your group, design a pattern to put on a traditional Native American object (pottery, tepee, rug, mask, beadwork, jewelry, blanket). Start by dividing the object into four equal areas.

4. Each of the four areas will have a unique shape.

   Area 1: Shape with exactly one line of symmetry.

   Area 2: Shape with exactly three lines of symmetry.

   Area 3: Shape with point symmetry.

   Area 4: Shape with any symmetry you like.

5. Apply a different transformation to each of the four shapes. Rotate, translate, reflect, and dilate.

6. If any of the shapes make a tessellation, that area of your piece will be filled with that tessellation. Do you think a dilation will tessellate?

7. Sketch some plans for your design.

615

Section 11B Review

1. What transformation is used in each pair of figures?

a.

b.

c.

The crescent shape is reflected across the y-axis.

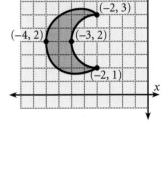

(−2, 3)

(−4, 2) (−3, 2)

(−2, 1)

2. List the corresponding vertex coordinates of the reflected figure.

3. What is the general rule for reflecting points across the y-axis?

4. A triangle with vertices at coordinates $(4, 6)$, $(−7, 2)$, and $(3, −3)$ is dilated with respect to the origin by a factor of 4. What are the vertex coordinates of the dilation?

5. Journal Suppose you had to give up one of the transformations but still wanted to be able to do all the same things with shapes that you could do before. Which one would you give up: Translation? Rotation? Reflection? Dilation? Explain your choice.

6. a. How many degrees can this design be rotated until it is rotated onto itself?

b. What kind(s) of symmetry does it have?

c. How many lines of symmetry does the figure have?

Test Prep

When you work with line symmetry, try to imagine folding the figure along the line of symmetry. The two halves should match exactly.

7. Which of the figures has a line of symmetry?

(A)   (B)   (C)   (D)

REVIEW 11B

Creating a Tessellation

A figure has rotational symmetry if it coincides with its original position after a rotation of less than 360°. All regular polygons have rotational symmetry.

The number of times a regular polygon coincides with its original position during a full 360° rotation equals the number of sides it has. For example, consider the equilateral triangle and a regular hexagon.

It is easy to create a tessellation by rotating a regular hexagon.

Create a tessellation using the equilateral triangle. Use a triangle with a different color on one side. Your tessellation should look like the one below.

1. How many 90° rotations will it take to complete one full rotation for a square? How many 72° rotations for a regular pentagon? How many 60° rotations for a regular hexagon?

2. What in nature resembles the tessellation of hexagons?

Chapter 11 Summary and Review

Graphic Organizer

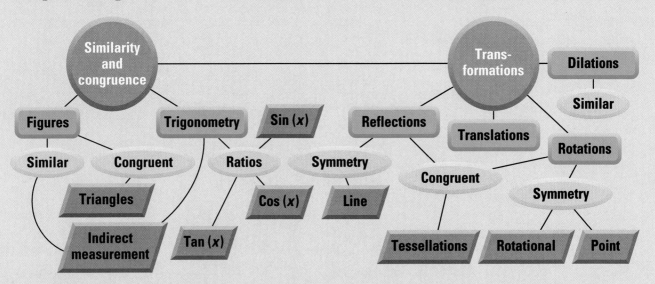

Section 11A Similarity and Congruence

Summary

- Two figures are **congruent** ($\cong$) if they have the same shape and size. Two figures are **similar** ($\sim$) if they have the same shape but not necessarily the same size. Corresponding angles and corresponding sides appear in both congruent and similar figures.

- You can use the **Side-Side-Side, Side-Angle-Side, Angle-Side-Angle,** and **Side-Angle-Angle** rules to determine congruence of two triangles.

- For an acute angle in a right triangle, the **adjacent leg** is the leg next to the angle and the **opposite leg** is opposite the angle.

- The **trigonometric ratios sine, cosine,** and **tangent** can be used for **indirect measurement** of triangles.

Review

1. The two pentagons are similar. Find the length x and the measure of $\angle 1$.

2. State whether the triangles are congruent; if they are, give the rule that justifies your answer.

3. Are the figures congruent?

10 cm
2 cm

9 cm
1.8 cm

4. Calculate each trigonometric ratio.

a. sin 60°   **b.** cos 30°   **c.** tan 45°

5. Use the lengths of the sides to write and evaluate the sine, cosine, and tangent ratios for the labeled angle.

1.75 m
6.25 m
A
6.0 m

6. In the figure, △*PQR* is similar to △*TSR*. Find the length of $\overline{RT}$.

Q
16 cm   24 cm
R
T
P   30 cm
8 cm
S

Section 11B Transformations

Summary

■ A **transformation** is a change in a figure that could be a **reflection, translation, rotation,** or **dilation.**

■ A figure has **symmetry** if it coincides with itself after a transformation. Three types of symmetry are: **line symmetry, rotational symmetry,** and **point symmetry.**

■ A **tessellation** is a repeating pattern of figures that covers a plane without gaps or overlaps.

Review

7. A figure has vertex coordinates $K(0, 0)$; $L(3, 1)$; $M(2, 4)$; and $N(0, 5)$. Find the coordinates of K', L', M', and N' after each transformation.

a. Reflection across the x-axis

b. Reflection across the y-axis

c. Rotation 90° counterclockwise

9. Which transformation has occurred? Are the figures similar? Congruent?

8. △*ABC* is translated 4 units right and 1 unit down. Find the coordinates of A', B', and C'.

10. Which are lines of symmetry?

M
Z   *N*
Y   *P*
X   *Q*
W

11. Can this tessellation be made using only rotations of a single triangle?

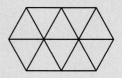

1. Are the figures similar?

2. Algebra In the figure, the rectangles are congruent. Find the values of x and y.

3. Are the triangles congruent? If so, state the rule that justifies your answer.

4. The top of a flagpole forms a 31° angle with a tourist who is 73 ft away from the base of the flagpole. How tall is the flagpole?

5. In the figure, $\triangle ACE$ is similar to $\triangle BCD$. If $\overline{CE}$ has a length of 18 cm, find the length of $\overline{CD}$.

6. $\triangle ABC$ with vertex coordinates of $A(2, 7)$; $B(0, 1)$; and $C(3, 4)$ has been reflected across the y-axis to produce $\triangle A'B'C'$. Give the coordinates of

  a. A'

  b. B'

  c. C'

7. The dog shape on the left was enlarged. Find the scale factor.

8. What polygons is the tessellation based on?

9. Calculate each trigonometric ratio.

  a. sin 24°

  b. cos 156°

  c. tan 88°

10. A figure has vertex coordinates $W(0, 0)$; $V(0, 4)$; and $X(2, 3)$. Find the coordinates of W', V', and X' after each transformation.

  a. Reflection across the x-axis

  b. Rotation 180° counterclockwise

Performance Task

Show how to make a tessellation using a concave quadrilateral such as the one shown. It may be helpful to cut five or ten identical shapes to see how they fit together.

Performance Assessment

Choose one problem.

A Triangle That's Not Quite Right

There is no Side-Side-Angle rule to show congruent triangles. Can you create one obtuse triangle and one acute triangle that would be "congruent" if such a rule existed? Explain your reasoning.

Palindrommytry

"Madam I'm Adam," "mom," "1881." These are all palindromes: phrases, words, or numbers that are the same when written backward or forward. What kind of symmetry do palindromes have? Give a few of your own examples of palindromes. Can you create a palindrome with two lines of symmetry?

A PUZZLING TESSELLATION

Jigsaw puzzles have entertained us all. Create a jigsaw puzzle piece that will tessellate. Repetitions of the piece should interlock with the others. Draw a picture to show your tessellation. Describe how you created the puzzle piece that tessellates.

The Task of a Mask

A mask is a sculpted face used for ornamentation or disguise. Masks, like most all faces, have one line of symmetry. List some features (for example, a nose) on a face and identify the type of symmetry each exhibits. Then, for a mask, draw a face with three lines of symmetry.

Entertainment

The object of Mancala, an African stone game, is to get more stones than the opponent. At each turn, players must consider the possible combinations of moves that can be made.

People of the World

In 1968, Shirley Chisholm was the first African-American woman elected to Congress. A former teacher, she fulfilled her pledge to her community to support education. This required her to analyze data to compare the possible ways of allocating funds.

Social Studies

At weddings, the custom of throwing the bridal bouquet to the unmarried female guests began in France in the 1300s. The chance of catching the bouquet depends on the number of people trying to catch it.

→ Science Link
www.mathsurf.com/8/ch12/science

→ Arts & Literature Link
www.mathsurf.com/8/ch12/arts

Science

Following much experimentation with various combinations of Siamese and Persian cats, breeders developed a new breed of long-haired cat—the much-sought-after Himalayan.

Arts & Literature

Three-line symbols called *trigrams*, commonly found in Asian art, are made of combinations of solid and broken lines. The ones on this flag symbolize heaven, earth, fire, and water. The Counting Principle can be used to determine how many ways these three-line symbols can be made.

KEY MATH IDEAS

You can count the number of ways a series of events can occur by using a tree diagram or the Counting Principle.

A permutation, or arrangement, is an ordered selection of objects. A combination is a selection of objects without regard to order.

The probability, or theoretical probability, of an event is the likelihood that the event occurs.

Experimental probability is the number of times the event occurs divided by the number of trials. Geometric probability is calculated by comparing areas, lengths, or other measures.

Conditional probability is the probability that event *B* will occur, given that event *A* has already occurred. The events may be independent events or dependent events.

CHAPTER PROJECT

Problem Solving

Understand
Plan
Solve
Look Back

Create a game that involves permutations and/or combinations. Use your knowledge of probability to make the game interesting. You may want to use cards, coins, spinners, number cubes, or just select numbers or objects from a hat. You might want the game to involve several players, or it could be a game of solitaire.

623

Checking for a Reasonable Answer

We often need to use calculators to solve problems with large numbers. But it is easy to enter incorrect numbers, forget parentheses, or miss a digit when writing the answer from the calculator screen. So it is important to look back at the reasonableness of your answer. Estimation and common sense are good guides to reasonableness.

Problem Solving Focus

Kirk is a volunteer for an environmental organization. These are some situations he has encountered.

State if each answer is "close enough," "too low," or "too high." Explain.

1 An acre, 43,560 ft^2, is set aside for a grove of trees. If the grove is a square region, how long should each side of the grove be?
Answer: 660 ft

2 A tree is 150 ft tall and has a diameter of 12 ft. The portion of usable wood from the tree is $\frac{4}{5}$. What is the usable-wood volume of the tree?
Answer: 1085 ft^3

3 There are estimates that rain forests are being cut down at the rate of 100 acres per minute. At this rate, how many acres are being cut down in a month?
Answer: 4,320,000 acres

4 Recycled paper is called "postconsumer." It costs $2.60 to produce 1000 sheets of 100% postconsumer paper and $3.20 to produce 1500 sheets of 20% postconsumer recycled filler paper. How much more does the 100% recycled paper cost to produce per sheet?
Answer: $0.05

SWIFTER, HIGHER, STRONGER

Thousands of people in the stadium, and millions more around the world, are cheering you on. The starter gun sounds, every muscle in your body strains, your lungs search desperately for air, and before you know it, you cross the finish line victorious. You're an Olympic champion, and the national anthem sounds as you accept the accolades of your country and the world. In the future, what do you think will be remembered about the Olympic Games held in Atlanta? The American gymnast who vaulted with an injured ankle and enabled her team to win the gold? The decathlon winner who, four years earlier, though favored to win, hadn't even qualified? Or the gold-medal swimmer who, because of exercise-induced asthma, sometimes passed out during vigorous workouts? Perhaps the individuals themselves won't be remembered. Maybe what will be remembered is their dedication and courage to perform their very best and never give up.

1 The number of women athletes in the 1992 Barcelona Games was 2708. In the Atlanta Games four years later, the number rose to 3779. What percent of increase is this?

2 In the Atlanta Games, Turkey's 141-pound Naim Suleymanoglu lifted 413 pounds. How many times his weight did he lift?

625

Tree Diagrams and the Counting Principle

▶ **Lesson Link**   In some situations, counting can be difficult. You know how to use multiplication to count square units in rectangles. A similar method can be used when counting choices. ◀

Explore | Tree Diagrams

The Way to School

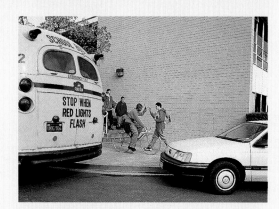

1. What different modes of transportation could you take to and from school?

2. Assuming you can take only one of these modes to school each day, how many different ways could you get to school?

3. Assuming you can take only one of these modes home from school each day, how many ways could you get home from school?

4. Make an organized list or drawing of all the modes you can use to get to school and back again (ignore whether you actually have your bike at school, for example). How many modes are there?

Learn | Tree Diagrams and the Counting Principle

To get to the 1996 Olympic Games in Atlanta, Jose could not get a direct flight from Shreveport, Louisiana. He had choices of connecting cities—Dallas, New Orleans, and Houston—and choices of airlines—Skies and Airway. You can show his options by making a table.

| Connecting City | Airline | |
	Skies	Airway
Houston	X	X
New Orleans	X	X
Dallas	X	X

From the list, you can count 6 choices. There are other ways to find this information. One way is to use a **tree diagram** . A tree diagram shows branches for each point where a choice is made. Each branch of a tree lists a possible outcome.

Example 1

Make a tree diagram to show all possible choices for the 3 connecting cities: Dallas, New Orleans, Houston, and the 2 airlines: Skies and Airway.

Connecting City	Airline	Choice
Dallas	Skies	Through Dallas on Skies
	Airway	Through Dallas on Airway
New Orleans	Skies	Through New Orleans on Skies
	Airway	Through New Orleans on Airway
Houston	Skies	Through Houston on Skies
	Airway	Through Houston on Airway

Try It

Jay has a choice of 4 flights from Newark to St. Louis and a choice of 3 return flights. Make a tree diagram. How many different pairs of flights can he take?

You don't need to make an organized list or a tree diagram. You may have noticed in Example 1 that:

$$3 \times 2 = 6 \text{ choices}$$

Connecting cities Airlines

COUNTING PRINCIPLE

If a situation can occur in *m* ways, and a second situation can occur in *n* ways, then these things can occur together in $m \times n$ ways.

Problem Solving TIP

Use the Counting Principle first. Then see if it makes sense to make a list or tree diagram to see the individual choices.

The Counting Principle also works for more than two situations.

Example 2

A computer-designed birthday card can be designed with 4 different messages, 7 different colors, and 5 different borders. How many different choices of cards do you have?

Using the Counting Principle, you have $4 \times 7 \times 5$ or 140 card choices.

Try It

Gifties has 10 types of wrapping paper, 12 colors of ribbons, and 3 different kinds of bows. How many gift-packaging options do you have?

Be sure that you understand the problem before using the Counting Principle.

Example 3

An Olympic stadium has 83,100 seats. Your ticket states, "Enter through the north gates." Gates A through E are on the north side and gates F through K are on the south side. How many ways can a ticketholder enter through a north gate and exit through any gate?

There are 5 north gates and 6 south gates. There are 5 ways to enter the stadium. To exit, there are 5 + 6 = 11 possible gates.

Using the Counting Principle, there are 5 × 11 = 55 ways to enter through a north gate and exit through any gate.

Try It

Animal researchers put identification tags on animals to study their habits. How many tag codes are possible?

May be any of 26 letters or 10 numbers (0–9)

May be any of 100 numbers (00–99)

Check | Your Understanding

1. Give an example of a situation in which the Counting Principle can be used, and one in which it cannot.

2. Suppose that there are 4 types of pizza sauce and *t* types of toppings. How many different 1-topping pizzas could be made?

3. How does a situation with 4 choices followed by 2 choices compare with the choices switched—2 choices followed by 4 choices? Give an example.

Practice and Apply

1. | Getting Started | At the Olympics, a deli ran a special on sandwiches. Here are the choices.

a. Copy and complete the diagram, showing all possible sandwiches.

b. How many different sandwiches are there?

Filling	Cheese	Bread
BBQ pork	Swiss	Wheat
Roast beef	American	Rye
	Jack	

Filling	Cheese	Bread	Sandwich
	Swiss	Wheat	Pork and Swiss on Wheat
		Rye	Pork and Swiss on Rye
BBQ pork	American	___	___
		Rye	Pork and American on Rye
	Jack	___	___
	___	___	___
Roast beef	___	___	___
	___	___	___

2. Beatrice took a red, a white, and a blue shirt and a red, a white, and a blue pair of shorts to the Olympic Games.

a. How many choices of shirts are there? How many choices of shorts?

b. Use the Counting Principle to find the number of different choices in outfits. You may want to check it by drawing a tree diagram.

4. Sports In major league baseball, there are 14 teams in the National League and 14 in the American League. How many different World Series match-ups (one team from each league) are possible?

3. How many different choices do you have in each situation?

a. 4 types of yogurt, 10 types of toppings (only 1 topping allowed)

b. 3 types of pizza crust, 2 types of sauces, 3 types of cheeses

c. 5 types of toast, 4 types of jams

5. Make a tree diagram to show the possible results of spinning both spinners.

PRACTICE 12-1

6. The Atlanta Committee for the Olympic Games provided Olympic athletes with 540 cases of tennis balls, each containing 24 cans, and each can containing 3 tennis balls. How many tennis balls were provided?

7. Geography Katrina is trying to get from Dallas to Abilene, through Fort Worth. There are 4 major highways from Dallas to Fort Worth and 2 from Fort Worth to Abilene. How many routes can she take?

8. Suppose your school has voted to wear uniforms. There are 3 colors of shirts and 3 colors of pants. Girls may also choose from 3 colors of skirts. How many uniform choices are there for boys? For girls?

The lunch menu from Rambo's Restaurant is shown. Use it to answer Exercises 9 and 10.

9. How many different lunch specials can be ordered?

10. **Test Prep** If Rambo's runs out of peas, how many different lunch specials could be ordered?

ⓐ 35　　ⓑ 24　　ⓒ 16　　ⓓ 8

$4.95 Lunch Special
Chicken or Pizza
Peas, Beans, or Carrots
Green Salad or Potato Salad
Soda, Coffee, or Tea

Problem Solving and Reasoning

11. Language Arts One word is to be chosen from each list. How many sentences can be made?

article	adjective	noun	verb	adverb
The	quick	dog	ran	quickly.
A	smelly	robot	slipped	badly.
	purple	king	cooked	
	scraggly		scratched	
			waited	

12. Communicate How many different people can be made with the flip book? How would you change it if you wanted to say "It makes 1000 different people"?

13. Describe a situation in which using an organized list or a tree diagram is more useful than using the Counting Principle.

— 8 different heads

— 8 different faces

— 8 different chins

Mixed Review

Solve. *[Lesson 3-7]*

14. $x - 10 < 12$　　**15.** $x + 4 > 6$　　**16.** $5x \geq 35$　　**17.** $4x - 2 \leq 14$　　**18.** $\frac{1}{2}x + 1 < 9$

19. Find the area of the paper used to make a snow cone that has a diameter of 3 in. and a height of 5 in. (use $A = \frac{1}{2} \cdot C \cdot s$). *[Lesson 9-5]*

Permutations and Arrangements

▶ Lesson Link You have learned about tree diagrams and the Counting Principle. You will now extend these concepts to counting situations in which order is important. ◀

Explore Permutations

Get in Line

Materials: 4 cards marked A, B, C, and D for each group

Each person in your group should take one card marked A, B, C, or D.

1. If the student with card A lines up alone, how many ways can this student line up?

2. If the students with card A and card B line up, how many ways can these 2 students line up?

3. Add the student with card C. Where can you slot this third student in line when the first 2 students are in order AB? When they are in order BA? How many ways are there for 3 students to line up? How does this relate to the number of ways to line up 2 students?

4. Add the student with card D. Where can you slot this fourth student in line when the first 3 students are in order ABC? When they are in the other orders? How many ways are there for 4 students to line up? How does this relate to the number of ways to line up 3 students?

5. Predict how many ways 5 students could line up.

You'll Learn …

■ to develop ways of counting in situations for which the order of items is important

… How It's Used

When determining the competition order of a team, the coach must be aware of the possible arrangements that could be made.

Vocabulary

arrangement

permutation

factorial

Learn Permutations and Arrangements

When looking at options or choices, you often look at the **arrangement**, or order, of people, letters, numbers, or other things. A **permutation** is an arrangement in which order is important. The permutation ABC is different from the permutation CBA. The Counting Principle can help you determine the number of choices or permutations.

Example 1

In the women's 4 × 100 m relay, the U.S. team was made up of Chryste Gaines, Gail Devers, Inger Miller, and Gwen Torrence. The coach decided that Gwen Torrence would run the anchor leg. In how many different orders could the coach have Gaines, Devers, and Miller run the first 3 legs?

Chryste Gaines   Gail Devers   Inger Miller   Gwen Torrence

For the first runner, there are 3 possibilities. Once a selection is made for the first runner, there are only 2 runners left from which to choose for the second leg. After that person is chosen, there is only 1 choice for the third leg.

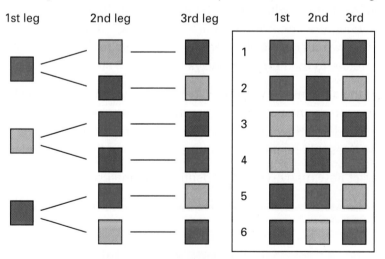

By the Counting Principle, the total choices are 3 · 2 · 1 = 6 ways.

There are 6 possible ways that the coach could order the 3 runners.

Try It

There were 8 lanes in which swimmers could compete in the 200 m butterfly races. How many different ways could the swimmers be arranged in the lanes?

Exponential notation is used to write a product when all of the factors are the same: $3 \cdot 3 \cdot 3 \cdot 3 = 3^4$. **Factorial** notation is used to write a product when the factors are consecutive whole numbers.

4 factorial is written as 4!, meaning $4 \cdot 3 \cdot 2 \cdot 1$.   0! is defined to be 1.

Example 2

Eight people were selected to carry the Olympic torch through downtown.

a. How many ways could the torchbearers be arranged in order?

Select all 8 torchbearers and see how many ways they can be arranged.

$8! = 8 \times 7 \times 6 \times 5 \times 4 \times 3 \times 2 \times 1 = 40{,}320$

There are 40,320 different ways to arrange the torchbearers.

b. How many ways could 3 of them be selected and arranged to carry the torch past three V.I.P. reviewing stands?

The ways to order 8 torchbearers are $8 \times 7 \times 6 \times 5 \times 4 \times 3 \times 2 \times 1$.

You only want to select and order 3 of the 8. The other 5 don't need to be arranged. Divide by the number of ways to arrange torchbearers who won't be passing the reviewing stands.

$$\frac{8!}{5!} = \frac{8 \times 7 \times 6 \times 5 \times 4 \times 3 \times 2 \times 1}{5 \times 4 \times 3 \times 2 \times 1}$$ Remove all common factors.

$$= 8 \times 7 \times 6$$

$$= 336$$

There are 336 ways to select and arrange the 3 torchbearers.

This makes sense because there are 8 people who can carry the torch past the first reviewing stand, then 7 who can carry it past the next one, and finally 6 who can carry it past the last one.

Try It

a. Evaluate 4!   **b.** Evaluate $(7 - 3)!$

c. A radio station has a contest. They name the top 10 songs, and listeners must tell the correct order of the top 5 songs to win. How many ways could a listener select and order 5 songs from a list of 10?

Example 3

Suppose you had to select and order parade vehicles and floats out of a group of 10. How many arrangements can you make if you select

a. 4 vehicles?

b. 5 vehicles?

c. 7 vehicles?

Scientific calculators have a factorial key, $\boxed{!}$.

a. For 4 vehicles, 6 vehicles are not selected.

$10 \boxed{!} \boxed{\div} 6 \boxed{!} \boxed{=} 5{,}040$

There are 5040 ways to select and arrange 4 vehicles.

b. For 5 vehicles, 5 vehicles are not selected.

$10 \boxed{!} \boxed{\div} 5 \boxed{!} \boxed{=} 30{,}240$

There are 30,240 ways to select and arrange 5 vehicles.

c. For 7 vehicles, 3 vehicles are not selected.

$10 \boxed{!} \boxed{\div} 3 \boxed{!} \boxed{=} 604{,}800$

There are 604,800 ways to select and arrange 7 vehicles.

Try It

a. How many ways are there to select and order 7 students to be hall monitors from a group of 9 student aides?

b. If you press 3 different buttons in the correct order, the door will open. How many ways are there to do this?

c. Suppose you had to select and order 3 students out of a group of 5 and assign them specific tasks for a class project. How many arrangements can you make? What if you could select 4 students? 5 students?

Graphing utilities usually have factorial as a math menu item.

MATH NUM HYP **PRB**
1: rand
2: nPr
3: ncr
4: !

Check Your Understanding

1. Explain what 5! means.

2. Of the functions you have studied—linear, quadratic, exponential, and so on—which does the factorial resemble? Why?

3. How does the number of ways to select and order 20 people out of 40 differ from the number of ways to order 40 people?

Practice and Apply

1. **Getting Started** The members of the gold-medal-winning U.S. archery team were Justin Huish, Butch Johnson, and Rod White. How many different ways could the coach have arranged the members' competition order?

Justin Huish

Justin < Butch ____ ____
       < Rod   ____ ____

Butch < ____ ____
      < Rod   Justin   Butch, Rod, Justin

____ < ____ ____
     < ____ Justin

   a. Complete the tree diagram to show the possible arrangements.

   b. How many arrangements are possible?

   c. What factorial could be used to count the arrangements?

2. Show all arrangements of the letters A, B, C, and D.

Evaluate.

3. $6!$

4. $(2!)(3!)$

5. $10!$

6. $(10 - 5)!$

7. $\dfrac{10!}{5!}$

8. $6(5!)$

9. $\dfrac{7!}{6!}$

10. $\dfrac{7!}{(7 - 3)!}$

11. **Career** Dusty, a disc jockey, has picked 5 songs to be played before the next commercial. How many ways can she order these songs?

How many ways can the letters in each of these words be arranged? (No letter is used twice.) The letters do not have to form a word.

12. GOLD

13. TRACK

14. MEDALS

15. GYMNAST

16. **Test Prep** Which formula would give the number of ways that r objects can be selected and arranged from a group of n objects?

Ⓐ $\dfrac{n!}{r!}$ Ⓑ $\dfrac{r!}{n!}$ Ⓒ $\dfrac{n!}{(n - r)!}$ Ⓓ $\dfrac{n!}{(r - n)!}$

17. **Chance** In the women's single-slalom kayak race, racers from the Czech Republic, France, and the U.S. won medals. If you didn't know which team won the gold, silver, and bronze, what are your chances of guessing the correct order?

PRACTICE 12-2

18. Cooking A white sauce can be made by slowly combining milk, flour, and melted butter in the correct order. How many orders are there? Guess the correct order. You may want to try it out!

20. Geography Fran wanted to visit New Zealand, Fiji, Australia, Bali, and New Guinea, but she was having trouble deciding the order. She tried to list all the orders. Why was she having trouble?

22. Mr. Lehr has 8 groups in his math class. Tomorrow, 3 of the groups will give their group-project reports. How many different ways can he select and order the groups?

19. Biochemistry To make an enzyme solution, Jay must pour the stabilizer, add the enzyme, and then add the reactant. He doesn't know which is which. What is the chance that he will mix them correctly?

21. Olympics There are 10 decathlon events: the 100 m run, long jump, shot put, high jump, and 400 m run on the first day; the 110 m hurdles, discus throw, pole vault, javelin throw, and 1500 m run on the second day.

a. In how many ways could the 10 events have been ordered?

b. In how many ways could the events on either day have been ordered?

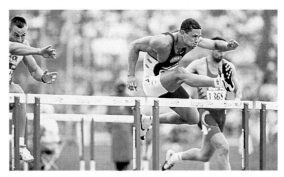

Problem Solving and Reasoning

23. Choose a Strategy Why are there fewer possible arrangements for the letters in the word LULL than the word LUGE? Which would you say has more possible arrangements, SALT or PEPPER? Why?

24. Critical Thinking Calculate the factorials 2! through 8!. Why do you think there is such rapid growth?

25. Communicate Nila picked 4 batteries out of 6 to use in her boombox. Does this situation describe a permutation? Explain.

Problem Solving
STRATEGIES

- Look for a Pattern
- Make an Organized List
- Make a Table
- Guess and Check
- Work Backward
- Use Logical Reasoning
- Draw a Diagram
- Solve a Simpler Problem

Mixed Review

Check each pair of ratios to see if a proportion is formed. *[Lesson 5-2]*

26. $\frac{3}{8}$ and $\frac{6}{18}$ **27.** $\frac{5}{6}$ and $\frac{10}{11}$ **28.** $\frac{47}{50}$ and $\frac{35}{39}$ **29.** $\frac{1}{3}$ and $\frac{27}{81}$

30. Decide whether the triangles are similar. *[Lesson 11-1]*

Combinations and Groups

▶ **Lesson Link**   You have learned about selections in which order was important. Now you will learn that in many situations order is not important. ◀

You'll Learn ...

■ to recognize unordered selections as combinations and to develop ways of counting in situations for which the order of items is not important

... How It's Used

Selecting Senate committee members involves combinations.

Explore | Combinations

What Difference Does It Make?

The U.S. team of LaMont Smith, Alvin Harrison, Derek Mills, and Arthuan Maybank won the gold medal in the men's 4 × 400 meter relay in the 1996 Summer Olympics.

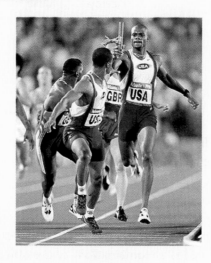

1. In how many ways could the lead runner and the anchor runner have been selected?

2. List the different arrangements of lead and anchor runner. Is order important in these selections?

3. A television station requested that any 2 of the runners appear together for an interview. How many different selections of 2 members of the team could be made? List the members.

4. How is the selection of 2 team members for an interview different from the selection of a lead runner and an anchor runner?

Vocabulary
combination

Learn | Combinations and Groups

Suppose your school holds an election for student council. Four students—Julie, Maria, Leroy, and Stephan—are running. The student with the most votes becomes president and the student with the second most becomes vice president. These are the possible outcomes of the election.

In this situation, order is important, so there are 4 · 3 = 12 possible outcomes.

But suppose the students with the top 2 votes simply become members of the council. It does not matter who of the 2 got the most votes; both become members. How does this change the number of outcomes?

President	Vice Pres
Julie	Maria
Julie	Leroy
Julie	Stephan
Maria	Julie
Maria	Leroy
Maria	Stephan
Leroy	Julie
Leroy	Maria
Leroy	Stephan
Stephan	Julie
Stephan	Maria
Stephan	Leroy

Council Members	
Julie	Maria
Julie	Leroy
Julie	Stephan
~~Maria~~	~~Julie~~
Maria	Leroy
Maria	Stephan
~~Leroy~~	~~Julie~~
~~Leroy~~	~~Maria~~
Leroy	Stephan
~~Stephan~~	~~Julie~~
~~Stephan~~	~~Maria~~
~~Stephan~~	~~Leroy~~

The outcome Maria/Julie is the same as Julie/Maria, so it can be eliminated. Leroy/Julie is the same as Julie/Leroy, so it is eliminated, and so on.

The number of outcomes drops from 12 to 6.

When the order is not important, the number of outcomes is reduced. A selection of a number of objects that forms a set of objects, without regard to order, is called a **combination** of the objects.

Example 1

Five students, Abby, Bonita, Chantall, Dani, and Eleni, are trying out for the dance team. There are slots for only 2 students. What are the different combinations of 2 students who could place on the dance team?

Make an organized list.

Abby/Bonita	Bonita/Chantall	Chantall/Dani	Dani/Eleni
Abby/Chantall	Bonita/Dani	Chantall/Eleni	
Abby/Dani	Bonita/Eleni		
Abby/Eleni			

There are 10 possible combinations of 2 students chosen from a group of 5.

Try It

A third slot opened up for the dance team. What are the possible combinations of students now? How many combinations are there?

Often the number of combinations will be too large for an organized list or a tree diagram. You can use the ideas that you learned about permutations to find the number of combinations.

On page 633, you found that to *select and arrange* 3 torchbearers from a group of 8, you didn't need to arrange the 5 unselected torchbearers. In this situation, you would divide 8! by 5! to find the number of permutations.

To find the number of ways to merely *select* 3 torchbearers from 8 torchbearers, you don't need to arrange the 3 selected torchbearers either. Divide 8! by the number of ways to arrange the *selected* torchbearers as well.

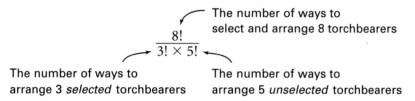

The number of ways to
select and arrange 8 torchbearers

$$\frac{8!}{3! \times 5!}$$

The number of ways to
arrange 3 *selected* torchbearers

The number of ways to
arrange 5 *unselected* torchbearers

Example 2

There are 20 paintings in a collection. How many ways can the following groups be selected? Write the answers in factorial notation.

a. 3 paintings

There are $\frac{20!}{3! \times 17!}$ ways to select 3 paintings.

b. 17 paintings

There are $\frac{20!}{17! \times 3!}$ ways to select 17 paintings.

Selecting 17 paintings is the same as selecting 3 paintings to leave out. The number of ways to do each is the same.

Problem Solving TIP

If the numerals in your denominator don't add up to the ones in your numerator, there's an error.

Example 3

For the all-around teams at the 1996 Olympics, 3 gymnasts were selected from each nation. The U.S. women's team had 6 gymnasts. How many different all-around teams could have been chosen?

Order is not important in the selection, so you are looking for a combination.

$$\frac{6!}{3! \times 3!} = 6 \boxed{!} \div \boxed{(} 3 \boxed{!} \boxed{\times} 3 \boxed{!} \boxed{)} \boxed{=} \textit{20}$$

There are 20 ways to select a group of 3 team members from the 6 gymnasts.

MENTAL MATH

If you realize that this is $6 \times 5 \times 4$ divided by $3 \times 2 \times 1$, and that the 6 cancels with the denominator, all that's left is 5×4.

Try It

How many selections of 4 team members could be made from a group of 6?

WHAT DO YOU THINK?

Four of 9 students will be selected to attend the MathCounts competition. How many different teams could be selected?

Ashley thinks ...

Order is not important. I am looking for the number of ways to select a group of 4 students from 9. I'll use my calculator.

$$\frac{9!}{4!(9-4)!} = 9 \boxed{!} \boxed{\div} \boxed{(} \boxed{4} \boxed{!} \boxed{\times} \boxed{5} \boxed{!} \boxed{)} \boxed{=} 126$$

There are 126 different teams.

Seung thinks ...

I'll list the factors. I can divide out 5! right away.

$$\frac{9!}{4! \times 5!} = \frac{9 \times 8 \times 7 \times 6 \times 5 \times 4 \times 3 \times 2 \times 1}{(4 \times 3 \times 2 \times 1)(5 \times 4 \times 3 \times 2 \times 1)}$$

$$= \frac{9 \times 8 \times 7 \times 6 \times \cancel{5 \times 4 \times 3 \times 2 \times 1}}{(4 \times 3 \times 2 \times 1)(\cancel{5 \times 4 \times 3 \times 2 \times 1})}$$

There are other common factors.

$$\frac{\overset{3}{\cancel{9}} \times \cancel{8} \times 7 \times 6}{\cancel{4} \times \cancel{3} \times \cancel{2} \times 1} = 3 \times 7 \times 6 = 126$$

There are 126 different teams.

What do you think?

Will one of the factorials always divide out?

Check | Your Understanding

1. How are combinations different from permutations? Why are there fewer combinations than permutations when selecting from a group?

2. How is choosing 2 from 7 related to choosing 5 from 7? Why?

Practice and Apply

Getting Started In which of these situations is order important?

1. Gold, silver, and bronze medals will be given to 3 of 8 competitors.

2. Certificates of merit will be given to 5 of 10 entrants.

3. Four of 10 students will be selected to each swim one stroke: butterfly, backstroke, breaststroke, or freestyle in the swim meet relay.

4. Four of 10 students will attend the Olympics in Sydney, Australia.

5. **Biology** In how many ways can 24 seedlings be selected from a group of 96 seedlings to test a growth enhancer? Write in factorial notation.

Evaluate.

6. $\dfrac{12!}{9! \times 3!}$ **7.** $\dfrac{10!}{5! \times 5!}$ **8.** $\dfrac{12!}{8!(12 - 8)!}$ **9.** $\dfrac{5!}{2!(5 - 2)!}$

10. In how many ways can 2 pizza toppings be selected from a group of 6 toppings?

11. **Consumer** How many ways could you select 3 possible components for a sound system from a tape deck, CD player, laser disc, equalizer, and surround-sound stereo?

12. After the class picnic, 10 of the 30 students are needed to clean up. How many different ways could they be selected?

13. There were 12 players on the 1996 U.S. Olympic basketball team. In how many ways could 5 starters be chosen? (Don't worry about player positions.)

14. **History** Henry VIII had 6 wives. How many ways could 2 of them be selected for portrayal in a documentary film?

15. A class is told that it should do only 8 out of 10 questions on the test. Is this the same as being told that it should omit 2 of the 10 questions?

16. **Literature** The most common type of poetry is lyric poetry which includes haikus, odes, elegies, sonnets, limericks, rondels, triolets, and villanelles. If you were assigned to write an essay describing 3 of these types of lyric poetry, how many ways could you select them?

PRACTICE 12-3

17. Chance To win a game, you must guess 6 numbers from the numbers 1–53. They must match 6 randomly selected numbers. Why is this game virtually impossible to win?

18. In Olympic diving, 7 judges award a score for each dive. The high and low scores are removed. In how many ways can 2 judges' scores be removed?

19. **Test Prep** A flower shop carries 12 types of flowers and sells a special Crazy 8 birthday bouquet using your choice of 8 different flowers. How many different ways can 8 flowers be selected?

ⓐ 96   ⓑ 495   ⓒ 12^8 ⓓ 40,320

Problem Solving and Reasoning

20. Critical Thinking How many ways can you give 10 swim-team members a snack if you have 12 snacks and each swimmer is to receive 1?

21. Communicate Suppose you select a group from 10 people. What size group has the most ways of being selected? Explain.

22. Choose a Strategy How many ways can groups of from 0 to 12 items be chosen from 12 items?

23. Math Reasoning How many different ways can you select 3 players from 10 for one basketball team, and then 3 from the remaining 7 for another team?

> **Problem Solving**
> # STRATEGIES
> • Look for a Pattern
> • Make an Organized List
> • Make a Table
> • Guess and Check
> • Work Backward
> • Use Logical Reasoning
> • Draw a Diagram
> • Solve a Simpler Problem

Mixed Review

Is the table an equal ratio table? If so, find the value of k, where $\frac{y}{x} = k$. *[Lesson 5-3]*

24.

x	3	6	9	12
y	4	7	10	13

25.

x	2	4	6	8
y	3	6	9	12

Determine whether each pair of figures is congruent. *[Lesson 11-2]*

26.

27.

> ### Project Progress
>
> Think about whether you want your game to involve permutations, combinations, or both. Which would make the game more difficult?

> **Problem Solving**
>
> Understand
> Plan
> Solve
> Look Back

You have seen many examples of counting situations. In this Connect, you will compute the combinations and permutations associated with the Olympic Games.

Swifter, Higher, Stronger

The interlocked rings of the Olympic symbol represent Africa, the Americas, Asia, Australia, and Europe.

1. In how many ways could the colors of the Olympic symbol have been arranged among the rings?

2. Let each group in the room be a "nation" in the Olympics. In how many orders can the groups march in the opening ceremonies?

3. In how many ways can the teams win gold, silver, and bronze in the first event? (Assume that each team can win no more than 1 medal.)

4. If only the top 3 teams can compete in the all-around competition, how many ways can they be arranged?

5. If the rules are changed and the top 4 teams can compete in the all-around competition, how many ways can they now be arranged?

6. In how many ways can the gold medal be awarded if each team competes in the first 5 events?

7. If 10 events are to be held, in how many different ways can the events be ordered?

8. Use one of the situations explored here. Show that choosing a group (combination), then ordering the group (permutation) is the same as selecting and ordering a group (permutation).

Section 12A Review

Evaluate.

1. 8!   **2.** 12!   **3.** $(10 - 3)!$ **4.** $(3!)(3!)$ **5.** $\dfrac{10!}{2!}$

6. $4(3!)$ **7.** $\dfrac{8!}{6!}$ **8.** $\dfrac{7!}{(7-4)!}$ **9.** $\dfrac{8!}{3! \times 5!}$ **10.** $\dfrac{6!}{2!(6-4)!}$

11. Make an organized list or tree diagram showing the possible outcomes of tossing 3 coins.

12. Make a tree diagram to show the possible outcomes of spinning the spinner twice.

How many ways can the letters in each of these words be arranged if no letter is used twice? The letters do not have to form a word.

13. SILVER   **14.** MEDALIST   **15.** WRESTLING

16. **Consumer** On his vacation, Fred wanted to take 6 tours, but he was having trouble deciding in what order to take them. How many different ways could he go on the tours?

17. **Olympics** In the heptathlon, there are 7 events—hurdles, high jump, shot put, 200 m dash, javelin throw, long jump, and 800 m run. These events are held in a certain order. How many different ways could these 7 events be ordered?

18. **Civics** A candidate will visit 9 of the 50 states the week before the election. How many ways can this be done? Write in factorial notation.

19. **Olympics** Mark Spitz won 7 gold medals in swimming at the 1972 Olympic Games in Munich. If he wanted to display the medals in a row on his wall, how many different ways could he arrange them?

20. Compare selecting 3 items from 7 if the selection is a permutation to selecting 3 items from 7 if the selection is a group.

Test Prep

Think about whether order is important.

21. For an international flight, how many different ways can 5 flight attendants be selected from 10 flight attendants?

Ⓐ 10×5 Ⓑ $10!$ Ⓒ $\dfrac{10!}{5!}$ Ⓓ $\dfrac{10!}{5! \times 5!}$

REVIEW 12A

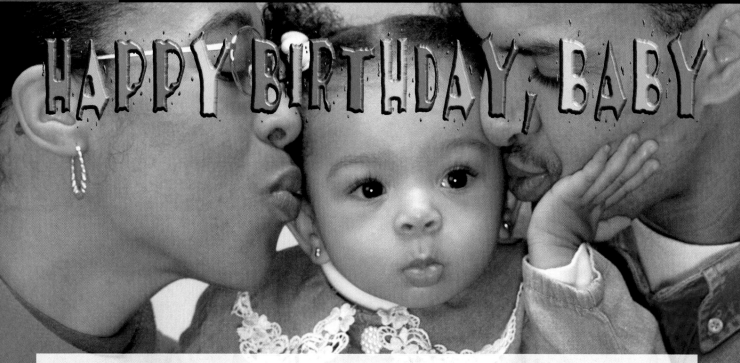

HAPPY BIRTHDAY, BABY

How many birthdays has the average person had? Actually, just one. All the other days you celebrate as birthdays are the anniversaries of that day. But "Happy Anniversary to You" is too difficult to sing, so we call them all birthdays.

You undoubtedly share this day with someone famous. Born February 17? Michael Jordan shares your birthday. Born May 16? So were Janet Jackson, Pierce Brosnan, and Tori Spelling.

We celebrate the birthdays of people important to our country, such as George Washington and Martin Luther King, Jr., with national holidays.

The day on which different people celebrate their birthdays is sometimes filled with coincidences. Five presidents were either born on, or died on, July 4.

Were you born alone or along with a brother or sister? When you were born, you had …

– 1 chance in 80 of being a twin,
– 1 chance in 6400 of being a triplet,
– 1 chance in 512,000 of being a quadruplet,
– 1 chance in 40,960,000 of being a quintuplet.

1 Do you share your birthday with anyone famous?

2 Martin Luther King, Jr.'s birthday is celebrated on the third Monday in January. Does this always fall on his birthday? Why do you think this is done?

3 Which has the greater chance of occurring, being born a twin or a quintuplet?

645

You'll Learn ...

■ to compute probability

... How It's Used

Probability is used to predict the place a hurricane will occur.

Vocabulary

experiment

outcomes

sample space

event

probability

▶ **Lesson Link** You have worked with methods for counting possible outcomes. Now you will learn to compute the chance that an outcome will happen. ◀

Explore | Probability

It's a Sure Thing

1. Draw a number line similar to this one.

| 0 | 0.1 | 0.2 | 0.3 | 0.4 | 0.5 | 0.6 | 0.7 | 0.8 | 0.9 | 1 |

If 0 indicates that something is impossible and 1 indicates that something is a sure thing, label points along this line that would show the chance of the following events occurring.

a. Rolling a 6 in a single roll of a number cube

b. Getting heads on a single flip of a coin

c. Selecting a pair of matching socks from a drawer, without looking, if there are two pairs of socks in the drawer

d. Drawing a card containing a vowel from a set of 10 cards containing the first 10 letters of the alphabet

e. Rolling a number other than 6 in a single roll of a number cube

2. Provide a rationale for each of your selections of position. Does each person in your group have the points in the same order?

3. Describe events you could place at 0 and at 1.

Learn | Probability

Suppose you toss a coin as an **experiment**. The coin can land on heads or tails, so there are two equally likely results or **outcomes** possible.

The set of all possible outcomes of an experiment is the **sample space**. Usually we are interested in the chance of a particular **event** occurring. This is called the **probability** of the event.

Probability can be expressed as a decimal, fraction, ratio, or percent.

$$P(\text{event}) = \frac{\text{number of outcomes in the event}}{\text{number of outcomes in the sample space}}$$

Examples

1 Jason and Alexander are playing a game with a number cube. If Jason rolls a *3 or more* on his next roll, he wins the game.

What are the outcomes in the sample space? Outcomes satisfying the event *3 or more*?

What is the probability of the event *3 or more*?

Sample space: 6 outcomes → 1, 2, 3, 4, 5, 6

Event *3 or more:*   4 outcomes →   3, 4, 5, 6

The probability of Jason rolling a *3 or more* on his next roll is $\frac{4}{6}$, or $\frac{2}{3}$.

2 Nicole likes to try to guess a person's birthday. What is the probability that she can guess the correct month of Jessica's birthday on the first try? Assume that it is equally likely for a person to have been born in any month.

There are 12 months in the year, so the number of outcomes in the sample space is 12. Jessica's birthday could only be during 1 month, so the number of outcomes in the event is 1.

$$P(\text{guessing correct month}) = \frac{1}{12}$$

Try It

For each situation, what are the outcomes in the sample space? What is the probability of the event?

a. If Alexander rolls a *5 or more* on his next roll of a number cube, he wins the game.

b. Will the next large Pacific earthquake occur *on a weekend*? (Assume that it is equally likely to occur on any day of the week.)

▶ **Science Link**

The Ring of Fire surrounds the entire Pacific Ocean with earthquake activity. It is the most active earthquake zone in the world.

The probability of an event occurring is always written as a number from 0 to 1.

When it is impossible for an event to occur, the probability is 0. When an event is certain to occur, the probability is 1.

Impossible   Certain

0 $\frac{1}{4}$ $\frac{1}{2}$ $\frac{3}{4}$ 1

Example 3

Suppose you get one spin on the spinner at the right. What is the probability that the spinner will land on ...

a. Red   **b.** Red or blue   **c.** Green   **d.** *Not* red

a. $P(\text{red}) = \frac{2}{5}$

b. $P(\text{red or blue}) = 1$ (certain)

c. $P(\text{green}) = 0$ (impossible)

d. $P(\textit{not}\ \text{red}) = \frac{3}{5}$

You can see that the probability of red plus the probability of *not* red is 1. The sum of the probability of an event occurring and the event *not* occurring is 1.

Remember

A **prime number** is an integer larger than 1 that is only divisible by itself and 1. **[Page 324]**

Try It

Find the probability that one roll of a number cube results in a

a. Prime number

b. Composite number

c. Number > 5

d. Number < 7

e. Fraction between 1 and 2

Check | Your Understanding

1. Explain the difference between an outcome and an event. Can an outcome be an event?

2. How does a probability of 25% compare with a probability of 0.4? With a probability of $\frac{1}{4}$?

3. If events A and B account for all of the possibilities in the sample space, what do you know about $P(B)$? Why?

Practice and Apply

1. **Getting Started** Find the probability of rolling a 2 on a number cube.
   a. List all of the outcomes in the sample space.
   b. How many outcomes are in the sample space?
   c. How many outcomes of rolling a 2 are in the sample space?
   d. Write a ratio using answers from **b** and **c** to find the probability.
   e. Express the probability as a fraction, decimal, and percent.

2. **History** Two U.S. Presidents, James Polk and Warren Harding, were both born on November 2. What is the probability of 2 people with November birthdays sharing the same birthday? (November has 30 days.)

List all outcomes in each sample space.

3. Rolling a number cube

4. Drawing a marble from a bag with 3 red, 2 green, and 3 blue marbles

Express the probability as a fraction, decimal, and percent.

5. Rolling an even number on a single roll of a number cube

6. Drawing a red sock out of a drawer that contains only red socks

7. Going to math class on New Year's Day

8. That a person's birthday is not on the fourth of July

9. **Test Prep** Which has the greatest probability of occurring?
   Ⓐ Tossing heads on a coin toss
   Ⓑ Tossing heads or tails on a coin toss
   Ⓒ Tossing a 6 on a number cube
   Ⓓ Not tossing a 6 on a number cube

10. On Jim's birthday, he chose a pet from a litter of dalmations. They were so cute, he just closed his eyes and picked one. If there were 3 males and 2 females, what are the chances that Jim's puppy is female?

11. **Science** Chromosomes determine whether a child is male or female. The probability of having 13 children that are all male is $\frac{1}{8192}$. What is the probability of having 13 children that are **not** all male?

The yellow and green sectors of the spinner are each $\frac{1}{4}$ of the spinner area.

12. What is the probability of spinning red?

13. Which two colors have equal probability?

14. What is the probability of not spinning green?

15. Number Sense Suppose you randomly select answers on a test. What is the probability of selecting the correct answer in each situation?

   a. Multiple choice question with 4 choices

   b. True-false question

16. Chance The *odds* of an event happening is the ratio of the ways it can happen to the ways it *cannot* happen. What are the odds of rolling a 3 with one number cube?

Problem Solving and Reasoning

17. Math Reasoning Two of these cakes are identical. Which are they? Suppose you had chosen two of them randomly. What is the probability that you would have chosen the two identical cakes?

Critical Thinking Answer "always," "sometimes," or "never."

18. An event that is certain _____ has a probability of 1.

19. An impossible event _____ has a probability of 1.

20. Communicate Explain the difference between *possible* and *probable*.

21. Explain why the probability of an event can never be greater than 1. Give an example of an event that has a probability of 1.

Mixed Review

Sketch each figure and find its volume. *[Lesson 9-6]*

22. A suitcase measuring 18 in. by 32 in. by 8 in.

23. A dumpster measuring 2 m by 1.5 m by 1.5 m

24. A box that is 3 cm by 4 cm by 3 cm

Are the triangles congruent? If so, state the rule that justifies your answer. *[Lesson 11-3]*

25.
4 cm   4 cm
60°   60°
3 cm   3 cm

26.
4 in.   4 in.
30°   30°

Experimental and Geometric Probability

▶ **Lesson Link** You have learned how to compute probabilities. Now you will see if what is likely to happen *does* happen. ◀

Explore | Experimental Probability

Materials: Shiny new nickels

Putting a Spin on It

1. Working in your groups, determine whose birthday is the latest in his or her birth month (for example, in a group in which students were born on the 12th, 3rd, 24th, and 19th, the 24th is the latest). Call this number *n*.

2. You will be spinning a nickel *n* times (24 times for the above). Write down how many times you expect to get heads.

3. Spin the nickel *n* times. Record the number of times you get heads. Is this the number you expected?

4. Divide the number of heads by the number of spins. Round to the nearest hundredth and write this as your probability.

5. What is the highest group probability? The lowest?

6. Tally the class results (total heads, total spins), and divide to find the class probability. Is this closer to what you expected?

You'll Learn ...

■ to use experiments to find probabilities

... How It's Used

Food manufacturers use market testing and probability to determine whether a recipe will be successful.

Vocabulary

theoretical probability

experimental probability

trial

geometric probability

Learn | Experimental and Geometric Probability

Sometimes it is easy to calculate the actual, or **theoretical probability**, of an event. When you roll a number cube, it is clear that each side has a $\frac{1}{6}$ probability of coming up. But for other situations, you may need to estimate the probability from survey or experimental data. The probability calculated by this method is called **experimental probability**.

The best way to understand experimental probability is to use it in a situation in which we know the theoretical probability and then compare the two.

Each time you perform an experiment, it is called a **trial** .

Example 1

a. What is the theoretical probability of rolling each possible sum when rolling a pair of number cubes?

Using the Counting Principle, there are 6 × 6 = 36 possible outcomes. You can draw a diagram or make an organized list to see all possible sums.

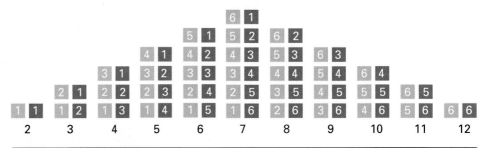

Theoretical Probabilities											
Sum	2	3	4	5	6	7	8	9	10	11	12
Outcomes	1	2	3	4	5	6	5	4	3	2	1
Percent	2.8	5.6	8.3	11.1	13.9	16.7	13.9	11.1	8.3	5.6	2.8

b. To find the experimental probabilities, roll a pair of number cubes 50 times and keep track of the sums that appear.

One student obtained these results:

Experimental Probabilities											
Sum	2	3	4	5	6	7	8	9	10	11	12
Outcomes	2	4	3	5	7	8	9	5	4	3	0
Percent	4	8	6	10	14	16	18	10	8	6	0

c. Compare these experimental results to the theoretical percents for sums from 2 through 12.

The percents of the experimental and theoretical probabilities are close. They would be much closer if the student had used a large number of trials.

Try It

a. What is the theoretical probability of tossing 2 heads, 1 head, and 0 heads when tossing a pair of coins?

b. To find the experimental probability, toss a pair of coins 50 times. Keep track of the number of times each result occurs.

c. Compare your experimental results to the theoretical percents.

The chance that a randomly selected person was born on leap day—February 29—is about 1 in 1461.

In many situations, it may be difficult or impossible to find the theoretical probability, so experimental methods are necessary.

Example 2

At many birthday parties, it is traditional to fill a piñata with treats and hang it from a tree. After being blindfolded and spun around a few times, guests are given 2 chances to break the piñata open with a bat or stick. When it breaks, there is a free-for-all for the treats.

El Burro manufactures piñatas. It would like the probability that a solid hit with the bat breaks the piñata to be about 8%. The company brings in children to test piñatas.

Complete the table to find the probability that a hit breaks each type of piñata. Which piñatas are ready to sell?

▶ **Language Link**

In Spanish, *piñata* means "pot." Originally, a clay pot was used to hold the treats, but now piñatas are made from wire, cardboard, and papier-maché.

Piñata Type	Number of Hits	Piñatas Broken	P(Hit Breaks Piñata)
Dragon	107	18	?
Bull	216	8	?
Burro	254	19	?

Dragon $P = \frac{18}{107} \approx 16.8\%$; bull $P = \frac{8}{216} \approx 3.7\%$; burro $P = \frac{19}{254} \approx 7.5\%$.

The burro piñatas are ready to sell.

Try It

Quality control is important in many businesses. BrightLights makes candles. BrightLights will tolerate a 0.5% defective rate for each package of candles (missing wicks, chips, and so on). Tests were run in different factories.

Complete the table to find the probability that a box contains defective candles. Which factories passed the inspection?

Factory	Number with Defects	Number of Packages Checked	P(Box Contains Defective Candles)
San Antonio	20	4534	?
Tulsa	27	5324	?
Uvalde	10	1095	?

If the number of packages produced at the San Antonio factory were 10,000 a day, how many would you predict would contain defective candles?

► History Link

In 1582, Pope Gregory XIII corrected the calendar, adjusting leap year to occur every 4 years—except for years divisible by 100, unless it is also divisible by 400.

Another way to determine probability is by using geometric models and comparing areas, lengths, or other measures. This is called **geometric probability**.

Example 3

A small prize is placed randomly in the birthday cake. It can be anywhere in the cake with equal likelihood. What is the probability that the prize is under one of the **iced edges**?

The area of the entire rectangle is 36 in. × 24 in. = 864 in². The center area is **30 in. × 18 in.**, or 540 in², so the area under the icing is 864 − 540 = 324 in².

The probability that the prize is in an edge piece is $\frac{324}{864}$.

324 ÷ 864 = **0.375**, or 37.5%.

Try It

A small prize is placed randomly in the birthday cake. It can be anywhere in the cake with equal likelihood. What is the probability that the prize is under one of the flowers?

Check | Your Understanding

1. Explain the difference between theoretical and experimental probability. Are probabilities quoted by doctors theoretical or experimental? Is geometric probability theoretical or experimental?

2. Carinna says that an experimental probability can exceed 1. Is this true? If so, give an example.

3. Suppose a quality-control tester at BrightLights tested 20 boxes, found defective candles in 1, and said the factory failed the test. Is this fair?

Practice and Apply

Getting Started Decide whether each probability is theoretical or experimental.

1. The probability that a bowler makes a strike is 30%.

2. The probability that a number cube lands on 6 is $\frac{1}{6}$.

3. Two coins are tossed 100 times. Two heads come up 23 times.

4. For his grandmother's 100th birthday celebration, Jeremy's mother asked him to find out what flavor cake each guest would prefer so she could begin cutting the 4 delicious cakes.

   a. What is the probability that a guest selected chocolate?

   b. What is the probability that a guest would choose lemon?

   c. What is the probability that the next guest would request a flavor other than carrot cake?

Flavor of Cake	No. of Requests
Chocolate	62
White	28
Carrot	22
Lemon	14

5. Geometry A player throws a marker onto the game board. It lands in a random location.

   a. What is the probability of its landing in the triangle?

   b. What is the probability of its landing outside the triangle?

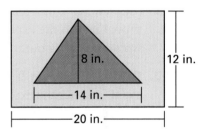

Toss 3 coins 50 times and make a table to record your results. Use the data to find the experimental probability of each event.

6. Tossing 3 heads and no tails   **7.** Tossing 2 heads and 1 tail

8. Compare the experimental probability of tossing 3 heads and no tails with the theoretical probability.

9. Geometry A particle travels around the perimeter of the hexagon and stops at a random location. What is the probability that it lands on the shortest side?

10. The day before her birthday, Shirin begged her mother to let her open one of her 7 gifts. With her mother's permission, she picked one to open, hoping it would be the radio she knew her father had bought her. Two of the packages were too small to be a radio. What is the probability that Shirin picked the radio?

11. Problem Solving Cliff surveyed his class to find the day of the month each person was born and organized his data in a stem-and-leaf diagram.

Stem	Leaf
0	1 3 5 7 7 8 8 9
1	1 1 3 5 6 7 7 7 8 9
2	0 0 1 2 2 3 4 6 6 7 8 9
3	0 0 1

   a. What is the probability that a student was born on the 17th?

   b. What is the probability that a student was born after the 29th?

   c. What is the probability that a student was not born on the 4th?

12. **Test Prep** Estimate the probability that a person was born in May.

   Ⓐ 8.5%   Ⓑ 12%   Ⓒ $\frac{11}{12}$ Ⓓ 60.1%

Problem Solving and Reasoning

13. Communicate Of 1000 patients, 600 were given a new medicine, and the rest were given a placebo (which has no effect). Of those given the medicine, 300 said their condition had improved, compared to 50 who received the placebo. Would you say the medicine is effective? Why?

14. 7 candles from a box of 24 regular candles were switched with "magic" candles that don't blow out. When Perry tried to blow out his 12 birthday candles, 5 of them remained lit. Compare the theoretical probability to the experimental probability that a candle would not blow out.

15. Critical Thinking If the theoretical probability of an event is 1, can the experimental probability be less than 1?

16. Math Reasoning What is the probability that the price of a birthday cake exceeds the median price for all birthday cakes? Explain.

Mixed Review

Find the volume of each prism after a dilation with a scale factor of 2. *[Lesson 9-7]*

17. 2 ft, 3 ft, 6 ft

18. 2 m, 2 m, 2 m

19. 8 in., 5 in., 5 in.

20. Evaluate the trigonometric ratios for $\angle BAC$. *[Lesson 11-4]*

656 *Chapter 12 • Counting and Probability*

PROBLEM SOLVING 12-5

Conditional Probability

▶ Lesson Link You have learned to compute probabilities of single events. Now you will learn how additional information and conditions affect probabilities. ◀

Explore | Conditional Probability

Food for Thought

Suppose that you have the following information about meal orders at a class function. You are working in the kitchen handing out meals on plates.

	Chicken	Vegetarian
Boys	73	11
Girls	52	29
Teachers	4	3

… How It's Used

Planning a large event requires considering many "what-ifs"—conditions and probabilities—so that risk is minimized.

1. What is the probability that a person ordered a vegetarian meal? What is the probability that any meal is for a teacher?

2. Is a vegetarian meal more likely to be for a boy, a girl, or a teacher? Is a chicken meal more likely to be for a boy, a girl, or a teacher?

3. Suppose a girl needs a meal. Is she more likely to have ordered chicken or vegetarian? Would you have been more sure or less sure of the meal selection if the person had been a boy? Why?

4. Suppose the first three teachers order a vegetarian meal. How sure would you be of the choice for the next teacher's meal?

Vocabulary
conditional probability

Learn | Conditional Probability

In many real-world situations, knowledge of one event affects your decisions about a second event. This is true in probability situations also. Often additional information leads to a more accurate ability to find the theoretical probability of an event.

Example 1

Suppose that you toss 2 coins. The first coin comes up heads.

a. What is the probability that you will toss 2 heads?

If you did not know anything about the first coin, the probability of 2 heads would be $\frac{1}{4}$. Because you know that the first coin is heads, then the sample space is reduced. There are now only 2 possible outcomes in the sample space. The probability of 2 heads, given that the first coin came up heads, is $\frac{1}{2}$.

1st coin   2nd coin   Outcomes

b. What is the probability that you will toss 2 tails?

Because the first coin came up heads, the probability that you will toss 2 tails is 0.

Try It

Suppose you roll two number cubes. The first cube comes up 1.

a. What is the probability that the sum of the two number cubes is 6?

b. What is the probability that the sum of the two number cubes is 8?

Problem Solving TIP

Rather than making an organized list, you may find it easier to draw a tree diagram to find the theoretical probability.

Conditional probability is the probability that, given that event A has already occurred, event B will occur. The fact that event A has already occurred reduces the sample space for calculating the conditional probability of B.

Example 2

Vanessa Mae, youngest person to record the Tchaikovsky and Beethoven Violin Concertos, shares a birthday with the legendary violinist Nicolò Paganini. Paganini was born in October of 1782.

a. What is the probability that you could guess her birthday randomly?

Since you know her birthday is in October, a month with 31 days, the probability is $\frac{1}{31}$.

b. What is the probability that she was born in a month that has exactly 30 days?

Because October has 31 days, the probability that she was born in a month with 30 days is 0.

Example 3

Movie reviewers Gene Siskel (born January 26) and Roger Ebert (born June 18) give each film they review "thumbs up" or "thumbs down." The table shows their ratings of 213 movies they reviewed between September 9, 1995, and July 27, 1996.

a. What is the probability that Roger would give a movie thumbs up? That Gene would give a movie thumbs up?

	Roger 👍	Roger 👎	Total
Gene 👍	80	20	100
Gene 👎	36	77	113
Total	116	97	213

Roger gave 116 of 213 movies thumbs up, so the probability is $\frac{116}{213} \approx 54\%$ that Roger would give a movie thumbs up. Gene gave 100 of 213 movies thumbs up, so the probability is $\frac{100}{213} \approx 47\%$ that Gene would give a movie thumbs up.

b. If Gene gives a movie thumbs up, what is the probability that Roger would too?

If **Gene** gives a movie thumbs up, the sample space is reduced. The probability is $\frac{80}{100}$, or 80%, that Roger would give it thumbs up too.

c. If Gene gives a movie thumbs down, what is the probability that Roger would give it thumbs up?

If **Gene** gives a movie thumbs down, the probability is $\frac{36}{113} \approx 32\%$ that Roger would give it thumbs up.

▶ **Career Link**

To become a movie critic, you can study film criticism at a university.

Try It

The results of a student survey are shown. First find the totals.

	Like Math	Don't Like Math
Calculators used in class	56	34
Calculators not used in class	35	25

a. What is the probability that a student selected at random would like math?

b. If you know that a student uses calculators in class, what is the probability that the student would like math?

Conditional probability can be shown geometrically. You know that a specific happening occurred in one region and you want to know the probability that it would occur in a smaller or intersecting region.

In the figure, the probability of a point being in square B is $\frac{1}{16}$. But if we know that the point is somewhere within square A, then the probability that the point is in square B is now $\frac{1}{4}$.

Example 4

Given that a point is inside the rectangle *RSTU,* what is the probability that it is inside square *ABCD*?

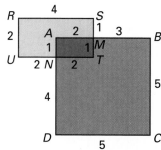

Because you know that the point is in rectangle *RSTU,* then it could possibly be in the rectangle *AMTN.* This rectangle is $\frac{1}{4}$ of the area of *RSTU,* so the probability that the point is in *ABCD* is $\frac{1}{4}$, or 0.25.

Try It

a. Given that a point lies in square *ABCD* above, what is the probability that it is inside rectangle *RSTU*?

b. What is the probability that a point within the large circle is also within the shaded region? Given that the point is within the small circle, what is the probability that it is within the shaded region?

Check | Your Understanding

1. Do new conditions always change the probability of an event? Explain.

2. Give an example of probability that increases given some condition. Give an example of probability that decreases given some condition.

3. Two number cubes are thrown. The first number cube shows a 2. What is the probability that the sum of the two number cubes is 9? Why?

Practice and Apply

1. **Getting Started** Suppose you spin the spinner twice.

   a. Make a tree diagram or an organized list to show the possible outcomes.

   b. How many possible outcomes are there?

   c. If the first spin lands on red, now how many possible outcomes are there?

   d. What is the probability that both spins will land on red?

2. Suppose you spin the spinner 3 times. What is the probability that it lands on green all 3 times?

Suppose that a fly lands on a checkerboard square. What is the probability that it lands…

3. On a red square?

4. On a square in the third row?

5. On a red square in the third row?

   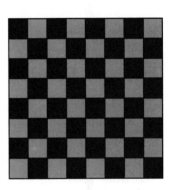

6. If you know that the fly landed on a black square, what is the probability that it landed on the bottom right corner square?

7. You roll a pair of number cubes in a board game. If the first cube comes up a 6, find the probability that the sum of the two number cubes is

   a. 6   **b.** 7   **c.** Greater than 10   **d.** Greater than 6

The graph shows the percent of people who have lost a job for various reasons.

8. **Career** Two employees are let go from an electronics company. What is the probability that both are let go due to negative attitudes?

9. **Math Reasoning** This graph represents 5000 people. About how many people were let go because they could not get along with others?

   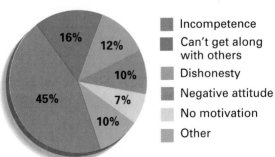

10. February 29 is sometimes referred to as Sadie Hawkins Day. Sadie was a character in Al Capp's comic strip *Li'l Abner*. Suppose one small spot on the comics page misprinted. If *Li'l Abner* was $\frac{1}{3}$ page and the Sadie Hawkins panel was $\frac{1}{6}$ of the comic strip, what is the probability that the misprint was on the Sadie Hawkins panel?

11. Consumer You are planning a pizza party and need a pizza parlor to provide the food. The results of the research on customer satisfaction of various pizza delivery services in your area are shown below.

	Satisfied	Not Satisfied	Total
Jay & Dee	12	6	18
The Coloseum	32	10	42
Peet-sa!	15	20	35
Total	59	36	95

What is the probability that if you choose a delivery service randomly from the ones shown ...

a. You will be satisfied?

b. You will be satisfied if you choose The Coloseum?

c. What is the probability that a person who was surveyed rated the Coloseum?

Problem Solving and Reasoning

12. Geometry If the inner circle has a radius of 2 in. and each ring has a width of 2 in., what is the probability of hitting a bull's-eye if a person's dart has hit in one of the black areas?

Critical Thinking Suppose a parachutist lands in the rectangular region shown.

13. What is the probability that the parachutist will land in a safe (light green) area, away from the corner trees and central fountain?

14. Communicate If she misses the trees, what is the probability that she will land in the safe area? Explain your strategy. What is the relationship between the sections of trees and the fountain?

Mixed Review

Find the volume of each solid. Use 3.14 for π. *[Lesson 9-8]*

15.

5 in.   12 in.

3 in.   12 in.

16.

40 cm

65 cm

17. Find the length of $\overline{XY}$ and $\overline{BC}$. *[Lesson 11-5]*

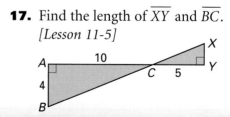

Dependent and Independent Events

▶ **Lesson Link**   You have learned about how one event can change the probability of another event. Now you will learn about whether one event can depend on another. ◀

Explore   Probability and Dependency

Point of No Return

Materials: Paper bag
3 Algebra tiles
Tape or dry marker

Mark the red side of two tiles and the yellow side of the third tile with tape or dry marker.

1. Without looking, take 1 tile out of the bag and record whether the red or yellow side is marked. Return the tile to the bag.

2. Take a second tile out of the bag and record whether the red or yellow side is marked.

3. As a class, make a table of the experimental outcomes.

	Second Tile	
	Red	Yellow
First Tile Red		
Yellow		

4. Repeat the experiment, but this time do not replace the tile.

5. Describe the effect of the first draw on the second draw in each case.

Learn   Dependent and Independent Events

Events that contain more than one outcome are called **compound events** . Sometimes the occurrence of one event affects the probability of a second event; sometimes it has no effect. If there is no effect, we say that the events are **independent events** .

If the events are not independent, the second event is a **dependent event** . You have considered several such situations in dealing with conditional probability earlier.

Example 1

Are these events independent?

a. The first roll of a number cube is 5, and the sum of the first two rolls is 4.

The second event is dependent on the first since the probability of rolling a sum of 4 changes to 0.

b. It is sunny and a movie theater changes its movies.

The fact that the sky is sunny has no effect on a theater changing its movies. The events are independent.

c. One person was born on May 27th and another was born on May 27th.

The birthday of the second person does not depend on the birthday of the first person. The events are independent.

Try It

Are these events independent?

a. It is raining and the parade is canceled.

b. You wear a Yankee cap, and the Yankees win.

If events A and B are independent events, then the probability of both A and B occurring is given by $P(A \text{ and } B) = P(A) \times P(B)$. This property for independent events is known as the **multiplication property** .

You could show the situation geometrically. If the probability of event A is $\frac{2}{5}$ and the probability of event B is $\frac{3}{4}$, then the probability of both event A and event B is $\frac{2}{5} \times \frac{3}{4} = \frac{6}{20}$, or $\frac{3}{10}$.

$A = \frac{2}{5}$

$B = \frac{3}{4}$

Example 2

Find the probability of flipping a coin and getting tails and then tossing a number cube and getting a number greater than 1.

The result of the coin flip does not influence the result of tossing the number cube. The probability of getting tails and tossing a number greater than 1 is $P(\text{tails, and roll} > 1) = \frac{1}{2} \times \frac{5}{6} = \frac{5}{12}$, or about 42%.

This can be shown by a tree diagram as well.

There are 12 possible outcomes; 5 satisfy the conditions, so the probability is $\frac{5}{12}$.

Example 3

Suppose you select a student at random. The probability that the student is either sex is 0.5 and the probability that the student is left-handed is 0.06. What is the probability that the student is a left-handed male?

P(male and left-handed) = 0.5 × 0.06 = 0.03. The probability of selecting a left-handed male is 3%.

Try It

At Artistes, 80% of the customers are female, and 43% make a purchase. What is the probability that a customer is a woman who makes a purchase?

When drawing a card from a deck, whether or not you replace each card affects the probability.

Example 4

a. A card is drawn and replaced. A second card is drawn. What is the probability that the first card is red and the second is blue?

b. Two cards are drawn (the first card is not replaced). What is the probability that the first card is red and the second is blue?

a. First card: $P(R) = \frac{4}{7}$ Second card: $P(B) = \frac{1}{7}$
P(red and blue) $= \frac{4}{7} \times \frac{1}{7} = \frac{4}{49}$ ($\approx 8.2\%$)

b. First card: $P(R) = \frac{4}{7}$ Second card: $P(B) = \frac{1}{6}$
P(red and blue) $= \frac{4}{7} \times \frac{1}{6} = \frac{4}{42}$ ($\approx 9.5\%$)

Try It

Two cards are drawn. What is the probability that both will be green if the first card is replaced? If it is not replaced?

Check Your Understanding

1. How is the independence of events important to a person using probability?

2. Why can you use the multiplication property to find the probability associated with a pair of independent events?

3. For event A, the probability is $\frac{1}{2}$; for B it is $\frac{1}{3}$; and for A and B, $\frac{1}{5}$. Would you say A and B are independent events? Explain?

Practice and Apply

1. **Getting Started** A number cube is tossed two times. Find P(even number, 6).

   a. Find the probability of rolling an even number.

   b. Find the probability of rolling a 6.

   c. Multiply the two probabilities and express your answer as a percent.

State whether each pair of events is independent or dependent.

2. A number cube is rolled twice.

3. Choose a marble, replace it, and choose a second marble.

4. Two children are born into a family—a girl, then a boy.

5. Your birthday is today and you have a birthday party.

Suppose that two marbles are drawn from the bag. The first marble is replaced before the second is drawn. Find each probability.

6. P(blue, yellow)   7. P(blue, blue)   8. P(green, **not** green)

Suppose that two marbles are drawn from the bag. The first marble is *not* replaced before the second is drawn. Find each probability.

9. P(blue, yellow)   10. P(blue, blue)   11. P(green, **not** green)

In the maze, a mouse picks his paths at random and continues toward the rooms marked A and B.

12. If the mouse reaches **2,** what is the probability that he ends in room A?

13. If the mouse reaches **3,** what is the probability that he ends in room B?

14. What is the probability that the mouse shown ends in room A? In room B?

15. **Industry** Suppose a security system and its backup each have a 97% chance of functioning correctly. If the systems are independent, what is the probability that they both fail?

16. **Test Prep** You buy a box of 50 birthday candles that has 10% red, 30% blue, 30% green, 20% yellow, and 10% white candles. If you pull 2 candles from the box, what is the probability that they are both blue?

Ⓐ 8.6%   Ⓑ 9%   Ⓒ 15%   Ⓓ 60%

17. You won a prize on your birthday.

a. If the prizes are chosen at random, what is your chance of winning the concert tickets?

b. If the first-place winner chose the graphing calculator, what are your chances of winning the concert tickets now?

PRIZES!

Concert Tickets
Graphing Calculator
Computer Game
3 Music CDs
Dinner for 2

Problem Solving and Reasoning

18. Critical Thinking Two different letters are selected from the word BIRTHDAY. The first letter is not replaced.

a. What is the probability that at least one letter is a vowel?

b. If the first letter selected is R, what is the probability that at least one letter is a vowel?

c. If the first letter selected is A, what is the probability that at least one letter is a vowel?

19. Communicate Explain how you could use the Counting Principle to find the probability of a compound event.

20. Chance You toss a coin three times and each time it comes up heads. What is the probability that it will come up heads on the fourth toss?

Mixed Review

Find the volume of each solid. Use 3.14 for π. *[Lesson 9-9]*

21.

11 in.

2.5 in.

22.

20 cm

8 cm

23. What are the coordinates of the point $(-1, -2)$ after being translated 2 units right and 4 units up? *[Lesson 11-6]*

Project Progress

Think about the probabilities you would want for your game. Can you use permutations or combinations to help you design your game?

Problem Solving

Understand
Plan
Solve
Look Back

TECHNOLOGY

Using a Graphing Calculator • Simulation

Problem: Simulate how often people arrive at a checkout counter. Estimate the probability that at least 2 people will show up at the same time within a 5-minute period.

You can use a graphing or scientific calculator to do this.

Suppose that the number of people arriving at a checkout counter each minute is given by the probabilities shown in the table.

Generate a random probability with your calculator. Find out how many people this represents using the last column of the table.

1 Complete the table (look for a pattern).

Number Arriving	Probability	Use
0	0.5	0 to 0.5
1	0.25	0.5 to 0.75
2	0.13	0.75 to 0.88
3	0.07	
4	0.05	

2 Press MATH, then choose **PRB** and **rand**. When you press ENTER twice, you get a random number between 0 and 1. Because this number is between 0.5 and 0.75, it represents 1 customer arriving.

3 Pressing ENTER 4 more times gives you 5 "minutes." For the numbers shown, 1, 1, 0, 0, and 0 customers arrived at the register. Two or more people did **not** show up within the same minute.

Solution: Generate several more 5-minute periods and record whether 2 or more people show up. To estimate the probability, divide the total number of times 2 or more people show up by the total number of 5-minute periods.

TRY IT

Suppose the probability that a basketball player makes a free throw is 0.710. Use a simulation to estimate the probability that she makes 3 out of 3 free throws.

ON YOUR OWN

▶ Try to simulate spins of a spinner numbered from 0 to 10.

In the Connect, you will apply your knowledge of probability to a famous birthday problem.

Happy Birthday, Baby

Your mission: Get through the room without finding two people with the same birthday. It should be easy, true? After all, there are 366 possible birthdays and only 20 to 30 of you.

Don't ask birthdays yet!

1. You will be the first student. Begin with one other student. What is the probability that you two share a birthday? Is this experimental or theoretical probability?

2. Assuming that you two do not share a birthday, how many birthdays remain that are open (not one of your birthdays)?

3. Add a third person. Does the birthday match either of your birthdays?

4. Continue adding a person at a time. What's happening to the probability of any pair sharing a birthday? Is the chance of each new person sharing a birthday with the others independent of the number of people already there?

5. Did you succeed in your mission? If there was a match, how many people did it take? How many matches were there in your class? Are you surprised?

6. If there were 370 people in the room, would there have to be a pair that share a birthday? Why?

Identify the sample space for each experiment, find the number of outcomes satisfying each event, and find the probability of each event.

1. Rolling a number cube with faces numbered 1 through 6. Events:

  a. Rolling a 5   **b.** Rolling a multiple of 2   **c.** Rolling a 7

2. Drawing a marble from a bag of 4 red, 2 green, and 3 blue marbles. Events:

  a. Drawing a red marble   **b.** Not drawing a blue marble

3. If you toss two number cubes, what are the following probabilities?

  a. $P(\text{sum of } 2)$ **b.** $P(\text{sum} > 9)$ **c.** $P(\text{sum of } 6, 7, \text{ or } 8)$

4. You draw two marbles from a bag of 3 red, 2 green, and 3 blue marbles. Find the probability if the first marble is replaced. Then find the probability if it is not replaced.

  a. $P(\text{red, then green})$ **b.** $P(\text{red, then red})$ **c.** $P(\text{red, then } \textbf{not} \text{ red})$

5. What is the probability of spinning yellow?

6. What is the probability of **not** spinning red?

7. If you spin the spinner twice, what is the probability of spinning red, then yellow?

8. If the first spin lands on red, what is the probability that both spins will land on red?

9. If one person is selected from a group to serve on a committee, does that affect the probability of the next selection? Why or why not?

10. Compare and contrast independent and dependent events.

Test Prep

Be sure to read the question carefully before you choose an answer.

11. What is the probability of a fly landing in square A if you know that it landed somewhere in square B?

  Ⓐ $\frac{1}{6}$ Ⓑ $\frac{1}{4}$ Ⓒ $\frac{1}{3}$ Ⓓ 1

REVIEW 12B

Probability of *A* OR *B*

When a number cube is rolled, it can't come up 2 and 5 at the same time. These are called *mutually exclusive* events—if one happens, the other can't happen. The probability of rolling a 2 OR rolling a 5 is just the sum of the probabilities.

In general, the probability of two mutually exclusive events is
$P(A \text{ OR } B) = P(A) + P(B)$.

Of 100 students, 90 take math, 80 take science. What is the probability that a student is taking math OR science (or both)?

If we were to simply add their probabilities, the result is greater than 1:

$$P(\text{math OR science}) \overset{?}{=} P(\text{math}) + P(\text{science})$$
$$\overset{?}{=} 0.9 + 0.8$$
$$\overset{?}{=} 1.7$$

But they are not mutually exclusive; you *can* take both math and science. You can see how adding in this case counts those taking math AND science twice:

To avoid this, the one extra math AND science group must be subtracted:
$$P(\text{math OR science}) = P(\text{math}) + P(\text{science}) - P(\text{math AND science})$$

Assuming that taking math and taking science are independent events:
$$P(\text{math AND science}) = 0.9(0.8)$$

So $P(\text{math OR science}) = 0.9 + 0.8 - 0.9(0.8) = 1.7 - 0.72 = 0.98$.

The probability that a student would take math or science is 0.98.

Try It
a. Two number cubes are rolled. What is the probability that either the first or second cube gives a 4?

b. What is the probability that, on a single draw, a heart or an ace will be picked from a deck of 52 cards? *Hint:* There are 13 hearts, 4 aces, and 1 ace of hearts.

671

Graphic Organizer

Section 12A   Counting

Summary

■ The **Counting Principle** states that if a situation can occur in m ways, and a second situation can occur in n ways, then these things can occur together in $m \times n$ ways. You can also use a table or **tree diagram** to count.

■ **Factorial** notation is used to write a product of consecutive whole numbers. 4! is 4 factorial, meaning $4 \times 3 \times 2 \times 1$. 0! is defined to be 1.

■ A **permutation,** or **arrangement,** is an ordered selection of objects. You can use the Counting Principle or factorials to count permutations.

■ A **combination** is a selection of objects without regard to order. The number of combinations is the number of permutations divided by the number of ways to arrange or order the *selected* objects.

Review

1. Make a tree diagram to show the possible results of spinning both spinners.

2. There are 5 roads from Morgantown to Shelbyville and 3 roads from Shelbyville to Tekton. How many routes are there from Morgantown through Shelbyville to Tekton?

3. Evaluate each expression.

　a. 5!　　**b.** $(6 - 2)!$　　**c.** $\dfrac{7!}{3! \times 4!}$

4. How many ways can the letters in PENCIL be arranged?

5. A club has 8 members. How many ways can a president, vice president, and secretary be chosen?

6. A Szechwan Chinese restaurant offers 10 entrees. How many ways can a family select 4 dishes to share?

Summary

- A **sample space** is the set of all possible **outcomes,** or results, of an **experiment.** An **event** is an outcome or a collection of outcomes.

- The **probability,** or **theoretical probability,** of an event is

  $$P(\text{event}) = \frac{\text{number of equally likely outcomes in the event}}{\text{number of outcomes in the sample space}}.$$

- The sum of the probability of an event occurring and the probability of the event *not* occurring is 1.

- **Experimental probability** is calculated using data from surveys or experiments. It is the number of times the event occurs divided by the number of **trials.**

- **Geometric probability** is calculated by using geometric models and comparing areas, lengths, or other measures. **Conditional probability** is the probability that event B will occur, given that event A has already occurred.

- If the occurrence of one event does not affect the probability of a second event, the events are **independent events.**

- The **multiplication property** states that, for independent events A and B, $P(A \text{ and } B) = P(A) \times P(B)$.

Review

7. What is the probability of rolling a 5 or more on one toss of a number cube?

8. What is the probability that a card chosen from a 52-card deck is one of the 4 jacks?

9. A radio station announces that there is an 80% probability of rain today. What is the probability that it will **not** rain today?

10. Roll a number cube 30 times. Record your results and calculate the experimental probability of rolling a 4.

11. A fly lands on the tablecloth shown. What is the probability that the fly lands on a green square?

12. The game of Scrabble® uses 100 letter tiles. There are 42 vowel tiles, of which 12 are E's. What is the probability that a tile chosen at random is an E, given that it is a vowel?

13. There is a hole in a green square of the tablecloth shown above. Find the probability that the hole is in the center square.

14. You roll a pair of number cubes and the first one comes up 3. What is the probability that the sum of the two number cubes is 9?

15. A bag contains 3 blue, 4 red, and 5 yellow marbles. Two marbles are chosen in order. Find $P(\text{yellow AND yellow})$ if

  a. The first marble is replaced before choosing the second.

  b. The first marble is **not** replaced.

16. A number cube is rolled twice. Find the probability that an odd number is rolled both times. Are these independent or dependent events?

1. Carmen's is having an outfit special. Buyers can choose one of 3 shirts, pants in one of 5 colors, and shoes in one of 2 styles. How many different outfits can a buyer choose?

2. The lunch special at Earl's Eatery includes soup or salad, and a choice of pasta, quiche, or sandwich. How many different lunch specials can be ordered?

3. Evaluate each expression.

   a. $7!$　　b. $\dfrac{8!}{5!}$　　c. $\dfrac{6!}{2!(6-2)!}$

4. How many ways can the letters of the word PHONE be arranged?

5. A disc jockey has chosen 6 songs he wants to play, but there is only enough time for 3 of them before the news. How many different ways can he select and order the 3 songs?

6. The debate club has 11 members.

   a. Find the number of ways to choose a committee of 3 members.

   b. Find the number of ways to choose 8 members to go on a trip.

7. What is the probability that a student chosen at random was born in March? Give your answer as a fraction, decimal, and percent. *Hint:* March has 31 days.

8. A pencil is chosen at random from 7 red, 3 blue, and 4 green pencils. List the possible outcomes in the sample space. What is the probability that the chosen pencil is green?

9. Cecilia rolled a number cube 60 times. Her results are shown. Give the experimental probability of rolling a 2.

Result	1	2	3	4	5	6
Number of Rolls	12	9	10	11	8	10

10. A wire is bent to make a trapezoid, as shown at the right. Find the probability that an ant crawling along the wire is on the 5 cm side.

11. Find the probability that the ant in Exercise 10 is on the 6-cm side, given that it is on one of the two parallel sides.

12. Julio was born on the 30th day of the month. Find the probability that he was born in October. *Hint:* All months except February have at least 30 days.

13. A card is drawn at random from a deck of 52 cards containing 13 diamonds. It is replaced and the cards are shuffled, and then a second card is drawn. Find the probability that both cards are diamonds. Are these *independent* or *dependent* events?

14. What would your answers be in Exercise 13 if the first card is **not** replaced?

Performance Task

Show several ways to find the number of 4-letter combinations from the word SAMPLE. Then write down all of the combinations in an organized list.

Multiple Choice

Choose the best answer.

1. If the value of k in $\frac{y}{x} = k$ is 8 and $x = 4$, what is the value of y? *[Lesson 5-3]*

Ⓐ 2   Ⓑ 16   Ⓒ 32   Ⓓ 64

2. Holly's Appliance Depot buys an oven for $600 and sells it for $750. What is the percent increase? *[Lesson 6-4]*

Ⓐ 20%   Ⓑ 25%

Ⓒ 80%   Ⓓ 125%

3. Which number is divisible by 9? *[Lesson 7-1]*

Ⓐ 6,829,269   Ⓑ 4,286,484

Ⓒ 9,238,832   Ⓓ 5,757,365

4. Find the angle supplementary to 73°. *[Lesson 8-4]*

Ⓐ 27°   Ⓑ 107°   Ⓒ 117°   Ⓓ 163°

5. Find the area of a circle with a diameter of 12 cm. Use 3.14 for π. *[Lesson 9-3]*

Ⓐ 37.68 cm²   Ⓑ 75.36 cm²

Ⓒ 113.04 cm²   Ⓓ 452.16 cm²

6. Subtract the polynomials. *[Lesson 10-7]*

$(2x^2 - 4) - (5x^2 + 3x + 4)$

Ⓐ $-3x^2 - 3x - 8$ Ⓑ $-3x^2 - 3x$

Ⓒ $-3x^2 + 3x - 8$ Ⓓ $-3x^2 + 3x$

7. What rule shows that the triangles are congruent? *[Lesson 11-3]*

Ⓐ Angle-Side-Angle   Ⓑ Side-Angle-Side

Ⓒ Side-Angle-Angle   Ⓓ None of these

8. $\triangle PQR$ is similar to $\triangle TSR$. Find the length of $\overline{TR}$. *[Lesson 11-5]*

Ⓐ 28.8 cm

Ⓑ 31.5 cm

Ⓒ 41.14 cm

Ⓓ 45 cm

9. What kinds of symmetry are in this figure? *[Lesson 11-8]*

Ⓐ Line symmetry

Ⓑ 90° rotational symmetry

Ⓒ Point symmetry

Ⓓ A and C

Ⓔ A, B, and C

10. A pizza parlor offers 3 sizes and 8 toppings. How many different 1-topping pizzas can be ordered? *[Lesson 12-1]*

Ⓐ 8   Ⓑ 24   Ⓒ 56   Ⓓ 336

11. A test requires students to choose 3 of the 5 essay questions. How many ways can the 3 questions be chosen? *[Lesson 12-3]*

Ⓐ 10   Ⓑ 15   Ⓒ 20   Ⓓ 60

12. Arlene flipped a coin 100 times and got 48 heads and 52 tails. What is the experimental probability of flipping tails? *[Lesson 12-5]*

Ⓐ $\frac{12}{25}$ Ⓑ $\frac{12}{13}$ Ⓒ $\frac{13}{25}$ Ⓓ $\frac{1}{2}$

13. You roll a number cube twice. What is the probability that you get a 4 on the first roll and an odd number on the second roll? *[Lesson 12-7]*

Ⓐ $\frac{1}{36}$ Ⓑ $\frac{1}{12}$ Ⓒ $\frac{1}{4}$ Ⓓ $\frac{2}{3}$

Chapter Review

Chapter 1 Review

1. Construct a line plot for the data set 43, 39, 51, 45, 40, 39, 49, 47, 42, 50, 39, 42, 44.

2. Make a stem-and-leaf diagram for the data set 28, 14, 29, 26, 35, 26, 19, 15, 19.

3. Find the mean, median, and mode of the data values 50.3, 41.2, 59.0, 46.7, 41.2, and 45.4.

4. Construct a box-and-whisker plot for the data set 3, 7, 2, 9, 4, 5, 2, 1, 0, 6.

5. Make a bar graph to show that a sandwich costs $4.00, a dessert $2.00, a drink $1.50, and a candy bar $0.50.

6. Describe a method for taking a random sample of customers in a bookstore.

7. Make a line graph for the following running times (in sec): 84 on September 5, 93 on September 10, 87 on September 15, and 82 on September 20.

8. Would a random selection of 200 people watching a movie premiere be a random sample of the population of moviegoers? Explain.

9. Read the bar graph to determine the number of each item in the music store.

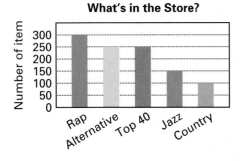

10. Read the line graph to determine the number of alternative CDs purchased by the music store each year.

11. Create a frequency table for the data set 4, 2, 5, 3, 2, 6, 5, 4, 5, 6, 2, 6, 4, 2.

12. Create a frequency table for the data set 1.5, 1.1, 0.8, 1.4, 0.9, 1.1, 1.5, 1.0, 1.3, 0.9, 1.5, 1.0, 1.3, 1.2.

13. Make a frequency table showing four occurrences each of 9.3 and 5.7, two of 1.5, and one each of 6.4 and 7.7.

14. Create a scatterplot and draw a trend line for the data set (1982, 10.3), (1984, 8.4), (1986, 11.4), (1988, 10.0), (1990, 13.5), and (1992, 14.2).

15. The U.S. government collected individual income taxes totaling $240 billion in 1980, $330 billion in 1985, $470 billion in 1990, and $590 billion in 1995 (estimated). Create a scatterplot and draw a trend line if possible.

16. One day in July, the temperature during the day was 89°F at 1:00 P.M., 92°F at 2:00 P.M., 94°F at 3:00 P.M., 96°F at 4:00 P.M., and 95°F at 5:00 P.M. Create a scatterplot for the data.

Chapter 2 Review

1. Find the absolute value of −93.

2. Find $|15| + |-23|$.

Compute.

3. −37 + (−29)

4. 73 + (−41)

5. −63 − 22

6. −38 − (−84)

7. −12 × 8

8. −54(−19)

9. 84 ÷ (−7)

10. −273 ÷ (−13)

11. 7 × −6

12. −4(12 − 19)

13. 4 × 11 − 56 ÷ (−8)

14. $5 - \dfrac{4(14 - 9)}{2}$

15. The temperature was −18°F and it went down 7°. What was the new temperature?

Give the coordinates of each point.

16. A

17. B

18. C

19. D

20. E

21. F

22. Write 8^4 in expanded form.

23. Write 12^5 in expanded form.

24. Write $9 \times 9 \times 9 \times 9 \times 9 \times 9$ in exponential form.

25. Write $2 \times 2 \times 2 \times 2$ in exponential form.

Evaluate.

26. $(-5)^3$

27. -4^0

28. -8^2

29. 1^8

Write each number in scientific notation.

30. Forty-two million

31. Seven thousandths

32. 835,000

33. 0.00000091

34. Write 6.31×10^6 in standard notation.

35. Write 2.97×10^{-4} in standard notation.

36. A microgram is 0.000001 g. Express this weight in scientific notation.

37. Venus is 67,200,200 mi from the sun. Express this distance in scientific notation.

38. The population of New Orleans, Louisiana, was 1,240,000 in 1990. Write this number in scientific notation.

39. A milligram in the metric system equals 0.0000022 lb. Write this number in scientific notation.

Chapter 3 Review

1. Using w for weeks and d for days, write a formula for the number of weeks in d days.

2. Find the area of a triangle with base 6.4 m and height 8.8 m. Use the formula $A = \frac{1}{2}bh$, where b is the base and h is the height.

3. Write an algebraic expression for "$12.50 each, plus $2.00 shipping and handling."

4. Simplify the expression $6(b - 3)$.

5. Evaluate the expression $5x + 2y$ for $x = -2$ and $y = 4$.

6. Evaluate the expression $-6x + 5y$ for $x = 3$ and $y = -2$.

Solve each equation.

7. $23 = m + 36$

8. $\frac{x}{3} = 12$

9. $z - 9 = 4$

10. $4y = 28$

11. The Pizza-n-More restaurant sells submarine sandwiches for $6 each and charges $2 for delivery. With $20, how many subs can you buy?

12. Are $x - 2$ and $4x$ equivalent expressions? Justify your answer.

Solve each equation.

13. $n - 40 = 47$

14. $x + 31 = 78$

15. $y \times 6 = 3.3$

16. $10 = \frac{2x}{3}$

17. $2.4 = 16z$

18. $7 = \frac{h}{42}$

19. $4x + 18 = 34$

20. $2x - 12 = 12$

21. The maximum height h (in ft) of an object thrown straight up from an initial height of a (in ft) with velocity v (in ft/sec) is given by the formula $h = a + \frac{v^2}{64}$. Find the initial height when $h = 36$ ft and $v = 32$ ft per sec.

Solve each inequality.

22. $y + 21 < 49$

23. $7.9 \geq \frac{2b}{5}$

24. $x - 14 > 32$

25. $12 \leq \frac{1}{2}y$

26. $w + (-2) \geq 32.5$

27. $\frac{k}{3} < 2.76$

28. $67 \geq h + 5$

29. $13 > \frac{3f}{6}$

Solve each inequality, then graph the solution.

30. $10 + 2x \leq 4$

31. $2y - 8 \geq -2$

32. $7 < \frac{x}{2}$

33. $3x - 1 > 3$

34. $\frac{x}{3} < 4$

35. $4x - 7 \leq 5$

36. $17 + 3x > 20$

37. $y + 14 < 12$

1. Find the value of y when $x = -2$ in the equation $y = -3x$.

2. Make a table of values for the equation $y = x - 9$. Use 0, 1, 2, 3, 4, and 5 for x.

3. Find the rule that relates x and y in the table. Then find y when $x = 28$.

x	1	2	3	4	5
y	4	8	12	16	20

4. Determine whether each ordered pair is a solution of $y = \frac{3}{2}x - 2$.

   a. $(2, 5)$ b. $\left(3, \frac{5}{2}\right)$ c. $(6, 9)$ d. $(8, 10)$

5. Give two solutions for the equation $y = 4x + 1$.

6. Graph the equation $y = 2x - 3$. Use 0, 1, 2, and 3 as x values.

7. A towing company charges a fee of $50 plus $2 per mile to tow a car. Graph the price charged. Use x for the number of miles towed.

8. Draw a line through the origin with the given slope.

   a. -2 b. $\frac{3}{4}$ c. $-\frac{1}{2}$

9. Graph the equation $y = -\frac{1}{4}x + 1$. Find the slope, the x-intercept, and the y-intercept.

10. For each line, find the slope, the x-intercept, and the y-intercept.

11. For each line, find the slope, x-intercept, and y-intercept.

    a. $y = 5x - 2$

    b. $y = -x + 1$

    c. $y = x - \frac{1}{2}$

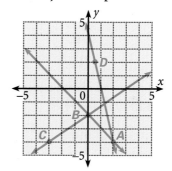

    a. Line through A and B

    b. Line through B and C

    c. Line through A and D

Solve each system of equations by graphing.

12. $y = 2x + 3$ $y = -\frac{1}{2}x - 2$

13. $y = x + 2$ $y = 2x + 1$

14. Econo Taxi charges $2 per trip plus $2 per mi. Super Taxi charges $5 per trip plus $1 per mi. For what number of mi is each cost the same?

Graph each inequality.

15. $y \geq 3x - 2$

16. $y < -\frac{1}{2}x - 1$

17. $y \leq x + 2$

18. $y > 2x - 1$

Chapter 5 Review

1. Write the ratio 5 to 6 as a fraction.

2. Draw a picture to show a ratio 4:3 of circles to squares.

3. Write all the ratios that can be made using the figure at the right.

4. Jean drives 248 mi in 4 hr and Paul drives 392 mi in 7 hr. Use cross products to determine whether these rates are equal.

5. Is the table an equal ratio table? If so, find the value of k.

x	6	12	18	24	30
y	5	10	15	20	25

6. Complete the table to create ratios equal to the given ratio.

5			20		30
8	16	24		40	

7. If the value of k in $\frac{y}{x} = k$ is 12 and $x = 25$, what is the value of y?

8. If the value of k in $\frac{y}{x} = k$ is 3 and $y = 12$, what is the value of x?

Solve each proportion.

9. $\dfrac{84}{48} = \dfrac{63}{m}$

10. $\dfrac{36}{81} = \dfrac{x}{324}$

11. $\dfrac{x}{102} = \dfrac{72}{136}$

12. $\dfrac{17}{x} = \dfrac{8}{32}$

13. Find the unit rate and create a rate formula for a rate of $1540 in 7 weeks.

14. Julie types 251 words in 4 min. Estimate how many words she would type in 15 min.

15. The ratio of jackets to shirts sold by Carla's Clothing Store is 6:17. In a two-week period, the store sold 136 shirts. About how many jackets were sold?

16. Last year, Central School had 420 students and 24 teachers. This year, there are 490 students. If the student-teacher ratio remained the same, how many teachers are there this year?

17. A scale drawing of a house is 3 in. tall and 13 in. across. If the scale is 1 in. = 4 ft, what are the dimensions of the actual house?

18. Find the missing measures in the pair of similar figures.

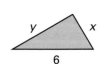

19. Find the unit rate for each situation.

a. $7.20 buys 18 candy bars

b. $0.50 for 100 paper clips

c. Traveled 120 miles in 2 hours

1. Use the information in the circle graph.

   a. What percent of the students watch 1 hr of television or less per day?

   b. What percent of the students watch 2 to 3 hr of television per day?

   c. What percent of the students watch 3 or more hr of television per day?

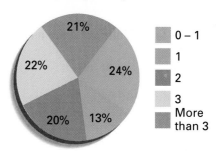

Hours Spent Watching Television per Day

21% 22% 24% 20% 13%

- 0 – 1
- 1
- 2
- 3
- More than 3

2. Write the fraction, decimal, and percent that describe how much of the figure is shaded.

3. Estimate the percent of the shaded region.

4. What number is 65% of 280?

5. Estimate 55% of 342.

6. Of the people at a concert, 12% bought a T-shirt after the show. If 156 people bought T-shirts, how many people were at the concert all together?

7. Find the total cost of a $110 stereo when its price is increased by 12%.

8. Estimate 37% of 248.

9. 15 is 24% of what number?

10. Pete's Boutique buys a sweatshirt for $24.95 and sells it for $39.95. What is the percent of increase?

11. A video normally sells for $29.95. Find its price during a 20%-off sale.

12. Abdul bought a book priced at $22.95. What was the tax rate if he had to pay $24.67 with tax?

13. Sharon earned $260 in simple interest on an investment in 5 yr. If the interest rate was 8%, what was her principal?

14. The price of a plane ticket can vary depending on the time of travel. Find the percent decrease for a ticket with a price of $210 in June and $145 in September.

15. Sal receives a discount on all purchases at the store where he works. He buys a radio for which the store originally paid $49.60. The store marked the price up 25% for retail, but Sal's price is $49.60. What percent discount did he receive?

16. Gina has a car valued at $4500. She sells it at an auction at an increase of 19%, but the auctioneer took 5% of the selling price. What amount did Gina receive when she sold her car?

Chapter 7 Review

1. Determine whether 184 is divisible by 2, 3, 4, 5, 6, 7, 8, 9, or 10.

2. Use a factor tree to determine the prime factorization of 504.

Determine the prime factorization of each number.

3. 21

4. 68

5. 117

6. 136

7. Find the GCF of 48 and 66.

8. Use prime factorization to find the GCF of 60 and 294.

9. Write the fraction $\frac{72}{104}$ in lowest terms.

10. Find the LCM of 24 and 30.

11. In one classroom, $\frac{4}{7}$ of the students are wearing T-shirts and $\frac{1}{3}$ of the students with T-shirts are wearing jeans. What fraction of the students are wearing both a T-shirt and jeans?

12. Rebecca does aerobics every three days and weight training every four days. Today she did both. In how many days will Rebecca again do both aerobics and weight training on the same day?

13. Write $\frac{14}{33}$ as a decimal and determine whether it is repeating or terminating.

14. Replace $\square$ with $>$, $<$, or $=$ to compare 10.9119 $\square$ 10.912.

15. Write 0.62 as a fraction in lowest terms.

16. Subtract $98.24 - 24.351$.

17. Add $4\frac{5}{8} + 11\frac{1}{2}$.

18. Divide $3\frac{4}{5} \div 5\frac{1}{6}$.

Write each decimal as a fraction in lowest terms.

19. 0.56

20. 76.892

21. $0.\overline{33}$

22. $1.\overline{64}$

23. Use prime factorization to find the LCM of 35 and 84.

24. Use prime factorization to find the GCF of 26 and 78.

Determine each square root.

25. $\sqrt{81}$

26. $-\sqrt{121}$

27. $\pm\sqrt{144}$

28. $-\sqrt{625}$

29. State whether 169 is a perfect square.

30. Find the square root of $\frac{36}{225}$.

31. Find the two consecutive integers that $\sqrt{89}$ is between.

32. What is the side length of a square with area 48 ft²?

33. Find $\pm\sqrt{361}$.

34. Find the missing side length for the right triangle.

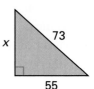

1. Convert 16 pt to qt.

2. Convert 6.2 m to cm.

3. What metric unit would you use for the mass of a bicycle?

4. Determine which measurement is more precise, 6 m or 605 cm.

5. Calculate 12.34 ft × 3.194 ft with the correct number of significant digits.

6. Find the complementary and supplementary angle measures for a 73° angle.

7. What are the latitude and longitude of Munich?

8. What is the position of Berlin relative to Frankfurt?

9. Classify 60° as a right, straight, obtuse, or acute angle.

10. In the figure shown,
  a. Which lines are parallel?
  b. Which lines are perpendicular?
  c. Which angle is a supplement to ∠A?

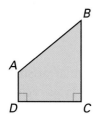

11. In the figure shown,
  a. Which angle is obtuse?
  b. Which angle is acute?
  c. Which angle is 90°?

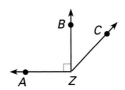

12. Draw the top view for the cube tower.

13. Classify the shape of this polygon by the number of sides. Then find the sum of the angle measures. [Hint: $180°(k - 2)$]

1. Find the perimeter and area of each polygon.

a.

14 in.
17 in.
15 in.
22 in.

b.

30 cm   16 cm
12 cm

2. Find the perimeter and area of

a. the polygon in Exercise 1a after a dilation by a scale factor of $\frac{3}{2}$.

b. the polygon in Exercise 1b after a dilation by a scale factor of $\frac{3}{4}$.

3. For the circle shown, find the circumference and the area.

11.3 m

4. Katie wears a ring that has a circumference of 2.36 in. Find the diameter of the ring.

5. Find the surface area of each figure.

a.

6 cm
2 cm

b.

10 ft
18 ft   8 ft

6. Find the slant height and the surface area of each figure.

a.

15 in.
8 in.

b.

18 ft   18 ft
13.5 ft
18 ft   18 ft
7.8 ft

7. Find the volume of each solid.

a.

16 m
9 m
7 m

b.

7 in.
6 in.

8. **a.** Find the volume of the solid in Exercise 7a after scaling two dimensions by a scale factor of $\frac{1}{4}$.

b. Find the surface area and volume of the solid in Exercise 7b after a dilation by a scale factor of 3.

9. Sketch a cylinder with a diameter of 3 in. and a height of 4 in. Then find its volume.

10. Sketch a triangular prism 6 cm in height. The triangular faces each have a base of 8 cm and a height of 4 cm. Then find its volume.

11. Find the volume of each solid.

a.

11 cm
25 cm   20 cm

b.

2.3 ft
2.3 ft
2.3 ft

12. A circular cone has a base area of 12 in². Find the volume of the cone if it's height is:

a. 3 in.

b. 12 in.

Chapter 10 Review

1. For the function machine shown,

Input	Multiply by 3	Output

   a. Find the output value for an input of 4;

   b. Find the input value for an output of -15.

2. What is a possible rule for the input and output shown in the table?

Input	3	5	7	9	10
Output	5	9	13	17	19

3. For the function rule $y = -4x - 1$, complete the table of values.

x	-1	0	1	2	3
y					

4. A ball is dropped from a height of 240 ft. Its height after t sec is given by $h = -16t^2 + 240$. Graph the function. When did the ball hit the ground?

5. Graph the functions $y = x^2$ and $y = x^2 - 2$ and explain their differences.

6. Graph the equation $y = 2x + 4$. Does the equation describe a linear function?

7. A car rental company charges $35 for each day or portion thereof. Graph this function.

8. Write the polynomial expression $4x^2 - 7x^4 + 2x - 1 + x^3$ in descending order. Find the degree of the polynomial.

Evaluate each expression for the given value of the variable.

9. $g^2 - 4g$ for $g = 2$

10. $2x^2 + 5x - 7$ for $x = -4$

11. $x^3 - x^2 + 6x - 2$ for $x = -3$

Simplify each expression. Write the resulting polynomial in descending order.

12. $3 - 6x + x^2 + x - 12 + 4x^3$

13. $2x - 9 + 4x^2 - x + 17$

Add or subtract each polynomial. Write each answer in simplest form.

14. $(y^2 - 7y + 4) + (3y^2 - y - 9)$

15. $(x^2 + 8x - 11) + (2x^2 + 3x - 1)$

16. $(-y^2 + 5y) - (2y^2 - 3y + 8)$

17. $(x^3 + 2x^2 - x + 4) - (x^3 - 2x^2 - 2x + 10)$

18. Find the total area of the region.

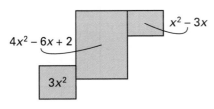

$4x^2 - 6x + 2$

$x^2 - 3x$

$3x^2$

19. The perimeter is $3x^2 - 4x + 9$. Find the missing side length.

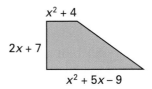

$x^2 + 4$

$2x + 7$

$x^2 + 5x - 9$

20. Find the area of a rectangle with a width of $3x + 4$ and a length of $2x^2$. Write the answer in lowest terms.

21. Multiply $-\frac{1}{3}t^2(3 - 12t)$.

1. The two trapezoids are similar. Find the length x and the measure of $\angle A$.

110°

16.8 m A

x

13.6 m   6.8 m

2. Are the figures congruent?

12 cm

3 cm   6 cm

20 cm

5 cm   10 cm

3. State whether the triangles are congruent; if they are, give the rule that justifies your answer.

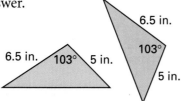

6.5 in.

103°

6.5 in.   103°   5 in.

5 in.

4. Use the lengths of the sides to write and evaluate the sine, cosine, and tangent ratios for the labeled angle.

65 ft

33 ft

30.5°

56 ft

5. In the figure, $\triangle DEF$ is similar to $\triangle GHF$. Find the length of $\overline{GH}$.

G

D 4.65 cm

F

3.1 cm

2.4 cm E H

6. Which are lines of symmetry?

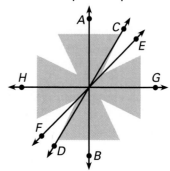

A C

E

H G

F

D B

7. Which transformation has occurred? Are the figures similar? Congruent?

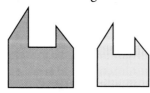

8. The trapezoid was reflected across the y-axis. Find the coordinates of points A and B.

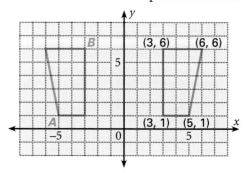

y

B (3, 6)   (6, 6)

5

A (3, 1)   (5, 1) x

−5   0   5

9. Can this tessellation be made using only rotations of a single polygon?

1. Make a tree diagram to show the possible results of spinning both spinners.

2. There are 6 different types of sandwiches and 5 different drinks. How many choices are there if only one sandwich and one drink are allowed?

3. Evaluate.

    a. $(4!)(2!)$ **b.** $(8 - 5)!$ **c.** $\dfrac{9!}{3!(9 - 3)!}$

4. How many ways can the letters of the word CAPTION be arranged?

5. Ten people are running in a race. How many ways can runners place first, second, and third?

6. A pizza parlor offers 12 different toppings for its pizzas. How many ways can a customer select 5 toppings for a pizza?

7. An office has 200 employees. How many ways can 15 employees be chosen to attend a conference? Use factorial notation for your answer.

8. What is the probability of rolling an odd number on one toss of a number cube?

9. What is the probability that a card chosen from a 52-card deck is one of the 13 hearts?

10. The probability that a tennis player will win a match is 60%. What is the probability that the player will lose the match?

11. Roll a pair of number cubes 25 times. Record the sums that appear and calculate the experimental probability of rolling sums greater than 9.

12. A dart is thrown at the target shown. What is the probability that the dart lands in a red area?

13. What is the probability that a card chosen from a 52-card deck is an ace, given that it is a diamond?

14. You roll a pair of number cubes and the first one comes up 5. What is the probability that the sum of the two number cubes is less than 8?

15. A drawer contains 6 black socks, 5 white socks, and 2 brown socks. Two socks are chosen in order. Find P(black, brown) if

    a. the first sock is replaced before choosing the second.

    b. the first sock is not replaced.

16. A gumball machine contains 16 blue, 22 white, 12 yellow, and 25 green gumballs. Find the probability of

    a. getting one white followed by one blue gumball.

    b. getting two yellow gumballs.

17. State whether Exercise 15 involves *independent* or *dependent* events.

18. A number cube is rolled twice. Find the probability that 4 is rolled both times.

Geometric Formulas

Rectangle

Area: $A = lw$

Perimeter: $p = 2l + 2w$

Square

Area: $A = s^2$

Perimeter: $p = 4s$

Parallelogram

Area: $A = bh$

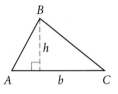

Triangle

Area: $A = \frac{1}{2}bh$

$m\angle A + m\angle B + m\angle C = 180°$

Trapezoid

Area: $A = \frac{1}{2}h(b_1 + b_2)$

Polygon

Sum of angle measures for
n-sided polygon: $S = (n - 2)180°$

Perimeter: sum of measures of
all sides

Circle

Area: $A = \pi r^2$

Circumference: $C = \pi d = 2\pi r$

Prism

Volume: $V = Bh$

Surface Area: $SA = ph + 2B$

Cylinder

Volume: $V = \pi r^2 h$

Surface Area: $SA = 2\pi rh + 2\pi r^2$

Measurement Conversion Factors

Metric Measures of Length

1000 meters (m) = 1 kilometer (km)

100 centimeters (cm) = 1 m

10 decimeters (dm) = 1 m

1000 millimeters (mm) = 1 m

10 cm = 1 decimeter (dm)

10 mm = 1 cm

Area

100 square millimeters = 1 square centimeter
$$(mm^2) \qquad (cm^2)$$

$10,000 \text{ cm}^2 = 1$ square meter (m^2)

$10,000 \text{ m}^2 = 1$ hectare (ha)

Volume

1000 cubic millimeters = 1 cubic centimeter
$$(mm^3) \qquad (cm^3)$$

$1000 \text{ cm}^3 = 1$ cubic decimeter (dm^3)

$1,000,000 \text{ cm}^3 = 1$ cubic meter (m^3)

Capacity

1000 milliliters (mL) = 1 liter (L)

1000 L = 1 kiloliter (kL)

Mass

1000 kilograms (kg) = 1 metric ton (t)

1000 grams (g) = 1 kg

1000 milligrams (mg) = 1 g

Temperatures in Degrees Celsius (°C)

0°C = freezing point of water

37°C = normal body temperature

100°C = boiling point of water

Time

60 seconds (sec) = 1 minute (min)

60 min = 1 hour (hr)

24 hr = 1 day

Customary Measures of Length

12 inches (in.) = 1 foot (ft)

3 ft = 1 yard (yd)

36 in. = 1 yd

5280 ft = 1 mile (mi)

1760 yd = 1 mi

6076 ft = 1 nautical mile

Area

144 square inches = 1 square foot
$$(in^2) \qquad (ft^2)$$

$9 \text{ ft}^2 = 1$ square yard (yd^2)

$43,560 \text{ sq ft}^2 = 1$ acre (A)

Volume

1728 cubic inches = 1 cubic foot

(cu in.)   (cu ft)

27 cu ft = 1 cubic yard (cu yard)

Capacity

8 fluid ounces (fl oz) = 1 cup (c)

2 c = 1 pint (pt)

2 pt = 1 quart (qt)

4 qt = 1 gallon (gal)

Weight

16 ounces (oz) = 1 pound (lb)

2000 lb = 1 ton (T)

Temperatures in Degrees Fahrenheit (°F)

32°F = freezing point of water

98.6°F = normal body temperature

212°F = boiling point of water

TABLES

Symbols

$+$	plus or positive	$\llcorner$	right angle
$-$	minus or negative	$\perp$	is perpendicular to
$\cdot$	times	$\parallel$	is parallel to
$\times$	times	AB	length of $\overline{AB}$; distance between A and B
$\div$	divided by		
$\pm$	positive or negative	$\triangle ABC$	triangle with vertices A, B, and C
$=$	is equal to	$\angle ABC$	angle with sides $\overrightarrow{BA}$ and $\overrightarrow{BC}$
$\neq$	is not equal to		
$<$	is less than	$\angle B$	angle with vertex B
$>$	is greater than	$m\angle ABC$	measure of angle ABC
$\leq$	is less than or equal to	$'$	prime
$\geq$	is greater than or equal to	a^n	the nth power of a
$\approx$	is approximately equal to	$|x|$	absolute value of x
$\%$	percent	$\sqrt{x}$	principal square root of x
$a{:}b$	the ratio of a to b, or $\frac{a}{b}$	π	pi (approximately 3.1416)
$\cong$	is congruent to	(a, b)	ordered pair with x-coordinate a and y-coordinate b
$\sim$	is similar to		
$^\circ$	degree(s)	$P(A)$	the probability of event A
$\overleftrightarrow{AB}$	line containing points A and B	$n!$	n factorial
$\overline{AB}$	line segment with endpoints A and B		
$\overrightarrow{AB}$	ray with endpoint A and containing B		

Squares and Square Roots

N	N²	√N		N	N²	√N
1	1	1		51	2,601	7.141
2	4	1.414		52	2,704	7.211
3	9	1.732		53	2,809	7.280
4	16	2		54	2,916	7.348
5	25	2.236		55	3,025	7.416
6	36	2.449		56	3,136	7.483
7	49	2.646		57	3,249	7.550
8	64	2.828		58	3,364	7.616
9	81	3		59	3,481	7.681
10	100	3.162		60	3,600	7.746
11	121	3.317		61	3,721	7.810
12	144	3.464		62	3,844	7.874
13	169	3.606		63	3,969	7.937
14	196	3.742		64	4,096	8
15	225	3.873		65	4,225	8.062
16	256	4		66	4,356	8.124
17	289	4.123		67	4,489	8.185
18	324	4.243		68	4,624	8.246
19	361	4.359		69	4,761	8.307
20	400	4.472		70	4,900	8.367
21	441	4.583		71	5,041	8.426
22	484	4.690		72	5,184	8.485
23	529	4.796		73	5,329	8.544
24	576	4.899		74	5,476	8.602
25	625	5		75	5,625	8.660
26	676	5.099		76	5,776	8.718
27	729	5.196		77	5,929	8.775
28	784	5.292		78	6,084	8.832
29	841	5.385		79	6,241	8.888
30	900	5.477		80	6,400	8.944
31	961	5.568		81	6,561	9
32	1,024	5.657		82	6,724	9.055
33	1,089	5.745		83	6,889	9.110
34	1,156	5.831		84	7,056	9.165
35	1,225	5.916		85	7,225	9.220
36	1,296	6		86	7,396	9.274
37	1,369	6.083		87	7,569	9.327
38	1,444	6.164		88	7,744	9.381
39	1,521	6.245		89	7,921	9.434
40	1,600	6.325		90	8,100	9.487
41	1,681	6.403		91	8,281	9.539
42	1,764	6.481		92	8,464	9.592
43	1,849	6.557		93	8,649	9.644
44	1,936	6.633		94	8,836	9.695
45	2,025	6.708		95	9,025	9.747
46	2,116	6.782		96	9,216	9.798
47	2,209	6.856		97	9,409	9.849
48	2,304	6.928		98	9,604	9.899
49	2,401	7		99	9,801	9.950
50	2,500	7.071		100	10,000	10

Trigonometric Ratios

Degrees	Sin	Cos	Tan
0°	0.0000	1.0000	0.0000
1°	0.0175	0.9998	0.0175
2°	0.0349	0.9994	0.0349
3°	0.0523	0.9986	0.0524
4°	0.0698	0.9976	0.0699
5°	0.0872	0.9962	0.0875
6°	0.1045	0.9945	0.1051
7°	0.1219	0.9925	0.1228
8°	0.1392	0.9903	0.1405
9°	0.1564	0.9877	0.1584
10°	0.1736	0.9848	0.1763
11°	0.1908	0.9816	0.1944
12°	0.2079	0.9781	0.2126
13°	0.2250	0.9744	0.2309
14°	0.2419	0.9703	0.2493
15°	0.2588	0.9659	0.2679
16°	0.2756	0.9613	0.2867
17°	0.2924	0.9563	0.3057
18°	0.3090	0.9511	0.3249
19°	0.3256	0.9455	0.3443
20°	0.3420	0.9397	0.3640
21°	0.3584	0.9336	0.3839
22°	0.3746	0.9272	0.4040
23°	0.3907	0.9205	0.4245
24°	0.4067	0.9135	0.4452
25°	0.4226	0.9063	0.4663
26°	0.4384	0.8988	0.4877
27°	0.4540	0.8910	0.5095
28°	0.4695	0.8829	0.5317
29°	0.4848	0.8746	0.5543
30°	0.5000	0.8660	0.5774
31°	0.5150	0.8572	0.6009
32°	0.5299	0.8480	0.6249
33°	0.5446	0.8387	0.6494
34°	0.5592	0.8290	0.6745
35°	0.5736	0.8192	0.7002
36°	0.5878	0.8090	0.7265
37°	0.6018	0.7986	0.7536
38°	0.6157	0.7880	0.7813
39°	0.6293	0.7771	0.8098
40°	0.6428	0.7660	0.8391
41°	0.6561	0.7547	0.8693
42°	0.6691	0.7431	0.9004
43°	0.6820	0.7314	0.9325
44°	0.6947	0.7193	0.9657
45°	0.7071	0.7071	1.0000

Degrees	Sin	Cos	Tan
46°	0.7193	0.6947	1.0355
47°	0.7314	0.6820	1.0724
48°	0.7431	0.6691	1.1106
49°	0.7547	0.6561	1.1504
50°	0.7660	0.6428	1.1918
51°	0.7771	0.6293	1.2349
52°	0.7880	0.6157	1.2799
53°	0.7986	0.6018	1.3270
54°	0.8090	0.5878	1.3764
55°	0.8192	0.5736	1.4281
56°	0.8290	0.5592	1.4826
57°	0.8387	0.5446	1.5399
58°	0.8480	0.5299	1.6003
59°	0.8572	0.5150	1.6643
60°	0.8660	0.5000	1.7321
61°	0.8746	0.4848	1.8040
62°	0.8829	0.4695	1.8807
63°	0.8910	0.4540	1.9626
64°	0.8988	0.4384	2.0503
65°	0.9063	0.4226	2.1445
66°	0.9135	0.4067	2.2460
67°	0.9205	0.3907	2.3559
68°	0.9272	0.3746	2.4751
69°	0.9336	0.3584	2.6051
70°	0.9397	0.3420	2.7475
71°	0.9455	0.3256	2.9042
72°	0.9511	0.3090	3.0777
73°	0.9563	0.2924	3.2709
74°	0.9613	0.2756	3.4874
75°	0.9659	0.2588	3.7321
76°	0.9703	0.2419	4.0108
77°	0.9744	0.2250	4.3315
78°	0.9781	0.2079	4.7046
79°	0.9816	0.1908	5.1446
80°	0.9848	0.1736	5.6713
81°	0.9877	0.1564	6.3138
82°	0.9903	0.1392	7.1154
83°	0.9925	0.1219	8.1443
84°	0.9945	0.1045	9.5144
85°	0.9962	0.0872	11.4301
86°	0.9976	0.0698	14.3007
87°	0.9986	0.0523	19.0811
88°	0.9994	0.0349	28.6363
89°	0.9998	0.0175	57.2900
90°	1.0000	0.0000	

Glossary

absolute position   Location given as coordinates. [p. 402]

absolute value   A number's distance from zero, represented by | |. Example: $|-8| = 8$. [p. 63]

acute angle   An angle measuring less than 90°. [p. 412]

Addition Property of Equality   If $a = b$, then $a + c = b + c$. [p. 141]

additive inverse   A number's opposite. The sum of additive inverses is zero. Example: 5 and -5 are additive inverses of each other. [p. 67]

adjacent leg   For an acute angle on a right triangle, the leg lying on one of the angle's sides. [p. 579]

algebraic expression   An expression involving variables, numbers, and operation symbols. Example: $2x + 17$. [p. 128]

alternate angles   Two angles formed by a transversal and each of the lines it crosses, on opposite sides of the transversal, either both interior or both exterior. [p. 417]

angle   A figure formed by two lines meeting at one point. [p. 410]

angle bisector   A line, segment, or ray that divides an angle into two congruent angles. [p. 413]

angle of rotation   The angle through which a figure turns during a rotation. [p. 594]

Angle-Side-Angle (ASA)   A rule used to determine whether triangles are congruent by comparing corresponding parts. [p. 575]

area   The number of square units contained in a figure. [p. 446]

arrangement   The order in which people, letters, numbers, or other things appear. [p. 631]

Associative Property (of Addition)   The fact that grouping does not affect the sum of two or more numbers. Example: $(a + b) + c = a + (b + c)$. [p. 69]

Associative Property (of Multiplication)   The fact that grouping does not affect the product of two or more numbers. Example: $(ab)c = a(bc)$.

bar graph   A graph using bars to represent the values of a data set. [p. 23]

base   On a three-dimensional figure, the top or bottom. [p. 462]

binomial   A two-term polynomial. [p. 533]

boundary line   On a graph of a linear inequality, the line separating points that are solutions from points that are not. [p. 207]

box-and-whisker plot   A visual way of showing median values for a data set. [p. 17]

center   The point that is the same distance from all points on a circle. [p. 456]

center of rotation   The point about which a rotation turns a figure. [p. 594]

circle   A plane figure whose points are all the same distance from its center. [p. 457]

circle graph   A graph in the form of a circle cut into wedges, also called a pie chart. [p. 274]

circular cone   A three-dimensional figure with a circular base and one vertex. [p. 469]

circumference   The distance around a circle. [p. 456]

circumscribed   A polygon with exactly one point of each side on the circumference of a circle. [p. 458]

coefficient   A constant by which a variable is multiplied. Example: in $12y$, 12 is the coefficient. [p. 146]

combination   A selection of objects from a set, without regard to order. [p. 638]

common denominator   A denominator that is the same for two or more fractions. [p. 345]

common factor   A factor shared by two numbers. Example: 7 is a common factor of 28 and 42. [p. 330]

common multiple   A multiple shared by two numbers. Example: 12 is a common multiple of 2 and 3. [p. 335]

Commutative Property (of Addition)   The fact that order does not affect the sum of two or more numbers. Example: $a + b = b + a$. [p. 69]

Commutative Property (of Multiplication)   The fact that order does not affect the product of two or more numbers. Example: $ab = ba$.

complementary   Two angles whose measures add up to 90°. [p. 412]

composite number An integer larger than 1 that is not prime. [p. 324]

compound event Event containing more than one outcome. Example: rolling first a 3 and then an even number with a number cube. [p. 663]

compound interest Interest based on both principal and previous interest. [p. 308]

compound statement A logical statement formed by joining two or more statements. [p. 163]

concave polygon A polygon with one or more diagonals lying outside the figure. [p. 424]

conditional probability The probability that an event B will occur, given that event A has already occurred. [p. 658]

cone A solid with one circular base. [p. 469]

congruent Two figures with the same shape and size. [p. 413]

conic projection A map projection that uses a cone shape to represent a spherical surface. [p. 499]

conjunction A logical set of statements joined by the word *AND*. [p. 163]

constant A number that does not vary. [p. 123]

constant of proportionality The quantity $\frac{y}{x}$ for two variables x and y whose ratio is constant. [p. 235]

convex polygon A polygon with all diagonals lying inside the figure. [p. 424]

coordinate system A set of intersecting number lines used to locate points. [p. 91]

coordinates A pair of numbers used to locate a point on the coordinate plane. [p. 235]

corresponding angles Matching angles on similar figures. The angles on the same side of a transversal that intersects two or more lines. [p. 417]

corresponding sides Matching sides on figures. [p. 565]

cosine For an acute angle x on a right triangle, the cosine of x is $\cos(x) = \frac{\text{adjacent leg}}{\text{hypotenuse}}$. [p. 580]

Counting Principle If a situation can occur in m ways, and a second situation can occur in n ways, then these things can occur together in $m \times n$ ways. [p. 627]

cross multiplication Multiplying opposite numerators and denominators of two ratios. [p. 243]

cross product The product of a numerator of one ratio with the denominator of another. [p. 229]

cube A 6-sided prism whose faces are congruent squares. [p. 479]

cylinder A three-dimensional figure with two parallel, congruent circles for bases. [p. 463]

cylindrical projection A map projection that uses a cylinder shape to represent a spherical surface. [p. 499]

degree For a polynomial, the value of the largest exponent of a variable. Example: the degree of $7x - x^3$ is 3. [p. 533]

dependent events Events for which the occurrence of one affects the probability of the other. [p. 663]

dependent variable The output variable for a function. [p. 513]

diagonal On a polygon, a segment connecting two vertices that do not share a side. [p. 423]

diameter The length of the segment that passes through the center of a circle and has both endpoints on the circle. [p. 457]

dilation A proportional reduction or enlargement of a figure. [p. 450]

direct variation When two variables are related by a constant ratio. [p. 555]

disjunction A logical set of statements joined by the word OR. [p. 163]

Distributive Property The fact that $a(b + c) = ab + ac$. [p. 83]

divisible Can be divided by another integer without remainder. [p. 324]

double bar graph A combination of two bar graphs, comparing two related data sets. [p. 24]

double line graph A combination of two line graphs, comparing two related data sets. [p. 25]

double stem-and-leaf diagram A stem-and-leaf comparison of two sets of data in a single diagram. [p. 7]

edge A segment where two faces of a polyhedron meet. [p. 461]

endpoint A point at the end of a line segment or ray. [p. 411]

equal ratios Ratios naming the same amount. Example: $\frac{6}{2}$ and $\frac{3}{1}$. [p. 227]

equation A statement that two numerical or variable expressions are equal. [p. 128]

equilateral triangle A triangle with three congruent sides. [p. 422]

equivalent equations Equations that are true for exactly the same variable replacements. [p. 141]

equivalent expressions Two expressions that always have the same value for the same substitutions. [p. 164]

evaluate To substitute values for variables in an expression and then simplify by applying the order of operations. [p. 128]

event A set of outcomes. Example: when a number cube is rolled, an event may be an even number turns up. [p. 646].

experiment In probability, any activity involving chance, like a coin flip. [p. 646]

experimental probability An estimated probability based on data from experiments or surveys. [p. 651]

exponent A raised number showing repeated multiplication. Example: $5^3 = 5 \cdot 5 \cdot 5$, where 3 is the exponent. [p. 96]

exponential function A nonlinear function in which an exponent is a variable. [p. 524]

exterior angles Angles formed by a transversal and the lines it crosses, outside of those lines. [p. 417]

face One of the polygon surfaces composing a polyhedron. [p. 461]

factor An integer that divides another integer without remainder. Example: 6 is a factor of 42. [p. 324]

factor tree A diagram showing how a whole number breaks into its prime factors. [p. 326]

factorial The product of all positive integers less than or equal to a number. Example: 6 factorial = 6! = $6 \cdot 5 \cdot 4 \cdot 3 \cdot 2 \cdot 1$. [p. 633]

formula A statement of a relationship among unknown quantities. Example: $P = 2(b + h)$. [p. 123]

frequency The number of times something occurs in a survey. [p. 38]

frequency table A table showing classes of things, a tally, and the frequency with which things occur. [p. 38]

function An input-output relationship giving only one output for each input. [p. 508]

Fundamental Theorem of Arithmetic All integers greater than 1 can be written as an unique product of prime numbers. [p. 325]

geometric probability A probability based on comparing measurements of geometric figures. [p. 654]

golden rectangle Rectangle with a length to width ratio of approximately 1.618. [p. 265]

greatest common factor (GCF) The largest number that is a common factor. Example: 15 is the GCF of 45 and 60. [p. 330]

height On a pyramid, the perpendicular distance from the base to the (opposite) vertex. [p. 466]

heptagon A seven-sided polygon. [p. 421]

hexagon A six-sided polygon. [p. 421]

histogram A type of bar graph where the categories are numeric. [p. 38]

hypotenuse The side opposite the right angle in a right triangle. [p. 374]

identity For any operation, the number that keeps another number the same. 0 is the additive identity, since $a + 0 = a$, 1 is the multiplicative identity since $a \times 1 = a$. [p. 141]

independent events Events for which the occurrence of one has no effect on the probability of the other. [p. 663]

independent variable The input variable for a function. [p. 513]

inequality A mathematical sentence involving $<$, $>$, $\leq$, or $\geq$. [p. 156]

inscribed A polygon with all its vertices on the circumference of a circle. [p. 458]

integers Whole numbers and their opposites: $\ldots -3, -2, -1, 0, 1, 2, 3, \ldots$. [p. 63]

interest Money paid for the use of money. [p. 308]

interior angles Angles formed by a transversal and the lines it crosses, between those lines. [p. 417]

inverse variation When two variables are related by a constant product. [p. 555]

irrational number A number, such as $\sqrt{2}$, that cannot be expressed as a repeating or terminating decimal. [p. 370]

isosceles triangle A triangle with at least two congruent sides. [p. 422]

latitude A measurement in degrees east or west from the prime meridian. [p. 90]

least common multiple (LCM) The smallest number that is a common multiple. Example: 48 is the LCM of 12 and 16. [p. 335]

like terms Terms in which the same variable is raised to the same exponent. Example: $3x^2$ and $9x^2$ are like terms. [p. 537]

line A one-dimensional figure extending forever in both directions. [p. 411]

line graph A line drawn through pairs of associated numbers on a grid, usually to show changes in data over time. [p. 24]

695

line of symmetry The line that divides a figure with line symmetry into two identical halves. [p. 605]

line plot A display of data that uses stacked X's to show how many times each data value occurs. [p. 7]

line segment Part of a straight line, with two endpoints. [p. 411]

line symmetry A figure has line symmetry if one half is the mirror image of the other. [p. 605]

linear equation An equation for which the graph is a straight line. [p. 182]

linear function A function whose graph is a straight line. [p. 514]

linear inequality A mathematical sentence involving $<$, $>$, $\le$, or $\ge$ whose graph is a region with a straight-line boundary. [p. 207]

longitude A measurement in degrees north or south from the equator. [p. 90]

lower quartile The median of the lower half of a data set. [p. 18]

mean The sum of a set of data values, divided by the number of values. [p. 11]

measure of central tendency A single value summarizing a set of numerical data. [p. 11]

median The middle value of a data set, when the values are arranged in numerical order. [p. 12]

metric system A system of measurement based on the meter, the gram, and the liter. [p. 390]

mode The most common value in a data set. [p. 13]

monomial A one-term polynomial. [p. 533]

multiple A product of a given integer and some other integer. Example: 35 is a multiple of 5, since $5 \cdot 7 = 35$. [p. 324]

multiplication property If A and B are independent events, then the probability of both occurring is given by $P(A \text{ and } B) = P(A) \cdot P(B)$. [p. 664]

Multiplication Property of Equality If $a = b$, then $ac = bc$. [p. 146]

multiplicative inverse If the product of two numbers is 1, each number is the multiplicative inverse of the other. Example: 6 and $\frac{1}{6}$ are multiplicative inverses. [p. 78]

mutually exclusive If either event A or B occurs, then the other cannot occur. [p. 671]

negative number A number less than zero. [p. 63]

negative slope The slope of a line slanting downward. [p. 191]

negative square root The opposite of the principal square root of a number. [p. 369]

net A pattern that could be folded to create a three-dimensional figure such as a prism. [p. 462]

nonlinear equation An equation whose graph is a curve rather than a line. [p. 213]

nonlinear function A function for which equal changes in x do not result in equal changes in y. [p. 518]

obtuse angle An angle measuring more than 90° but less than 180°. [p. 412]

octagon An eight-sided polygon. [p. 421]

opposite leg For an acute angle on a right triangle, the leg lying across from the angle. [p. 579]

opposites Two numbers on opposite sides from zero and the same distance from zero, such as 3 and -3. [p. 62]

Order of Operations The rules telling what order to do operations in: Do any operations inside grouping symbols, exponents, multiplications and divisions and additions and subtractions. [pp. 83, 97]

ordered pair A pair of numbers, such as $(-2, 8)$, used to describe a point in a coordinate system. [p. 91]

origin The point $(0, 0)$ in a coordinate system, where the x-axis and y-axis intersect. [p. 91]

outcome One of the possible equally likely results of an experiment. [p. 646]

outlier An extreme value in a data set, separated from most of the other values. [p. 12]

parabola A U-shaped or upside-down U-shaped curve, the graph of a quadratic function. [p. 518]

parallel lines Lines in a plane that never intersect. On a graph, lines with the same slope. [p. 197]

parallelogram A quadrilateral with two pairs of congruent sides. [p. 423]

pentagon A five-sided polygon. [p. 421]

percent A ratio comparing a number to 100. Example: 63% means $\frac{63}{100}$. [p. 274]

percent decrease The decrease in an amount expressed as a percent of the original amount. [p. 300]

percent increase The increase in an amount expressed as a percent of the original amount. [p. 294]

perfect square A number with an integer square root. [p. 364]

perimeter   The distance around a figure. [p. 444]

permutation   An arrangement in which order is important. [p. 631]

perpendicular   Lines forming a right angle. [p. 416]

perpendicular bisector   A line, segment, or ray that is perpendicular to a line segment and divides the line segment into two congruent parts. [p. 416]

pi (π)   The ratio of a circle's circumference to its diameter: 3.14159265... . [p. 457]

point symmetry   Point symmetry is a kind of rotational symmetry. A figure has point symmetry if it rotates onto itself after a rotation of 180°. [p. 607]

polygon   A figure formed by three or more points joined by line segments. [p. 421]

polyhedron   A three-dimensional figure composed of polygons. [p. 461]

polynomial   An algebraic expression that is the sum of one or more terms. [p. 532]

population   The collection of all things to be studied in a survey. [p. 32]

positive number   A number greater than zero. [p. 63]

positive slope   The slope of a line slanting upward. [p. 191]

power   A number that can be written as a product of equal factors (or, in other words, as an integer with an integer exponent). Example: $32 = 2^5$. [p. 96]

precision   The exactness of a measurement, determined by the unit of measure. [p. 396]

prime factor   A prime number that divides another integer without remainder. [p. 325]

prime factorization   A number written as a product of prime factors. Example: $120 = 2^3 \cdot 3 \cdot 5$. [p. 326]

prime number   An integer larger than 1 divisible only by itself and one. The primes start with 2, 3, 5, 7, 11, ... [p. 324]

principal   An amount of money deposited or borrowed, on which interest is paid. [p. 308]

principal square root   The positive square root of a number. [p. 369]

prism   A polyhedron with vertical sides whose bases are congruent and parallel. [p. 462]

probability   The chance that a particular event can occur. [p. 646]

proportion   An equation stating that two ratios are equal. [p. 229]

pyramid   A polyhedron with one base, on which all other faces are triangles meeting at a single point. [p. 466]

Pythagorean Theorem   For every right triangle, the sum of the squares of each leg equals the square of the hypotenuse. [p. 374]

quadrant   One of the four regions into which the x- and y-axes divide the coordinate grid. [p. 91]

quadratic function   A function where the value of x is squared. The graph of a quadratic function is a parabola. [p. 518]

quadrilateral   A four-sided polygon. [p. 421]

quartile   One of the numbers dividing a data set into equal fourths. [p. 17]

radical sign $\sqrt{}$, the symbol for the square root of a number. [p. 364]

radius   The distance from the center of a circle to any point on the circle. [p. 456]

random sample   A sample chosen in such a way that every member of the population has an equal chance of being included. [p. 33]

range   The difference between the highest and lowest values in a data set. [p. 6]

rate   A ratio in which two quantities using different units of measure are compared. Example: 76 dollars per 8 hours. [p. 224]

ratio   A comparison of two quantities by division. [p. 222]

rational number   A number that can be written as a ratio of two integers, such as $\frac{2}{3}$. [p. 344]

ray   Part of a straight line, with just one endpoint. [p. 411]

real numbers   All rational and irrational numbers. [p. 370]

reciprocal   One divided by a number. The number and its reciprocal are multiplicative inverses. [pp. 78, 357]

rectangle   A quadrilateral with four right angles. [p. 423]

reflection   A transformation that flips a figure over a line. [p. 594]

regular polygon   A polygon with all sides and all angles congruent. [p. 424]

relative position   Location given in relationship to another place. [p. 402]

repeating decimal   A decimal with a repeating digit or group of digits on the right, like 5.787878... . [p. 345]

rhombus   A parallelogram with four sides of equal length. [p. 423]

right angle   An angle measuring 90°. [p. 412]

right triangle   A triangle with one right angle. [p. 374]

rise   For a line on a graph, the vertical change for a given horizontal change, or run. [p. 191]

rotation   A transformation that turns a figure about a point. [p. 594]

rotational symmetry   A figure has rotational symmetry if it rotates onto itself after a rotation of less than 360°. [p. 606]

run   For a line on a graph, the horizontal change used to find the vertical change, or rise. [p. 191]

sample   The part of the population examined in a survey. [p. 32]

sample space   The set of all possible outcomes of an experiment. [p. 646]

scale   The ratio of measurements in a scale drawing to the measurements of the actual object. [p. 256]

scale drawing   A drawing showing the shape of an object exactly, but not the actual size. [p. 256]

scale factor   The ratio of new dimensions to old dimensions after a dilation. [p. 450]

scalene triangle   A triangle with no congruent sides. [p. 422]

scatterplot   A graph showing a set of points based on two data sets. [p. 43]

scientific notation   Writing a number as a power of 10 times a number whose absolute value is less than 10 but greater than or equal to 1. Example: $0.097 = 9.7 \times 10^{-2}$. [p. 102]

sequence   A patterned arrangement of numbers. [p. 113]

Side-Angle-Angle (SAA)   A rule used to determine whether triangles are congruent by comparing corresponding parts. [p. 575]

Side-Angle-Side (SAS)   A rule used to determine whether triangles are congruent by comparing corresponding parts. [p. 575]

Side-Side-Side (SSS)   A rule used to determine whether triangles are congruent by comparing corresponding parts. [p. 575]

significant digits   In a measured quantity, the digits representing the actual measurement. [p. 397]

similar   Having the same shape but not necessarily the same size. [p. 259]

similarity ratio   The ratio between corresponding side lengths on similar figures. [p. 565]

simple interest   Interest based on principal alone. [p. 308]

simplified   A polynomial containing no like terms. [p. 538]

simplify   To reduce the complexity of an expression by applying the order of operations. [p. 128]

simulation   An experimental model used to find probability. [p. 668]

sine   For an acute angle x on a right triangle, the sine of x is $\sin(x) = \frac{\text{opposite leg}}{\text{hypotenuse}}$. [p. 580]

slant height   On a pyramid, the perpendicular distance from one edge of the base to the vertex. [p. 466]

slope   For a line on a graph, the rise divided by the run. [p. 191]

solution   The variable replacement making an equation true. [p. 128]

solution of a system   The variable replacements making all equations in a system true. [p. 202]

solve   To find the variable replacement that makes an equation true. [p. 128]

sphere   A solid whose points are all the same distance from its center. [p. 479]

square   A rectangle with four sides of equal length. [p. 423]

square root   The square root of N is the number that when multiplied by itself gives N. Example: 9 is the square root of 81. [p. 364]

stem-and-leaf diagram   A display of data that uses the digits of the data numbers to show the shape and distribution of the data set. [p. 7]

step function   A function in which different rules are applied to different input values. The graph of a step function is made up of unconnected pieces. [p. 525]

straight angle   An angle measuring 180°. [p. 412]

substitute   To replace a variable with a specific value. [p. 123]

supplementary   Two angles whose measures add up to 180°. [p. 412]

surface area   On a polyhedron, the sum of the areas of the faces. [p. 461]

survey   A study that requires collecting and analyzing information. [p. 32]

symmetry   A figure has symmetry if it coincides with itself after some transformation. [p. 605]

system of linear equations   Two or more linear equations considered together. [p. 202]

tally A quick record of a count taken during a survey. [p. 38]

tangent For an acute angle x on a right triangle, the tangent of x is $\tan(x) = \frac{\text{opposite leg}}{\text{adjacent leg}}$. [p. 580]

term A number in a sequence. [p. 113]

terminating decimal A number with a fixed number of digits. [p. 345]

terms A part of a polynomial containing a variable with a whole-number exponent and coefficient. [p. 532]

tessellation A repeating pattern of figures that covers a plane without gaps or overlaps. [p. 610]

theoretical probability The actual probability of an event. The ratio of the number of equally likely outcomes in the event to the number in the sample space. [p. 651]

transformation A movement of points that affects all points of a figure. [p. 594]

translation A transformation that slides all points of a figure the same distance in the same direction. [p. 595]

transversal A line crossing two or more other lines. [p. 417]

trapezoid A quadrilateral with exactly one pair of parallel sides. [p. 423]

tree diagram A tree-like diagram on which each branch shows a possible outcome of a situation. [p. 626]

trend A pattern formed by points on a scatterplot. [p. 43]

trend line A line that approximately "fits" points forming a trend in a scatterplot. [p. 43]

trial One experiment. [p. 652]

triangle A three-sided polygon. [p. 421]

trigonometric ratios Ratios of the side lengths of a right triangle, related to the measures of the triangle's acute angles. [p. 580]

trinomial A three-term polynomial. [p. 533]

unit rate A rate in which the second number in the comparison is one unit. Example: 300 million meters per second. [p. 224]

U.S. customary units A system of measurement units, including the inch, the pound, and the gallon, widely used in the United States. [p. 390]

upper quartile The median of the upper half of a data set. [p. 18]

variable A symbol, such as x, that represents an unknown quantity. [p. 123]

Venn diagram A visual aid that shows relationships by grouping things into sets. [p. 422]

vertex On an angle or a polygon, the point where the two sides intersect. On a polyhedron, the intersection point of three or more faces. [pp. 410, 421, 461]

vertical angles Angles on opposite sides of the intersection of two lines. [p. 418]

volume The number of cubic units in a solid. [p. 476]

x-axis The horizontal number line in a coordinate system. [p. 91]

x-coordinate The first number in an ordered pair used to locate a point in a coordinate system. [p. 91]

x-intercept A point where a graph crosses the x-axis. [p. 196]

y-axis The vertical number line in a coordinate system. [p. 91]

y-coordinate The second number in an ordered pair used to locate a point in a coordinate system. [p. 91]

y-intercept A point where a graph crosses the y-axis. [p. 196]

Zero Property of Addition The sum of an integer and its additive inverse is 0. [p. 67]

Selected Answers

Chapter 1

1-1 Try It

Leaf	Stem	Leaf
	0	9
	1	2 4 7
9 8 6 3 2	2	1 1
6	3	

1-1 Exercises & Applications

1. a. 5 **b.** 3 or 12–15 **c.** 13; 15
3. Range: $2 to $7

5. Range: 8 to 33

Stem	Leaf
0	8
1	2 6 8
2	2 3
3	3

7.

Leaf	Stem	Leaf
2	12	
	13	
5	14	
0	15	
5	16	0
	17	
5 5 5	18	0 0 0
	19	
5	20	0
	21	5
	22	0
	23	
	24	3

9.

Stem	Leaf
5	0 3 7
6	6
7	5 5 6
8	1
10	1
11	7

13. 437 **15.** 50,000
17. 7,030,000 **19.** 725 **21.** 8803
23. 6109 **25.** 10,500

1-2 Try It

Mean: $9; Median: $7.50

1-2 Exercises & Applications

1. a. 774 **b.** 9 **c.** 86 **3.** Mean: 180; Median: 174; Mode: None
5. Outlier: 31; Revised mean: ≈ 11.4; Revised median: 10.5
7. Mean: 91 million people **9.** C
11. Mean: $5.80 **13.** Eight hundred fifty-six **15.** Four thousand eight hundred twenty-six
17. Forty-five thousand six hundred
19. Three million seven hundred forty-six thousand seven hundred
21. 726 **23.** 398 **25.** 3854
27. 4848

1-3 Try It (Example 1)

a. 20 or 0–20 **b.** Median: 4
c. Lower quartile: 2; Upper quartile: 10 **d.** One-quarter of the 12- to 15-year-olds have been to a music store between 10 and 20 times.

1-3 Try It (Example 2)

Between 16 and 18

1-3 Exercises & Applications

1. a. 100; 90 **b.** 95 **c.** 93 **d.** 99
e.

3. Between 20 and 24.5

5.

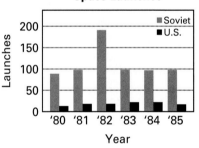

Possible answer: The middle half of the data has a range of 1524 to 2515. **7.** With outliers **11.** 18,486
13. 19,886 **15.** 558,448
17. 274,752 **19.** 43,640
21. 37,000 **23.** 46,400

1-4 Try It (Example 1)

a. 1990 **b.** 1994

1-4 Try It (Example 4)

1-4 Exercises & Applications

1.

Earnings of Book Publishing

3.

Number of Postmasters in U.S.

Probably stayed the same. **5.** D
7. Yes; all the data would still be
shown. **9.** 26 **11.** 36 **13.** 7 R11
15. 578, 735, 2378, 4321 **17.** 4257,
4527, 4725 **19.** 642, 654, 664, 684

Section 1A Review

1. Mean: 3.8; Median: 5; Mode: 5

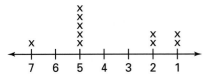

3. 140,400 km^2; 6.47 million

5.

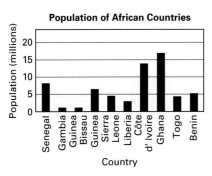

7. (44 × 6595 + 7462) ÷ 45 =
(about) 6614 fans

1-5 Try It

a. 679 **b.** No: a person who is on-
line had a better chance of being
surveyed than a person who is not.

1-5 Exercises & Applications

1. City households; 2301 **3.** U.S.
state governors; Random
5. Country music fans; Not random
7. No; Sample is too small.
9. a. Women **b.** 7244 **11.** No;
Possible answers: Only people who
respond to surveys responded.
13. Possible answer: Advertisers
want to influence buyers, not users.
15. 56,460 **17.** 974,352

1-6 Try It (Example 1)

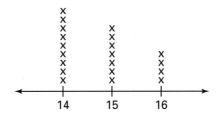

1-6 Try It (Example 2)

1-6 Exercises & Applications

1. a.

1993 Population

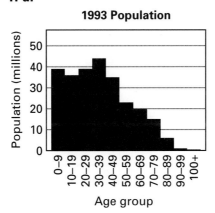

b. No, the frequency table gives
intervals instead of exact ages.
c. A histogram

5.

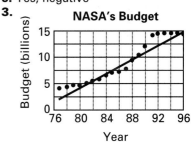

7. 2,066,592 **9.** 5,975,692
11. 1,758,591 **13.** 1,367,888
15. Mean: ≈ 55.44; Median: 64
17. Mean: 75.5; Median: 75.5

1-7 Try It (Example 1)

As the total waste increases, the
amount recycled increases.

1-7 Try It (Example 2)

a. No **b.** No relationship

1-7 Exercises & Applications

1. a. No trend **b.** Yes, positive
c. Yes, negative
3.

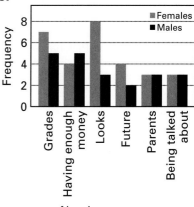

$17 billion **5.** D **9.** Yes
11. 891,488 **13.** 15,251,067,288
15. 77,732,551,971

701

1-8 Try It

a. How many hours do you spend on homework each week?
b. Possible answer: Pick names randomly.   **c.** Possible answer: A box-and-whisker plot.

1-8 Exercises & Applications

1. a. U.S. teenagers   **b.** To get U.S. teenagers to buy more of the company's shoes.   **c.** No, since New Yorkers might have different music tastes than the rest of the country.
3. Possible answer: What sports do you participate in?   **5.** Possible answer: How many TVs are in your home?   **7.** B   **11.** 32,768
13. 161,051   **15.** 7,311,616

Section 1B Review

1. a. Not random; Every 1st through 49th car.   **b.** Not random; Students who aren't the student's friends.
3.

Wait time (sec)	Frequency
0–60	4
61–120	6
121–180	3
181–240	1
241 +	1

Yes; The average wait time is about 112 seconds.   **5.** D

Chapter 1 Summary & Review

1.

2.

Stem	Leaf
0	67
1	334
2	1227

3. 16; 15.7; 14.9
4.

5.

6.
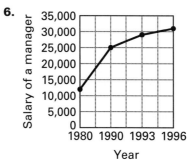

7. Answers may vary.   **8.** No, not all American adults read *TV Guide*.
9. Fiction: 1400; Non-Fiction: 1600; Reference: 1200; Multimedia: 500; Periodicals: 200   **10.** 1985: 200 books; 1986: 250 books; 1987: 300 books; 1988: 400 books; 1989: 300 books; 1990: 200 books

11.

0	1
1	1
2	3
4	1
5	3
6	2
7	2

12.

1	1
2	1
3	3
5	2
6	1
7	3
9	2

13.

1.57	2
2.45	1
2.74	1
5.35	3
7.39	1

14.

15.

16.

Chapter 2

2-1 Try It (Example 1)

a. 3   **b.** −$3   **c.** 0

2-1 Try It (Example 2)

17, −17

2-1 Try It (Example 3)

Belgium, Denmark, France

SELECTED ANSWERS

702

2-1 Exercises & Applications

1. a.

b. −4   **c.** −4, −1, 0, 2, 3   **3.** 42
5. 0   **7.** Possible answer:
Temperature on a winter day is 25°
below zero.   **9.** Possible answer:
Owe $60.   **11.** Possible answer:
Deducted 75 points.   **13.** D   **15.** =
17. <   **19.** >   **21.** >   **23.** 18
25. 2   **27.** 19,340 ft   **29.** C
31. Possible answer: −$0.08
33. Random

2-2 Try It (Example 1)

a. 8   **b.** 2   **c.** −2   **d.** −8

2-2 Try It (Example 4)

a. 11   **b.** −22

2-2 Exercises & Applications

1. a. −2 + 2 + (−4) + (−3) + 5
b. (−2 + 2) + [(−4) + (−3)] + 5
c. 0 + (−7) + 5   **d.** −2   **3.** 3 + −5 =
−2   **5.** −62   **7.** −6   **9.** −142
11. −48   **13.** −125   **15.** A
17. Never   **19.** Always   **21.** 327
gold bars   **25.** It will be on the 29th
floor. (Maybe the 30th floor because
many buildings do not have a 13th
floor.)
27. No trend

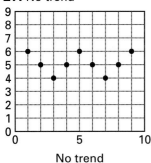

No trend

29. Women   **31.** People who live in
warm climates.

2-3 Try It (Example 2)

a. −12   **b.** −12   **c.** 12   **d.** 12

2-3 Try It (Example 3)

a. −31   **b.** Rose 25 ft

2-3 Exercises & Applications

1. a. −2   **b.** 9   **c.** −10   **3. a.** 12 +
−24 = −12   **b.** −24 + −12 = −36
c. 24 + 12 = 36   **d.** −12 + 24 = 12
5. −148   **7.** −110   **9.** 967   **11.** −2
13. −48   **15.** 420   **17.** No
19. 1165°F   **21.** D   **23. a.** >; 5 is
added on the left.   **b.** <; 5 is added
on the right.
25.

Stem	Leaf
3	2 4 8
4	1 2 2 6
5	3 8

2-4 Try It (Example 1)

−$10.00

2-4 Try It (Example 3)

a. $\frac{1}{-8}$ **b.** $\frac{5}{2}$ **c.** $\frac{3}{-8}$

2-4 Exercises & Applications

1. a. 78   **b.** −78   **3.** 48   **5.** −48
7. −12   **9.** −12   **11.** −14   **13.** 2
15. 0   **17.** −140   **19.** 0   **21.** −9
23. 0   **25.** 14   **27.** 28   **29.** C
31. $61 loss per month   **33.** 100
35. Commutative   **37.** −14°F
39. a. Positive   **b.** Negative
41. $47\frac{2}{3}$; 47

2-5 Try It (Example 1)

10

2-5 Try It (Example 2)

a. −24   **b.** −792

2-5 Exercises & Applications

1. a. Multiplication   **b.** Addition
c. Division   **d.** Addition   **3.** 22, 22
5. −12, −12   **7.** −9, −1   **9.** 90
11. −81   **13.** $36.44   **15.** 20
17. 1   **19.** 2°   **21.** 100 + 24 ÷
(3 + 1) = 106   **23.** −5 × (3 + 3 × 6) =
−105   **25.** 1.8 in.   **27.** Possible
answers: 3 ÷ 3 = 1; $\frac{3+3}{3+3}$ = 1; 3 − 3 +
3 ÷ 3 = 1   **29. a.** 36(100 + 1)
b. 50(100 − 1)   **c.** (50 − 1)13
d. (100 − 2)42
31.

78   85.5   92   97.5   115

33.

Length (in.)	Frequency
1–8	6
9–16	4
17–24	8
25–32	3
33–40	5

Section 2A Review

1. a. 10°, 20°, 30°, 40°, 50°   **b.** −10°,
−20°, −30°, −40°   **c.** 10°, −10°; 20°,
−20°; 30°, −30°; 40°, −40°   **d.** 50°
e. −40°   **3.** −612   **5.** −1,326   **7.** 3
9. −9   **11.** 100   **13.** 10   **15.** 0
17. −500   **19.** −3   **21.** 5   **23.** −1
25. 682,650   **27.** C

2-6 Try It (Example 1)

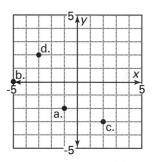

2-6 Try It (Example 2)

A is (2, 4); The low tide was 2, the
high tide was 4.

B is (−4, −1); The low tide was −4,
the high tide was −1.

C is (−7, −1); The low tide was −7,
the high tide was −1.

D is (0, 3); The low tide was 0, the
high tide was 3.

2-6 Exercises & Applications

1. a. *x*   **b.** Left; −2 is negative.
c. *x*   **d.** Down; −4 is negative.
2–5.

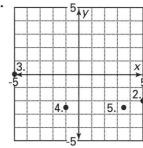

7. (1, 3) **9.** (−2, −3) **11.** (6, 0)
13. G **15.** K **17.** 24° S, 46° W
19. 19° N, 73° E
21.

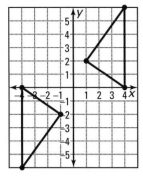

23. (−1, 2), (1, 4), (1, 0), (3, 0), (3, 4), (5, 2); Hexagon **25. a.** II **b.** I
c. III **d.** IV **29.** 317 **31.** 22

2-7 Try It (Example 2)

a. 625 **b.** 759,375 **c.** −8

2-7 Try It (Example 3)

a. 4 **b.** 18 **c.** 255 characters

2-7 Exercises & Applications

1. a. 8 **b.** 4 **c.** 4 **d.** 4,096 **3.** 9
5. 64 **7.** 8 **9.** 125 **11.** 24,900 mi
and 9860 mi **13.** 49 **15.** 1
17. −1 **19.** 16 **21.** 1 **23.** 0
25. −20 **27.** 11 ft **29.** 8, −8
31. 3 **35.** Random **37.** 6
39. −38

2-8 Try It (Example 1)

a. 326,000,000; 3.26×10^8
b. 98,000,000; 9.8×10^7

2-8 Try It (Example 2)

$15 \times 1,000,000$; 1.5 ⊠ 10 ⌃ 7

2-8 Try It (Example 3)

a. 96,000,000,000
b. −3,800,000,000,000
c. 10,200,000,000,000

2-8 Exercises & Applications

1. a. 28,000,000 **b.** 7 **c.** 7
3. 9.36×10^8 **5.** 8.11×10^7
7. 1,200,000,000 **9.** 74,400,000
11. 9,140,000,000 **13.** 18,000,000
15. a. 3.4×10^5; $10^5 > 10^4$ **b.** 8.9×10^5; $8.9 > 3.95$ **c.** 1.2×10^2; −4.6 is

negative **d.** 1.1×10^8; $10^8 > 10^7$
17. 130,200 km; 143,000 − 12,800
19. a. 10,536 hr **b.** 6.3216×10^5
min **27.** −12 **29.** −74

2-9 Try It (Example 2)

a. 1×10^{-6} **b.** 3×10^{-5}

2-9 Try It (Examples 3–4)

a. 0.000000003 or 3.0×10^{-9}
b. 8 ÷ 1,000,000 = 8 ⊠ 10 ⌃ 6 +/−

2-9 Exercises & Applications

1. a. 0.00035 **b.** 4; right **c.** −4
3. C **5.** 4.55×10^{-3} **7.** 2.54×10^{-1} mm **9.** 7×10^{-5} m
11. 0.000000001 **13.** 3×10^{-4}
15. 0.00000004004 **17.** −0.00021
19. a. 4.4×10^2 **b.** 1.95×10^{-3}
c. 1.5×10^{-2} **d.** 9.8×10^{-7}
21. 0.000000000316 m **23.** b, a, c, d **27.** −48 **29.** −60 **31.** −4
33. 6

Section 2B Review

1. 33° S, 71° W
3–6.

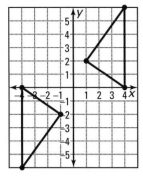

7. 16 units² **11.** 475,000
13. 4,140,000 **15.** 0.00019 **17.** d, a, b, c

Chapter 2 Summary & Review

1. 43 **2.** 4 **3.** 57 **4.** 34 **5.** −144
6. 2,088 **7.** 8 **8.** −8 **9.** 15
10. −24°F **11. a.** (4, 1) **b.** (0, −2)
c. (−2, 3) **12.** A(−5, −5), B(−1, 0), C(3, −2) **13.** $4 \times 4 \times 4 \times 4 \times 4 \times 4$
14. 7^4 **15.** 15 **16.** −27
17. 3.5×10^5 **18.** 2×10^{-4}
19. 0.0000725 **20.** 378,000
21. 7.76×10^7 **22.** 3.4×10^{-6}
23. 9×10^{-6} mm **24.** 9.5×10^5 gal

Cumulative Review
Chapters 1–2

1. D **2.** A **3.** C **4.** B **5.** C **6.** B
7. C **8.** C **9.** B **10.** A

Chapter 3

3-1 Try It (Example 3)

a. 2.5 hr; ≈ 1.4 hr; ≈ 0.65 hr
b. Yes; The temperature will be −5°C, which is below freezing.

3-1 Exercises & Applications

1. $r = \frac{d}{t}$; 200 mi/hr **2.** $t = \frac{d}{r}$; 4 min
3. $d = rt$; 165 mi **4.** $r = \frac{d}{t}$;
4.55 m/min **5.** 3515 **7.** 3136
9. 68 **11.** $0.99 **13.** ≈ 107.8 mi/hr
17. C **19. a.** 4.72 hr; 5.26 hr;
5.68 hr **b.** No

3-2 Try It

a. 20 **b.** 8

3-2 Exercises & Applications

1. a. 16 **b.** 640 **c.** 890 **3.** 336
5. 102 **7.** 95 **9.** 2196 **11.** 7
13. 4 **15.** −20 **17.** −5 **19.** 66
games **21.** 12.5 times **23.** B
25. a. $A + 0.5Z$ **b.** Yes
27. Mean: 40.64; Median: 42.8
29. 0 **31.** 13 **33.** 2 **35.** 4

3-3 Try It (Examples 1–2)

a. If b is the weight of the humming-bird, then $100,000b$ is the weight of the ostrich. **b.** $C = 100 + 2s$; $124, $140, $196

3-3 Try It (Example 3)

$4.5 + y$; $0.05(4.5 + y) = 0.225 + 0.05y$ miles

3-3 Exercises & Applications

1. c **2.** a **3.** e **4.** d **5.** b **6.** f
7. $3t$ **9.** $\frac{i}{36}$ **11.** $9n = 10n - n$
13. $m = (a + b + c) \div 3$
17. a. About 670 mi/hr **b.** About 675 mi/hr **c.** Yes **21.** 7 **23.** 4
25. 0 **27.** −19

Section 3A Review

1. 50 **3.** 169 **5.** $\approx$ 52.6 mi/hr
7. 390 **9.** 105.6 **11.** 36 **13.** 12
15. -9 **17.** $120 + (5 - 2) \cdot 85$;
$\approx$ 375 g **19.** C

3-4 Try It

a. 18 **b.** 21 **c.** 505 **d.** -145
e. -7 **f.** $-12°F$

3-4 Exercises & Applications

1. Take 3 blocks from each side.
2. Take 3 blocks from each side.
3. Add 5 to each side. **5.** Add 6 to
each side. **7.** 15 **9.** 15 **11.** 37
13. 6 **15.** -7 **17.** 37 **19.** $7\frac{1}{2}$
21. 32 **23.** 70 watts **25.** 139
27. a. $500 + x = 5500$; 5000 watts
b. $100 + x = 3000$; 2900 watts
31. 11 **33.** 6

3-5 Try It

a. 9 **b.** -180 **c.** 21

3-5 Exercises & Applications

1. Divide by 10. **2.** Multiply by 6.
3. Multiply by 4. **4.** Multiply by $\frac{3}{2}$.
5. 3 **7.** 9 **9.** 32 **11.** 6.8 **13.** $\frac{1}{2}$
15. 90 **17.** 1 **19.** 20 **21.** -15.5
23. 12.5 **25.** 0.05 **27.** A
29. $\approx 41\frac{2}{3}$ hr **31.** About 53 times
as efficient. **35.** People with tele-
phones **37.** -54 **39.** -6

3-6 Try It (Examples 1–2)

a. 5 **b.** 6.5 **c.** 30 **d.** 30

3-6 Try It (Example 3)

$9x + 10 = 75$; ≈ 7.22 months

3-6 Exercises & Applications

1. Add 5 **2.** Subtract 6 **3.** Add 3
4. Subtract 5 **5. a.** 5, 5 **b.** 24
c. 6 **7.** 7 **9.** -1 **11.** 6 **13.** 3
15. 20 **17.** 42 **19.** 9 **21.** 0
23. 180 kWh **25.** 127.5 hr **27.** C
31. 2 hours **33.** $42.05; $32.94
35. -17 **37.** -3 **39.** 16
41. 1331 **43.** -1

3-7 Try It

a.

b. $x \geq 5$

3-7 Exercises & Applications

1. $x \leq 20$ **2.** $x \geq 20$ **3.** $x > 20$
4. $x < 20$ **5.** C **7.** $x > 6$ **9.** No
11. Yes

13. $x > 4$

15. $x \geq 11$

17. $y \leq 5$

19. $p \geq 8$

21. $z \geq 5.25$

23. $n \leq 6\frac{2}{3}$

25. $x \leq 0.5$ ft **27.** At least $120
33. 73,200,000 **35.** 9,373,400,000,000
37. 1.6384×10^4 **39.** 1.44×10^4

Section 3B Review

1. 25 **3.** 15 **5.** 60 **7.** 60
9. 188.9 kWh
11.

13.

15. 84 **17.** 108 **19.** Because the
two bears eat up to 105 lb/day.
21. B

Chapter 3 Summary & Review

1. $m = \frac{d}{f}$ **2.** $5.95x + 3.00$

3. 15.625 cubic centimeters
4. $-5w + 35$ **5.** -74 **6.** $b = 516.6$
7. $p = 16$ **8.** 440°F **9.** Only for
$x = 3$ **10.** $b = 91$ **11.** $n = 34$
12. $w = 4.68$ **13.** $0.0825 = x$
14. $140 = k$ **15.** $R = 14.4$ ohms
16. $x = 5$ **17.** $v < 38$ **18.** $7.28 \leq z$
19. $h \geq 5$

Chapter 4

4-1 Try It (Examples 1–2)

d	A
0	0
1	50
2	100
3	150

4-1 Try It (Example 3)

$y = 30x$; $y = 1500$ when $x = 50$

4-1 Exercises & Applications

1. a. $y = 12x$ **b.** $y = 12 \times 5$
c. $y = 60$ **3.** 8 **5.** -5
7.

x	0	1	2	3	4	5
y = −6x	0	−6	−12	−18	−24	−30

9.

x	0	1	2	3	4	5
y = x − 8	−8	−7	−6	−5	−4	−3

11.

x	0	1	2	3	4	5
y = −10x	0	−10	−20	−30	−40	−50

13.

x	0	1	2	3	4	5
y = x − 15	−15	−14	−13	−12	−11	−10

15. $y = -7x$; -140
17. $y = x - 3$; 17
19.

x	1	2	3	4	5
y	3	4	5	6	7

23.

g	10	20	30	40
f	20	40	60	80

b. $f = 2g$, where g is the number of gallons and f is the maximum number of fish. **25.** 12 **27.** −419 **29.** 8^6

4-2 Try It (Examples 1–2)

a. No **b.** Possible answer: (4, 0), (6, −1)

4-2 Try It (Example 3)

a. $150 **b.** $1735

4-2 Exercises & Applications

1. a. Yes **b.** Yes **c.** No **3. a.** Yes
b. No **c.** Yes **5. a.** No **b.** No
c. Yes **7. a.** No **b.** Yes **c.** Yes
9. a. No **b.** No **c.** Yes
11–17. Possible answers given:
11. (0, 2), (1, 3) **13.** (0, 3), (1, 5)
15. (0, 2), (2, 12) **17.** (1, 8), (2, 7)
19.

Number of Toppings	Price
1	$ 8.25
2	$ 9.00
3	$ 9.75
4	$10.50

21. Possible answer: (20, 12), (30, 13), (40, 14) **23. a.** $y = \frac{1}{4}x$ **b.** 75 pounds
c. 800 pounds **25.** They are all ordered pairs in which the x-coordinate and y-coordinate are equal.
27. 46 **29.** 0 **31.** C

4-3 Try It (Example 1)

Possible points on line: (2, 5) and (4, 7)
For (2, 5), $5 = 2 + 3$
For (4, 7), $7 = 4 + 3$
Possible point not on line: (0, 5)
For (0, 5), $5 \neq 0 + 3$

4-3 Try It (Example 2)

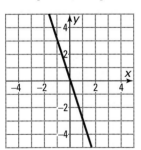

4-3 Exercises & Applications

1. 1; 2; Does
a.

b. Yes

3.

5.

7.

9.

11.

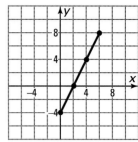

Graph is linear.

13.

Graph is not linear.

15.

17. a.

x	1	2	3	4
y	22	24	26	28

b. Yes

c.

19. $c = 2p$, where c is cubic feet of space needed and p is pounds of scraps added per day.

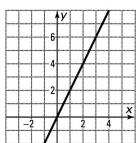

21. 360 **23.** -0.01 **25.** 4.107×10^5 **27.** 9.4×10^{-2}

Section 4A Review

1. 56 **3.** 3

5.

x	0	1	2	3	4
y	0	−3	−6	−9	−12

7.

x	0	1	2	3	4
y	0	2.5	5	7.5	10

9. a. No **b.** Yes **c.** No
11. $y = 4x$; 240

13.

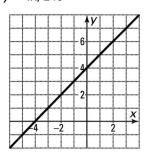

15. C

4-4 Try It (Example 1)

0.35; No

4-4 Try It (Example 2)

-2

4-4 Try It (Example 3)

a.

b.

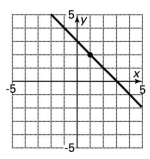

4-4 Exercises & Applications

1. Rise; Run **2.** 4, 2, 2 **3.** $\frac{1}{8}$
5. $-\frac{1}{5}$ **7.** $\frac{2}{5}$ **9.** $\frac{4}{3}$

11.

13.

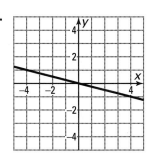

15. $\frac{1}{12}$ **17.** $\frac{\text{rise}}{\text{run}}$ is about 0.6

19. a. $\frac{1}{4}, \frac{1}{2}, \frac{2}{5}, \frac{1}{4}$ **b.** Diamond Peak and Bear Valley **21.** Horizontal: $\frac{\text{rise}}{\text{run}} = \frac{0}{\text{run}} = 0$; Vertical: $\frac{\text{rise}}{\text{run}} = \frac{\text{rise}}{0}$, and division by 0 is not defined.

23. -41 **25.** $A = 63$

4-5 Try It

a. 3; 2; -6

b. $-\frac{1}{2}$; 8; 4

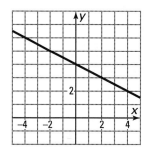

4-5 Exercises & Applications

1. 2; 4; $\frac{1}{2}$ **2.** -4 **3.** 2 **5.** 2; -1; 2
7. 1; 0; 0

9. 2; 3; -6

11. $-1; 0; 0$

13. $5; -\frac{2}{5}; 2$

15. $\frac{1}{2}; 4; -2$

17. A

19.

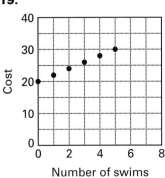

21. 1800 ft; 450 ft per hr   **25.** -46
27. 90   **29.** 40   **31.** 6

4-6 Try It

a. 2 rides   **b.** 10 rides

4-6 Exercises & Applications

1. a. Yes   **b.** Yes

3.

$(-1, 1)$

5.

$(0, 3)$

7.

$(6, 9)$

9.

No solution

11.

Each side has 6 oz on it.   **13.** For 5
times, the cost is the same either
way. For 6 times, the cost is $55 for
the first plan, but $60 for the second.
So she should take the first plan.
15. The cost is $48 in either case. It
doesn't matter.   **17.** -48 **19.** -8
21. $D + 4$ **23.** $2p + 17$

4-7 Try It (Examples 1–2)

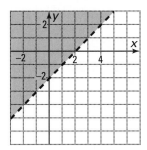

4-7 Try It (Example 3)

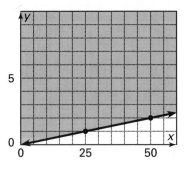

At least 11 teachers

4-7 Exercises & Applications

1. D   **2.** C   **3.** A   **4.** B   **5. a.** No
b. No   **c.** No

7.

9.

11.

13.

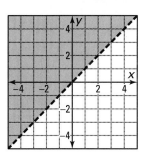

15. y = teachers, x = students
17. $n \geq 4x$, where n is the number of calories and x is the weight in grams.

19.

21. No
23.

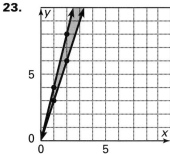

27. 8^2 **29.** 2^3 **31.** 32 **33.** 3
35. 0.06 **37.** $-\frac{1}{8}$

Section 4B Review

1. 2; 1; −2
3.

5.

(2, 1)

7.

9. $y > 2x$

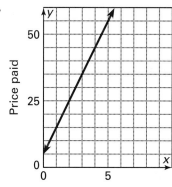

11. Substitute the coordinates for the ordered pair into the equation or inequality. If the resulting statement is true, the ordered pair is a solution.

Chapter 4 Summary & Review

1. $y = -15$
2.

x	0	1	2	3	4	5
y	4	5	6	7	8	9

3. $y = -7x$; $y = -161$ **4. a.** No
b. Yes **c.** No **5.** Possible answer: (0, 15), (5, 0)
6.

7. a.

b.

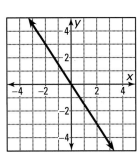

8. a. Slope $-\frac{1}{2}$; x-intercept -2; y-intercept -1 **b.** Slope $-\frac{3}{2}$; x-intercept 2; y-intercept 3   **c.** Slope 2; x-intercept $-\frac{3}{2}$; y-intercept 3

9. Slope $\frac{3}{5}$; x-intercept 5; y-intercept -3

10.

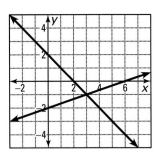

$(3, -1)$ **11.** 8 months

12. a.

b.

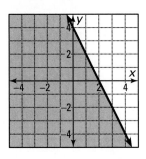

**Cumulative Review
Chapters 1–4**

1. B   **2.** D   **3.** D   **4.** B   **5.** C   **6.** B
7. B   **8.** C   **9.** A   **10.** C   **11.** C
12. A   **13.** B   **14.** D   **15.** B

Chapter 5

5-1 Try It (Examples 1-2)

a. 4 to 9; 5 to 9; 4 to 5; 5 to 4; 9 to 4; 9 to 5   **b.** 1:9

5-1 Try It (Example 3)

a. ≈ 0.82   **b.** ≈ 62,500,000

5-1 Exercises & Applications

1. a. 3:4   **b.** 4:7   **c.** 7:4
3. a.

b.

5. No   **7. a.** 8:25   **b.** 21:7 or 3:1
c. 25 to 7; 7 to 25   **9.** 3:2   **11.** 2:5
13. 3:5   **15. a.** 4:5   **b.** 5:1   **c.** Yes;
When amount of stored memory
increases, available memory

decreases.   **19.** 6.94×10^{-3}
21. 1×10^{-9} **23.** $x = 35$
25. $x = -6$

5-2 Try It (Examples 1-2)

a. 3; 5; 20; 150

b.

Tickets	20	40	60
Cost ($)	5	10	15

≈ $11

5-2 Try It (Example 3)

a. No   **b.** Yes

5-2 Exercises & Applications

1. a. $\frac{12}{36}$ **b.** $\frac{24}{72}$ **c.** $\frac{1}{3}$ **d.** $\frac{2}{6}$ **e.** $\frac{8}{24}$
3. 4; 6; 8; 10   **5.** C   **7.** =   **9.** ≠
11. ≠   **13.** ≠   **15.** No   **17.** Yes,
$\frac{50}{14,400} = \frac{120}{34,560}$ **21. a.** Triangle
b. Painting   **c.** Steam
d. Proportion   **23.** $A = 121$
25. $F = 57.2$ **27.** $x = 54$

5-3 Try It (Example 1)

a. $\frac{4}{1}$, $\frac{8}{2}$, $\frac{12}{3}$, $\frac{16}{4}$, $\frac{20}{5}$ **b.** 40; 80
c. If y = number of pages and
x = time, $y = 4x$.

5-3 Try It (Example 2)

a. $k = 2$
x 5 10 15
y 10 20 30

b. 2; They are the same.

5-3 Try It (Example 3)

a. The graph does not show a
proportional relationship.

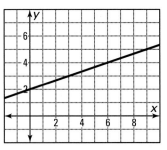

b. The graph shows a proportional relationship.

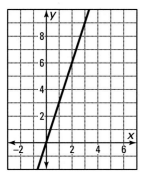

5-3 Exercises & Applications

1. a. $\frac{y}{x} = 3$ **b.** $\frac{y}{x} = 10$ **c.** $\frac{y}{x} = 0.5$
3. Yes, $k = 6$ **5.** Yes, $k = 11$ **7.** 5
9. 2; 2 cost $5.34 and 3 cost $8.01
11. a. 5 **b.** $k = 5$ **c.** $p = 5h$
d. $85.00
13.

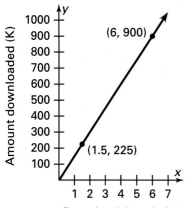

15. 69 **17.** 175 **19.** Yes **21.** Yes

Section 5A Review

1. $2{:}6 = 1{:}3$ **3.** 1:5 **5.** $\neq$ **7.** $\neq$
9. 18, 27, 45, 54 **11. a.** 3:2
b. Word proc. to video games.
c. Educ. programs to homework.
13. C

5-4 Try It

5000 films

5-4 Exercises & Applications

1. a. 7×3 **b.** 21 **c.** 21 **d.** $5\frac{1}{4}$
3. $\frac{12}{x} = \frac{8}{2.50}$ **5.** 75 **7.** 12 **9.** B

11. D **13.** 8 **15.** 31 **17.** 20
19. 8 **21.** C **23.** No; $\frac{2}{22} \neq \frac{1}{7}$
25. $\approx$ 23 ft **27.** $x = 3$ **29.** $x = 3\frac{1}{3}$
31. 24 cm, 20 cm, 12 cm
33. 2.3884×10^5 **35.** -42 **37.** 5

5-5 Try It (Example 1)

$1,368

5-5 Try It (Example 2)

75 ounces for $8.99

5-5 Try It (Example 3)

a. 2880 frames; 25 seconds
b. $F = 30s$; 300 seconds (5 min)

5-5 Exercises & Applications

1. a. 30 **b.** $d = 30t$ **c.** $d = 30 \cdot 7$;
$d = 210$ mi **3.** 40 words per
minute; $W = 40m$ **5.** 55 miles per
hour; $M = 55h$ **7.** $40,000 per day;
$C = 40,000d$ **9. a.** $2.88 per lb
b. $3.59 per lb **11.** $\approx$ 10.5 **13.** A
6 oz box for $1.25 **15.** $\frac{1}{4}$ lb for $2.00
17. Yes; The average height of each
floor is about 12.2 ft **21. a.** about
400 **b.** Hire 35 more teachers
23. 0.0084 **25.** Possible answers:
(1, 6); (2, 7) **27.** Possible answers:
(1, −5); (2, −4)

5-6 Try It

120 frames; 30 fps

5-6 Exercises & Applications

1. a. 360 **b.** 5 **c.** 12 **3.** A and B
5. a. $\approx$ 95.3 million **b.** $\approx$ 953,000
7. $\frac{2}{4} = \frac{4}{8}, \frac{4}{8} = \frac{8}{16}, \frac{8}{16} = \frac{16}{32}, \frac{2}{4} = \frac{16}{32}, \frac{2}{4} = \frac{4}{16}, \frac{4}{16} = \frac{8}{32}, \frac{2}{8} = \frac{8}{32}, \frac{2}{16} = \frac{4}{32}, \frac{4}{8} = \frac{16}{32}$
and all reciprocals of these.
9. 236 in. **11.** 840 ft

5-7 Try It (Example 3)

Possible answer: 1 in. = 10 ft

5-7 Try It (Examples 4-5)

12.5

5-7 Exercises & Applications

1. a. Shape; Size **b.** Sizes; Shape
3. 1200 mi **5.** $\approx$ 2520 mi **7.** 30 cm
9. 13.425 cm **11.** $\frac{1}{32}$ in. **13.** 24 ft
15. 10.8 **17.** $b = 15$, $c = 9$, $a = 10$
21. About 24 in. **23.** $x = -16$
25. $r = 45$

Section 5B Review

1. $\frac{10 \text{ bottles}}{x} = \frac{6 \text{ bottles}}{1.99}$; $x = 3.32
3. 80 **5.** 40 **7.** 560 **9.** Possible
answer: $P = 22.5n$ **11.** $a = 2.5$;
$b = 4$; $c = 2$ **13.** 5 ft

Chapter 5 Summary & Review

1. $\frac{3}{7}$

2.

3. Red area to total area: 2:5. Total
area to red area: 5:2. Blue area to
total area: 3:5. Total area to blue
area: 5:3. Red area to blue area: 2:3.
Blue area to red area: 3:2. **4.** Not
equal **5.** No
6.

4	8	12	16	20	24
5	10	15	20	25	30

7. $x = 60$ **8.** $u = 77$ **9.** 3 gallons
per hour; $g = 3h$, where g is the
number of gallons and h is the number of hours. **10.** About 350 mi.
11. 231 pairs of blue shoes.
12. 5166 comedy videos. **13.** 7.5 ft
tall and 17.5 ft across. **14.** $x = 12$;
$z = 22.5$

Chapter 6

6-1 Try It (Example 3)

a. 82% **b.** 12.5% **c.** 50%
d. 12.5% **e.** 0.6%

6-1 Try It (Example 4)

a. $\frac{12}{100} = \frac{3}{25}$; 0.12 **b.** $\frac{45}{1000} = \frac{9}{200}$;
0.045 **c.** $\frac{200}{100} = 2$; 2.00

6-1 Exercises & Applications

1. a. $\frac{74}{100} = \frac{37}{50}$ **b.** 0.74 **c.** 74%
2. a. $\frac{1}{4}$ **b.** 0.25 **c.** 25%
3. Possible Answer:

5. 80% **7.** 120% **9.** 0.35% **11.** $\frac{49}{50}$; 0.98 **13.** $\frac{3}{40}$; 0.075 **15.** $\frac{7}{5} = 1\frac{2}{5}$; 1.40 **17.** $\frac{3}{400}$; 0.0075 **19.** No; The risk is too high. **21.** 20% off; It is the largest reduction. **23.** 70%; 20%; 10% **25.** 90% of 50 = 45; The student answered 45 correctly. **27. a.** 50%; 25%, 50%, and 75%. **b.** You scored better than 9500 students.

6-2 Try It (Example 3)

1. a. 12.5% **b.** 36 **c.** 90

6-2 Try It (Example 4)

3200 oz = 200 lb

6-2 Exercises & Applications

1. $\frac{12}{x} = \frac{40}{100}$ **3.** 4 **5.** 22 **7.** $33\frac{1}{3}$% **9.** 200% **11.** 20 **13.** 1.25 **15.** 435 students **17. a.** 16 passengers **b.** 104 **c.** U.S. **19.** 1% **21.** Iron **23.** 30% **25.** $\frac{(a + b + c + d)}{4}$; Answers may vary.

6-3 Try It (Example 1)

a. 180 **b.** 60

6-3 Try It (Example 2)

About 80 or 90 mg

6-3 Try It (Example 3)

a. About $33\frac{1}{3}$% **b.** About 250 students

6-3 Try It (Example 4)

About 35–40%. The top part is about 25%. The bottom part is half of that or 13%. 25% + 13% = 38%.

6-3 Exercises & Applications

1. a. $\frac{1}{3}$ **b.** $\frac{1}{5}$ **c.** $\frac{1}{100}$ **d.** $\frac{1}{10}$ **3.** 25% **5.** 98% **7.** 14 **9.** 4 **11.** 30% **13.** 67% **15.** > **17.** < **19.** 0.3 g **21.** B **23.** It cannot be determined. About 75% of his serves are in bounds. **27.** $y = 19$ **29.** $p = -2$

31.

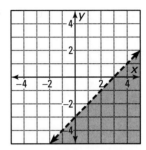

Section 6A Review

1. a. $\frac{4}{5}$; 0.8; 80% **3.** 67% **5.** 1450% **7.** 0.72; $\frac{18}{25}$ **9.** 0.1275, $\frac{51}{400}$ **11.** 0.56, $\frac{14}{25}$ **13.** 25% **15.** 12 **17.** 20% **19.** 12.5 **21.** About 60% **23.** D

6-4 Try It (Examples 1-2)

a. ≈ 50% **b.** $79.13

6-4 Try It (Example 3)

4593

6-4 Exercises & Applications

1. a. $1.20 **b.** $17.19 **c.** $17.19 **3.** 100% **5.** 17% **7.** 14% **9.** $909.42 **11.** $21 **13.** ≈162 cm **15.** January **17.** ≈ 596% **21. a.** 1.2 oz **b.** 1.44 oz **c.** 12% **23.** 3:5; 3:8; 5:3; 5:8; 8:3; 8:5

6-5 Try It (Example 1)

$12.23

6-5 Try It (Example 2)

20%

6-5 Try It (Example 3)

$279.75

6-5 Exercises & Applications

1. a. 78% **b.** 70% **c.** 80% **d.** 60% **3.** 8% **5.** 18% **7.** 9% **9.** $1.91 **11.** 29 **13.** $31.25 **15.** C **19. a.** $78.80; $80.38 **21.** = **23.** =

6-6 Try It (Example 2)

a. $81.72 **b. i.** $38.40 **ii.** $42.00

6-6 Try It (Example 3)

20%

6-6 Exercises & Applications

1. a. 150% **b.** $90 **c.** $90; $133\frac{1}{3}$% **d.** $120 **3.** 25 **5.** 75 **7.** 100 **9.** 2 **11.** $49.94 **13.** $121.50 **15.** $100.31 **17.** 25% **19. a.** 1350 **b.** About 11% **21.** 12 notes **23.** 37.5% **25.** $y = 19$ **27.** $a = -3$ **29.** $p = -\frac{1}{3}$ **31.** 17.4 **33.** 0.1

Section 6B Review

1. 25% decrease **3.** 0% (neither) **5.** 33% increase **7.** $109.97 **9.** 8% **11.** $44.10 **13.** $239.50 **15.** $600 **17.** No

Chapter 6 Summary & Review

1. $\frac{4}{5}$; 0.8; 80% **2. a.** 16% **b.** 24% **c.** 60% **3.** 161 **4.** 75 **5.** 225 **6.** About 20% **7.** About 10% **8.** About 40 **9.** About 37.2% **10.** 6.5% **11.** $24.36 **12.** $221 **13.** About 75% **14.** $2400 **15.** $139,872 **16.** About 23.1%

Cumulative Review
Chapters 1–6

1. B **2.** A **3.** B **4.** D **5.** C **6.** B **7.** B **8.** C **9.** A **10.** C **11.** C **12.** D **13.** C **14.** B **15.** B **16.** A

Chapter 7

7-1 Try It (Example 1)

a. 2 only **b.** 2, 3, 4, 5, 6, 8, 10 **c.** 2, 4 **d.** 3, 5

7-1 Try It (Example 2-3)

a. $2 \times 3 \times 3 \times 3$ **b.** $2 \times 2 \times 3 \times 11$
c. $2 \times 2 \times 59$ **d.** $2 \times 3 \times 59$

7-1 Exercises & Applications

1. Prime **3.** Composite **5.** Prime
7. 3, 9 **9.** 2 **11.** 3, 9 **13.** 2
15. 2, 4, 8 **17.** 1, 2, 4, 8, 11, 22, 44,
88 **19.** 1, 2, 4, 5, 10, 20, 25, 50, 100
21. $2 \times 3 \times 3 \times 3$ or 2×3^3 **23.** 2^7
25. $2 \times 2 \times 5 \times 11$ or $2^2 \times 5 \times 11$
27. $3 \times 5 \times 5 \times 5$ or 3×5^3
29. 5×101 **31.** D **33.** $n = 81$
35. $w = 1250$ **37.** $2^3 \times 3^2 \times 5$
39. 34 **41.** Possible answers: $3 = 2^2 - 1$; $7 = 2^3 - 1$; $31 = 2^5 - 1$
43. Possible answers: 24, 36, 48, 600
45. B **50.** 37.5 hr or 37 hours and
30 minutes

7-2 Try It (Example 2)

a. 6 **b.** 7 **c.** 4

7-2 Try It (Examples 3-4)

a. 5 **b.** $\frac{3}{4}$

7-2 Exercises & Applications

1. a. 1, 3, 9, 27 **b.** 1, 3, 5, 9, 15, 45
c. 1, 3, 9 **d.** 9 **3.** 4 **5.** 7 **7.** 9
9. 30 **11.** 8 **13.** 4 **15.** 14 **17.** 5
19. 12 **21.** 2 **23.** $\frac{2}{5}$ **25.** $\frac{1}{4}$
27. $\frac{9}{10}$ **29.** $\frac{2}{3}$ **31.** $\frac{6}{11}$ **33.** 210,
512, 915, 972 **35.** $18 = 2 \times 3^2$
37. A **39.** Possible answers: 4 and
7; 15 and 16; 9 and 20. **41.** 1; Yes
43. Slope = 2; x-intercept = 2;
y-intercept = -4. **45.** Slope = -3;
x-intercept = $\frac{8}{3}$; y-intercept = 8.
47. Slope = -7; x-intercept = 0;
y-intercept = 0.

7-3 Try It (Example 2)

a. 30 **b.** 147 **c.** 9384

7-3 Try It (Example 4)

a. $\frac{6}{21}$ and $\frac{14}{21}$ **b.** $\frac{28}{48}$ and $\frac{15}{48}$

7-3 Exercises & Applications

1. a. 8, 16, 24, 32, 40, 48, 56, 64, 72,
80 **b.** 12, 24, 36, 48, 60, 72, 84, 96,
108, 120 **c.** 24, 48, 72 **d.** 24

3. 40 **5.** 60 **7.** 144 **9.** 60 **11.** 84
13. 88 **15.** 744 **17.** 60 **19.** 7000
21. 3432 **23.** $\frac{4}{6}$ and $\frac{1}{6}$ **25.** $\frac{3}{8}$ and $\frac{6}{8}$
27. $\frac{20}{36}$ and $\frac{15}{36}$ **29.** $\frac{45}{60}$, $\frac{40}{60}$, and $\frac{42}{60}$
31. $\frac{28}{252}$, $\frac{72}{252}$, and $\frac{105}{252}$ **33.** Every 90
days. **35.** A **37.** Multiply the two
numbers; their product is the LCM.
38. Possible answers: A 10 3 6 rectangle **41.** $(-3, 8)$ **43.** $(4, -1)$
45. 176% **47.** 0.5% **49.** 320%
51. 0.3% **53.** 640% **55.** 275%
57. 0.2%

Section 7A Review

1. 2, 3, 6, 9 **3.** 2, 4, 5, 8, 10 **5.** 2, 4
7. $5^2 \times 19$ **9.** $2^4 \times 3^2$ **11.** GCF, 1;
LCM, 36 **13.** GCF, 3; LCM, 120
15. $\frac{3}{5}$ **17.** $\frac{3}{7}$ **19.** $\frac{2}{3}$ **21.** 12
23. 24 **27.** A

7-4 Try It (Example 3)

a. $0.8\overline{3}$; Repeating **b.** 0.125;
Terminating **c.** 0.75; Terminating

7-4 Try It (Example 4)

a. $\frac{15}{100}$ or $\frac{3}{20}$ **b.** $2\frac{6}{10}$ or $2\frac{3}{5}$ **c.** $\frac{46}{1000}$ or
$\frac{23}{500}$

7-4 Try It (Example 5)

a. $2\frac{13}{99}$ **b.** $\frac{8}{33}$

7-4 Try It (Example 6)

a. $-4\frac{1}{3} < -4.3$ **b.** $2.07 < 2\frac{1}{7}$

7-4 Exercises & Applications

1. a. 210 **b.** $-\frac{140}{210}$, $\frac{175}{210}$, $\frac{0}{210}$, $-\frac{120}{210}$,
$\frac{189}{210}$, $-\frac{42}{210}$, $\frac{35}{210}$ **c.** $-\frac{140}{210}$, $-\frac{120}{210}$, $-\frac{42}{210}$,
$\frac{0}{210}$, $\frac{35}{210}$, $\frac{175}{210}$, $\frac{189}{210}$ **3.** < **5.** < **7.** >
9. < **11.** 0.44; Terminating
13. $0.\overline{285714}$; Repeating **15.** $\frac{9}{20}$
17. $4\frac{14}{25}$ **19.** $2\frac{1}{3}$
21.

7-5 Try It (Example 1)

a. 111.63 **b.** 36.75 **c.** 527.05
d. 3.74

7-5 Try It (Example 3)

a. $2\frac{1}{2}$ **b.** $5\frac{5}{6}$

7-5 Try It (Example 4)

a. $-5\frac{1}{4}$ **b.** $14\frac{5}{24}$

7-5 Exercises & Applications

1. a. $\frac{24}{30}$, $\frac{25}{30}$ **b.** $\frac{49}{30}$ **c.** $1\frac{19}{30}$
3. -160.713 **5.** 164.14 **7.** $-\frac{1}{4}$
9. $-\frac{2}{15}$ **11.** $10\frac{2}{5}$ **13.** $4\frac{4}{7}$
15. $-14\frac{43}{60}$ **17.** $n = -1\frac{1}{2}$ **19.** $n =$
$11\frac{1}{4}$ **21.** 3.29 miles per second
23. $\frac{1}{20}$ **25.** B **29.** $x = \frac{3}{4} + \frac{3}{8} - 1\frac{1}{4} =$
$-\frac{1}{8}$ **31.** $x = 17$ **33.** $k = -54$
35. $r = -4.9$ **37.** $n = -2.2$
39. 43%

7-6 Try It (Example 1)

a. -3.6 **b.** 56.1697

7-6 Try It (Example 2)

a. 2.24 **b.** $-68.\overline{18}$

7-6 Try It (Example 3)

a. $-3\frac{31}{48}$ **b.** 22

7-6 Try It (Example 4)

a. 4 **b.** $4\frac{1}{2}$

7-6 Exercises & Applications

1. a. $\frac{13}{4}$ **b.** $\frac{78}{4}$ **3.** 0.0072 **5.** 0.032
7. $\frac{1}{9}$ **9.** $-2\frac{1}{3}$ **11.** $\frac{1}{6}$ **13.** $1\frac{67}{115}$
15. $\frac{9}{14}$ **17.** $1\frac{2}{7}$ **19.** 150 **21.** $\frac{5}{114}$

23. The sea cow **25.** Ana
27. 3.14084507; 3.14285714
29. $\frac{3}{8}$ **31.** Possible answer: $\frac{11}{50}$
33. Possible answer: $-\frac{62}{72}$ **35.** $12 + n$
37. $36k$ **39.** 150 **41.** 40

23. ≈ 4,524,518 square miles

25. $\frac{1}{4}$ × 100 gallons   **27.** A   **29.** No

31. No; Possible answer: If both of the numbers are < 1, their product would have to be < 1.   **33.** $x = 9$

35. $x = -44$ **37.** $x = -41$ **39.** $x = 21$ **41.** 33%   **43.** 19%

Section 7B Review

1.

3.

5. 0.75; Terminating

7. $11.\overline{714285}$; Repeating

9. 4.7; Terminating   **11.** $3\frac{1}{200}$

13. $\frac{364}{999}$ **15.** 7.42   **17.** −0.1326

19. $\frac{1}{24}$ **21.** $1\frac{5}{8}$ **23.** $-\frac{1}{6}$ **25.** 15

27. $x = -\frac{2}{15}$ **29.** $x = \frac{3}{7}$ **31.** D

7-7 Try It (Example 1)

a. Yes   **b.** No   **c.** Yes   **d.** No

7-7 Try It (Example 2)

a. 12   **b.** 21   **c.** 50   **d.** 91

7-7 Try It (Example 3)

a. 3 and 4; 3.2   **b.** 4 and 5; 4.6
c. 5 and 6; 5.5   **d.** 8 and 9; 8.9

Try It (Example 4)

a. $\frac{5}{8}$ **b.** $\frac{10}{25}$ **c.** $\frac{11}{18}$ **d.** $\frac{6}{15}$

7-7 Exercises & Applications

1. a. $\frac{\sqrt{9}}{\sqrt{144}}$ **b.** $\frac{3}{12}$ **c.** $\frac{1}{4}$ **3.** Yes

5. No   **7.** 5 and 6   **9.** 8 and 9

11. 5 and 6   **13.** $1\frac{1}{2}$ **15.** $\frac{3}{5}$

17. ≈ 230.22 meters   **19.** 9, 10

21. 12 in.   **23.** 7.5 seconds

25. 8 feet   **27.** Possible answers:
(1 • 2 • 3 • 4) + 1 = 25 = 5^2; (2 • 3 • 4 • 5) + 1 = 121 = 11^2; (3 • 4 • 5 • 6) + 1 = 361 = 19^2; (5 • 6 • 7 • 8) + 1 =

1,681 = 41^2; (6 • 7 • 8 • 9) + 1 = 3025 = 55^2 **29.** Yes   **37.** $\frac{11}{66}$ **39.** $\frac{3 \text{ ft}}{1 \text{ yd}}$

7-8 Try It

a. Irrational   **b.** Rational; −30
c. Rational; ±74   **d.** Irrational

7-8 Exercises & Applications

1. a. 9.7467943   **b.** Irrational

3. Irrational   **5.** Irrational

7. Irrational   **9.** Irrational

11. Rational   **13.** 3.873   **15.** 9.950

17. 15.875   **19.** 44.721   **21.** 21.354

23. ≈ 5.48 in.   **25.** 6.5 m   **27.** 22 ft × 22 ft   **29.** A   **31.** 1; 4: 1, 2, 4; 9: 1, 3, 9; 16: 1, 2, 4, 8, 16; 25: 1, 5, 25; 36: 1, 2, 3, 4, 6, 9, 12, 18, 36; 49: 1, 7, 49; 64: 1, 2, 4, 8, 16, 32, 64; 81: 1, 3, 9, 27, 81; 100: 1, 2, 4, 5, 10, 20, 25, 50, 100. Possible answers: They all have an odd number of factors.

33. 38.3 miles; No; They would see about 54.2 miles.   **35.** $y = 39$

37. $y = 17$

39.

x	0	1	2	3	4	5
y	−3	−2	−1	0	1	2

41.

x	0	1	2	3	4	5
y	−4	−3	−2	−1	0	1

7-9 Try It (Example 1)

a. $c = 5$ in.   **b.** $h ≈ 17.69$ cm

7-9 Try It (Example 2)

a. $a ≈ 9.16$ m   **b.** $a ≈ 10.39$ ft

7-9 Try It (Example 4)

a. $a ≈ 5$ in.   **b.** $c ≈ 8.367$ m

7-9 Exercises & Applications

1. a. $12^2 + 16^2 = c^2$ **b.** 144 + 256 = c^2; 400 = c^2 **c.** $c = 20$ cm
3. $a ≈ 21.07$ **5.** ≈ 7.2 ft   **7.** 1600 ft
9. C   **11.** Yes   **13.** Yes   **15. a.** 9 ft
b. ≈ 12.728 ft   **17.** Possible answers: (2, 1); (6, 3)   **19.** Possible answers: (10, 6); (15, 9)
21. $x = 66$ **23.** $x = 1$

Section 7C Review

1. No   **3.** No   **5.** Yes   **7.** ≈ 8.25
9. $\frac{2}{5}$ **11.** −6   **13.** ±3.5   **15.** −3

17. Rational   **19.** Rational

21. ≈ 5.66 in.   **23.** 21 cm

25. ≈ 2.06 ft   **27.** $m = 15$

Chapter 7 Summary & Review

1. Divisible by 2, 3, 6, and 9

2. 924 = 2^2 × 3 × 7 × 11   **3.** 3   **4.** $\frac{3}{4}$

5. 75   **6.** 60   **7.** 0.1875;

Terminating   **8.** 3.806 > 3.8059

9. $\frac{3}{25}$ **10.** 18.478   **11.** $5\frac{1}{18}$ **12.** $\frac{57}{80}$

13. No   **14.** $\frac{5}{6}$ **15.** 7 and 8

16. ≈ 5.657 cm   **17.** ± 23   **18.** −27

Chapter 8

8-1 Try It (Examples 1-2)

a. 32,000 m   **b.** ≈ 1.96 mi

8-1 Try It (Example 3)

a–d. Possible answers: **a.** mL
b. min   **c.** lb   **d.** kg

8-1 Try It (Example 4)

a–d. Possible answers: **a.** m^2
b. mm^3 **c.** g   **d.** mi

8-1 Exercises & Applications

1. a. $\frac{1 \text{ mi}}{5280 \text{ ft}}$ **b.** ≈ 5.5 mi   **3.** mi
5. mL   **7.** kg   **9.** 2,500,000 mL
11. 4 lb   **13.** 5 qt   **15.** 15.66 g
17. A   **21.** in^2 **23.** Composite
25. Prime   **27.** Composite
29. Composite   **31.** 14   **33.** 1
35. 3   **37.** 2

8-2 Try It (Example 2)

a. 2638 ft   **b.** 197.5 cm   **c.** 35.75 in.

8-2 Try It (Example 3)

a. 2   **b.** 6   **c.** 1   **d.** 5

8-2 Try It (Example 5)

a. 14.1 g; 3   **b.** 9.8 mL; 2   **c.** 47 in.; 2   **d.** 22 m; 2

8-2 Exercises & Applications

1. a. 3   **b.** 3   **c.** 6   **3.** 2   **5.** 5
7. 235 cm   **9.** 0.25 L   **11.** 3.30 hr

13. 44 mi **15.** 49 m² **17.** 13° C
19. 42,600 m **23.** 21 **25.** 55
27. 104 **29.** 60
31.

33.

35. $2\frac{17}{100}$ **37.** $\frac{1}{2}$

8-3 Try It (Example 2)

a. 4 blocks east **b.** $c - 17$

8-3 Try It (Examples 3-4)

a. Brazil **b.** 30° N, 90° W

8-3 Exercises & Applications

1. 10C **3.** Salt Lake City Municipal Airport No. 2 **5.** Northeast **7.** 4° latitude; ≈ 1° longitude **9.** Mt. Everest **11.** About 395 mi **13.** About 200 mi **15.** Answers may vary **17.** Possible answer: Distance between longitude lines decrease as you get closer to the north and south poles because they all intersect at the poles. **19.** East **21.** 55 mi/hr **23.** $6 per hr **25.** ≈ 2.3 children per home **27.** 3.115 **29.** 140.256 **31.** $2\frac{2}{3}$

Section 8A Review

1. Liter **3.** cm² **5.** ≈ 4.08 hr **7.** 2,500,000 mL **9.** 28 oz **11.** 1 **13.** 3 **15.** 1.89 L **17.** 3499 in. **19.** 13.6 g **21.** 93 cm² **23.** China **25.** C

8-4 Try It (Example 1)

a. 145° **b.** 52°

8-4 Try It (Example 2)

Acute

8-4 Try It (Examples 3-4)

a. 47.3° **b.** 72°

8-4 Exercises & Applications

1. a. 53°; 53° **b.** Yes **3.** Acute **5.** Acute **7.** Acute **9.** Straight **11.** Obtuse **13.** 68° **15.** 80.9° **17.** 60° **19.** 90° **21.** 120° **23.** 135° **25.** 162° **27.** 105° **29.**

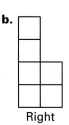

T   V

31.

R   V

33. C **35.** 157° **37.** 60° **41.** $x + y = 180$; $y = 180 - x$; $y = 109°$ **43.** They are congruent. The same two lines form the sides for both angles. **45.** 240 **47.** $8 **49.** 3 **51.** 27.51

8-5 Try It (Example 1)

∠DQK and ∠GRL; ∠KQE and ∠FRL

8-5 Try It (Examples 2-3)

a. 146° **b.** 146° **c.** 34°

8-5 Exercises & Applications

1. a. 4; 6; 8 **b.** 1; 3; 5 **3.** 1 and 8; 2 and 7 **5.** Possible answers: 1 and 4; 2 and 3; 5 and 8; 6 and 7 **7.** 130° **9.** 130° **11.** 139° **13.** Alternate exterior angles **15.** 47° **17.** parallel **19.** congruent **23.** $m\angle 3 = 75°$; $m\angle 4 = 55°$; $m\angle 5 = 50°$; $m\angle 6 = 125°$; $m\angle 7 = 130°$ **25.** $x = 4$ **27.** $x = 5$ **29.** $\frac{63}{64}$ **31.** 1.78

8-6 Try It (Examples 1-2)

a. 5 in. **b.** 5 in. **c.** 60°, 60°, 60°

8-6 Try It (Examples 3-4)

a. 114° **b.** 114° **c.** $\overline{QS}$

8-6 Try It (Examples 5-6)

Regular convex hexagon

8-6 Exercises & Applications

1. a. 84° **b.** 96° **3.** Irregular convex hexagon **5.** Irregular convex octagon **7.** False **9.** True **11.** 71° **13.** 61° **15.** 720° **17.** 1080°

19. a. Triangles and rectangles **b.** Pentagons and hexagons **21.** n **23.** A concave polygon must have at least 4 sides.
25.

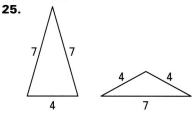

The length of the third side could be 4 in. or 7 in.; There are two possible triangles. **31.** 7 **33.** 13 **35.** 4 **37.** $\frac{3}{11}$

8-7 Try It

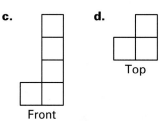

8-7 Exercises & Applications

5. Possible answer:

7.

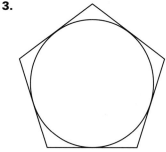

(Note: the figure at position 7 is a star-like shape.)

9. A   **17.** Irrational   **19.** Irrational
21. Rational

Section 8B Review

1. Acute   **3.** Acute   **5.** Right
7. 32.5°   **9.** 130°   **11.** 130°
13. d   **15.** b   **17.** Pentagon
19. Parallelogram   **21.** Their
shapes are the same but the base
plan has the number of units
stacked up written on it.

Chapter 8 Summary & Review

1. Liter   **2.** 192 oz   **3.** 438 ft
4. 36.1 cm²   **5.** 40° N; 83° W
6. About 235 mi south
7. Complement: 52°; Supplement:
142°

8.

3	4	3	4
1	2	3	4

9. a. $\overline{AB}$ and $\overline{CD}$ **b.** $\overline{AB}$ and $\overline{BC}$ or
$\overline{BC}$ and $\overline{CD}$ **c.** $\angle D$ **10.** Obtuse
11. 540°

Cumulative Review, Chapters 1-8

1. C   **2.** B   **3.** A   **4.** C   **5.** B   **6.** A
7. D   **8.** A   **9.** C   **10.** C   **11.** D
12. A   **13.** C   **14.** C   **15.** D   **16.** A

Chapter 9

9-1 Try It (Examples 2–3)

a. 2.12 in.   **b.** 22 m

9-1 Try It (Example 5)

a. $10\frac{5}{6}$ yd²   **b.** 34.4375 cm²

9-1 Try It (Example 7)

a. 105 mm²   **b.** 390 in²

9-1 Exercises & Applications

1. a. $A = (\frac{1}{2})(5.5) \cdot 4$ **b.** $A = 11$ cm²
3. 25 cm; 39.0625 cm²   **5.** 24 m;
24 m²   **7.** ≈ 35.2 cm; ≈ 52 cm²
9. 64.4 m; 237.475 m²   **11.** 15.75
cm; 11.8125 cm²   **13.** $13\frac{1}{3}$ ft; $11\frac{1}{9}$ ft²
15. a. 80 ft   **b.** 384 ft²   **17.** 5; ≈ 6.4
19. ≈ 47.4 cm   **21.** 37 ft   **23. a.** 20
cm   **b.** Find the area of the triangle
and multiply it by 5.   **25. a.** 6 by 8,
4 by 12, 3 by 16, and 2 by 24
b. 6 m by 8 m; 2 by 24   **27.** 9%
29. 142%   **31.** No   **33.** Yes

9-2 Try It (Examples 1–2)

5

9-2 Try It (Example 4)

$p = 31\frac{1}{2}$ m and $A = 61\frac{1}{4}$ m²

9-2 Exercises & Applications

1. a. $b = 16.8$ cm; $h = 24$ cm
b. 201.6 cm²   **3.** 57.6 ft; 138.24 ft²
5. 42 m; 81 m²   **7.** 9 cm; 3.9 cm²
9. 250 m²   **11.** A   **13.** Enlargement
15. Perimeter increases slightly, but
the area doubles.   **17.** 2 ft²   **21.** 80
23. 400   **25.** 1.5 m   **27.** $16\frac{1}{3}$ ft

9-3 Try It (Example 2)

a. 1.73 m   **b.** ≈ 10.86 m

9-3 Try It (Example 4)

a. ≈ 50.24 cm²   **b.** Yes

9-3 Exercises & Applications

1. a. 4 cm   **b.** ≈ 50.24 cm²
3.

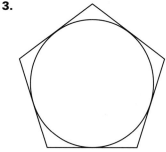

5. ≈ 28.26 m   **7.** ≈ 31.4 mi
9. ≈ 33.17 ft²   **11.** ≈ 7.5 km²

13. ≈ 39 in.   **15.** ≈ 785,000 ft²
17. The circumference for a full
circle would be 188.4 ft, so for a
semicircle the perimeter would be
half of that plus 60 ft, or 154.2 ft;
The area of a full circle would be
2826 ft², so the area of a half-circle
would be 1413 ft².   **21. a.** 15.6 cm²
b. 93.6 cm²   **c.** ≈ 113.04 cm²
d. 19.4 cm²   **23.** 70%   **25.** 10%
27. 5   **29.** 3

9-4 Try It (Example 1)

22 in²

9-4 Try It (Example 2)

a. $A ≈ 50.2$ in²   **b.** $A ≈ 150.7$ in²
c. $SA ≈ 251$ in²

9-4 Exercises & Applications

1. a.

b. 3 × 6 = 18, 3 × 10 = 30, and
6 × 10 = 60   **c.** 216 m²
3. 201.5 in²

5. $37\frac{1}{2}$ ft²

7. $116\frac{3}{4}$ yd

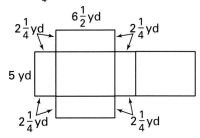

9. 8 in² **11.** 336 in² **13.** 324 cm²
15. 816 in² **17.** $2(bh + hw + bw)$
19. a. Cylinder B; It has the same area on its side as two cylinder As put together, and it has more area on the ends. **b.** Cylinder B; Two cylinder As could be put inside it with room to spare. **21.** 100%
23. Obtuse **25.** Right **27.** Acute

9-5 Try It (Example 1)

a. Square pyramid **b.** 8 cm
c. ≈ 8.5 cm **d.** ≈ 25.5 cm²
e. ≈ 138 cm²

9-5 Try It (Example 2)

a. 11 ft **b.** ≈ 2.6 ft **c.** ≈ 16.5 ft²
d. ≈ 53.4 ft²

9-5 Exercises & Applications

1. a. 4 **b.** 252 ft² **c.** 252 ft² each
d. 1008 ft² **3. a.** 11.2 in. **b.** 291.2 in² **5.** 384 ft² **7.** D **9.** ≈ 423.9 ft²
11. Possible answer: The height is like one of the legs of a right triangle and the slant height is like the hypotenuse. **13.** The pyramid
15. 7, 9; If the base of a pyramid has k sides, then the pyramid has $k + 1$ faces. **17.** 1, −3, 3 **19.** −2, 0, 0 **21.** 3, 0, 0 **23.** 4, $\frac{5}{4}$, −5
25. 2, 3, 4, 5

Section 9A Review

1. Perimeter **3.** Prism **7.** 34 in.;
$61\frac{3}{4}$ in. **9.** $13\frac{1}{2}$ ft; $7\frac{7}{8}$ ft² **11.** 59 ft;
192 ft² **13.** 6480 m² **15.** 2014 cm²

9-6 Try It (Example 2)

a. 205.8 cm³ **b.** $274\frac{5}{8}$ in³

9-6 Try It (Example 3)

246 ft³

9-6 Exercises & Applications

1. a. 12 **b.** 60 **3.** 663 m³
5. $99\frac{3}{4}$ yd³ **7.** $27\frac{13}{16}$ ft³
9. 6000 ft³

11. $\frac{4}{9}$ of a cent per in³
13. ≈ 113.04 cm³
15. 125 cm³; $V = s^3$

17–18.

L	W	H	V	A
1	1	36	36	146
1	2	18	36	112
1	3	12	36	102
1	4	9	36	98
1	6	6	36	96
2	2	9	36	80
2	3	6	36	72
3	3	4	36	66

19. The prism with dimensions 1 in. × 1 in. × 36 in. has the greatest surface area. The prism with dimensions 3 in. × 3 in. × 4 in. has the least. **21.** Both items have a volume of 648 in³. The book will not fit in the box because of its 9 in. length.
23. Yes **25.** No **27.** 1080°
29. 360°

9-7 Try It (Example 1)

a. 120 in³ **b.** 480 in³ **c.** 1920 in³

9-7 Try It (Example 2)

a. 5375 ft³ **b.** 5.375 ft³

9-7 Exercises & Applications

1. a. $\frac{1}{8}$ **b.** 45 ft³ **3.** 5184 in³
5. 6048 in³ **7.** 13.824 m³ **9.** D
11. 785,000 cm³; 0.785 cm³, $\frac{1}{1,000,000}$
13. a. Speedy Shipping **b.** No; E-Z Shipping would be cheaper for a 10 in. × 10 in. × 10 in. package, for example. **15. a.** Possible answer: $\frac{1}{30}$, which makes the model 18 in. long—a suitable size for a class project. **b.** 404 in² not including the floor **c.** 720 in³
17. a. Yes **b.** Yes **c.** Yes **19.** 13

9-8 Try It (Example 1)

a. $3\frac{1}{2}$ in. **b.** 7 in² **c.** 49 in³

9-8 Try It (Example 2)

a. ≈ 310.86 cm³ **b.** ≈ 2289.06 in³

9-8 Exercises & Applications

1. a.

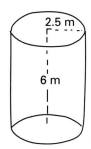

b. ≈ 19.625 m² **c.** ≈ 117.75 m³
3. ≈ 254.34 cm³ **5.** ≈ 565.2 cm³
7. ≈ 2893.824 cm³ **9.** 0.09 m³
11. ≈ 753.6 in³ **13. a.** 221,174 m³
b. 25,277 m² **15.** The tallest prism will have the greatest volume; The shortest will have the least; Since the volume of a prism is the base area times the height, the volume will be proportional to height.
17. (2, −3) **19.** (−5, 4)

9-9 Try It (Example 1)

V ≈ 39.25 m³

9-9 Try It (Example 3)

a. 50 m³ **b.** 126 in³

9-9 Exercises & Applications

1. a. $12\frac{1}{4}$ ft² **b.** $16\frac{1}{3}$ ft³ **3.** 36 cm³

5. 56 ft³ **7.** ≈ 94.2 cm³ **9.** ≈ 11.9 mm **11.** 680 cm³ (This is only an approximation, since part of the cone actually sticks into the cylinder.) **13.** The pyramid **15.** $h^2 + 81 = 225$ $h = 12$ in. **17.** 6280 cm³ **19.** 64 **21.** 64 **23. a.** Yes **b.** No **25. a.** Yes **b.** No

Section 9B Review

1. 561 in³ **3.** ≈ 48.2304 cm³ **5.** 1296 m³ **7.** 560 in³ **9.** ≈ 1515 cm³ **11.** 27 in³ **13.** 50.24 in³

Chapter 9 Summary & Review

1. a. $p = 26$ cm; $A = 28$ cm² **b.** $p = 16$ in.; $A = 14$ in² **2. a.** $p = 78$ cm; $A = 252$ cm² **b.** $p = 6.4$ in.; $A = 2.24$ in² **3.** $C ≈ 52.1$ cm; $A ≈ 216$ cm² **4.** ≈ 45 ft **5. a.** ≈ 149.2 ft² **b.** 1710 cm² **6. a.** $s = 13$ in.; $SA = 360$ in² **b.** $s = 25$ m; $SA ≈ 1884$ m² **7. a.** $V = 125$ cm³ **b.** $V = 7350$ ft³ **8. a.** $V ≈ 184$ in³ **b.** $V = 192.5$ cm³ **9. a.** $V = 120$ cm³

b. $V ≈ 83.7$ in³

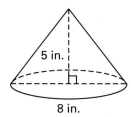

10. a. $V = 5$ cm³ **b.** $SA = 114,562$ ft²; $V = 2,521,050$ ft³ **11. a.** $V = 13.5$ m³ **b.** $V = 27$ m³ **12. a.** $V = 24$ ft³ **b.** $V = 6$ ft³

Chapter 10

10-1 Try It (Example 1)

$110; Yes; 10 hours

10-1 Try It (Example 2)

Yes; For any given number of Buddy Biscuits, there is only one price.

10-1 Try It (Example 3)

a. Yes; Input n yields output n^2
b. No; There are two output values for 1 and two output values for 2.

10-1 Exercises & Applications

1. a. 4 **b.** 8 **c.** Multiply by 3 and subtract 4 **d.** 14 **3.** −2.25 **5.** 1.75 **7.** 16 **9.** −16 **11.** Multiply by 2 and subtract 1 **13.** C **15. a.** Calories burned = minutes × 13.5; 202.5; 270; 405; 607.5 **b.** About 22 min **c.** Yes; Yes; Each input value yields only one output. **17.** Yes; For any given time there is only one height **19.** Take the absolute value. **21.** 23% **23.** 30%

10-2 Try It (Example 2)

a. Yes; The graph is a straight line.
b. Money earned = $4 × number of shirts sold; 9 shirts; Yes; The number of shirts determines the amount of money earned.

10-2 Exercises & Applications

1. a. y **b.** x **c.** $y = -2$, $y = 3$, $y = 8$ **3.** 11, 10, 9, 8, 7 **5.** B **7.** Yes **9.** No **11. a.** $d = 34.5t$ **b.** 69 mi, 207 mi, 345 mi **13.** No; Inputs −1 and −2 each have two output values. **15. a.** $c = 6.5n + 18$ **c.** Yes **19.** 12 in., $4\sqrt{3} ≈ 6.9$ in² **21.** Perimeter can't be determined, 230 cm²

10-3 Try It (Examples 1–2)

a.

b.

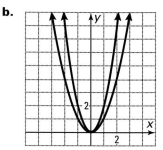

The graphs have the same general shape, but the $2x^2$ graph is skinnier.

10-3 Try It (Example 3)

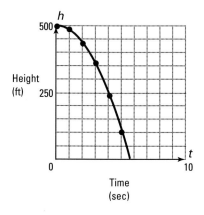

10-3 Exercises & Applications

1. Neither **3.** Linear
5.

Same general shape, but varying widths.

7.

Same shape, but one opens up and one opens down.

9. F   **11.** D   **13.** B   **15.** C
17. The canyon is 400 ft deep; The value is negative because the function represents height measured from the canyon's rim.   **21.** 27
23. 66 cm

10-4 Try It (Examples 1–2)

a.

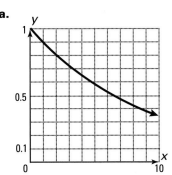

0.66, 2.12   **b.** About $7\frac{3}{4}$ hours

10-4 Try It (Example 3)

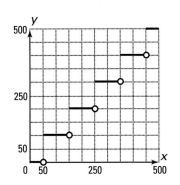

10-4 Exercises & Applications

1. B   **3.** C

5.

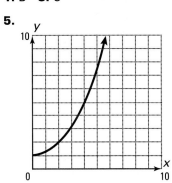

7.

9. There will be $1000 \times 2^1 = 2000$ butterflies after 1 year, $1000 \times 2^2 = 4000$ butterflies after 2 years, $1000 \times 2^3 = 8000$ butterflies after 3 years, and $1000 \times 2^{10} = 1{,}024{,}000$ butterflies after 10 years.   **11. b.** Step
13. Quadratic   **15.** Linear
17. a. \$1402.55   **b.** 11 years
19. a. Increase   **b.** Decrease for $x < 0$, increase for $x > 0$
c. Increase   **d.** Decrease
21. Exponential, increasing
23. $10 - 2n$ **25.** 12π m, 36π m^2
27. 5.8π m, 8.41π m^2

Section 10A Review

1. -10 **3.** 0   **5.** -2 **7.** C
13. Yes; Each x value corresponds to only one y value.

15.

Similar: All three functions are increasing to the right of the origin. Different: $y = x$ is a straight line, $y = x^2$ curves up at both ends (and so is decreasing to the left of the origin), and $y = 4^x$ is nearly flat on the left and curves up on the right.

17. a.

Time (sec)	Height (ft)
0	0
1	-16
2	-64
3	-144
4	-256
5	-400
6	-576
7	-784
8	-1024

b. 256 ft; Height is measured from ground level.

10-5 Try It (Examples 1–2)

$-4x^2 + x + 22$

10-5 Try It (Examples 3–4)

a. 5, -34 **b. i.** ≈ 2.09 ft^3
ii. ≈ 134 ft^3 **iii.** ≈ 23.8 m^3

10-5 Exercises & Applications

1. a. 3   **b.** 1   **c.** 2   **3.** Trinomial
5. Binomial   **7.** $2x + 4$; 1   **9.** $-x^4 - x^3 + x^2$; 4   **11.** -3 **13.** 51   **15.** 6;
910   **17.** 3; -5 **19.** 175.9 in^2
21. B   **23. a.** 85,486 ft^2
b. 2,350,879 ft^3 **25.** $V = ns^3$ where s is the side length and n is the number of boxes.   **27.** 0, 1, 5, 14, 30; The differences are the perfect squares 1, 4, 9, 16.   **29.** 105
31. 180   **33.** 3584 cm^2

10-6 Try It (Examples 1–2)

a. $7x^2 + 7x + 1$ **b.** $-11n^2 - n - 9$
c. $3x^2 + 8x - 10$

10-6 Try It (Example 3)

$2x^2 + x - 11$; 199

10-6 Exercises & Applications

1. a. Descending   **b.** Like terms
c. Distributive   **3.** Already simplified   **5.** $7m^2 - 3m$ **7.** $4a + 6$
9. $-2x^2 + 1$ **11.** $13x^2 + 4x - 7$
13. $4x^2 - x + 9$ **15.** A   **17.** $x^3 + 5x^2 + 4x^2 + 7x$; $x^3 + 9x^2 + 7x$;
582 ft^3 **19.** $2x^2 + 13x + 20$
21. $3x^2 + 13x + 11$ **23.** Possible answer: $4x - 3x + 2x - x$
25. No; Should be $7x$

27. a. Incorrect; Added exponents, forgot to add coefficients.
b. Incorrect; Added exponents.
c. Correct; Added coefficients but not exponents. **d.** Incorrect; Forgot to add coefficients. **29.** 36 **31.** 9
33. $\approx 30.8 \text{ cm}^2$

10-7 Try It (Examples 1–2)

a. $2x^3 - 1$ **b.** $2x^3 + 6x^2 + 6x - 5$

10-7 Try It (Example 3–4)

a. $-70p^2 + 1495p - 300$; $7650
b. $6x - 5$

10-7 Exercises & Applications

1. a. x^3 **b.** $-4x^2$ **c.** $-2x$ **d.** $7x^5$
e. -27 **3.** $-x^4 + 2$ **5.** $-3x^3 - 2x$
7. $x^5 - 2x - 9x^3 + 3$ **9.** $2x^2 + 4x - 1$ **11.** $-4m^2 + 4m - 1$
13. $2v^3 - 8v^2 + 6v - 1$ **15.** $a^3 - 6a^2 + 2a - 3$ **17.** $11x^2 - 2x + 1$
19. $12x^2 + 4x + 3$ **21.** $x^2 - 3x + 3$
23. $x^2 + 4$ **25.** $10t - 8$ **27.** No; She dropped the variable.
31. $2x^5 + 2x^4 + 3x^2 - 2x + 1$
33. $2 \cdot 3^2 \cdot 5$ **35.** $3 \cdot 29$ **37.** $3 \cdot 5^3$
39. 232.56 m^3

10-8 Try It (Example 2)

1. a. 5^6 **b.** 8^3 **c.** x^8 **d.** $-32x^6$

10-8 Try It (Example 3)

a. $-10x^6 - 12x^3$
b. $6x^4 + 10x^3 - 2x^2$

10-8 Try It (Examples 4–5)

a. 3.5×10^{11} **b.** 4.94×10^{12}

10-8 Exercises & Applications

1. a. $x \cdot x \cdot x \cdot x$ **b.** $x \cdot x \cdot x$ **c.** 7
d. x^7 **3.** 4^7 **5.** $6r^6$ **7.** $-24d^{10}$
9. $20f^{15}$ **11.** $3b^5$ **13.** $-6t + 6t^3$
15. $15g^7 - 10g^6 + 25g^5 + 40g^4$
17. $2m^2 + 4m$ **19.** 9.92×10^9
21. 8.16×10^6 **25. a.** 2.47×10^{11}
b. 5.89×10^{10} **c.** 8.55×10^9
d. 5.89×10^{11} **27.** $3^6 = 729$; a^6
29. a. Subtract exponents
b. $2^1 = \frac{8}{4} = 2$ **31.** 25 **33.** 3
35. 884.736 m^3

Section 10B Review

1. Binomial, two terms.
3. Monomial, one term. **5.** 1; $8x - 6$ **7.** 5; $-x^5 + x^2 - x$ **9.** 7; $x^7 - 3$
11. Already simplified **13.** $10x + 5$
15. $2x^2 + 4x - 1$ **17.** $p^2 - 2p - 9$
19. x^6 **21.** $-20x^{10}$ **23.** $y^2 + 3y$
25. $x^6 + 5x^4$ **27.** C

Chapter 10 Summary & Review

1. a. -18 **b.** 4 **2.** Multiply by 3 and add 1.
3. Yes

4. Answers may vary.

5. 64 ft

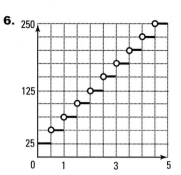

6.

7. $-4x^3 - 7x^2 + 3x + 5$ **8. a.** 18
b. 12 **9.** $5x^3 - 5x^2 - 3x + 14$
10. $4p^2 - 1$ **11.** $4x^2 + 2x + 5$
12. $x^2 - x - 5$ **13.** $6x^3 - 9x^2 - 2x + 15$ **14.** $g^2 + 8g + 3$
15. $6x^3 - 15x^2$ **16.** 4.14×10^{14}
17. $-15u^5 + 21u^4 - 12u^3$

Cumulative Review
Chapters 1–10

1. D **2.** D **3.** C **4.** B **5.** D **6.** A
7. B **8.** C **9.** B **10.** C **11.** A
12. B **13.** D

Chapter 11

11-1 Try It (Example 2)

a. $\frac{8}{5}$ **b.** 118°

11-1 Try It (Example 4)

a. Yes **b.** No

11-1 Exercises & Applications

1. a. $\frac{1.5}{3.0} = \frac{1.8}{3.6}$ **b.** Yes, $(1.5)(3.6) = (3.0)(1.8) = 5.4$ **3.** Yes **5.** 1 in.:50 ft **7.** A **9.** $64x^2$ **11.** Each cable forms a different angle measurement where it intersects the road.
15. Factors: 1, 2, 3, 6, 11, 22, 33, 66; Prime factors: 2, 3, 11 **17.** Factors: 1, 2, 3, 4, 6, 8, 12, 16, 24, 48; Prime factors: 2, 3 **19.** 12 **21.** 5.01
23. -17

11-2 Try It (Example 2)

No

11-2 Try It (Example 4)

a. $\overline{HI}$ **b.** $\frac{5}{8}$ in. **c.** 120°

11-2 Exercises & Applications

1. a. The corresponding sides are not congruent.   **b.** The corresponding angles are congruent.   **3.** 6 mm   **5.** Yes   **7.** 8   **11.** They are congruent.   **15.** 8   **17.** 10   **19.** Yes   **21.** Yes

11-3 Try It (Example1)

No.

11-3 Try It (Example 3)

Yes; The SAS rule.

11-3 Exercises & Applications

1. a. $\overline{QS}$ **b.** $\overline{RS}$ **c.** $\angle Q$ **d.** $\angle R$ **e.** $\angle S$ **3.** Yes; The SSS rule.   **5.** Yes; The SAA rule.   **7.** Yes; The SAS rule   **9. a–c.** Answers may vary.   **11.** The SAS rule.   **13.** Not necessarily; The triangles are the same shape (i.e., similar) but not necessarily the same size.   **15.** 60   **17.** 10   **19.** 60

11-4 Try It (Example 1)

a. $\overline{KM}$ **b.** $\overline{ML}$ **c.** $\overline{KL}$

11-4 Try It (Example 2)

a. $\frac{4}{5}$ **b.** $\frac{4}{3}$

11-4 Try It (Example 4)

a. ≈ 11.78 m   **b.** ≈ 12.79 m

11-4 Exercises & Applications

1. a. Opposite   **b.** Adjacent   **c.** Tangent   **d.** ≈ 38.87 in.   **3.** sin = $\frac{1}{\sqrt{2}}$, cos = $\frac{1}{\sqrt{2}}$, tan = 1   **5.** ≈ 618.8 m   **7.** ≈ 10.4 ft   **9.** B   **11.** ≈ 3035 ft   **13.** sin(60°) ≈ 0.866, cos(60°) = 0.5, tan(60°) ≈ 1.732 **15.** $2\frac{1}{50}$ **17.** $4\frac{6}{25}$ **19.** $9\frac{9}{10}$ **21.** Exponential   **23.** Linear

11-5 Try It (Example 2)

7 cm

11-5 Try It (Example 3)

1.$\overline{66}$ ft

11-5 Exercises & Applications

1. a. 16 cm   **b.** $m\overline{EG}$ = 14.4 cm   **3.** ≈ 11.58 in.   **5.** D   **7.** ≈ 387.32 yd   **9.** Possible answer: Since $\angle A$ is congruent to the corresponding angle of the triangle for which s is the hypotenuse and 10 ft is the length of the adjacent side of that angle, solve the equation $\frac{10}{s}$ = cos(22°).   **11.** 4   **13.** Because most trigonometric ratios are irrational numbers, the results involving them are approximate rather than exact.   **15.** 0.176   **17.** $\frac{7}{16}$ **19.** $-3x^2 + 2x + 5$; 2   **21.** $-x^3 - x^2 + 3x - 3$; 3

Section 11A Review

1. 6 in.   **3.** Yes, SAA   **7.** 3290 ft

11-6 Try It (Example 1)

$(-2, -2)$, $(-5, -2)$, $(-5, -1)$, $(-3, 0)$; $(2, 2)$, $(5, 2)$, $(5, 1)$, $(3, 0)$

11-6 Try It (Examples 3-4)

a. $(-3, 1)$; $(-1, 1)$; $(-3, 4)$; $(-1, 4)$ **b.** $(-1, -2)$; $(-4, -2)$; $(-1, -3)$; $(-2, -3)$; $(-2, -5)$; $(-4, -4)$

11-6 Exercises & Applications

1. a.

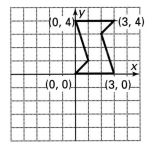

c. $(0, 0)$, $(0, 4)$, $(3, 4)$, $(3, 0)$ **3.** Rotation   **5.** The y-axis   **7.** C   **9.** A reflection   **11.** No transformations of the word "TRANSLATE" as a whole will work. Each letter must be reflected and rotated separately.   **13.** No; A parallelogram and a trapezoid are not congruent.   **15.** 381.98   **17.** $\frac{16}{63}$ **19.** 0.68   **21.** $87\frac{1}{9}$ **23.** $x^3 + 7x^2 - 2$

11-7 Try It (Example 2)

a. $(-12.5, -5)$; $(-7.5, 5)$; $(-2.5, 10)$; $(2.5, 10)$; $(7.5, 5)$; $(12.5, -5)$ **b.** $(-2\frac{2}{3}, 0)$; $(0, 2\frac{2}{3})$; $(2\frac{2}{3}, 0)$; $(0, -2\frac{2}{3})$

11-7 Try It (Example 4)

a. $\frac{1}{5}$ **b.** 5

11-7 Exercises & Applications

1. 2 and 3   **3.** Reduction, $\frac{2}{3}$ **5.** B   **7.** ≈ 4.8 **9.** The result will be a lizard 11.75 cm long and 6.25 cm wide.   **11.** 12   **13. a.** The quotient is 2 in every case.   **b.** Yes   **15.** $E'' = (8, 0)$, $F'' = (10, 6)$, $G'' = (5, 8)$, $H'' = (0, 6)$, $I'' = (2, 0)$ **17.** $\frac{2}{3}$ **19.** $\frac{8}{9}$ **21.** $2x^3 - 4x^2 + 2x - 5$ **23.** $-x^2 - 5x - 2$

11-8 Try It (Example 3)

a. Four   **b.** Yes; 90°

11-8 Try It (Example 5)

Rotational and point symmetries

11-8 Exercises & Applications

1. a. $\overleftrightarrow{BY}$ **b.** $\overrightarrow{PX}$ **c.** $\overleftrightarrow{QW}$ **3.** C   **5.** 120°, 240°, 360°   **7.** Ten   **9.** Horizontal line through E.   **11.** No lines of symmetry.   **13.** Yes; Yes; The deer in the top two rows are congruent.   **15.** You can't because the deer in each row are looking in different directions.   **19.** Irrational   **21.** Rational   **23.** 5.762 $\times 10^{14}$ **25.** 5.39×10^7

11-9 Try It (Example 4)

a. Yes   **b.** Yes   **c.** No

11-9 Try It (Example 5)

90

11-9 Exercises & Applications

1. a. No   **b.** Yes   **c.** No   **3. a.** Triangles, squares, hexagons.

b. Possible answer: They do not fit together to cover the plane without gaps or overlaps.   **5.** 4000
7. a. Equilateral triangles
b. Trapezoids   **c.** Regular hexagons
9. a. Yes   **b.** Yes   **c.** No   **d.** Yes
15. ≈ 15.9 in.   **17.** $x = 80$ **19.** 24.5

Section 11B Review

1. a. Rotation   **b.** Translation
c. Reflection   **3.** For each point (x, y) the reflected point is $(-x, y)$.
5. Possible answer: Give up translation, which can be replaced by two successive rotations with different axis points, or by two reflections with parallel reflection lines. The other option: Give up rotation, which can be replaced by two successive reflections using intersecting reflection lines.   **7.** B

Chapter 11 Summary & Review

1. $x = 18$ in.; $m\angle 1 = 135°$
2. Congruent by SAA   **3.** Not congruent   **4. a.** ≈ 0.87   **b.** ≈ 0.87
c. 1   **5.** $\sin \angle A = \frac{1.75}{6.25}$; $\cos \angle A = \frac{6}{6.25}$; $\tan \angle A = \frac{1.75}{6}$ **6.** 15 cm
7. a. $K'(0, 0)$; $L'(3, -1)$; $M'(2, -4)$; and $N'(0, -5)$ **b.** $K'(0, 0)$; $L'(-3, 1)$; $M'(-2, 4)$; and $N'(0, 5)$ **c.** $K'(0, 0)$; $L'(-1, 3)$; $M'(-4, 2)$; and $N'(-5, 0)$
8. $A'(1, -1)$, $B'(1, -2)$, $C'(3, -2)$
9. Dilation; Yes; No   **10.** $\overleftrightarrow{MW}, \overleftrightarrow{PY}$
11. Yes

Chapter 12

12-1 Try It (Example 1)

Possibilities are: Flight 1 return A, flight 1 return b, flight 1 return C, flight 2 return A, flight 2 return B, flight 2 return C, flight 3 return A, flight 3 return B, flight 3 return C, flight 4 return A, flight 4 return B, flight 4 return C.

12 pairs

12-1 Try It (Example 2)

360

12-1 Try It (Example 3)

3600

12-1 Exercises & Applications

1. a. Possibilities are: Pork and Swiss on wheat, pork and Swiss on rye, pork and American on wheat, pork and American on rye, pork and jack on wheat, pork and jack on rye, beef and Swiss on wheat, beef and Swiss on rye, beef and American on wheat, beef and American on rye, beef and jack on wheat, beef and jack on rye.   **b.** 12   **3. a.** 40   **b.** 18
c. 20
5.

7. 8   **9.** 36   **11.** 240   **15.** $x > 2$
17. $x \le 4$ **19.** ≈ 24.6 in²

12-2 Try It (Example 1)

40,320

12-2 Try It (Example 2)

a. 24   **b.** 24   **c.** 30,240

12-2 Try It (Example 3)

a. 181,440   **b.** 60   **c.** 60; 120; 120

12-2 Exercises & Applications

1. a. Possibilities are: Justin, Butch, Rod; Justin, Rod, Butch; Butch, Justin, Rod; Butch, Rod, Justin; Rod, Justin, Butch; Rod, Butch, Justin
b. 6   **c.** 3!   **3.** 720   **5.** 3,628,800

7. 30,240   **9.** 7   **11.** 120   **13.** 120
15. 5040   **17.** 1 in 6   **19.** $\frac{1}{6}$
21. a. 14,400   **b.** 120   **23.** LULL has repeated letters; SALT has 4! = 24 arrangements, and PEPPER has 3! = 6.   **25.** No; Order is not important.   **27.** No   **29.** Yes

12-3 Try (Example 1)

Abby / Bonita / Chantall
Abby / Bonita / Dani
Abby / Bonita / Eleni
Abby / Chantall / Dani
Abby / Chantall / Eleni
Abby / Dani / Eleni
Bonita / Chantall / Dani
Bonita / Chantall / Eleni
Bonita / Dani / Eleni
Chantall / Dani / Eleni
10 combinations

12-3 Try It (Example 3)

15

12-3 Exercises & Applications

1. Yes   **2.** No   **3.** Yes   **4.** No
5. $\frac{96!}{24! \times 72!}$ **7.** 252   **9.** 10   **11.** 10
13. 792   **15.** Yes   **17.** The chances of winning are 1 in $\frac{53!}{6! \times 47!}$, or 1 in 22,957,480.   **19.** B   **21.** 5 people, since the value of $\frac{10!}{r!(10 - r)!}$ peaks when r is half of 10.
23. 4200   **25.** Yes; $k = \frac{3}{2}$ **27.** No

Section 12A Review

1. 40,320   **3.** 5040   **5.** 1,814,400
7. 56   **9.** 56   **11.** 3 heads, 2 heads and 1 tail, 2 tails and 1 head, 3 tails
13. 720   **15.** 362,880   **17.** 5040
19. 5040   **21.** D

12-4 Try It (Examples 1–2)

a. 1, 2, 3, 4, 5, 6; $\frac{1}{3}$ **b.** Sun, Mon, Tues, Wed, Thur, Fri, Sat; $\frac{2}{7}$

12-4 Try It (Example 3)

a. $\frac{1}{2}$ **b.** $\frac{1}{3}$ **c.** $\frac{1}{6}$ **d.** 1   **e.** 0

12-4 Exercises & Applications

1. a. 1, 2, 3, 4, 5, 6 **b.** 6 **c.** 1 **d.** $\frac{1}{6}$
e. $\frac{1}{6}$; 0.1666...; $16\frac{2}{3}$% **3.** 1, 2, 3, 4,
6 **5.** $\frac{1}{2}$, 0.5, 50% **7.** 0, 0, 0%
9. B **11.** $\frac{8191}{8192}$ **13.** Yellow, green
15. $\frac{1}{4}$; $\frac{1}{2}$ **17.** First in top row, third
in bottom row; 1 in 36 **19.** Never
25. Yes

12-5 Try It (Example 1)

a. 2 heads: $\frac{1}{4}$; 1 head: $\frac{1}{2}$; 0 heads: $\frac{1}{4}$
b. Answers may vary. **c.** There
should be $\approx$ 25% of 2 heads, 50% of
1 head, and 25% of 0 heads.

12-5 Try It (Example 2)

San Antonio is the only one that
passed; You would expect to find
defective candles in $\approx$ 44 boxes out
of 10,000.

12-5 Try It (Example 3)

$\frac{4}{27}$

12-5 Exercises & Applications

1. Experimental **2.** Theoretical
3. Experimental **5. a.** $\frac{7}{30}$ **b.** $\frac{23}{30}$
7. About $\frac{3}{8}$ **9.** $\frac{2}{27}$ **11. a.** $\frac{1}{11} \approx$ 9%
b. $\frac{1}{11} \approx$ 9% **c.** 1 **13.** Yes **15.** Yes
17. 288 ft³ **19.** 1600 in³

12-6 Try It (Example 1)

a. $\frac{1}{6}$ **b.** 0

12-6 Try It (Example 3)

a. $\frac{91}{150} \approx$ 60.7% **b.** $\frac{28}{45} \approx$ 62.2%

12-6 Try It (Example 4)

a. $\frac{2}{25}$ **b.** $\frac{1}{18}$; $\frac{1}{2}$

12-6 Exercises & Applications

1. a. red, red blue, blue yellow,
yellow green, green red, blue
blue, red yellow, red green, red
red, yellow blue, yellow yellow,
blue green, blue red, green
blue, green yellow, green green,
yellow **b.** 16 **c.** 4 **d.** $\frac{1}{16}$ **3.** $\frac{1}{2}$
5. $\frac{1}{16}$ **7. a.** 0 **b.** $\frac{1}{6}$ **c.** $\frac{1}{3}$ **d.** 1
9. 800 people **11. a.** $\frac{59}{95} \approx$ 62.1%
b. $\frac{32}{42} \approx$ 76.2% **c.** $\frac{42}{95} \approx$ 44.2%
13. $100 - \frac{9\pi}{100} \approx$ 72% **15.** 90 in³
17. $XY = 2$; $BC \approx 10.77$

12-7 Try It (Example 1)

a. Dependent **b.** Independent

12-7 Try It (Example 3)

34.4%

12-7 Try It (Example 4)

a. $\frac{4}{49}$ **b.** $\frac{2}{42}$

12-7 Exercises & Applications

1. a. $\frac{1}{2}$ **b.** $\frac{1}{6}$ **c.** $\approx$ 8.3%
3. Independent **5.** Dependent
7. $\frac{1}{4}$ **9.** $\frac{1}{10}$ **11.** $\frac{4}{15}$ **13.** 1
15. 0.09% **17. a.** 1 in 5 **b.** 1 in 4
21. 71.96 in³ **23.** (1, 2)

Section 12B Review

1. Sample space: 1, 2, 3, 4, 5, 6
a. 1 outcome; Probability: $\frac{1}{6}$ **b.** 3
outcomes; Probability: $\frac{1}{2}$ **c.** 0 out-
comes; Probability: 0 **3. a.** $\frac{1}{36}$ **b.** $\frac{1}{6}$
c. $\frac{4}{9}$ **5.** $\frac{1}{4}$ **7.** $\frac{1}{8}$ **9.** Yes; There is
one less person left to pick from.
11. D

Chapter 12 Summary & Review

1.

2. 15 **3. a.** 120 **b.** 24 **c.** 35
4. 720 **5.** 336 **6.** 210 **7.** $\frac{1}{3}$ **8.** $\frac{1}{13}$
9. 20% **11.** $\frac{13}{25}$ **12.** $\frac{2}{7}$ **13.** $\frac{1}{13}$
14. $\frac{1}{6}$ **15. a.** $\frac{25}{144}$ **b.** $\frac{5}{33}$ **16.** $\frac{1}{4}$;
Independent events

Cumulative Review
Chapters 1–12

1. C **2.** B **3.** B **4.** B **5.** C **6.** A
7. D **8.** D **9.** D **10.** B **11.** A
12. C **13.** B

Credits

Photographs

Cover/Spine Don Mason

Front Matter **iii** GHP Studio* **iii(background)** John Banagan/The Image Bank **v-xviT** GHP Studio* **xviiiTL** Roy Morsch/The Stock Market **xviiiR** Peter Menzel/Stock, Boston **xviiiB** Marc Chamberlain/Tony Stone Images **ixT** Ken Karp* **xixB** Ken Karp,* Dennis Geaney* & Parker/Boon Productions and Dorey Sparre Photography* **xxii** Ken Karp* **xxiii** Ken Karp* xxv Ken Karp* **xxvi** Michael Rosenfeld/Tony Stone Images **xxviiL** David Young Wolff/Tony Stone Images **xxviiCL** Hans Reinhard/Bruce Coleman Inc. **xxviiCCL** Frank Siteman/Stock, Boston **xxviiCCR** Robert Pearcy/Animals, Animals **xxviiCR** Peter Vandermark/Stock, Boston **xxviiR** Fritz Prenzel/Animals, Animals

Chapter 1 **2-3(background)** Suzanne Murphy/Tony Stone Images **2L** Bruno De Hogues/Tony Stone Images **2TR** Culver Pictures 2B Ken Karp* **3T** CNRI/SPL/Photo Researchers 3B Cheryl Fenton* **4T** The Image Bank **4B** Jenny Thomas* **5** Cheryl Fenton* 6 Ken Karp* **7T** Blair Seitz/Photo Researchers **7B** John Scheiber/The Stock Market **8** Ben Van Hook/Duomo **9** Gabe Palmer/The Stock Market **10** Greg Pease Photography **11** Jim Pickerell/Stock, Boston **12T** SPL/Photo Researchers **12B** Lyle Leduc/Liaison International **13** Michael Skott/The Image Bank **14L** Ken Karp* **14R** Dennis Geaney* **15** Jenny Thomas* **16** Chuck Savage/The Stock Market **17L** GHP Studio* **17R** Jose L. Pelaez/The Stock Market **18** John Elk III **20** Ben Simmons/The Stock Market **21T** Mark Reinstein/Uniphoto Picture Agency **21B** SIU/Visuals Unlimited **22** Randy Duchaine/The Stock Market **22L** Cheryl Fenton* **23** Cheryl Fenton* **25** NASA/Stock, Boston **26** George Haling/Photo Researchers **27L** Popperfoto/Archive Photos **27R** Mitchell Layton/Duomo **31** Cheryl Fenton* **32L** Bob Daemmrich/Uniphoto Picture Agency **32C** Cheryl Fenton* **32R** Cheryl Fenton* 33 Ken Karp* **35** Photo 20-20 **37L** Cheryl Fenton* **37R** Bodhan Hrynewych/Stock, Boston **39** David R. Frazier Photolibrary **40T** George East/Visuals Unlimited **40B** Gene Gray/Transparencies, Inc. **41L** Dennis Geaney* **41R** Ken Karp* **42** Ed Lallo/Liaison International **43** Burrows/Liaison International **45** Space Telescope Science Institute/NASA/SPL/Photo Researchers **46** Bob Daemmrich/Tony Stone Images **47** Barros & Barros/The Image Bank 48 M. Antman/The Image Works **49** Cheryl Fenton* **50** Ken Karp* **52** NASA/Mark Marten/Photo Researchers **53** Geoffrey Nilsen Photography* **57T** Cheryl Fenton* **57BL** Cheryl Fenton* **57BR** Romilly Lockyer/The Image Bank

Chapter 2 **58-59(background)** Ralph A. Clevenger/Westlight **58TL** Tournament of Roses **58TR** Tony Stone Images **58B** Fred Bavendam/Peter Arnold, Inc. **59T** Jose Fuste Raga/The Stock Market **59BL** John Cancalosi/Peter Arnold, Inc. **59BR** Larry Ulrich/Tony Stone Images **60T** Zig Leszczynski/Animals, Animals **60B** Bruce Hands/Tony Stone Images **62L** Ed Bock/The Stock Market **62R** Bernard Boutrit/Woodfin Camp & Associates **64** Mark Harwood/Tony Stone Images **65** Phil Schofield/Tony Stone Images **66** Cheryl Fenton* **67** David Madison/Duomo **68** Ken Karp* **69** Kenneth Eward/BioGrafx/Photo Researchers **70** Robert E. Daemmrich/Tony Stone Images **71T** Western History Collections, University of Oklahoma Libraries **71B** Peter Poulides/Tony Stone Images **72L** Robert Frerck/Woodfin Camp & Associates **72R** Ken Karp* **73** Jenny Thomas* **74** Mitchell Layton/Duomo **75** J. L. Bulcao/Liaison International **76TL** Edmondson/Liaison International **76TR** NASA/Mark Marten/Photo Researchers **76B** Jim Cambon/Tony Stone Images **77L** GHP Studio* **77R** Richard Megna/Fundamental Photographs **78** James Wilson/Woodfin Camp & Associates **79** Frank White/Liaison International **80** Jan Halaake/Photo Researchers **81** David Madison/Tony Stone Images **82L** David Madison/Duomo **82TR** Harald Sund/The Image Bank **82BR** Cheryl Fenton* **84L** Parker/Boon Productions and Dorey Sparre Photography* **84R** Ken Karp* **85** R. Rathe/FPG International **88** H. R. Bramaz/Peter Arnold, Inc. **89TL** Douglas Faulkner/Photo Researchers **89TC** Alain Evrard/Photo Researchers **89TR** Warren Morgan/Westlight **89CL** Connie Coleman/Tony Stone Images **89C(background)** Thomas Wiewandt/Masterfile **89CR** Michael Busselle/Tony Stone Images **89BL** Anthony Cassidy/Tony Stone Images **89BC** Neil Gilchrist/Panoramic Images **89BR** Mark Joseph/Tony Stone Images **90L** Bob Daemmrich Photos, Inc. **91** Yu Trung Dung/Liaison International **92** National Geographic Image Collection **94** Demetrio Carrasco/Tony Stone Images **96** Francois Gohier/Photo Researchers **96R** GHP Studio* **97** Clyde H. Smith/Peter Arnold, Inc. **98** Dennis Geaney* **100** Paula Lerner/Woodfin Camp & Associates **101** Nancy Simmerman/Tony Stone Images **102** John Eastcott-Yva Momatiuk/Woodfin Camp & Associates **104** Piero Codato/Camera Photo/Liaison International **105** Sovfoto/Eastfoto **106L** Andrew Syred/SPL/Photo Researchers **106R** Terry Eiler/Stock, Boston **107** Gunther F. Bahr/AFIP/Tony Stone Images **108T** Wernher Krutein/Liaison International **108B** Prof. P. Motta/Dept. of Anatomy/University "La Sapienza", Rome/SPL/Photo Researchers **109T** Robert Brons/BPS/Tony Stone Images **109B** Diane Schiumo/Fundamental Photographs **110** Dr. Jeremy Burgess/SPL/Photo Researchers **111T** Warren Morgan/Westlight **111CL** Thomas Wiewandt/Masterfile **111CR** Michael Busselle/Tony Stone Images **111BC** Neil Gilchrist/Panoramic Images **111BR** Mark Joseph/Tony Stone Images **113** Geoffrey Nilsen Photography*

116 John Lund/Tony Stone Images **117** S. Lowry/Univ. Ulster/Tony Stone Images

Chapter 3 **118T** John Mitchell/Photo Researchers **118BR** Dallas & John Heaton/Stock, Boston **118BR** Steve Dunwell/The Image Bank **119T** NASA **119B** Peter Souhwick/AP/Wide World Photos **120** Jenny Thomas* **121** Brownie Harris/The Stock Market **121(inset)** Cheryl Fenton* **121(background)** W. Cody/Westlight **122L** Mark Wagner/Tony Stone Images **122C** Superstock **122R** Jerry Wachter/Photo Researchers **123** Archive Photos **124** Richard Kaylin/Tony Stone Images **125** Archive Photos **126L** Kaoru Ishie/Nature Production **126C** D. Cavagnaro/DRK Photo **126R** M. P. Kahl/Bruce Coleman Inc. **127** Cheryl Fenton* **128** David R. Frazier Photolibrary **129** Ken Karp* **132** Broderbund Software, Inc. **133** Richard Megna/Fundamental Photographs **134L** AP/Wide World Photos **134R** Ray Pfortner/Peter Arnold, Inc. **136L** AP/Wide World Photos **136R** Ross Harrison Koty/Tony Stone Images **137** Brownie Harris/The Stock Market **137(inset)** Cheryl Fenton* **138** Frank Schneidermeyer/Oxford Scientific Films **139** Bob Shaw/The Stock Market **140** M. Rutherford/Superstock **141** Michael Dwyer/Stock, Boston **142** Larry Mayer **145** Michael Dalton/Fundamental Photographs **146** Alain Eurard/Liaison International **147L** Dennis Geaney* **147R** Parker/Boon Productions and Dorey Sparre Photography* **148** Dennis Geaney* **149L** Ray Stott/The Image Works **149R** Tony Stone Images **150** Isaac Geib/Grant Heilman Photography **151** Torin Boyd/Liaison International **152** Superstock **154** W. H. Black/Bruce Coleman Inc. **155L** Ed Wheeler/The Stock Market **155R** Jenny Thomas* **157** Antman/The Image Works **158** Larry Mayer **159** Jenny Thomas* **161** Bob Shaw/The Stock Market **162** Keren Su/Tony Stone Images **167C** Tony Stone Images **167B** William R. Sallaz/Duomo

Chapter 4 **168-169(background)** Joanne Lotter/Tom Stack & Associates **168TL** Paul Chesley/Tony Stone Images **168TR** Superstock **168BC** M. Gadomski/Bruce Coleman Inc. **168BR** M. Antman/The Image Works **169T** Art Wolfe/Tony Stone Images **169C** U.S. Postal Service **169B** Superstock **170** Liza Loeffler* **171** Jenny Thomas* **172** Roger Tully/Tony Stone Images **173T** Jenny Thomas* **173B** Ron Kimball **174** Herbert W. Booth III/Liaison International **175** Jean-Michel Labat/Jacana/Photo Researchers **176** Hans Reinhard/Bruce Coleman Inc. **177L** Jenny Thomas* **177C** Jenny Thomas* **177R** Paul S. Howell/Liaison International **179** Leonard Lee Rue III/Animals, Animals **180** Tony Cordoza/Liaison International **181** Holt Studios International (Nigel Cattlin)/Photo Researchers **182L** Ken Karp* **182R** Gerard Lacz/Animals, Animals **184** Dennis Geaney* **185** Adolfo Previdere/Bruce Coleman Inc. **186** Ken Karp* **187** Jenny Thomas*

CREDITS

Ltd.   **659** Jon Randolph/Tony Stone Images
661 Camerique/The Picture Cube   **662** Andrew M.
Levine/Photo Researchers   **663L** Ken Karp*
663R Larry Lawfer/The Picture Cube   **664** Ed
Birch/Unicorn Stock Photos   **665** Ken Karp*
666 Ken Karp*   **669R** Ken Karp*   **669L** Cheryl
Fenton*   **671** Geoffrey Nilsen Photography*

*Photographs provided expressly for Scott
Foresman - Addison Wesley

Illustrations

Christine Benjamin: xxixa, 33c, 42a, 57b,
129e, 263c, 269d **Joe Heiner Studio:** all icons
and borders **Paul Koziarz:** 324a, 325a, 326a,
339a, 369a, 444c, 445a, 448n, 450b, 452c, 454h,
456c, 459b, 459j, 464h, 466b, 476b, 480b, 486b,
487a, 492a-d, 497a-c, 497g, 498a-c, 498f-i, 565b,
566b, 567f, 578a, 578b, 581b, 585c, 585d, 586c,
588f, 589b, 592e, 600a, 605b **Maryland
Cartographics:** 93b. 401a. 402a-c, 403a, 404a,
405a-c, 406a, 408a, 420a, 437d, 438a, 499a, 499b,
683a **Helene Moore:** 344a, 378b **Andrew
Muonio:** 132a, 144a, 161c, 274b, 509b, 630a,
666b, 666c **William Pasini:** 11a, 15b, 30a, 76c,
102a, 112a, 131a, 257b, 260a, 289e, 333a, 350a,
479h, 636a **Precision Graphics:** All illustrative
technical artwork throughout; all generated electronically. **QYA Design:** 465a **William
Rieser:** 368a, 373b, 375d, 377g, 379a-c, 395a,
396a, 398b, 420b, 426a, 451b, 463a, 508b **Rob
Schuster:** xxviiia, 34a, 34b, 75b, 90a, 99i, 103a,
140a, 141a, 143a, 143b, 176a, 191e, 193b-d, 201a,
338a, 338b, 342a, 377e, 377f, 381a, 551b, 574a,
628b, 630b, 654a, 654c **Susan Todd:** 599a, 606e-
g, 607a-c, 608e, 609c, 610a, 616e, 621a **Joe
VanDerBos:** 167d **Tom Ward:** xxiva, 650d
Jil Weil: 5b, 17b, 19a, 31b, 44b, 48a

Index

A

Absolute position, 402, 405
Absolute value, 63–65, 68, 94, 102, 131, 359, 369
Acute angle, 412, 414, 434, 465, 579, 583, 592
Acute triangle, 614
Addition
    in algebraic expressions, 128, 130–131, 133, 135, 138, 154, 162, 176, 181, 238
    of decimals, 351, 362, 568, 589
    in equations, 140–144, 150–153, 162, 173, 175, 178, 180, 188, 199, 210, 232, 255, 261, 290
    in formulas, 126, 138
    of fractions, 352–353, 362, 568, 589
    in inequalities, 156–159, 238
    of integers, 67–71, 82–86, 88, 100, 136, 194, 199
    of polynomials, 537–541
    of whole numbers, 10, 13–14, 36, 46
Addition Property of Equality, 141
Additive identity, 141
Additive inverse, 67, 69, 74, 141, 151, 542–543, 546, 604
Additive Inverse Property. *See* Zero Property of Addition
Adjacent leg, 579–580, 582–583, 586
Advertising, 38, 47, 274, 293
Agam, Yaacov, 218
Agriculture, 395–396, 491
Air traffic control, 195
Algebra. *The development of algebraic skills and concepts is a key goal of this math program and is found throughout the book.*
    absolute value, 63–65, 68, 80, 88, 94, 102, 131, 186, 359
    addition property of equality, 141
    additive identity, 141
    additive inverse, 67, 69, 74, 141, 151, 542–543, 545–546, 604
    Additive Inverse Property. *See* Zero Property of Addition
    algebraic expression, 68–70, 73–80, 82–83, 85–86, 88, 96–105, 107–111, 128–131, 133–138, 150, 154, 162, 176, 181, 186, 191–194, 199, 205, 210, 238, 349, 354, 359, 527, 532, 534–535, 540, 551–552, 554, 568
    associative property, 69, 78
    binomial, 533, 535, 539, 554
    boundary line, 207–209
    coefficient, 146–147
    Commutative Property, 69, 74, 77–78
    compound statement, 163

conjunction, 163
constant, 123–126, 538, 555
coordinate, 91, 235, 329
coordinate grid. *See* coordinate system
coordinate plane. *See* coordinate system
coordinate system, 91–95, 112, 159, 181–185, 190–193, 196–200, 203–204, 207–213, 234–238, 255, 279, 285, 290, 311, 329, 368, 406, 431, 435, 514, 517
degree of polynomial, 533, 535, 554, 589
dependent variable, 513, 530
direct variation, 555
disjunction, 163
Distributive Property, 83–88, 134, 426, 537, 549
equation, 128, 130, 135, 138, 140–154, 157, 159, 162, 172–176, 178–181, 183–188, 196–200, 202–204, 210–213, 226, 232, 234, 238, 246, 251, 255, 261, 279, 285, 290, 310, 328, 334, 339, 353–354, 360, 373, 378, 400, 415, 426, 459, 471, 480, 496, 514, 516–517, 522, 526–527, 536, 541, 573
equivalent equations, 141
evaluating, 85, 88, 97, 99, 128–130, 138, 150, 154, 162, 176, 181, 238, 496
exponent, 96–100, 102–104, 107–112, 154, 176, 181, 186, 210, 213, 532–533, 537, 550–552, 554
exponential function, 524–525, 527
formula, 123–126, 133–138, 160, 399, 426, 479–480
functions, 508–512, 514–517, 519–522, 524–525, 527, 530, 534, 554, 568, 573, 578, 583
graph. *See also* coordinate system
graph of exponential function, 524, 526, 530
graph of inequality, 156–158, 162
graph of linear function, 514–515, 517, 521, 526, 530, 578
graph of quadratic function, 518–522, 530, 578
graph of step function, 525, 530
independent variable, 513, 530
inequalities, 156–159, 162–163, 206–210, 212, 238, 279, 486
input, 508–512, 514–517, 525, 530, 568
integer, 63–71, 73–88, 91–95, 97–100, 102–105, 110, 136, 144, 149, 154
inverse property of multiplication, 78
inverse variation, 555
latitude, 90–93, 112
like terms, 537–540, 543–545

linear equation, 182–188, 196–200, 202–204, 211–213, 516
linear function, 514–516, 520, 527, 555
linear inequality, 206–210
longitude, 90–93, 112
matrix, 547
monomial, 533, 535, 547, 549, 551, 554
Multiplication Property of Equality, 146
multiplicative inverse, 78–79, 146–147
multiplying powers with like bases, 548
negative exponent, 107–112
negative number, 63–71, 73–81, 83–86, 88, 91–95, 97–100, 104–105, 110, 175, 180–181, 183, 185, 188, 192–194, 196–199, 204–205, 207, 209–210, 213
negative slope, 191–192
nonlinear equation, 213, 518–524
nonlinear function, 518, 524
opposites, 62, 64–65, 67, 73–74, 88, 186
order of operations, 82–83, 87, 97, 534
ordered pair, 91–95, 112, 159, 178–185, 188, 191–193, 196–197, 202–203, 207, 210, 212–213, 304, 333, 480, 496
origin, 91–92, 192–193, 212, 234, 236, 261, 406, 431
output, 508–512, 514–517, 530, 568
parabola, 518–520, 522
parallel lines, 197–198, 200, 212
polynomial, 532–541, 543, 545–547, 549–550, 554, 589, 604
positive number, 63–66, 68–71, 73–81, 83–86, 88, 91–95, 97–100, 104–105, 110, 175, 180–181, 183, 185, 188, 192–194, 197–199, 204–205, 207, 209–210, 213
positive slope, 191–192
power. *See* exponent
quadrant, 91–92, 94–95, 112
quadratic function, 518–519, 521–522, 527
reciprocal, 78–79, 146–147
rise, 191–194, 196–200, 203–204, 207–213, 235, 435
rule, 174–176, 188, 509–512, 514, 516, 522, 568
run, 191–194, 196–200, 203–204, 207–213, 235, 435
scientific notation, 102–105, 107–112, 159, 186, 226, 246, 251, 550–551, 554, 609
shape, 421
simplifying, 128–131, 133–137, 538–541, 543–546, 549, 554, 599
slope, 191–194, 197–200, 203–205, 207–217, 233–238, 261, 279, 329, 334, 431, 435, 471

INDEX

INDEX

INDEX

536, 541, 551, 568, 573, 592, 599, 614, 616, 630, 644, 650, 656, 670
Journalism, 22
Joyner-Kersee, Jackie, 560

K

Kayaking, 206

L

Land-use planning, 129, 190, 193–194, 258, 354, 624
Language, 13, 91, 183, 191, 286, 489, 532, 601, 653
Language arts, 226, 535, 630
Language Link, 13, 91, 183, 191, 286, 489, 532, 601, 653
Latitude, 90–93, 112, 403–406, 499
Law enforcement, 20, 39, 299, 401
Least common denominator, 337, 342, 352
Least common multiple (LCM), 335–342, 400, 578
Like terms, 537, 539–540, 543–545
Line, 411, 414, 419, 434
Line graph, 24–28, 44, 46, 50, 76
Line of symmetry, 605–609, 616
Line plot, 7–9, 30, 38–39, 126
Line segment, 411, 414–415, 426, 434
Line symmetry, 605–609
Linear equation, 182–185, 197, 212–213, 516
Linear function, 514, 520, 527, 555
Linear inequality, 207–208
Literature, 236, 464, 585, 641
Literature Link, 236, 585
Logic, 232, 329, 405
Longitude, 90–93, 112, 403–406, 499
Lower quartile, 18–20, 53. *See also* Quartile

M

Map projections, 499
Marine navigation, 588. *See* Navigation
Math Link, 514
Math reasoning, 10, 41, 46, 135, 154, 159, 176, 181, 186, 210, 255, 279, 310, 329, 354, 360, 378, 395, 400, 406, 415, 431, 455, 460, 465, 480, 496, 536, 552, 568, 573, 578, 589, 609, 614, 642, 650, 656, 661
Matrix, 547
Mean, 11–16, 30, 81, 131, 285
Measurement
  absolute position, 402, 405
  latitude, 403–406
  longitude, 403–406
  metric system, 390–394, 398, 408, 455
  precision, 396–400, 408
  relative position, 402, 405–406
  significant digit, 397–400, 408, 460
  U.S. customary units, 390–395, 398, 408, 455

Measures of central tendency
  mean, 11–16, 30, 81, 131, 285
  median, 12–16, 18–20, 30, 53, 81, 131
  mode, 13–16, 30, 40
Mechanical engineering, 364
Median, 12–16, 18–20, 30, 53, 81, 131
Medicine, 21, 36, 42, 108–109, 127, 222, 252, 369, 656
Mental Math, 74, 78, 180, 224, 230, 259, 275, 282, 287–288, 509, 543, 639
Meteorology, 125, 142, 160, 195, 420, 592, 607
Metric system, 390–392, 394, 408
Microbiology, 106–111, 257, 524
Mixed numbers
  adding, 351–353, 362
  comparing, 347–349, 362, 400
  to decimals, 362
  decimals to, 346, 348
  dividing, 357, 359, 362
  equivalent, 354
  multiplying, 357–359, 362
  to percents, 292
  repeating decimals to, 347–348
  simplifying, 400
  subtracting, 351–353, 362
Mode, 13–16, 30, 40
Model building, 261, 466, 469, 486, 492, 498, 585, 591
Modular arithmetic, 381
Monomial, 533, 535, 547, 549, 551, 554
Motion, 507
Mountain biking, 194
Mountain climbing, 199
Movies, 16, 18, 210, 243, 246–247, 250–251, 253–255, 257, 261, 263, 329, 659
Multiple, 324, 329, 336, 339
Multiplication
  in algebraic expressions, 96–100, 128, 130–131, 133–135, 138, 154, 176, 238
  of decimals, 356, 359, 362
  in equations, 146–153, 162, 175, 180, 188, 226, 255, 261, 310
  in formulas, 123, 125–126, 134, 138
  of fractions, 357, 359, 362
  in inequalities, 157–158, 162, 238
  of integers, 77–78, 80–81
  of polynomials, 548–551
  in problems involving percents, 281–285, 295–299, 301–310, 314
  in ratios and proportions, 228–231, 240, 243–246, 248–250, 253–255, 257–261, 264, 310
  of whole numbers, 21, 41, 46, 50, 210
Multiplication Property
  of equality, 146
  for independent events, 664–665
Multiplicative inverse, 78–79
Multiplying powers, 548
Music, 18, 35, 37, 148, 300, 306, 310, 590, 633, 635
Musical instruments, 574, 605
Mutually exclusive events, 671

N

Native American arts and crafts, 593, 595–596, 598, 602, 604, 606–610, 614–615
Nature, 409
Navigation, 389, 393, 499, 579, 588. *See also* Marine navigation
Negative exponent, 107–112
Negative fraction, 352
Negative number, 63, 66, 71, 79, 81, 88, 196
Negative slope, 191–192
Negative square root, 369, 371
Net, 429–431, 433, 462, 464, 467, 512
Newton, Isaac, 168
Nonagon, 426
Nonlinear equation, 213
Nonlinear function, 518, 524
Number line, 12, 63–64, 68, 70, 73, 88, 144
Number sense, 21, 65, 71, 75, 80, 104, 110, 138, 205, 279, 289, 292, 368, 455, 460, 465, 479, 486, 495, 589, 650
Nutrition, 140, 273, 275–278, 280–281, 284, 287–291

O

Obtuse angle, 412, 414, 434, 465, 614
Oceanography, 72
Octagon, 421, 425, 460, 522, 571, 573
Octagonal pyramid, 471
Odd number, 325, 342
Odds of an event, 650
Olatunji, Babatunde, 320
Olympics, 27, 400, 630, 633, 635–637, 639, 641–644
Operation sense, 85, 400, 491
Opposite leg, 579–580, 583
Opposites, 62, 64–65, 67, 73–74, 88, 186
Optics, 260
Order of operations, 82–83, 87, 97
Ordered pair, 91–95, 159, 178–185, 188, 196–197, 202–203, 207, 210, 212, 304, 333, 496
Origin, 91–92, 192–193, 212, 234, 236, 261, 406, 431
Outcome, 637–638, 644, 646–649, 652, 658, 664, 670
Outlier, 12, 14–16, 19, 21
Output, 508–512, 514–517, 530, 568

P

Packaging, 464–465, 475–482, 485–488, 490, 495–498, 553
Paleontology, 523, 584
Parabola, 518–520, 522
Parachuting, 662
Parallel lines, 197–198, 200, 212, 416, 418, 423–424, 435, 588
Parallelogram, 423, 425, 446–449, 569, 572, 598, 614

INDEX

INDEX

U

V

W

X

Y

Z

INDEX